MAGILL'S
LITERARY ANNUAL

1980

MAGILL'S LITERARY ANNUAL

1980

*Essay-Reviews of 200 Outstanding Books
Published in the United States during 1979*

_____

With an Annotated Categories Index

Volume One

A-In

Edited by
FRANK N. MAGILL

SALEM PRESS
Englewood Cliffs

LIBRARY OF CONGRESS CATALOG CARD NO. 77-99209

ISBN 0-89356-280-7

First Printing

PRINTED IN THE UNITED STATES OF AMERICA

PREFACE

MAGILL'S LITERARY ANNUAL, 1980, comprising essay-reviews of two hundred outstanding books published in 1979, is the fourth two-volume version of the MASTERPLOTS annual one-volume series that began in 1954 and continued yearly until the changeover in 1977. This year's edition provides studies of books in various categories as follows: fiction, 53; poetry and drama, 21; literary criticism, 8; history, 39; general biography, 23; literary biography, 14; autobiography, memoirs, letters, 16; essays, 17; science, 7; current affairs, 2. Eighty-eight individual contributors provided the critical analysis and commentaries that comprise this work.

The range of fiction was broad in 1979, running from Alan Saperstein's MOM KILLS KIDS AND SELF, a "news report" type novel depicting the breakdown of the family in today's America, to Gilbert Sorrentino's MULLIGAN STEW and Stephen King's supernatural thriller THE DEAD ZONE. Somewhat more conventional are Joseph Heller's GOOD AS GOLD, Gabriel García Márquez's IN EVIL HOUR, John Barth's very clever LETTERS, John Hawkes's strange but well-controlled THE PASSION ARTIST, and Muriel Spark's wryly written TERRITORIAL RIGHTS. Other novels of note published during the year include those by Bernard Malamud, James Baldwin, David Madden, Philip Roth, Kurt Vonnegut, John Wain, Wallace Stegner, and William Golding.

Short fiction fared extremely well during the year, with such excellent representatives as collections by Sholom Aleichem, Paul Bowles, Mario Vargas Llosa, Ian McEwan, Isaac Bashevis Singer, V. S. Pritchett, John Updike, William Faulkner (the uncollected stories, an excellent tool for Faulkner research), and F. Scott Fitzgerald, this volume edited by Matthew J. Bruccoli and containing one story never before published.

Poetry was also represented by some excellent volumes in 1979. Louis Zukofsky's "A"—a long career-ending sum-up by a major poet—appeared during the year. Other fine volumes include Dave Smith's GOSHAWK, ANTELOPE, a work whose themes may remind some readers of Robinson Jeffers; Howard Moss's elegant NOTES FROM THE CASTLE, wherein the persona speaks as a sophisticate; James Dickey's THE STRENGTH OF FIELDS, a fine production from a gifted poet; Pulitzer Prizewinner Anthony Hecht's THE VENETIAN VESPERS, whose long and brilliant title poem highlights the volume; and WIND MOUNTAIN, the third section of Fred Chappell's "novel in verse" and the best part thus far. John Ashbery, Derek Walcott, and John Hollander, also published volumes in 1979, and THE POEMS OF STANLEY KUNITZ, 1928-1978 appeared during the year.

Not much new drama was published in 1979, though three works are surely worthy of note: THE ELEPHANT MAN by Bernard Pomerance, NIGHT AND DAY by Tom Stoppard, and Lanford Wilson's 5TH OF JULY, the first part of a trilogy.

The year 1979 saw an abundance of excellent essays published. Among the noteworthy collections were V. S. Pritchett's THE MYTH MAKERS, Isak Dinesen's DAGUERREOTYPES AND OTHER ESSAYS, Joan Didion's THE WHITE ALBUM, and OF POETRY AND POETS by Richard Eberhart. C. H. Sisson's THE AVOIDANCE OF LITERATURE: COLLECTED ESSAYS provides an excellent evaluation of American (and other) poets; Irving Howe's CELEBRATIONS AND ATTACKS covers thirty years of Howe's critical writings; Douglas R. Hofstadter's GÖDEL, ESCHER, BACH: AN ETERNAL GOLDEN BRAID represents an interesting approach to "interdisciplinary" discussions; and in ON LIES, SECRETS, AND SILENCE Adrienne Rich issues a strong appeal for the dethroning of men in favor of women to control society. Also, in THE EIFFEL TOWER AND OTHER MYTHOLOGIES, the recently deceased Roland Barthes offers a collection attempting to show what Barthes's philosophy of language is all about; and in MEDUSA AND THE SNAIL we can gain some fascinating ideas from an M. D. about nature, life, and the human condition.

The fields of literary criticism and literary history provided some excellent subjects for study. One of these is Leon Edel's BLOOMSBURY: A HOUSE OF LIONS. Another is THE MADWOMAN IN THE ATTIC: THE WOMAN WRITER AND THE NINETEENTH-CENTURY LITERARY IMAGINATION, by Sandra M. Gilbert and Susan Gubar. Other titles worthy of mention include Grant Webster's THE REPUBLIC OF LETTERS: A HISTORY OF POSTWAR AMERICAN LITERARY OPINION, Timothy Materer's VORTEX: POUND, ELIOT, AND LEWIS, and A REVOLUTION IN TASTE by Louis Simpson, a work concerned with changes in American cultural and poetic tastes since the 1930's.

Among the excellent literary biographies that enlivened the year were those of Albert Camus, Jorge Luis Borges, Heinrich and Thomas Mann, Joseph Conrad, Thornton Wilder, Ivan Turgenev, Sara Teasdale, Stendhal, and an account of D. H. Lawrence's unsettled years in England during World War I. Those who do not demand light reading will find Jean Orieux's VOLTAIRE a rewarding experience.

Those readers who prefer a more intimate approach to their literary figures should examine the letters of Flannery O'Connor (THE HABIT OF BEING), THE LETTERS OF VIRGINIA WOOLF, Volumes IV and V, the Nabokov-Edmund Wilson letters, the Steinbeck-Pascal Covici letters, THE LETTERS OF D. H. LAWRENCE (the first volume of a projected seven), and THE LETTERS OF LEWIS CARROLL, VOLUME ONE. For a change of pace there is the first volume of Henry Kissinger's WHITE HOUSE YEARS.

Biography continues to be popular with the reading audience and there were many interesting works to fill the need in 1979. In BERNARD BERENSON: THE MAKING OF A CONNOISSEUR, Ernest Samuels gives a full portrait of this brilliant Italian Renaissance expert. Public life provided the background for several excellent works: David Burner's HERBERT HOOVER: A PUBLIC LIFE; Edmund Morris' THE RISE OF THEODORE ROOSEVELT; and Robin Reilly's WILLIAM PITT THE YOUNGER, perhaps England's greatest prime minister. Another British figure, important for his explorations, came in for attention during the year through Kenneth Lupton's MUNGO PARK THE AFRICAN TRAVELER. Robert E. Conot's A STREAK OF LUCK removes some of the aura of magic from the achievements of Thomas A. Edison and shows him as a brilliant and determined man who used others to help him perfect his major inventions. John D. Gates, in THE DU PONT FAMILY, offers another example of how brilliance, determination, and inventiveness could bring great success quickly when America was younger.

General reader interest in history continues—fueled by the media who incessantly tells us of the present and thus make us want to know more of the past as well—and the number of books on history published in a year now runs into the thousands. Unfortunately, there is space to deal with only fifty-three of them in our 1980 Annual, of which the following titles form a representative dozen for varying tastes: THE BARBARY COAST: ALGIERS UNDER THE TURKS, 1500-1830; THE BRETHREN: INSIDE THE SUPREME COURT; THE BRINK: CUBAN MISSILE CRISIS, 1962; THE DEVIL'S HORSEMEN: THE MONGOL INVASION OF EUROPE; DUST BOWL: THE SOUTHERN PLAINS IN THE 1930s; THE END OF THE WAR IN ASIA (WW II); FRANKLIN D. ROOSEVELT AND AMERICAN FOREIGN POLICY, 1932-1945; FROM *Brown* TO *Bakke*, THE SUPREME COURT AND SCHOOL INTEGRATION: 1954-1978; GERMAN REARMAMENT AND THE WEST, 1932-1933; HITLER VS. ROOSEVELT: THE UNDECLARED NAVAL WAR; MUNICH: THE PRICE OF PEACE; and THE PALESTINE TRIANGLE: THE STRUGGLE FOR THE HOLY LAND, 1935-48.

Science now holds great interest for many general readers, and publishers are making available to the reading public more and more books that treat scientific progress in "nonscientific" terms. Several of these works are dealt with in the 1980 Annual, among them, THE EIGHTH DAY OF CREATION: THE MAKERS OF THE REVOLUTION IN BIOLOGY, by Horace Freeland Judson; MIND AND NATURE: A NECESSARY UNITY, by Gregory Bateson; PREHISTORIC AVEBURY, by Aubrey Burl; and Carl Sagan's BROCA'S BRAIN: REFLECTIONS ON THE ROMANCE OF SCIENCE.

Those familiar with the three earlier editions of MAGILL'S LITERARY ANNUAL may notice that no "Sources for Further Study" sections appear in the current work. After three years of testing, it has been decided that these review references serve no useful purpose in our volumes, and thus they have been discontinued. The same information, in an even broader scope, is readily available in the reference room of almost every library.

As usual, the task of selecting for inclusion in this Annual a mere two hundred titles from the many thousands of books published in the year just past has been a challenge not without awe. We earnestly trust that our staff has been able to include some works of special interest to you.

FRANK N. MAGILL

LIST OF TITLES

LIST OF TITLES

page

TITLES BY CATEGORY

_____

ANNOTATED

FICTION

xxi

LITERARY CRITICISM
LITERARY HISTORY

HISTORY

CONTRIBUTING REVIEWERS FOR 1980 ANNUAL

J. Stewart Alverson

Peggy Bach

Terry Alan Baney

Carolyn Wilkerson Bell

Gordon N. Bergquist

Gary B. Blank

Harry Brand

Peter Brier

John R. Broadus

Kenneth T. Burles

Jack L. Calbert

John C. Carlisle

David B. Carroll

John R. Chávez

Gordon W. Clarke

John Cleman

Ronald D. Cohen

Dawn Paige Dawson

Phyllis DeLeo

Ellen Devereux

R. H. W. Dillard

Leon V. Driskell

John W. Evans

John P. Ferré

W. Bryan Fuermann

Betty Gawthrop

Roger A. Geimer

Robert Gish

Christine Gladish

Gabriel Gonzalez

William E. Grant

Alan G. Gross

Max Halperen

Patricia King Hanson

Stephen L. Hanson

Gary L. Harmon

Robert L. Hoffman

Jeffry Michael Jensen

Henderson Kincheloe

Paul B. Kern

David Kubal

Angelika Kuehn

Heinz R. Kuehn

Anthony Lamb

Saul Lerner

Elizabeth Johnston Lipscomb

Mark McCloskey

Agnes McDonald

Paul D. Mageli

Robert E. May

Walter E. Meyers

Jim W. Miller

Zenobia Mistri

Leslie B. Mittleman

Paul Monaco

Gordon R. Mork

Sheldon A. Mossberg

Joan Taylor Munger

Keith Neilson

Guy Owen

Deba P. Patnaik

L. W. Payne

Doris F. Pierce

James Pringle

Anne C. Raymer

John D. Raymer

Margaret Raynal

Bruce D. Reeves

Michael S. Reynolds

Richard Rice

Michael C. Robinson

Karl A. Roider, Jr.

Larry S. Rudner

Richard H. Sander

Steven C. Schaber

Margaret S. Schoon

Don W. Sieker

Leon Stein

Henry Taylor

William B. Toole III

Lance Trusty

Stuart Van Dyke, Jr.

Richard A. Van Orman

John N. Wall, Jr.

Thomas N. Walters

Mary C. Williams

Susan Wells

John Wilson

MAGILL'S
LITERARY ANNUAL

1980

"A"

Author: Louis Zukofsky (1904-1978)
Publisher: University of California Press (Berkeley). 826 pp. $16.95
Type of work: Poetry

A lengthy and imaginative work which the poet dedicated more than forty-five years to completing and in so doing solidified his position as a major contemporary poet

Two years after he taught English at Columbia, Louis Zukofsky produced his long poem, *The*, in 1926—a long poem in partly conventional blank verse which uses the technique of multiple voice and verbal collage. Inspired by his technical experiment for more daring and dramatic results, Zukofsky "started to think of *"A"* as soon as I had finished *The*," as he writes in a letter to his friend, Lorine Niedecker. About 1927, he began with a sketch— a plan of the form with section titles for a poem in twenty-four parts. This plan suggests that he originally envisioned *"A"* as more than *The*, but not of the length and scope of the final version of *"A"*, while he also made a table of difficulties to be overcome in the writing of the poem. In an interview on May 16, 1968, he answers, *""A"* is written at various times in my life when the life compels it. That also means that my eye is compelling something or my ears compelling something; the intellect is always working with words." This statement underlines three significant and crucial features found in *"A"*— the visual imagination, the aural power, and the quality of intelligence at work. It also indicates that the motivation behind the writing of the poem has been the very life of the poet.

Predetermined by the number of parts or movements ("the 'curve' of it in twenty-four movements") and undetermined as to the specific form or content, *"A"* is a staggering record of creative dedication, concentration, and richness spanning a period of more than forty-five years of life. 1 was written in 1928 and 23 during 1973-1974, although the final movement, 24, was done in 1968 with Celia Zukofsky's arrangement. These twenty-four parts—"A kind of childlike/Play this division/Into 24" (12)—display a variety of poetic strategies and formal virtuosity, which demonstrates that within Zukofsky's "childlike play" there is an astute and inventive mind in operation. For example, Part 24 is a Masque in five-part score with music (Handel's "Harpsichord Pieces"), drama, story, thought, and poem—the last four items are in an arrangement of four voices from Zukofsky's writings; 21, a translation of Plautus' *Rudens*, but for the chorus-speeches, is in five-word lines, and 18 is totally in eight-word lines; 9, like 7 of seven sonnets arranged in a canzone form, combines an exquisite sonnet-sequence and double canzone; 13 is a "partita" verbally imitating the rhythms in Bach's Violin Partita in D minor; 19 has twenty-five pages of Spenserian stanzas following eight quatrains of two-word lines; 17, "A Coronal," is a collage of quotations from William

Carlos Williams and Zukofsky's writings. 12 is the longest movement, with 135 pages, and here is 16 in its entirety:

> An
> > inequality
> > windflower.

Even though in his May, 1968, interview Zukofsky remarks, "I don't know about the structure of *"A"*. I don't care how you consider it . . . ," a dominant preoccupation or element in the poem is his concern for and engagement with the form and language. William Carlos Williams, in his Note to the Kyoto edition of *"A" 1-12*, rightly points out that Zukofsky "is a poet devoted to working out by intelligence the intricacies of his craft," and that "the major aim is not to show himself but that order that of itself can speak to all men." Therefore, Zukofsky has always, Williams maintains, devoted his care to "the spiritual unity of the world of ideas." His entire corpus reflects this keen engagement with the craft and ideas. From the very beginning of *"A"*, Zukofsky strikes the note: "A round of fiddles playing/Without effort" and "longing for perfection." One could find a definition of *"A"* in movement 5: "One song/Of many voices" and "Words ranging forms." He further elaborates on his craft in 6:

> The melody! the rest is accessory:
> My one voice. My other: is
> An objective—rays of the object brought to a focus,
> An object—nature as creator—desire
> for what is objectively perfect
> Inextricably the direction of historic and contemporary particulars.

Again in the same movement: "Environs-the sea,/The ears, doors;/The words—/Lost—visible." He repeatedly talks about poetics—his poetics in particular. 12 opens with a discussion on shape, rhythm, and style, then moves to "Measure, tacit is"; finally,

> I'll tell you.
> About my *poetics*—
> > music
> > speech
>
> An integral
> Lower limit speech
> Upper limit music

14 further extends and expands his poetics to the ultimate statement: "lower limit speech/upper limit music/lower limit music/upper limit *mathemata*."

In terms of the total construction, *"A"* is not an absolute success; it does not have the strength of *Paterson* or *The Cantos*. In spite of elegant and exquisite passages such as the opening sonnet in 7, parts of movements 6, 7, and 8 seem to obfuscate the content and meaning; movement 17, too, fails in its collage form; *Rudens* (21) is rather dull and appears to be not quite integral; and, 24, the "Masque," not only disappoints us as an effective final movement, but also gives the impression of being too deliberate and troublesome to read. Minor inaccuracies occur; for example, Bach did not have twenty-two children (scholars say he had twenty), nor was "The Passion According to Matthew" composed in 1729 (it was written in 1727, according to Bach specialists). In 6 Zukofsky asks: "Can/The design/Of the fugue/Be transferred/To poetry?" On the whole, *"A"* is more of a fugal experiment; the poet may not seem to be totally triumphant "to master/music and related matter" (8). But he has "Journeyed/With an impulse to master" with humility, courage, and dedication. "A poetics," says 12 "is informed and informs—/ Just *informs* maybe—the rest a risk." In this "risk"—daring—lies Zukofsky's strength and greatness; it is the singular value of his particular perception and communication. It is not so much a matter of innovation, but more a matter of inquiry and order of expression—"That order that of itself can speak to all men."

This concept of "order" is inseparable from Zukofsky's sense of form—his use of language, his measure, and his style. In 12 he writes, "The order that rules music . . . /harmony"; in 6, "We need beauty in everything, . . . /Well made and well thought out"; in 8, "Or sweetness: where there is more light than logic./A full number of things in a very few words"; and, in 12, "A sound akin to mosaic:/A rhythm of eyes." Zukofsky's subtle and elegant mind could turn out such startling imagery and expressions as "The Treasury is like a spittoon" or "The seals pearled for a minute/In the sun as they sank" (6) or "One sky is rich in us,/Undivided" (12) or "pine needles/frost tomorrow's/ sun." Hugh Kenner points out the "structural eloquence" in *"A"*, the rigorous way with language which gives the poem a "weightless structure" by the use of shorter lines, more tension, fewer words, "brief twinkling phrases," and the "miraculous verbal transaction, shaped and shapely words by their joinery achieve meaning," as in the opening lines of movement 7 or the "hummingbird" lines in 12.

Lorine Niedecker feels Zukofsky's "greatest gift" is in "transmuting events into poetry" through the idea of recurrence ("All art is made, I think, out of recurrence," writes Zukofsky) as in the case of the idea of "journey." Mirrors, flowers, horses, sea, and "inwreathed" amply illustrate the idea of recurrence in the poem, as does the thematic orchestration in 8 of eight different themes—history, labor, physics, mathematics, poetic craft, Christ's burial, and the nature of things—already enunciated in movements 1-7. Zukofsky's musical sense in *"A"*—"aurality and its relation to measure," to quote Duddy—has been pointedly demonstrated by Thomas A. Duddy in his essay "The Measure of Louis Zukofsky." Dembo, on the other hand, discusses

Zukofsky's "objectivist" poetics and his remarkable mastery of style. "The eye is a function of the ear and the ear of the eye." suggests Zukofsky. In "thinking with the things as they exist," he has achieved not only in structure and organization of the poem, "A", but also in the use of language, a remarkable fusion of melopoeia, phanopoeia, and logopoeia—in his words, "Cadence plus definite language equal the full meaning."

In Zukofsky's use of line endings, submerged half rhymes, spaced intervals and words, there is a distinct kinetic relation between the speech—meaning—and the sounds—music. It is not only "music heard, but seen"; the words are, as William Carlos Williams would call, "mordents"—"words in more or less sentence formation . . . in a wider relationship to the composition or musicality." The parsimony of adjectives, the predicative force in a whole phrase or lines without a verb, nouns and adjectives turned to verbs, the elliptical articulation and the imagery, not so much a visual image as "tangible ideation," create in "A" such an orchestration of aural or musical power that the words generate "energies which make for meaning." The very opening of the poem sets the tone and texture: "A/Round of fiddles playing Bach." In his A Test of Poetry, Zukofsky suggests, "Poetry convinces not by argument but the *form* it creates to carry its context." So "A" achieves a complex ascending clarity from speech to music to "mathemata"—toward the "rested totality" Zukofsky talks about with regard to his Objectivist poetics. In 2, Zukofsky writes,

> The music is in the flower
> Leaf around leaf ranged around the center;
> Profuse but clear outer leaf breaking on space,
> There is space to step to the central heart:
> The music is in the flower,
> It is not the sea but hyaline cushions the flower.

In movement 8, he states, "If you know all the qualities of a thing/You know the thing itself;/Nothing remains but the fact/The said thing exists without us." Further, he writes, "bringing together facts/which appearances separate:/all that is created in a fact/is the language that numbers it,/The facts clear,/breath lives/with the image each lights." In his celebration and perception of the world, Zukofsky, like Wittgenstein (whose name and ideas he often uses in the poem), not only strips language of bewitchment but strips his poem of inauthentic values and sentiments as well.

As this stupendous poem weaves personal and historical facts and themes, and as it celebrates Paul and Celia, his son and wife, in particular, Zukofsky's "intelligence moved by passion," to quote his words on Apollinaire, notates another parallel movement with speech, music, and mathemata: "Knowledge/Identity/Idea/Negation" (13). As he states in 12, "To re-collect *Be* as an archetype of bees/And neglect his *to not-be*/A verb which he has—/No more than it would have done for an/ancient Hindu." But this ascension toward "negation" is not nothingness, a denial of life and world, a rejection of intellect or imagination. It is, in fact, "to move on to the beginning." The poem begins with A and ends with Z (not counting the appended movement 24), encompassing "moonwort:/music, thought, drama, story, poem/park's sunburst—animals, grace notes—/z-sited path are but us" (23). This is the "simple mathematics"—the "divine arabesque"—of the poem, and "What stirs is/his tracing a particular line," that reveals Zukofsky's humility, humanity, and awareness of the fourth dimension, "the dimension of stillness," that he so admired in Ezra Pound. *"A"* includes ALL and, in its fugal movement, progresses to THE ultimate knowledge—"One single number should determine our life:1" (12) and one single alphabet: A—and "the grace that comes from knowing" (11).

> Reject no one
> and
> Debase nothing.

Deba P. Patnaik

AARON BURR
The Years from Princeton to Vice President
1756-1805

Author: Milton Lomask (1909-   )
Publisher: Farrar, Straus and Giroux (New York). 443 pp. $17.50
Type of work: Biography
Time: 1756-1805
Locale: Colonial and post-Revolutionary America

A detailed study of the life and character of one of America's most enigmatic and controversial political figures

> *Principal personages:*
> AARON BURR, Vice-President of the United States during Jefferson's first term as President
> JONATHAN EDWARDS, a Puritan divine and Burr's grandfather
> THEODOSIA BARTOW BURR (née PREVOST), Burr's first wife
> THEODOSIA BARTOW BURR, his daughter
> ALEXANDER HAMILTON, Secretary of State under George Washington's Administration; killed by Burr in a duel on July 11, 1804
> GENERAL JAMES WILKINSON, Governor of the Louisiana Territory, 1805-1806

Few public figures in the history of America have provoked as much controversy as Aaron Burr. He has been maligned, misunderstood, labeled adventurer and traitor, and, quite recently, romanticized in a fictional biography. The general public, for the most part, still tends to think of him as the man who callously killed Alexander Hamilton in a mismatched duel. Those who recall their American history more clearly may remember Burr as the provocateur who engineered an unsuccessful conspiracy against the United States aimed at creating for himself a western empire from Spanish and American territories beyond Louisiana. Few of us have a clear picture of this brilliant, compelling, and enigmatic American, and historian Milton Lomask has attempted to close this gap. In a new study of Aaron Burr, Lomask addresses himself to a sympathetic and thoroughly documented biography grounded in carefully detailed scholarship. Although Lomask is no apologist for some of the more controversial actions of his subject, he does provide some convincing arguments which help explain Burr's erratic behavior, much of which seemed contradictory and self-destructive.

In addition to revising the imperfect portrait of Burr which many of us carry, Lomask is concerned with the man's political and legal morality, which, on several occasions, tested the strength and flexibility of the newly created American government. With the nation barely in its second decade, Burr questioned the authority of the executive office, forced the drafting of a Constitutional Amendment, and challenged a Federal Circuit Court with Chief Justice John Marshall presiding to redefine the meaning of treason.

Lomask also investigates other aspects of Burr's life and provides a vivid account of this revolutionary patriot, military figure, state representative, financier, and public servant. In addition, the intellectual and cultural life of pre- and post-Revolutionary America is reviewed, with Burr's contribution carefully assessed. Not only is Lomask a qualified biographer, but he also faithfully re-creates the age in which Burr flourished before his ignominious exile in 1805. Of particular interest are the regional studies of New Jersey, Connecticut, and New York—states in which Burr lived and worked before rising to the position of Vice-President during Jefferson's first presidential term.

Aaron Burr was born into a distinguished New England family in 1756. His maternal grandfather, Jonathan Edwards, was the Puritan divine who organized the Great Awakening during the 1740's. This religious revival kindled intense fervor among its followers, who emphasized the power and impatience of God and the total depravity of man. Edwards was Colonial America's prophet of doom and hellfire, and his movement had an enormous influence on the quality of religious life in mid-eighteenth century America. Burr's father was also a clergyman, but he was better known for his contribution to Colonial education, not religion. During the year of Aaron's birth, Reverend Burr became president of the College of New Jersey, soon to be renamed Princeton University. Aaron's own education took place at Princeton, and although he showed considerable scholastic promise during the early years, he was unwilling to exert himself, graduating in 1772 without distinction. His restless disposition led to several career indecisions and nearly four years of semi-idleness. His parents had died during his infancy, so he was denied the strong guidance of a Puritan father, an influence which might have urged him to pursue a religious vocation.

When the New England governments rebelled against the authority of George III and the Continental Congress ordered the formation of an army, Burr's career dilemma was temporarily resolved. He enlisted in General Richard Montgomery's volunteer unit, which had orders to march from the Colonies into Canada, capture Montreal, then join General Benedict Arnold's forces to storm Quebec. The military strategy of the Canadian campaign, which included neutralizing British bases and preventing Northern units from joining with those in the South, was not entirely successful. Montgomery and Arnold were denied Quebec, but they did manage to contain a large British force for nearly a year. Burr's own conduct during the campaign was exemplary, and he was cited for bravery under fire.

Concerned that more decisive battles were being waged within the Colonies, Burr requested a transfer to the Continental Army's New York City headquarters. Under the direct command of General George Washington (neither man was much impressed with the other), Colonel Burr was charged with protecting all of Westchester County. He looked upon his duties contemptuously and was convinced that Washington had exiled him to watch over dairy cows and turnstiles while the Continental Army readied itself for crucial battles elsewhere. In 1779, Washington approved his resignation, whereupon Burr returned to Connecticut, resumed his courtship of Theodosia Bartow Prevost, and earnestly began his study of the law. Within four years he had married Miss Prevost, opened a highly successful law practice in New York City (at 3 Wall Street, "next door but one to the City Hall"), and became one of the most skillful and respected attorneys in the region.

Burr's growing reputation as a lawyer attracted considerable attention, and those who were planning the future of New York State invited him to join their circle. In the late 1780's, Burr was elected to the State Senate, and he continued to serve and represent the interests of New Yorkers for the next ten years. It was during this period that Burr, the preeminent Federalist, revealed his genius for administrative organization and his ability in creating powerful coalitions. These skills, and his reputation for sound political sense, led to the formation of a "Burr for President" movement in 1796. Although unsuccessful, the attempt served notice to the nation that Aaron Burr was a powerful political figure capable of gaining wide support.

The election of 1800 verified this broad support for Burr—he was selected as Thomas Jefferson's vice-presidential running mate. Although the Republicans were clearly the victors, it was uncertain which of these two candidates was to be president, as Burr and Jefferson collected an identical number of electoral votes. The Constitution did not provide official guidance for this unprecedented eventuality, so the House of Representatives was forced to resolve the matter. On February 17, 1801, Jefferson was finally elected President. The prolonged political maneuvering during this period nurtured the growing antagonism between Burr and the Jefferson/Hamilton camp. Although Burr fully understood the significance of his secondary standing on the presidential ticket, he did not let this knowledge interfere with his desire to exploit the legal uncertainties of the Constitution. Because of these uncertainties, Congress considered it prudent to prevent such an embarrassment from recurring. The Twelfth Amendment, which provided for separate voting in the Electoral College for president and vice-president, was quickly passed.

The electoral problems in 1800 had damaging repercussions for the new nation. The President and Vice-President hated each other, and Burr complained bitterly that Jefferson intended to destroy him. Lomask suggests that Jefferson's imperious manner toward Burr and his open distrust of the Vice-President might have inspired some of Burr's more questionable actions, including the Hamilton duel, Burr's flirtation with the formation of a Northern Confederacy, and his abortive conspiracy in the South which led to his arrest, trial, and self-exile.

Milton Lomask's critical biography reveals the complex nature of Aaron Burr's personality in an admirable manner. Furthermore, the author convincingly investigates the cause and motive for much of Burr's strange behavior, especially in matters of public life. For example, the tragic events leading to and including the duel with Alexander Hamilton at Weehawken, New Jersey, are carefully reevaluated, and it is Lomask's conclusion that Burr did not behave in an entirely dishonorable manner. Indeed, the popular notion that Hamilton contemptuously refused to fire his weapon (one Hamiltonian defender would have us believe that Hamilton did not know how to operate a firearm) is seriously challenged. A far more convincing account of that day is provided by the author: two extremely proud and ambitious men faced each other to defend their honor; each sought to destroy his opponent, and one was the better shot.

Perhaps of equal interest to the modern reader is Lomask's highly detailed and sensitive portrayal of Burr the family man. This aspect of Burr's life reveals a person deeply devoted to his wife and daughter who performed his paternal duties honorably and in keeping with the highest expectations of the age. In addition, Burr chose to supervise personally the education of his daughter, a fatherly prerogative more commonly bestowed upon sons. In so doing, he gave more than lip service to the radical notion of the day that women were educable.

Lomask does not resolve the mystery which shrouds all of Burr's peculiar conduct. He does, however, investigate fully and sympathetically the first sixty-one years of this brilliant and often unstable patriot. The biography is a clearly written, well-organized study which illuminates a great and controversial American. In *Aaron Burr: The Years of Exile* (in progress), Lomask studies the aftermath of the Weehawken tragedy, Burr's conspiracy, and the sensational trial which followed. There is every reason to believe that this subsequent volume covering Burr's remaining years will be equally readable and informative.

Don W. Sieker

ACCOUNTING FOR GENOCIDE
National Responses and
Jewish Victimization during the Holocaust

Author: Helen Fein
Publisher: The Free Press (New York). 468 pp. $15.95
Type of work: History
Time: 1939-1945
Locale: Europe

An analysis of the Holocaust from the standpoint of national responses to the isolation, persecution, and destruction of the Jewish community of Europe

Accounting for Genocide: National Responses and Jewish Victimization during the Holocaust by Helen Fein claims to be "an application of historical sociology, not a conventional history." For this reason, the book suffers from schizophrenia, gravitating from well-written and often eloquent history to the turgid and almost incomprehensible language of sociology. Because the book attempts to be a sociology of the Holocaust, it apparently seeks to derive sociological principles from the experience and to use sociological principles to comprehend that tragedy. A problem from such an approach is that the author is really extrapolating from a single point. In order to avoid such a charge, Fein briefly includes a discussion of Turkish annihilation of the Armenians in 1915. Inclusion of this example of genocide does little to universalize Fein's sociological principles or to comprehend the Holocaust, and the few pages on which she considers the Armenians could well have been eliminated from the book.

To a great extent the Nazis were able to destroy the Jewish population of Europe because they developed and rationalized a bureaucracy and a technology of death in which humanity was ignored. The humanity of Jews was denied, and Jews were abstracted into raw material to be processed. This process is poignantly described in R. Rubinstein's *The Cunning of History* and, most importantly, in Raul Hilberg's *The Destruction of the European Jews*. Hilberg's brilliant account of the technology of destruction remains a classic study of the Holocaust and of man's inhumanity to man. Fein recognizes that the Final Solution depended on an abstraction of man: "Only by focusing on the identity of the victim and that of the perpetrator can we strip the mask of ideology and the accounting mechanisms used by perpetrators to disguise their responsibility." However, this is precisely what is wrong with Helen Fein's book. By attempting to devise a sociology of the Holocaust and laws or principles to explain what happened, Fein seeks to derive abstractions that quite deliberately ignore the identity of the victim and focus, instead, on a "calculus" or "mechanism" of genocide.

Moreover, the abstract language that Fein employs to give the appearance of being scientific is problematic; it ignores humanity and compassion to convey an impression that a machine and not a person has written portions of this book. Readers are treated to such statements as "If Jews were included by the dominant group within the nation-state as members with equal rights, the likelihood of Jewish victimization should be negatively related to the intensity of solidarity among members of the state." Frequent use of language of this sort, especially in the first half of the book, makes the account unpalatable, if not indigestible.

The author's effort at deriving principles of human interaction from the historical events of the tragedy leads to the denial of freedom and capriciousness in history. Fein argues that what happened during the Holocaust had to have happened. Yet, choices were made to persecute Jews, to refuse to assist them, to murder them. The results were not inevitable. Men could have made other choices from those they made. For example, Fein attempts to test the thesis that "differences among nation-states in the percentage of Jews victimized are positively and regularly related to the intensity of German control. When German control was greater, there were more Jewish victims than when German control was less." First, such statements belabor the obvious. The reader, for example, is told "one's chances of escaping many raids decline successively in a geometric ratio as raids multiply if one relies on chance alone. The evader is the person who has escaped the first raid, and the second and the third (and so on), successively." (Fortunately, the author did not feel it necessary to explain that the person ceases to be an "evader" when he gets caught.) Second, such statements attempt to create inevitable principles out of the events of the Holocaust. Third, they attempt abstraction about events that can only be abstracted at the cost of their impact on students of the Holocaust. This is all done to give the appearance of an objective and neutral science of the Holocaust when in fact the book advances little beyond existing historical accounts, such as those of Hilberg, Nora Levin, and Lucy Dawidowicz.

While Fein could criticize Hilberg, Levin, Dawidowicz and others because they are not theoretical enough—an appropriate critique of the works of a historian by a sociologist—it can also be argued that Fein attempts to be too theoretical—an appropriate criticism of the works of a sociologist by a historian. Fein should accept the commandment that "thou shalt not commit a social science." Such a commission becomes particularly problematic when the result is obfuscation and confusion of a subject that requires description with delicacy, clarity, and compassionate understanding.

Fein's effort at developing a sociology of the Holocaust fortunately occupies only a portion of her book. When she moves from sociology to historical description, the book improves. Her summaries of secondary and primary sources and her many long quotations from primary sources present the ideas of others clearly and develop an important line of argument.

Fein's description of the responses of the Christian Churches to the victimization of the Jews is an excellent study of the literature. The author correctly points to the particular unwillingness of the Vatican to criticize their deportation and murder. Even local clergy were frequently far more yielding and sensitive than the Vatican to the plight of the Jews. In those cases in which national churches took a forthright stand in behalf of assisting Jews, as did the Lutheran Church of Denmark and Stefan, Metropolitan of Sofia, and Patriarch of Bulgaria, Jewish lives were saved. The successes of those Christian religious leaders who aided the Jews forces a condemnation of those who remained indifferent or who chose to assist in the destruction of the Jews.

Fein's description of the Judenräte and the literature dealing with this phenomenon is very interesting. The point that Fein stresses is that the process of isolating or segregating Jews and stripping them of their rights and belongings was performed by the nation-state and not by the Judenräte. Some leaders of the Judenräte were better and some were worse; some were corrupt and others were honest. However, Jews were victimized primarily by the state rather than by this agency. The sources of victimization were the isolation of the Jews and Germany's decision to exterminate them. To dwell on the role of the Judenräte in this process, according to Fein, is to ignore reality.

Some of the European states attempted to defend the Jews. Fein describes the ways in which Denmark refused to tolerate discrimination. As the Nazis put more and more pressure on Denmark, the Danish government remained convinced that Jews must be protected. When deportation of Jews was mandated by Germany, the Danes tried to send as many of them as possible to Sweden. A complex network of assistance was provided by the Danish population with the Danish police aiding, rather than deterring, the escape of the Jews. The situation in Belgium differed considerably from that of Denmark. German defeat of Belgium was followed by isolation of Jews and stripping them of their jobs, rights, and property. Deportation began in 1942 and encountered some resistance from both Jews and non-Jews. The resistance was not as great as in Denmark, but it was significant. Major resistance to Jewish deportation from Bulgaria was widespread and involved the government, the Orthodox Church, and the non-Jewish population. As may be seen in the examples of Denmark, Belgium, and Bulgaria, non-Jewish resistance to victimization of the Jews contributed greatly to Jewish survival.

Such opposition to victimization was absent among the Allied powers. Fein repeats and summarizes much of the discussion of Allied apathy and indifference that may be read in Henry Feingold's *The Politics of Rescue*, Arthur D. Morse's *While Six Million Died*, D. S. Wyman's *Paper Walls*, Saul S. Friedman's *No Haven for the Oppressed*, and other such works. The United States could have aided Jews fleeing Nazi persecution and destruction by permitting immigration and encouraging it among the Allies. The United States decided not to provide such assistance. The United States could have imposed sanctions on Germany to assist the Jews. Again nothing was done.

Not only did the United States not aid Jewish immigration, but immigration laws were also enforced in a way designed to keep them out of the United States. The United States participated in international refugee conferences (Evian in 1938, Bermuda in 1943) to convey the appearance without the reality of aiding the Jews. The Department of State's opposition to assisting Jews was deliberate, conscious, and conspiratorial. Only in 1944, after the annihilation of most of Europe's Jews, was the War Refugee Board created to help Jews in Europe. The United States government's nonaction and indifference toward European Jews was simply a reflection of the apathy and lack of concern on the part of American citizens, both non-Jewish and Jewish.

While the British government was generally indifferent to their plight, far more Jewish refugees were admitted to Great Britain during World War II than were admitted to the United States. The British White Paper of 1939 closed Palestine to Jewish immigration in order to satisfy and pacify Arabs of the Middle East. Lacking Palestine as a refuge, Jews died in Nazi death camps. Fein points out that the British were not really as indifferent to the Holocaust as were Americans. For this reason, the British government did not represent the wishes of its people on this issue as the United States government did. Of the major Allies, the Soviet Union provided some protection for Russian and other Jews fleeing from the Germans. This was done informally, and the official policy of the Soviet Union toward them was, like that of the United States and Britain, indifference.

If the Allies were apathetic to the Holocaust, the neutral countries were not. Swedish officials did as much as possible to rescue and welcome Jews. Sweden openly accepted Jewish refugees and intervened diplomatically in their behalf when necessary. Spain did not take such initiatives, but accepted any and all Jewish refugees, intervened to save Spanish Jews from deportation from Greece, and protested Jewish deportations from Hungary in 1944. They were not welcome in Switzerland, where anti-Semitism paralleled that in Germany. Here again is support for the argument that assistance and cooperation saved Jews, while apathy condemned them.

If the response of the world to the plight of Jews was not always very supportive, acting alone in their own behalf was also not very effective. The major example that Fein cites is the Warsaw Ghetto uprising. Describing in detail the uprising from *Notes from the Warsaw Ghetto: The Journal of Emmanuel Ringelblum, The Warsaw Diary of Chaim A. Kaplan*, Mary Berg's *Warsaw Ghetto*, Alexander Donat's *The Holocaust Kingdom*, Tovia Borzykowski's *Between Trembling Walls*, Vladka Meed's *On Both Sides of the Wall*, and other such accounts, Fein paints the picture of the Warsaw Ghetto, persecution of the Jews, deportation and death, and the heroic and desperate uprising that eventually was crushed by the Nazis. The story is very well told in the words of the Jewish participants, but Poland was not a place of Jewish survival. In 1939, Poland contained one of the largest Jewish populations in

Europe. By 1945, fewer than 2½ percent of the Jewish population survived to return to Polish soil, and of the Jewish inhabitants of Warsaw, only one in one hundred evaded German capture.

Fein's book concludes with a description of the Netherlands and Hungary, based on diaries. While many such documents are available for the Netherlands, including Anne Frank's *The Diary of a Young Girl*, there are only two sources for Hungary: the diary of Eva Heyman and Elie Wiesel's autobiographical novel, *Night*. The descriptions of life under the Nazis in the Netherlands and Hungary are very well presented. While the Netherlands provides many illustrations, it is exceedingly difficult to generalize about conditions in Hungary on the basis of two sources, one of which is unashamedly fictionalized. However, as with other nations of Europe where non-Jews attempted to aid Jews, Jewish lives were saved; when non-Jews were indifferent or hostile, Jews died.

Helen Fein's book is an important historical description that clearly establishes the relationship between national responses to Jewish victimization and the reality of that victimization during the Holocaust. The author's explanation of genocide places heavy responsibility for the destruction of Jews on the apathy and indifference of the nations of Europe and the Allies. The victimization was a product of the isolation of Jews. When isolation was not permitted by European nations, Jews were not victimized and survived; the apathy or hostility of nations meant their annihilation. In spite of its inadequacies, *Accounting for Genocide* is a significant contribution to the literature of the Holocaust.

Saul Lerner

ALBERT CAMUS
A Biography

Author: Herbert R. Lottman
Publisher: Doubleday & Company (Garden City, New York). Illustrated. 753 pp.
  $16.95
Type of work: Literary biography
Time: 1913-1960
Locale: Algeria, France, and New York

The first biography of Albert Camus

> *Principal personages:*
> ALBERT CAMUS
> CATHERINE CAMUS, his mother
> SIMONE HIÉ, his first wife
> FRANCINE CAMUS (NÉE FAURE), Madame Albert Camus, his second wife
> MARIA CASARÈS, an actress, his lover and friend
> MICHEL GALLIMARD, son of his publisher, a friend

Addressing a symposium on the art of biography hosted by the National Portrait Gallery in Washington, Leon Edel proposed a method "related to the methods of Sherlock Holmes and also to those of Sigmund Freud." The biographer, Edel said, must seek "the figure under the carpet, the evidence in the reverse of the tapestry, the life-myth of a given mask." He concluded this remarkable lecture (later collected in *Telling Lives: The Biographer's Art*, edited by Marc Pachter) by urging biographers to learn from modern painters, who

> moved from the splendid verisimilitude of Rembrandt's self-portraits to a kind of UR-portrait. In the recreation of lives, we have reached a time when we must, like these painters, give a new account of ourselves. We must not flinch from the realities we have discovered; we must realize that beyond the flesh and the legend there is an inner sense of self, an inner man or woman, who shapes and expresses, alters and clothes the personality that is our subject and our art.

The life of Albert Camus, now that we have Herbert R. Lottman's massive account of it, would seem to be an ideal subject for Edel's ideal biographer. At the peak of his success, a Nobel laureate in Literature at forty-three (only Kipling had been younger), he was suffering writer's block, "years of it (even if screened from public view by an abundance of ancillary activity)." A relentlessly moral writer, a man revered by many as the conscience of his generation, he was in private often quite different: clever, cynical, charming, and apparently a tireless womanizer. A colonial, and born into the working class (his mother could neither read nor write), he never lost a sense of solidarity with the oppressed, yet he was also driven by an enormous personal ambition: in his mid-twenties, he had outlined elaborate long-range plans for his *oeuvre*.

Camus presents a striking case, then, of the tension between the public "mask" and the animating "inner sense of self." To give a coherent account of Camus' life, a biographer must, in Edel's words, write "the life of his subject's self-concept. . . ." This is not to countenance the excesses of contemporary "psycho-history," nor should we quibble with the biographer of Henry James over a bit of psychological jargon. Camus' "self-concept" or "life-myth" is the figure under the carpet, the pattern without which there is no intelligible whole. Without this imaginative re-creation, a biography falls short of art. Camus still lacks such an empathic study.

Meanwhile, the standard will be Lottman's work. Not only is it the first biography of Camus in English, it is also the first biography of the man anywhere. Although this is not an "authorized" biography, it gives evidence of years of painstaking research, and Lottman did have the cooperation of Madame Albert Camus. The thirty-five black-and-white photographs include a number of family pictures, beginning with photos of Camus' mother and father.

Albert Camus was born on November 7, 1913, in Mondovi, Algeria. His parents were both descended from early settlers in Algeria. His father, Lucien Auguste Camus, was called up for service in the Zouaves soon after Albert's birth. Wounded in the Battle of the Marne, he died on October 11, 1914. Thus, Camus was reared by his submissive mother (who was "traumatized" by her husband's death) and by her harsh, dominating mother. Two uncles— his mother's brothers—and Albert's brother, Lucien, completed the household.

Lottman devotes considerable attention to these early years, and makes much of Camus' "Spanish blood" (his mother was Spanish). In part this is simply to balance the public image of Camus in France (well over half his life was spent in Algeria), but Lottman was also influenced by the novel, *le Premier Homme* (The First Man), which Camus left unfinished at his death. (The manuscript was in a briefcase which was flung from the car in his fatal accident.) Camus referred to this novel—of which some eighty thousand words exist—"not jokingly," Lottman says, as his *War and Peace*. Camus' most autobiographical work, *le Premier Homme* (which has not been authorized for publication) is "a painstakingly detailed description of the sorrows and joys of growing up in French Algeria, in the shadow of a mythical father. Camus had thought of calling his book *Adam*."

Fortunately, as a schoolboy Camus was singled out as a promising student. With encouragement from an exceptional teacher, he passed an examination which won for him a scholarship, allowing him to attend high school. Like Samuel Beckett, another writer who settled in France and later won the Nobel Prize, Camus was a soccer player, a better than average goalie. His active participation in the sport stopped when he came down with tuberculosis soon after his seventeenth birthday, but he continued to report on soccer games many years later.

Tuberculosis changed the direction of his life: "time for reading and reflection, forced by the exigencies of a long convalescence." During the next few years, Camus achieved a university degree (which would have qualified him for teaching were it not for his tuberculosis), became active in the theater (which he strayed from but never left thereafter), and began what was to be a lifelong if intermittent career in journalism. He also joined the Communist Party for a short time—discreetly, Lottman observes. In the midst of all this activity he was writing; in the spring of 1935 he began to keep the journal which he continued until his death; in 1937, he began *la Mort heureuse* (*A Happy Death*), his first novel, which was published posthumously.

In 1934, Camus married a young woman named Simone Hié. Lottman's account of this marriage and its breakup two years later, which he considers crucial to the formation of Camus' mature character, is typical of the author's inadequacy in interpreting his materials. "At the beginning she was by all accounts a ravishing girl," Lottman says of Simone. (About six hundred pages later the reader is briefly introduced to a nameless but "ravishing young woman" who, if such a coy paragraph can be decoded, was Camus' favorite mistress during the last year of his life. By then it is a familiar story: another "ravishing" or "stunning" companion.) Simone Hié was also "a flirt, worse, a vamp. If she was seldom caught wearing the same dress twice, she never wore anything under her dress, and *that* was rather exceptional at the time." She also took drugs, more and more frequently.

When discussing the breakup of the marriage, as seemed inevitable from the beginning, Lottman pontificates in his worst prose: "From now on Albert Camus would wear the stigma of his burnt marriage, face the full impact of his essential solitude." He goes on to account for Camus' womanizing: "Almost as if taking revenge for the wounds inflicted by Simone, he was also punishing himself by refusing the comfort and the reassurance of a single, enduring liaison."

Lottman's analysis is hardly persuasive, but—more important—it seems never to have occurred to him to ask *why* Camus chose to marry Simone Hié. "Camus believed at the time that he could rescue her": that is as far as Lottman goes. Such failures of interpretation—starting with failures to ask the right questions—cripple this biography. For the most part, Lottman simply surrounds an "event" in Camus' life with testimony from various contemporaries.

Not long after his break with Simone, Camus began working on his "triptych": *l'Étranger* (*The Stranger*), *le Mythe de Sisyphe* (*The Myth of Sisyphus*), and *Caligula*, the works that would make him famous. In 1940, he went to France to work for the newspaper *Paris-Soir*. He married an Algerian-born girl, Francine Faure, in December, 1940; laid off by the newspaper, he had to return to Algeria in 1941. *The Stranger* was published in 1942 by Gallimard, the reigning literary publisher in France. Although early reception of the novel was muffled by the war, *The Stranger* won critical praise, including a long, laudatory essay by Jean-Paul Sartre.

Camus' subsequent career is well-known. *The Stranger* became the most widely read, most influential European novel in the 1950's and 1960's. His work in the Resistance and his postwar influence through the newspaper *Combat* have been in currency with the essays collected in *Resistance, Rebellion and Death* and other volumes. As a representative of "existentialism," from which he kept detaching himself, to no avail, he was exported to America, where his name appeared everywhere—in seminars, in sermons, in newspaper columns. His death in a car accident—he was riding in a sports car driven at high speed by his friend Michel Gallimard—seemed to many observers a perfect symbol of the Absurd.

Lottman's biography has been seized upon by a number of reviewers eager to debunk Camus. Many of these critics—apparently oblivious to the headlines—have been particularly scornful in their dismissal of Camus' courageous stand on the Algerian question: he refused to support the Nationalists because he could not accept the tactics of indiscriminate terrorism. There is life enough in Camus' books to provoke such attacks—life enough, now that the fuss over existentialism has died down, to reward any readers who want the books for themselves. These readers will be grateful to Herbert Lottman for this comprehensive study of the life of Albert Camus.

John Wilson

ALBERT EINSTEIN: THE HUMAN SIDE
New Glimpses from His Archives

Author: Albert Einstein (1879-1955)
Edited by Helen Dukas and Banesh Hoffmann
Publisher: Princeton University Press (Princeton, New Jersey). 167 pp. $8.95
Type of work: Letters
Time: 1898-1955
Locale: The United States, Germany, and Switzerland

A small group of letters from the Einstein archives which show a side of the mathematical genius not often seen by the general public

In the popular view, the image of Albert Einstein, without doubt the greatest scientific mind of our century, is that of the recluse, complete with disordered, flowing white hair and somewhat disheveled clothing. To a certain extent, that image has validity; certainly Einstein was a kind of recluse, living in a world of physics, deep in the recesses of high-level abstraction.

Helen Dukas and Banesh Hoffmann present a different image of the man, however, an image unknown to most of us: that of "the human side" of the theoretical physicist. Dukas was Einstein's secretary from 1928 until his death in 1955, and since then she has been a trustee of his literary estate and archivist of his papers. Hoffmann, Professor Emeritus of Mathematics at Queens College, CUNY, worked with Einstein on research for the general theory of relativity. A few years ago, Dukas and Hoffmann collaborated on the prizewinning biography, *Albert Einstein: Creator and Rebel*. This time they have taken examples from Einstein's personal correspondence to show his concerns in nonscientific as well as scientific areas.

Born in Ulm, Germany, in 1879, Einstein's first fascination with science came as the result of a gift from his father—a compass. As its needle always pointed north, Einstein grasped both the truth of the laws of nature and the demonstrability of those laws. By the age of twelve, he was reading scientific books, and by nineteen he was studying in Zurich, Switzerland. Even at that age he saw his work as his only real goal in life. In a letter to his sister, he wrote: "I have never permitted myself any amusements or diversions except those afforded by my studies. . . . If everybody lived as I do, surely the writing of romantic novels would never have come into being."

Following that period of study, Einstein worked briefly as a private tutor in Switzerland and became a Swiss citizen; from 1902 to 1909, he worked as an examiner in the Swiss Federal Patent Office. Amazingly enough, it was while working as a civil servant that Einstein proposed his theory of Special Relativity and the Mass of Energy, in 1905. Einstein developed this theory, which had as much influence on modern astronomy and atomic science as any in the last three hundred years, in the hours after work. His letters give a clue to the kind of mind which can function in this way, for in 1918 he wrote to a friend that he had originally planned to become an engineer but found "intolerable" the idea that he would have to apply "the inventive faculty to matters that make everyday life more elaborate—and all just for dreary money-making." Obviously, one must do something in life to earn a living, but that can easily be a secondary concern. For Einstein, thinking, "thinking for its own sake," was the important thing in life. In the same letter he indicated that when he had no special problem to work with, he would re-construct proofs which he had long known of mathematical and physical theorems. "There is no goal in this," he said, "merely an opportunity to indulge in the pleasant occupation of thinking. . . ."

Einstein admitted in his correspondence that he appeared to be a hermit, but he also knew he was "a man possessed . . . hoping to unearth deep secrets." Even for Einstein such a struggle was difficult, sometimes seemingly "beyond my powers," but more importantly it was rewarding "because it makes one immune to the distractions of everyday life."

Letters such as these and others presented by the editors support the image of a recluse, a man with a vast mental capacity who marched in the academic procession commemorating the 350th anniversary of the University of Geneva wearing his straw hat and his everyday suit. It is the other letters, however, which support a different image of Einstein than is generally held: that of Einstein as a humanist.

In 1919, in response to a query about his reasons for working in science, Einstein wrote that he was motivated "by an irresistible longing to understand the secrets of nature and by no other feelings." Such a statement is not surprising from a man of his intellectual capacity. However, the most impor-tant comment in that same letter comes from a remark Einstein felt compelled to make, even though his questioner had not requested it. Immediately fol-lowing his explanation of his scientific motivation, he added: "My love of justice and the striving to contribute towards the improvement of human conditions are quite independent from my scientific interests." This is the other side of Einstein that the editors want to present.

Einstein was a deeply moral man, having written to his sister in 1935 that "the foundation of all human values is morality." When he became director of theoretical physics at the Kaiser Wilhelm Institute in Berlin in 1914, he became a German citizen again. Thus, his views on morality have a unique side when seen in terms of the historical events of his time.

When elected to membership in the Kaiser Leopold German Academy of Scientists in 1932, Einstein answered the standard biographical questionnaire about his birth by saying he was "born the son of Jewish parents," although anti-Semitism was already blatant in Germany. Within months, the Nazis took control of the nation, Einstein's citizenship was revoked, his property was confiscated, and former colleagues who supported his theories became doctrinaire, party-line critics—all because he was "born the son of Jewish parents." By 1934, when he wrote an article for an American magazine about the nature of tolerance, even Einstein must have begun to despair. He addressed the subject in terms of tolerance of the individual by society and by the state, and he evidenced concern about a time when the state might become all-powerful and the individual "its weak-willed tool," for then "all finer values are lost." The events of Nazi Germany must have been in his mind as he wrote.

A request to write about tolerance may seem a strange one to make to a theoretical scientist, but it was only one of many unusual requests Einstein received after he had become a famous figure. One of the most delightful aspects of this book is the insight given into how Einstein handled these requests. For example, a sixth-grade girl wrote him in 1936 asking if scientists prayed. His reply, written in simple terms for her, could stand as a manifesto for a kind of deistic humanism. He had written almost ten years earlier that he could not conceive of a "personal God," one who becomes involved in the daily affairs of individuals, but admitted he admired "the infinitely superior spirit" that the scientist could comprehend in reality. To his adolescent correspondent he wrote that the laws of nature seemed to deny the value of prayer, "a wish directed to a supernatural Being," but that those same laws made him feel there was a spirit manifest in the laws quite superior to that of man, and that led him to a "religious feeling of a special sort." To his 1927 correspondent he had added: "Morality is of the highest importance—but for us, not for God." Perhaps the best understanding of his religious views comes in a brief comment by the editors. "He evaluated a scientific theory by asking himself whether, if he were God, he would have made the Universe in that way."

The Nobel Prize-winning physicist was human in other ways too. He could become irritated by an accumulation of little things over the years. In 1949, he wrote to a friend who was disturbed at being misquoted, assuring him that it happened to everyone. Einstein said there had been so many "brazen lies and utter fictions" attributed to him that he would have long since gone to his grave had he paid attention to them. He was not prepared, either, for having to be on guard about "every casual remark," which was sure to be "snatched up and recorded." Had he known such would occur, he said, "I would have crept further into my shell."

The editors give us only a too-small glimpse of Einstein's humor, which appears to have been sharp. He once wrote: "How wretchedly inadequate is the theoretical physicist as he stands before Nature—and before his students!"

The most sobering element in this little book about "the human side" of Einstein is his thought about the changes in the world brought about by increased scientific knowledge. Although many of these changes have been positive, giving increased knowledge of the laws of nature, one direct result of his work—the atomic bomb—must be viewed as a negative outcome. As far back as 1917, Einstein was concerned that the era had become "monstrously amoral," that the "lauded technological progress . . . is like the axe in the hand of the pathological criminal." In 1946, with Hiroshima and Nagasaki a part of world history, Einstein wrote of his concern about the "horrifying deterioration in the ethical conduct of people" as a result of the "mechanization and dehumanization of our lives," which in turn was "a disastrous byproduct" of scientific and technical developments. "Nostra culpa!" he wrote, "I don't see any way to tackle this disastrous short-coming. Man grows cold faster than the planet he inhabits." With its potential for the annihilation of the human race, if not the physical destruction of the earth, one "disastrous byproduct" of his work—the atomic bomb—surely must have weighed heavily upon his mind, although there was nothing he could do to control the results of scientific and technological discoveries.

Although *Albert Einstein: The Human Side* does not qualify as a biography, it provides fascinating insight into this great scientist, even for someone not well-acquainted with the details of his life.

John C. Carlisle

ALEXANDER HAMILTON
A Biography

Author: Forrest McDonald (1927-   )
Publisher: W. W. Norton and Company (New York). 464 pp. $17.50
Type of work: Biography
Time: 1757-1804
Locale: The northeastern United States

An analysis of Alexander Hamilton's life and contributions to American history

Principal personages:
ALEXANDER HAMILTON, American Revolutionary leader and first Secretary of the Treasury
ELIZABETH SCHUYLER, his wife
GEORGE WASHINGTON, Commander in Chief of the Colonial army and first President of the United States
THOMAS JEFFERSON, first Secretary of State and third President of the United States
AARON BURR, third Vice-President of the United States and political rival of Hamilton which led to a duel where Hamilton was killed
JOHN ADAMS, second President of the United States

The Federalist era is important and interesting not only because the present constitutional foundation of the United States was laid in these years, but also because of the personalities who participated in this historic process. The first President of the United States, George Washington, was a man of simplicity and impeccable integrity; his Secretary of State, Thomas Jefferson, possessed democratic visions; and his Secretary of the Treasury, Alexander Hamilton, was an administrative genius. Washington's Vice-President and successor as president, John Adams, added the leavening of political cynicism to the times, while the opportunistic scoundrel Aaron Burr lurked in the background. These men established a nation while at the same time embodying every possible political position and argument.

Hamilton was born and reared in the British West Indies, but had the good fortune to escape the sloth of those islands to enroll at King's College (now Columbia) in New York City in 1773. There he began reading eighteenth century political and economic theory, which inspired him to write in favor of the revolutionary cause of the American colonists. He served in the Revolutionary War and, always anxious to connect himself with persons of importance, managed to get on Washington's staff and to marry Elizabeth Schuyler, a member of a distinguished New York family. At the termination of the conflict, he set up a law practice in New York City, where he often defended loyalists attempting to recover property confiscated during the Revolution.

Hamilton was appalled by the chaotic and selfish nature of American society, which almost lost the revolutionary struggle to Britain, and all of his life he maintained a lively interest in political and economic debates occurring on both sides of the Atlantic. Naturally he entered political life. He participated in the Annapolis convention of 1786, was elected to the New York legislature in 1787, and attended the Philadelphia constitutional convention that same year. He did not take a central role in the drafting of the constitution, although his speeches at Philadelphia indicate that he favored a strong and centralized monarchical form of government for the United States. He was the author of approximately two-thirds of the essays in the *Federalist*, which sought to sway public opinion in favor of ratification of the constitution.

Washington was not a man of great intellect, but he was intelligent enough to know that he needed talented men to help him launch his administration and get the country off on the right foot. Hamilton had demonstrated his abilities while serving on Washington's staff during the war, and hence the president called on him to head the treasury, an appointment which enabled Hamilton to put into effect many of the ideas he had gathered over the years. Hamilton wanted the new nation to repudiate its colonial heritage, wherein a handful of landowners and slaveowners, mostly on the basis of inherited wealth, presided over a stagnant and backward society; he envisioned a dynamic, commercialized, and industrialized country where persons with a talent for creating wealth would govern. He believed that the United States government, properly constituted and supported by propertied elements, would provide the vehicle to transform American society along the lines that he envisioned; hence he introduced initiatives at the treasury on public credit, a national bank, and on manufactures.

In his Reports on Public Credit (1790), Hamilton proposed to Congress that the United States government establish its credit by funding the debts of the states and of the defunct Confederation; that is, he wanted to pay the interest on the debts and gradually pay off the principal with a sinking fund. These debts had for all practical purposes been repudiated during the revolutionary period, leaving American money markets in chaos. Hamilton argued that funding them would at once establish the credit of the government and bind the creditor classes to the government, thus creating a permanent national debt. Such a debt would permanently establish machinery for the transfer of surplus private funds into public and, then in turn, private economic ventures. He also proposed the creation of a national currency in conjunction with the funding of the debts and sent Congress a Report on a National Bank (1790) proposing the establishment of a Bank of the United States, which would be charged with establishing a currency and credit system to aid the economic and financial development of the country. In 1791, his Report on Manufactures proposed a protective tariff to subsidize struggling American industries.

Money, banking, and credit are unfortunately subjects of passionate interest to most people, while few really understand either how these systems work or what possibilities for both good and evil are inherent in such schemes. Hamilton's proposals naturally touched off a storm in Congress, and an opposition of Southern agrarian interests emerged, headed by James Madison of Virginia. After Hamilton agreed that the national capital would be located on the banks of the Potomac River near the lands of these planters, most of his ideas, with the exception of the protective tariff, were adopted and signed into law by Washington.

Hamilton's programs produced the prosperity that he had envisioned; the chaos and inflation of the revolutionary period were finally turned around into stable and solid economic growth. These accomplishments were shortly threatened by the outbreak of war between revolutionary France and Britain, since Hamilton's system rested on the restoration and growth of orderly trade with the mother country and on the collection of import duties to support the activities of the federal government. The United States was also a debtor nation and needed access to the credit markets of Holland which were threatened by French actions. Hamilton counseled Washington to repudiate the alliance with France dating from the American Revolution and to seek a close association with Britain; the President followed Hamilton's advice by issuing a Neutrality Proclamation and sending John Jay to London to negotiate differences with Britain stemming from the revolutionary settlement. Jay's Treaty repaired Anglo-American relations and averted war; Senate approval was extremely difficult, since many American grievances were not satisfied by the treaty, but that approval was finally won.

Hamilton presided over renewed prosperity but personally received very little of it, being a salaried official of the United States government. Hence, feeling that his task essentially was accomplished, he resigned in 1795 and returned to his New York law practice in an effort to repair his private fortunes. Successful in this endeavor, he also continued to advise Washington and the cabinet, and largely composed Washington's Farewell Address for him. He never approved of John Adams, who did not share his vision of a modern industrialized America, and worked against Adams' candidacy in the presidential elections of 1796 and 1800. Adams was elected as Washington's successor in 1796, but in 1800 failed to achieve a majority of the electoral votes.

Historians have generally agreed that Adams possessed many negative characteristics; suspicious of people in general, he really did not belong in politics, even in the eighteenth century, and often neglected the presidency to the point of irresponsibility. He retained Washington's cabinet, which undoubtedly was influenced greatly by Hamilton (although McDonald denies this), and spent entirely too much time at his home in Massachusetts. However, the situation in Europe eventually demanded that he take charge of his office, and once roused he did take the bull by the horns. Following Jay's Treaty, relations with France steadily deteriorated, and Adams' attempts to negotiate with that nation resulted in the infamous XYZ Affair, wherein emissaries of the French government demanded a bribe from the United States as a condition for negotiations. Adams published the correspondence relating to this incident, and a francophobe war fever, which quickly got out of hand, swept the country. Hamilton's response to all this apparently amounted to a scheme to plunge the United States into war against France, since he advocated an American attack upon Spanish Louisiana and Florida. Spain was allied with France, and such an action would effectively have brought the United States into the war on the side of Britain. The national outcry for war against France and for the raising of an army also enabled Hamilton to seek a position of command for himself, which he received with Washington's support.

Adams concluded that Hamilton was using the war hysteria to advance his own political career and that war with France would be an unmitigated disaster for a struggling new nation. He therefore decided to try for negotiations with the French once more, and since the politics of the revolution had shifted yet again, this time he was successful; war was averted with the Franco-American Convention of 1800. This peace arrangement ended Adams' relations with Hamilton as well as his chances for reelection. McDonald's portrait of Adams as an unbalanced and fanatical opponent of Hamilton does not fit with these acts of statesmanship.

No candidate achieved a majority of the electoral votes in the presidential election of 1800, and the election was sent to the House of Representatives for settlement. Adams had no hope of election after Hamilton disowned him, nor did Hamilton have the strength to put through his own choice, Charles Cotesworth Pinckney. The real decision was between Thomas Jefferson and Aaron Burr, two very dissimilar leaders of the opposition to Hamilton's economic and foreign policies. Hamilton concluded that Burr was a political charlatan and that Jefferson would be preferable as president, since once in office his rhetoric would necessarily be tempered by economic and political realities. Hence he brought sufficient pressure on his supporters in the House to effect Jefferson's election, which permanently destroyed his position among Adams' supporters. Burr was selected as vice-president, after having attempted every trick to make himself president in place of Jefferson, whom he had earlier agreed to support. Burr's position within Jefferson's Administration was thus undermined from the start and eventually resulted in his decision to reenter New York politics. Hamilton opposed his New York efforts and made certain statements which resulted in a duel between the two men and Hamilton's death in 1804.

Hamilton's programs were to a considerable extent undone by Jefferson and his successor James Madison, but following the War of 1812 many of them were revived, only to be undone again by Jackson in the 1830's. They were revived a second time by Lincoln and the Republicans during the Civil

War and brought to full fruition during the decades of Republican ascendancy following the destruction of slavery. McDonald regrets that Hamilton's reputation and philosophy have waned during the twentieth century, and that once again Americans prefer stagnation and dependency to individuality and dynamic growth. This statement about Americans may be true, but the reasons underlying such a development are not simple. Hamilton's system rose to success on a great, spacious, and resourceful continent which only awaited population, development, and the proper government to grow. In the course of the twentieth century all this has changed: America is now an overly populated nation with declining resources, confronting a world in which every nation faces problems equally severe, and in most cases much more severe, than her own. Hence, no nation is in a mood to give over its resources cheaply, and most Americans quite naturally feel increasingly helpless before such a situation. It should be possible to reorganize and overcome this predicament, but more will be needed than Hamilton's ideas on encouraging individual initiative or Jefferson's on upholding individual freedom. Both of these concepts are still important ingredients in maintaining human freedom, but they alone will not solve the problem of organizing and taming the gigantic public and private bureaucracies, both national and international in scope, which at once provide us with our standard of living and threaten our individual freedoms and initiatives.

Jack L. Calbert

THE ANARCHISTS' CONVENTION

Author: John Sayles
Publisher: Little, Brown and Company (Boston). 313 pp. $9.95
Type of work: Short stories
Time: The present
Locale: The United States, Indonesia, and Vietnam

A collection of fifteen short stories which reveals glimpses of a special segment of modern American society: the losers

This collection of stories is animated by a cast of characters of rich and fascinating diversity. They are not attractive characters, at least not in the usual sense of being people one would like to know. In a success-oriented society, as the United States is, the losers are by definition a repellent lot. And these are stories about the losers, the people operating outside the guidelines for success, the people lacking access to the mainstream middle class, or opting out for one reason or another. They are anarchists, by choice or by circumstance, living in a state of confusion or disorder and at odds with the mores and rules of society. Some are victims, caught up in a web of circumstances beyond their control and struggling for survival in a grim and absurdly cruel world where one may be first rejected and then punished for being an outcast. Those who are not victims are the defiant ones, the people who turn their backs on the social order and their prescribed role to seek a different way—to follow a dream.

This book of stories is truly an anarchists' convention. A stunning assortment of losers is gathered together here, where we may join them in their stories for an interlude of revelation, an episode of crisis, or a brief moment of compassionate understanding. The fifteen stories in this collection are divided into three groups. The first group, comprising six stories, is a kaleidoscope of impressions of a remarkably diverse group of characters. The jungles of Indonesia, a town in Vietnam, and the broad expanse of the United States are the settings, but the people could be from anywhere, going anywhere. They are transients, forming brief superficial attachments, wistfully yearning for something they lack, whether it be affection, achievement, or excitement.

There is a special pathos in many of the stories, for the theme of rejection recurs again and again. Michael, in "The Cabinetmaker," plots his furtive departure from Laura, who is ardently hopeful about a new and lasting relationship after the breakup of her marriage. Janey conquers a 7-10 split as a heroic gesture of defiance against her impending lonely old age ("The 7-10 Split"); but the reader knows, as does Janey, that the loneliness and the aging will overwhelm her in time, as they have her friend and mentor, Evelyn. The subtlety and complexity of the human spirit is also depicted well in "Schiffman's Ape," where the critical situation is resolved through displacement. The bowling game and the observations of the ape are the symbols of the crises and resolutions which engage these characters' efforts. The characters are very human; their strengths are barely staunch enough to support their frailties, and their pathos is almost but not quite outweighed by their irritating ways. The excitement of these stories arises from the characters' passionate commitment; they are totally committed, whether by choice or circumstance, to the course of events taking place. They have no reservations, no second thoughts. The outcome is thus more devastating, because, since the commitment is total, the loss is also total. Rejection, loneliness, and inadequacy are the threads from which the tales are woven. The characters are young and old and mostly poor; they share the same wistful needs, and they bear their misery with a dignity and forbearance which ennobles them.

Sayles is adept at writing about both the young and the old, but he clearly feels most at home with youth, and his second group of stories has as the central character a teenage boy coming to maturity and an understanding of the world through his various encounters and travels. The set of six stories takes the youth from the East coast to the West, and the stories narrate his progress much in the manner of the traditional apprenticeship novel; the only difference is that these stories are episodic and are clearly intended to stand alone. "Bad Dogs" introduces Brian to the treachery of some dogs and some girls. In "Hoop" he learns about the attitudes and actions of men and boys and is confirmed in his isolation and singularity. The third story documents his decision to leave, and sketches the leave-taking scene with his mother. The brief, incomplete constructions of the sentences, the lack of transitions, and the inability of the mother and son to communicate are all superbly meshed into a stylized, staccato rhythm—a throbbing impulse to escape, which is nearly as incoherent as is his explanation to his mother of where he is going and why. The final three stories in this section document encounters with bizarre characters Brian meets in his travels, as they gamely or even defiantly cope with the struggle for existence.

The final group of three stories depicts the destruction of three lives—one literally, one through abuse, and one through annihilation of a dreamworld. The story of Tan documents the degradation of a young Vietnamese girl whose survival is secured only by her acquiesence to being used by various men. Her progressive loss of identity and self-respect are devastating, and the final surrender of her sense of self is equated with her consenting to have her eyes operated on so that she will look less oriental. Her identity is the real treasure she is losing, but it is accompanied by the loss of a cache of opium which had been implanted in her breasts, opium which she regards as "the last of Vietnam locked inside her." This sensitive narrative documents the series of events which progressively undermines the girl's sense of self-worth and finally destroys her hope for any better future. The viewpoint of the impassive, objectively detached narrator reinforces the theme of helplessness and the conception of Tan as the victim struggling alone to survive the cruelties of men and society. This story, like many of the others, is also rich in implied social criticism. These people struggle against or cope as best they can with a system which is harsh toward misfits, and both scornful and vindictive toward those who reject its system and its values.

The final story in the collection, "I-80 Nebraska, m.490-m.205," won an O. Henry Prize for excellence. It is a narrative related through the conversations of truckers talking over their CB's as they skirt Lincoln and head on out into the black Nebraska night. The truckers and the "smokies" are being taunted by a trucker whom they can neither identify nor find. The clues over the CB, the guesses and frustrated attempts to find and identify the mysterious Ryder P. Moses, culminate in a wild and dogged chase down the interstate to the inevitable doom of the mischievous and inventive wraith of the highway—who is also, as it turns out, a pill-popping loner on his final high.

The other story in this final group details the closing night's performance of a theater which had been dedicated to playing old classic movies. The nostalgia and the grim tasks the manager must perform as he executes the changeover to an "adult" movie house are interwoven with painful precision. The story indicates that the movies serve as a microcosm for the changes going on in society as a whole. We are moving, it suggests, from a simpler, more wholesome view of life to a sordid one motivated largely by greed.

Sayles has a gift for matching personalities to situations. His people seem inevitably suited to their circumstances; they act, react, and interact with never a false move or an unpredictable gesture. Mastery of dialogue is perhaps Sayles' best single achievement. He has a cultivated ear for dialect, which is especially well represented in "Home for Wayfarers." He also reproduces an authentic rhythm and idiom of speech which befits his characters superbly. The CB conversations are particularly compelling examples, but this quality is generously present in all of his stories. There is little humor in this collection. One finds occasional flashes of wit, but more often the tone is ironic and somewhat bitter.

John Sayles has given us a series of intense and vivid confrontations with a group of people who are strong, resilient, and brave because they must be. He presents them with gentle compassions and clear-eyed realism. His hallmark is authenticity; his strength is dialogue; his greatness is the hungry passion for life which illuminates these tales.

Betty Gawthrop

AS WE KNOW

Author: John Ashbery (1927-   )
Publisher: The Viking Press (New York). 118 pp. $12.50; paperback $7.95
Type of work: Poetry

A fine collection by one of America's premier poets which delves into what it means to be conscious

"There is another world," writes the French poet Paul Eluard, "and it is in this one." Plotting itineraries from *Some Trees* through *The Tennis Court Oath*, *Rivers and Mountains*, *Fragments*, and *The Double Dream of Spring*, and from *Three Poems* through *Self-Portrait in a Convex Mirror*, *The Vermont Notebook*, *Houseboat Days*, and finally *As We Know*, one finds Eluard's idea as the central and interconnecting theme in the corpus of Ashbery's poetic work. The first poem, *Litany*, in the present collection of poems opens: "For some one like me/The simple things/Like having toast or/Going to church. . . ./Like having wine and cheese,/The parents of the town/Pissing elegantly. . . ./The casual purring of a donkey" as well as "The/Snapdragons consumed in a wind" do "rouse me from my accounts." He is fully aware of the "lived eventualities/That torment our best intentions" and "the epidemic of the way we live now"—the "disorderly house" of our "drab existences." Yet he wishes "to retain my kinship/To the rest," while keeping "my difference," as he writes in *Litany*.

Although he writes in "The Preludes" that he is "trapped in the principle of the great beyond" in this checkerboard space of our world, he says, "I no longer have any metaphysical reasons/For doing the things I do." And while, in the same poem, he concludes that "we are all ushered in—/Into the presence that explains," in "Their Day" he realizes that

> From these boxed perimeters
> We issue forth irregularly. Sometimes in fear,
> But mostly with no knowledge of knowing, only a general
> But selective feeling that the world had to go on being good
> to us.

In "Haunted Landscape," Ashbery comments,

> But you wanted to know why so much action took on so
> much life
> And still managed to remain itself, aloof, smiling and
> courteous.
> Is that the way life is supposed to happen? We'll probably
> never know.

Combined with a "passionate intelligence," a deep, self-reflective, exploratory attitude and a skeptical honesty sustain *As We Know*, instead of any kind of metaphysical reverie or speculative enchantment. With an incredible range of inventive vocabulary and verbal postures reminiscent of John Berryman, Ashbery continues his "immense journey" (*Fragments*) in the midst of "intimidated solitude and isolation" (*Fragments*), and, he says in the *Self-Portrait in a Convex Mirror*, "deep into the midst of things." *Some Trees* talks of "We see us as we truly behave," but in this volume the focus is on "as we know." Even then there is that skepticism, tentativeness, and a meditative humility in Ashbery's thinking—"We shall never recognize our true reflections," and "One can never change the core of things" (*The Tennis Court Oath*). Because of this sense of reality and self, his powerful and dense long poem, *Litany*, ends not in any kind of speculative flight or metaphysical abstraction, but on a mundane note.

Even though Ashbery claims words are the "total environment" and "An idea I had and talked about/Became the things I do," the final lines in "Tapestry" raise a different question: "As words go crying after themselves,/leaving the dream/Upended in a puddle somewhere/As though 'dead' were just another adjective." Yet *"Fools rush into my head, and so I write,"* Ashbery remarks in *Litany*. To tell, to communicate, to express becomes unavoidable and urgent for the poet.

> We must first trick the idea
> Into being, then dismantle it,
> Scattering the pieces on the wind,
> So that the old joy, modest as cake, as wine and friendship
> Will stay with us at the last, backed by the night
> Whose ruse gave it our final meaning.

It is no wonder, then, that Ashbery's last book of poems before *As We Know* had already anticipated the first poem of the present collection, *Litany*.

Despite the "unprepared knowledge/Of ourselves" and *"Antithesis chirping/To antithesis,"* despite "meaningless/Rolling and lurching" in this "ambiguous space" of our existence, Ashbery, the indefatigable beginner, does not escape into silence. This is because existence "is a part of all being, and is . . . to be prized" (*The Double Dream of Spring*). Nor does he indulge in lyric abstraction. As *"Histoire Universelle"* states, "To free speech is an aspect of the dream and of Dreamland/In general that asserts an even larger/View of the universe. . . ." Further, he states in *Litany* that "In the beginning of speech the question/Of frontiers is taken up again." So, when we return to "As We Know," we return to the "small capitulations/Of the dance." "Life is not really for the squeamish either." Articulation, communication, the power of the word becomes for Ashbery a holy and human essential—"There is a central crater/Which is the word." After all, litany is a chant, a song, that connects two and more.

Litany as well as several other poems in the volume do not lead us to any

climactic ascensions, but dare us to epiphanic "ecstasy and apprehension"—
an intensification of momentary consciousness and an exploration of history,
reality, and life. Ashbery defines his poetry in the *New York Quarterly* interview as "consciously trying to explore consciousness." There is, one could
say, a radical corporeality and radical immaterialism in these poems which
we have already experienced in his *The Double Dream of Spring* and *Self-
Portrait in a Convex Mirror*. *Litany*, a variation on the original theme, is also
an improvisation on other recurrent motifs—time, history, flux, death, beginning, voyaging, knowing, and writing. The diastolic movement of this two-
columned, seventy-page-long poem creates a mood of destiny, transformation, and equilibrium. The "carnivorous/Way of these lines is to devour their
own nature, leaving/Nothing but a bitter impression of absence, which as we
know/involves presence." The language and style of the poem appropriate
a kind of daringness, materiality, and sublimity. Ashbery appears, in his own
words, as an "adventurous acolyte" offering us a "task and vision, vision in
the form of a task" on "the threshold of so much unmeaning, so much/Being"
(*Fragments*). What is remarkable is that the poem becomes its own creation,
a means of transformation and awareness: "code names for the silence," both
"in an explosion of surprise" and by a "great implosion," in the words of the
poem.

In the same *New York Quarterly* interview, Ashbery explains his own methodology of writing poetry. "My poetry," he remarks, "doesn't have subjects";
so, "fluidity of thought rather than objects of thought" informs it, and frequently the poems comment "on themselves . . . therefore the methodology
occasionally coincides with the subject." *Litany* resonates with such meditations as the personal and "the other" and the particular and the general
interpenetrate and the poem acquires another dimension—of recognition,
cognition, and recollection. The italicized column of the poem in its second
movement is devoted to an intense reflection on poetry and criticism and
their significance in our lives. Poetry is constantly happening, and so is criticism, for both are inextricably connected with us and in us; and the "*tale/Is
still so magnificent in the telling*" in the face of uncertainties and failures. This
telling is conjugated with the concept of the thing itself, be it an object or
idea—"The artifice lets it become itself,/Nestling in truth."

Regarding joy, Ashbery writes, "it was not joy/But rather something more
like the concept of joy,/I was able to experience it like a fruit/One peels,
then eats." Peeling and participating, reaching into the very kernel:

> There comes a time when the moment
> is full of, knows only itself.
> ....
> ....
> To know itself, and to know everything else
> As well, . . .

This is the "sudden moment of maturity," which is "suffused with a kinetic/ purpose." The purpose, according to Ashbery, is the question of the "frontier"—his own question: *"But what shall clean me within?"* And his answer, total and epiphanic, is: *"The way to nothing/Is the way to all things."* Not a matter of epistemology, but of *kenosis*, which is "something like/Grace, in the long run, which is what poetry is."

Deba P. Patnaik

ASHES
Poems New & Old

Author: Philip Levine (1928-   )
Publisher: Atheneum Publishers (New York). 66 pp. $4.95 (paperback)
Type of work: Poetry

A combination of poems which comprise a remarkably unified statement about losses, about being lost, and about being found

Ashes surpasses anything Philip Levine has done before, confirming both the craft and commitment of his previous seven books. Critics who have cited his "horror poems" in previous books and sometimes found his recitation of "the barbarities of our time" little more than old-fashioned will be startled at Levine's use of horror in *Ashes*. Muting his voice, varying his forms, and building upon repeated words and images, Levine takes the reader through a series of increasingly painful tensions to sum up a significant part of what it means to be sensitive to life in the final quarter of the twentieth century. Consistently tough and precise, the poems in *Ashes* mean what they say, but they suggest far more than they say. In the poems, the reader finds a poet both real and palpable.

The poet of *Ashes* avoids the exhibitionism of the confessional writers, but he does not hesitate to reveal a person and a personality. His total craft gives us the theme of his book and the person of the poet. Never does the reader feel that he should respond because the poet has bared himself; instead, the reader is likely to respond because the poet has struck the reader's nerve. At the same time, Levine's book avoids the merely skillful. The effect is cumulative, and the reader may have difficulty accounting for his emotional response. One critic, speaking of this quality of Levine's work, observed that analysis seems beside the point—one wants to quote whole poems. So sensitively and adroitly do these poems cohere that one wishes to quote an entire collection.

Levine has ordered older poems from a private press book, *Red Dust* (1971), to play against new poems which provide a personal, but not confessional, story line of a man moving from fatherlessness to fathered, from lost to found. The personal gains are hard-won; they do not represent the poet's cheering himself up. The book's conclusion is poignantly tentative, but amounts to a small victory—what the late Robert Frost would call a "momentary stay against confusion." *Ashes* reaches, and earns, a place to begin from.

In 1963, American novelist John Hawkes defined the avant-garde and specified its quality of "coldness, detachment, ruthless determination to face up to the enormities of ugliness and potential failure within ourselves and the world around us." Hawkes added that the avant-garde writer brings to this exposure "a savage or saving comic spirit and the saving beauties of language." Hawkes describes perfectly what Philip Levine's poems accomplish.

Ashes arises from an age of displacement and rootlessness. The poet's sensibility has been shaped by the fact of the destructive power of the atomic and hydrogen bombs, and, unlike writers who came after him, he has not yet come to live comfortably in an age of apocalypse. Levine has no ideology to offer, no formal elaborations intended to comfort; he has only the awareness of "enormities of ugliness" and the possibility of beauty, both natural and verbal. What Levine offers is adequate.

Ashes summons up much of the malaise of the present, but the book's central consciousness, the poet, is working toward understanding. He is not content with vague complaints or with heroic stances. The "I" of these thirty-two poems scarcely resembles the professionally neurotic confessional poet anxious to announce his or her personal ontological anguish. In crafting the individual poems and the larger poem of the total book, the author of *Ashes* obviously learned about himself and his world and can therefore teach. This teaching takes the form of shared experience; the poet resists didacticism as well as confessionalism. One must be grateful when craft leads to even partial resolution.

Thirteen of the poems in *Ashes* come from *Red Dust*; the rest are new, but the totality does not appear contrived. Levine has not "padded out" a book with either new or old poems. The old and the new function together, for Levine has created new poems to provide a context for the sense of loss and anger apparent in the older poems. He weds the whole through persistent but subtle reiteration of words and images. The result is a landscape and mindscape both familiar and strange. The older poems generalize; the new ones particularize and make personal.

The lack of a father and the search for a father unify the story line of *Ashes*, and recurring words and images underline that unity. The opening poem, appropriately called "Fathers," states the theme. It also introduces images important throughout. The setting is Michigan, famed for its cars; the earth is "sick on used oils." Rain brings both fear and hope. The poet—a child at forty-three—finds his father beside "a mason jar of dried zinnias," but he turns away from what he has found. The poem ends with an imperative—"Don't come back." The last poem, "Lost and Found," resolves this conflict.

"Clouds," an older poem, follows "Fathers" and opens with an allusion to zinnias and includes images of oil and rain. With his opening poems, Levine establishes themes which the rest of the book will develop. Few of the poems in Part I are new, but all serve the book's total scheme. "The Miracle," for example, gives impetus to the yellow and golden imagery which recurs throughout the book; the poem treats a mother's acceptance of a son's death and the impact of that acceptance upon another son, who at the end looks out on the world he "always sees" and thinks "it's a miracle." *Ashes* is full of such miracles, all made real.

The middle poem in Part I, "The Rains," brings back the fear of loss, death, and abandonment established in the opening poem, but it also looks forward to the gains of the final poem, "Lost and Found." Further, "The Rains" balances against "The Water's Chant," a poem which begins the build-up of Part II. These interrelationships are intricate but effective; they are what we have come to expect of Philip Levine's books.

In "The Rains," a child fears flood and is comforted because Papa has said it will not flood. Still, the child wonders how he will get home from school, and, once home, alone ". . . calling/out the names/of those I lived with," he thinks the cold empty house is all he has—until he hears a brother stamping his boots on the mat. Later in the poem, the poet and his wife walk in silence among the pines in a world they cannot see and which they have "sourced" by not giving enough love. The world, dark "with oils and fire," remains one they could "have come to call home." This is not the only poem in which Levine calls attention to possibilities. The final poem in Part I, "Any Night," ends with the statement about a child "far from home, lost" that "he could be happy."

At the end of "The Rains," husband and wife are hand in hand (as father and child will be in the book's final poem); they move toward identity—the joy or sadness they have no name for. At the moment of transcendence, their faces stream with "the sweet waters/of heaven." Later, in "The Water's Chant," the poet's prayer for death concludes with an act of communion and with acceptance of the mundane. Resonance of imagery, the insistence of golden color, the swaying eucalyptus tree, a cumulative effect of many poems, prepares for the final triumph and intensifies its rightness.

Two new poems conclude Part I and extend the book's plot line. The penultimate poem ("I Won, You Lost") gives us a "yellow parlor," "an old man's room," to which the poet returns realizing "Something is missing." What is lacking is "the music a boy would laugh/at until it went out." This poem prepares for the finality of childhood's loss, and of death—both stated in the book's climactic poem, "Lost and Found."

The last poem in Part I ("Any Night") imagines a time when the birds "learned/to fly backwards" and thus ended the "chorus of love." Again, Levine speaks of loss—the absence of song, which drives the poet to sing and to think of a boy who "could be happy." That boy is perhaps the poet, who prays now—not for death, as in "The Water's Chant," but that "in time/ we find our lives."

Ashes moves toward a time in which all of us can find our lives, and by doing so be able to give enough love that the world will not be soured. Part II opens with a poem called "Starlight," which returns the reader to the father-son theme. The poet, age four, is with his father on a warm evening. The child does not understand his father's question "Are you happy," but smells tiredness on his father's breath. "Starlight" transports the reader to a magical "as though" state. At the poem's end, the father holds the child as though the stars "might find a tall, gaunt child/holding his child against the promises/of autumn, until the boy slept/ never to waken in that world again." The father and child are one under the stars, but neither can wake to the world's potential.

In "Lost and Found," the final poem in *Ashes*, the poet has "come home from being lost," and the father, "the one I searched for," is home too. We, "father and child/hand in hand, the living and/the dead, are entering the world." The entire volume has worked toward the acceptance expressed in the final poem. To prepare for that poem, Levine began to intensify with a tersely surreal poem called "The Red Shirt," the epigraph of which speaks of unread poems as "dust, wind, nothing, 'like the insolent colored shirt he bought to die in.' " The epigraph is from Vargas Llosa. A shirt to die in, Levine's red shirt, is also one to live in while waiting to die. The poem is a wonderful blend of logic and illogic, of the carefully perceived and the irrationally imagined. The final lines of "The Red Shirt" return the reader to Levine's preoccupation with stones and other mute things—a field of "great rocks weeping,/and no one to see/me alone, day after/day in my red shirt."

The creation may be insensible, as Levine clearly imagines it, but our dying takes place in the world with no one to see. Perhaps we should not call it dying, but living. Levine seeks no easy affirmation, and the next several poems challenge the reader to endure the reality necessary for both living and dying. The poem, "On a Drawing by Flavio," refers to, but does not depend upon, the cover illustration for *Ashes*, by Flavio Costantini, which obliges the poet and reader to identify with the Rabbi of Auschwitz. The horrors of the twentieth century return, but again the poet insists on acceptance of the body even as it is "closing on/death." The poet realizes that the Rabbi's face is his own and that the Rabbi's "tapering fingers" reach for "our father's hand/long gone to dirt." The Rabbi's fingers hold "hand to forearm,/ forearm to hand because/that is all that God/gave us to hold."

The point is clear; we may and must hold to the things of this world, for that is what God gave us. We cannot whimper to God. The poet manifests his concern. In "The Water's Chant," he felt for his brother thickened and aged by meaningless work. In "Ashes," he felt for migrant workers, but, at final analysis, Levine tells us that the Self must accept identity and enter the world. That entry occurs in "Lost and Found," and the book ends triumphantly.

What has Levine accomplished? He has personalized, without trivializing, his general awareness of loss and displacement. He has tied together thirty-two poems with personal diction and syntax. He has made real a world of zinnias, eucalyptus trees, oil, a world of yellow and yellowing, of gold and golden. He has linked a bruised river with people bruised by the sun. He has revitalized the quest for a father and the meaning of life which accepts the world, but does not compromise.

In *Ashes*, Philip Levine has ritualized loss and has made *being found* a profound human experience. Levine has made a book which speaks to today.

Leon Driskell

THE AVOIDANCE OF LITERATURE
Collected Essays

Author: C. H. Sisson
Edited by Michael Schmidt
Publisher: Carcanet Press/Persea Books (New York). 581 pp. $20.00
Type of work: Essays

Sisson's essays, arranged in chronological order, covering topics from social and political criticism to literary criticism

C. H. Sisson's *The Avoidance of Literature* gives the educated, considerate reader much to consider. The point of view of the essays is conservative amid the growth of twentieth century British liberalism. The work of a poet, it touches the heart of twentieth century poetry (including the work of Pound, Eliot, and Yeats). It probes the thoughts and growth of Sisson the poet, finding some poetic truths while documenting a nonacademic rhetorical stance markedly consistent in its development. Editor Michael Schmidt presents readers with an interestingly mixed collection of C. H. Sisson's works, obviously hoping to expose the British poet-critic-essayist's varied concerns. Consequently, more than forty years of reviews, essays, editorials, and introductions comprise the volume (which excludes Sisson's poetry and fiction). Arranged chronologically with a few exceptions, these writings assess twentieth century life and literature from an interesting perspective through some of the century's most turbulent years. While Sisson's views are decidedly British, those of a conservative Tory, they are, if anything, sharp identifications of what has pricked the conscience of modern Britain. Throughout the volume, Sisson calls for a firm order, one based in long-established traditions, one mindful of the immense Anglican heritage, and one including the monarchy, strong state-church relationships, and a bountiful literature.

To this literature, Sisson, being a poet, often turns for an essay subject. He especially reveres Ezra Pound, and he borrows heavily from Pound's intellect. In Sisson's development, T. S. Eliot also figures prominently, as do Ford Madox Ford and Wyndham Lewis. Schmidt goes so far as to say that these four "define the tradition in which Sisson writes." Readers will find Sisson astute in examining this formidable tradition because he is precise in extracting key concepts to synthesize.

Sisson's critical method is to reveal an author's background to place his work in historical and social perspective. Sisson knows that literature cannot be separated from the world of the producer and the world of the reader, and he knows that his approach enriches our understanding; but he avoids ironclad proclamations about sources and influences. Rather, he approaches each work with commonsense questions about where the author was, whom he had encountered, how these encounters might have led to certain effects in the literature, and what implications those effects hold for later readers.

He thus reveals something of the prejudices of the writer, something about how the mind was likely to assimilate and embellish particular events or influences. In the cases of Eliot and Pound, where literary debts and influences become badges of accomplishment and textual notes are a matter of course, Sisson's approach takes us a long way toward understanding subtleties in the works. A poet himself, Sisson sensitively penetrates the maze of influences and personal bits of detail. Avoiding overindulgence in fact-finding and extra detail for its own sake, he instead clarifies literary allusions by establishing their contexts.

The sensitive approach becomes a sensible approach, revealing the developing trends in an author's work. Of Pound, for example, Sisson says, "his crucial didactic works are essential for anyone who wants to understand the aims of his poetry and the nature of his contribution to the poetry of the century." Pound, after all, was the most eclectic of readers and exerted immense influence on his contemporaries. (Sisson notes the revisions in Eliot's *The Waste Land* and Yeats's debts in his later works as evidence.) Pound, furthermore, read with vision and was able to give his own and others' verse the occasional infusion that would change poetry's direction in the twentieth century. Sisson says, for example, that Pound's work with Chinese and Japanese translations provided an "aid to concentration of language," an idea central to Pound's poetic formulations and what was to be called the Imagist movement. This concentration had far-reaching effects and surely appears in Yeats's work after the period Yeats and Pound spent together, when Pound, working on Ernest Fenollosa's notes, enthralled Yeats with the Japanese Noh theater.

Whatever the effect Pound's reading had on others, it remains clear that delving into obscure texts was his passion. Also clear are his severe standards and sharp reactions. The "great merit of Pound's work," according to Sisson, is "that he declares unashamedly what does not interest him and searches out, sometimes in unlikely corners, work which is capable of contributing to the pleasure and the poetics of his own time." To an extent, Sisson shares this great merit and bluntly states his own preferences.

At one point, for example, in "Some Reflections on American Poetry," Sisson almost echoes Pound when he says, "I have never been an academic and happily have not had to read very far in poets who do not interest me." Generally uncomplimentary to all nineteenth century American poetry, he does commend a few poems by Edgar Allan Poe for their incomparable effects, but toward Whitman he is scathing. Whitman appears to him an untidy lout, "a lout of the western Protestant decadence, not of a civilization still refining itself." Sisson wants to put Emily Dickinson in a class with Christina Rossetti, "herself a writer of great unevenness." But for some reason, he singles out Herman Melville's poetry for praise, liking "a quality of liveliness, a sense that it is the real world he is celebrating, and that he cares for the people he is celebrating." Sisson's comments, which are those of a fairly conservative British poet and critic, will strike most American readers as odd, although many readers are likely to agree with his judging of most nineteenth century American poets as "eminently dispensable."

Sisson's comments on twentieth century American poets are just as pointed and certain to stir mixed reaction. He admits bluntly that he cannot "stomach" Wallace Stevens, while recognizing how inflammatory such a statement is. That he finds Stevens' work "pernicious" is interesting to consider, but he chooses not to explain except to say he "can imagine few less rewarding tasks than disentangling the threads of what [Stevens] thought he had to say." Later Sisson elaborates reasons for not being very aware of a great many American poets and for not paying those he has encountered much attention. He believes one's contemporaries and juniors have neither stood the test of time nor the test of influence, except with notable exceptions, and so are less awe-inspiring than they might be. He mentions a list of eight rather well-known modern and contemporary American poets, only to dismiss them with, "it would have made no difference to me if they had not written." Citing Dante, he asserts that the critical reception of such poets is inconsequential for lacking temporal distance. (In fact, he seems to disparage American critics generally for taking themselves and contemporary American poetry too seriously.) Sisson does name six poets who have given him some degree of pleasure— William Carlos Williams, Robert Frost, John Crowe Ransom, Marianne Moore, Allen Tate, and H. D.—although he qualifies several of these selections.

Sisson's prejudices are evident, his Tory bearing firmly intact as he moves to conclude his reflections with an interesting assertion: that no division exists between English and American poetry. He maintains that "a literature is the literature of a language," and that "the phenomenon of literary separatism is based on shifts of the centres of political power, and nothing else." According to Sisson, such shifts and any geographical distance from England do not deny the tradition of English literature, and poets who attempt to deny that tradition weaken their stance. Perhaps at no other point in *The Avoidance of Literature* so much as in "Some Reflections on American Poetry" is Sisson's remoteness from America and Americans so noticeable.

Readers who want to understand Sisson's relation to tradition and the remoteness of his stance should follow editor Schmidt's advice to read the essays "Natural History" and "Autobiographical Reflections on Politics" at the outset. As Schmidt says, this will "help to define a voice and the source and character of its authority." Ultimately, perhaps, these may be the most interesting essays in the collection. Taken together with scattered statements from other essays in the book, these two pieces reveal a developing poet behind the essayist, the man of letters within a strong tradition. Throughout his career, Sisson has asserted the necessary task of all educated men: to participate in the world of action. That the literary realm gives a somewhat distorted view of truth Sisson recognizes, and at one point, in an essay on William Barnes, he says, "the avoidance of literature is indispensable for the man who wants to tell the truth." He holds literary art in high esteem, however, even though he recognizes its limited powers in the current age. In "Natural History" he expresses this relationship: "in some sense poetry is secondary, a series of glimpses on a journey, which you would not have had if you had taken another journey. Nonetheless, most of the business of life is trivial by comparison."

For Sisson, a sort of double life enshrouds the artist, and it is to penetrate this duplicity that the poet must work. For Sisson, telling the truth has considerable importance; it becomes a key tactic in this act of penetrating and of establishing the artist's foundation. When he gives advice to young writers, it concerns the nature of literary truth: "write about something about which you have some truth to tell." Later he presents a sort of credo: "to know when one has some truth to tell is in a way the whole tact of the poet—a sort of shyness he has to use in his own mind." Considering Sisson's reverence for Pound and Eliot and his conservative leanings, readers will recognize the implications of such statements. Much in contemporary art seems not to be the telling of truths.

Furthermore, from Sisson's perspective, twentieth century liberalism has failed to develop from truthful perceptions of the world. In his essay called "The Case of Walter Bagehot," for example, Sisson takes strong exception to E. M. Forster saying that his world is "really a pleasure-garden, for those who care for that sort of pleasure and can afford high walls to live behind." He objects, it seems, to the lack of credibility within Forster's brand of liberalism. Moreover, he certainly implies a moral objection when he says that liberalism

> reached an intense florescence under the roof of King's College, Cambridge, in the twentieth century, when personal relations, without even the degree of natural realism which is imparted by the phenomena of heterosexuality, were amusingly believed to hold a primacy over the prejudices not only of religion but of patriotism.

Sisson's conservative stance is evident, but evident, too, is his belief that the corporate affairs of men demand realistic attention if the literary man is to speak the truth. He sees Forster's liberalism as fragile because "liberalism does not flourish except within safe frontiers," and the world described by Forster and his circle is indeed an isolated, safe one "that allows a few soft people so to amuse themselves, and to consume what others have sweated or got themselves killed for."

Sisson's comments mark him as clearly opposed to idyllic notions, especially concerning the foundations of political thought; but he seems to desire a clear separation of issues literary from issues political. In an editorial from *PN*

Review, for example, he addresses the entire problem of censorship and freedom of expression, a struggle prevalent in the twentieth century, finding it peripheral to literature's development. He asserts: "the right to say things which are politically and morally offensive has more to do with politics and commerce than with literature." This comment underscores Sisson's conservative stance and remains consistent with his concern for the preservation of the English inheritance.

Undeniably, this inheritance rests upon a base of good writing, and in this tradition, too, Sisson participates. His fluid style finds its rhythms easily, although there are instances when sentence structure gets overcomplicated; Sisson reads best when he gets closest to the reader in a reserved informality and worst when he strikes a somewhat pedantic tone. Even in his most literary investigations, however, he avoids delving too technically and manages to meet the layman's needs. No matter what his subjects, he treats them sensibly in the reserved manner so characteristically British yet with insights uniquely his own. Sisson's essays should be read by more readers than probably will read them, especially American readers. He speaks with a voice not often heard on this continent and balances the demonstrably narrow vision presented by writers more widely read, such as Forster. While his eloquence and witty humor fall short of Forster's, Sisson, it seems, manages in *The Avoidance of Literature* to present some truth, and for that his readers will find a use.

Gary B. Blank

THE BAKKE CASE
The Politics of Inequality

Authors: Joel Dreyfuss and Charles Lawrence III (1943-   )
Publisher: Harcourt Brace Jovanovich (New York). 278 pp. $8.95; paperback $3.95
Type of work: History
Time: 1972-1978
Locale: The United States

An analysis of a landmark Supreme Court Decision concerning "reverse discrimination"

Principal personages:
ALLAN BAKKE, a man who was denied admittance to the University of California at Davis Medical School
PETER STORANDT, Assistant Dean of Student Affairs at U. C. Davis
REYNOLD H. COLVIN, Bakke's attorney in the case
ARCHIBALD COX, the lawyer who represented U. C. Davis before the Supreme Court

This book is an extraordinarily lucid and perceptive account that analyzes more than the legal dimensions of this landmark case. Of the copious writing that has been done on the *Bakke* case, it is one of the few that gets close to the principals in this legal drama and probes underlying human and societal issues shrouded by convoluted trial arguments and tactics. The authors brilliantly contend that "reverse discrimination" and race were not the fundamental issues. Rather, the broader questions were the increasingly limited number of career opportunities offered to the middle class, the fierce competition for access to those available, and the growing consensus among white Americans that the nation's once rampant racial inequality had been resolved.

Allan Bakke's case was simple and direct. He argued that the University of California at Davis Medical School, in an attempt to correct racial injustices of the segregated past, had set aside sixteen places in each entering class for members of minority groups. Because he was white, Bakke was prevented from competing for those sixteen places. He contended that because his grades and test scores were higher than those of many minority students, he was better qualified to become a physician; but his aspirations had been thwarted by the issue of color.

Thus, the *Bakke* case posed a serious dilemma for America's white majority. It represented a confrontation of two basic concepts: equality as a theoretical right and equality as a reality. To make a place for those held back for generations by discrimination, some members of the majority would have to give way. To critics of affirmative action, this "reverse discrimination" was simply unjust; but to do nothing was to sentence entire generations of black, brown, and poor people to suffer permanently the effects of inequality.

The authors present the case on several levels. They attempt to describe the key characters in the drama, namely the attorneys who represent the case's respective sides. This biographical-journalistic dimension is supplemented by a firm grasp of the facts in the case and the trial strategies adopted by the contending parties. Finally, Dreyfuss and Lawrence probe the large societal issues raised by the case and reflect upon the changes in American racial dynamics during the 1970's.

The first one-third section of the book is the strongest; it details the case through its review by the California Supreme Court. The author's prodigious research unearthed some intriguing, thought-provoking aspects of its history. For example, the authors reveal that Peter Storandt, the university's thirty-year-old Assistant Dean of Academic Affairs, had a central role early in the drama. His meetings with Bakke and their exchange of letters no doubt encouraged the prospective student to sue. He provided a sympathetic ear, crucial information about the school's admission procedures, and important advice on the legal strategy Bakke would follow thereafter.

The authors' tedious analysis of the school's admissions policies and procedures point out the arbitrariness and subjectivity of the system. The ramulose procedure may in fact have discriminated against Bakke on the basis of his age (Bakke was in his early thirties when he applied). Furthermore, the dean, in deference to political and class considerations, could override the procedure and virtually admit whom he wanted. It is unfortunate that the authors do not further explore the inequities in the school's admissions.

The authors also offer some titillating criticism of the handling of the case by the university's attorneys. The lawyers were seemingly hampered by an ambivalence about the central issues. Reynold Colvin, Bakke's talented and homespun Jewish lawyer, is given high marks for his shrewd handling of the case and his dogged devotion to his client's fundamental interest. It is clear from the book that Bakke's decision to sue was based upon a genuine desire to become a doctor; he was neither a seeker of publicity nor a dupe of a lawyer's efforts to pursue a landmark case. Until the very eve of the initial trial, Colvin attempted to negotiate Bakke's admittance, but the university relentlessly sought a ruling on the constitutionality of the admissions program.

The essence of the case was whether race or ethnicity could be taken into consideration in selecting applicants for the medical school. The authors chronicle the litany of missed opportunities by the university's lawyers that aided Bakke's victory in the Yolo County Court. The judge ruled that there was no compelling public purpose to be served by granting preference to minority students. Thus the program at Davis violated the equal protection clause of the United States Constitution.

The authors' handling of the case by the California Supreme Court is the most disappointing part of the book. The drama is cast as a conflict between two principal judges, and the discussion of the case's facts and issues becomes tedious and redundant. A majority of the California Supreme Court ruled that the Constitution is color-blind and that race should never be considered. Thus, it was implied that minorities were asking for more than their fair share of protection. As a result, the university's three major arguments—that special admissions policies would result in more professional diversity and make doctors generally sensitive to the needs of minorities; that an increase in minority doctors would provide more services to minority communities; and that minority doctors would have a greater rapport with patients of their own race—were rebuffed.

This discussion is followed by two additional weak and probably misplaced chapters. The first is an unfocused discussion of "The Continuing Significance of Race" that offers a simplistic overview of civil rights legislation since the Civil War as well as the interpretation of the Fourteenth Amendment. The conclusion regarding the growing divergence of perceptions of discrimination between whites and blacks should have been compressed and more tightly reasoned. The chapters on "The Best Doctors" convincingly shows that many of the sixteen minority students admitted did well in medical school; it also attempts to show the bitter irony the term "reverse discrimination" represents to black Americans who have struggled hard to achieve civil rights. Nevertheless, here as elsewhere, the authors never specifically address the question of whether Bakke's individual rights were violated. The success of the minority students does nothing to resolve this dilemma.

Dreyfuss and Lawrence regain their stride in "The Solicitor's Brief," an insightful examination of the Carter Administration's response to the case. They recount the political problems the case posed for the White House and detail the influence Stuart Eizenstat tried to exert on the Justice Department. The brief filed with the Supreme Court by the Justice Department supported affirmative action programs. Ironically, the two top blacks in the Justice Department were initially opposed to this type of preferential treatment, for they believed that affirmative action programs could cheapen the achievements of minorities.

Perhaps the most vivid chapter in the book covers the presentations before the Supreme Court. It is a well-crafted blend of personalities, legal issues, and courtroom drama. The narrative is skillfully interspersed with testimony. One watches the respective issues unfold as lawyers present their arguments and are periodically interrupted with sharp questions from the justices. The talented and urbane Archibald Cox, who handled the university's case, is observed at times awkwardly fumbling for appropriate responses to the justices. Cox's defense largely comes off as too abstract. Colvin, on the other hand, stuck to the facts in the case and was more agile in his interchange with the Court.

The case caused a deep cleavage of opinion in the Court and was resolved by a compromise crafted by Justice Lewis Powell. On June 29, 1978, the Court's decision was announced by Powell, which straddled the two camps in the Supreme Court. It ruled that Bakke had been wronged by the Davis Medical School, but also stated that it was legitimate to use race as a factor in selecting applicants. Thus, the authors term the Court's action a "Solomonic decision" in which each side received half a loaf, and they are somewhat critical of the justices for taking such a "political" or timid stance in the case. The Supreme Court had disappointed the public by its failure to take a definitive stand on the issues that would provide guidance to school administrators and others.

The *Bakke* case, as the authors note, reflected the fundamental change that had taken place in the country's perception of race relations. The problem posed was no longer a matter of granting rights to everyone but of allocating a limited number of opportunities. The country had clearly shifted away from the economic and political generosity that made the civil rights movement so successful in the 1960's. At the case's core was a basic difference in people's perceptions of America: most whites believed that our major racial problems had been solved, but most blacks did not.

This book stands as the definitive treatment of the *Bakke* case. With sharp insight, Dreyfuss and Lawrence illustrate the fact that race and social inequality still remain America's greatest, yet unresolved dilemmas.

Michael C. Robinson

THE BARBARY COAST
Algiers Under the Turks, 1500-1830

Author: John B. Wolf (1907-   )
Publisher: W. W. Norton and Company (New York). 364 pp. $16.95
Type of work: History
Time: 1500-1830
Locale: North Africa and the Mediterranean

Describes the sixteenth century struggle between Christians and Muslims for control of the Mediterranean, life in the Regency in Algiers, the condition of the Christian slaves there, and the eventual triumph of European power in the seventeenth and eighteenth centuries

> *Principal personages:*
> AROUDJ REIS, founder of the Regency in Algiers
> KHEIR-ED-DIN BARBAROSSA, greatest corsair in the sixteenth century
> CHARLES V, Holy Roman Emperor and ruler of Spain

John Wolf's *The Barbary Coast* has proven to be most timely. In considerable detail, Wolf recounts the Islamic-Christian warfare which occurred over control of the Mediterranean from the sixteenth to the nineteenth century, concentrating on the corsair community in Algiers. No reader can put down Wolf's book without realizing that the antagonism and distrust which now poison the relationship between Teheran and Washington are only the latest manifestation of a struggle which has endured for centuries. The work causes salutary reflection on both the underlying structures of human existence and the individual actions which create conflict anew. At a moment when relations with the Islamic world are so strained, this book is a valuable lesson in history. However, *The Barbary Coast* is not an easy book to read. Wolf covers more than three hundred years and includes seemingly endless naval battles, treaties, and hijackings carried out by a succession of what to the general public must be extremely obscure personages. To a reader unable to place most of this activity in a familiar historical and cultural context, the narrative becomes tedious and one-dimensional. The cumulative result is instructive, but the pedagogical method is overly monotonous.

John Wolf is a noted scholar who has long been respected for his work in European history. Especially well-known for a biography of Louis XIV, he has contributed a volume to the Langer History of Europe series and has also written a history of France from 1815 to 1940. Well-versed in the intricacies of events in Europe, Wolf has wandered somewhat off his beaten track in *The Barbary Coast*, attempting to analyze a part of the globe separated from the ideas and symbols which move the West. Although he has done his homework, he is not an expert in the Islamic world, nor does he have the deft hand of a Fernand Braudel in dealing with the Mediterranean. He does have an interesting subject, though, and he is right in pointing out that it is not widely known.

There are several aspects to Wolf's book. One theme which recurs is the private vendetta between Spain and North Africa which dates back to the Muslim conquest of Iberia in the eighth century and continues throughout the period of Wolf's interest. This conflict was an intimate and bitter one. At the end of the fifteenth century, Christians finally recaptured all of Spain. The result of the reconquest and the Inquisition was the expulsion of hundreds of thousands of Muslims (as well as many Jews) to North Africa. Throughout the sixteenth century, there was a great thirst for revenge on the part of the displaced Muslims, leading to incessant strife. Small parties would raid the Spanish coast, pillaging and taking prisoners. The Spanish government in turn organized larger-scale ventures to conquer North Africa and put an end to the terrorism. This remorseless feud continued for a long time, and relations between Spain and the corsairs of Algiers were always worse than those with France or England.

A second theme is the more epic struggle which pitted Christians against Muslims for control of the Mediterranean. The Christian success in Spain was more than countered by the rise of the Ottoman Turks and the conquest of Constantinople in 1453. The Turkish thrust then carried them far into Europe, all the way to Vienna in the sixteenth century, as well as to Algiers in the Western Mediterranean. The Barbary Coast thus became an important component in the great contest between Christian Europe and the Islamic world.

A third focus for Wolf rests on life in Algiers itself. It was a peculiar arrangement. At the top was a government run by Turks recruited annually from Anatolia who were discouraged from having contact with the native Berbers and Arabized Berbers who made up the local population. At the bottom were the thousands of Christian slaves who had been captured by the corsairs. Admittedly, this mixture was unusual, and Wolf is correct to point out its interest.

Finally, the book concludes with the long years of piracy and decay of the seventeenth and eighteenth century. The West had halted Turkish expansion, and as its mastery of technology accelerated, it asserted its superiority over the Muslims. The corsairs in Algiers became increasingly restricted in their ability to plunder seagoing commerce, and as funds and slaves dried up, so did their prosperity. Finally, this decadence reached such a stage that in 1830, the French were able to land troops on the beaches outside the city and march in virtually uncontested.

The Barbary Coast begins in the early sixteenth century with the Spanish setting up forts in many of the towns along the North African Mediterranean coast. Concurrently, a group of adventurers from the Levant, led by Aroudj, arrived in the Maghreb. Although basically pirates, their being Muslims made them more acceptable to the local inhabitants, and they were thus able to establish their dominance in a number of towns along the troubled coast. Aroudj expanded his power, taking Algiers, and then, moving westward, he came into direct conflict with Spanish troops and lost his life in the battle. Aroudj's brother, Kheir-ed-din, then decided that the best way to defend Algiers was to become part of the Ottoman Empire. His petition was accepted by Sultan Selim I, bringing the Ottoman Turks into the region. Janissaries were sent out to serve as the new army, and the first Spanish attempt to dislodge Kheir-ed-din was unsuccessful when twenty-six out of forty ships were wrecked in a storm. Because of mounting problems in Europe, war with France, the Protestant Reformation, and rebellion in Spain, the Hapsburg ruler, Charles V, was unable to revenge his defeat in North Africa immediately. A second attempt undertaken in 1530 failed as well.

With the Turkish defeat at Vienna in 1529, the Ottoman Sultan decided on a new tactic. He would challenge Spain in the Western Mediterranean and then invade the Iberian peninsula in order to prevent the Hapsburgs from combining forces in the defense of Central Europe as they had just done. The first step of the new strategy was the conquest of Tunisia, accomplished in 1534, but the next year, Charles V took it back. The Turks, with the help of the Algerian corsairs, then began challenging Venice and Spain for dominance in the Ionian Sea and southern Italy.

In 1541, the Spanish in turn decided once and for all to take Algiers. Thirty-six thousand soldiers, two thousand horses, and 465 ships set sail for the Barbary Coast. Once established in the harbor of Algiers, however, a violent storm struck again, destroying much of the fleet, and Charles V was forced to withdraw. This third failure assured the safety of Algiers, but did not resolve the battle for the Mediterranean.

The next two decades were characterized by frequent skirmishes, with the major shift in power coming with the Turkish capture of Tripoli in what is now Libya. Neither side could dislodge the other from their major strongholds, but both were free to carry on piracy. Finally, in 1565, the Ottomans decided to take the offensive by attacking Malta, one of the bases for the Christian marauders. This time, it was the Turks who landed forty thousand men, but the Knights of St. John, who controlled the island, had a strong position and were determined to hold out. They resisted doggedly, until the Turks finally withdrew in September, before bad weather set in.

The Turks were not ready to quit, however, and set their sights on Cyprus. Cyprus was in Venetian hands, but the Pope intervened to create the Holy Alliance, which brought Spain into the war on Venice's side. This confrontation was the occasion for the celebrated Battle of Lepanto of 1571, in which the Turkish navy went down to defeat. Wolf does not seem to feel that the battle was as decisive as some historians have judged, but it was a blow for the Turks and the Algerian corsairs, who dominated the Ottoman fleet. Proof that the Turk was still a threat came three years later when, under the leadership of corsair Admiral Euldj Ali, the reconstructed navy took Tunis from the Spanish. This triumph was the Turks' last hurrah, however, for decay soon set in for the Ottoman Empire, and it no longer threatened the conquest of the Western Mediterranean. Nevertheless, the corsairs at Algiers continued their personal plunderings.

After recounting the titanic duel of the sixteenth century, Wolf turns to the regency in Algiers and analyzes its form of government. There were several power centers. The janissaries, land troops recruited from Asia Minor and the Levant, were one, while the corsair or pirate admirals who made up one of the essential elements of Ottoman naval strength were another. The corsair leader was generally a charismatic figure who was deeply involved in the highest levels of naval strategy for the entire empire and thus was generally able to dominate the local scene. With the decline of Ottoman power, a shift took place in leadership, since the Constantinople connection was no longer strong enough to guarantee control in Algiers. The position of the janissaries and the corsair admirals was strengthened, and Algiers politics became much more of a local affair. The janissaries controlled the hinterlands and extorted taxes from the recalcitrant tribes, while the corsairs sallied forth in search of loot. One of the prime treasures they found was slaves.

Wolf does not argue much with a missionary who wrote in 1630 that there were twenty-five thousand male and two thousand female slaves in Algiers; they were all Christians, and Spaniards and Italians were the most common victims. Probably as many as five to six hundred thousand slaves were sold in Algiers from 1520 to 1660; more than two hundred thousand were taken between 1660 and 1830. This is an average of three to four thousand per year in the first period and of less than two thousand per year in the latter period. Slaves were valuable in more ways than one. The wealthy could be ransomed off handsomely, in the manner of some of today's hostage-taking. The captives were taken to the markets, where they were auctioned, with the ones who could bring a ransom fetching the highest prices; the rest were sold as laborers. English, French, and Dutch captives might hope to be released through treaties between Algiers and their respective governments, but Spaniards, Portuguese, and Italians had little hope of ever regaining freedom. Redemptionist fathers collected money in Europe, but could never get enough to free the bulk of the slaves. There were periodic revolts, but none were successful. Conditions varied depending on one's master, but Wolf does not believe they were as bad as the treatment Africans received in the Americas. Some slaves renounced their religion and were able to make good in Algiers in one position or another; females not infrequently married Muslims. Cervantes, however, himself a slave, described their lot as "sad and miserable . . . a harsh and rude slavery, in which labors were long and happiness short and fugitive . . . purgatory in life, hell in the living world. . . ."

As might be expected, slave trading and the disruption of commerce could not continue without European reaction. Wolf describes the attempts made by the various powers from 1600 to 1830 to end this piracy in great detail; the general pattern was that the rising curve of European might and the declining curve of corsair strength intersected at varying times, at which points it no longer became feasible to capture vessels brazenly. For most of the seventeenth century, it was possible to play off England, Holland, and France, who were often mutual enemies, in order to keep raiding the shipping of at least one of these countries, but by the eighteenth century even this gambit did not work. Hostility with Spain was always more serious, and very little attempt was made to accede to Spanish diplomacy. In 1775, the Spanish tried to land at Algiers once again, but their own mistakes defeated the enterprise. Hostage-taking went on massively during these centuries, and diplomatic frustration was great.

Finally, the lack of pirate treasure impoverished the Regency to the point that it became easy prey for the fast-developing European nations; it was only a question of time before one successfully descended upon her. In France, the reactionary King Charles X, eager to reinforce his monarchy, decided on a military adventure for "*la gloire*" in 1830. His troops took Algiers easily enough, but unfortunately for the King, the people of Paris rose up and overthrew him a few days later.

There is a lesson in Wolf's book. Today's hostilities do not date from yesterday, but repeat a long-established pattern. Also important is the understanding that the recent injustices of Western imperialism mask the more distant wrongs of Ottoman imperialism and Barbary slavery.

Stuart Van Dyke, Jr.

THE BASS SAXOPHONE

Author: Josef Škvorecký
Translated from the Czech by Káča Poláčková-Henley
Publisher: Alfred A. Knopf (New York). 209 pp. $8.95
Type of work: Two novellas, prefaced by a memoir
Time: The Nazi Occupation and the 1950's
Locale: Czechoslovakia

A superbly translated collection of two novellas and a memoir which celebrate the anarchic freedom of jazz and the elegiac power of storytelling

With few exceptions, Eastern European writers have met with indifference in America during the postwar decades, yet far from being merely provincial, the experience of the Eastern Europeans is now exemplary, for this is a time in which every writer, as Saul Bellow has said, is living on the periphery; there are no more literary capitals. No writer better exemplifies the alert, omnivorous intelligence and the stubborn integrity characteristic of the best Eastern European artists than Josef Škvorecký. He has published Czech translations of many American writers, including William Faulkner, whose stylistic influence is apparent in *The Bass Saxophone*, but also "marginal" figures such as Ray Bradbury and Raymond Chandler. Such choices reveal Škvorecký's taste for popular art, his disdain for authority, and his flair for discovering usable material: with writers as various as Italo Calvino and Peter Handke, he has seen the potential energy in peripheral genres.

Although he is hardly known in America, several of Škvorecký's books have been translated into English, including *All the Bright Young Men and Women*, his richly anecdotal "personal history" of the Czech cinema. Škvorecký grew up watching films every day: his father was the director of one of two movie theaters in his hometown, Nachod. A close friend of Miloš Forman, he contributed in various ways to a number of New Wave films. Before the Soviet invasion of Czechoslovakia in 1968, Škvorecký had published some ten books while working as an editor and translator; he frequently dueled with Zhdanovite toadies, and his first novel, *The Cowards* (1958; English version published 1970), was the subject of an orchestrated critical attack. Soon after the invasion he emigrated with his wife to Canada, where he is currently Professor of English and Film at the University of Toronto. In 1980 he was awarded the Neustadt International Prize for Literature.

The Bass Saxophone, Škvorecký's finest work available in English, collects two novellas published separately in Czechoslovakia: "Emoke" (1963) and "The Bass Saxophone" (1967). The novellas are prefaced by a substantial memoir, "Red Music," which introduces Western readers to the jazz cult in Nazi-Occupied Eastern Europe. "Red Music" also introduces the themes which the novellas will repeat with variations, particularly in "The Bass Saxophone." The memoir begins: "In the days when everything in life was fresh—

because we were sixteen, seventeen—I used to blow tenor sax. Very poorly." Those opening sentences establish Škvorecký's characteristic tone, at once elegiac and ironic.

Red Music was the name of the band in which Škvorecký played as a teenager in the Nazi Protectorate of Bohemia and Moravia. The name, he explains, had no political connotations, but was chosen in analogy to Blue Music, a band from Prague, without any awareness of the musical connotations of "blue." This comical ignorance was typical of the jazz cult, who mistranslated the name of one band leader as "The Duke of Ellington" and tried to decipher enigmatic song titles ("Struttin' with Some Barbecue") by consulting a pocket Webster's. But what they lacked in information, they made up for in passion: Škvorecký saw a Swedish jazz film, *Swing it, magistern!*, "at least ten times."

"Red Music" is much more, however, than a memoir of an adolescence which, despite its bitter incongruities, more or less resembled the experience of youths in New York or Los Angeles. In Škvorecký's hands, the jazz cult in war-torn Eastern Europe becomes a potent, multilayered symbol. "Cult" is not a word casually chosen: again and again in the memoir—and in the novella, "The Bass Saxophone"—Škvorecký speaks of jazz in religious terms, calling it "that international language of an innocent cult"; circulating sheet music and jazz lore in underground publications, the cult "served the sacrament that verily knows no frontiers."

The religious language emphasizes the nature of the conflict between the jazz cult and the "authorities," first the Nazis, then the Communists (whom Škvorecký calls "the bishops of Stalinist obscurantism," at once sustaining the religious motif and parodying the familiar abusive epithets which still issue from *Tass* and *Pravda*). This conflict, Škvorecký insists, is not what it first might appear to be. It is not essentially political, nor is jazz—"no matter what LeRoi Jones says to the contrary"—essentially a form of protest. Jazz, like any true art, is an anarchic, explosive expression of "creative energy," akin to the prodigious energies of the natural world. In any totalitarian regime, this spontaneous uncontrolled energy will be registered as a threat, and will be ruthlessly suppressed. "Red Music" and "The Bass Saxophone" document this suppression with great passion and with an unerring instinct for the mordantly suggestive detail. Škvorecký paraphrases, from memory, an "unseemly Decalogue" of regulations issued in wartime Germany and translated into Czech, aimed at orchestras which included jazz in their repertoire. The regulations strictly prohibited, for example, "all mutes which turn the noble sound of wind and brass instruments into a Jewish-Freemasonic yowl. . . ."

However, totalitarian regimes are only the most obvious, the most blatant examples of the abuse of authority. The jazz cultists are "missionaries possessed of faith without ideology, indeed a faith which cancels ideologies." A faith in what, then? In "creative energy"? How does one practice such a faith? These are the themes, the conflicts, the questions which have always preoccupied Škvorecký. The privileged role of youth in his work is not reducible to the natural defiance with which youth meets authority. Youth is simply good because it is fresh, energetic, curious, open—not yet stupefied and hardened by suffering, by indifference, by routine. Thus art, for Škvorecký, is fundamentally elegiac—"literature is forever blowing a horn, singing about youth when youth is irretrievably gone"—and his two novellas, "Emoke" and "The Bass Saxophone," are the purest, most concentrated expression of his art yet to appear in English.

"Emoke" has been mistakenly labeled as a parable by several critics, and has even been linked with Kafka, presumably because of the Czech connection. In fact, it is a traditional novella, in its verisimilitude and in its structure, with the episodic development, the focus on a single conflict, the action limited in space and time, and the symbolic resonance which are characteristic of that form. It is a first-person narrative with no distinction implied between author and narrator, and minimal chronological displacement. Škvorecký's formal originality (which can only be artificially separated from the original sensibility which informs all his work) lies in his fusion between the traditional novella and the meandering digressive Faulknerian sentences—the first such sentence includes the word "susurrus," in sly acknowledgment of the master—which are the most striking stylistic traits of both "Emoke" and "The Bass Saxophone." The result is a fresh, distinctive style which contrasts favorably with that of a work such as Gabriel García Márquez's *The Autumn of the Patriarch*, where the Faulknerian impulse to say it all in one sentence meets with insufficient resistance.

The plot of "Emoke," like that of many great works of fiction, is banal in summary. The narrator, a young man of thirty, unmarried, goes in August for a week's vacation to a People's resort in Communist Czechoslovakia. His profession is not specified; a well-educated man, he will return to an office in Prague. At the resort he shares a garret with a lecherous, ignorant country schoolteacher, fifty years old with a wife and three children, who begins the first night bragging about his sexual conquests. The narrator himself is currently and messily involved with a married woman named Margit, but in response to the schoolteacher's prying—perhaps to shut him up, perhaps to establish his manhood—he changes her name to Irene, makes her a widow, and says that he intends to marry her before Christmas.

With that seemingly trivial exchange—accomplished in the first page of the story proper—the machinery of the plot begins to turn. Among the other vacationers at the resort there is a beautiful young widow, a Hungarian woman named Emoke. Her marriage to a crude, violent man was very unhappy, and long before his death she had turned to a strange blend of Christianity, parapsychology, and theosophy. If the schoolteacher is man reduced to a bestial state, Emoke represents the opposite extreme, a pathological repression of man's physical nature. Yet when the narrator sits down at the piano and plays some blues, she comes alive.

The narrator's conflict is simple. He sees through the fog of mysticism, sees that he has Emoke in his power despite herself, like an "ensnared little woodland animal." But he also sees that an ephemeral relationship would destroy her. He can save her before she is irrevocably lost in spiritualism, but he is reluctant to commit himself. His choice is to be fully human, or something less than that. He vacillates, but on the last night, inspired by music and fueled by wine, he dances with Emoke and sings to her, opening his heart to her in a passionately improvised blues.

Emoke believes him. But when he returns from the toilet and a chat with the bandleader, she is dancing with the schoolteacher, her face gone dead while he urgently talks to her. The narrator has a photograph of his "fiancée" and her little girl in his identity folder, a photograph he had shown to the schoolteacher that first night.

Fiction in the great tradition, from the nineteenth century masters through *Dr. Zhivago*, often runs on the mysterious, fateful power of seemingly trivial actions or "coincidences." The point is not to minimize human responsibility but, on the contrary, to suggest the seriousness and the terrible power of human freedom. Škvorecký might well have ended his story on the dance floor, but instead he added a long coda: on the train ride home, the narrator gets his revenge by humiliating the schoolteacher, exposing his inability to perform simple reasoning in a guessing game similar to the familiar Twenty Questions. In this long, excruciating scene, the narrator himself is a cruel beast. Once back in Prague, he takes up with Margit again and does not write to Emoke or visit as he had promised. He sinks into indifference, "that indifference that is our mother, our salvation, our ruin," but never forgets Emoke entirely: "I wonder, I wonder, I wonder."

"The Bass Saxophone" is a companion piece to "Red Music," a dense narrative on the same themes which were later explicitly elaborated in the memoir. The action of the novella is concentrated in a single evening. The story begins at twilight in a town in wartime Czechoslovakia. Again, the plot is set in motion by chance. The narrator, an eighteen-year-old youth, is standing in front of a hotel when he notices an old man dragging a big black case from a bus parked nearby. The case happens to fall open, revealing a rare (but not imaginary) instrument: the bass saxophone. The instrument belongs to a traveling German band—Lothar Kinze with His Entertainment Orchestra—who are to perform that night at the rabid, threatening insistence of the local Nazi commandant. Their saxophone player is lying in a hotel room in a stupor—sick? hung over?—and they must find a substitute. Fortunately for them, the instrument-case just happens to fall open, and a jazz-crazy sax-playing youth just happens to catch a glimpse of the bass saxophone.

The story is dominated by images of this magnificent, bizarre instrument: a mastodon, a bishop's staff, a giant hookah. The bass saxophone symbolizes the primitive, anarchic power of art: its sound is prehistoric, the cry of a dying dinosaur, the voice of a melancholy gorilla—metaphors at once powerful and absurd, because art shatters decorum. Its tone is infinitely sad, because art is essentially elegiac. The narrator overcomes his diffidence—should he play with Germans?—and performs with Lothar Kinze's orchestra, because he is an artist, or wants to be one, and artists are outcasts, like this traveling freak-show of a band: a woman with a nose like a carnival mask, a man whose legs have been amputated below the knee, a blind hunchback, a one-eyed giant with an artificial leg, and a beautiful girl with a torn voice.

In the novella's climactic scene, the bass saxophone player appears in the middle of the schmaltzy performance for the German community of the town, reclaims his instrument, and begins to honk: a terrible, somber music. In a torrent of images, Škvorecký accomplishes the near-impossible: he makes sound live on the page, so the reader can hear the struggle of this anonymous Charlie Bird, with his "leaden crown of thorns of gray hair." Only when the narrator returns to the band's hotel room to retrieve his things—the bass saxophone is still wailing—does he begin to understand the message he has just heard. A light is on in the bathroom—"a light I hadn't turned on"—and a trail of blood leads to the tub of pink water. Škvorecký trusts his readers—who, as he is, are practiced readers of detective stories and crime fiction—to remember the "dazzling white cuffs of a gauzy material" which the saxophone player wore under loose cuffs when he seized his instrument. The narrator begins to understand "that desperate scream": it will come to him at odd moments in the years ahead, penetrating the thick skin he has grown in self-defense, reminding him of "dream, truth, incomprehensibility: the memento of the bass saxophone."

John Wilson

BAY OF PIGS
The Untold Story

Author: Peter Wyden (1923-   )
Publisher: Simon and Schuster (New York). Illustrated. 352 pp. $12.95
Type of work: History
Time: March, 1960-April, 1961
Locale: The United States, Cuba, Guatemala, Nicaragua, and the Carribean Sea

A comprehensive account of the disastrous Cuban exile invasion of Cuba, in April, 1961, which was sponsored by the United States Intelligence Agency

> *Principal personages:*
> FIDEL CASTRO, Dictator of Cuba, 1959-present
> DWIGHT D. EISENHOWER, President of the United States, 1953-1961
> JOHN F. KENNEDY, President of the United States, 1961-1963
> ALLEN W. DULLES, Director of the Central Intelligence Agency, 1953-1961
> RICHARD M. BISSELL, JR., Deputy Director of Plans, Central Intelligence Agency, 1958-1962
> COLONEL JACK HAWKINS, Military Commander of the CIA Cuba Project, November, 1960-April, 1961
> GRAYSTON LYNCH, Hawkins' chief subordinate
> COLONEL STANLEY BEERLI, Director of Air Operations of the CIA Cuba Project, November, 1960-April, 1961
> "PEPE" SAN ROMÁN, CIA-appointed Commander of the Cuban exile Brigade
> ARLEIGH BURKE, Chief of Naval Operations during the Kennedy Administration.

The launching of so-called "covert operations" by the United States Central Intelligence Agency has been praised by some Americans as essential to the national interest and damned by others as immoral. In *Bay of Pigs: The Untold Story*, Peter Wyden, a professional journalist and writer, has written a definitive account of one of the most poorly managed of all the CIA covert operations: the abortive Cuban exile landing at the Bay of Pigs, in April, 1961. The author ably re-creates the atmosphere of overconfidence and wishful thinking which produced this debacle.

Wyden has put a considerable amount of effort into doing the research for this book. He has interviewed everyone from the highest United States Government official to the humblest common foot soldier. He was able to talk not only with Cuban exiles and American intelligence officers, but also with the men on the other side: Cuban Dictator Fidel Castro and the militiamen who did so much to defend his regime against the exile invaders. Besides relying on interviews, the author has also made use of hitherto secret CIA documents, which he succeeded in getting declassified only after two-and-a-half years of struggle.

Wyden shows that it was in March, 1960, during the administration of

President Dwight D. Eisenhower, that the CIA was authorized to plan covert activities against the new Dictator of Cuba, Fidel Castro, who was already showing himself to be strongly sympathetic to Russia and to Communism. Although Allen W. Dulles was the head of the CIA, it was his subordinate, Deputy Director of Plans (Director of Covert Operations) Richard M. Bissell, who was placed in charge of the Cuba project. Under Bissell's direction, training camps for anti-Castro Cuban exiles were set up in the friendly Central American state of Guatemala, and an airstrip was built there also. Exile airmen received training from CIA pilots.

Richard Bissell, a former Yale University Economics Professor, had, Wyden shows, both a reputation for brilliance and a gift for persuading people. His sole military experience prior to this time had been the organizing of U-2 airplane reconnaissance flights over Russia. Yet it was this man who, in November of 1960, decided, on his own initiative, to escalate the Cuba project from a mere infiltration scheme to a full-fledged plan for invasion.

An American Marine officer and veteran of Iwo Jima, Colonel Jack Hawkins, became CIA military commander of the project; his chief subordinate was the former soldier Grayston Lynch. Colonel Stanley Beerli became the project's head of Air Operations. The commander of the exiles' Cuban Brigade, "Pepe" San Román, was appointed by the CIA project leadership. The Central American state of Nicaragua secretly allowed the CIA to use part of its territory as a staging area for the planned invasion.

In January, 1961, John F. Kennedy became President of the United States. In order to win the new President's support for the Cuba project, Bissell blithely assured him, over and over again, that the Cuban people would rise in revolt against Castro the moment the exile invasion force landed. Wyden severely criticizes Bissell for having seriously underestimated the popularity of Fidel Castro within Cuba, the fervor and bravery of his Cuban supporters, and the effectiveness of his measures of repression.

From the beginning, Wyden makes clear, the planning and organization of the Cuba project were incredibly amateurish. Because of the desire of the CIA for secrecy, there was no arrangement for recording in writing either the original plan or later modifications of it. As a result, there was little coordination of effort between the CIA and other branches of the government, including the Defense Department. Except for Bissell, few people, even in the CIA itself, knew exactly what had been approved and why. Bissell himself, eager to see the exile invasion carried out at almost any price, agreed to a series of arbitrary changes which fatally weakened the original plan.

The author of these changes was President Kennedy. The President, the author shows, was not the dashing young knight of the Camelot legend, but an indecisive, often confused, and inexperienced chief executive. He was torn between a strong desire to take vigorous action against the Western Hemisphere's first Communist government and an unrealistic hope that the United

States could succeed in overthrowing that government while keeping its own role in the operation absolutely secret. In his behind-the-scenes account of the agonizing debates in the President's Cabinet over the invasion plan, the author shows how, step by step, the original plan was completely twisted out of shape.

The first change concerned the site of the landing. According to the original plan, the landing was supposed to take place near the city of Trinidad. At a Cabinet meeting held in March, 1961, however, President Kennedy, fearful that this plan would be too spectacular, asked for a change in the landing site away from that populous city to a less heavily populated region. By changing the landing site to the Bay of Pigs, the author points out, the CIA planners unwittingly made it impossible for the exile invaders to flee to the mountains and survive as guerrillas in the event of an initial defeat. Trinidad was quite close to the Escambray Mountains, where guerrillas could survive for a long time. The Bay of Pigs was separated from these mountains by eighty miles of swamp. Although the CIA planners were unaware of it, the people of the Bay area were quite pro-Castro; the area was the Cuban Dictator's favorite resort. Right up until the invasion's disastrous end, however, Kennedy continued to believe that the exile invaders could easily escape to the mountains if they had to.

At several key Cabinet meetings held in early April of 1961, President Kennedy gave his final approval to the CIA-sponsored invasion, while tinkering with yet another crucial element of the plan: air power. Bissell had wanted the CIA's exile-piloted B-26 airplanes to knock out Castro's air force all at once in a single surprise attack on the very day of the invasion, Monday, April 17. To allay Kennedy's fears about the possible exposure of the American role, however, the Deputy Director of Plans decided to schedule two limited air strikes; one on the Saturday before the invasion, the other on the day of the invasion itself. Although this change sacrificed the vital element of surprise, it might, it was thought, make the whole enterprise look more Cuban and less American. To make the American role look even less obvious, Kennedy made, on April 14, another decision: only six planes should fly on these air strikes instead of the sixteen originally planned.

On Saturday, April 15, the Cuban exile pilots launched a series of attacks on Castro's air force bases. One of their number landed near Miami, Florida, where he announced that he was a defector from Castro's air force. This ruse, however, soon seemed likely to be exposed. Newspaper photographs of the nose cone of this pilot's B-26 showed that it was quite different from that of Castro's B-26's. The Russians asked for a United Nations meeting to discuss American aggression against Cuba, and it soon began to look as if American involvement in the strikes would be bared for all the world to see.

Haunted by this fear, Kennedy made, on the Sunday of April 16, 1961, yet another fateful decision. He canceled the second air strike, which had been planned to coincide with the invasion itself. He did so even though the first strike had by no means completely destroyed Castro's air force. Bissell, the author shows, did try to get the President to change his mind about the cancellation of the second air strike, but he was unwilling to press him on the issue. He was happy that his own brainchild, the exile invasion, was actually going to take place at all. The operation had become too visible for the American role to be kept secret, yet too limited to have any real hope of success.

On the morning of April 17, 1961, the exile Brigade, consisting of 1,543 men, stormed ashore at the Bay of Pigs. Contrary to all CIA expectations, the invasion failed utterly. Throughout the battle, Castro's air force retained complete command of the skies. By Wednesday evening, April 19, the invaders had been thoroughly defeated. Some of them were killed; a few escaped by boat; but the majority were captured by Castro's forces. The captives would not be ransomed and sent back to the United States until December of 1962.

The CIA had expected a Cuban rebellion against Castro and massive defections from Castro's armed forces; but neither of these things took place. In his portraits of soldiers and airmen who fought for Castro, the author makes it clear just how loyal, resourceful, and daring the Cuban Dictator's supporters really were. The inhabitants of the Bay of Pigs area, Wyden shows, regarded the invasion not as an act of liberation, but as an attack on their homes and families.

While showing a high regard for the courage of Castro's men, Wyden by no means denigrates the record of the soldiers of the exile Brigade. Many of them, he shows, fought with considerable bravery against overwhelming odds. He sees the exile soldiers as courageous and naïve men who placed a childlike faith in the lavish promises of American air cover given them by their CIA advisers. They were not aware until it was too late of Kennedy's resolve to keep American military involvement in the invasion at a minimum. Kennedy, the author concludes, simply used the exiles as "tools" and then discarded them.

The American military's role in the invasion, Wyden shows, was much greater than has been previously supposed. Two ships of the American Navy, the *Essex* and the *Eaton*, were sent to the Bay of Pigs with their names painted over to escort the landing craft of the invaders. They were, however, never permitted to do anything else.

For, after an agonizing Cabinet meeting, held in the early hours of Wednesday morning, the President, overruling opposition from Chief of Naval Operations Admiral Arleigh Burke, stuck to his earlier decision: no American air or naval involvement in the battle was to be permitted. Thus, American sailors and airmen had to watch helplessly offshore, as Castro's forces destroyed the tiny anti-Castro Brigade. While empathizing with the feelings of rage and frustration of the American personnel on the scene, Wyden also implies that such American restraint was absolutely necessary if World War III were to be avoided.

A major part of the blame for the Bay of Pigs disaster, according to the author, lies with Richard M. Bissell, the Deputy Director of Plans. It was Bissell's gung ho spirit, the author believes, which captured Kennedy's imagination and won his approval for the Cuba project. Yet Wyden does not view Bissell as either sinister or villainous. Instead, he sees him as a brilliant and fundamentally decent man who was led astray by his overconfidence and by his ardent ambition to become CIA Director as quickly as possible.

Wyden tries to explain to the reader why nobody in Kennedy's Cabinet was willing to point out to the President those flaws in the invasion plan which seem so obvious in retrospect. Too many men in the Cabinet, the author concludes, placed being loyal team players above speaking their minds frankly. Those few men who did have doubts about the wisdom of the operation were too intellectually inclined to have much influence on an Administration whose main theme was activism. The officers of the Joint Chiefs of Staff, the author shows, felt uneasy about the whole operation from the very beginning; yet they too were unwilling to carry their questioning of the plan beyond a certain point once they knew that the President was strongly in favor of it.

Underlying much of the planning of the operation against Castro, Wyden sees a kind of racist arrogance which could not accept the possibility that foreigners, especially those with darker complexions, could possibly be as competent and capable as Americans. Thus, the men of the CIA greatly underestimated both the popularity of Castro and the strength of his air force. It was the same sort of racist arrogance which, the author believes, would later cause the United States so much trouble in Vietnam.

Wyden's well-written, blow-by-blow account reads as briskly as a good novel. He provides excellent physical descriptions and short biographical sketches of all of the major and minor CIA officials and American military men who helped guide the operation. Unfortunately, however, the narrative frequently skips around from one theater of action to another, and even jumps back and forth chronologically at times. This jerkiness does not make the narrative impossible to follow, but it can be distracting. Some of the anecdotes, while interesting, are not really necessary to the telling of the story. A short chronology in the front of the book, listing key dates in the evolution of the Cuban invasion scheme, might have made the whole patchwork plan easier for the reader to comprehend.

Wyden's book does, however, contain a good number of other aids for the reader. There are two maps, one of the Bay of Pigs invasion site, the other of the Trinidad invasion site originally envisaged by the CIA. There are photographs of all the major participants in the drama: American military men, CIA men, and Cabinet officials; Fidel Castro, leading officers of the Cuban armed forces, and ordinary citizens of the Bay of Pigs area whom the author interviewed; the Cuban exile politicians of Miami, Florida; and the Cuban exile soldiers of the Brigade. The book contains an excellent critical bibliography. Although there are no numbered footnotes, there are chapter notes at the back of the book, giving the sources, oral and written, used for each chapter.

Paul D. Mageli

BEEN IN THE STORM SO LONG
The Aftermath of Slavery

Author: Leon F. Litwack (1929-   )
Publisher: Alfred A. Knopf (New York). 651 pp. $20.00
Type of work: History
Time: 1861-1870
Locale: The American South

A major historian's reconstruction of a critical decade in the history of black Americans which traces the interplay between the hopes and ambitions of the freedman and the manipulation of powerful social and economic pressures by racist Northern and Southern power brokers

> *Principal personages:*
> ABRAHAM LINCOLN, sixteenth President of the United States, 1861-1865
> FREDERICK DOUGLASS, ex-slave and recruiter for the Union Army
> JEFFERSON DAVIS, President of the Confederate States of America, 1861-1865

For a hundred years in thousands of classrooms, the Civil War era was simply and satisfactorily explained by a durable legend which portrayed the Old South as a sinful region that held slaves and "destroyed the Union." Fortunately, Jehovah intervened on behalf of the United States causing Saints John Brown and Abraham Lincoln to smite the evildoers with fire and sword, preserve the Union, and abolish slavery. After a brief Reconstruction, during which both sides agreed to forgive but not forget "the late unpleasantness," America proceeded with her grand destiny. The middle years of the nineteenth century, then, formed a seamless fabric, tied to Dred Scott and Fort Sumter at one end, and Frederick Douglass, freedom, and national unity at the other.

If this charming *Gone with the Wind*-type tale is true, then how do we account for the patently unfree status of the freedman following these events? How do we assess the appalling poverty of the freedman in, for example, 1880? Have we digested the results of closer studies that reveal blacks to be relatively poorer in 1900, when America boasted a wealthy middle class, than in 1800, when most Americans were farmers? Can we speak of true political liberty for blacks even after the Civil Rights movement ("Reconstruction II") in a society afflicted by moldering ghettoes and rural poverty?

Historians of black Americans discern a temporary, shallow advancement of black political rights during the early years of Reconstruction, followed by a Jim Crow-dominated age of white supremacy which, protected by a broad intersectional understanding, endured until the middle of our century. Indeed, most strides toward black equality have been made since World War II. Is it possible that the Civil War and Reconstruction arrived and departed, leaving black life little changed, save by a brief moment of promise and hope?

Did that era witness and condone a mere pack of tricks played on gullible fieldhands by racist Northern and Southern whites? These are tough questions, but the answers may best explain the precipitate rise and fall of black liberty after "emancipation," a tragic pattern of events brilliantly traced in Leon Litwack's *Been in the Storm So Long*.

Litwack's story begins in the war years with the growth of white "insurrectionosis"—a deep fear of servile rebellion that infected the entire Confederacy. "What if they rise?" was the bedrock question in the Southern white mind as Union soldiers, including two hundred thousand ex-"contrabands," invaded the South. On plantation after plantation, they joyously recited the shallow promises of the Emancipation Proclamation, led three cheers for Father Abraham, and marched away. "I surely would rise, were I a slave," concluded Jefferson Davis' people, and the white rebels sourly awaited the day of black rebellion.

Clearly, the slave held the key to the war and thus, to the Southern cause. One hint of rebellion, one backcountry uprising by some rustic Denmark Vesey or Nat Turner, would have sent Lee's invincibles pelting homeward in a mad dash to preserve family and property. However, ignoring the atmosphere of nervousness and even stark fear that permeated the South, blacks remained docile. They clearly understood the issues at hand, but steadfastly refused to break either custom or their masters' heads. Blacks spoke of freedom and the future with intelligence garnered from rumors, secret networks, and an occasional newspaper. They grumbled, worked slowly, and waited. Perhaps victims of their own conservatism, slaves—beyond those under arms (and so free) or serving as military laborers—failed to change the course of war.

The slave emerges in Litwack's re-creation as a tolerant Southern traditionalist, ruled by monumental patience; only the actual arrival of Union forces triggered the expected ritual of "make free." Some portable property was then redistributed and a few hogs and chickens sacrificed in an appropriate celebration. Then the "hands" settled down to await future events in the "quarters" with an uncertainty shared by "Massa" in the "Big House."

There was no grand Independence Day for slaves, no *uhuru* distributed in village squares and plantation yards. Slavery died piecemeal during the hot summer of 1865, dissected by the slow hands of bored Union troops, cowed masters, and complacent Freedman's Bureau functionaries. The old order was apparently gone, as Litwack demonstrates in a welter of "farewell" addresses delivered before assembled freedmen by ex-owners, but the nature of the new order was unclear. What were the *real* rules and boundaries? No one knew, and racist Yankee overlords rarely enlightened their expectant charges. Massa became Boss or Cap'n, the whip was symbolically retired, and young blacks went to town in new finery to marvel at stores, railroad depots, and crowds of people. Then harsh reality destroyed the moment:

crops had to be planted immediately, and it happened that fieldwork was to continue as a black occupation. Throughout the South during the 1865 growing season, freedmen plowed, sowed, and harvested as before, all the while wondering what freedom meant. Doubtless they recalled that ten percent of the Union army was recruited among Southern blacks, and that a full third of them had been swept away in storms of iron and lead. Heroic deeds, however, had again failed to purchase true freedom, and four million ex-slaves labored on in the fields and barns of an unrepentant South.

What was "freedom?" Blacks knew the answer was not complicated—"fo'ty acres and a mule." Land was the key to liberty, not Bureau agents and windy speeches "from de cotehouse steps." The overarching tragedy of Reconstruction was the failure of the Bureau of Refugees, Freedmen and Abandoned Lands to provide land for the landless. A forgiving presidential pardon policy, coopted officials, and the unrelenting drive of Southern whites for home rule and *status quo antebellum* precluded black acquisition of the means to become free people in a free society. Their dream faded in icy tests of will between landed planters and poverty-stricken ex-slaves. Southern blacks were neither Santo Domingan firebrands nor outraged Sepoys; they pressed their cases peacefully, and lost. Keys to the plantation were surrendered, and with them, all hope for land and rights. Thus, when the dust of war and peace had settled, the South was little changed. Free blacks still hoed someone else's corn, chopped the man's cotton and husked his rice, and wondered what had gone wrong. Loyalty to the Union in war and sweet reasonableness in peace had failed to earn equal seats at the table of liberty.

The new order—white supremacy coupled with steadily increasing exploitation of blacks—was perhaps uglier than slavery, which at least had had the virtue of openness. By 1870, most freedmen had accepted reconfirmation of their roles as mudsills of the South. Later generations would recognize the monolithic racism of nineteenth century white America and concede that the abolition of slavery was only an episode in the long struggle for democracy.

Late twentieth century historians understand that Lincoln—the real Lincoln, not "Father Abram"—was honest and correct: the Civil War *was* a war to preserve the Union, and the abolition of slavery was scarcely more than a symbolic political gesture, a necessary means to a greater, nationalist end. This postwar synthesis was comfortably ratified in 1877 by the Grand Old Party. Having buried their abolitionist past, Republicans bargained with a renascent Southern Democracy, traded the black man for the White House, and closed the debate.

So ended an unstable age, blessed with white compassion and forgiveness that extended even unto national agreement that blacks should never again be permitted to divide whites. That ghastly synthesis, which endured until World War II, remanded the freedman into slavery (with the proviso that the South, respecting tender Yankee sensibilities, would call it something else).

Thus, the essence of the peculiar institution continued until tractors, new crops, and migration ended black peonage.

For a century, American historians have analyzed the black role in Reconstruction. Their conclusions have generally reflected the dominant views of their own era. Most have traced broad histories, heavily salted with white issues and leaders and only lightly peppered with black individuals. After the turn of the century, William Dunning, Claude Bowers, and Woodrow Wilson portrayed a rudderless black race, childlike yet brutal, freed too soon and inherently condemned to failure. Later writers of the caliber of W. E. B. Dubois, Kenneth Stampp, and John Hope Franklin corrected this baleful thesis, but still wove their stories around whites, parties, and movements.

In contrast, *Been in the Storm So Long* is a history of freed men and women, of ordinary black people, their white tormentors, and their friends. Its author, Leon Litwack, emerged as a major historian of black Americans in 1961 with the publication of *North of Slavery: The Negro in the Free States, 1790-1860*, an examination of antebellum racism in the "free" states. Later works (two anthologies and a text) have confirmed his status. *Been in the Storm So Long* is a remarkable addition to the history of Reconstruction (a period that reconstructed little beyond the Republican Party); it is our finest account of the human side of the story. It borders on old-fashioned narrative history, permitting slaves and slaveholders to tell their stories in their own words. Litwack explains a short moment at the close of our national trauma, for he has wisely chosen to limit himself, following a concise analysis of the later war years, to the first years of "peace." In so doing, he has re-created the high tragedy of the first optimistic moments of the new era and, in the next instant, the bleak horror of the reconstruction of slavery.

Litwick's style is commendably calm after a decade of hot rhetoricians. Yet the text is charged and dramatic, above all a moving tale that reveals as much about whites as blacks. The author's sources are manifold and impeccable. Blacks tell their stories in early accounts and in the indispensable narratives collected by scholars and the WPA during the 1920's and 1930's. Planters, more literate and leisured souls, speak to us through diaries, journals, and published writings. Unforgettable images crowd every page. Richmond slave trader Robert Lumpkin watches his world and business crumble in 1865, marries a former slave, and walks off the pages of history. Jourdon Anderson duns his ex-master for back wages and requests that he thank George Carter for "taking the pistol from you when you were shooting at me."

Leon Litwack has researched and written a superb, highly readable book. *Been in the Storm So Long* is a fine Pulitzer Prize-winning study of a crucial moment in our history and a sharp look at the origins and nature of the racism that still festers in America a century later.

Lance Trusty

A BEND IN THE RIVER

Author: V. S. (Vidiadhar Surajprasad) Naipaul (1932-   )
Publisher: Alfred A. Knopf (New York). 278 pp. $8.95
Type of work: Novel
Time: The late 1970's
Locale: Africa and London

A realistic exploration, through the perceptions of representative characters, of the ordinary effects on human lives and cultural mores brought about by the violent attempts of an emerging African nation to establish its political identity while avoiding deeply resented European influences

> Principal characters:
> SALIM, the narrator, a young Indian merchant
> METTY, his half-breed clerk who marries an African woman
> FERDINAND, a young African student selected for leadership in the new regime
> INDAR, Salim's successful, egotistical Indian friend
> THE PRESIDENT
> RAYMOND, the white intellectual writing the President's history
> YVETTE, his wife, with whom Salim has an affair

Should a reader come first to the work of V. S. Naipaul through his fictional *A Bend in the River*, it might prove helpful to identify the author's base of attitude as reflected in the titles of his nonfiction works. These titles signify the author's profound sense of dislocation, of being bereft: *India: A Wounded Civilization*, *The Overcrowded Barracoon*, *The Loss of El Dorado*, *The Middle Passage*, and *An Area of Darkness*.

Naipaul is uniquely equipped to reflect upon bereavement. Indian by blood, Trinidadian by birth, Briton through his choice of home, and an exile through his experience and spirit, Naipaul is concerned with the loss of old dreams and old definitions—the loss of what formerly seemed to be guiding verities. A man of no single nation, his allegiances held in abeyance, he casts a dark and perceptively ironic eye on his varied worlds. He sees with awful clarity the doddering old and the brutally new. For him, the old world is a dream only vaguely, though poignantly recalled. Through his vision, the contemporary world, though irresistibly real, emerges as either dusty and stupidly dull, filled with the failure of old European concepts, or horrifyingly cruel and confused, lacking any consistent, workable ideals. His psychological landscape is as bare and as existentially frightening as any created by Albert Camus, for example, or by Paul Bowles.

A novel, therefore, set in an emerging country deep in the interior of Africa provides Naipaul with a perfectly staged arena for his characters to blunder around in while trying to understand their purpose and their relationships with one another. Beneath Naipaul's uncompromising stare, Africa is no longer Conrad's romantic and mysterious "heart of darkness"; rather, it is a blindingly illuminated, demystified landscape of an immense, relentless, and jungled slum. Characterized equally by chance beauty and brutality, the landscape is as passive as a lizard in the sun, unblinking in the face of murder, greed, waste, and futility. Caught in this landscape's strange sterility, victimized randomly by gang warfare and by pointless fertility and the profligacy of nature, Naipaul's characters do not move themselves. Bereft of volition, they are moved only by chance events, by perverted or misperceived old dreams, by their era's lack of a sense of either the past or the future.

For Naipaul's characters, historically linear constructs such as "the future" and "the past" have been irrevocably lost or have become nightmares. For these people all that is left is a juiceless twentieth century version of Mister Kurtz's earlier "horror" to be passively endured. Though there are villainous acts in this novel, significantly, there are no true villains. Conversely, there appears absolutely no possibility for the heroic; the time and the place undercut any intended extreme acts. One moment Salim, the novel's narrator, muses that he is tired of submitting to Fate; he dreams of being in charge. The next moment he acknowledges emptily the fact that a force he calls a "tide of history," forgotten by his contemporaries and found only in books by Europeans he has yet to read, has already swept over him. Now he can only wait passively for another tide of history—this time, perhaps, to wash him away.

Salim tells his story in retrospect, seeming stolidly unconscious of his precarious position, at the time of the telling, as a chance survivor of another of history's convulsive tides. His first comment, his astonishingly arrogant observation that "the world is what it is," and that men who are—who allow themselves to be—*nothing*, do not belong in it, is consistently belied by his own impotent behavior in the rest of the narrative. All his actions are merely allowed by caprice. None of them is productive, for him or anyone else. At the novel's conclusion, for example, he escapes by sheer chance the coming warfare, which would have surely included his extermination. Although Salim sees much, he clearly fails to see that Fate has deigned his survival. He has not been anything through his own force. He cannot see that when the time is right, when Fate decrees, he will be nothing.

Naipaul seems to be suggesting that Salim's existence—barely a dot in the wave of human history—is representative of those other, only slightly larger moments in time we take so seriously: those cultural upheavals which are ultimately as temporal and as unaffecting as Salim's capricious billeting for awhile at a certain bend in a certain river. He implies that what we call history is actually no more than a bend in the immense river of time.

Precisely because of this enormous view and this theme of the smallness of man's actions in the face of larger history, Naipaul's novel is a darkly comic one. Caught in the need to care, he finally must laugh at that impulse. His tone of voice, his calculated understatements, and his sardonic laughter at the heavens thus resemble strongly those of, say, Graham Greene or Evelyn Waugh. Naipaul, however, though sharing their mastery of English prose style, differs from these men in not having been allowed to be a part of the European tradition except as an objective observer. His sense of loss thus is determinedly less particular, more general, but nevertheless poignant; as a result, it is often more powerful in its evocation of the anomalous relativity of individual experience within human history. Strangely—because he differs from Waugh's final nihilistic mirth; because he does not share Conrad's nostalgic wish for Kiplingesque heroes; and because he does not agree with Greene's reliance upon religion—Naipaul most reminds us of the anarchistically purified views of the British novelist Alan Sillitoe in his *A Tree on Fire*, or of the American film director Francis Ford Coppola in his *Apocalypse Now*. For Naipaul to have his powerless Salim declare his refusal to be nothing in the world, even while relating events in his world which have inexorably rendered him a nothing—*and* to have him refuse to acknowledge the fact of his nothingness—is a classically poignant statement about the human condition. Salim, like other humans, notes that humans demonstrably *are*—therefore, they seem bound to maintain that they are important. Naipaul's novel, however, concludes with the river flowing off into a larger darkness beyond the realm of the human heart, into the unknown, beyond any individual's momentary "bend."

Naipaul's mastery of English prose and his grasp of contemporary emotional and historical concerns combine to make his work of lasting value. *A Bend in the River* is destined to be one of the most memorable statements, fictional or otherwise, about the emerging third world nations. It is to his credit that, while writing about the larger machinations of history, he never relegates his characters to the roles of merely illustrating types. His characters are vitally alive; they are so vividly engaged in the novel's events that they can be viewed clearly both as individuals in a contemporary setting and as representatives of various human concerns in a more symbolic landscape of history.

Salim, for example, is both a vividly individual character as well as a representative of all the culturally, politically, and emotionally displaced men of our history. He does his best, but sadly, he does not know much; he has little education and less wisdom. When he sees how inevitably paltry his efforts are, he tells himself the necessary lies to keep on going. In a representative moment, Salim lies in bed amid the squalor of his mid-Africa, friendless, hopeless, and unconsciously defiant of reality, as he whiles away grimy hours by looking at the glossy pages of European magazines depicting frothy dreams of the past—or of a fantastic present if not already doomed, then certainly not accessible to him. Belonging nowhere, Salim finds himself simultaneously envious and resentful of nearly all those around him whether they are his servants or his masters.

One of those people "beneath" him whom Salim envies is the briefly seen

Zabeth, the African woman who is primitively, innately sure of herself, of her visceral power and place. She does not appear to think. She acts; she rarely speaks. In her presence, Salim asks himself questions to which there are no answers. He is powerless to act; he is pointlessly verbal. Zabeth is as inscrutable as the jungle into which she merges. Salim, his furrowed brow all too readable, can hide nowhere. Cursed with the cerebral ability to see imaginatively beyond himself, Salim thus finds himself at the advantage of a woman intellectually his inferior, but, in his world's reality, his superior. Thus, symbolically, Salim, like much of the complex, sophisticated world, finds himself dependent upon and mystified by the reemerging primitive, nonverbal elements around him.

Another effective character among the many hauntingly memorable ones in this novel is a young would-be intellectual, the black student, Ferdinand. He is another figure who learns he belongs nowhere. Because of his identified intelligence and subsequent European education, Ferdinand is forcibly wrenched from his youth and from the iron-age practices to which he was born. Pressed into the service of the new black president, he is thrust into the deadly complexities of attempting the imposition and maintenance of altered European political structures on his less intelligent brethren. Ultimately Ferdinand loses all; he cannot identify fully with his ruthless leader's sophisticated rationales for slaughter, nor can he—or his country—ever return to the simplicities previously known. Somewhere behind Ferdinand and Salim both, Zabeth is a shadow, blindly strong but nevertheless vulnerable to the twentieth century's machine guns and napalm.

Thus Naipaul, through the lives of such representative characters, underlines his apocalyptic vision of the primary agony of our age: the simultaneous knowledge of the need for, and the recognition of the inability of, men to merge gracefully the best of past and present toward a more purposeful future. As an imaginative documentation of observable history, *A Bend in the River* is eerily disquieting, beautifully crafted, and powerfully controlled; it functions first as an emotionally subjective record of human endeavor and second as an unemotionally objective measure of that endeavor surveyed against the largest of all the scales we know: time.

Thomas N. Walters

BERNARD BERENSON
The Making of a Connoisseur

Author: Ernest Samuels (1903-   )
Publisher: Harvard University Press (Cambridge). 477 pp. $15.00
Type of work: Biography

Traces the development of a poor Lithuanian Jew from his humble origin to his recognition as the foremost connoisseur of Italian Renaissance art

Principal personages:
BERNARD BERENSON
MARY SMITH COSTELLOE, an art collaborator and later Berenson's wife
CHARLES ELIOT NORTON, an eminent Harvard art professor
EDWARD WARREN, a wealthy college friend of Berenson and an art collector
"MRS. JACK" ISABELLA STEWART GARDNER, chief patron for whom Berenson collected many masterpieces
BERTRAND RUSSELL, Berenson's brother-in-law
OSCAR WILDE, one of Berenson's many literary acquaintances

Bernard Berenson: The Making of a Connoisseur, the first volume of a major critical biography of Berenson, covers the first forty years of his life, culminating in his triumphal tour of the United States in 1904 when he was recognized as a great art critic and feted by many of the important literary, social, and artistic leaders of the time.

Berenson, the eldest child in a family of unorthodox Lithuanian Jews, was ten when he came to America in 1875 with his immigrant family. A precocious and studious boy, he entered the famed Boston Latin School where he earned money tutoring other students. He found the Boston Public Library and became a voracious reader. For two years, from age sixteen to age eighteen, he worked so steadily at his studies "without resting *one* day," as he told one of his older comrades in 1883, that toward the end of his first semester at Boston University he was "more of a walking ghost, a somnambulist, than a rational creature."

His ambition was to become a writer as well as a scholar, and he was convinced that he must study at Harvard, which he entered after completing his first year at Boston University. His biographer says that Berenson's awareness was all inward and literary, and that he seemed to feel that life for him must be a kind of intellectual footrace for which he must train himself to outrun the others. His small stature and delicate frame ruled out any distinction in rough competitive sports.

When he entered Harvard in 1884, the intellectual stir there aroused Berenson's ambitions to the highest pitch. The challenging excitement of Harvard inspired in him a lifelong gratitude, and he willed his art treasures and papers to Harvard seventy years later. He had many eminent professors, but the courses which had the greatest impact upon his later career were those he took under Charles Eliot Norton, Boston's dictator of art. Norton guided proper Bostonians into an appreciation of Italian art, and it was here that Berenson made the acquaintance of "Mrs. Jack," Isabella Stewart Gardner, who was to play a large role in his future career as patron and client.

While at Harvard, Berenson converted to Christianity, joined the Episcopal Church, and was baptized by the famous Phillips Brooks. Five years later, in 1891, steeped in the religious art of the Renaissance in Italy, he converted again, this time to the Catholic Church, into which he was formally received by the abbot of the monastery of Monte Oliveto. His youthful interest in religion declined, however, and throughout his later life he considered himself a "lapsed Catholic."

Berenson applied for a Parker Travelling Fellowship in order to broaden his study of art and literature abroad, but he did not receive it. This setback aroused his influential friends. Thomas Sergeant Perry, onetime instructor at Harvard and one of the leaders of Boston's literary life, rallied a group of sponsors including himself, "Mrs. Jack" Gardner, Edward Warren, and Professor Ferdinand Bocher to make up a purse equivalent to the seven hundred dollars awarded to the Parker Fellows. Warren had sponsored him for entrance into Harvard and was now studying at Oxford; his wealthy family had long been identified with the Museum of Fine Arts in Boston. His fast friendship with Berenson continued with their joint desire to make Boston a world center of Italian art. Berenson's sponsors had great faith in his genius and enabled him to continue his studies long past the one-year limit.

In 1888, Berenson met and fell in love with Mary Costelloe, the wife of Frank Costelloe, an English lawyer. He wrote in his diary that this meeting "became the determining factor in the rest of my life and career." Mary left her husband and two little girls and eventually, after Frank's death, married Berenson in 1900. Their relationship was so close that *Bernard Berenson* is almost as much her story as that of her husband.

Samuels describes Mary as being undeniably handsome with a Junoesque figure and vivacious charm and intelligence. Having been brought up a strict Quaker, she continued in adult life to use the traditional "thee" and "thou," as one notes in many passages which Samuels quotes from her extensive correspondence. Yet in other ways, perhaps influenced by her life with Berenson, she departed from her early Quaker training. A year older than Berenson, she had attended the Harvard Annex (later Radcliffe) when he was a Harvard student, although they had not met. She met and married the Englishman Frank Costelloe in 1885 upon graduation, and soon afterward her wealthy Pennsylvania family moved to England. It was at their country estate, Friday's Hill, that Berenson first met Mary.

The inhabitants of Friday's Hill lived independently of Victorian social strictures, and Mary's mother took over the care of the two small granddaughters so that Mary could travel and research with Berenson. Her mother, Hannah Smith, was an avowed feminist who, when told of Mary's plans to marry Berenson (as reported by Mary's brother), "took it very sensibly although she can't help despising a woman, who when she has had the luck to become a widow, deliberately chooses to marry again." At first Robert Smith, Mary's father, had scorned Berenson as a "penniless Bohemian," but in 1895 he converted his allowance to her into an annuity. He never welcomed Berenson but he died in 1898 before they were married. He did not dislike Bertrand Russell, however, who married his other daughter, Alys. It was Lady Russell, Bertrand's grandmother, who was then displeased.

Mary, an enthusiastic and energetic collaborator in art matters, was an apt student who wrote and lectured with ease, reinforcing Berenson's theories. She undertook to turn Berenson's aesthetic passion into practical channels, but wrote nearly fifty years after their first meeting: "Perhaps I was, after all, wrong to try to turn this creature, so rarely gifted for enjoyment of a not ignoble kind, into the 'worker.'"

Berenson's ambition to write had not produced the results that his sponsors had hoped for. In a letter to Mrs. Gardner of April 28, 1889, he said, "What I shall do, I do not know, almost anything for a living," and he explained that his wealthy friend, Edward Warren, had offered to subsidize his further study. Warren had already begun to count on Berenson for advice on his art purchases. Berenson confided to Mrs. Gardner that when he returned to Boston, "I shall be picture-wise then and perhaps that will enable me to turn an honest penny." As she had been most anxious for him to publish, she abruptly stopped her help and correspondence, and it was five years before she would again become Berenson's friend.

Mary acted as Berenson's secretary and in addition kept a comprehensive account of all their business and social affairs. Her diary was to prove an invaluable source to the Berensons' biographer. During a stay in Florence, Mary wrote to her mother in May, 1894, "I've been having a square stand-up fight, and have come out at the end victorious, but a little battered." She was referring to a love affair with a new acquaintance, Hermann Obrist, a sculptor. Bernard and she were committed to the principle that they were both free agents unbound by ordinary conventions, but when Mary grew flirtatious, there was a rift, though it was soon mended with Mary saying she was sorry.

Bernard and Mary attracted many of the interesting personages of their time. She wrote in her diary on June 24, 1894, that she had taken Oscar Wilde to call on Vernon Lee's brother and that "Oscar talked like an angel and they all fell in love with him, even Vernon who had hated him almost as bitterly as he hated her." Oscar had said that "he liked people without souls or else with great peace in their souls." He had met Berenson at Oxford in 1886 and had exclaimed, as Berenson recorded, that "I was completely

without feeling, that I was made of stone." Now, eight years later, he asked
Berenson whether he "really felt anything or really dreaded anything." "I
told him," replied Berenson, "I felt and dreaded ennui and that I preferred
death. He pretended that that would make him forgive all my cruelty and all
my 'moral' qualities." After Wilde's sensational trial in 1895, the Berensons
never saw him again.

Berenson keenly wished to regain Mrs. Gardner's good opinion. When he
finally published a book of art criticism, *The Venetian Painters*, he sent her
a copy with the humble note that he had let the time go by without writing
to her because he had not had anything to show her that would change the
opinion she had had of him when she ended their correspondence. She was
instantly mollified, and renewing her friendship with Berenson could not have
come at a more opportune time since she had recently inherited two million
dollars from her father.

Samuels gives a detailed account of every negotiation undertaken by Berenson to secure art treasures for Mrs. Gardner; he is responsible for most
of the major paintings which make Fenway Court in Boston such a remarkable
museum. She was married to a millionaire as well as being fabulously wealthy
in her own right. Berenson paid court to her in letters which sometimes seem
to give off the scent of fulsome flattery from a client seeking a reward.
"Whatever comes," he writes on one occasion, "I shall always worship you
without exception as the most life-enhancing the most utterly enviable person
I have ever had the good fortune to know." And again, "I know not how to
describe you, but a miracle certainly, a goddess and I, your prophet."

Mrs. Gardner was apparently a person removed from reality who expected
homage from everyone. She headed the list of celebrities who turned out to
entertain Berenson and Mary when they returned to the United States in
1904 for a six-months tour. The millionaire collectors of Beacon Hill came
to them for counsel: Cabot, Coolidge, Kidder, Peabody, Parkman. They met
railroad magnates, Charles T. Yerkes, William Laffan (editor of the *New York
Sun*), J. Pierpont Morgan, and a host of other dignitaries in Chicago, Detroit,
and Philadelphia. Investing in art was fashionable, and what better guide
could they get than Berenson?

On their marriage, Berenson and Mary had moved to a hill outside Florence
and into Villa I Tatti, which would become world famous. In his Preface
Samuels tells of visits to I Tatti and of seeing Berenson, age ninety-one, in
1956. All through the account of this first flowering of the celebrated art critic
are hints of future conquests and events. The next volume is eagerly anticipated.

Ellen Devereux

THE BEST OF SHOLOM ALEICHEM

Author: Sholom Aleichem (1859-1916)
Edited by Irving Howe and Ruth R. Wisse
Publisher: New Republic Books (Washington, D. C.) 276 pp. $12.50
Type of work: Short stories
Time: The late nineteenth and early twentieth centuries
Locale: Western Russia and Eastern Europe

A collection of twenty-two of Sholom Aleichem's stories of Jews living in Russia and Eastern Europe prior to World War I

These stories, set only fifty to one hundred years ago, seem to speak to the reader almost from another world. The persecutions which dispersed a fragile community of Jews also drove the author to Europe and New York. He continued his prolific writing career, using a disarmingly folksy narrative style to delight readers with his gentle humor and instruct them in the uncertainties and cruelties of daily life. Aleichem writes of the Jewish tradition of Eastern Europe just before it disintegrated and became the nurturing soil of modern Jewish life. His use of folklore and the oral tradition give his stories the impact of immediacy and the heartwarming intimacy of a personal conversation. The reader is there in the *shtetl*, and Aleichem is there with him as the friendly guide pointing out the sights.

Aleichem describes an insular and cohesive society. As the editors point out in the Introduction, the comic levity is a viewpoint imposed by the author on situations permeated by change, anxiety, and guilt. There is in this marvelously funny collection of tales a pervasive and cumulative experience of misery, guilt, and fear. The humor is possible especially because these characters are not daunted by their conditions; they face them with dignity, hope, and outrageously comic manipulations. The author's sharp wit is constantly probing the foibles, pretensions, assumptions, and characteristics of the culture of this people. In his adaptation of the folktale "The Haunted Tailor," he not only narrates the simple story but also elaborates on it, amplifying the personalities and gently ridiculing the follies of the tailor, his wife, and the townspeople with wit and charm. Aleichem's insistence that he cannot state the moral of the story slyly puts the burden of doing so upon the reader.

These stories exude an abundance of humor in many guises, from the innocent merriment in the tales of "From Mottel, the Cantor's Son," to the folly of misguided outrage in "Dreyfus in Kasrilevke," and to the bittersweet chuckle of compassion at Tevye's dreams of wealth in "The Bubble Bursts." However, a sense of pain also underlies many of the stories, and the humor takes a darker turn. Later tales—such as "The Krushniker Delegation," which recalls memories of a too-recent and too-painful past—foreshadow the use of humor so prevalent today. Although wretchedness, poverty, humiliation, and frustration provide his subject matter, Aleichem develops his material in such a way that the folly of his characters' behavior becomes the focus, rather than the pain of their experience. This poetic distance, or detachment, makes the pain bearable and the humor possible.

However, Aleichem's distance is always controlled and conscious. A skilled craftsman, he allows the point of view and the moral he is delivering to determine the shape of each story. Because he writes about the things, people, and situations he knew so intimately and loved so well, his personality and his good-natured, witty, warmhearted delight in people pervade his stories. He includes himself in the final story, telling of his own forgetfulness and inadvertent confusion in the course of a lecture tour and of his wife's wryly humorous response; he is able to poke fun at himself as well as others because his humor is never vicious or destructive. Rather, he depicts his characters with gentle, wry, ironic, and compassionate humor. He captures East European Jewish culture as a vivid, bustling, struggling, engaging reality; through their anger, joy, fear, hope, and tenderness, the people in these tales exhibit a dignity which ennobles their strivings.

The group of stories about Tevye the dairyman trace his fortunes, and indeed those of his entire Jewish community, from a settled, stable period, through a series of changes and misfortunes, to his eviction from his homeland and the scattering of his kindred. Tevye's comic role is largely sustained by his language. His misquotations, puns, and creative interpretations provide such a magnificently vigorous and original vision of life that he becomes a folk hero, an embodiment of the spirit of an entire nation of people caught up in a time of change and loosening of the bonds of tradition. Aleichem's extraordinary facility at creating dialogue—reproducing the quality and tone and phraseology of the common speech—is perhaps nowhere so well sustained as in the monologue "The Pot," in which the poor widow overwhelms the rabbi with her endless questions.

The tales are uneven in length; some are scarcely more than an elaborated joke or an expanded anecdote, while the longer ones become short stories in a genuine sense of full development. The selections, however, are representative and well chosen, and the translators have managed to preserve the sparkle, wit, and gentle irony of the originals. The Introduction, formulated as a series of letters between the editors, is well conceived and provides useful insights into the author's life and his writings. This volume not only offers the best of Sholom Aleichem, but also tempts one to read more works by this writer who offered laughter to a civilization in a time of agonizing upheaval and change.

Betty Gawthrop

BIRDY

Author: William Wharton
Publisher: Alfred A. Knopf (New York). 310 pp. $8.95
Type of work: Novel
Time: The mid-1930's and World War II
Locale: Philadelphia

A vividly told fantasy about a young boy and his visions of flight and freedom told through the memories of his best friend

> *Principal characters:*
> BIRDY, an individual who seeks freedom in a fantasy world
> AL, his best friend and the narrator

In the universe created by human dreams, an entire world can be designed and inhabited. In some cases, the obsessive nature of the dream/fantasy can become the base out of which a fiction can be made. In William Wharton's carefully structured first novel, one is introduced to the magical mind of "Birdy," a character whose fantasies become the stuff of his actual life. Although one only meets Birdy through the eyes of his best friend, Al—a tough Sicilian kid who, like Birdy, grows up in a working-class Philadelphia neighborhood before World War II—the long, detailed flashback sequences present enough material so that Birdy becomes as real as the memories that evoke his image.

Birdy is first met when his friend Al, a wounded soldier recently returned home at the end of the war, is called to the psychiatric ward of an army hospital. Al is asked to try and get his friend Birdy, also a veteran, to emerge from what seems to be a psychotic state of mind: an obsessive way of acting like a bird that has confounded Birdy's psychiatrist. It appears that Birdy has retreated into a world known only to himself. Al sees Birdy clad in thin, white hospital pajamas, squatting birdlike in the middle of his cell. He does not speak to Al; in fact, he shows no sign of recognition. "The way he squats," Al states, "you'd think maybe he just might spring up, flap his arms a few times and fly out that window he's got his eye on." Al senses that the only way he will be able to open any sort of communication with Birdy is by reminding him of their shared childhood memories. It is at this point in the novel that one is introduced to the mysterious mind of Birdy, one developed out of a loving fascination with all types of birds.

The long, detailed passages following the initial encounter with Birdy alternate between Al's own memories of Birdy's youth and equally long narratives written from Birdy's point of view. Thus the past is reconstructed, tracing Birdy's fascination with the flight patterns of birds from the late 1930's when Birdy, at thirteen, first becomes entranced by pigeons, until that point in the present when Birdy's birdlike identity results in his incarceration in the hospital.

Almost all of the novel's action takes place in the Philadelphia neighborhood where Al and Birdy grow up. Birdy is the product of parents defeated by the circumstances of their birth and their near-poverty. Known by his parents only as a kind of strange presence inhabiting an upstairs bedroom, Birdy is unloved. Al, too, is a child of the working class, with a violent Sicilian father who works as a plumber and is given to fits of hysteria when provoked by Al. Both sets of parents ignore their sons and, quite naturally, the two boys turn to each other for the comfort and security missed at home. Birdy's mother, "a first class bitch," according to Al, extends her hateful feelings to anyone in the neighborhood who attempts to intrude on her privacy. She, as Al notes, has been secreting away all of the baseballs knocked into her backyard from the baseball games played in an adjacent field. While the novel's narrative is centered around the boys' attitudes, the reader's attention is also drawn to the secondary characters' influence on Al and Birdy, as both boys rebel against the constraints placed on them by their parents and the harsh atmosphere of the parochial school system.

Birdy's maturation begins when he decides to raise canaries and learns, through the experience, that he can live a life outside of his environment. As he becomes devoted to the birds, Birdy begins to imagine the world in which his birds exist. He devises a grand fantasy about his favorite bird, Perta. He loves her softness, and, in the striking passages where he attempts to understand his feelings, he willfully injects his own existence into the world of Perta and her companions. Birdy, in short, becomes one with the objects of his love; he imagines himself as a canary, with all of the affectations and emotions he has by now attributed to his "family." "I'm really in love with Perta now," Birdy thinks. "She's so dainty, so quick, so skilled." Soon the aviary itself begins to expand to include a large part of Birdy's backyard and income as his affection for Perta and her "children" continues to grow.

As Birdy becomes absorbed in his created dreams, the reader is introduced to detailed descriptions of the habits and flight patterns of birds, which, despite their seeming unimportance, play a large role in Wharton's description of Birdy's new universe. Birdy's boy-world, understood to be devoid of love and, with the exception of his friend Al, companionship, suddenly takes on a wondrous resonance. At one memorable point in the narrative of Birdy's dreamworld, Birdy-as-canary actually mates with Perta. The boy awakes to find that he has ejaculated in his sleep and, in his postnocturnal consciousness, discovers he is satisfied with his memories because they seem unlike any kind of transitory dream.

Through the prism of Birdy's mind, one is introduced to a magical world where life and death take on new meaning. Birdy's relationships with his birds—and with Perta in particular—are no more than the sustained longing of a human being cut off from love and security. Along with Al, Birdy is forced to grow up in a world that is, for better or worse, about to come apart: the boys find no solace at home, in institutions, or in the army that finally inducts them to fight in a war. At the same time, the two boys' longing for security and meaning can be seen when one considers how much they grow to dislike the institutions that are supposed to help them: each finds little more than entrapment at the hands of nuns, teachers, parents, and army personnel. The world is a place that must be escaped in some way.

In the grip of his own aspirations for freedom, Birdy attempts to flee the "real world" where he unhappily is placed. Through the freedom he dreams about within the aviary—a freedom that is also "practiced" by Birdy-as-canary—he also begins to understand how reality intrudes even in the most idyllic of worlds. Birdy meets tragedy when a cat kills his beloved Perta. He begins to mourn his loss, "to fly in slow motion," and soon he is "flying alone" in his dreams. Yet despite the tragedy, Birdy is at one with himself, understanding that life is to be lived only for the moment, and peace comes when any loving creature is prepared to accept each moment as important. "I begin to sense a strange restlessness in myself," Birdy thinks. "Even when I'm flying I'm thinking of something else and I don't know what it is. Then I know. I'm feeling the urge to flock and migrate. Is it in the other birds or is it only me? Is it the dream birds, too?"

The dream is shattered for Birdy, and for Al as well, when the two boys are drafted. Al is sent to the European front, while Birdy is stationed in the Pacific. Al's experiences are horrible, and he learns to confront death, mutilation, and fear. In much the same way as he was forced to come to terms with the discomfort of his home life, Al sees how badly the world operates. The pressures of seeing men killed or made catatonic by the war causes Al to become "scared deep into my bones." Al wants to get a "psycho discharge" because he is "scared of even being scared." Wharton devises a graphic battle scene in which most of Al's squad is killed; they are wiped out in horrible ways by exploding mortar shells, or disfigured to the point where several of his squad are no longer recognizable. Al, too, is wounded, and because of the seriousness of his injury, he is shipped back home for treatment.

Al and Birdy meet in the army's psychiatric hospital and, after a sustained period, begin to communicate. The two friends begin to explore Birdy's visions, his past, and their shared sense of wonder at being alive after seeing so much destruction. A feeling of ease grows between the two men as each begins to understand the degree of lunacy necessary to survive in a world that makes war an ongoing part of human existence. Al and Birdy are out of the system now, the system that, as the army psychiatrist Weiss notes, has to be lived in and accepted.

Birdy contains passages which combine beautifully written observations with humor and pathos, as Warton successfully creates a unique fictional universe. One begins to believe in Birdy's world and to accept his moralistic frame of reference. Birdy wants a new world and freedom, and he wants it to continue. "And that's the way it ends?" Al asks Birdy at the novel's end.

"Not really," Birdy responds. "It's never that easy. Nobody gets off that way. But it's worth trying."

Larry S. Rudner

BLANCO

Author: Allen Wier (1946-   )
Publisher: Louisiana State University Press (Baton Rouge). 234 pp. $9.95
Type of work: Novel
Time: The mid-1950's
Locale: Blanco, Cotulla, and San Antonio, Texas

The story of the disintegrating lives of a family caught in the physical, emotional, and spiritual emptiness of west Texas, and of their search for real connections in a landscape of disconnection and for freedom in the cage of the flesh

> *Principal characters:*
> JUNE MARRS, a thirty-two-year-old woman
> TURK MARRS, her forty-five-year-old brother
> EUNICE MARRS, their talkative mother
> ARMON MARRS, their father, dead twenty years
> CAGE, June's new husband
> ROBERT ALLEN, Turk's friend
> SALLY, Turk's love

The Spanish word *blanco*, as the epigraph to Allen Wier's first novel reminds us, is a remarkably complex word, referring at once to aspects of the physical world and, at the same time, to an absence within that physicality: "white; fair (complexion); blank; yellow (cowardly); white (person); coward; white star, white spot (on horse); target; aim, goal; interval; hole, empty; blank space." That *Blanco* should be the title of this novel is, then, particularly apt, not only because its events center around the tiny town of Blanco, Texas, but also because it is informed by the tension within the word, the tension between an inescapable physicality and an equally unavoidable sense of absence in that physical world. The characters in the novel are as fully physical as any in modern literature, of the earth earthy, bone and sinew and skin, prey to age and illness, victims of gravity and the tethers of life in the flesh. But at the same time, they are alone and empty, each one in himself, each one from each other, lost in space within and without.

"No ideas but in things," William Carlos Williams seems to be shouting in the background of this novel, and its foreground is filled with things, the things of ordinary lives: garbage cans and tin roofs, pink Christmas tree ornaments and new Buicks, calendars on the wall and dead armadillos on the road, cigarettes and coffee, automatic photo booths and doctor's waiting rooms, chicken excrement and shotguns. And yet for all these things, the most telling (and striking) thing about the landscape of this novel, inner and outer, is its emptiness. These people whom we come to know so well seem almost cut off from the reality of the world around them, the world that is draining them and emptying them minute by minute. They drive cars and see themselves reflected in the windshield or the rearview mirror; they are almost smothered in the man-made colors around them (orange, pink) but they seldom focus on the colors of the natural world; they write their names in dust (Turk does, June does) as though to assert their belonging in this world they can scarcely believe to be real.

Turk Marrs, forty-five years old, heavy, nearsighted, still living at home with his mother, working here and there, at the filling station or mowing the cemetery grass, tries to come to grips with his isolation from the living world. He thinks of his father, dead now for twenty years and buried in the cemetery where Turk earns some of his living, and he wonders what he looks like now, what his physical father looks like, for Turk has no sense of anything that might last beyond the flesh:

> Was his hair turned white? Did he still have a white handkerchief sticking out of his breastpocket? Half moons on each fingernail? A knot on his second finger from bearing down so hard on his pencil? Where were all the ways that made a man stored up? Was all that lost, just because time kept moving? There seemed to be no such thing as sudden death, we all pass away a little more every day, drifting like sand down a dry hillside, giving up our lives like loose grass, slowly wearing down, losing our shape, carried away by rains and steady wind.

With the loss of his father, who told tales of his ancestors, the pioneers with courage and life so much a part of them, and who told tales of himself and his friends and of Turk and June themselves, Turk loses the past itself. He is stranded in the moving present where he can only stand still, come from nowhere he can remember, going nowhere he can see, only wearing down, losing shape, drifting down.

His sister June has a larger sense of herself, knowing that she is more than her body, able to imagine herself drifting up and away from her collapsing flesh "through the trees like smoke leaving a burned-up log." Her imagination fails her, however, when she must deal with that flesh in collapse. She can imagine a gynecological examination as a visit to a room with overstuffed furniture, but even as her fancy saves her from the shame and fear of the fact, it renders her inanimate and dehumanized. Later, when she is having serious and painful trouble with her sexual organs, she cannot bear to know what is the matter, preferring her desperate dreams of blood and violence to the potentially bloody fact.

Both June and Turk seek some freeing action, some moment of turning, some second when they may gain control of themselves and their lives. They seek this action in their dreams, but only find themselves pegged down there as well; June dreams once that she is literally staked out in the median of a highway and left to graze. They seek this action in their imaginative flights, but too often the imagination betrays as well, leads them into grotesque disfigurations of the present rather than saving visions of possible futures. They lack what Coleridge called the esemplastic power of the imagination, that vital process which dissolves, diffuses, and dissipates in order to re-create; they are left only with what he called Fancy, which "must receive all its materials ready made from the law of association."

Much of the source of their imaginative failure, of their failure to use imagination as the re-creator of their lives, lies in a failure of language in their lives and thoughts. Their mother Eunice is a talker; she has used talk as an escape from the confines of her life for years; she surrounds herself in gossip and speculation and opinion:

> It seemed she had spent her life listening to other people talk. Their stories were her stories, they made up her life for her. When she was alone or unhappy she would listen to the stories and imagine a different life. As she got older she made up stories of her own and found out that her imagination could make her totally free. She could become anyone, do anything, be anywhere.

Her children—plunged into this apparently endless stream of talk and seeing how, for all her fantasizing, Eunice is trapped in herself and her life, ailing and complaining, not free at all for all her talk—retreat into a nearly inarticulate mode of thought and speech. They think in associational images, cut off both from their father's language of tradition and history and from their mother's continual verbal present. They both seek a language with which to express the things they feel and yearn to understand, but their effort breaks down in sound play as inarticulate and associational as their imagistic thoughts.

> Turk: "The pig, the pink pig café. Pink pig, pink pie, pink eye. To say she had pretty, pretty eyes. Pig, prig, plink, prink, pink, prick. To please, to please let him put his pink prick, to put it in her pink."
> June: "Cage cut his neck. Nicked his neck, neckid nick on his neck. Coffin, coffee in the kitchen, coughing. Coughing up blood, coffee break, break neck, neck broke, dead throat, blood goat."

Turk feels that something must be done, that something is happening to him, but he can never express what the "something" is. He even fears that language and talk would literally destroy all the "feelings" which he knows he has, even if he cannot express or understand them. Like a Sherwood Anderson or early Hemingway character, Turk fears language and its ability to falsify feeling and real understanding, but, ironically, it is his inability to speak what he feels, to name it and know it, that causes him to explode into violence when he finds three Mexicans robbing the filling station at which he works. He kills the Mexicans because he had to do "something," and then he kills himself by dropping a wheelless car onto himself as he had earlier imagined Cage doing to him. He sees himself and his reality poorly, and, because he is unable to articulate what little he does see clearly, even his fancies and daydreams turn to ugly fact, to the sudden death that he did not believe ever happened to anyone.

Imagination, lacking the articulate power to reshape fact into new future, turns in on itself, becomes mere Fancy, recombining the given reality into other forms of itself, never really changing a thing. Armon Marrs played at suicide, hanging himself from a tree, catsup on his lips, and stated thereby the limits of his life—the vital past that snaps shut like a trap in Blanco County. Turk and June inherit his death-centered fantasies. Turk dreams of Cage's killing him as he works under a car; June kills Cage time and time again in her fantasies, smashing his car on the highway, having his heart crimp and stop on the sidewalk, choking him to death on a hunk of steak. June murders herself as well, imagining car wrecks with Cage, imagining that the doctor has stolen what was valuable in her body and left a metal instrument behind, imagining herself bleeding, bleeding, bleeding until she floats in her own blood. Turk murders Cage in his dreams, and Cage, the dullest and least imaginative person in the novel, imagines his father holding out a dripping pigsfoot to him when he has sex with June, sucking June's ear and driving himself to furious orgasm with the image of the pigsfoot in his mind.

Language fails, and the imagination fails. Turk watches his own reflection in glass, and he decides that if the reflection took his place no one would ever notice the difference. June leaves blurry photographs of her breasts and bare belly (taken in the automatic photo booth) all over the bus station and in a waiting empty bus. Cage remembers flushing away the bits and pieces of his father's pornographic picture collection after his death. Dismemberment shatters their lives; they yearn for wholeness and connection, but they are too wounded by emptiness, by the "madness of space," to be able to find it or create it imaginatively. They need to do something, but they do not know what the something is.

Turk kills the Mexicans and then himself. Eunice continues to talk and write letters, to pity herself and fill herself with the illness and failure of the lives around her. Cage transforms everything he touches into shabby success, into a reality as vulgar as the Texaco station he allowed to be built right in his own yard for the money and the "convenience." June, seriously ill and pain-ridden, but determined not to see a doctor about it, starts the new year by not taking down the pink-lit Christmas tree in her house; it stands as an emblem of meaninglessness to her. (Earlier she had talked her friends into accepting the minister's invitation in church, while she held back herself, unable to believe or to take any action of belief.)

At the end of the novel, her father long dead, her brother recently dead, isolated from her mother and her husband, June drives around the beltway around San Antonio, a closed circle, but one that does deny the lesson of that pink window in her house. She drives fast, the wind tearing at her clothes, stripping her like a snake of its old skin, a snake "finally working free of its old dead skin and darting onto new spring grass, its senses awake to new life." June drives her fierce circle but races on "into new territory."

Perhaps at the end of the novel, June will, for all the ambiguity of those images (snake and closed circle, spring grass and new life), find a new territory and a language with which to deal with it. The dead lie behind her as she encircles her own dead life like an Apache around the trapped wagons; June drives on, having killed Cage in her fantasies time and again and possibly able now to revive herself with an imagination freed of the need for further violence. The novel does not answer that question except in the vitality of its own language, in the richness of its own images, and in the openness of its own imagination.

Allen Wier is a young writer of genuine ability, possessed of a craft worthy of his vision. In *Blanco*, he has explored the Badlands of the human spirit, the blank spaces where white stars may come to birth. It is exciting to consider what new territory he will explore in the books that lie ahead, the maps he will draw for us, the flora and fauna he will describe, the astonishing blossoms which will open for us in the filled spaces of his pages.

R. H. W. Dillard

BLOOMSBURY
A House of Lions

Author: Leon Edel (1907-   )
Publisher: J. B. Lippincott Company (New York). 288 pp. $12.95
Type of work: Literary history

A well-organized, sympathetic history of the Bloomsbury group by a respected literary biographer and historian

> *Principal personages:*
> VIRGINIA WOOLF, famous English author and co-founder of the Hogarth Press
> LEONARD WOOLF, English publicist and co-founder of the Hogarth Press
> CLIVE BELL, English critic of art and literature
> DESMOND MCCARTHY, English author and critic
> LYTTON STRACHEY, English author
> JOHN MAYNARD KEYNES, English economist
> VANESSA BELL, (NÉE STEPHEN), wife of Clive Bell
> THOBY STEPHEN, her brother

Within the last decade, Bloomsbury has become a profitable cottage industry. The books on Virginia and Leonard Woolf seem unlimited. We now have five volumes of Virginia Woolf's letters, three volumes of her diaries, three volumes of previously unpublished reviews and essays, two biographies, numerous critical studies of her fiction, five volumes of Leonard Woolf's autobiography, a reissuance of his novel, *The Wise Virgins*, and several accounts of their marriage and their publishing house, the Hogarth Press. Similarly, Michael Holroyd has written an unnecessarily lengthy two-volume biography of Lytton Strachey, and this same thoroughness is now being applied to the Bloomsbury painters, other members of the Bloomsbury circle, tangential Bloomsbury figures such as E. M. Forster, Lady Ottoline Morrell, Dora Carrington, and to miscellaneous personages and events conveniently labeled Bloomsburyana. With such a deluge of publications, many of which in all fairness have contributed significantly to our understanding of a group of people who shaped the modern movement in English letters, biography, painting, and economics, one might remark: "Not another book!"

To anyone already familiar with the jokes, anecdotes, gossip, bedroom histories, and general goings-on among the Bloomsbury set, such a remark could justifiably apply to Leon Edel's *Bloomsbury: A House of Lions*. Edel tells us in his Introduction that he began his study of Bloomsbury nearly twenty years ago, but his monumental work on the five-volume biography of Henry James kept him from finishing the book until well after Bloomsbury had been discovered as a popular literary commodity, and others had already told Edel's tale. But for those who are uninitiated Bloomsburyites, or who enjoy watching a master biographer apply his considerable skills to a familiar story, or who wish to know more about the less well-known Bloomsbury figures, Edel's book will serve as a well-organized, nearly always interesting introduction to his subject. In it Edel provides a Bloomsbury chronology; a Bloomsbury checklist which, like the price of gold, seems to change daily; a section devoted to those who were and were not "Bloomsbury"; a set of wonderful pictures heretofore unpublished; and a neatly woven series of psychological portraits of the circle as it unfolded. It is, on the whole, an enjoyable if not very original effort.

Edel argues that what has come to be known as Bloomsbury developed over three phases. The first, he rightly states, began at Cambridge in 1900. For it was here, amidst the dining halls, bedrooms, classrooms, and walkways of King's College and Trinity College, that the male members of Bloomsbury— Leonard Woolf, the righteous, hard-working, social-minded Jew on scholarship; Clive Bell, the robust, easygoing landed gentleman who early displayed a keen eye for visual details; Desmond McCarthy; Lytton Strachey, the gangling homosexual whose fondness for history foreshadowed his career in historical biography; John Maynard Keynes; and Thoby Stephen, the son of Sir Leslie Stephen, editor of the *Dictionary of National Biography*—first met. They studied together, exchanged ideas as well as boyfriends, and dedicated their lives to the principles of G. E. Moore, the British philosopher and adviser to the Apostles, a secret society to which all but Clive Bell belonged. In fact, Edel suggests, Moore became the cornerstone of Bloomsbury: "that of a cultivation of the art of friendship, made possible by a certain homogeneity of mind that invites closeness yet safeguards independence— and 'social' awareness, and a desire to probe the common enjoyment of the Beautiful."

By 1906, the male core of Bloomsbury had graduated, and Thoby Stephen decided to re-create the weekly Apostles' meeting with a mini-Cambridge in London. On Thursday nights, he and his friends would congregate in Bloomsbury at No. 46 Gordon Square, the townhouse he now shared with his sisters, Vanessa and Virginia Stephen. It was here amidst the *haute bohème* world of the Stephen household that the center of Edel's story takes hold: "No. 46 Gordon Square very quickly became the center, the heart of the Bloomsbury of our story."

Two factors contributed to the successful perpetuation of the Cambridge life in Bloomsbury. First, the majority of the group had modest, independent incomes which gave them the freedom from all responsibility except that to which they were all homogeneously most interested: a passionate involvement with ideas, conversation, rebellion against Victorian standards and modes of behavior, laughter, a narcissistic sense of their own self-importance, and a commitment to art and social reform. Equally important, however, were the talents and personalities of the Stephen girls, who, at first reluctantly but then enthusiastically, turned the post-graduate Apostle group into a coeducational experience.

Vanessa Stephen was blessed with a wonderful gift of energy and a single-minded purpose in life: to turn whatever she saw, felt, or experienced into plastic expression. It was this passion for art as well as her monolithic presence, her careful attention to domestic details, and her thorough enjoyment in being a well-rounded emancipated woman which made her, almost inevitably, the earth-mother figure for the Bloomsbury group. Her sister Virginia, by contrast, was ethereally beautiful, psychologically fragile, nervous around men, and uncertain about her womanhood. Yet she possessed a talent for words which made her by 1906 a frequent contributor to the *Times Literary Supplement* and a conversationalist equal to any among the group for her cleverness, intelligence, and bitchiness. Although at first uncomfortable around Thoby's friends, Virginia gradually became a central part of the Thursday night gatherings. Edel's discussion of Vanessa's character and the role she played in the early stages of Bloomsbury makes for enjoyable reading and is one of the few original portraits in his story. His summary of Virginia's psychological development, on the other hand, though always perceptive and well-written, suffers from the constraints he has set for himself. Too much of the material pales in range and critical insight by comparison to other biographical portraits of Virginia Woolf, in particular Phyllis Rose's *Woman of Letters: A Life of Virginia Woolf*. Nevertheless, Edel describes the nascent years of Bloomsbury with obvious fondness and a clear understanding of its personalities.

If the first stage of Bloomsbury's history, which concluded with the premature death of Thoby Stephen and the marriage of Vanessa and Clive Bell, was a period of introductions and delayed adolescence with homosexual men and young virgins passionately discussing the Good and the Beautiful, the second phase was one of deepening friendships, greater candor, and shared sexual relations. After the Bells took over No. 46 Gordon Square as their home, Virginia and her younger brother Adrian, about whom Edel says very little, moved to No. 29 Fitzroy Square where, on alternate Thursday nights, they hosted the group's discussion meetings. By this time, Edel remarks, Bloomsbury was producing the "most brilliant and fantastic conversations that one can hear anywhere in England."

It was also yielding greater intimacies. Virginia, jealous of Vanessa's marriage, carried on an asexual, yet verbally passionate, affair with Clive while Vanessa, hurt by Virginia's behavior and bored with Clive's, fell in love with Roger Fry, who was, according to Edel, "standard" Bloomsbury: Clifton (Thoby's preparatory school), King's College (Keynes' college), a member of the Apostles, an art historian of the first rank, and a painter of considerable abilities. Having quickly been assimilated into Bloomsbury society, Fry made celebrities of the group with his now famous Post-Impressionist show at the

Grafton Galleries in 1910. Meanwhile, John Maynard Keynes took on Duncan Grant, Lytton's cousin, as his lover; the two were integrated into the group when they moved to No. 38 Brunswick Square, which Virginia had established as a high-brow commune after her relations with Adrian became impossible to continue. Next, Leonard Woolf, having resigned from the foreign service and being encouraged by Lytton (who himself had momentarily succumbed to love fever when he proposed to Virginia), married Virginia in 1912. By 1913, then, Bloomsbury had grown up, a fact which Leonard Woolf, fresh from his years in the Ceylon jungles, was quick to perceive: "What was so new and exhilarating to me in Gordon Square . . . was the sense of intimacy and complete freedom of thought and speech, much wider than in Cambridge of seven years ago, and above all including women." What was new, in effect, was that Bloomsbury had become an intimate circle of Bohemian artists and intellectuals who seem to have adored one another's company.

The final phase of Bloomsbury began shortly before World War I, in which all but Keynes, McCarthy, and the Woolfs were pacificists, and ended in 1920 when Bloomsbury began exercising lionlike influence over English life and thought. It was during this final phase that Bloomsbury earned its permanent place in English intellectual history.

Lytton Strachey, who had struggled during the first two phases of Blooms- bury to find a form in which to use his pointed, mocking sentences in the manner of his mentor, Voltaire, decided in 1913 to write a series of silhouettes of great Victorians. By 1918 he had finished *Eminent Victorians,* a book which instantly made him famous and which reshaped biography as a literary form. What Strachey accomplished, Edel points out in the finest critical section of the book, was to incorporate for the first time the ideas of Freud into historical analysis and to reduce massive amounts of biographical material into a form noted for its economy and brilliant turn-of-phrase. In the years to follow, Strachey would add to his success with the publications of *Queen Victoria* and *Elizabeth and Essex*, which solidified his position as England's eminent biographer. On Strachey's contribution to English letters and his affair with Dora Carrington, the boy-girl painter with whom he spent his later life, Edel is at his best.

Equally influential was John Maynard Keynes who, having assisted Lloyd George at the Paris Peace Conference, published in 1919 *The Economic Consequences of the Peace*, which created an enormous sensation and estab- lished Keynes not only as a brilliant economist with political foresight, but also one whose economic theories were firmly rooted in the liberal humanism of Bloomsbury. For Keynes the years ahead were ones of triumph, culmi- nating in his peerage and the publication of his masterly *Treatise of Money* which helped "lift Britain out of its depression and aid Roosevelt in launching his New Deal." Of all the Bloomsburyites, Keynes has had the greatest influence on the greatest number of people.

Although Strachey and Keynes achieved the greatest notoriety during this final phase, the other Bloomsbury figures were wielding considerable influence in their own fields. Virginia Woolf, who would in the 1920's establish herself as one of the foremost novelists of this century, published *The Voyage Out* (1915) and *Night and Day* (1919) and with her husband set up the Hogarth Press, which established a notable position in publishing history. Leonard, too, published two novels, *The Village in the Jungle* (1913) and *The Wise Virgins* (1914), and side by side with the Webbs helped to build the Fabian Socialist Movement in England. Duncan Grant and Vanessa Bell were finally recognized by the London galleries after the War as artists of the first rank, and their mentor, Roger Fry, shored up his writings in *Vision and Design* (1920) and *Transformations* (1926), which had an influence on English Art History equal only to Clive Bell's *Art* (1914) with its all-important catchpenny phrase, "significant form." By 1920, then, Bloomsbury had, through its hard work and extraordinary talent, fostered the modern movement in English letters, art, economics, and politics. Although the group would continue to meet in Gordon Square and Brunswick Square, they dispersed at this time to lead separate lives in the country. For Edel, their final years is another story.

Edel admits that as Bloomsbury became influential it generated a number of critics, including Henry James, Wyndham Lewis, and D. H. Lawrence, who saw the circle as nothing more than a self-perpetuating admiration society filled with rude busybodies, bad-mannered egoists, and self-indulgent lesbians and homosexuals. Edel dismisses such claims as the work of jealousy, paranoia, and shortsightedness. Bloomsbury, he concludes, should be judged solely for what it achieved: breaking the barriers of reticence and sex; giving friendship and conversation a new dimension; and creating a body of work which shaped the way Englishmen felt and thought. In his uncritical praise of the group, he seems to imply that great artistic achievements overshadow any personal flaws that Bloomsbury might have had.

This bias gets Edel into trouble. Describing the conversation of Bloomsbury as the most fantastic and brilliant in England, for example, Edel argues his position not from substantive sources but from his own wish-fulfillment:

> "Brilliant and fantastic conversation" has a way of not getting itself recorded. When it is recorded by accident or design, it sounds strangely discontinuous and fragmented. It needs cigarette smoke, gestures, colors, a ballet of body postures, smiles natural and artificial, the nuances of verbal warmth or venom. Accounts of Bloomsbury parties across the years . . . sound like intellectual parties anywhere. We must take it on trust that they were remarkable.

Why must we trust? Granted, Bloomsbury was remarkable, but bright people can be just as boring, just as cruel, and just as cliquish as lesser minds. Similarly, in striving to show us how superior Bloomsbury was, Edel stretches credulity with his frequently embarrassing comparisons. He likens talk in

England to certain moments in Rome and to Athens, presumably under Socrates, and the birth of Angelica Bell to the reenactment of the Nativity:

> . . . a baby, a daughter, was born at 2:00 A.M. on Christmas Day, the first Christmas of the peace. In the Charleston of that Yuletide it was as if some Sussex Nativity Play were being enacted. There were assorted attendants and at least one Wise Man, Maynard Keynes, who helped the thirty-three-year-old father, Duncan Grant, during his hours of anxiety. . . . In the frosty dawn, when her travail was over, Vanessa might have felt that hovering angels had attended, for she named her daughter Angelica.

It is ironic that in purple passages such as this, Edel, who has devoted much of his life to Henry James, whose novels dramatize impressionable Americans abroad, should in his latest work reveal himself to be a perfect subject for the Master's hand.

There is, however, another irony to the publication of Edel's book as well as all of the other Bloomsburyana coming out weekly. These works come at a time when the values and achievements of Bloomsbury are under revision if not in disrepute. John Maynard Keynes may have changed the way Britain and the United States have spent government money over the past fifty years, but in this neoconservative period, his economic ideas are being rejected by all but the most diehard, social-spending liberals. Duncan Grant, Vanessa Bell, Roger Fry, and Clive Bell may have made a major movement of Post-Impressionism, but their style and theories of art are, with the possible exception of the current fad for pattern painting, no longer practised in this postminimal age. Lytton Strachey's use of Freud in interpreting history has been enormously influential, but his successors have clearly turned away from the Strachian biographical form for more old-fashioned, massive, unwieldy biographies. One need only mention Ellmann on Joyce, Painter on Proust, Holyrod on Strachey, and Edel, himself, on James. Of all the Bloomsburyites, Virginia Woolf alone continues to impress and to emerge as one of the supreme artists of this century.

Finally, perhaps most importantly, Bloomsbury's life style seems not only impossible to re-create in an age of dwindling trust funds and fashionable equalitarianism, but it also is in retrospect hypocritical. For all of their liberalism and desire to rebel against outmoded forms and values, the members of Bloomsbury were, if anything, lovers of middle-class comfort, recipient inheritors of the privileges of the English class system, less than heroic in their manner of pacifism, inbred and snobby, and exclusive in the worst way. Although Edel is right to point up their superior virtues and achievements, his failure to focus on this other, less admirable side seriously limits the merits of his story. As a consequence, his version of Bloomsbury is a highly romantic one, a perfect summer's read on the deck chair.

W. Bryan Fuermann

BLUE WINE AND OTHER POEMS

Author: John Hollander (1929-   )
Publisher: The Johns Hopkins University Press (Baltimore, Maryland). 71 pp. $8.95
Type of work: Poetry

One of America's most skillful poets grapples with the puzzling relationship that exists between art and life

John Hollander is a poet of great learning and skill whose knowledge and mastery of the English lyric has made him one of the outstanding craftsmen among contemporary poets in the English language. What he calls in his *Vision and Resonance* "the modality of verse" is the augmenting force behind his verbal virtuousity—his sense of rhyme, meter, wordplay, line, and other formal intricacies. The aural quality of his verse is striking, as is evident in such volumes of his poetry as *The Night Mirror* and *Spectral Emanations*. His sophisticated humor and satire and his playfulness and wit in *Town and Country Matters* and *Reflections on Espionage: The Question of Cupcake* lend an immediate appeal to his poems. The emblematic poems in *Types of Shape* display Hollander's wit and fancy. His last collection of poems, *Spectral Emanations*, aroused excitement and expectations. Unfortunately, *Blue Wine and Other Poems* does not promise much, although these poems are less verbose, Latinized, allusive, and of less knotted syntactical patterns.

This volume essentially consists of short lyrics and four longer poems— "Blue Wine," "The Train," "Monuments," and "Just for the Ride." There are poems on painting and sculpture exploring the interaction of art and life. Dream continues to be a major motif in this collection; and the poet is still concerned with memory, questions of reality, and the problems of creativity. "The New Notebook," one of the few better poems in the book, exemplifies Hollander's poetic strength:

> These faintly reassuring lines,
> Gray and reasonably spaced in a field of fainter gray
> We may as well call white —
>
> Are they the traces of tradition?
> Are they in themselves the tradition being nearly at one
> With the words that walk them?
>
> Or do our forebears silently inhere
> In the very characters we feel to be so fresh
> (Shaken from morning leaves
>
> Or struck from the dry night rock
> Or shaken like tears of joy from a dancer on the hill)
> Falling into their places

In the newly blued space
Between those lines merely unused yet and unable
Themselves to rule?

We shall see where we make them
Take us, as guides or as the faint shadows by whom we walk
Hand in hand with ourselves.

The poet's tentativeness and the challenge of writing have been conveyed
with remarkable economy and lyrical power in this poem. A sense of questioning is dominant throughout the book, although it often appears that the
rhetorical device of questioning is as overused as that of exclamatory O. An
image such as two buses that kiss for a moment in passing seems rather trite
and easy, but "Just for the Ride" is a sustained reflection on the choice of
the road, when at the end of journeying "the unchosen/Alternatives seem
more vivid/Than the way taken." The poem displays Hollander's masterful
manipulation of metrical and rhythmic variations; however, it does not fully
satisfy because, somehow, one gets the impression that Hollander has not
grappled with the deeper conceptual and philosophical issues inherent in such
a treatment with adequate depth. In fact, this is the major disappointment
of *Blue Wine and Other Poems*. A kind of withdrawal or refusal to encounter
life and to experience headlong in a deep and passionate manner—a lack of
enough rich substance—fails the poems. Added to that is some sort of vagueness and obscurity in these poems. One senses glimmerings of intense and
deep ideas, but the language does not quite cohere to communicate depth,
intensity, and clarity. That is the problem with poems such as "Another Sky,"
the sequence called "Pictures in a Gallery," "*Deja-Vu*," "The Train," and
"Blue Wine."

The title poem is witty and fanciful, the line structure and movement
skillful, and expressions like "reality is so Californian" somewhat startling;
yet the thrust of the poem is not clear. Even the closing image, "clear cup
of his own eye," seems facile and trite, and the concluding stanza peters out
despite the heavy suggestiveness in the opening lines of the stanza. Hollander
seems strangely prone to such tendencies. Take, for example, the last lines
in "Some of the Parts." The image of "lying in the sun like the pieces of some
dream" following "Remembering which, in the swarm of noon's/ Tiny-winged
exigencies, will flake apart the promise/ Of it" makes very little effect or
point. The last two lines in an otherwise compact lyric, "Land and Water,"
give the impression of being an intrusion forced to some mysterious effect.
Expressions such as "flagrant nights," "Olympian squibs," and "to ogle the
acute scintillations of/All the countless seen and unseen others" give a feeling
of vagueness and wordiness to "What Was Happening Later at Night." "The
Train" has some exceptional passages—stanzas 3 and 6, for example—but
it gives out a sense of metaphysical posturing and lack of concentration which

one does not find in his other long poems, "The Head of the Bed" (in *Tales Told of the Fathers*) and "New York" (in *Country Matters*).

With regard to his art poems in this volume, one has to admit that they do not have the strength and richness of his "Kranich and Bach" or the engaging quality of his *Reflections on Espionage*. Although the ultimate impact of these poems in *Blue Wine and Other Poems* is not as drastic as the last line of "Last Echo" in the volume—"No more than a cold rhyme"—the overall sense is not of meditative intensity or conceptual seriousness. "August Carving," "Monuments," "At the End of the Day," "The New Notebook," and "Just for the Ride" are the most effective and successful poems in this latest collection by John Hollander.

Deba P. Patnaik

THE BOER WAR

Author: Thomas Pakenham (1933-   )
Publisher: Random House (New York). Illustrated. 718 pp. $20.00
Type of work: History
Time: 1899-1902
Locale: South Africa

A history of the turn-of-the-century British-Boer conflict

Principal personages:
> JOSEPH CHAMBERLAIN, British Secretary for the Colonies, 1895-1903
> (GENERAL) LORD KITCHENER (LATER EARL), Chief of Staff to Field Marshal Sir Frederick Sleigh Roberts, 1899-1900; British Commander in Chief for South Africa, 1900-1902
> PAUL KRUGER, President of South African Republic (the Transvaal), 1883-1902
> SIR ALFRED MILNER (LATER LORD), British High Commissioner for South Africa, 1897-1905

Afrikanerdom originated with the migration of seventeenth century Dutch Calvinists to the Cape of Good Hope at roughly the same time English Calvinists migrated to America. The Afrikaners chose an out-of-the-way part of the earth in which to build their version of Jerusalem; consequently, it took centuries for the world to catch up with them, if indeed such a thing ever has occurred. At the tip of Africa these Afrikaners hewed out a puritanical society which has shown a tough resiliency to the few outside interferences that have come its way. Britain annexed the Cape of Good Hope to her empire at the close of the Napoleonic wars, since the Cape was important in terms of controlling world shipping lanes, but in the course of the nineteenth century she failed to achieve mastery of the Afrikaners themselves. In the twentieth century she lost what authority she ever exercised over them as well as strategic control of the Cape.

By the end of the nineteenth century the British had granted self-government to the Afrikaners of Cape Colony and Natal, while two independent Afrikaner or Boer (the Dutch word for "farmer") republics, the South African Republic (the Transvaal) and the Orange Free State, had emerged in the interior. These two independent states were an irritant for a variety of reasons. President Paul Kruger of the Transvaal presided over and spoke for a beleaguered Boer society, which had been literally invaded by Uitlanders (non-Dutch persons) following the development of the largest gold mining complex in the world in the Witwatersrand. Kruger and the Boers refused political rights to these Uitlanders, rightly fearing that they would be swamped if the franchise were extended to all these immigrants. Consequently, the Uitlanders had no voice in such things as the rates charged by the Netherlands South African Railway Company, which possessed the only rail link to the outside.

They also blamed the Boer government for what they held to be outrageously high wage rates paid black African labor in the mines.

The British and world monetary systems of the late nineteenth century were dependent upon gold, and "gold bugs" such as Cecil Rhodes and Alfred Beit had enormous influence with the British government. These South African mining millionaires backed the extension of the franchise to the Uitlanders and formed an alliance with the British High Commissioner, Sir Alfred Milner, to demand the franchise from the Boers. Milner assumed a very aggressive attitude and demanded voting rights for all Uitlanders having five years' residence in the Boer republics. The Secretary for the Colonies, Joseph Chamberlain, backed Milner's demands with an equally aggressive stance.

Kruger eventually offered the franchise after seven years' residence, but this was insufficient given Milner's and Chamberlain's belligerence. Tensions accelerated, and the Boers gave an ultimatum to the British warning against the reinforcement of the latter's South African garrison. Thus the Boer War, the longest, costliest, bloodiest, and most humiliating war that Britain fought between the Napoleonic wars and World War I, broke out. Eventually half a million British soldiers were tied down trying to conquer 87,000 Boers. It was a war in which the Boers possessed definite advantages, given the difficult terrain, the long lines of communications for the British, and a countryside hostile to the British and friendly to them. The Boers also employed modern rifle fire very effectively, and the war foreshadowed the looming horror of World War I with its usage of rifles, machine guns, and trenches. The British were totally unprepared for the conflict, and their army was initially paralyzed by a personal feud between Sirs Redvers Buller and Frederick Sleigh Roberts, which led to awful blunders. Buller eventually hammered out a victory strategy.

Pakenham has written the first full-scale history of the war since 1910 and has exhausted his subject in terms of original research; he probably runs five thousand names across six hundred pages. During the first stage of the confrontation, the Boers took advantage of British weakness and unpreparedness to attack Natal from the Transvaal as well as northern Cape Colony from the Orange Free State. Northern sections of Cape Colony also rebelled against the British and joined the Boers. During Black Week (December 10-15, 1899), the Boers besieged Ladysmith, Mafeking, and Kimberley, and the British suffered reverses at Spion Kop in January, 1900. General Kitchener then took complete charge of the second phase of the conflict, relieved the besieged towns, beat the Boer armies in the field, and advanced along the railroads. Bloemfontein, capital city of the Orange Free State, was occupied by the British in February, 1900, while Johannesburg and Pretoria, Transvaal centers of gold mining and government respectively, were taken in May and June, 1900. Kruger fled Pretoria for Europe.

Toward the end of 1900, the Boers began a guerrilla war against the British which lasted some fifteen months. Boer commandos led by Christiaan Rudolf de Wet and Jacobus Hercules De la Rey harassed British army bases and communications. Jan Smuts advanced within fifty miles of Cape Town. Large rural areas of the Transvaal and Orange Free State were out of British control. Kitchener's response was to erect barbed wire and blockhouse fortifications along the railroads in an effort to protect British positions, a tactic which largely failed to do the job. He then set out on a scorched earth policy, burning and destroying Boer and African farms thought to be supporting the guerrilla movement. The inhabitants of these farms were rounded up and put in concentration camps located alongside the railroads. These camps were miserably run and unhygienic, and were soon swept with disease and epidemics. Twenty to twenty-eight thousand civilians died in them, and the conscience of Britain was stirred. In the end, some seven thousand of perhaps 87,000 Boers died resisting the British, and Kitchener's methods paid off; the Boers accepted the loss of their independence at the Peace of Vereeniging (May, 1902).

Probably 100,000 black Africans served both sides in the conflict, and over twelve thousand of these perished in the British camps alone. Blacks clearly paid the heaviest price of the war and its aftermath. Article Eight (clause nine) of the peace agreement provided that no native franchise would be required in South Africa until *after* the introduction of self-government. Article Eight protected the constitutions of the two former Boer republics, and Milner agreed to this arrangement confident that massive British immigration and liberalization would follow on the heels of an aggressive policy of development, which he personally planned to administer. However, a subsequent scheme to import Chinese labor to work the gold mines created a controversy, wherein Britishers joined with Afrikaners against his administration, and he resigned as high commissioner in 1905. British immigration of a magnitude sufficient to dwarf the Afrikaners never did materialize, and Article Eight was incorporated into the constitutional foundations of the Union of South Africa (1909). Once the Afrikaners achieved self-government they did not grant the franchise to nonwhites and instead secured legislation in 1924, 1934, and 1948 which delivered South Africa into the hands of apartheid, a system of total segregation of the races and of white supremacy. Criticism within the British Commonwealth of these policies caused South Africa to leave that organization in 1961, ending forever Milner's version of a prosperous South Africa within the British community.

Today the Boers face a final war of independence, one that is of concern to the entire world. South Africa is more than ever situated in a strategic location, which watches over world shipping lanes and produces gold and an array of minerals for a gold and mineral hungry world. It remains an open question as to whether a white, puritanical society, even one with a long history of cohesion and perseverance, adept at police state methods, and perhaps in possession of a nuclear capability, can indefinitely maintain control of nonwhite worker races that are increasingly more numerous than their white governors.

Jack L. Calbert

BREAKING RANKS
A Political Memoir

Author: Norman Podhoretz (1930-   )
Publisher: Harper & Row Publishers (New York). 375 pp. $15.00
Type of work: Memoir
Time: 1946-1978
Locale: The United States

The story of an intellectual's growth from traditional liberalism, through political radicalism, and finally to a redefinition of liberalism in contemporary terms

> *Principal personages:*
> NORMAN PODHORETZ, an intellectual, author, and editor of *Commentary*
> PAUL GOODMAN, an author and proponent of radical ideas
> JASON EPSTEIN, an editor of the radical *New York Review of Books*
> LIONEL TRILLING, an old-line liberal, author, and intellectual
> DANIEL P. MOYNIHAN, an intellectual and politician in the liberal tradition

Breaking Ranks is an intellectual odyssey; it is also an exercise in self-justification. It starts with the author's espousal of the liberal anti-Communism of the 1940's and 1950's with its emphasis on benevolent government centralization, salutary economic growth, and integration as a solution to racial problems. It shows Podhoretz's conversion at the close of the 1950's to the radicalism that was to characterize much of the 1960's, a radicalism which attacked these positions. This memoir deals centrally, however, with the author's "breaking ranks"—his dismissal of 1960's radicalism as a self-defeating sham—and his attempt to define a new position in terms of his own interests as an American and as an intellectual.

When Podhoretz began his career as editor of *Commentary* in 1960, he immediately altered its ideological direction by publishing Paul Goodman's *Growing Up Absurd*, serialized in the magazine's first three issues. This spirited critique attacks American society as a creator of obstacles for people who want to satisfy "certain elementary needs of the human spirit—for useful and necessary work to do, for sex without shame or guilt, for a community to be loyal to." In his support of Goodman and his desire to criticize American society and its public values, Podhoretz was at odds with his teacher and mentor, Lionel Trilling, and at one with his friend, Jason Epstein, whose *New York Review of Books* was on the forefront of radical ideology preferring a Communist victory in Vietnam, suspecting American motives at home and abroad, and glorifying youthful irresponsibility as political idealism.

Podhoretz, however, soon began to distance himself both from traditional liberalism and from new-style radicalism. This distancing can be seen in his essay "My Negro Problem—and Ours" and in his first book of memoirs, *Making It*. In "My Negro Problem—and Ours," Podhoretz gives vent to his pessimism about integration: all blacks hate whites and all whites are "twisted and sick" in their feelings about blacks. Moreover, blacks "hate whites not only—or perhaps not even primarily—for social and political reasons, but also for psychological and spiritual ones." This essay attained some notoriety, but *Making It* actually became notorious. Published in 1968, *Making It* was a memoir of the author's craving for and attainment of success as a member of the New York intellectual community. His attitude toward success was essentially positive: it was right to want it and a pleasure to have it. Podhoretz's affirmation provoked intense hostility. As one example among many, his friend, novelist and social critic Norman Mailer, who has praised the book in private, damned it in public as a "blunder of self-assertion, self-exposure and self-denigration."

This concerted attack on Podhoretz's views was only a skirmish in a major war: the bid for power and ideological supremacy on the part of the radical movement. A "New Class" of the educated and prosperous were "making a serious bid to dislodge and replace the business and commercial class which had on the whole dominated the country for nearly a century." For all its supposed interest in the poor and the blacks, the radical movement which this class energized had one concern only: "to aggrandize its own power." It was a movement that did not so much represent youth as use them for its own purpose as "commandos" and as a symbol "implying that [the movement was] the wave of the future." Even the great linguistic scholar Noam Chomsky could be dishonest enough to attack those who disagreed with him on Vietnam as "no better than Nazi war criminals." Chomsky and other leaders of the antiwar movement used language to intimidate, so that "those who continued speaking up in favor of American policy were isolated and even excommunicated by students and colleagues alike."

This intellectual meretriciousness forced Podhoretz "to break political ranks." To be loyal to radicalism was to betray intellectual standards, to give up the right to make valid distinctions and follow where truth leads. Therefore, in the early 1970's, *Commentary* made its break with the movement; movement policy was called little more than the mindless generation of turmoil, and the movement's chief intellectual organ, the *New York Review of Books*, was labeled as morally reprehensible yellow journalism of the left with no regard for the truth. Although Podhoretz claims that the purpose in this attack was "a deepening of the society's sense of things, the refinement of its consciousness, the enhancement of its cultural life," in fact, he was developing and defending his new political point of view. In foreign policy, he was anti-Communist, believing that only a strong American defense policy could protect the free world. He had few doubts that our foreign policy was conducted on a higher moral plane than that of the Soviets. In domestic matters, he objected to the refusal of the young "to assume responsibility for themselves by taking their place in a world of adults." Supporting traditional

American values of hard work and the politics of self-interest, he valued competition and success, but not to the point of eliminating the New Deal programs that eased the lot of the poor and the unemployed. He felt strongly about equal opportunity but was against affirmative action when it meant that race or ethnic background superseded merit.

Podhoretz eventually had an opportunity to put his political ideas into action. In 1976, Daniel Patrick Moynihan, an intellectual with views Podhoretz could support, became a popular figure because of his outspoken patriotism and his bluntness: for example, he called Idi Amin of Uganda a "racist murderer." Moynihan was persuaded to run in New York's Democratic Senatorial primary; he won in the primary and then in the election defeated his Republican opponent, James Buckley. He began "to define a liberal alternative . . . to the left and . . . to the right and to prove that this alternative commanded more popular support than either." To Podhoretz, Moynihan's victory was a hopeful sign that this country was still capable of political common sense.

Podhoretz's political odyssey from traditional liberalism through the new radicalism toward a redefinition of liberalism in terms of contemporary political realities is worthy of attention. It will help to clarify an era many have lived through but few have understood. *Breaking Ranks* is one man's story shaped by inevitable biases, but it carries weight and enlists conviction because of Podhoretz's determined honesty about his motives and his mistakes. Despite his false starts and his frustrations, he hopes for and dreams of a better America which is truer to itself.

Alan G. Gross

THE BRETHREN
Inside the Supreme Court

Author: Bob Woodward and Scott Armstrong
Publisher: Simon and Schuster (New York). Illustrated. 467 pp. $13.95
Type of work: History
Time: 1969-1976
Locale: The United States

A description of the functioning and internal operations of the Supreme Court of the United States from 1969 to 1976

> *Principal personages:*
> HUGO BLACK, Justice of the Supreme Court appointed by Franklin D. Roosevelt in 1937; resigned in 1971
> WILLIAM O. DOUGLAS, Justice of the Supreme Court appointed by Franklin D. Roosevelt in 1939; resigned in 1975
> EARL WARREN, Chief Justice of the Supreme Court appointed by Dwight D. Eisenhower in 1953; resigned in 1969
> JOHN M. HARLAN, Justice of the Supreme Court appointed by Dwight D. Eisenhower in 1954; resigned in 1971
> WILLIAM J. BRENNAN, JR., Justice of the Supreme Court appointed by Dwight D. Eisenhower in 1956
> POTTER STEWART, Justice of the Supreme Court appointed by Dwight D. Eisenhower in 1958
> BYRON WHITE, Justice of the Supreme Court appointed by John F. Kennedy in 1962
> ABE FORTAS, Justice of the Supreme Court appointed by Lyndon Johnson in 1965; resigned in 1969
> THURGOOD MARSHALL, Justice of the Supreme Court appointed by Lyndon Johnson in 1967
> WARREN E. BURGER, Chief Justice of the Supreme Court appointed by Richard M. Nixon in 1969
> HARRY A. BLACKMUN, Justice of the Supreme Court appointed by Richard M. Nixon in 1970
> LEWIS F. POWELL, JR., Justice of the Supreme Court appointed by Richard M. Nixon in 1971
> WILLIAM H. REHNQUIST, Justice of the Supreme Court appointed by Richard M. Nixon in 1971
> JOHN PAUL STEVENS, Justice of the Supreme Court appointed by Gerald R. Ford in 1975

The Brethren is, as the subtitle suggests, an effort to comprehend the inner functioning of the nation's highest court; it is important because it represents the first major attempt to understand the inner workings of the Supreme Court from 1969 through the 1975 term. It also at times exposes, denigrates, and ridicules members of the Supreme Court and the ways in which their decisions are made. Criticism is undertaken without citing sources and is based upon misrepresentation, inaccuracy of description, and unjustified attribution of motives. Finally, the effort of Woodward and Armstrong to besmirch the public perception of members of the Supreme Court is purposeless and tasteless.

The Brethren provides a description of the many cases considered and the decisionmaking process in each of the terms of the Supreme Court from 1969 through 1975. This was a critical period in the history of the Court, for it encompassed the transition from the Warren Court to the fully developed Burger Court. The transition is depicted almost as a regression, with a high-minded and exceptionally competent Earl Warren being replaced by a mediocre Warren Burger. One by one, the towering figures of the Warren Court either resign or manifest triviality and pettiness under Burger. Advocacy of the defense of liberty gives way to political conservatism. Through all of this, Woodward and Armstrong describe, characterize, and criticize in a neutral journalistic language designed to convey the impression of objectivity.

In the authors' view, Earl Warren had for fifteen years been the leader and spirit behind a judicial revolution in behalf of liberty, while Warren Burger was the selection of a Nixon Administration seeking to undermine that revolution. In actuality, after his appointment as Chief Justice, Burger attempted to modernize and improve the system of physical facilities of the Supreme Court and to open lines of communication between the Supreme Court and the legal establishment in the United States. According to Woodward and Armstrong, however, Burger's role in decisionmaking was manipulative, incompetent, and politically conservative. For example, he sought to eliminate or reduce busing for purposes of racial integration; he attempted to reduce the rights of prisoners; and he supported the death penalty. The tag "conservatism," for Woodward and Armstrong, explains most positions that Burger took. The authors insist that "The Chief provided no intellectual leadership." Moreover, in "legal analysis, he was grossly inadequate." In addition to Burger's "intellectual inadequacies" and "inability to write coherent opinions," the style of the Chief Justice was "overbearing and offensive." Altogether, Warren Burger "was a product of Richard Nixon's tasteless White House, distinguished in appearance and bearing, but without substance or integrity. Burger was abrasive to his colleagues, persistent in ignorance, and, worst of all, intellectually dishonest."

Woodward and Armstrong portray the Chief Justice as highly manipulative in the assignment of the writing of opinions. Burger prevented important "cases in criminal law, racial discrimination, and free speech" from going to the liberals on the court, Justices William O. Douglas, William J. Brennan, and Thurgood Marshall. He deferred his own opinions in conference and took any side he wished in order to be in the majority and therefore able to assign cases to the Justices he wished. He freely switched his view back and forth while an opinion was being written in order to exert maximum influence. For example, in *Chandler* v. *Roudebush* (1975), before the unanimous decision was announced, the Chief Justice had changed his vote five times. Woodward and Armstrong paint an unflattering portrait of Burger which they stress repeatedly throughout *The Brethren*.

Not only do Woodward and Armstrong describe Burger with severity, but their treatment of the other Justices can be equally critical, as well. While Thurgood Marshall's greeting to Burger, "What's shakin', Chiefy baby?," injected humor into the Court, Marshall is presented as a man who had very great difficulty formulating satisfactory opinions. The authors' treatment of Douglas is likewise unfortunate. Burger's efforts to direct opinions away from Douglas and to prevent him from assigning the cases that were part of his judicial prerogatives must have been very difficult for Douglas. The story is one of almost constant frustration generated primarily by the Chief Justice. The final tragedy of Douglas' stroke, his physical and mental decline, his desperate struggle to stay on the Supreme Court, and his eventual resignation are described with a wealth of detail, particularly about his physical and mental health, that is obscene and tasteless. Evidently the Woodward-Armstrong brand of journalism favors titillating the public over maintaining standards of decency.

The book's treatment of Justice Hugo Black's gradual deterioration is not as cruel as its depiction of Douglas, but again the description goes beyond the bounds of propriety. Of other Justices that *The Brethren* describes critically, Harry Blackmun is presented as a man perpetually confronted with an inferiority complex; Byron White as a rather inconsistent loner who could, at times, be brilliantly analytical; and William Rehnquist, the Court's knee-jerk conservative, as a man willing to misconstrue and distort facts and decisions to attain his ideological objectives.

The heroes of *The Brethren* are the Justices who represent the center, who achieve the compromises needed to arrive at decisions, and who control the Court. Justice William Brennan's liberal-centrist role evaporated as conservatives were appointed to the Court under the Nixon-Ford Administrations. Brennan was forced ever more into a defense of liberalism. By the end of the period covered by the book, he had, with Marshall, become a voice crying in the wilderness that could generally be ignored. In his isolation, Brennan assumed a posture that denied compromise and, hence, ceased to be very effective.

The Brethren is most kind in its treatment of Justice John M. Harlan, whose views were invariably conservative. Harlan frequently assumed a conservative-centrist role on the court as he utilized brilliant skills of scholarly precision in an attempt to achieve compromise on the Supreme Court.

The genuine centrists of the Court are Potter Stewart and Lewis F. Powell. Exceedingly capable, these justices have been able to produce constructive opinions that have drawn other members of the Court into the center and have maintained that center. The Woodward-Armstrong account of their consistent resourcefulness, moderation, and good sense conveys more than a mere description of tactics. The Justices of the center have brought some sense of community and compromise to the Court. Neither a Nixon Court nor a Burger Court, from 1969 to 1975 "the major opinions had been the achievement of the center coalition." All of the Justices, even the very competent John Paul Stevens who enters the Court only in the last pages of *The Brethren*, had to recognize that "The center was in control."

The importance of the center was reflected in the opinions of the Court. For example, the 1971 Supreme Court decision upholding court-mandated busing for Charlotte, North Carolina, was an opinion written by Burger. It was, in fact, a document to which almost all of the Justices eventually contributed. Capital punishment was an issue that was long debated and agonized over. The Justices (except Marshall) were unwilling to abolish the death penalty, but were also unwilling to accept responsibility for the deaths of the prisoners on death rows throughout the nation. The result was a fifty-thousand-word, 243-page, five-to-four decision recognizing that some but clearly not all death penalty laws were unconstitutional. State legislators who insisted on a death penalty had to weigh alternatives carefully. The issue arose again, most significantly in the 1975 term, and again produced much agonizing on the part of the Justices.

Efforts of the Burger Court to restrict obscenity and pornography foundered on consideration of the First Amendment; therefore, the Court was unable to assume, to the displeasure of Burger, a position that significantly curtailed its distribution. In the same way that the center could often produce a clear decision, it could also prevent one. The Court tried to arrive at a clear decision on abortion. Blackmun struggled for many months with a decision based on the formula that the right to abortion decreases and the interest of the state to protect the fetus increases as a pregnancy progresses from the first trimester to the second and, subsequently, to the third. This appeared to be a brilliant compromise that satisfied the Court, but on such a heated topic as abortion, any decision would have generated general antagonism from one or another side in the controversy. This was exactly the result.

Jumping from one case to another during each term, the Woodward-Armstrong volume makes little attempt at analysis. The book is less interesting than it might have been with a somewhat different format. The long and sustained description of Watergate, the Nixon tapes, and the issue of executive privilege is, in contrast with much of the rest of the book, a particularly exciting and well-presented section.

The major issue relating to Watergate involved executive privilege. The Watergate Special Prosecutor, Leon Jaworski, urged the Supreme Court to require that President Richard Nixon turn his taped conversations over to Jaworski. The President's attorney, James St. Clair, insisted on executive privilege, saying that the President was immune from criminal prosecution and was not required to submit evidence to the Special Prosecutor. St. Clair held that the President could be impeached, but otherwise could not be subjected to a criminal investigation. When the case was considered in conference, from the outset there was unanimity (Rehnquist withdrew from the case) with almost each Justice actually contributing significantly to the writing of the decision. The interaction of the Justices on this case is a fascinating story and is one of the highlights of the book. The final vote was eight to zero against President Nixon; two and a half weeks later, the President resigned. Again, the final decision was based on compromise and the domination of the court by its center. Woodward and Armstrong successfully support their view of the importance of the center on the Burger Court.

The authors are not so successful in other aspects of the book. The attribution of authorship of opinions is not always correct. Justice Douglas and not Brennan was the author of *Brady* v. *Maryland* (1963). In *DeFunis* v. *Odegaard*, Douglas is said to have taken a particular position on an opinion when he actually took the opposite view. The book contains other similar inaccuracies. Sources represent a problem in this book. Invariably much information is attributed to the law clerks working for the various Justices. However, nowhere are sources cited, and reviewers who have spoken directly with law clerks have discovered that in many important instances Woodward and Armstrong are wrong in their descriptions, frequently misinterpret events, and sometimes misconstrue facts. Occasionally former clerks deny what Woodward and Armstrong describe.

Furthermore, it is not clear how Woodward and Armstrong arrived at their descriptions of the Justices' feelings toward one another. For example, the source for Justice Powell's determination "to bend over backward to maintain good personal relations with all other justices" is unclear. This kind of unsubstantiated opinion can be found throughout the book. Detailed conversations among the Justices are revealed as they discuss cases in Court conferences. The only problem here is that only the Justices are present in conference and Woodward and Armstrong simply cannot know the specifics of such confidential conversations; they claim to reveal the innermost thoughts and sentiments of the Justices with no factual support and no citation of sources. In the quasi-objective language of the book, Burger manipulates, Stewart compromises, Marshall relaxes, and White does his "own thing." Invariably the view of the Justices is harsh, as Woodward and Armstrong ascribe to intrigue many of their actions and motives. Much in this account is merely character assassination—especially the treatment of Chief Justice Burger.

How, then, is one to evaluate *The Brethren*? First, it is a conscious effort to demonstrate that the Justices of the Supreme Court have feet of clay and that the hallowed Court is a very human and often nasty institution; the book is exposure for the sake of exposure. Such an approach might even be acceptable were it not for the constant stream of inaccuracies throughout the book, the pretense of being able to read the secret thoughts and conversations of the Justices, and the constant use of anonymous sources that readers are expected to believe. Claiming to be an objective account, *The Brethren* is, in reality, a hatchet job that ignores journalistic standards of truth and intellectual integrity. Saddest of all, in its merciless depiction of the decline of Black and Douglas and in the ridicule that is placed in the mouths of Justices to describe other Justices, the book lacks decency. Profound ethical questions are raised by this book about the nature of such journalism. It seems clear that *The Brethren* says far more about Woodward and Armstrong that it says about the Supreme Court and its Justices.

Saul Lerner

THE BRINK
Cuban Missile Crisis, 1962

Author: David Detzer (1937-   )
Publisher: Thomas Y. Crowell (New York). Illustrated. 299 pp. $11.95
Type of work: History
Time: 1960-1962
Locale: The United States and Cuba

A broadly based study of the ingredients which collectively produced the threat of war between the United States and Russia over the placement of offensive missiles on the island of Cuba during the John F. Kennedy presidency

> *Principal personages:*
> FIDEL CASTRO, Premier of Cuba, 1959-
> JOHN F. KENNEDY, President of the United States, 1961-1963
> NIKITA KHRUSHCHEV, Premier of the Union of Soviet Socialist Republics, 1958-1964
> ROBERT MCNAMARA, Secretary of Defense in the Kennedy Administration
> JOHN MCCONE, Director of the Central Intelligence Agency in the Kennedy Administration

With the possible exception of the assassination in Dallas in November, 1963, no single event of the John F. Kennedy presidency has attracted more scholarly attention than the Cuban missile crisis in the fall of 1962. The handling of that dilemma and its inherent effects upon subsequent international developments is widely regarded as the high watermark of the Kennedy Administration. While it can certainly be claimed that the image and style of the Kennedy years have left a stronger legacy than specific administration achievements, the impact of those fateful days in October, 1962, clearly altered the flow of world trends.

Much has been written regarding the sequence of events during that relatively brief crisis by those individuals closely connected with it. Notable figures ranging from Soviet Premier Nikita Khrushchev to Attorney General Robert F. Kennedy to NBC reporter Elie Abel have offered their recollections of the matter in print. In each instance, the available commentaries have shed an added perspective on the handling of the problems and the nature of decisionmaking. Yet each of these firsthand accounts has focused upon those aspects of the crisis that the author observed while largely ignoring the larger questions of history.

David Detzer examines the Cuban missile issue in a somewhat broader context. Although a substantial portion of the text records the daily happenings when the crisis was at its peak—approximately from October 14 to October 28—a larger effort is made to examine the reasons for the Russian placement of offensive missiles in Cuba and the attitude of the Kennedy Administration toward Castro's regime.

Detzer, a professor at Western Connecticut State College whose most notable previous work was a look at the Korean War period in *Thunder of the Captains*, employs a writing style which borders on that of mystery thrillers. Dialogue quotations and attempts at a description of the environmental scenes make for a casual style which is eminently readable in the manner of escapist novels. Yet considerable research has gone into the verification of these presentations, as the concluding chapter notes amply demonstrate. When problems emerge in Detzer's work, they arise from his own assumptions, which are liberally sprinkled throughout.

The initial third of Detzer's book is, in some ways, its most distinguishing feature. Considerable pains are taken here to present a portrait of the leading figures involved in the Washington-Moscow-Havana triangle and also to create the mood for the eventual missile confrontation. A prologue of some length strives to set the tone by remembering the New York City visits of Khrushchev and Fidel Castro in September, 1960. Both arrived in the United States for the purpose of making addresses to the United Nations Assembly, although the U.N. speeches themselves are not the focal point of Detzer's study. Instead, the visits are used here as a vehicle to paint a period image of Castro and his entourage in terms of their gruff life-styles, shifting hotel residences, and even the social implications of their sprouting beards. The simultaneous arrival of the Soviet Premier in New York is garnished with a glance at Khrushchev's background, including his origins in the peasant class and his rise to a central position in the Russian Communist Party.

To build upon these opening images, the author then devotes considerable time to a look at Cuba's past, its cultural styles by 1960, and a quick-paced biography of Fidel Castro in conjunction with a record of the shortcomings of the insensitive Batista regime of the late 1950's. Through Detzer's presentation, Castro is portrayed as a vibrant revolutionary largely divorced from any strict ideological code or doctrine. While falling short of ever becoming the romanticized figure of Che Guevara in the mid-1960's, Castro nevertheless was further removed from the intellectualism of a Lenin. If Castro and Khrushchev can be said to have had anything in common, it would be their humble origins and their determination to succeed. Both were survivors who relied more upon instinct and ambition than upon rigid revolutionary formulae. Detzer illustrates this point by quoting Khrushchev as having once told press reporters, "Life is a great school. It thrashes you and bangs you about and teaches you."

The personalities of Khrushchev and Castro, however, are only a segment of the author's study. Considerable emphasis is also given to the growing disenchantment of the United States toward Castro's Communism. The American public's initial sense of hope which accompanied Castro's overthrow of the Batista government in Cuba gradually disappeared as crude outdoor arena trials were held convicting Batista loyalists. Coupled with these incidents came a flood of horror stories from Cuban exiles and refugees to Florida, and the increasingly Communistic slant of Castro's own public statements.

With his treatment of the Kennedy Administration, Detzer's observations begin to be based upon questionable assumptions. Although his evaluation of the Bay of Pigs fiasco in 1961 as a CIA misreading of Castro's status and the temperament of the Cuban population is valid, Detzer's attempt to penetrate Kennedy's motives is more controversial. In describing the new President, the author notes Kennedy's pre-Castro vacationing on the island and suggests that pleasant memories of Cuba became tarnished in Kennedy's mind by the presence of a Marxist-oriented regime controlled by rowdies. Such an appraisal depicts Kennedy's attitudes as surprisingly bourgeois.

More valid, however, is Detzer's attention to Kennedy's fear (expressed to *New York Times* columnist James Reston) that Khrushchev might interpret the Bay of Pigs disaster as a sign of Kennedy's inexperience and lack of resolve, especially insofar as the invasion was poorly orchestrated and not promoted by the participation of actual United States troops. That the Bay of Pigs failure angered Kennedy is a viable conclusion which subsequent Administration actions seemingly justify. Beyond this, however, Detzer feels compelled to draw the analogy of the common Kennedy family symbol: competitive touch football. Regarding the Kennedy temperament, he concludes that "one didn't lose at touch football; one certainly shouldn't lose in Cold War contests." Detzer's use of such an equation borders on the sophomoric.

There can be little argument that Castro and Communism in Cuba became a near obsession with many high-ranking members of the Kennedy Administration. Secretary of Defense Robert McNamara admitted as much to a later Senate Select Committee studying United States intelligence activities, and, on another Senate committee report, McNamara is recorded as once openly proposing Castro's assassination. In particular, the CIA was actively involved in a range of bizarre clandestine attempts to hasten Castro's downfall, especially after the more direct approach failed in the Bay of Pigs. The CIA method was to tamper with Cuban economic conditions to such an extent that a homegrown Cuban uprising would end Castro's control on the island. How deeply involved in these covert CIA schemes the Kennedy Administration's planners were is a matter Detzer feels less secure about; but he concludes that this was "presumably the New Frontier's" agreed-upon strategy and not just a case of Agency pastimes.

In any event, the obvious United States attempts to topple or at least pressure his government led Castro to conclude by the summer of 1962 that a more developed military invasion of his island was reasonably imminent. Aside from the CIA tamperings, of which Castro may or may not have been fully cognizant, there were the more readily observable matters of United States military maneuvers in the Caribbean and the easily charted fluctuations in the mood of Miami's Cuban population. Detzer uses matters such as these to explain why Russia took the risk of placing missiles on the island.

Naturally, many suggested explanations for the Soviet missile decision have been offered both at the time of the crisis and in its aftermath. Although Detzer deals in some depth with all of the likely possibilities, his suggestions suffer from the same problem that all Cold War histories face: the lack of access to Soviet official documents. What few sources are available, such as Khrushchev's own memoirs, are admitted by the author to be so frequently jumbled that the entirety of the evidence is suspect. To Detzer's credit, however, those assumptions which he does put forth are not presented as absolutes but rather as a collection of viable scenarios.

Unlike some writers seeking the same answers, Detzer does not present one overriding reason for the Russian missile policy but instead offers three seemingly pertinent ones: the dangerous Soviet strategic military position in relation to the United States, the use of Cuban missiles as a bargaining point regarding West Berlin, and the feasibility of a full-scale United States military invasion of Cuba. Detzer considers the first of these three reasons the most important and therefore gives it the greatest elaboration. The author argues strongly in a lengthy summary of United States missile development programs during the 1950's that, despite the 1960 election campaign debate over the existence of a "missile gap" favoring the Soviets, the United States was in fact significantly ahead. Through the efforts of individuals such as Albert Wohlstetter at the RAND Corporation, the United States had begun to pull away substantially from the Soviets in technological advances and had established not only a good second-strike nuclear capability, but also the means to deal a potentially crippling first-strike on the Russian arsenal. Certainly such a situation was not readily apparent to many Americans who were transfixed by the glamour of the Russian satellite launchings. Yet the sophistication of the United States missile program augmented by the deployment of a nuclear submarine fleet was far in excess of Russia's early 1960's weaponry. For the Soviets to regain a competitive level would require a massive financial commitment at a time when Russia's agricultural production was in an embarrassing state, and might require considerable time.

As such, Detzer believes that Khrushchev began by April of 1962 to see the placement of a Russian missile base in Cuba as an interim strategy. Detzer further theorizes that any high-level Russian official opposition to Khrushchev's notion may have come from the lack of precedent in Soviet policy for having sent this type of sophisticated weaponry far beyond Russia's own borders. Nevertheless, the establishment of strategic missiles in Cuba would not only buy time for Russia to enhance its development programs, but would also alter the balance of power to the point that the Western presence in Berlin could become negotiable, and the likelihood of any United States assault on Cuba would be forestalled. In addition, Detzer adds that such a step might have had the bonus impact of diffusing China's growing criticism that Russia had become revisionist, exchanging hard-line Marxism for an unassertive policy of peaceful coexistence.

After discussing the question of Russian motives, Detzer turns his attention to the nature of the United States response; again, he presents a variety of possible theories. He focuses mostly on the bureaucratic orientation of American foreign policy. The gathering, assimilation, and evaluation of pertinent data from a mass of inconsequential and erroneous information is offered as a key ingredient in the months of delay before any genuine Administration fears were aroused. The author interestingly notes that the Administration had a file five inches thick on missiles in Cuba three years before the Soviets sent any missiles there. Clearly, the file was based upon random bits of hearsay from Cubans, CIA operatives, and various observers, but the collection dealt with such a sensitive situation, and one being keenly monitored by the Administration, that it could not be dismissed lightly. Detzer awards John McCone, Director of the CIA, the distinction of being the first high-ranking official to suspect that the missiles were in Cuba by August of 1962; this was at least two months before President Kennedy was presented with hard evidence by McGeorge Bundy, the Administration's National Security Adviser.

Perhaps because the tangles of bureaucratic shuffling are a common feature of foreign policy, Detzer does not really fault the Administration for its gradual consensus-building methods prior to the decision to blockade Cuba. On the whole, Detzer's coverage of the nerve-racking two weeks during which the Kennedy-Khrushchev confrontation occurred is a relatively standard presentation of now well-documented events. Kennedy is also dutifully praised by the author for showing restraint in not pushing Khrushchev or seeking to humiliate the Soviets once the Kremlin had served notice that it would dismantle the Cuban sites.

More notable, however, are the author's comments on whether the crisis could have been avoided altogether. Insofar as 1962 was an American election year and Kennedy was battling to answer Republican criticisms over the Administration's lackluster Cuban policy (especially from New York Senator Kenneth Keating), Detzer suggests that Khrushchev had a tendency to overestimate the importance of American elections. Seemingly this observation is meant to imply that the Soviets feared that Kennedy would take a hard line against Cuba, possibly to the point of invading the island, in order to salvage Democratic Party political prospects. Regrettably, Detzer does not provide any real illustrations to back up this suggestion. He merely introduces it as a blanket characteristic.

Somewhat more peculiar is Detzer's conclusion that had Kennedy made clear "his total opposition to strategic weapons in Cuba before the Spring of 1962, the crisis could have probably been avoided." The oddity of such a theory becomes greater when one recalls the lengths to which the author has earlier argued that Khrushchev faced a nuclear missile balance-of-power dilemma with the United States. In addition, Detzer observes that Kennedy was of the opinion that Khrushchev never put much value on words in comparison to actions, and that, in any event, the legacy of the Bay of Pigs and the Kennedy-Khrushchev Vienna Summit Conference in 1961 suggested a President who was weak.

To say that David Detzer's book is frequently undermined by faulty or insupportable assumptions does not fully detract from the worth of the presentation. For many, *The Brink* will provide a good, compact survey of the crisis that brought the world closer to nuclear war than ever before. There remains, however, a continuing need for the motivations behind the policies and decisions to be more authoritatively recorded.

Terry Alan Baney

BROCA'S BRAIN
Reflections on the Romance of Science

Author: Carl Sagan (1934-   )
Publisher: Random House (New York). 347 pp. $12.95
Type of work: Science

A thought provoking work which celebrates the power and potential of the human mind and man's quest for knowledge

In 1880, a French neurosurgeon and anthropologist named Paul Broca died. His brain was carefully removed and preserved in a bottle which is still housed in the Musée de l'Homme in Paris among countless other brains Broca had collected and studied during his successful anatomical career. Bypassing the irony of Broca's final repository, Carl Sagan uses this brain as a starting point and thematic symbol for his collection of articles, *Broca's Brain: Reflections on the Romance of Science*. Having dealt with the evolution of our species in his 1978 Pulitzer Prize-winning book *The Dragons of Eden*, Sagan here reveals his appreciation for the inner genius of mankind and its outward manifestation in the exploration and description of our world.

Carl Sagan is a respected astronomer whose work has won numerous scientific awards and has been translated into many languages. He is also becoming respected by the general public for his ability to share his scientific knowledge with the lay person while conveying his enthusiasm for the joys of discovery and creativity. The subtitle of this book clearly defines its pervasive theme. To Sagan, the pursuit of knowledge is exciting and exhilarating in every field, and his goal is to strike a responsive chord in the reader. In five main sections, he discusses intellectual explorations in astronomy, pseudoscience, cosmology, and religion, along with minor excursions into science fiction, psychology, extraterrestrial life, government·policy, and popular beliefs and customs.

Despite the impossibility of fully understanding the entire universe of knowledge, this volume celebrates the attempts of scientists and other creative thinkers to unravel the laws of nature and the universe. This search for knowledge means that each new theory or idea must meet the tests of scientific inquiry before it can be fully accepted. Scientific knowledge develops in stages. The discovery of factual information is an important step, but we also depend upon the synthesis and development of theories to explain the relationships of those facts to one another. The testing and retesting of facts and theories as new discoveries are made is essential to the growth of knowledge. Once a theory is accepted without such testing, growth stops. To demonstrate this tenet, Sagan gives numerous examples of how various missions into space in recent years have confirmed previously developed theories of cosmologists. With some clear, specific evidence, these scientists can now proceed with more assurance than was possible before. This type of proof is as necessary today as it was for Galileo in his struggle to prove the heliocentric theory of Copernicus.

Theories which cannot withstand continual close scrutiny in the light of new discoveries should be dismissed. A major section of *Broca's Brain*, "The Paradoxers," is an exposé of popular and scientific theories which fit into this category, such as the lost continent of Atlantis, UFO's, dream precognition, and ESP. Continuing his argument and giving an example of how such theories should be tested, Sagan devotes a long chapter to a detailed critique of the theories presented in Immanuel Velikovsky's *Worlds in Collision* (1950). Velikovsky theorized that celestial catastrophies have been, and still are, the major shaping force in the universe, using various mythologies and scientific theory to support his contention. Sagan's point is that such controversial work deserves detailed criticism rather than casual dismissal in order to test fully all of the facts and theories presented. Without such painstaking analysis, it is impossible, Sagan argues, to dismiss any argument. All new ideas should be welcomed and examined. Another less ponderous example of Sagan's method is his refutation of the mathematical method by which a numerologist has proven himself to be God. Throughout these chapters, Sagan's approach is at once critical of the theories on a factual basis, but supportive of the creative, exploratory intellect inherent in their design.

The author's respect for curiosity and intuitive genius is well documented, along with his knowledge of many scientific fields. Following his initial introduction of Paul Broca, he describes at length the enormous accomplishments of fellow scientific heroes Albert Einstein and Robert Goddard, and many other contributors in passing. This continual display of scientific achievement throughout the volume is stimulating and provocative. Sagan uses every opportunity to propose new questions on the basis of proven theories and to indicate the directions for future experiment and thought. In many respects, the book epitomizes its own theme, encouraging others to continue the quest for knowledge while celebrating the considerable information we have already amassed. Sagan is very obviously an optimist.

Broca's Brain is generally enjoyable to read as well, although the quality varies. Many chapters were previously published as separate articles and were collected here with additional chapters linking them together. The inconsistencies mainly arise from the variety and range of subjects Sagan approaches, showing his scientific knowledge in some, while favoring his intuitive speculation in others. Even in the detailed mathematical explanations, however, he rarely fails to make his point with a concise and simple clarity. Scientific reviewers appreciate his enthusiasm, his considerable scientific and mathematical ability, and his support of their pursuits, while the lay person is amused, enlightened, and challenged. In the sections in which he is obviously outside his field—those dealing with religious faith, psychic phenomena, or psychological theory—he is more open to criticism. To his credit, he is careful to label his speculation as such, and he would probably welcome a thorough critique and examination of the issues he raises.

A primary reason for Sagan's popularity as a writer is his ability to draw upon a wide variety of sources, highlighting his ideas with amusing stories and apt quotations in combination with a witty literary style. Although this facile manner of writing can sometimes be overly cute (at one point he refers to a small asteroid as a "worldlet," for example), this anecdotal quality is generally appealing. It is encouraging that a respected astronomer can stoop to a pun relating the work and name of cosmologer J. Richard Gott in discussing various theories on the nature and origin of the universe. His personal notes about Einstein, Goddard, Isaac Asimov, and others are equally diverting.

Sagan can also be accused of small provincialisms, such as assuming parallel cultural and technological development on other planets, and regarding life as always carbon-based. In his final chapter, his discussion leads him to "suppose" that the experience of birth trauma may be a primary factor in a future scientist's choice of cosmological theory. This fanciful theory may be totally untested and somewhat humorous, but it causes one to ponder its implications and the nature of our psychological development.

Broca's Brain is an important book whose value will continue to serve students and other interested readers as a stimulating tribute to the power and potential of the human mind. It could easily inspire a young scientist to seek answers to any of the many questions Sagan poses, or help a future Einstein feel more confident about his or her abilities and interests, despite lack of academic success. A third major contribution is Sagan's appeal in several chapters for increased government and popular support for science education and space exploration. Whether or not his arguments will result in improved monetary support, he has produced a convincing and compelling testament to the view that the destiny of the human race is to continue progressing, and that to extend the limits of knowledge is our most rewarding challenge.

Christine Gladish

THE BROTHERS MANN
The Lives of Heinrich and
Thomas Mann 1871-1950 and 1875-1955

Author: Nigel Hamilton
Publisher: Yale University Press (New Haven, Conn.). 422 pp. $16.95
Type of work: Literary biography
Time: 1871-1955
Locale: Germany and the United States

The joint biography of Heinrich and Thomas Mann, two of Germany's most distin-guished writers in the twentieth century

> *Principal personages:*
> HEINRICH MANN, German author and political leftist
> THOMAS MANN, German author and recipient of the Nobel Prize
>   for Literature
> JOHANN HEINRICH MANN, their father
> JULIA MANN (NÉE DA SILVA-BRUHNS), their mother
> KATJA MANN (NÉE PRINGSHEIM), Thomas' wife

In this, Nigel Hamilton's first major work, we have for the first time a biography of two writers, each celebrated in his own right, but all the more interesting because they happen to be brothers. What is more, they lived through an extraordinary period of their country's history, from the imperial state of the Kaisers through World War I and the Weimar Republic. Both were forced into exile in World War II, living in Southern California, where Heinrich Mann died in 1950, while his younger brother Thomas returned to Europe and died in Zurich in 1955.

The joint biography is of further interest because the relationship of the two brothers was itself important for their work and provides a key to un-derstanding some of their themes. The two were rivals in their early years, when, for a time, Heinrich was the more famous; and they passed through a period of conflict over their opposing political views in World War I, in which Thomas was a spokesman for the conservative, patriotic German po-sition, while Heinrich was pro-French, internationalist, and pacifist. The two eventually reconciled and were united in their opposition to Hitler's regime, as they were united in exile. Finally, during the war years and the postwar period, Thomas' fame grew steadily, as he became accepted as one of the great writers of the twentieth century, while Heinrich's reputation dwindled to the point that he is known outside of Germany, if at all, only as the author of the story of "The Blue Angel," the film made famous by Marlene Dietrich. In spite of these unequal reputations—and surely few critics would claim for Heinrich a status anywhere near equal to that of his more celebrated brother—as a pair, the two men do constitute what is probably the most distinguished literary brotherhood in modern literary history; this book is therefore of great value to anyone interested in German literature or in the cultural development of modern Germany. Indeed, Hamilton is by profession a historian, and his book is perhaps weakest in its literary criticism, although his wife, who died shortly after its completion, was German and a literary specialist, and contributed her expertise to the work.

Since Thomas Mann based so much of his early work on his own family, the background of the brothers is familiar to anyone acquainted with the novel *Buddenbrooks*. The Mann family was a member of the patrician class of the North German city of Lübeck and had grown prosperous as merchants; one of its members achieved the rank of Senator, and the family occupied one of the most impressive homes in the city. The business acumen of the family was waning, however, and it is significant that neither Heinrich nor Thomas had the slightest intention of entering the family business. Both were supported by their mother, who was more sympathetic to the arts than their father, who in his testament left instruction that both boys should be discouraged from a literary career. Upon his death, however, the firm was dissolved, and the mother moved to Munich, an artistic and literary center that figures frequently in the works of Thomas as the symbolic opposite pole to Lübeck—the two cities representing the two sides of his own personality.

The polarity that lies at the heart of so much of Thomas' work is evident in the relationship between the two brothers. Heinrich, the elder, was the iconoclast, the rebel, the one who had to be the first to defy his father, and whose works reflect this opposition to the social structure. Thomas, younger, was less aggressive and more conventional both in the social and the literary world. Heinrich's first works are satirical, grotesque, and at times shocking, while Thomas' first great novel, *Buddenbrooks*, is virtually old-fashioned—slow-moving, descriptive, expansive in the style of the nineteenth century, and exhibiting the irony that was to become one of Thomas' defining characteristics. This dichotomy characterized them throughout their lives. Thomas would marry well, have a large family, and grow wealthy and famous, while Heinrich remained isolated, marrying twice but both times unsuccessfully, and at the end living off a subsidy from his younger brother.

This basic split in personalities and values lies at the heart of their famous quarrel, which placed them on opposite sides of public opinion in Germany during World War I. Heinrich, a liberal, opposed the war and spoke out against it. His essay on Zola in 1914 contained a not-well-veiled criticism of Thomas, who was busily producing patriotic pieces defending Germany and German culture as an almost mystical value against the civilization of France and seeing in the war a struggle of values in which Germany must emerge the superior. Thomas was greatly offended, and the two reached an open break. Following the war, when public opinion turned to favor the liberal antiwar position, the younger generation especially saw in Heinrich a spokesman for their ideals of internationalism, social criticism, and antimilitarism. His works achieved their greatest popularity during this period, and were reprinted and highly praised. On the occasion of his fiftieth birthday in 1921, he was celebrated as one of Germany's great writers, while Thomas was in decline, having backed the losing side and having compromised both himself and in effect his work as well, with its detached ironic tone. Thomas acknowledged that his older brother had in fact discerned more clearly than he, and a reconciliation was effected, at a time when they were more or less equals.

From this point, however, Thomas' career ascended rapidly. In 1924, *The Magic Mountain* appeared, a work of world stature which elevated Thomas into the front rank of European authors, and in which a central theme is the ongoing debate between characters representing opposing political and cultural viewpoints. In these debates, the very foundations of European values are probed and analyzed, and it is as if Thomas is rehearsing not merely the quarrel with his brother, but the intellectual foundations of the broader questions that underlie the whole history of modern European political thought. The education of the protagonist is in effect the education of Thomas himself, and he ends by assuming the position of the brother and sending his protagonist down from the mountain into the conflict of the world, committed to fight for the humane values he has come to espouse. Although this work was perhaps the one which established Thomas' stature, it was for *Buddenbrooks* that he was awarded the Nobel Prize in 1929.

As the Weimar Republic came under increasingly greater attack from the forces of dissolution, both brothers devoted themselves to its defense and to activity against the rising Nazi Party. Yet even here, the difference in their temperaments is evident. Thomas was working on his great *Joseph* cycle, and even after he was warned not to return to Nazi Germany from Switzerland where he was resting, he could not bring himself to speak out strongly against the Nazis for fear of jeopardizing the publication of the *Joseph* novel in Germany. It was three years before he broke this self-imposed silence. The story of the exile of the two brothers in the United States is a particularly interesting section, with Thomas again the more successful of the two. This portion of his life finds its way into the latter sections of the Joseph series, providing a kind of homage to Franklin D. Roosevelt and the New Deal as a model for Joseph as caretaker of Egypt during the famine.

Heinrich Mann continued to work, but his later works did not receive the attention accorded those of Thomas. It was not until after the war that he found a new audience, in Eastern Europe, where he was one of the few German writers whose statements had been in harmony with the views of the socialist states arising there. His works were published in East Germany, and he was invited to settle there. It was probably less ideological differences than sheer inability to take up a new life that led Heinrich to remain in California. Thomas felt a need to return to Europe, partly because of his uneasiness over the intolerance he experienced in the era of Joseph McCarthy, when his refusal to condemn Communism outright was regarded with suspicion and hostility by his critics here. He saw a potential for the development of a kind of national paranoia which had led to the Fascist nightmare of Germany, and he spoke out quite critically of this trend in America. Thus, it was in Europe that Thomas passed his last years, although even there he was not without his critics among the younger generation which had lived through the war and resented his comfortable exile. Nevertheless, the appearance of his last works was greeted with enthusiasm, and he was showered with honors.

Inevitably, much of the attention in a work on the two men must gravitate toward Thomas, who stands with James Joyce and Marcel Proust as one of the giants of modern European literature. Yet Hamilton is fair in his evaluation of the two men and seems in fact to prefer Heinrich, not as a writer, but as a human being. His passion, warmth, and openness do make him in ways more appealing than the more reserved, private, methodical Thomas, who was inclined to be pompous and pedantic. This work is rich in documentary evidence on both men, letting them speak for themselves. Many of these materials have only recently become available; in fact, some materials are still in preparation, but Hamilton has had access to major collections in the Heinrich Mann Archives in East Berlin and the Thomas Mann Archives in Zurich, along with newly published correspondence and materials in the memoirs of contemporaries. Both Heinrich and Thomas left autobiographical materials, but surprisingly there has been no full-length treatment of either author in English; thus, this book serves a most important function. The format of *The Brothers Mann* is not particularly attractive, using small type and dense pages; nor are the translations of the German sources always graceful. Nevertheless, the book is an impressive work and certainly provides a significant documentation of the relationship of these two figures to each other, to their country, and to their times. A literary historian will find much that is valuable here in the way of background to the novels and stories, though little on the works themselves as literature. The lives of these two men are in a sense exemplary, and just as Thomas Mann moved in his career to a style that invested every account with mythic resonances, so one may see in the difficult relationship of these two greatly (though unequally) talented brothers a reflection of the intellectual dilemmas of modern Europe and a paradigm of the potential responses of European intellectuals to the challenges of this century.

Steven C. Schaber

BURGER'S DAUGHTER

Author: Nadine Gordimer (1923-   )
Publisher: The Viking Press (New York). 361 pp. $10.95
Type of work: Novel
Time: The recent past
Locale: Chiefly South Africa, but also France and England

A moving account of the consequences of South Africa's racist society, especially as they are reflected in the life of a young woman who is the daughter of two white people who die in prison for their efforts on behalf of the cause of black liberation

> *Principal characters:*
> ROSA BURGER, the daughter
> LIONEL BURGER, her father
> BERNARD CHABALIER, her French lover

Nadine Gordimer weaves a number of themes together in this book to produce a moving narrative which dramatizes the cost of South Africa's racist social policies. The setting is the segregated society of South Africa in all its complexity. With spies for the white government everywhere, life is a constant struggle within rigid limitations on personal movement, personal relationships, and social and professional opportunities. Against this backdrop we meet Lionel Burger, a doctor turned Communist, who early in the book dies in prison where he is being held for his efforts in behalf of black liberation. His death leaves his daughter alone in the world, her mother having died earlier as a consequence of her own imprisonment on similar charges.

Rosa, faced with all the usual complexities of growing up and finding her own sense of identity, discovers that her personal problems are complicated by her status as the daughter of a hero, since she is the object of constant government surveillance. Trained from youth in the complex need for duplicity and secrecy, Rosa finds that her own life must be surrounded by a web of deceit. As a result, she finds that she cannot attain the kind of self-expression that is her right as a human being. She is not free to be spontaneous; every action must be guarded and self-consciously planned in terms of how it will appear to others. Not sure that she shares her parents' dedication to the black cause, she finds that others expect this of her. Unable to embrace her past, she learns that she cannot escape it either, since she is forbidden to leave the country.

At the end of a long effort, she finally gains a one-year travel permit to go to Europe, as long as she avoids contact with people whom the government has reason to suspect of antigovernment sympathies. While in Europe, she discovers what it is like to live in a country where one does not have to be ashamed of a white skin. She also discovers new perspectives on her past when she visits a woman who was married to her father before he married her mother. Here, also, she meets and becomes the lover of Bernard, through whom she finds a sense of self, as well as the space and time to feel and think for herself, to experience life on her own, and to cast off the shackles of her past. With Bernard, life for Rosa becomes, for the very first time, sponta- neous, open, and free of the constraints of others' expectations. Her past comes home to her, however, in a chance meeting with a South African black man in London whom she had known at home as a child. His rage at the condition of his people in a sense brings back to Rosa the family tradition of resistance to racism; at the end of the book, she is back in South Africa in jail, finally following in her parents' footsteps.

Gordimer's novel is a sustained exercise in mood-painting; alternating in narration between Rosa herself and an unknown omniscient narrator, the work evokes powerfully the experience of South African society and Rosa's journey to self-discovery within and without it. The novel is a haunting and lyrical work; much of its focus comes in the contrast between Gordimer's two narrative stances. The external narrator suggests Rosa's remoteness from life; throughout these passages we feel that we see her at a distance. This sense of separation between reader and character is carried over into Rosa's own comments early in the novel, as we get the feeling of a woman acutely self- conscious, distanced from self, and incapable of any depth of feeling or spontaneity of behavior. Later, as she leaves South Africa and enters into her European odyssey, we find ourselves coming closer and closer to her as she learns to experience herself and her world with an ease and freedom impos- sible earlier in her life.

The book's ending however, is painfully ironic. The voice at the end is that of the narrator; Rosa again retreats from us as we see her once more sub- merged into the ambiguities and confinements of others' views of her—both friends and foes—as well as the literal confinements of a South African jail. We are left with questions—is her return to her homeland an acceptance of her parents' views freely arrived at and made possible by her one taste of freedom? Or, in spite of her new experiences in France, is she, finally, so much a prisoner of a closed society that she cannot make her escape? Perhaps the narrator would have the reader take the former view, for we are told explicitly that Rosa's new sense of self makes it possible for her to hear the pain of her black acquaintance, as if for the first time. Yet we are left with tantalizing ambiguities.

What must be said about this work is that it brings home in powerful ways the realities of apartheid—its incredible cost in human terms to all, black or white, who are caught up in its oppressive and confining snares. The author has provided a vivid picture of a society at once foreign and yet hauntingly familiar to Americans; the sensitive reader can share with Rosa the triumphs and tragedies of living in such a society. *Burger's Daughter* is an evocative and moving work, one not soon forgotten.

John N. Wall, Jr.

CANARIS
Hitler's Master Spy

Author: Heinz Höhne (1926-   )
Translated from the German by J. Maxwell Brownjohn
Publisher: Doubleday & Company (Garden City, New York). Illustrated. 703 pp.
$15.95
Type of work: Biography
Time: 1887-1945
Locale: Europe, primarily Germany

A biography of the chief of military intelligence (the Abwehr*) in Nazi Germany, who was involved in anti-Hitler plots and was hanged by the SS*

> *Principal personages:*
> WILHELM CANARIS, chief of military intelligence in Nazi Germany, 1887-1945
> ADOLF HITLER, Führer of Nazi Germany, 1933-1945
> HANS OSTER, an army officer, second in command under Canaris
> HEINRICH HIMMLER, head of the SS and of all police forces in Nazi Germany, 1936-1945
> REINHARD HEYDRICH, onetime naval officer who became second in command to Himmler, 1937-1945

Admiral Wilhelm Canaris, head of German military intelligence (the *Abwehr*), has attracted the attention of several biographers and at least one moviemaker. Words such as "inscrutable," "cryptic," and "enigmatic" seem to fit him well. On the one hand, he was a dedicated naval officer who fought for his country in two world wars using his considerable naval and intelligence skills to further the military goals of Imperial and National Socialist Germany. On the other hand, he was involved in the opposition to Hitler and Nazism. He provided cover for anti-Hitler activities by several subordinates through his control of the apparatus of military intelligence. Some have seen him as the "guardian angel" of the German resistance, or even more generously as its "inspiration, patron, and brains."

Heinz Höhne provides us with a very balanced picture of this remarkable man. A West German journalist on the staff of the massive news magazine *Der Spiegel*, Höhne has several other books to his credit, most notably *Order of the Death's Head: The Story of Hitler's SS*. In the lengthy work reviewed here, he tells us three stories. One is the biography of a patriotic officer who trained for the Kaiser's navy, hated the revolution which overthrew the Second Reich, and served the Third Reich with professional competence. The second story is that of World War II espionage and counterespionage, intricate in its detail and more fascinating than any James Bond thriller because we see its careful documentation. Third, and perhaps most gripping of all, is the story of the opposition and resistance to Hitler in the very highest circles in Berlin. As Höhne develops these three stories, he shows how an understanding of each is vital to the comprehension of the other two. These three stories will be discussed below in reverse order.

The history of the resistance to Hitler has been the object of intensive research by several excellent historians. Nevertheless, certain problems remain, both because some of the facts are in dispute and because interpretations on such crucial questions as motivation vary widely. By its very nature, a conspiracy leaves no clear trail of documentary evidence behind it. Post-1945 testimony is open to challenge as being self-serving, because once the Führer's Reich had ignominiously fallen, many wanted to clear their names. Nevertheless, Höhne is able to show conclusively how Canaris was opportunistically loyal to the regime until 1938, when the dismissal of Generals Blomberg and Fritsch through a trumped-up scandal brought him to question Nazi rule. The outbreak of war and the extermination policy of the *Einsatzgruppen* (SS murder squads) in Poland aroused both his moral indignation and his fears that Hitler had led Germany into a conflict which it could not win. Therefore Canaris protected his subordinates Hans Oster, Hans von Dohnanyi, Josef Müller, and others, who plotted Hitler's overthrow and who made contacts abroad on behalf of the resistance. He remained personally uninvolved, and he apparently kept himself intentionally ignorant of the details of their activities.

Höhne points out that an important factor in the attitudes of the opposition was the distinction in German law between *Hochverrat* (high treason) and *Landesverrat* (betrayal of the country to a foreign enemy). The first was limited to plotting against a particular regime; many a military officer, including Canaris, thought this was quite appropriate during the Third Reich, given Hitler's own revolutionary disregard of the due process of law. Betrayal of the country to a foreign enemy, however, was considered to be a heinous crime by Canaris and most of his fellow officers. He was quite willing to aid subordinates in establishing surreptitious connections with foreign powers for diplomatic purposes, but he became enraged when he discovered that Oster and others were willing to bring about Hitler's fall by aiding the enemy in order to hasten the defeat of German armies. In retrospect such distinctions seem a bit forced, at least to Americans, but to Canaris and men of his background they were very important.

By the time the resistance set off the bomb under Hitler's map table on July 20, 1944, Canaris had been dismissed from the *Abwehr* and given a meaningless desk job far from the chain of command. He was entirely uninvolved in that plot. As Himmler's men cast out the net for all potential opponents of the regime, Canaris was arrested too. It was only late in the war, however, during the defense of Berlin, that a safe of documents fell into Gestapo hands which proved him guilty of contact with the opposition between 1938 and 1943. On Hitler's orders there was a hasty "trial" at Flossenbürg concentration camp, and the Admiral was promptly hanged, along with Oster and the Protestant theologian Dietrich Bonhoeffer, only a few days before the United States Seventh Army liberated the area.

Our understanding of German intelligence and counterintelligence prior to and during World War II will be much improved by the publication of this book. We see Canaris as the clever espionage agent who was put in charge of a rapidly expanding organization in 1934. He loved to be directly involved in intelligence activities. Time and time again he would leave Berlin to visit his agents in the field and to be directly involved in espionage operations. The most startling revelation in the book is that Canaris is reputed to have met secretly with William J. Donovon, head of the American O.S.S., and Stewart Menzies, chief of British intelligence, in Santandar, Spain, in the summer of 1943. (The evidence Höhne cites for this meeting is limited; historians still have some research to do on this point.)

Admiral Canaris was better as an agent, however, than as an administrator. Höhne shows that Canaris' *Abwehr* had only uneven successes. The author refers to "a tidal wave of blunders" which finally swamped the Admiral and his organization. His failure to predict the United States Anzio landing in Italy virtually finished his career. Since 1933, Himmler, Heydrich, Ribbentrop, and other Nazi figures had been working to destroy the independence of the *Abwehr* and to integrate it into a centralized intelligence agency under party control. Höhne deals skillfully with this drama of interdepartmental rivalry, often played out against the backdrop of superficial comradeship. (Heydrich and Frau Canaris played first and second violin, respectively, in a neighborhood string quartet.) The inadequacies of *Abwehr* performance, which were evident by early 1944, nearly destroyed the case for its continued independent existence.

The biographical approach which Höhne uses to tie these stories together is well suited to explain many of the enigmas of this fascinating man. Why did Canaris serve the Nazi state so long and, generally speaking, so well, while at the same time involving himself with those who plotted its downfall? Some previous biographers have uncritically praised him for his anti-Nazi activities and ignored his inconsistencies. Critics, on the other hand, have doubted his motives and his courage. Höhne shows that as a career officer trained in the tradition of the Imperial Navy, Canaris behaved in ways which were neither unique nor surprising. He had no ideological commitment to National Socialism, but neither was he a friend of democracy. He believed he had a realistic view of world politics, and that view led him to the conclusion that Hitler was leading his fatherland to moral and military disaster. Like many in the opposition, he wanted to rid Germany of Hitler in order to preserve a state dominated by conservatives like himself. When this goal began to appear increasingly unrealistic, he took the fatalistic position that the historical drama had to be played out to its inevitable conclusion of defeat. Yet to the end, foreign enemies remained enemies, and orders were orders.

Höhne builds his book on the researches of such fine scholars as Harold C. Deutsch and Peter Hoffmann, adding information he has gathered from unpublished and published sources during two decades of work on the Third Reich. Unlike many journalists, however, he uses interviews with survivors only sparingly. The care with which he has assembled his material, as well as the freshness of a certain amount of it, has led him to a judicious, well-formed, and often exciting picture of his subject and the context in which he lived and acted. Not every historian will agree with Höhne on every point, but the overall picture is very believable.

The volume is competently translated by J. Maxwell Brownjohn and includes numerous useful aids such as charts, a glossary, and a bibliography, as well as the usual index and complement of photographs. If Canaris could see the book, one thing would probably appeal to his ironic turn of mind. In the German original, the title was *Canaris: Patriot im Zwielicht* (literally translated, "Patriot in Twilight"). The book jacket of the Doubleday American edition reads *Canaris: Hitler's Master Spy*. It is clear that the admiral was a spy of great skill and occasionally even brilliance. But as chief of military intelligence, he hardly proved himself a master. Moreover, as an individual he was not ever really "Hitler's." He retained the professional disdain for politics endemic among the German officer corps from the first to the last. That independent professionalism led him to accept Hitler in the first place, to shield those who plotted against the Führer between 1938 and 1943, and ultimately to fail in his attempts to dislodge Hitler and his henchmen from power in order to save his nation from paying the bills which fell due because of Nazi megalomania.

Gordon R. Mork

CANDIDO
Or, A Dream Dreamed in Sicily

Author: Leonardo Sciascia (1921-   )
Translated from the Italian by Adrienne Foulke
Publisher: Harcourt Brace Jovanovich (New York). 133 pp. $7.95
Type of work: Novel
Time: 1943 to the present
Locale: Sicily, Turin, and Paris

A surreal novel about Candido Munafò's growth to awareness in modern-day Italy

> *Principal characters:*
> CANDIDO MUNAFÒ, the protagonist
> FRANCESCO MARIA MUNAFÒ, a lawyer
> MARIA GRAZIA MUNAFÒ, Candido's mother
> JOHN HAMLET DYKES, an American Captain
> ARCHPRIEST LEPANTO, later Don Antonio
> CONCETTA, a nurse
> GENERAL ARTURO CRESSI, a Christian Democrat
> POALA, the General's housekeeper
> FRANCESCA, Candido's cousin and mistress

Sciascia's *Candido: Or, A Dream Dreamed in Sicily* reflects the disillusionment and despair that man experiences in the process of trying to live a meaningful life. Like his great progenitor Voltaire, Sciascia re-creates a situation for discovery. Candido's surreal growth to manhood shows the universe (Sicily) regularly and horribly malfunctioning at all levels. This disease appears in the family, church, and government. Everywhere dishonesty, misery, and injustice rule. Sciascia asks many of Voltaire's questions and sheds a twentieth century view on them. He asks, man, are you for real? How do I live my life? How do I find essence in my existence? These questions are answered as the absurdity of the universe, in which Candido lives, becomes apparent.

Candido's experience in the family unit is rocky and barren. He is born amidst man-made catastrophe—bombardment; his father, Francesco Munafò, a lawyer, miraculously escapes destruction. As he revels in his escape, he is struck by the virtue of the words candid, white, and pure; he feels reborn, and in the light of the shattering experience he names his son Candido.

Candido's mother is no pillar in the family structure. She even refuses to breast-feed him, "unlike all mothers in that period." Then she proceeds to fall in love with an American Captain, John Hamlet Dykes. Incredibly, Munafò begins to believe Candido is Hamlet's son, even though the child is born about the time of the American's arrival. Maria Munafò soon leaves her husband and child. As Candido grows up, his straightforwardness and honesty prove to be destructive. His simplicity causes havoc when he unwittingly causes the suicide of his father. Soon, he is dubbed "a little monster."

Candido now lives with the "General," his maternal grandfather, a Fascist turned Christian Democrat. Sciascia uses this setting to give his readers a perspective of the meaninglessness of the Italian political scene. Candido observes the events around him as he contemplates life; he analyzes the pieces of the puzzle more than the possible final products. At all times he speaks on issues as he perceives them. Much of what he says is shocking to his nurse Concetta, who goes to see Dr. Pangloss's substitute, Archpriest Lepanto. They decide to watch him; but, in a subtle fashion, Candido takes over the role of observer, watching and analyzing as Lepanto tries to observe. In a subtle role reversal, the Archpriest discovers nothing while Candido discovers that the Archpriest needs reeducating and enlightenment. In the process a deep affection is kindled.

Under Candido's influence, the Archpriest becomes more human, honest, and involved, as seen in his unusually direct way of dealing with a legal scandal involving a profligate priest who has been murdered by an irate father, a respectable lawyer in the community. Honesty gains Lepanto little, however, since both the bishop and the peasants deplore his truthfulness and reject him. Lepanto resigns as Archpriest and becomes known as Don Antonio. As he resigns, he parodies the Church: " 'I am the way, the truth, and the life,' but sometimes I am the blind alley, the lie, and death." Thus, religion offers little solace and encourages hypocrisy. Candido's moral education is complete.

Candido next tries a retreat to the soil. When he tries to improve farming techniques, the peasants on his land reject him; next, he fails in his attempts to give his land to the peasants. Soon he realizes the ludicrousness of his attempt to live close to the earth.

Candido's political education begins soon after he forms a sexual partnership with Paola, the General's young housekeeper, and both he and Don Antonio join the Communist Party. Like many of the Italian intelligentsia of the time, they regard Communism as a replacement for a Church that has none of the virtues it should have. Much of the Communist literature bores him, but he enjoys Gramsci. His need for a center forces him into embracing Communist thinking because he feels capitalism carries man toward disintegration, yet he enjoys reading Hugo, Zola, and Gorki, all imaginative writers.

The Communist Party fails Candido. When he tries to donate a piece of land to the municipality for a hospital, he is rejected because the land offers little opportunity for scheming and profiteering. Next, Candido is deserted by both his mistress and the Party, and his father's family cheats him out of his property. As he is leaving for Paris with his cousin, Francesca, Candido realizes the impossibility of living a fruitful life in Sicily. He tells Francesca, "Do you know what our life is, yours and mine? It's a dream dreamed in Sicily. Perhaps we're still there, and we are dreaming."

The novel closes as surrealistically as it begins. Candido accidentally meets his mother in a Parisian café, and she perfunctorily invites him to visit her in America. He refuses. "Here you feel that something is about to end and something is about to begin. I'd like to see what should come to an end come to its end." The sense of ending in Kermodian terms seems imminent. For Frank Kermode, the end of one era of thought intersects and ushers in the beginning of a new time. Hopefully, in Paris, the home of reason, Candido will see a viable new light being born.

Candido: Or, A Dream Dreamed in Sicily demands attention. Deceptively light in treatment, it attacks all establishments. Sciascia's novel has some autobiographical roots. Occasionally, Italian political parties back a well-known figure like Sciascia. Sciascia accepted the nomination for a local position with the purity of Candido, served eighteen months on the council, realized its ineffectiveness, and resigned. His disenchantment with the system finds its way into Candido's land gift. Corruption is replete. However, this attack is only part of a universal disenchantment with Italy, and, beyond that, systems everywhere.

Sciascia's question, "Man are you for real?" is tied up with the shifting realities shown in the book. The surreal beginning sheds light on the purpose of the novel. Candido is born in a grotto, and the Christian overtones are obvious: this Christ-figure makes a second coming to save a world threatened by destruction, hypocrisy, and corruption. Like Joseph, Munafò doubts Maria's fidelity, while Concetta calls Candido her baby Jesus. However, she soon calls baby Jesus a little monster. By the age of five, Candido knows everything about his father, who resembles Joseph and who knows nothing about his own son.

Sciascia's experience with crime mysteries adds deftness to his prose as the narrative progresses. The book pivots on discovery; reality constantly shifts as the narrative progresses, and in the process the reader and Candido are educated. In his father's office, Candido listens to a murderer confess to a crime for which an innocent man has been arrested by his friend's father. The simplicity of the prose is deceptive. We are told that the murderer confesses so that he can get advice about how he should behave if the innocence of the innocent man were to be recognized and the suspicions of the Carabinieri were to fall on him. The upshot of this is that Candido tells his friend and the Carabinieri, and the lawyer kills himself, not for harboring a criminal or hampering justice, but because he feels he has failed his profession and his code of conduct. Thus, the legal profession is shown to be underhanded and operates with corrupt systems and codes.

Everywhere, standards and concepts have lost their validity; the possibility of discovering laws of conduct and ultimate value disappears; man is directed away from good. Even someone as religious as Concetta, who has spoken of the murder with horror, tells Candido she would like to cut out his tongue for telling. Contradictory messages abound. Candido's innocence appears evil and is treated as evil. The General's political background and party shifts are smoothly handled. Although the General belongs to the Christian Democrat Party, his bedroom overflows with Fascist memorabilia. When Candido innocently asks if the General's Fascist past was an error, the general furiously declares that the Fascists and Christian Democrats are the same. Ironically, the General, who knows little loyalty to kin or party, is deeply wounded when he sees himself down ten places in the 1948 election, and he accuses Candido of betraying him. This easy shift in standards and values becomes commonplace as the novel progresses.

If Candido dreams of finding substantial integrity in the Communist Party, he is also mistaken. Sciascia reveals the secretive and distorted life of the stagnating Communist Party. Like the Church, it speaks to no one; empty and devoid of purpose, it floats along. When he tries to complain to the Party about Zucco, who tries to get a bribe for negotiating a land deal, the Party does nothing.

Sciascia relates the history of a lost and corrupt Italy—and world—so lost that Candido-Christ cannot save it. In the author's note, Sciascia specifically refers to the present age as being one of heavy times. His book shows that modern man has unparented himself, lost his values, his norms, his laws, and his religion. In the process an innocent like Candido tries to find solace and refuge in Paris, the city of reason, where he hopes he can best "cultivate his garden" and find essence in his life. He waits, however, for an end to brutish reason and for the beginning of a new age, one in which man does not arrange his realities to appear as illusions; where he does not fear the demands made on him by his family, society, or religion; where emptiness does not reign; and where there is room for a second coming.

As Sciascia says, this book was meant to be light. It is that, but the lightness is deceptive. It suits the illusion/reality theme, the double shifting perspective which is typical of surrealism. Perhaps Archbishop Lepanto's mocking of the Church service best fits Sciascia's message: ". . . sometimes I am the blind alley, the lie, and death."

Zenobia Mistri

CANNIBALS AND MISSIONARIES

Author: Mary McCarthy (1912-   )
Publisher: Harcourt Brace Jovanovich (New York). 369 pp. $10.95
Type of work: Novel
Time: 1975
Locale: New York, Paris, Holland, and the interior of two large airplanes flying over Europe and the Atlantic Ocean

The story of a hijacked airplane and its captors and its prisoners which explores the psychological dimensions of terrorism while it reveals the complexities of human reactions to direct and prolonged contact with physical danger

> *Principal characters:*
> FRANK BARBER, an Episcopal priest
> GUS HURLBUT, a retired Episcopal bishop
> SOPHIE WEIL, a young American journalist
> AILEEN SIMMONS, a middle-aged American president of a woman's college
> VAN VLIET DE JONGE, a member of the Dutch Parliament
> JAMES CAREY, a United States Senator
> VICTOR LENZ, an American college professor
> DR. CAMERON, a Scottish lecturer at Oxford University
> JEROEN, GREET, HORST, ELFRIDE, YUSUF, HUSSEIN, AND AHMED, hijackers

Cannibals and Missionaries falls into an easily recognizable category of narratives, the tale of a "ship of fools." The basic plot device is a straightforward one: take a more or less representative cross section of humanity, isolate it from the rest of the world, subject it to a crisis of some sort, and see what happens. The group will then serve as a microcosm of all society, of all humanity. The form is at least as old in Western literature as the late middle ages; at present it is experiencing a revival in disaster motion pictures of the *Airport* or *Poseidon Adventure* variety.

McCarthy's "ship" is a modern airliner; her "fools," a group of liberals sent to Iran to investigate government atrocities. Most of the group are Americans; they include an American priest of the Episcopal Church who is in trouble with his congregation for having a black radical preach in his parish, an elderly Episcopal bishop, a college professor with connections with the CIA, a Senator who supposedly ran against McGovern for the Democratic presidential nomination, a liberated Jewish woman journalist, and an unmarried woman college president who immediately begins to survey the group for a new sexual partner. Joining the group in Paris to give a more international flavor are a Dutch politician and a lecturer at Oxford.

Also along on this journey, but riding in first class while the committee sits back in tourist, is a group of wealthy American art collectors on their way to look at the treasures of Iran. They get included in the body of hostages after Charles Tarrant, an aging homosexual art collector, is overheard by one of the hijackers bragging about the vast private collections of his fellow travelers. The price for release of the collectors is delivery of their paintings to the terrorists; the price for the rest of the party includes the usual release of political prisoners, coupled with the demand that Holland end its association with NATO.

Early in the trip, the Americans' only concern is with who actually is coming on the trip; no one wants to be the only one along, for there seemingly is safety in numbers on an expedition like this one. De Jonge, however, more sensitive to the complexities of European and Middle Eastern politics, is anxious about trouble from the start. He sees a secret agent of the Shah in every seat and is not really surprised when the plane taking them from Paris to Tehran is hijacked. Oddly, the plane does not continue on to some friendly Arab country, but winds up in Holland, where the prisoners are transferred by commandeered helicopter to a rented farmhouse on land which has only recently been reclaimed from the sea. After being forced by their captors to push the helicopter into a barn, the prisoners set up housekeeping in the farmhouse and await the result of negotiations for their release.

They get bored, they get dirty, they worry about a dwindling food supply, they fall in love with each other, they put up with inadequate and awkward toilet facilities, and they play Bridge with homemade cards. When asked to make recordings to facilitate the release of their paintings, the wealthy passengers debate the ethics of such a move for a few pages, but finally give in; as a result, they are soon set free. With the government of Holland refusing to yield on its relationship with NATO and the terrorists beginning to fight among themselves, Jeroen, the leader of the terrorists who has fallen in love with a painting by Vermeer, blows up the paintings, himself, most of the hijackers, and most of the prisoners as well.

The chief problem with this book is that McCarthy is unable to make us care very much about any of her characters. She tries to bring them alive for us by having each of the main characters tell parts of the story in turn, but they remain two-dimensional and unconvincing. Their concerns are superficial at the outset, and their experiences do little to improve them. Only Frank, the priest, and Aileen, the college president, survive unscratched; at the end of the book, they fly back to America and comment on the need to give youth hope so that more will not turn from despair to violence. Frank at least realizes that he is incapable of responding to his adventures with more than platitudes; the problem with this book is that McCarthy is capable of no more profound response either.

The book offers other possibilities; McCarthy might have offered an indictment of Western society's inability to cope with violence. She might have offered a subtle study of men and women in the face of violence. She might have used the role of art in the book—itself an attempt at a work of art—to explore the relationship between Western attitudes toward art and the Western response to Third World demands. Perhaps she set out to do these things, but what we have in *Cannibals and Missionaries* is a banal and boring novel, filled with half-developed characters, stock situations, a plot overburdened with loose ends and unresolved issues, and a contrived and forced ending. At the end, we know little more about terrorism and its effects, and care less. If, as Aileen says at the end, Western civilization has become a mini-bottle of bourbon served on a KLM jetliner, then perhaps we do not deserve to survive our current crisis. Many of us feel it is a lot more than that, and that it is well worth saving, but we find little evidence for such an argument in Mary McCarthy's novel.

John N. Wall, Jr.

CELEBRATIONS AND ATTACKS
Thirty Years of Literary and Cultural Commentary

Author: Irving Howe (1920-   )
Publisher: Horizon Press (New York). 256 pp. $14.95
Type of work: Essays

A collection of book reviews and writings from the last thirty years by one of America's foremost contemporary literary critics

Now that Edmund Wilson and Lionel Trilling are dead, Irving Howe is America's reigning man of letters. Indeed, it is difficult to think of anyone who seriously challenges his position. Malcolm Cowley and Alfred Kazin should perhaps be considered for the honor, but it is now questionable whether they are of Howe's stature in the field. The literary critics, besides Howe, who speak with the most authority outside the academic journals, are, curiously, British—men such as George Steiner, V. S. Pritchett, and Denis Donoghue. The professors are addressing only themselves on increasingly specialized topics, and the creative writers, with the exception of John Updike, are not doing any notable criticism.

When one compares the previous generation, roughly spanning the years 1935 to 1965, with the present in terms of critical achievement, one has the feeling we are in a kind of latency period. During that earlier time, we not only witnessed the birth and flourishing of such brilliant journals as the *Partisan, Kenyon,* and *Hudson* reviews, and *Commentary,* but we also enjoyed the writings of critics, besides Wilson and Trilling, such as Philip Rahv, William Philips, Dwight MacDonald, Mary McCarthy, John Berryman, Delmore Schwartz, Isaac Rosenfeld, Randall Jarrell, Allen Tate, R. P. Blackmur, Richard Chase, and Robert Penn Warren. This is not even to mention T. S. Eliot, who continued to write prose into the 1940's and 1950's. From our present vantage, it is apparent that that age was the great one of criticism in American literature.

It is perhaps idle to speculate, at least here, about the causes of the lacuna; but it does not have to do with anything so dramatic as the "death of criticism." In fact, much very able work, both scholarly and general, is being done; but no major critics, with the exception of Irving Howe, have emerged to teach us how to look at literature and culture in new and provocative ways. Certainly it is possible that we are haunted by the weight and scope of the fathers, unwilling to compete with their achievement, choosing other territories. It is also true that real doubts have been raised in regard to the efficacy of literary criticism to say anything significant about culture. The social sciences, along with their offshoot, literary structuralism, have gained the ascendancy. Besides, rational mind in general is looked upon with a good deal of skepticism.

The credentials of an *homme de lettres* must, of course, include more than literary criticism in the narrow sense of the phrase. Wilson and Trilling, for example, not only addressed themselves to fiction and poetry, but also to biography, history, politics, and culture in general. Both of them wrote fiction as well. As Matthew Arnold taught us, the true critic takes all knowledge as his province, expanding the notion of literature to embrace "the best that is known and thought," and not, as it is now more often understood, to include just works of the fictive imagination. Criticism itself is essentially a discovery of knowledge, and an effort to establish truths more adequate than the current ones, rather than a mere aesthetic judgment. It is, moreover, as Arnold also believed, a social act in the way it is preoccupied with the health of the body politic, and particularly with the welfare of the mind in its function of making society.

It is in this Arnoldian sense that Irving Howe is a critic, and it is because of the breadth and achievement of his work that he deserves to be regarded as a man of letters. Just where he will stand in relation to his predecessors is a judgment best postponed, for we require more of a perspective, made possible only in time, to pass it. At any rate, the current book under consideration, *Celebrations and Attacks*, does not provide an opportunity to make such an evaluation, since it is, for the most part, a collection of book reviews, writings of the moment rather than of study and reflection. Howe's reputation now stands solidly on three collections of literary essays (*The Critical Point: On Literature and Culture*, *Decline of the New*, and *Politics and the Novel*); a book of cultural commentary (*Steady Work*); three critical studies (*Thomas Hardy*, *William Faulkner: A Critical Study* and *Sherwood Anderson*); and, primarily, on his magnificent history of New York Jews, *World of Our Fathers*. In addition, early in his career, he coauthored histories of the American Communist Party and of the UAW. His most recent book is a monograph on Trotsky. Finally, while he is a Professor of English at City University of New York, he is also the editor of the distinguished socialist journal, *Dissent*.

Celebrations and Attacks, even though it represents his work over a thirty-year period, does not begin, then, to indicate the cogency of Howe's thought. With the exception of the introductory essay, "Strangers," an informal and partly autobiographical account of the development of the American Jewish critic, and the concluding piece, "Literature and Liberalism," in which he insists on the continuing pertinence of the liberal tradition, the book contains short articles, both animadversions ("attacks" is too strong a word in most cases), and approvals (again, "celebrations" rather overstates his approach) on contemporary writing. The celebrations outweigh the attacks by a wide margin, with the latter appearing more frequently during the 1950's, decreasing in the 1960's, and disappearing, with two exceptions, in the 1970's, when Lillian Hellman particularly awakens his ire.

The same gradual lessening of polemical anger can also be seen throughout his entire career. In the 1950's, Howe, passionately committed to left-wing politics, enlivened a cultural atmosphere that was far too tame for his taste, although it was much more lively than we now think. Even his literary criticism of the time, specifically *Politics and the Novel*, was combative, a tone he later regretted. During the latter part of the 1960's, he was dismayed by the irrationality of the rebellious students and by the emergence of the counterculture. In the next decade, however, while he was no more pleased by the direction of society, he assumed a more disinterested manner and extended a generosity toward the villains of culture, both past and present. In other words, he relaxed his will, a virtue he probably learned at least partly from the example of and in his developing friendship with Lionel Trilling. It is this *lâcher prise*, which angered many on the New Left, that now characterizes Howe's mind and work, a growth all too infrequently seen among American intellectuals.

As recorded in *Celebrations and Attacks*, Howe's displeasure has been elicited by the fiction of Philip Roth, Norman Mailer, J. D. Salinger, and Robbe-Grillet; by the criticism of Leslie Fiedler, Carlos Baker, and Quentin Anderson; and by the political ideas of Richard Chase and Lillian Hellman—all judgments that he would still, no doubt, stand by. His celebrations include the fiction of Ralph Ellison, Bernard Malamud, William Faulkner, Isaac Singer, Richard Wright, J. F. Powers, John Williams, and James Hanley; the criticism of Wilson and Trilling; and the politics of Norman Thomas, a man whom he praises highly, saying at one point that he "was the only great man I have ever met, and if I never meet another I will not feel deprived."

Whether manifested in fiction, criticism, or political thought, Howe rejoices in the mind's willingness to grant and to involve itself with familiar social reality. He will not abide abstraction, and he deplores the unwillingness of mind to give shape to its materials. In Salinger's fiction, for example, he finds love "but no sex and little of those social contingencies through which men must realize their love." Besides, as he continues, "There is . . . a premature readiness to dismiss the familiar social world without either a hard struggle against it or a true retreat from it." In the instance of *Goodbye, Columbus*, the failure shows itself in Roth's inability to perceive the true complexity of Jewish tradition and the diversity of contemporary Jewish life. (On the other side, it could be argued that Howe fails to perceive the genuine sympathy and even love Roth extends to the Patemkins, and overlooks the irony that Roth directs at his cynical protagonist when he ridicules the Patemkins and his own family.) *Barbary Shore* draws a fiercer displeasure from him, for in the novel Mailer does not admit to the difference between Russian Communism and American capitalism. He simplemindedly equates the two, the result of ideology overcoming experience. Howe concludes,

> The trouble is that Mailer has come to his radicalism a little late: he does not really know in his flesh and bones what happened to the socialist hope in the era of Hitler and Stalin,

and that is why he can refer so cavalierly to democracy and carry on like a stale pamphleteer.

The fiction he approves of is solidly grounded in social reality, fully cognizant of its time and circumstance. In black writers such as Ellison and Wright; in Southern novelists such as Faulkner and Flannery O'Connor; in Catholics such as Powers and, again, O'Connor; and in Jewish writers such as Malamud and Singer, Howe recognizes a relief from the easy despair in and rejection of ordinary life, which forms the message of so much contemporary fiction. He values what might be called the imagination of piety, which feels its own inadequacy when confronted with the mystery of the usual, allowing the possibility that its resistance to form and conception may testify to the strength of the human spirit.

It is precisely the absence of a similar kind of humility that marks bad critics and political ideologues. In the performances of the self-dramatizers, who are frequently on the lookout to catch or create a trend, one sees the mind enamored of itself, not of reality, not of the "object as it really is." They are like Fiedler, who lacks, according to Howe, the

> gift of character—which is essential to the critic: the willingness to subordinate his own schemes and preconceptions to the actualities of a particular novel or poem, the love or generosity which persuades a critic to see the work in its own terms and not to bend it to his personal or ideological needs. Another way of saying this is that the critic needs a conscience.

That conscience, which makes its ultimate appeal to reality and refuses to acquiesce in any illusion, no matter how comfortable, has its modern origins in the Enlightenment, in the fiercely independent and liberal minds of Voltaire, Diderot, and Johnson. It is this tradition, carried on in the nineteenth century by Goethe, Arnold, and Sainte-Beuve, and in the twentieth century by Freud, Wilson, Orwell, and Trilling, that Howe seeks to preserve, celebrate, and finally represent. It was the forsaking of that intellectual ideal and the embrace of the Soviet myth, defended with so much distortion and sentimentality by Lillian Hellman in *Scoundrel Time,* that has been instrumental, according to Howe, in undermining a genuine American socialism. That abandonment might also account for the hatred of ordinary reality and the flight into self which typifies contemporary art. It certainly explains the phenomenon of the antinovel and the French rejection of experience for paradigm; and it may even help us to understand the weakening of criticism that has taken place during the last two decades.

Such a cultural condition can make it difficult to hear a voice as reasonable as Howe's. Since he has no grand critical theory to propound, nor any quick cures to hawk, his ideas have little chance in the pandemonium of the moment. Not only in Forster's India does the noise of the Marabar caves drown out all rational discourse. Yet (if we might permit ourselves one illusion, the same one Freud did), although reason is quiet in making its demands, it is stubbornly insistent, and at last it will be heard. To believe otherwise is to invite the empty silence that inevitably follows the noise. And more than anything else, Howe abhors that silence.

David Kubal

CHARMED LIVES
A Family Romance

Author: Michael Korda (1933-   )
Publisher: Random House (New York). Illustrated. 498 pp. $12.95
Type of work: Biography
Time: The first half of the twentieth century
Locale: Hungary, England, and the United States

A biography of the Korda family, especially the brothers Alexander, Zoltán, and Vincent, and the latter's son Michael

Principal personages:
ALEXANDER KORDA, eminent film director and producer
ZOLTÁN KORDA, his brother and a director
VINCENT KORDA, their brother, a renowned art director
MICHAEL KORDA, Vincent's son and author of the book

Charmed Lives combines many of the elements of a successful book about rich and glamorous moviemakers. It is biographical, being a recounting of the lives of the famous Korda brothers, Alexander, Zoltán, and Vincent, and it is autobiographical in its discussion of the early life of the author, Michael Korda, Vincent's son, as he grew up in the presence of many of the world's most famous film personalities. It is also highly peppered with gossip, social history, and self-analysis, all of which usually ensure a book's place on the best-seller list.

Korda is well qualified to write such a book on many counts. Being one of the principals of this biography/autobiography, he had first hand information as well as meaningful insights into the complex lives of the Korda family. As an author of nonfiction material who has written three previous books (*Male Chauvinism!*, *Power!*, and *Success!*, Michael Korda is an accomplished writer who did not need to rely on a ghost writer to make his story intelligible, as is frequently the case among Hollywood biographies. In recent years, best-selling biographies of stars or important directors have fallen into three general categories: highly inflamatory biographical exposés; reminiscences of life and romances as told by a celebrity to a ghost writer; or discussion of a famous person by an offspring such as *Mommie Dearest* by Christina Crawford or *Haywire* by Brooke Hayward.

Although the last category would seem the most appropriate for *Charmed Lives*, it is to the author's credit that he does not succumb to the temptation of adding yet another psychological horror story to the list of those already in print. Instead, he successfully combines aspects of all three of these categories. Korda recounts his own life from early childhood to young adulthood without bitterness or maliciousness despite a rather unsettled and unhappy youth. Born in October, 1933, Korda was shuffled between London, Hollywood, and various boarding schools in the 1930's and 1940's as a result of the circumstances of being not only the son of art director Vincent Korda, but also, more importantly, the nephew of producer and impressario Alexander Korda.

Although the book is a family biography, Alexander looms large in the study. The book's title comes from a statement made by Alexander's third wife and widow, Alexa, made shortly after her husband's death. She told the twenty-two-year-old Michael that Alexander had not led a "charmed life"; and although Michael protested that he never thought that his uncle did lead such a life, his book belies his protest, depicting Alexander as the sun around which the entire family, including Michael, revolved. When Michael was sent to school, for example, it was his uncle rather than his father who decided to which school he would be sent; even though Alexander never appeared overly fond of his nephew—or, indeed, of any children—he was nevertheless the head of the family. However, while his brothers usually complied with his wishes, they also managed to undermine his authority in small ways. One incident which illustrates this pattern involved Alexander's attempt to coerce Vincent into keeping a chauffeur. Vincent opposed such trappings of wealth and initially refused. Alexander got his way, however, by instructing the chauffeur in private to plead with Vincent, to intimate that he needed employment desperately, and to claim that this position was his only prospect. The ploy succeeded, playing as it did upon Vincent's belief in hard work and his sympathy with the plight of the unemployed chauffeur. Vincent gained a small moral victory in the end, however, by refusing to ride in a Rolls-Royce or Daimler, insisting first on a small, economical European car, and later on an American Ford. This dispute was typical of many in which Alexander usually prevailed as a result of his strong will, his personal charisma, and the closeness of the Hungarian family.

Charmed Lives is most entertaining when it chronicles the careers of the Korda brothers; particularly interesting are the portions of the book which follow Korda's move from England to the United States on the eve of World War II, and his filmmaking for the British government. *That Hamilton Woman* (1941), entitled *The Lady Hamilton* in Great Britain, was Korda's first American film. It was made on the direct order of Prime Minister Winston Churchill, who requested a propaganda film which would both appeal to British audiences and at the same time rally American support for the British cause. The result was a stirring love story about one of Britain's greatest heroes, Lord Nelson, and his mistress Lady Emma Hamilton, played by Laurence Olivier and Vivian Leigh. The film was a success and led to Alexander's knighthood, despite the fact that he was, at the time, severely criticized for deserting Britain, his adopted country (he was Hungarian born), in its time of greatest need. Although the Korda brothers made a number of successful films in the United States, they gradually made even more British films and eventually returned to England, where they finished their careers.

Throughout this account, Alexander Korda emerges as an interesting, char-ismatic figure who was extraordinarily domineering and selfish, no matter how creative and successful he was. Perhaps Alexander's marital problems best illustrate this point. Thrice married, Korda's domestic life was always stormy. His first wife, Hungarian actress Antónia Farkas, whose real name was Maria, was involved in an endless series of lawsuits against him after their divorce, one of which continued against his estate. The author barely knew his uncle's second wife, Australian actress Merle Oberon; thus he offers little information about her or the marriage except to indicate that the couple's careers, the difference in their ages, and geographic separations led to their divorce. Alexander's third wife, Alexa, is one of the most filled-out characters of the book. Michael himself was in love with her at one time, although she never returned that love and their relationship never became physical or serious. She was years younger than Alexander and seemed to be more aware of his shortcomings than any other member of the family. Because she did not revere his memory, and married an "ordinary" Englishman soon after Korda's death, the rest of the family resented her.

Likewise, Vincent Korda had rather tenuous relationships; he cared more for his work than for his wife or child. Michael describes his father as being almost happy about his divorce from his wife Gertrude, as it would leave him more time to devote to his work. Vincent was never affectionate toward his son, although he always took an interest in such things as his education. None of the three brothers seemed to have a need for domestic happiness; instead they created wonderful films, both together and separately, which will hold interest far longer than any stories about their lives.

The book is least successful when it delves into young Michael's own life and thoughts; readers are less likely to be interested in the author's experi-ences as a young man than they are in the lives of film stars and producers. Korda has some amusing reflections—his first memory of Los Angeles is that of an orange juice stand shaped like an orange—but his introspection bogs down an otherwise interesting social biography. Oddly enough, Alexander Korda never seemed to have much to do with his nephew; yet the young man was obsessed with him. After Alexander's death, Michael brooded about the loss, but it was more because of his reliance on his uncle than because of personal grief. To him, Alexander was a godlike figure who was the prime mover of his life. Particularly in the final portions of the book, dealing with Michael's attempt to "find himself," after Alexander's death, in the Hungarian Revolution of 1956, the reader's interest wanes. It is the stories, humorous anecdotes, and bits of gossip about well-known personalities that hold the book together and make it worth reading. The author's own youthful problems and self-analysis, however meaningful they might be in another context, simply cannot compete for the reader's attention with the fascinating story of the Kordas' charmed lives.

Patricia King Hanson

CHRISTOPHER ISHERWOOD
A Critical Biography

Author: Brian Finney (1904-   )
Publisher: Oxford University Press (New York). Illustrated. 336 pp. $13.95
Type of work: Literary biography
Time: 1904 to the present
Locale: Europe, primarily England and Germany, and the United States

A study of Isherwood's writings set in the context of his life, prepared by a man who has had Isherwood's cooperation in gaining access to relevant information, as well as Isherwood's permission to give an honest account

Christopher Isherwood, a minor novelist, was a member of that group of English writers who first began to attract attention in the years following World War I. A close friend of W. H. Auden and Stephen Spender, Isherwood shared with both men a devotion to leftwing politics and homosexuality. Growing up in a world which taught them prewar values, they were too young to participate actively in the war which destroyed those values. A sense of being unprepared both by training and experience for postwar Europe shaped the lives and work of all these men; Isherwood's work, which is always autobiographical in approach, is perhaps as good a guide as we have to the kinds of influences to which these writers responded.

Isherwood is best known for his stories which evoke vividly the decadent world of Weimar, Germany, that climate in which Hitler and his Nazi Party rose to power. His strongly drawn characters of Sally Bowles and others of that world are etched in the American consciousness through the powerful performances of Liza Minnelli and Joel Grey in the movie *Cabaret*. Yet this material is only a small part of Isherwood's important work, a point which Brian Finney makes clear in this skillfully written literary biography.

Finney's approach is straightforward; illuminating discussions of Isherwood's works are interspersed with chapters of biography. Finney has been aided in his efforts by the direct cooperation of Isherwood, who now lives in Los Angeles with Don Bachardy, his lover for the last three decades. One benefit of this alliance between writer and scholar is a marked candor in Finney's accounts of Isherwood's homosexual orientation and life-style. Finney pulls no punches; he explores the possible origins of Isherwood's sexual preference and describes openly and without apology the series of lovers Isherwood has known. Isherwood is a militant homosexual; one of his regrets, according to Finney, is that his earlier work is not as open as his later writings about this aspect of his personality.

In fact, one of the interesting problems faced by Finney in writing this book derives from Isherwood's candor. One must surmise that openness about Isherwood's homosexuality is almost a requirement for anyone writing about him who would want the man's help in such an endeavor. Yet there are those whose lives are connected with Isherwood's who are still alive and do not want such exposure. With Auden, Finney has no problem; Auden's homosexuality was a subject of public knowledge before his death. As a result, Finney can state openly that Isherwood and Auden were once lovers. In the case of Spender, however, Finney is more circumspect, stating only that at one point Isherwood spent some time with one of Spender's old boyfriends. The reader is left, as in days of less candor, reading between the lines, trying to understand the significance of asides about men sharing a private language and experience. One wonders, finally, whether candor in such matters is really an improvement.

In any case, Isherwood's life took him through the (seemingly usual in such cases) boyhood world of absent father and domineering mother, the English Public School with its floggings, and the university with its cliques and coteries of bright, imaginative young men. Isherwood left Cambridge without a degree; his early journeys to Berlin, it turns out, were to find a world in which homosexuality was more accepted and beautiful young men were more accessible at the many "boy-bars" the city provided. His later career found him emigrating to America with Auden and taking up residence in California, where he became a devotee of Eastern religion and pacifism. There he has lived since the late 1930's, continuing to write novels while sustaining himself financially through work on film scripts. His most recent works include *Kathleen and Frank*, a biography of his parents, and *Christopher and His Kind*, an autobiography of the Berlin years, both of which have attained strong critical acceptance.

Finney's aim in this work is to put Isherwood's writings in their biographical context; to a large extent he succeeds. His only failing has to do with the amount of material he must condense into the relatively narrow scope of what is, in these days of the massive biographies, really a very short book. Too often his biographical accounts amount to little more than a catalog of names, dates, and places; we are given little sense of the ethos, little feeling for setting, for the mood and tone of the places and people Isherwood has known.

In a real sense, Isherwood's homosexuality dominates the work. This is understandable, in the light of his present militancy on the subject, yet it raises problems. Isherwood is important, important enough to receive this kind of treatment, primarily because he is a writer. Part of Finney's agenda in this work is to attract for Isherwood's later work the kind of attention lavished on his Berlin writings. Yet Finney himself often questions whether the more open emphasis on Isherwood's homosexuality in his later books is a strength or a weakness. It may well be that his underplaying it in the Berlin stories and other early writings allows a more fully human response to the world to emerge, a perspective with a wider appeal than the more narrowly focused concerns of the later work. Surely the homosexual stance is as valid and real a way of being in the world as any other; yet the homosexual world is such that it creates its own language and style of living among its members. To stress that side of its writers' experiences may well limit their ability to convey a whole vision of human life, as well as limit the range of their appeal to the larger world which contains people of all sexual persuasions. It is probable that the works by Isherwood which will endure will be precisely those in which the author's sexual preference is not the central issue, but which instead are concerned with the more common human experiences which unite us all.

Be that as it may, Finney has written a helpful and concise guide to Isherwood, one that, within its limits, is a model of one way of writing literary criticism. While it may not widen the range of Isherwood's readership, it will satisfy those who wish to know more about the world of literary England in the 1930's and after. It will serve to clarify the details of Auden's early career. It will also stand as the definitive account of the life and literary career of a man who has been a minor but important part of the literary life of our age.

John N. Wall, Jr.

THE COLLECTED POEMS

Author: Muriel Rukeyser (1913-1980)
Publisher: McGraw-Hill Book Company (New York). 588 pp. $17.50
Type of work: Poetry

A Whitmanesque record of social and personal concerns from the 1930's to the present

Muriel Rukeyser's work suggests what might have happened to Whitman's had he lived in her own day. To begin with, one of the main resources of her poetry is social and political idealism, and whereas Whitman's work sanctioned freedom and the abundant energies of America in the mid-1800's, Rukeyser's documents the absence of freedom and the deterioration of these energies in the twentieth century. Rukeyser substitutes a Freudian view of motive and a Jungian view of history for Whitman's transcendentalism, but both poets are breathless to affirm that all things are useful, to which Rukeyser adds an enthusiasm for what she calls "new beginnings." Finally, like Whitman, Rukeyser passionately identifies the history of her own meanings with that of the world's at large; there is, in fact, a Whitmanesque thrust in her work to translate the world and herself into each other.

Impending war concerns Rukeyser's earlier work, as in "Night Flight: New York," where airplanes become "a swoop of bare/fatal battalions." In "For Fun," she accuses herself of not speaking out when the omens of war are clear, even in the violence of nature itself ("Correspondences"). In her later "Delta Poems," she speaks of children and adults burned to death in the Vietnam War, and, as in her earlier work, she remembers in her later poetry "that core of all our lives"—the Spanish Civil War ("Neruda, the Wine").

Throughout her career Rukeyser has attacked political oppression. In her early "Three Sides of a Coin," the guests make light of political issues at a cocktail party, but Rukeyser chastizes this indifference and the status quo that supports it. The list of the heroes of rebellion she praises is long, and includes figures such as Marx, Ann Burlak, Martin Luther King, Jr., and Malcolm X. "The Lynchings of Jesus" shows how "sweet generous rebels" are destroyed in the name of law, and "Breaking Open" shows how man puts on in the name of reason the various guises of the torturer. Yet beyond man's cruelty and for its victims, Rukeyser finds hope.

Modern life, often in the name of progress, thoughtlessly disrupts locales and maims people. "Sand-Quarry with Moving Figures" sees, beyond the mere clearing of land to build houses, "the land ruined,/exploded, burned away, and the fiery marshes bare." The lives of coal miners are brutalized by their work ("The Tunnel"), and in a series of poems, many in the form of reports and witness statements, Rukeyser presents hundreds of mine workers in the "Gauley Tunnel" slowly dying of silica poisoning, the hard time they have getting even minimal compensation, and the power of nature turned against itself and man by technology. Observing city life itself, Rukeyser points out that it blights us by telling us to want what it has to sell and by bullying us into behaving as though nothing were wrong with our times.

Social ills are also imposed on people in the form of Freudian disjunctions in childhood: "the parents quarrel," treating each other like "favorite" children, until their real children see the mother as a father and grow up yearning for a mother ("The Victims, a Play for the Home"). In this climate of injury, one ends up either "gasping into a pillow/ . . . to nobody anywhere" ("Burning Bush") or using sex as a sort of sleeping pill. One's need, in fact, becomes so great it frightens him and he cannot accommodate it ("First Elegy. Rotten Lake"). As for fear itself, Rukeyser says we grow up with it, fearing first authority, then sexual rejection, and finally "the overarching wars and poverties" ("The Gates," X).

There is, however, below the Freudian stratum where we are "broken," a mythic stratum where we feel complete and find, Rukeyser suggests, "the symbols of worship" which help to rescue us from guilt ("The Key"). Even war has this mythic aspect in that it illuminates, and connects us with, perennial cycles of struggle, death, and birth ("Endless"). Rukeyser's ontology also says that "all exists in all. We hold/All human history" ("The Wards"); when she talks about the "collective unconscious," she sees it as this history surfacing in us asleep or awake, and she calls for it to be articulated ("Breaking Open").

From the beginning Rukeyser's work has upheld the power of self to deal with, not hide from, the world's incredible energies and the antipodal nature of form itself; after all, "we bloom upon this stalk of time," she says in "Night Flight: New York," exposing thereby an optimism equal to Whitman's, and moving toward an ethic which charges us to "Rebel against torment" ("Night-Music"), go out to offered love, and oppose and work to cure social ills. When she insists in "Born in December," "There is an entrance we may always find," she echoes what she wrote much earlier in "Eighth Elegy. Children's Elegy": "The new world comes among the old one's harms," for the children of victims remake the world for themselves. In such a world as Rukeyser would have it, disguises and old dogmas are scrapped, women (because they are adept in the forms of suffering) would exceed the roles historically imposed on them "sex and spirit" would be the same ("The Six Canons"), men and women would nourish one another, people would be guided by their deepest inclinations and concepts, and self (*a la* Whitman) would go beyond the limits with which mere identity afflicts it.

To work toward this condition we must, Rukeyser admonishes, take risks. Failure may imbue and death conclude all that we are and do, but there are no changes, no "new beginnings," without them. Her prescription for human behavior comes down to a life which makes use of everything in it (including fear), lets go when it ought to, and intimately knows itself as a process.

Besides a mode of social testament, Rukeyser's poems are also records of the archetypal episodes of her own life. She leaves home ("This House, This Country"); she goes through a spiritual illness that nothing outside her can cure ("Panacea"); she finds herself her own worst enemy ("Clouds, Airs, Carried Me Away") and, in a later change in her life, "without resource" ("A Birth"); she bears a child, hungers for an absent lover, and wakes to herself as "a violent woman in the violent day/Laughing" ("Waking This Morning"); she feels death taking hold of her ("Desdichada") and remembers her parents "never touched" her ("More Clues"); she loses her parents and a sister, leaves one husband and takes another (perhaps a lover) who is a "dark outlaw" ("Double Ode," IV); she hangs on to sex and life after a stroke ("Resurrection of the Right Side"); she even goes to prison ("Breaking Open").

It is through discomforts and damages like these that Rukeyser feels joined to the human world in general and justified in her description of it. The ultimate tone she applies to her own case, however, (as she does to existence itself) is uplift. In her first book (1935), she says, "I will be open" ("Effort at Speech Between Two People"), and in her last (1976), she says, "my young look still blazes from my changing" ("Poem"). Nature and the direction through it may not have her name on them, but she is impelled to give herself generously to them just the same ("Then I Saw What the Calling Was"). Often seeing herself reflected in the "newborn," she is willing to start over again, unhampered by used-up directions and undismayed by the opacity of new ones. She trusts that the pieces in her will come together of their own accord ("The Poem as Mask"), and she is alert to the genesis she cannot control: "Something again/is beginning to be born./A dance is/dancing me" ("Recovering").

Wanting, as she says in her Preface, to excise nothing from the observations, feelings, decisions, and growth she has set down lest she betray them in the name of art, Rukeyser defends the sprawl and clutter of her book—which includes mostly free but often premodern formats and an array of genres under single titles and multiple subtitles, from the journalistic report and the biomythical narrative to the epistle and the lyric. It may be hard to sit still for the impassioned redundancies, and sometimes hard to sort out the details this abundance makes for, but as with Whitman one must be willing to wait for the best moments in Rukeyser's poetry; two such moments are "St. Roach," which shows a sense of humor mostly absent from her work, and "Ms. Lot," which exchanges the almost Wagnerian density of much of her work for an undecorated, idiomatic style affording new life to an old theme.

Mark McCloskey

COLLECTED STORIES, 1939-1976

Author: Paul Bowles (1911-   )
Introduction by Gore Vidal
Publisher: Black Sparrow Press (Santa Barbara, California). 417 pp. $14.00; paperback $6.00
Type of work: Short stories
Time: The twentieth century
Locale: North Africa, New York, Latin America, and Thailand

A collection of thirty-nine stories by an American expatriate author which reveals experimentation, variety, and sometimes brilliance

Paul Bowles, one of America's most unusual authors of novels and short stories, has gained a considerable critical reputation (but only a limited popular following) by writing not about his native country but principally about North Africa, where he has lived most of his life. He first visited Africa in 1931, returned in 1932 and again in 1934, and finally made Tangier, Morocco, his home in 1947 (with an alternate home on an island near Ceylon). Thus it is not surprising that most of his short fiction, like his novels and travel writings, reflects his fascination with North African landscape, climate, people, languages, and customs.

Of the non-African stories in *Collected Stories*, only two clearly derive from Bowles's brief stays in New York. Several others grew from his living for a time in Mexico after his marriage to the writer Jane Auer and from his travels in Latin America and the Far East. The few American characters in the stories are usually seen living abroad.

The thirty-nine stories (two of them novellas) in *Collected Stories* exhibit experiments and changes of style and technique as well as a variety of locales and characters. Favorite themes—such as the contrasting of "civilized" and primitive characters, the altering of consciousness through drugs, and the friendship of dissimilar persons—are repeated a number of times during the thirty-seven years between the earliest and the latest stories. Violence is sometimes seen, especially in two of Bowles's best-known stories, "A Distant Episode" and "The Delicate Prey"; but it is more often implied without being described as, for instance, the rape of the woman tourist in "Under the Sky" and the strangulation murder of the Frenchman Royer, which has been predicted early in the novella "The Hours After Noon" and which occurs at the story's end. Very few of Bowles's characters are sympathetically portrayed. In fact, he seems often to have less interest in character than in scene. Dialogue is spare in most stories, and character is revealed more by authorial reporting and by action than through talk. Plotting is frequently slight and many stories stop abruptly, leaving the reader wondering what Bowles's purpose was in writing them.

Such early stories as "The Scorpion" and "By the Water" Bowles looked upon as experiments in automatic writing or "surrealism," by which he meant beginning to write and then putting down whatever came to mind with no idea what the outcome might be. As a result, the stories do seem to picture a surrealistic dreamworld. Bowles would later change his mind about this kind of writing, remarking on one occasion, "I don't think one could follow the Surrealist method absolutely, with no conscious control in the choice of material, and be likely to arrive at organic form."

The first four stories in *Collected Stories* are all African, and two contain a theme that appears again and again in Bowles's fiction: people's need or desire to communicate and their inability to do so. In "Tea on the Mountain," a lonely American woman novelist living in Morocco takes tea on a picnic with two Moroccan boys, learns from one of them a few facts about native life and customs, and returns to her hotel as uncomprehending of an alien culture as the boy, who has spoken of taking tea with her in America and bringing back "cinema stars and presents from New York."

"A Distant Episode," which has been often anthologized, is a much more successful story. An unnamed professor, a linguist interested in North African dialects, wishes to buy some camel-udder boxes as curios and is told to visit a group of fierce Requibat tribesmen camped in the desert. He is captured and his tongue is cut out. Dressed fantastically in several belts with dangling, jangling tin can tops, he is sold as a living toy. Finally, after the professor has failed to leap and cavort as expected, his buyer kills a Requibat in revenge, and the wildly bellowing and suffering man runs into the desert toward the setting sun. The theme of the failure of representatives of two cultures to communicate is reinforced by the irony of a linguist who has lost his tongue and who at the close seems to an amused Foreign Legion soldier who takes a potshot at him only a "holy maniac."

In "Pages from Cold Point," perhaps the best of Bowles's Latin American stories, another professor appears. Norton, having resigned his American university position after the death of his wife Hope, has taken his sixteen-year-old son Racky with him to live in an isolated house on a Caribbean island. Disgusted with modern civilization and contemptuous of his teaching profession, he wishes to escape both and to live a quiet life of aimless pleasure and no accomplishment except the writing of a few pages in his journal. Norton now loathes his older brother who in youth was his homosexual partner, and guilt-ridden Charles thinks Norton unfit to have custody of Racky. On the island, unknown to Norton, Racky seeks out men and boys, including young Peter, his father's gardener. After a policeman's warning that Racky is a bad influence and following a fight between Racky and Peter, Norton finds his own bed occupied by his nude son. The seduction succeeds, but Norton buys off Racky by setting him up in Havana with an apartment and a new convertible, and Norton returns to his idle, empty life at Cold Point.

Bowles's fictional method in "Pages from Cold Point" differs from that which he used in "A Distant Episode," in which the professor is seen largely from the outside. Norton tells his own story through his journal and frankly reveals himself as a hedonist whose ambition in life is to do nothing and who declares himself happy doing it. The homosexuality in the story is less sensational today than when it was first published in 1949, but there is still a shock effect when Norton finds Racky in his bed and quietly joins the boy, who may or may not be sleeping.

Between 1946 and 1949, Bowles published several stories with a variety of Latin American locales. In "The Echo," the scene is a mountain coffee plantation in Colombia where a young American woman, Aileen, visits her mother with whom Prue, an artist, is living. Aileen dislikes Prue and is repeatedly rude to her, until her mother tells Aileen that she must leave. Prue, after several tries at being friendly toward Aileen, playfully flicks a little water into her face on the morning of her departure and is violently attacked. Aileen's furious scream echoes back to her from across a gorge, but the scream also echoes one which had come earlier from a native hut into which Aileen had hurled a rock after a young Colombian peasant had spurted a stream of water into her face. The brown-skinned native's scream of pain after the response to his insult to the white foreigner has been echoed by the white woman's scream of rage and release after her reaction to what had been intended as a mere joke. Aileen's unexplained earlier resentment of Prue appears motivated by a lesbian attachment between Prue and her mother.

The cultural chasm which divides Costa Rican aristocrats and the poor Indians who serve them is seen in "At Paso Rojo," in which Lucha, a middle-aged city woman, is visiting her uncle's ranch with her sister Chalía. "Indians, poor things, animals with speech," Lucha remarks to Don Federico, and later she advises him that Indian boys "need a strong hand and no pity." The theme of an old maid's sexual frustration and its aftermath is combined with that of cultural snobbery when Chalía vainly tries to seduce an Indian ranch boy and afterward takes a cruel revenge.

The professor in "A Distant Episode" is a linguist who anticipates no special difficulty in understanding an African tribal dialect and who thus moves toward his own destruction. There is a near parallel to him in "Pastor Dowe at Tacaté." Dowe, a minister well-versed in the dialect of a Latin American Indian tribe, wishes to bring Christianity to the benighted pagans through his sermons delivered in their language. They listen politely but do not understand and really are interested only in hearing a worn record of "Crazy Rhythm" played on a small phonograph and in the salt which he can get for them. In the end, Dowe is given a small girl as his wife, being warned by his Indian assistant that he must accept her according to tribal custom. As the tongueless professor in the earlier story had fled into the desert, the frightened pastor plunges into the jungle. There he is enclosed in physical darkness just as his mind is imprisoned in the gloom of his ignorance of the Indians whose souls he has wanted to save.

Most of Bowles's stories published from 1950 on are African, and one of the best is "The Delicate Prey," although some readers have objected to what they have regarded as Gothic horrors in the series of murders, two of which are described in brutal detail. The artfully controlled narrative compresses action, description, and spare dialogue into a small space. Young Driss accompanies his two uncles, who are leather merchants, on a dangerous trip across the Algerian desert toward distant Tessalit. Members of the Filali tribe, they are later joined by a Moungari whom Driss eyes doubtfully, although the traveler seems jolly and friendly. Promising good gazelle hunting, the Moungari lures first one uncle and then the other over the desert hills to seek the delicate prey. The phrase takes on a double meaning as lustful Driss envisions the pleasures that await him at journey's end:

> In the advancing heat he dozed, his mind playing over a landscape made of soft thighs and small hard breasts like sand dunes; wisps of song floated like clouds in the sky, and the air was thick with the taste of fat gazelle meat.

The uncles do not return and Driss imagines what has happened. Despite his vigilance he is ambushed, sexually mutilated, and then raped by the Moungari, who later servers his windpipe and hides the body among rocks. Many days afterward, other Filali merchants in Tessalit exact revenge for the triple murders and the theft of the travelers' leather by burying the Moungari up to his head in the desert sand to await the rising sun.

Bowles regards himself as primarily a writer, but he is also a composer—he wrote the music for Tennessee Williams' *Summer and Smoke*—and he uses music as an integral part of many of his Latin American and African stories. Music is brilliantly incorporated into the structure of "The Delicate Prey." Early in the journey, Driss plays on a small flute "whatever sad songs he could call to mind." When the first uncle leaves to hunt, he goes off "singing a song from Tafilalet; it was about date palms and hidden smiles. For several minutes Driss heard snatches of the song, as the melody reached the high notes. Then the sound was lost in the enveloping silence." Before Driss is ambushed, he hears the Moungari singing far away. After the Filali have put the Moungari into what will be his sandy grave, he pleads for release, "But he might have been singing a song for all the attention they paid to his words." At the close of the story, "The wind blew dust along the ground into his mouth as he sang."

Bowles's two novellas show some of his best writing. In "The Hours After Noon," conversation and interior monologue are used effectively for thematic development and character portrayal. Among its multiple themes are cultural snobbery in Mrs. Callender, who is suspicious and contemptuous of Moroccans; generational conflict in Mrs. Callender and her daughter Charlotte; sexual perversion in M. Royer; the relationship between cumulative memory and basic character in Mrs. Callender and Royer; and tribal protection of property in the Moroccans at El Menar, who murder the Frenchman before he can spoil the sale value of a little brown girl.

The second novella, "The Time of Friendship," is in one respect most unusual for a Bowles story: both leading characters are sympathetically portrayed. Fräulein Windling, a Swiss teacher, for many years has spent her winter vacations at an Oasis in the Algerian desert, but on her last visit she is told that she must leave because of the French-Algerian war. For three years she has befriended an Algerian boy, Slimane, who is now fourteen. Each respects and cares for the other despite their different religious beliefs and cultural backgrounds. Slimane rides with her to catch the train at Colomb-Bechar that will take her away from her beloved desert forever. After the train has started, she looks at the address Slimane has given her, realizes he has run away to become a soldier, and sadly hopes he will be "among the fortunate ones, an early casualty." A quick death will save him the painful loss of his beautiful innocence and idealism.

While writing his first novel, *The Sheltering Sky* (1949), and again in the 1960's, Bowles experimented with drugs and their effects on artistic creativity by smoking kif and eating majoun, both derived from hemp. In the four strange African stories which resulted from the later experiment he achieved only an indifferent success. The protagonists of all the stories are young kif smokers, and the drug leads them variously to commit injustice, robbery, and murder.

A number of Bowles's later stories, in which he consciously imitates the tales told orally by illiterate kif smokers, employ a different style from his earlier writing. With simple vocabulary, short sentences, primitive superstition, and even the transformation of a man into a snake, they are less impressive on the printed page than they perhaps would be as oral tales.

The collection of Bowles's short fiction into a single volume should bring the stories a wider recognition than they have had in the past. The best of them deserve rereading; many of the others have at least the interest of novelty and the introduction of scenes, characters, and customs from a part of the world little known to most Americans.

Henderson Kincheloe

THE CONFEDERATE NATION
1861-1865

Author: Emory M. Thomas (1939-   )
Publisher: Harper & Row Publishers (New York). Illustrated. 384 pp. $15.00
Type of work: History
Time: 1861-1865
Locale: The United States, Europe, Mexico, and the high seas

An overview of the Confederate experience, stressing the degree to which the American South, achieved in war an independent nationality

> *Principal personages:*
> JEFFERSON DAVIS, President of the Confederacy
> ROBERT E. LEE, Confederate general and key military adviser to Davis
> ROBERT BARNWELL RHETT, SR., a key secessionist who failed to achieve status in the Confederacy
> PIERRE G. T. BEAUREGARD, Confederate general in both the East and the trans-Appalachian West
> PATRICK CLEBURNE, Confederate general who recommended freeing the slaves as a means to achieve Southern independence
> JOSEPH E. JOHNSTON, controversial commander who quarreled with Davis
> STEPHEN MALLORY, Confederate Secretary of the Navy who sponsored ironclad ships as a means of countering Union naval superiority

The Confederate Nation marks a significant literary marriage: the uniting of Harper & Row's always competent *New American Nation Series* with the writing finesse and insights of Emory M. Thomas, a highly respected authority on the Southern Civil War experience by virtue of his *The Confederacy as a Revolutionary Experience, The Confederate State of Richmond: A Biography of the Capital,* and other writings. The work constitutes an exciting contribution to our understanding of the South.

Despite the voluminous literature on the Confederacy, Thomas' study answers a definite historiographical need. New findings in the 1970's about diverse facets of the Civil War South, such as the wartime deterioration of slavery, structural problems in the Army of Tennessee, and the motivation for secession, require a fresh overview of the "Confederate Nation." Were such an assimilation of materials all that Thomas' work achieved, it would be well worth the effort; and though Thomas does present a very competent summary of the Southern wartime experience in its land, sea, diplomatic, political-administrative, and social aspects, his study is most noteworthy for its interpretive flair.

Thomas focuses upon the degree to which the Confederacy succeeded, in its brief history, in becoming a legitimate and distinct nation. To pursue this idea, he begins logically by assessing the roots of Confederate nationality in

a substantial three-chapter analysis of the Old South and the secession movement. Although he acknowledges that Southerners were Americans as well
as Southerners and that the South constituted a diverse society including a
significant yeoman class, he nevertheless aligns himself firmly with that school
of historical thought which has defined the antebellum South as a unique part
of the United States.

Thomas argues that the Old South constituted "a unique social economy
combined with a distinctive 'mind,' religious spirit, life style, and culture. . . ."
He stresses—in the manner of historian Rollin G. Osterweis—how romanticism led to jousting tournaments and appreciation of Sir Walter Scott rather
than Northern-style reform movements; how slavery, "physical circumstances," and a "folk culture" led to militarism, the *code duello*, and a personal
emphasis upon violence which sought expression in the "classically Southern
act" of Preston Brooks's caning of Charles Sumner; how slaveholding undermined the work ethic in the South; how the staple-crop Southern economy
retarded industrialization and urbanization; and how a minority status within
the Union led to a genuine (rather than merely tactical) appreciation of the
states' rights political philosophy. Thomas agrees with historians such as
Eugene D. Genovese who have argued that despite Southern participation
in international trade, the Southern mentality was essentially precapitalist.
Like Genovese, Thomas emphasizes the paternalistic side of the plantation
system: emotions and a sense of responsibility toward one's slaves interfered
with the natural functioning of slave markets, and planters expressed a sense
of noblesse oblige "toward their farmer neighbors." Racial solidarity and self-
interest committed most Southern plain folk to a political and economic
system dominated by the aristocratic slaveholders. Wilbur J. Cash's argument
that many Southern planters were but a generation removed from the frontier
is countered with a reminder that planters believed in the landed aristocratic
ideal no matter how coarse their manners, and that they pursued class interests.

Within this schema, secession is presented as an essentially conservative
movement intended to preserve a status quo. Thomas concurs with Michael
P. Johnson's recent study of secession in Georgia, which contended that planters controlled the secession movement and that they feared not only the
threat from Yankee "money-grubbers" (Thomas' words) to slavery and racial
calm but that they also worried about a potential challenge to slavery from
the poorer classes within the South. To prove the conservative implications
of secession, Thomas emphasizes that Southern radicals who would have
altered society by such programs as reopening the African slave trade did
not control the Confederacy. Thus, the notorious radical South Carolina
leader, Robert Barnwell Rhett, Sr., could not gain the presidency. The Confederate constitution, moreover, was a conservative document; and Jefferson
Davis demonstrated in his inaugural address that the Confederacy was con-

trolled by practical men rather than doctrinaires by stressing that Southerners had not overturned "the system of our Government" despite their invoking the right of revolution to justify their course of action. It is unfortunate that Thomas tarnishes his argument slightly by citing John A. Quitman's failure to appear in the Mississippi delegation to the Montgomery Convention as part of his evidence that the Confederacy left the radicals behind. Quitman had died over two years earlier.

According to Thomas, the emergence of a distinct Confederate nationality in wartime was the product of adversity on the battlefield during the interim between victory at Bull Run in July, 1861, and the Peninsula campaign near Richmond in the spring of 1862. Most Civil War historians have stressed Union difficulties during this period, particularly George B. McClellan's problems in mounting a significant threat against the Confederate capital. Thomas, however, focuses upon the Southern losses at Roanoke Island; the Confederate withdrawal from Missouri after Pea Ridge; the forfeiting of Kentucky after the occupation of Columbus and the defeat at Mill Springs; the defeat in West Virginia; the Union landings at Port Royal, South Carolina, and Ship Island near the mouth of the Mississippi; the Henry-Donelson disaster; and various Union thrusts on the Mississippi River.

"Confounded" by disaster, Jefferson Davis and other Confederate leaders launched a program of remedial reform which, in a subtle sense, undermined the nature of the Old South society and produced a new nationality. The scope of this change has already been delineated in depth in Thomas' *Revolutionary Experience* and need only be summarized here: individualism and civil liberties were undermined by the draft and powers granted to Davis to suspend the writ of habeas corpus and declare martial law; state-controlled industrialization was effected; and women descended from their pedestals and joined the war effort in noncombatant ways. The Confederacy did not discard all prior values. Thomas believes that even the wartime Confederate industrialists rejected the acquisitive, entrepreneurial value structure of their counterparts in the North. Nevertheless, a new and legitimate nation had been forged which, after diplomatic adjustments, victory at Chancellorsville, stalemate in Tennessee, naval success on the Mississippi River and at Galveston, Texas, ran at "full tide" in the early months of 1863. It was also a nation which had developed a cultural life far less sterile than portrayed in most prior accounts. Thomas defends the "creative expression and intellectual vitality" of the Confederacy by emphasizing technological breakthroughs like Matthew Fontaine Maury's torpedo mines and the operational submarine *Hunley*, and the richness of diaries, letters, and newspapers of the time. Moreover, a new class consciousness was emerging among the yeoman and laboring classes as they found themselves replacing aristocrats in military command and facing food shortages and runaway inflation.

Confederate nationality, however, quickly unraveled as the battlefield and diplomatic situation seriously deteriorated beginning in the summer of 1863. Following Gettysburg, Vicksburg, Missionary Ridge, and the termination of the Confederate mission to England, and amidst rampant inflation, it was impossible to maintain unity and faith in the cause. Thomas describes the rising anti-Davis bloc in the Confederate Congress, desertions in the army, desperate military thrusts such as Jubal Early's brutal raid on Chambersburg, Pennsylvania, and the retreat into religious revivalism. Nevertheless, the concept of Confederate nationality persisted to the very end of the war. When Jefferson Davis and the Confederate War Office issued General Order Number Fourteen freeing all slaves who enlisted in the Confederate army, that had forfeited the main pillar of their heritage "in order to achieve Southern self-determination."

Could different policies have salvaged the Confederate crusade? Thomas, in arguing that the "hard truth was that law and policy could not tap resources which did not exist," seems to be suggesting that victory could not be attained given the Northern superiority in manpower and natural resources. Adjustments such as efficient taxation, railroad nationalization, and a functioning two-party system would have strengthened the Confederacy. But Thomas periodically observes that European aid and perpetual nationhood depended on the battlefield. Since he presents the Davis and Lee offensive-defense strategy as intelligent and refuses to side with those historians who have attacked Davis and Lee as insensitive to the trans-Appalachian West, it appears that Confederate defeat was inevitable. Thomas' approach will trouble those who feel that command decisions in Richmond caused the loss. He is surprisingly charitable, for instance, toward Jefferson Davis' handling of the Vicksburg question and the disastrous replacement of Joe Johnston with John B. Hood at Atlanta. Given war weariness in the North in 1864—Lincoln was quite dubious about his own chances of reelection—Johnston's strategy of judicious retreat to prolong the war might have provided the South's best hope.

If Thomas' analysis of the Confederacy has a serious flaw, however, it is that, for the sake of clarity, he overdraws his portrait of Southern distinctiveness. While it would be absurd to suggest that the Old South represented a carbon copy of the Old North, the cultural ties binding the two sections were firmer than Thomas' narrative implies. Thomas misleads readers by citing the "relatively high numbers of Southern military schools and militia units that took seriously the study and profession of arms" as proof of a sectional proclivity to "corporate violence." Actually, military schools were a Northern invention, and many were located in the North. Several of the most famous Southern institutions, such as Virginia Military Institute and The Citadel were dependent upon state arsenal appropriations and represented in part a means to guard state arms. As for the militia, most militia periodicals were Northern publications, and the antebellum North had its fair share of volunteer militia units. The Zouave idea originated in Chicago. While Thomas acknowledges William R. Taylor's work on antebellum literature, *Cavalier and Yankee*, he neglects Taylor's findings that Northern novelists such as James Fennimore Cooper idealized the Southern aristocracy and that many fictional works by antebellum Southerners satirized, rather than glorified, the plantation world. Thomas implies that Southern authors almost uniformly projected a romanticized picture of plantation living. Actually Northerners read Sir Walter Scott as well as Southerners, and Thomas gives too much emphasis to the strain of chivalry in the South. One can read antebellum Southern letters for years before encountering an account of an actual visit to a jousting tournament.

Likewise Thomas might have given more emphasis to the common racial views held by Northerners and Southerners. Racism, as James A. Rawley has shown in his work on the Kansas controversy, became a vital underlying mechanism behind the Northern political stance. Thomas underestimates the common North-South conviction that European revolutions around midcentury were an offshoot of the American experience of 1776 and subsequent republican example. Thomas says that when Southerners witnessed European revolution at midcentury, they "identified with the old order instead of the new." Yet the Vicksburg *Tri-Weekly Whig*, as was typical of much Southern opinion, cheered on the Louis Kossuth revolution in Hungary, calling Kossuth gallant. Furthermore, once the Civil War came, as David Donald has shown in his recent synthesis, *Liberty and Union*, the Confederacy and the Union responded to the challenges of conflict in remarkably parallel ways, further verifying their common shared characteristics.

Thomas' study constitutes a short history. Some readers will be troubled by the innumerable aspects of Civil War Southern life, such as Delaware's attitudes on secession, prison camps, and Russian policy toward the Confederacy which are treated in a sentence or two, or not at all. Page limitations rule out exhaustive treatment of campaigns and battles. Thus Thomas gives no indication that command confusion between Edmund Kirby Smith and Braxton Bragg seriously undermined their invasion of Kentucky in the summer of 1862, and the Confederate invasion of New Mexico passes in two sentences. Other readers will differ with minor matters of judgment, such as the implication that James Mason was a suitable appointment for the key mission to Great Britain.

However, *The Confederate Nation* is as comprehensive and well informed a treatment as might be expected given the constraints of the Harper & Row series; shrewd analysis and lush writing, moreover, establish the book as a minor masterpiece. Sensitive to irony and paradox, Thomas observes an Old South ruled by men rather than law yet dependent on legalism at the national level; a Confederacy striving to take the offensive but fighting best when on the defensive; a diplomatic corps insisting that the Union blockade was a paper blockade, yet claiming that European nations should intervene in the Civil War because the blockade interrupted their cotton supply; a nation of farmers going hungry; and a Southern ministry invoking the righteousness of the Confederate cause while William Quantrill killed innocent Union civilians in Lawrence, Kansas. Much of Thomas' descriptive prose is unforgettable (such as his sensual depiction of Charleston Harbor as a geographical expression of the female anatomy), and he manages to include lucid, concise profiles about virtually every important Confederate personality without seriously impairing the flow of his narrative. His brief description of Confederate-Indian relations as a microcosm of the wider Southern diplomatic problem marks only one way he recasts old material in a fresh new light.

Emory M. Thomas, in his *The Confederate Nation*, has made a significant contribution to the postcentennial continuation of literature about the Old South society and its Civil War expression. Like the "Lost Cause," the centennial seems to gain momentum with the passing of time.

Robert F. May

CROSSROADS OF DEATH
The Story of the Malmédy Massacre and Trial

Author: James J. Weingartner (1940-   )
Publisher: University of California Press (Berkeley). 274 pp. $14.95
Type of work: History
Time: 1944-1951
Locale: Belgium, Germany, and the United States

An analysis of a brutal World War II incident, the killing of some seventy American war prisoners by an SS unit, and the war crimes trials which followed it

> *Principal personages:*
> JOCHEN PEIPER, Colonel in the elite "Leibstandarte SS Adolf Hitler" and head of the military unit which killed the American prisoners
> SEPP DIETRICH, a long-time Nazi activist and commanding General of the "Leibstandarte SS Adolf Hitler"
> WILLIAM R. PERL, United States Lieutenant assigned to the investigation and prosecution staff dealing with the accused SS men
> WILLIS M. EVERETT, JR., United States Colonel, appointed defense counsel for the accused SS men
> JOSEPH MCCARTHY, Senator from Wisconsin

Late in 1944, Hitler took one last gamble to win World War II by a renewed *Blitzkrieg* in Belgium. To Americans, the conflict was known as the "Battle of the Bulge." One particular incident of that brief campaign stood out in the minds of many Americans. An advancing SS armored unit had herded more than seventy GI prisoners of war into an open field just south of the town of Malmédy and turned their machine guns on them. Several individuals had lived to tell about the ordeal by feigning death. The physical evidence of the killings had been gathered by United States Army inspection teams who came upon the frozen and snow-covered bodies when the German offensive failed and the United States Army advanced once more. The disarmed corpses were bullet-ridden, some with their frozen hands still above their heads. If any Americans needed to be reminded of the ruthlessness of the SS troops, the "Malmédy Massacre" provided the grisly evidence.

As the war drew to an end, the sometimes lethargic, sometimes precipitous machinery of United States military justice sought out the perpetrators of the deed. The unit in question was identified as the Battle-Group-Peiper, named after its dashing young Commander, Colonel Jochen Peiper. On May 16, 1946, seventy-four officers and men of the Waffen-SS (SS-military, as opposed to the police or purely political SS) were put on trial before an American military court. Seventy-one men, including Peiper himself, were members of the erstwhile Battle-Group-Peiper; the other three, including SS General Sepp Dietrich, were higher up the command structure. They were accused of a criminal conspiracy and the murder of 538 to 749 American prisoners of war and over ninety Belgian civilians. Ironically, the trial took place in Dachau; the accused were incarcerated in the infamous concentration camp. By July 18, 1946, the trial was completed, and the defendants all found guilty of "violations of the laws and usages of war." Forty-three men, including Peiper, were sentenced to death; the rest, including Dietrich, were sentenced to prison.

The story, and Weingartner's carefully researched and well-written account of it, might have ended there, but it did not. The American colonel who had been assigned to defend the accused SS men, Willis Everett, was convinced that an injustice had been done. A prominent Atlanta attorney in civilian life, he began a series of legal and political maneuvers which were to lead to a Senate investigation of the Malmédy trial and eventually to freedom for all the defendants. Everett had at first approached his task of legal defense at Dachau with considerable distaste; but soon he became convinced that the United States Army's case against his clients was seriously flawed. Clearly the seventy-two American corpses in the field near Malmédy proved that a war crime had taken place there. The several hundred other alleged murders were not as well-documented; some appeared to Willis to be the result of double counting and exaggerated estimates, while other deaths could be attributed to legitimate battlefield casualties. In fact, there was considerable evidence that Peiper's unit had treated many of its prisoners very correctly, thus undercutting the prosecution's contention of a criminal conspiracy to kill as many prisoners as possible. Everett also came to the conclusion that the sworn written confessions of the accused, upon which much of the Army's case rested, had been obtained under conditions of physical and psychological duress by men like Lieutenant William Perl, an American officer of German-Jewish background and a one-time refugee from Nazism. Not only did Willis believe that this evidence was invalid on technical legal grounds, but he also believed that large parts of it were falsified and therefore implicated many of the wrong men.

Everett's campaign led to a Senate investigation in which Joseph McCarthy of Wisconsin played a role. Not yet as well known as he would become during his investigations of alleged Communist conspiracies, the Senator nevertheless showed the penchant for flamboyant rhetoric and questionable procedures which would lead to his censure. Perversely, he stressed charges of physical brutality to the SS men, including the damaging of numerous genitals. Through innuendo he played upon latent nativist and anti-Semitic prejudices in America by emphasizing the role of men such as Lieutenant Perl.

Weingartner shows that the Senatorial investigation gave additional notoriety to the Malmédy Massacre and trial, but that the eventual commutation of all the death sentences probably had less to do with the rhetoric of Senator McCarthy than with the shifts in the international balance of power. By 1951, when the last of the death sentences was reduced to life imprisonment, the United States feared the Waffen-SS no longer; the threats to the American way of life were coming from elsewhere. In 1955, Sepp Dietrich was released from prison, and the following year, Jochen Peiper, the last of the imprisoned defendants, was given his freedom.

James Weingartner, a well-trained and highly competent American scholar, who was but four years old when the seventy-two Americans were killed at Malmédy, has written an excellent study of the event and its aftermath. His book is more complete and more balanced than Charles Whiting's journalistic *Massacre at Malmédy* (1971) while being equally readable. Weingartner's earlier work, *Hitler's Guard: The Story of the Leibstandarte SS Adolf Hitler, 1933-1945* (1974), has thoroughly familiarized him with the primary sources and secondary literature on the SS. In this new book, he has added significant research into American occupation policies and into the dynamics of United States history during the postwar period. He is candid and even colorful in his description of the men and events with which he deals, whether German or American. Some readers might take offense at his implication that the Malmédy shootings were nothing more than a "tragic error" or a "product of a set of military circumstances which could have created pressures for the shooting of prisoners in any army." Yet his book is in no way an apology for the SS. He graphically shows how the training of the Nazi elite in *Härte* (ruthlessness, hardness) conditioned the men under Peiper's command to act as they did. On the other hand, Weingartner shows us something of the quality of American military justice: cases are not tried and reviewed in a vacuum, but within a public and political context which directly affects the outcome.

Rarely does Professor Weingartner refer to the American experiences in the Vietnam War, which must have been on his mind when he researched and wrote this book. However, if it is proper for academic historians to restrain themselves when they feel inclined to historical comparisons, it is equally proper for active citizens and policymakers to keep such things firmly in mind. *Crossroads of Death* is no antimilitary polemic; it is the kind of careful but meaningful book which raises questions worthy of consideration by scholars, by students, by military leaders, and by the reading public. Of the millions who died in the conflagration which we call World War II, the seventy-two GI's at Malmédy were an infinitesimally small proportion. However, this brief book on that incident and its aftermath raises broad and significant questions which need to be pondered.

Gordon R. Mork

THE CUBS AND OTHER STORIES

Author: Mario Vargas Llosa (1936-   )
Translated from the Spanish by Gregory Kolovakos and Ronald Christ
Publisher: Harper & Row Publishers (New York). 139 pp. $10.00
Type of work: Novella and short stories
Time: The 1950's or unspecified
Locale: Peru, primarily Lima and its environs

A collection of stories focusing on the "rites of passage" into manhood, especially those of the Peruvian upper class

The Cubs and Other Stories includes a novella written by Mario Vargas Llosa in 1965 and six of his early short stories written between 1953 and 1957. Except, in some respects, for "On Sunday," the short stories, completed before the author was twenty-two years old, do not compare in quality with the novella, entitled "The Cubs." Thematically, however, the entire collection deals in interesting ways with coming of age, especially with the "rites of passage" experienced by upper-class Peruvians approaching manhood. In virtually every story, boys or youths encounter danger or death in tests that they and their peers subconsciously feel they must meet before they can go on with the living and reproduction of life. The challenge to danger is an essential element of these rites because to be a man traditionally means to engender and protect life, a role constantly challenged by death. Repeated failure to meet and transcend such tests denies meaning to the life of the youth who fails, since he cannot fulfill what seems to him the natural purpose of his existence.

In addition to themes, "On Sunday" and "The Cubs" share surroundings—the upper-class neighborhoods of Lima and its environs. In general the atmosphere is paradoxically one of anxious boredom; the need for excitement, to break the seemingly endless days experienced by the young, fills the air. In that atmosphere arise the challenges that become rites of passage. For Miguel, the protagonist of "On Sunday," the excitement and tests come when he becomes enamored of a girl named Flora. Rejected when he asks her to be his steady, he becomes livid on learning that rather than go to the movies with him, she intends to visit the home of his friend and rival, Rubén. Out of this adolescent, melodramatic opening, Vargas Llosa builds a surprisingly touching story of a youth learning, in desperation, self-assertion and courage. To prevent Rubén from going home where he would meet with Flora, Miguel challenges his imposing rival to a drinking contest that soon leads to a more serious trial.

In a thoroughly realistic style, Vargas Llosa describes Miguel's successful struggle against Rubén, the elements, and especially himself. The beer-guzzling ending in a draw, the intoxicated youths continue their confrontation, now only secondarily concerning Flora, in the cold winter sea. Challenging

Rubén, a champion swimmer, to a race in the dangerous waters, Miguel finds himself in a contest with death for both his own life and his friend's. Struck by a cramp, Rubén calls for help, and Miguel, himself already close to drowning, conquers his own fear of death and pulls the other boy to safety. Miguel, therefore, proves his manhood, not merely by equaling Rubén in a drinking bout or beating him in a reckless race, but by preserving life through the strength of his own character. Moreover, he confirms his newly won manhood by hiding the fact of the rescue from their friends to avoid humiliating Rubén. In this way, Miguel preserves Rubén's dignity, allowing the latter to prove himself at some other opportunity. Although "On Sunday" lacks sufficient originality in structure, plot, and imagery, Vargas Llosa's effective psychological portrait of Miguel foreshadows the fine characterization in the author's mature novella, "The Cubs."

While Miguel successfully completes his rite of passage and looks forward to fulfillment in life, P. P. Cuéllar of "The Cubs" is sadly denied that fulfillment despite his constant contention with the dangerous and with death itself. Rites of passage being socially mandated, Vargas Llosa's use of neighborhood youth as a chorus to narrate Cuéllar's life gives an appropriate perspective to the novella. Using a complex innovative technique, the author writes from the point of view of the first person plural, giving the impression that an entire group, rather than a representative individual, tells the tale. Despite this, individual voices from past and present come to the fore as if in a conversation interspersed with recordings of dialogue from Cuéllar's life. Out of all this talk emerges the main character, first a child—possessing the intelligence, industriousness, and physical abilities valued by society—then an adult— underemployed, rebellious, and isolated. Cuéllar's failure as an adult, in his society's terms, results from a horrible attack he suffered as a boy.

Emasculated by a Great Dane, Cuéllar finds the way to manhood forever closed to him. As a result of his castration, he becomes obsessed with the rites of passage to the state that he can never sexually fulfill; for example, immediately after recovering from the attack, he loses interest in his studies and becomes preoccupied with soccer, a masculine endeavor. As Cuéllar grows older, the inevitable problems arise from his incapacitation and the expectations of society. The increasing isolation and despair he feels, as each of his friends becomes attached to a woman, completely infect the reader. To compensate for his physical loss, he begins to surf daringly, to drive and drink wildly. These masculine, though often antisocial contests with danger continue until Cuéllar unexpectedly falls in love. For a time, he behaves himself as he hopelessly woos Terry Arrarte; but knowing the relationship can never come to fruition, he fails to commit himself and finally loses her. He returns to his crazy ways—dangerous swims, deadly car races—unable to transcend the rituals of adolescence into maturity. Eventually he drifts away from his boyhood friends as they marry and settle down. His death in an auto accident comes as no surprise and is actually a relief. Far from being tragic, Cuéllar's death evokes only pity, for it asserts nothing; affirming no values conducive to life, he dies as meaninglessly as he lived.

Although not nearly as moving as "On Sunday" or "The Cubs," "The Challenge," another of Vargas Llosa's early stories, also deals with the pervasive Latin American concern over machismo. A knife fight becomes the confrontation with death that a youth, Justo, must face on his way to manhood. The significance of such confrontations as rites of passage latently sanctioned by society is especially apparent in this story. Symbolism plays an important role in the basically realistic plot, which consists simply of the spreading news that there will be a fight and the fight itself. The characters themselves are more important as tokens than as personalities, as symbols of the generations that have faced or must still confront death. The narrator, Julian, represents the adult male, and is father of a baby described as deathly asleep; Leonidas, an old man, represents the sanctions of tradition and presides over the rite of passage that his son, Justo, must endure. Unlike Miguel of "On Sunday," Justo unfortunately dies during his trial; but, unlike the protagonist of "The Cubs," he dies meaningfully. While Cuéllar's death is a release, even an escape, from a fruitless life constantly testing himself for manhood, Justo's death assures him of his own manhood, of his willingness to fight for the protection and reproduction of life which he holds dear. He transcends the kind of test that Cuéllar can only repeat with no feeling of success.

In "The Leaders," Vargas Llosa writes of a confrontation less dangerous, but as significant as those of the stories already discussed. Angered by the arbitrary policies of their principal, the secondary students of a wealthy boys' school lead a brief strike against the administration. This revolt against authority serves as a mass rite of passage to manhood for all the boys, but especially for the leaders who face the danger of expulsion. Realistic, like basically all the stories in the collection, "The Leaders" is most interesting as a study of developing manhood in a sociopsychological setting. Two boys, the narrator and Lou, stand out against the other characters, who are rather undifferentiated; the competition between these two for supremacy runs parallel to the conflict with the principal. In the beginning virtually the entire school supports the strike despite the principal's threats, but when Lou uses force against those who disagree, dissension breaks out in the ranks. Confronted with his macho tactics, other boys assert their own masculinity, and violence erupts, destroying the solidarity necessary for a successful strike. The narrator, having counseled patient persuasion in dealing with the dissenters, is furious with Lou and challenges him to a fight. At this point, however, both suddenly realize that their own macho drives to prove themselves superior have cost them victory against the administration. Nevertheless, knowing that they have both bravely confronted authority and danger, they recognize each other as men and transcend their confrontations by finally accepting each other as friends.

Unlike the stories set in urban areas that comprise the rest of this collection by Vargas Llosa, "A Visitor" and "The Younger Brother" lack authenticity of atmosphere. Easily the poorest of all the stories, these two tales take place in rural settings during unspecified periods; the characters are sketchy, the language and plot structure, uninspired. On the other hand, thematically, the two compare well with the rest of the collection; the theme of manhood and the rites of passage to that state also appears in the rural stories in thought-provoking patterns. In "A Visitor," the author selects an adult male, rather than a boy or youth, as his main character. However, this male, called the Jamaican, has not achieved manhood, regardless of any tests he may have faced in the past, because he betrays the life of a former ally to the authorities in return for his own release from jail. Furthermore, he is terrified when at the story's conclusion the authorities, having captured the fugitive, abandon the Jamaican to certain death at the hands of the fugitive's friends. Even though the main character doubtless faced danger many times during his illegal activities, he clearly never transcended these tests to become a man who encourages and defends life.

"The Younger Brother" is clearly a product of the author's apprenticeship; that story reflects the *costumbrismo* popular in Latin American literature during the nineteenth century, a movement emphasizing local landscapes, customs, history, and peoples. Accompanying the local color was often a concern with social and political reform, a concern echoed in this story. The theme revolves around the horror experienced by Juan—a youth recently returned to his family's hacienda after years in the city—when he realizes that he has killed an innocent Indian for the alleged rape of his sister. Having avenged this "rape," Juan believed he had proven himself as much a man as his older brother, a rugged rancher. On learning that his sister had lied about the Indian and that his brother is unconcerned about the consequences of that lie, Juan goes into a rage, mounts a skittish horse normally beyond his ability as a rider, and then frees a group of Indians imprisoned in the hacienda's stockade. At this point, having supported life by condemning the oppression of the Indians, Juan seems to have achieved true manhood; however, after his outburst he returns to the embrace of his family and its society, indicating that he does not transcend the rite of passage. His oppressive society sees him as a man for having asserted his will, not for his defense of the Indians. Because of this, that society prevents him from becoming a true giver and protector of life.

In the Preface to this collection of short stories, Vargas Llosa remarks, " 'The Grandfather' is out of key in this suite of adolescent and *machista* stories." Despite this, "The Grandfather" can readily be interpreted as an account of an initiation to manhood subconsciously arranged by an old man for his grandson. The apparently senile grandfather, doubtless to avenge some trick perpetrated against him by his grandson, places a skull with a candle inside in a dark garden path where the boy must walk. Just as the boy appears, the old man furtively ignites the candle, sending beams of light through the skull's eyes, nose, and mouth—successfully frightening the boy. Symbolically, the grandson thus confronts death, probably for the first time; significantly, the author leaves no doubt that the candle is a phallic symbol, reinforcing the image of the grandfather's prank as a preliminary rite of passage to manhood.

Because *The Cubs and Other Stories*, in a period of rising feminism, may seem lacking in universality, a broader interpretation of Vargas Llosa's "masculine" rites of passage must at least be noted. While he may deal specifically with those rites testing a male's ability to protect life, obviously males have no monopoly on its preservation and reproduction. Every culture acknowledges this and has rituals at adolescence for women, usually emphasizing fertility and the cultivation of life. Although the emphasis may be different, adolescent rites, whether feminine or masculine, are microcosms of the struggle for existence itself. This being the case, *The Cubs and Other Stories* can also be analyzed as literature about life as a rite of passage between nothingness and death.

John R. Chávez

CULTURAL MATERIALISM
The Struggle for a Science of Culture

Author: Marvin Harris (1927-   )
Publisher: Random House (New York). 381 pp. $15.00
Type of work: Anthropology

An explication of the principles of the cultural materialist approach to anthropology and a comparison of this approach to the major competing schools of cultural analysis

In his popular works, *Cows, Pigs, Wars and Witches* and *Cannibals and Kings: The Origins of Cultures*, Marvin Harris established himself as the major spokesman for the cultural materialist approach to anthropology. In *Cultural Materialism*, he outlines the principles of his anthropological practice and compares his approach to alternative methodologies in anthropology in order to make a case that "cultural materialism leads to better scientific theories about the causes of sociocultural phenomena than any of the rival strategies that are currently available." Although primarily addressed to the professional anthropological community, Harris' work will appeal to almost any reader seriously concerned with the study of cultures.

The point of departure for cultural materialism is Karl Marx's statement that "the mode of production in material life determines the general character of the social, political, and spiritual processes of life. It is not the consciousness of men that determines their existence, but on the contrary, their social existence determines their consciousness." Although acknowledging his debt to Marx, Harris modifies Marx's basic principle in some important ways to make it sufficiently inclusive to describe all aspects of cultural phenomena. Fundamentally, he rejects the idea of dialectical contradictions central to dialectical materialism in favor of a more empirical and scientific analysis of "systemic interactions between thought and behavior." Philosophically, Harris points out, "dialectical materialism" is predicated on Hegelian principles while his own "cultural materialism" derives from the epistomological assumptions of "David Hume and the British empiricists—assumptions that led to Darwin, Spencer, Tylor, Morgan, Frazer, Boas, and the birth of anthropology as an academic discipline."

Marx also failed, according to Harris, to give equal attention to the mode of reproduction as he did to the mode of production, even though these two aspects of culture are equal as shaping powers. Nor was Marx aware of the modern anthropological distinctions between "emic" aspects of culture, in which the native informant offers the ultimate criteria for judging the adequacy of anthropological observations, and "etic" approaches, which make the scientific observer the best judge of cultural phenomena. Simply put, the "emic" approach studies a culture on its own terms while "etic" approaches study cultures from the outside using scientific principles. "Frequently, etic operations involve the measurement and juxtaposition of activities and events

that native informants may find inappropriate or meaningless." Harris stresses
the separate study of emic and etic aspects of culture because:

> . . . research strategies that fail to distinguish between mental and behavior stream events
> and between emic and etic operations cannot develop coherent networks of theories
> embracing the causes of sociocultural differences and similarities. And a priori, one can
> say that those research strategies that confine themselves exclusively to emics or exclusively
> to etics do not meet the general criteria for an aim-oriented social science as effectively
> as those which embrace both points of view.

Using his elaborated Marxist perspective and the etic-emic distinctions,
Harris arrives at the universal cultural principles which shape the cultural
materialist approach to anthropological research:

> To begin with, each society must cope with the problems of production—behaviorally
> satisfying minimal requirements for subsistence; hence there must be an *etic behavioral
> mode of production*. Second, each society must behaviorally cope with the problem of
> reproduction—avoiding destructive increases or decreases in population size; hence there
> must be an *etic behavioral mode of reproduction*. Third, each society must cope with the
> necessity of maintaining secure and orderly behavioral relationships among its constituent
> groups and with other societies.

Since cultural materialists believe disorder to be most likely to result from
economic processes which allocate labor and distribute material products,
"one may infer the universal existence of *etic behavioral domestic economies*
and *etic behavioral political economies*." Finally, there is an etic behavioral
superstructure which encompasses acts based on speech and symbolic processes. As further simplified by Harris, this system lumps the modes of production and reproduction together as the *infrastructure* of a culture while the
domestic and political economy together make its *structure*. The *infrastructure*
and *structure* combine with the behavioral *superstructure* into an interdepen-
dent tripartite scheme of social organization.

These etic aspects of culture are paralleled by comparable emic components, but the latter are of lesser importance to cultural materialism than the
former. This relative importance is based on a theory of "infrastructural
determinism" which states that the etic infrastructure (modes of production
and reproduction) generally determines a society's etic structure (political
and domestic economy) which in turn determines its emic behavioral and
mental superstructure.

Harris' most important departure from classical Marxist principles is his
insistence on equal status for modes of reproduction with those of production.
For Harris, "There is no more important aspect of production than reproduction—the production of human beings," and "the failure to accord the
development of the technology of population control a central role in the
evolution of culture does great damage to the credibility of both classical and

new-wave Marxist principles and theories." In addressing the questions of why populations increase, Harris demonstrates the importance of reproduction by arguing that increases of technological capability frequently have not been utilized to save labor or reduce the amount of time required to gain basic subsistence, but rather are put "to increasing the energy throughout, which in turn has not been used to improve living standards but to produce additional children," often with the effect of decreasing the quality of life. Such seemingly perverse behavior, Harris argues, can best be accounted for by allowing reproduction equal force with production in shaping cultural directions.

Cultural materialism has been particularly subject to the criticism that it subordinates the human capacity for thought to mechanically deterministic social forces. In response, Harris argues that:

> . . . in asserting the primacy of the behavioral infrastructure over the mental and emic superstructure, cultural materialism is not addressing the question of how technological inventions and other kinds of creative innovations originate in individuals but rather how such innovations come to assume a material social existence and how they come to exert an influence on social production and social reproduction.

Conscious thought, he suggests, is important in helping people chart their individual paths through the social maze, but the maze itself is determined by material conditions. As Schopenhauer put it, "We want what we will, but we don't will what we want."

In an example which incorporates elements of ideology, domestic organization, and modes of production, Harris compares the success of the current women's movement to the relatively slight changes in the social system wrought by the youth rebellion of the 1960's. Although fueled by a strong revolutionary, anticapitalist sentiment, the ideas of the latter movement "had absolutely no effect upon the structure and infrastructure of U. S. capitalism, and even their survival and propagation within the superstructure now seems doubtful except insofar as they enhance the profitability of corporations that sell records and clothes." The women's movement, on the other hand, though it has used consciousness-raising as a tool for liberating women, has also benefited from important changes in the infrastructure:

> One cannot argue that political-ideological struggle by women was responsible for the vast shifts in technology, production, demand for cheap labor, rise of cities, and increased cost of rearing children . . . which provide the functional infrastructural conditions upon which the propagation and amplification of modern feminist political-ideological struggle is premised.

These examples are not randomly chosen. Harris is at his best using the tools of cultural materialism to trace the evolution of political units from the most primitive pre-state societies to a variety of more complex sociopolitical systems. "At the heart of the cultural materialist theoretical corpus is a set of theories dealing with the origin of the principal varieties of pre-state societies, the origin of sexism, classes, castes, and the state, and the origin of the principal varieties of state level systems." Looking at the developed countries, and especially the United States, as the population declines because of the high cost of rearing children and the minimal long-term benefits to their parents, Harris arrives at a bleak picture:

> In the United States this is happening at the same time that resources are being depleted and domestic capital is flowing overseas at an increasing rate in search of cheap labor, leading to inflation and the necessity for having two wage earners per middle-class family. From this we get quite plausibly the generation gap, the flamboyant redefinition of sex roles, delayed marriages, "shacking up," communes, homosexual couples, and one-person families. And from the general closing down of the American dream, which was founded on the rape of the previously unexploited resources of an entire continent, we get the revival of religious fundamentalism, astrology, and salvation in or from outer space.

To this catalog of results of a decaying infrastructure, Harris adds "as a final ideological product . . . the growing commitment of the social sciences to research strategies whose function it is to mystify sociocultural phenomena by directing attention away from the etic behavioral infrastructural causes." More than half of *Cultural Materialism* is devoted to a comparison of Harris' theories with those of such other major schools of anthropology as sociobiology, dialectical materialism, structuralism, structural Marxism, psychological and cognitive idealism, eclecticism, and obscurantism. Underlying these comparisons, which assert the superior ability of culturalism materialism to account for the causes of complex sociocultural phenomena, is Harris' sincere conviction that, if solutions are to be found to complex social problems, they will be arrived at through scientific analysis and objective understanding of how cultures work. "The time is ripe," Harris maintains, "to replace the incohate and unconscious paradigms under whose auspices most anthropologists conduct their research with explicit descriptions of basic objectives, rules, and assumptions."

Harris' skepticism toward unscientific approaches to culture study reflects his conviction that, while every effort should be made to understand the thinking of other peoples, "we cannot stop at that understanding. It is imperative that we reserve the right not to believe their explanations. Most of all we must reserve the right not to believe ruling class explanations." Though said in regard to the Aztec, Harris would maintain the same principle in regard to the study of any culture, including our own. "If it be anthropology to struggle against the mystification of the causes of inequality and exploitation," he writes, "long live anthropology."

It is in Harris' concern with the political dimensions of culture which lead to exploitation and injustice that we see under his own scientific objectivity the image of a true humanist whose search for truth is an expression of love for mankind. "To erect a barrier between truth and love is to wantonly degrade and limit human nature," he writes. *Cultural Materialism* erects no such barrier.

William E. Grant

THE CULTURE OF NARCISSISM
American Life in an Age of Diminishing Expectations

Author: Christopher Lasch (1932-   )
Publisher: W. W. Norton and Company (New York). 268 pp. $11.95; paperback $2.95
Type of work: Sociology
Time: The present
Locale: The United States

A colorful but superficial picture of the "me-first-and-only" society that the author feels controls the nation, woven together by strands of history and Freudian psychology

In this latest work, Christopher Lasch continues his polemic against a politically and intellectually "bankrupt" liberalism, which he calls "the political theory of the ascendant bourgeoisie," which "long ago lost the capacity to explain events in the world of the welfare state and the multinational corporation." The bankruptcy has brought a decline of "competitive individualism." In its place, "feel good" therapy has given us a society of narcissists out to satisfy the desires of the moment with little thought for the future.

In the course of the book, Lasch analyzes the problems of workers and managers, professional sports, and schools; explains the reasons behind the collapse of parental authority in the American family (his previous book was subtitled *The Family Besieged*); offers insights into the deep-seated masculine fears which cause the middle-class war between the sexes; and presents a multifaceted image of a society which has no hope for the future. And he does it all with an unquestioning faith in the Freudian explanations of all behavior.

Certainly there are many economic, political, and social problems in contemporary American society. Few observers of the culture would argue with some of Lasch's statements, but as with most platitudes, these pronouncements are strong on generalities and weak on documentation. That is, what he writes looks substantial on the surface, but often that surface turns out to be a hollow shell. Such an approach leads to at least two major problems in his persuasive technique and one major failing in his total argument. (Before continuing, a definition is needed. Just who or what is a narcissist? It is difficult to summarize, but according to Lasch, the narcissist is a "superficially relaxed and tolerant . . . psychological man [who] forfeits the security of group loyalties . . . demands immediate gratification and lives in a state of restless, perpetually unsatisfied desire." These are the dominant qualities of our society in Lasch's view, so the "he" of a comment about a narcissist also means the "we" of contemporary society.)

The first problem involves the extreme positions the author takes in his sociological and psychological attacks upon American society. Perhaps he must be so shrill in his harangue; perhaps he feels such "overkill" is necessary to awaken us. Lasch is an academic, a historian from the University of Rochester; hence, one of the major sins of the narcissist, as detailed by Lasch, is that he no longer cares about the past. That is, the narcissist has no sense of history, of the continuity of time and society, and seemingly he does not want such a continuity. He is indifferent to the past, and that indifference, "which easily shades over into active hostility and rejection," is the "proof" of the cultural bankruptcy of our society.

If we have no sense of the past, we also no longer care about the future, that is, a time beyond our own expected life span. "People busy themselves . . . with survival strategies, measures designed to prolong their own lives, or programs guaranteed to ensure good health and peace of mind." Somehow it is slightly improper to attempt to prolong life, in the author's view.

But if we are to achieve a concern for the future, if we are to reverse the narcissistic trend, might not one way be to attempt to live longer in order to help make things better? If we do not care about the future, why jog or diet or avoid carcinogens? Why do protestors picket against nuclear plants? They are concerned that a plant may explode and cause immediate damage to lives and property, and, at the same time, they are fearful that slow, accidental leaks or low-level (and legal) emissions may cause long-range genetic damage to persons living close to the plants, damage which may not appear for generations. Why do other groups form to protect whales or seals or birds if there is this total lack of care about the future which Lasch attributes to all of society?

The behaviors Lasch superimposes upon all of society may in fact be the actions of some people. However, his examples of narcissists are heavily skewed toward "the beautiful people," the celebrities, and it is not justifiable to say that all of society has lost its sense of values and directions just because the *nouveau riche* and the disco groups seem to have done so. Yet Lasch makes such sweeping generalities his stock approach. Thus he can say that "self-absorption defines the moral climate of contemporary society" and that "the poor have always had to live for the present, but now a desperate concern for personal survival, sometimes disguised as hedonism, engulfs the middle class as well." The economic problems of the middle class lead to second jobs, moonlighting, working wives, and repairs on the old car instead of the purchase of a new one. To call such activities "hedonistic self-absorption" is unfair and unjust.

Another sociological discussion which predicates all behavior upon the observed actions of a few comes in Lasch's explanation for the collapse of parental authority in our society. He cites instances, case studies, perhaps, of parents who "rely on doctors, psychiatrists, and the child's own peers to impose rules on the child and to see that he conforms to them." Thus when the child will not eat his spinach or liver or take her vitamins, the parent says the doctor ordered it, or if the child is "unruly," he is whisked off to the psychiatrist. Note, there are no qualifiers in Lasch's statements, no indications that what he means is that *some* parents *may* refer to outside authority *occasionally*. He simply says this is what parents do, and he leaves the reader to draw the logical conclusion that all parents do these things, that all parents have lost the ability to establish rules for their children.

This example of the decline of parental authority exposes another of Lasch's extreme positions, that of proposing a Freudian basis for and explanation of all behavior. "The decline of parental authority reflects the 'decline of the superego' in American society as a whole." Lasch is not a psychiatrist; he is a historian, a writer who wishes to pass judgment on the state of society on the basis of his research and his own opinions.

He must be credited with having read friend and foe alike. He knows their works well enough to mention Riesman's "other-directed" type, Whyte's "organization man," Horney's "neurotic personality of our time," and Fromm's "market-oriented personality." However, all such potential causes of and answers for contemporary social problems are dismissed by Lasch as simply as he dismisses Fromm. "Like many social scientists, Fromm exaggerated the degree to which aggressive impulses can be socialized; he saw man as entirely a product of socialization, not as a creature of instinct whose partially repressed or sublimated drives always threaten to break out in all their original ferocity." In other words, Fromm and the other non-Freudians simply are wrong; the views of Freud and the Freudian proponents simply are right.

The Culture of Narcissism is Lasch's book, of course, and he may do what he wishes to do, even when it is to project Freudian solutions upon societal problems. But when the effect of such projections will be more complications rather than solutions to the problem, perhaps Lasch and his Freudian cause-and-effect analysis needs to be tempered by other viewpoints as well.

Such an analysis is what takes place in the chapter entitled "The Flight from Feeling: Sociopsychology of the Sex War." The problems which face women and men at a time when one-third of all marriages end in divorce and when women earn 59¢ for each dollar earned by men for comparable work and when more and more men are experiencing occasional, temporary impotence cannot be solved by falling back upon "easy" Freudian etiology. According to Lasch and the authorities he cites, impotence, for example, is caused by the "apparently aggressive overtures of sexually liberated women." Perhaps some men, faced with a "sexually liberated" female, might well be frightened into temporary impotence, but with increasing frequency, impotence seems to be caused, too, by job-oriented stress and worry and by environmental situations. Whether stress and worry or work-related causes are more to blame or less to blame for impotence than some Freudian cause is not the point; what is of concern is that Lasch presents *only* the Freudian reasons.

"Women's sexual demands terrify men because they reverberate at such deep layers of the masculine mind, calling up early fantasies of a possessive, suffocating, devouring, and castrating mother." This statement summarizes, for Lasch, the reason for all interpersonal difficulties between men and women. Since these problems are located in the subconscious structure of the mind, there is little to be done to solve them, short of individual psychoanalysis—if one wishes to solve the problem, that is. Lasch says: "The abolition of sexual tensions is an unworthy goal in any case; the point is to live with them more gracefully than we have lived with them in the past."

The sociopsychological extreme, then, is one major problem the reader faces with this book. Another significant problem shows through in Lasch's much-lauded chapter, "The Degradation of Sport." As with many of his comments, the generalizations about American professional sports—high salaries, commercialization, long seasons—would find agreement in a wide range of audiences. But when he states that sports are degraded because they are trivialized, that crowds are more violent today because they do not "abide by the conventions that should bind spectators as well as players," and that the "conventions that formerly restrained rivalry even as they glorified it" have collapsed, but never gives examples of these "conventions," the second major problem becomes apparent.

Underlying every analysis, every generalization, and every specific he offers is a strong conservative bias, whether it takes an economic or behavioral outlet. Lasch never admits to his bias, but anyone who speaks of "conventions" of the past without defining them is espousing a conservative, elitist position, and if one must ask for definitions, one does not belong.

Such bias also leads him to produce generalizations, and nowhere is this weakness, this proclivity, more apparent than in the chapter on education, "Schooling and the New Illiteracy." When rudimentary knowledge was all most citizens needed, the home or the one-room, frontier "blab" school, where all the students in all the various grades recited their lessons simultaneously, was adequate. The local school no longer is a one-room affair, however, but it still is the most readily available social institution for many people. Hence the local school is an easy target for social commentators, and the public school system must bear the brunt of some of Lasch's most hollow and/or contradictory generalizations.

> The whole problem of American education comes down to this: in American society, almost everyone identifies intellectual excellence with elitism. This attitude not only guarantees the monopolization of educational advantages by the few; it lowers the quality of elite education itself and threatens to bring about a reign of universal ignorance.

A few of the major problems with this book are seen in the preceding comments. Most of them would be bearable if they were not compounded by the even larger major failing: Lasch's volume is all diagnosis, with no prescription for cure. How can these multiple problems be solved? What can institutions and individuals do to effect needed changes? Lasch says they can "take the solution of their problems into their own hands" by creating their own "communities of competence"—whatever that may mean. This is the only suggestion, the only answer he gives.

Finally, the author says in his Introduction that he is writing about a "way of life that is dying—the culture of competitive individualism." All his discussions sound as though this culture already is dead, as though he is delivering the eulogy to individualism. But, on the final two pages, he admits "the will to build a better society . . . survives," and along with that will, society still shows the "traditions of localism, self-help, and community action." In addition, "the moral discipline formerly associated with the work ethic still retains a value independent of the role it once played in the defense of property rights."

If this is true, why did Lasch not contrast these traditions with the narcissistic and illogical behaviors of the persons he discusses as examples of the problem he would have us believe plagues all society? Perhaps he does not want the reader to know until the end that all is not lost. That is, he wants nothing to mitigate his jeremiad. In the end, his procedure serves only to weaken his argument.

John C. Carlisle

DAGUERREOTYPES AND OTHER ESSAYS

Author: Isak Dinesen (1885-1962)
Publisher: University of Chicago Press (Chicago). 229 pp. $12.95
Type of work: Essays
Time: 1938-1960
Locale: Denmark, Germany, England, and New York City

A collection of essays and radio talks by Denmark's most distinguished modern writer of fiction

The Baroness Karen Blixen was born as Karen Christentze Dinesen in Rungsted, Denmark, daughter of a Danish officer who also served as a leftist member of parliament and wrote books on hunting as well as his military experiences. He committed suicide when she was ten, causing Karen to experience a traumatically unhappy childhood. She came to idealize her dead father and to imitate his pattern of life by uniting adventurous action with a writing career. Her mother, who came from a wealthy mercantile family, took Karen to her own mother's home after the Baron's death, and insisted that her daughter be reared in the Unitarian faith, which is unusual in Denmark.

Karen was largely brought up by governesses and taught fluent English and French, literature, art, and history. In 1904, she studied English at Oxford; in 1910, painting in Paris. In 1912, she lived in Rome with a cousin and conceived a lifelong love for Italy, in which she was to set many of her stories.

In 1913, Karen became engaged to a cousin, the Swedish Baron Bror von Blixen-Finecke. An uncle persuaded them to emigrate to Kenya, and they bought a six-thousand-acre coffee farm near Nairobi in 1914, shortly before their marriage. They were divorced in 1921, whereupon she managed the plantation alone, with her ex-husband preferring the life of a big-game hunter. In 1931, the Depression and consequent collapse of world coffee prices forced her to lose the farm. She returned sadly to Denmark, where she turned to a writing career in her mid-forties, with her brother supporting her for two years while she worked on the group of stories that was to be published in 1934 as *Seven Gothic Tales*.

The Baroness reverted to her maiden name for her authorial identity and prefixed to it the Old Testament pseudonym "Isak," meaning "the one who laughs." She recalled Sarah, in Genesis, who laughed when she finally bore a son in her old age after a lifetime of barrenness. Karen felt that her first book was *her* late-born child, and was jubilant that she had been able, through the power of her literary talent, to recover from the twin loss, in 1931, of not only her farm but also the love of her life.

Dinesen describes him in *Out of Africa* (1937), a prose pastoral that unites autobiography with myth. He was Denys Finch-Hatton, younger brother of a wealthy earl, handsome as the proverbial Greek god, a poet, pilot, and hunter, and a man of courage, culture, and moral probity. They would hunt together, read the Greek and Latin classics together in the original languages, and she would play Scheherezade to him in the evenings, sitting cross-legged and inventing stories. Denys died in a crash of his plane several months after her last coffee crop had failed.

The most spectacular period of Isak Dinesen's literary career is represented by her first three books: *Seven Gothic Tales*, *Out of Africa*, and *Winter's Tales* (1942), on which the substance of her reputation rests. *Seven Gothic Tales* remains her most popular work, attracting readers by its fantastic, extravagant, highly mannered, and perverse qualities. Dinesen often produced patterns and meanings beyond the intent of her characters, who lose their naturalistic identities and become marionettes in some higher, mystical scheme whose nature they do not comprehend. In the first story of *Seven Gothic Tales*, "Deluge at Norderney," four characters are stranded by a flood in a sinking farmhouse. They begin a dance of wit which increases steadily in imaginative intensity. The author uses this complex tale to mock aestheticism and rationalism as opponents of instinct and realistic experience, employing three inset stories for this purpose. Both comic and tragic tones assume increasing dimension during the night these people spend together, making the farm's hayloft the setting for the free play of their masquerades and imaginations. All four meet death, but they transcend it through a self-realization rarely matched in literature.

After *Winter's Tales* Dinesen's art suffered a hiatus of fifteen years, interrupted only by a novel, *The Angelic Avengers*, a mystery which she had published in 1946 under the name of Pierre Andrézel, and would not acknowledge for years. Then, in her seventies, Dinesen published two volumes of stories, *Last Tales* (1957) and *Anecdotes of Destiny* (1958), and a collection of African reminiscences, *Shadows on the Grass* (1961). Two additional story collections have been published posthumously, *Ehrengard* (1963) and *Carnival* (1978), with most of the last volume consisting of tales rejected as substandard for publication by their fastidious author.

Daguerreotypes and Other Essays is a mixed bag in quality. Its title essay was originally published by itself in 1951, and was first delivered on the Danish radio. In it Dinesen examines the differences between the aristocratic past and the populist present. The nineteenth century woman, who presided over religion and poetry, was either a guardian angel, housewife, *bayadère*, or witch. Dinesen approves of these classifications, and is aghast at contemporary efforts to undermine ritual and prestige for the sake of equality and comfort. To shake the "grand temple of human dignity" that the old order constitutes is to behave like Samson—and be crushed in the crash of the pillars of responsible aristocracy. However, Dinesen does try to adjust to the new order as gracefully as she can. When a nephew of hers told her he wanted to spend a year traveling around the world, hitching rides and occasionally taking jobs on freighters, she subsidized a course in tattooing for him so he would have a good opportunity to earn food-and-board money on his way. Moreover, she concludes, tattooing is an ancient art that includes a sense of ritual and mystic motifs; its clientele includes not only seamen but kings.

The longest selection in this anthology consists of "Letters from a Land at War." Dinesen explains in an introduction that three Scandinavian newspapers had commissioned her in the fall of 1939 to spend a month each in London, Paris, and Berlin, and to write for them four feature articles from each city. She first went to Berlin, where she largely resided from March 1 to April 2, 1940. On April 9, with the author back in Denmark to write her Berlin articles, the Germans occupied the country and, of course, made it impossible for her to travel to London and Paris. Hence the "Letters" deal only with Germany, concentrating on Berlin but also including Bremen.

Dinesen admits that she pulls some of her punches in her reports on Germany in the spring of 1940: Denmark had, after all, to respect the sensitivity of her powerful German neighbor. Hence she makes no direct mention of Hitler or other Nazi chieftains, or of the Nazis' anti-Semitic campaigns. She does satirize the Nazis' cult of social realism in art as middle-class escapism into a silly heroic idyll, with the heavy-set young maiden developing into an amply proportioned young mother, exuding milk, honey, and piety. She also chides the Germans for lacking a sense of humor: it is anathema to them because they regard it as "a heresy directed against the sole means of salvation—that is, belief in the omnipotence of the will." These tremendous exertions of will both impress and depress Dinesen. She admires German architectural achievements, the meticulous organization of women for state-ordered occupations, and the nation's disciplined dedication to causes. She prefers, however, her notion of God to the German belief in the materialist force of the human will, and she mistrusts the Germans' transcendental dedication to such tasks as the transformation of people's souls.

The main defect of these essays is their discursive chattiness, their lack of a sharp focus or sustained argument. In a 1953 talk, "Oration at a Bonfire," she begins by discussing feminism, but soon admits that this is a topic she does not understand and has never concerned herself with. She then becomes vaguely autobiographical, stating her belief that the inspiring exchange between men and women has been history's most powerful determinant, creating "what is characteristic of our aristocracy: courageous exploits, poetry, the arts, and the refinement of taste." She never examines closely any of the socioeconomic problems women have had (and continue to have) in a male-dominated society. Instead, she offers her traditional preference for separate roles of the sexes: "A man's center of gravity, the substance of his being, consists in what he has executed and performed in life; the woman's, in what she is." Let women take for their ideal the Virgin Mary, who offered up her existence so that God could become Man. How a modern woman can bridge the gap between Mary's passivity on the one hand, and management of a coffee plantation and a writing career on the other, Dinesen never explains.

She offers a more satisfactory response in a 1960 essay, "On Mottoes of My Life." There she tells us that she has sailed the course of her life under several mottoes. The first was, *Navigare necesse est, vivere non necesse!*, originally uttered by Pompey to encourage his timid crew to brave high seas. She translated the motto to her own needs: "It is necessary to farm, it is not necessary to live." Then she adopted the motto of Finch-Hatton's family: "*Je responderay*," and held herself answerable for every circumstance of her life. After Dinesen had lost nearly all in Africa, she adopted the motto, "*Pourquoi pas?*," which guided her in her writing life. She admits she cannot fully account for its meaning or power; but it did encourage and inspire her.

In the 1950's, Dinesen's health, never sturdy, became the central problem of her life. She underwent two serious spinal operations, and a third in which most of her stomach was removed, reducing her weight to below seventy pounds. Photos taken of her during these years resemble a hooded, fragile gnome, her eyes black with kohl. Yet she managed not only to keep writing but also to travel and give readings from her books. She deeded her estate, Rungstedlund, to the Danish nation, with the proviso that it be used as a bird sanctuary open to the public. She died there, of general weakness and malnutrition, on September 7, 1962.

Harry Brand

DARKNESS VISIBLE

Author: William Golding (1911-   )
Publisher: Farrar, Straus and Giroux (New York). 265 pp. $10.95
Type of work: Novel
Time: 1940's to the present
Locale: England and Australia

In this novel, William Golding explores in a modern setting of violence and cruelty the theme of Christian apocalypse

> *Principal characters:*
> MATTHEW (MATTY) "SEPTIMUS" WINDRAVE/WINDROVE/WIND-
> GRAVE, a visionary, saint, or lunatic disfigured by fire
> SOPHY STANHOPE, a dark-haired beauty driven by an impulse for
> violence
> TONI (ANTONIA) STANHOPE, her twin sister, a political terrorist
> MR. PEDIGREE, a homosexual schoolmaster at the Foundlings
> School
> SIM GOODCHILD, a bookseller
> EDWIN BELL, his friend, a schoolmaster

Like all of William Golding's novels, *Darkness Visible*, his most recent major fiction, treats as a fable, or didactic moral tale, aspects of the theme of Christian salvation. In his 1962 essay entitled "Fable," reprinted in *The Hot Gates and other occasional pieces* (1966), Golding explicitly describes the beliefs that control his purposes as a moralist:

> Man is a fallen being. He is gripped by original sin. His nature is sinful and his state perilous. I accept the theology and admit the triteness; but what is trite is true; and a truism can become more than a truism when it is a belief passionately held.

The author's artistic credo applies most directly to *Lord of the Flies*, his first and most popular book, but in different ways it applies as well to his later novels. In *Lord of the Flies*, Jack and his fellow hunters, isolated from civilized society, revert to a primitive condition of "original sin." Similarly, in *The Inheritors*, Golding's fable of the inherent evil in human nature which extends to man's ancestors, the murderous Cro-Magnon (*Homo sapiens*) people who exterminate their gentle rivals, the Neanderthals. In other novels, Golding exposes the folly of man's prideful belief in his rationality. For example, Christopher Martin (*Pincher Martin*), a naval officer in wartime, is blown into the North Atlantic after a submarine attack; swimming to a jutting rock, he supposes that, through the powers of his reason and imagination, he might survive. But the reader learns that his damnation has already taken place and that, after a momentary struggle, during which his entire story unfolds in his mind, he has drowned ignominiously. Similarly, in *Free Fall*, Sammy Mountjoy makes a Faustian decision that eventually destroys both his freedom and his soul; the novel explores the precise moment when his damnation through pride had occurred. Against the pattern of human sinfulness, folly, and pride, Golding always establishes obscure fables of Christian redemption.

In *Darkness Visible*, Golding's religious fable is perhaps least obscure, for the "darkness" of the title represents Christian mysteries that become visible for the faithful through revelation. As experienced by Matthew "Septimus" Windgrave (one of his several names), the revelation is fearsome, a human holocaust, a metaphor of fire. From fire, indeed, he emerges—a mere child, naked, nearly burnt to death in an incendiary bomb attack on London during World War II. An anonymous victim of the ravages of senseless cruelty, he is patched together by plastic surgeons, still hideously marked, then turned back into the world as a freak. At the Foundlings School in Greenfield, he stands apart from the other children, alienated as much by his scrupulous moral uprightness as by his physical appearance.

Ironically, Matty's ugliness becomes a reverse symbol for his inner spiritual perfection. To his respected schoolmaster Mr. Pedigree, an aging pederast who is dangerously attracted to beautiful boys, he is an object of horror. To his employers he is a harmless drudge who deserves to be exploited. And to girls, he is either the source of revulsion or pity. So he turns to the voices of his spiritual masters. They assure him that he has a divine, although darkly understood, mission. After he returns to England following his travels in Australia, where he had been symbolically crucified, he begins to keep a journal of his spiritual meditations. Slowly, from the revelations of his masters, he comes to perceive, though not yet as perfectly visible, the shape of his mission.

Contrasted to Matty, disfigured by fire, are the beautiful but wayward twins, Sophy and Antonia Stanhope. Even as children, both are attracted to evil, which they see as "weirdness." Mature, they use their physical beauty as a mask to conceal their inner corruption. Toni runs off to become a model in London, disappears from England, trains with Palestinian and Cuban terrorists, then returns to her sister as a hardened revolutionary. Sophy, even more depraved, flings herself upon men for casual sex, becomes bored by her own moral vacuousness, and finally settles with a gang of toughs, restless for petty adventures. When Toni enlists herself in a kidnap-ransom scheme that might involve a lucrative reward, Sophy is more excited by her sadistic notion of the outrage than of any mere promise of wealth.

The child marked for the kidnapping, a Middle-Eastern youth of mysterious origins, had been attending the exclusive Wandicott School. He now becomes the focus not only of the Stanhope girls' criminal plot but also of Matty's revelations. The spiritual voices tell Matty that he must ready himself for a selfless act. As the drama moves quickly to its apocalypse, a chorus of witnesses, the feckless but innocent Sim Goodchild and Edwin Bell, try to piece together with their deficient human understanding the divine purpose. Yet they fail, well-meaning though they are, to comprehend the meaning of

Matty's final redemption. To save the child from the act of outrage, he must return to fire; he immolates himself as a final sacrificial holocaust. Thus darkness becomes fully visible: through the fable of apocalypse, Christian salvation becomes possible.

Carefully crafted, suspenseful, and consistent, *Darkness Visible* is a worthy technical achievement for the author of *Lord of the Flies* and *The Spire*. On both thematic and psychological levels, however, the novel falls short of the high level of Golding's best fiction. With the theme of redemption, one suiting the talents of Graham Greene, a less melodramatic, less hortatory presentation would seem necessary. Serious, indeed humorless, Golding at times unintentionally parodies his own subject. For example, the Australian aborigine who stomps upon Matty's genitals in a scene intended to represent the hero's crucifixion (or mock crucifixion) is named Harry Bummer. Bummer comes upon Matty in the desert, famished, surrounded by "large black ants running at his feet" (we recall the ant-martyrdom of Celia in T. S. Eliot's *The Cocktail Party*) and crying out for water. Bummer notices with disdain that Matty has a Bible, then leaps to his feet with this execration: "Fucking big sky-fella him b'long Jesus Christ!" In another climactic scene in which Golding's language similarly appears inappropriate to maintain the serious mood that he intends to establish, Sophy wields a knife at a rabbit trapped in a latrine. Hysterically she imagines that the rabbit is, instead, the kidnapped child: "She felt an utter disgust at the creature itself sitting there on the stinking loo, so disgusting, eek and ooh, oh so much part of all weirdness from which you could see the whole thing as ruin. . . ."

Just as Golding betrays his theme at times by inappropriate language, he also fails to make many of his characters psychologically credible. Matty never truly comes to life. Only with the introduction of the evil Stanhope twins does the novel sustain a vitality. Their wickedness is far more engaging, from the point of view of fiction, than Matty's suffering sanctity. Bored, vicious, and calculating, Sophy is perfectly realized as a type. Yet Golding burdens even her uncomplicated character with language beyond her capabilities: "A truth appeared in her mind. *The way towards simplicity is through outrage.*" Better for Sophy to commit outrage than to philosophize about it. Similarly, at the end of the novel, Golding places into Pedigree's consciousness ideas that the reader would not expect him to develop. In a Resurrection scene, Matty has returned to his old schoolmaster, seemingly has blessed him, offering the pederast a momentary grace. Then Pedigree, in a passage that shows Christian charity, accepts Matty's sacrifice; but his thoughts are profound beyond those we would expect of this dreary man.

To Golding, it is Pedigree, not Matty or the Stanhope girls, who is central to the existential problem. Matty, a modern John the Baptist who makes way for the redeeming child, is holy beyond ordinary human possibilities; the twins are contrastingly evil, as diabolical as Matty is good. Yet Pedigree is flawed, the Old Adam, neither wholly good nor wholly evil. Although his tendencies are toward homosexual love for boys, he suffers remorse for the excesses of his imagination. Moreover, he at least has the power to love, even though his eroticism runs counter to societal norms, and he has the power to choose. To Golding, freedom permits the terrible existential choice of good or evil. Caught between the antipodes, Pedigree must choose a way for himself. In his decision he has been aided, for at least a moment's grace, as a result of the supernatural intercession of Matty. To Golding, such an apocalypse, one that makes darkness visible, has already been offered to all Christians.

Leslie B. Mittleman

DARROW
A Biography

Author: Kevin Tierney
Publisher: Thomas Y. Crowell (New York). Illustrated. 490 pp. $16.95
Type of work: Biography
Time: 1857-1938
Locale: The American Midwest, primarily Chicago

A workmanlike study which introduces Clarence Darrow as an undistinguished student with a maverick's restlessness who learns to fight for the underdog in Chicago where, as a trial lawyer, he defends some of the most notorious people of his day

> Principal personages:
> CLARENCE DARROW, one of America's outstanding trial lawyers
> JOHN PETER ALTGELD, a writer whose pamphlets about the rights of the disenfranchised caused considerable controversy and inspired Darrow early in his career
> OSSIAN SWEET, a Detroit black, charged with the murder of a white, who was represented by Darrow in a landmark case
> JOHN T. SCOPES, a Tennessee schoolteacher tried for teaching Darwin's evolutionary theory
> EUGENE V. DEBS, an Indiana-born socialist and labor movement organizer who led some of America's first great labor strikes during the late nineteenth century
> RICHARD LOEB AND NATHAN LEOPOLD, JR., two murderers whose sentences Darrow had reduced from death to life imprisonment

Author Kevin Tierney, who presently teaches law at the University of California's Hastings College in San Francisco, has written one of the most complete studies to date of America's foremost trial lawyer: Clarence Darrow, the courtroom spellbinder who defended the most unpopular causes and personages of his day, including organized labor, anarchists, child murderers, and blacks charged with murdering whites. In *Darrow: A Biography*, the myth of Darrow, brave defender of the weak and hated, is given considerable reinforcement. For here is the battler of legend, who, although struggling against an army of enemies bent on his destruction or humiliation, wins case after case: the Loeb-Leopold "thrill murder" affair, the John Scopes "Monkey Trial" in Tennessee, the *Ossian Sweet* case in Detroit. On the other hand, one sees Darrow in a different light than that in which he is usually portrayed. He is presented as a frustrated writer yearning to be part of the Chicago Renaissance group of poets and novelists; as a victim of bad luck, judgment and timing; and as a midlife failure.

The twists and turns of Darrow's life were dramatic, with astonishing success followed by terrible defeat which, in turn, was followed by phoenixlike recovery. In fact, it could be said that Tierney's principal aim in writing about Darrow is to demonstrate how supremely hard it was for him to win not only a name for himself but also the respect of fellow colleagues, many of whom were repulsed by his sense of superiority. A lesser man would have been broken by any one of the sizable defeats life dealt Darrow. However, his will and large heart, combined with a love of courtroom debate, made him the "people's champion" late in life.

From tiny Kinsman, Ohio, an unincorporated hamlet not even appearing on maps of the day, Darrow started his life's quest in solid Horatio Alger fashion, having neither prosperous or well-connected parents nor a decent school record upon which to rely. Tierney stresses that Darrow's skepticism, his obstinacy, and his at times vehement unconventionality were there from the outset, as was his ambition to forge ahead no matter what or who stood in his way. Since anything which restricted his capacity to learn firsthand about the world and its workings angered him, it was only a matter of time before he spurned Kinsman's dull ways and headed for law school at the University of Michigan. Nevertheless, even a university setting was too predictable and orderly for Darrow, too isolated from the combative real world he wanted so much to be part of, so he left.

Out in the world, unknown by it but ready to be known, Darrow learned law his own way through doing rather than by diligent study. First he went to Youngstown, where he passed the bar examination, then to Andover, and finally to Ashtabula, Ohio, where he became active in politics, falling under the sway of reformer John Peter Altgeld's essay, "our Penal Machinery and Its Victims," a tract defending the legal rights of society's lower-class.

After a time, Darrow's restlessness led to his making the final big move of his life when he journeyed to Chicago, the new metropolis teeming with life, possibilities, and problems. Immediately upon his arrival there in 1887, he allowed Chicago to be the one schoolmaster he would listen to. The city would, in turn, teach him some of life's cruelest lessons and force him to assert his brilliance and ability.

At the time of Darrow's arrival, Chicago was already a swollen giant of a city with a population hovering around the one million mark; it was well-known for its wild, unruly populace and incredible growth rate. As Tierney points out, "No other place challenged its preeminence in actuality or prospects. America's young hopefuls assessed Chicago as the city of the future." So important, in fact, had the city become by the end of the nineteenth century that some believed the nation's capital would be moved from Washington, D.C., to Chicago, the continent's center.

The rebuilding of Chicago meant a great surge of cheap labor coming to the city from Eastern Europe and elsewhere, labor at first easily exploited by capitalists such as George Pullman or meatpackers Armour and Swift. Laboring men and women were so poorly treated that unionization was the only thing to which they could turn to help them receive the wages and hours they needed; and it was such unionization that led to the brutal Haymarket Riot of 1886 in which "unionist" anarchists supposedly threw a bomb, killing onlookers and police alike. That the "plot" leaders were so quickly condemned to death by hanging bothered, among others, Clarence Darrow. In fact, it was that decision by the Illinois court that led Darrow into the unionist cause and the fight for the rights of the laboring man.

By listening to Chicago's finest legal authorities speak, by immersing himself in books and articles written about Chicago, by acquainting himself with the city's streets and neighborhoods, and by introducing himself to those who were well-connected or in important city posts, Darrow gradually, albeit painfully, pulled himself out of obscurity and into the limelight.

Above all others, it was the idol of his youth, John Peter Altgeld, who offered help by making sure his novice lawyer friend Darrow found enough wealthy clients to begin his practice. Although no saint (he embodied "a peculiar mixture of idealism and ruthlessness"), Altgeld wanted to do a good turn for a person of Darrow's talents and cast of mind who appreciated the fight he was making for individual rights in Illinois.

Darrow became prosperous as his horizons widened. Yet despite his early success, he continually quarreled with colleagues, adopting the attitude (foreign to most attorneys) that "he who opposes my client in the courtroom is no friend of mine." Miffed by Darrow's presumption and his penchant for seeing colleagues as enemies, many members of the Chicago bar avoided him. Later, when Darrow was in need of help from fellow lawyers, scarcely a handful were interested enough in him to give assistance. All in all, Darrow, as Tierney indicates, went out of his way to hurt his reputation. It was not until the 1920's that he would be well received again in legal circles.

Among the early cases which caused considerable bad feeling between Darrow and other lawyers was the so-called "Debs's Rebellion" at the Pullman Company just outside of Chicago. Here, federal troops fought and fired upon striking members of Eugene V. Debs's Railway union which then caused the workers to burn and vandalize Pullman property. Caught between his instinctive loyalty to underdog causes like that of the workers and his disapproval of union terrorist activities, Darrow finally decided to side with the latter against the former and, in so doing, had to give up his lucrative connection with the Chicago and Northwestern Railroad. As he stepped out of the railway company's office, he found his true vocation. According to Tierney, the first major case Darrow undertook, the one involving Eugene V. Debs's defense, set the pattern for his future undertakings. Darrow's zest for defending Debs was grounded in his dislike of institutions and his corresponding admiration for those who confronted institutions and made them tremble.

Darrow put everything he had into his early cases, most of which involved the "little man" versus the corporation: the Kidd case which had to do with an alleged "worker conspiracy" against the president of a Wisconsin lumber company; the 1912 defense of Pennsylvania anthracite coal miners; the defense of Western Federation of Miners Secretary-Treasurer William Haywood, accused of murdering Governor Steunenberg of Idaho; and the McNamara case in which union members were said to be responsible for the bombing of the *Los Angeles Times* office, to name but some of the most notable cases.

What dazed prosecutors in case after case was Darrow's splendid ability to come up with precisely the right phrase which would sway a jury or convince a judge. Likewise, his tenacity and talent for drawing out difficult witnesses were extraordinary. Even in an age of oratorical giants, Darrow had no peers.

Although used to success, Darrow, at age fifty-five found it slipping away. The labor movement which he had so assiduously defended turned on him after the McNamara bombing case in Los Angeles. Here, as in the earlier Pullman strike, workers used violence to obtain justice and, by so doing, alienated Darrow. Sickened by the bombing of the *Los Angeles Times* and tired of defending those who praised such acts, Darrow began to see himself as a middle-aged failure too depressed and humiliated to carry on his life's work. Adding insult to injury was his indictment as a briber of a juror in the McNamara case. Friends and enemies alike noticed the changes stealing over Darrow; his voice cracked, he looked wan and disoriented, he drank too much, and he sought human contact too seldom. In short, he appeared to be what he himself felt he had become: a washout.

According to Tierney, it was not so surprising that few people rushed to Darrow's defense after the bribery charges had been lodged against him, for he had done little to endear himself to people in positions of authority. Many, in fact, detested him. Although in the end, he was acquitted of the bribery charges, Darrow never quite recovered from the incident. To both him and others, the case proved that even a great lawyer could be brought low if he made a serious miscalculation.

Brought low but not defeated, Darrow slowly pieced together his broken life and rid himself of his depression with the help of a few friends and strangers who stood by him. For a time, no one wanted to join Darrow's firm or be associated in any way with the man. Yet in time, socialist lawyer Peter Sissman joined him, and later, cases started coming his way again. In the initial stages of his rise from defeat, Darrow defended numerous poor black clients as well as a few well-known ones such as Frank Lloyd Wright. It was at this time that Darrow thought most seriously about leaving Chicago for New York, but nothing came of it.

In Tierney's estimation, the greatest push in Darrow's later career came from World War I, a conflagration which "would act as a catalyst to the rehabilitation of his reputation . . . that would propel him from the outer to the innermost circles of power." Siding with "gallant, little Belgium" against an invading German army, Darrow shocked his pacifist friends by his sudden conversion from dove to hawk. Indeed, radical friends like Eugene Debs were appalled by Darrow's insistence upon the notion that the war was a kind of holy crusade, regarding the conflict as nothing more than a terrible bloodbath created by bloated capitalists. Although Darrow lost some friends in leftist circles, he garnered considerable admiration from America's socio-political establishment, support which would come in handy in the future. He made public statements which agreed with those made by President Wilson, urging Americans to go fight for "civilization." Ironically, even though Darrow's reputation was restored by his fervent support of the Allied cause, he became disillusioned about that cause late in the war, discovering that the atrocity tales he earlier believed to be true were, in large part, fabrications aimed at getting America into the conflict.

Darrow's recovery was all but accomplished by war's end in 1918, for many prewar conflicts which he had had with people were by now forgotten; he could begin his career anew. He was helped in another way as well. As a lawyer, he was "the beneficiary of the revolution in morals and manners that the war had accomplished." To the new generation, whatever moral indiscretions he might have been party to in the McNamara case were overlooked as insignificant.

Crime in Chicago was in its world-famous heyday during the postwar decade, an era which seemed to encourage the commission of greater, more heinous crimes than were previously committed. Darrow, who earlier defended only those he believed to be innocent of the crime for which they were charged, was now defending anyone, principally on the grounds that "no one was guilty" of anything. In Tierney's eyes, this meant that Darrow no longer believed in justice, but rather in nothing at all. Darrow admitted as much, saying that "the playing of the game is the forgetting of self, and we should be game sports and play it bravely to the end." In order to best "play the game," he represented a rogue's gallery of people during the 1920's, persons summarily judged guilty by the nation's news reporters and by the public at large. Chicago's notorious gangsters known for their cold-blooded killings were defended by Darrow, as was Fred Lundin, the campaign manager for Chicago mayor "Big Bill" Thompson, a man thought to be in the employ of mobsters. Lundin was acquitted of the charge of stealing nearly one million dollars from public funds, through Darrow's efforts.

Nevertheless, the biggest, most publicized case to date was the 1924 Loeb-Leopold murder trial in which Richard Loeb, son of a Sears, Roebuck & Company executive, and Nathan Leopold, Jr., son of rich Jewish parents, were charged with the "thrill murder" of Bobby Franks, a young schoolboy targeted for execution at random. Overnight, Loeb and Leopold became internationally known villains whose guilt was assumed. All of the evidence in this important case—the rented car, the chisel used to kill Franks, some rope purchased at a hardware store, a blood-soaked carpet—damned the accused killers. Moreover, their alibis, given separately, failed to correlate. Nathan Leopold said it best: "What could a lawyer do now? They [the prosecutors] had all the facts—all the facts."

Darrow, faced with such poor prospects, decided to take a risky course and plead his clients guilty in hopes that the judge might not give them the death penalty. Using psychiatrists as witnesses, Darrow got what he set out for: the young men's lives were spared. The verdict was one of the highest points in the attorney's life; a vast public now awaited every big case in which he would participate, and his every speech was analyzed carefully.

Soon after the Loeb-Leopold victory came another courtroom spectacular: the Scopes "Monkey" case involving the right of a teacher to teach Charles Darwin's evolutionary theory if he so chose. Fundamentalistic Christians had passed a law in Tennessee forbidding the teaching of Darwin's theory of evolution, and John T. Scopes was arrested for breaking the law by expounding upon Darwinism in his classes. The case strongly appealed to Darrow's antireligious bent as well as to his sense of fair play. Additionally, he had long before lost patience with small-town values when they were forced upon people whose values were different.

The *Scopes* case not only gave Darrow the chance to expose the fraud he felt was involved in religious fundamentalism, but also the opportunity to needle his old opponent, William Jennings Bryan, the lawyer and orator whom Darrow found to be an addlebrained windbag. Bryan, however, was a fine match for Darrow, as Tierney points out in detail; however, Tierney goes along with other historians who have pointed out that Bryan very often would lose control of himself and become maudlin, "bathetic," and overwrought. As Tierney also shows, the *Scopes* affair really represented a rearguard attempt by a fading group of Christian conservatives to revert to simpler times prior to the widespread acceptance of Darwinian theory. In that sense, the case was not all Darrow made it out to be. Out of the trial came a "slap-on-the-wrist" penalty for John Scopes and a victory for the forces of modernity; it also caused an enlarging of Darrow's already sizable public. He had made the State of Tennessee and its representative Bryan seem absurdly out-of-date; yet he, too, seemed to be fighting old, worn-out causes—or at least, so Tierney believes.

Later would come more victories such as the acquittals of Detroit black Ossian Sweet, the light sentences afforded the defendants in Hawaii's *Massie-Fortescue* case, and the release of the New York anti-Fascists, Calogero Greco and Donato Carrillo.

All the while he was enjoying victories, Darrow was, according to Tierney, losing his vigor and his driving moral spirit to old age's advances. His last battles were against President Franklin Roosevelt's New Deal. Ironically enough, it was Roosevelt who decided to appoint Darrow to be chairman of the National Recovery Review Board, an appointment which the financially strapped attorney acceded to, although he felt the Board was a bad thing for the country. While Chairman, Darrow fought against governmental interference, something which bewildered his colleagues to the point of exasperation.

In fact, Darrow chose to investigate the New Deal in order to purge it of errors. Such protest as he made eventually did their work, resulting in the Supreme Court's ruling against the NRA in a major decision of the day.

The NRA matter was the last major case in which the aging lawyer wished to become involved. After 1935, Darrow's condition disintegrated very rapidly, so much so that he was driven to have monkey glands inserted in his body in an attempt to rejuvenate him. He also searched for a successor, someone who would and could carry on his good fight against oppressors, but there was no one of his stature to take over his work now that his career had come to a close.

Tierney does a satisfactory job of acquainting us with Darrow the giant killer who himself became a giant. It is no wonder that he had such a difficult time finding anyone who had his same rhetorical skills and emotional drive. That one could have failed so often in life and yet gone back into the maddening fray of court battle time and again and win time and again is remarkable. Yet Clarence Darrow is, as Tierney assents, more than remarkable: he has become an American institution long to be remembered with fondness and awe.

John D. Raymer

DA VINCI'S BICYCLE

Author: Guy Davenport (1927-   )
Publisher: The Johns Hopkins University Press (Baltimore, Maryland). Illustrated.
    185 pp. $12.95; paperback $4.95
Type of work: Short stories

Ten stories about various historical figures and moments, famous and obscure, with illustrations by the author

Da Vinci's Bicycle is Guy Davenport's second collection of stories. His first, *Tatlin!* (1974), introduced a new form of the short story, as distinctive as that of Borges or Barthelme and already widely imitated. Since the publication of *Da Vinci's Bicycle*, his brilliant fictions have continued to appear in journals and little magazines (see particularly "Christ Preaching at the Henley Regatta," *North American Review*, June, 1979; and "The Death of Picasso," *Kenyon Review*, Winter, 1980), and a third collection, *Eclogues*, is forthcoming.

Sentence by sentence, Davenport's stories are built with a sure hand and unfailing excellence. It is this quality which led John Gardner (*On Moral Fiction*) to number Davenport among the few contemporary writers who will outlast the century, "if sheer precision and uncompromising artistry count." Davenport is that good, yet the terms of Gardner's praise—however just— are forbidding: "uncompromising artistry" might suggest the extreme intransigence and the willful private language of a writer like the German novelist Thomas Bernhard, who has said that anyone who claims to understand his books is a liar. Davenport invites understanding—one of his favorite words is "clarity"—whether he is layering an allusive elliptical text or doing a bit of slapstick in the manner of Eudora Welty, one of his acknowledged masters. He never neglects the oldest, simplest pleasures of fiction: the pleasure of surprise, the pleasure of the strange and new ("A hero without a journey is like a saint without a vision . . ."), the delight in *naming*.

Davenport brings many talents to his fiction: he is an accomplished painter and draftsman, a classicist and a translator, a scholar of modern literature, and a dedicated classroom teacher. None of these talents is irrelevant to an understanding of his art—in a sense they constitute his apprenticeship, since he did not begin the first story in *Tatlin!* until he was forty-three—but the particularly strong link between his painting and drawing and his writing should be singled out. Like *Tatlin!*, *Da Vinci's Bicycle* is illustrated with a number of drawings by Davenport. Writing about his own fiction, Davenport has said: "A page, which I think of as a picture, is essentially a texture of images," and he notes that "to write" and "to draw" are the same verb in Greek. Readers should come to *Da Vinci's Bicycle* with that visual expectancy and receptiveness which is usually reserved for the darkness of the movie theater.

Da Vinci's Bicycle, then, is a collection of stories which share an imagistic method and a common theme: "the instinct to forage," Davenport calls it, the insatiable human desire to *know*. "The pervasive idea of this work is, as Bernard Sylvestris said in the twelfth century, that man was created to understand the world." Understanding begins with wonder, with curiosity; curiosity begins with the title: Da Vinci's bicycle? Davenport supplies a drawing, and the information that he derived it from *The Unknown Leonardo*, where in turn it was taken from a recently discovered drawing by an eleven-year-old apprentice of a bicycle "drawn or perhaps built by Leonardo." This bicycle satisfies Davenport's taste for fragments: "I like things that almost don't exist." The title story in *Tatlin!* was based on scraps of knowledge about the Russian Constructivist, Vladimir Tatlin, most of whose works have been lost, and about whom very little is known. There is no story in *Da Vinci's Bicycle* corresponding to the title, but the bicycle appears in two of the stories, principally in the first story of the book, "The Richard Nixon Freischutz Rag." This brief story interweaves three "plots": President Richard Nixon visiting China and talking with Chairman Mao; Leonardo Da Vinci in his workshop; and Gertrude Stein and Alice B. Toklas visiting Assisi.

This barebones summary is adequate to outline Davenport's characteristic procedure: he invites the reader to make connections between seemingly unrelated elements. Thus, while Leonardo rhapsodizes about the voyage of Columbus, knitting East and West, the reader has in mind Mao receiving Nixon. And soon after Leonardo has imagined a phalanx of bicycles "bearing lancers at full tilt," Davenport jump-cuts to the bombing orders Richard Nixon gave before flying to China, including "a thousand targets in Laos and Cambodia bombed by squadrons of B-52's."

Da Vinci's bicycle becomes an extraordinary symbol of human knowledge, of the "instinct to forage," in which good and evil seem inextricably tangled. Leonardo in his workshop is Man the Knower. He sees the hidden harmonies of nature's laws, and, like Newton, who filled volumes with his interpretations of Daniel and the Apocalypse, sees occult harmonies in history. The bicycle itself testifies to this perception of harmony and order, for as long as the machine remains in motion it will stay in balance, "as the flow of a river discouraged a boat from wandering." Yet Leonardo's reverie takes a sudden turn when he sees cyclists going into battle, trumpets blaring. This image is both wonderfully comic and tragically prophetic: the B-52's which Nixon sent over Cambodia and Laos were the cumulative handiwork of a thousand lesser Leonardos, generations of men seeking to know, to understand. The "instinct to forage" is perhaps the instinct which moved Adam and Eve to tragic knowledge.

Decoding the title of *Da Vinci's Bicycle* in this fashion is ponderous and slow: a reader of the book will make these connections effortlessly as he goes. Indeed, one is always making connections while reading Davenport's fiction, connections between multiple "plots" within a given story; connections between stories, as images, ideas, and characters reappear or undergo metamorphosis; and even connections between books (readers of *Tatlin!* will welcome the return of Adriaan van Hovendaal in "The Death of Picasso," which will appear in the forthcoming *Eclogues*). There is nothing quite like it in fiction.

Davenport himself prefers to call his stories *assemblages*, and this is not an affectation. The term, taken from the history of modern art, accurately describes his methods, not only his use of historical materials and his imagistic texture but also the structure of his fiction: "I first saw a way to plot stories by studying the films of Stan Brakhage, where an architectonic arrangement of images has replaced narrative and documentation." His stories are often quite literally assembled, consisting of two or more "plots" which never converge in the narrative. These assemblages are his invention, his distinctive contribution to the short story form, but he is also a master of more conventional straightforward storytelling.

Of the ten stories in *Du Vinci's Bicycle*, three are longer, deeper works: "C. Musonius Rufus," "Au Tombeau de Charles Fourier," and "A Field of Snow on a Slope of the Rosenberg." The remaining seven stories maintain the high standards of the major works in an extraordinary variety of forms and voices. One of the most gentle and charming of these, "The Wooden Dove of Archytas," is an assemblage of two plots. In the first, Archytas the Pythagorean, a contemporary of Plato, launches a steam-powered wooden dove. The account of this event, narrated by a Greek schoolboy, alternates with the second plot: in postbellum backwoods South Carolina, a Presbyterian lady and her proud "house nigger" watch with condescension and fascination while some Indians who live in the remnants of the slave compound chant for the soul of a dove which was accidentally killed. "Dovey about to fly," one of the Indians explains. "Her soul go up. It be happy where she go." Another gem among the shorter pieces is "Ithaka," which is not properly a "story" at all; it is a brief recollection of a day Davenport and two friends spent in Rapallo with the aged Ezra Pound and his companion, Olga Rudge. Narrated in a flat style which contrasts sharply with Davenport's usual preference for rich diction and complex rhythms, "Ithaka" pictures a figure now familiar from many accounts—silent, anguished, self-condemned—with great simplicity and power.

The three longer stories consider, from three utterly different perspectives, the meaning and the consequences of man's "instinct to forage." The first of the three, "C. Musonius Rufus," had its origin in a line from Ezra Pound's *Pisan Cantos*: "Honor to the tough guy, Musonius." Musonius, Davenport learned, was a first century Stoic philosopher condemned by Nero to slave labor. Only six of his sayings survive. The first voice in the story, however, is not that of Musonius. This voice from the afterworld ("I huddle upon the wild rose, wait with the moth upon the wall, still as time") quickly identifies itself: "I am the emperor Balbinus kept in a jug." Balbinus, whose reign as emperor was the shortest in the history of Rome, was murdered by a rival faction, as he recalls in the story. Speaking from the life after death, he is learning humility before the order of things and a sense of fellowship with all of creation. His body, he explains, never leaves its jug, yet "I have thrust myself into a sunflower and washed in its basil green. Near deep iron I have shuddered and gone numb." Instructed by beneficent spirits, the Consiliarii, he achieves sufficient understanding by the story's end to "live in the oak Volscna, who is a thousand years old. Trees are people I have learned." In all literature, there is no more beautiful imagination of the afterlife.

But there is also the voice of Musonius: the story proceeds by switching back and forth between the two voices, first Balbinus, then Musonius. The voice of Balbinus is lyrical; he is preoccupied with bees and mice, with flowers and trees. The voice of Musonius is raucous, bitter, Rabelaisian, unyielding in its integrity. He speaks of his pupils—a cobbler, a Senator, a slavewoman, a scamp—of the habitual cruelty of Rome, where crowds laugh at crucifixions. He works on the chain gang, digging with his bare hands. Such are the consequences when men's intuition of order goes awry, when men begin to impose their order on the world and on other men, substituting authority and contempt for humility and understanding.

Thus, the third and final element of the assemblage in "C. Musonius Rufus" is a single scene, inserted without transitions, of Mussolini entering Rapallo with all the pomp of an emperor; Ezra Pound receives him with respect and—as recounted in the *Cantos*—reads from his poetry. "How amusing!," says Mussolini. This scene takes up a recurring theme in *Da Vinci's Bicycle*. Again and again in the book we see artists who are susceptible to man-made schemes for order, who can idealize tyranny; we also see artists tempted to become little dictators themselves, like Gertrude Stein, who "cut her hair short to look like a Roman emperor and to be modern." In this perversion of the desire for order, however, artists are only representative of all men.

The last story in *Da Vinci's Bicycle*, "A Field of Snow on a Slope of the Rosenberg," is one of the finest Davenport has written. It is a first-person narrative, not an assemblage of voices: the narrator is Robert Walser, a Swiss-German writer (1878-1956) better known in Europe than in America, although even there his work has not received its due. (Apart from the intrinsic value of Walser's fiction, it should be read for its influence on Kafka, an influence more significant than many staples of Kafka criticism.) After some early successes, Walser wrote in poverty, without a public, without a publisher. In 1929, at his sister's urging, he committed himself voluntarily to a psychiatric clinic; in 1933 he moved to an asylum in Switzerland, where he spent the rest of his life, writing no more.

Although "A Field of Snow on a Slope of the Rosenberg" includes a good deal of comedy, the story finally confronts its readers with the naked weariness of a human soul. Walser's vision is not so different from that of the afterlife in "C. Musonius Rufus": "It says in the pages of Mach," Walser tells a psychiatrist, "that the mind is nothing but a continuity of consciousness. It is not itself a thing, it is its contents, like an eye and what it sees, a hand and what it holds." The psychiatrist's response (which recalls Mussolini's response to Pound) is to call this "a charming poetic image." For Walser, however, it is no image; it is a lived reality, and his perception of the mind as a "continuity of consciousness" ("It is nothing else at all, at all"), so similar to the perception vouchsafed to the emperor Balbinus by his angelic counselors, erodes the security of personality: Walser was diagnosed as a schizophrenic.

The agony of living with this perception is evident in the two drawings of Walser which accompany the story. Early in the story there is a drawing of him as a young man, head tilted, eyes angled away from the viewer. Late in the story, one turns the page to meet a much older man face to face, looking straight into his tormented eyes. Can this be the same man? One can only verify that by looking up the book about Walser which includes the two photographs which were Davenport's models. But Walser might ask: what is the point of the question? The story ends with Walser taking one of his habitual long walks: "I think they said at the table that today is Christmas. I do not know." A reader who is curious to read Walser firsthand will find his novel *Jakob von Gunten*, translated by Christopher Middleton, who mentions in his Introduction that Walser died on Christmas Day while out on a walk.

John Wilson

THE DAY AMERICA CRASHED

Author: Tom Shachtman (1942-   )
Publisher: G. P. Putnam's Sons (New York). 336 pp. $10.95
Type of work: History
Time: October 24, 1929, and immediately before and after
Locale: The United States

*A history of the hour-by-hour events of the stock market Crash on October 24, 1929,
with an emphasis on its effects on individuals from all segments of society*

> Principal personages:
>   CHARLES E. MITCHELL, Director of the Federal Reserve Board of
>   New York and Chairman of the board of National City Bank in
>   1929
>   RICHARD WHITNEY, a broker for leading New York bankers

The revival of interest in the Great Crash of the stock market in 1929 in the year of its fiftieth anniversary has coincided with the publication of a highly readable account of that event, *The Day America Crashed*, by Tom Shachtman. Shachtman is not a professional historian but a documentary filmmaker who has written films for the commercial and public television networks, a playwright, and a dialogue writer for foreign films. He writes good history, however, concerning himself not only with the Crash itself but also with its short- and long-term causes and effects. He also demonstrates an understanding of the sociological impact of the Crash on segments of the American public. His enviable literary style and sense of timing and continuity undoubtedly are reflective of his experience as a filmmaker and playwright. As a result, his book will appeal to the general reader as well as the student, sociologist, and historian.

The author's motive for writing this book, clearly outlined in his Introduction, is to clarify what happened on October 24, and immediately before and after, with special emphasis on some of those individuals who were directly affected by it. The Great Crash is a subject that has long been minimized in American history textbook accounts. Indeed, many textbook writers devote little more than a paragraph to an event that marked a watershed in American history. Secondary and college teachers also often demonstrate a hesitancy to devote adequate attention to this event. Reasons for this appear to vary from a lack of understanding of the economic and financial conditions that produced and characterized it to an inadequate appreciation of its significance. Shachtman is convinced that this event must be studied if one is to have a full understanding of human nature in general and the American character in particular in a time of crisis. This was, after all, an event which directly affected between fifteen- and twenty-five million people who represented stockholders and their families. The Crash's impact as a trigger of the Depression affected everyone. It was also a direct and painful rebuff to the widely held American conviction that, through luck and a little investment gambling, everyone could become rich. It demonstrated, in 1929, that rising prosperity is not inevitable—a lesson Americans are now learning anew. The scope of Shachtman's book is national, although he concentrates by necessity on the activities taking place on Wall Street. It is also neither socially nor geographically discriminatory; the author investigates the impact of the Crash on the mill worker and automobile mechanic as well as the Wall Street financier and broker, on black and on white, on men and women, young and old, and in various sections of the nation.

Shachtman has chosen "Black Thursday," October 24, 1929, as the day to chronicle. Tradition has often identified October 29, as the day of the Crash, but decided decline really began five days earlier. Although the 29th was a worse day on the New York Stock Exchange than the 24th—indeed it was the worst the Exchange ever experienced—it was essentially anticlimactic. Most had already been driven from the market with staggering losses beginning five days earlier, and the shock had come on the 24th. On the 29th, those who thought they might weather the storm were swept away. The world of illusion created by many Americans was indeed destroyed on October 24, and thus Shachtman's choice of that day as his center of concentration is fully justified.

After providing an illuminating overview of conditions and attitudes in America at the time of the Crash, the author continues with a detailed hour-by-hour chronicle of the day, moving from one center of action to another, and a brief view of the evening. In the late 1920's, America, as Will Rogers cogently expressed it, went on a "financial drunk." Modern methods of production and enormous consolidation and centralization were working to create an America of rising material expectations which were being quickly satisfied. Almost everyone, through outright purchase or buying on the installment plan, could acquire the conveniences of modern living: electric irons, vacuum cleaners, washing machines, refrigerators, and cars. In 1929, twenty-three million cars were on the road serving a population of 125,000,000. Novelties which had been introduced during the past decade included pyrex, cellophane, celanese, rayon, dry ice, neon signs, sound motion pictures, air-conditioned theaters, and, of course, radio. America had become a nation of consumers, prosperity reigned supreme, and everyone hoped to share in it.

Businessmen were the high priests of this new prosperity, and the New York Stock Exchange was its temple. Initially regarded as a place where funds could be invested in anticipation of modestly rising values and good dividends, the stock exchange had become the center of frenzied speculation. Contributing to this trend were government monetary and tax policies which encouraged industrial expansion and investment, and banks eager to invest their depositors' funds in stocks and to sell stocks through their security affiliates. Margin buying, investment trusts, excessive company profits, and the growing illusion that quick fortunes could be made in the market with a minimum of labor also played key roles. Everyone was encouraged to invest in the market in anticipation of a quick profit. Stock values continued to rise, and President Coolidge, shortly before leaving office in early 1929, encouraged the speculative fever by asserting that stocks were still cheaply priced. In late March, there was a brief period of panic when the Federal Reserve Board, which had not denied its opposition to continued speculation, met daily and, although issuing no statements, caused many to fear a tightening of credit. This produced a pronounced drop in stock prices on March 25, and early on March 26. The bull market rebounded and tensions were relieved, however, when Charles E. Mitchell, an investment banker and Director of the New York Federal Reserve Board, announced that his National City Bank would make necessary loans at reasonable interest rates to prevent liquidation. The Federal Reserve Board's continued silence was taken as an indication that it had capitulated to Mitchell and to continued speculation. Mitchell was awarded the chairmanship of the National City Bank for his actions and the nation continued to delude itself into believing that conditions could only improve.

Americans had and continued to fool themselves, as Shachtman expertly explains, by accepting as truths what were really fictions. A stock exchange has no permanent and unchanging reality. It is nothing more than a place where people agree to barter on the future of certain business enterprises. A share of stock is a piece of paper, a statement of part ownership in a corporation that offers no guarantees to its holder. Both these fictions will operate beneficially if a third fiction is accepted: that there will always be a buyer for a stock at near, and hopefully above, its present market quotation. This "idea," rather than law, of supply and demand had been used to explain why the market had risen so spectacularly during the late 1920's. When there was a shortage of stocks, or of a certain stock, the demand forced its price up. If no buyer could be found at a higher price, then surely the pool of potential buyers could increase as the price of the stock began to drop, and the holders could sell without great loss. But what if suddenly there were no buyers even at a moderately lower price? This is what began to happen in late October, 1929, and, as it did, the world one had created on the basis of trust in these fictions began to crumble under his feet. One's life-style, which had been predicated on the maintenance and even increase of stock values, was suddenly seen as ephemeral. Stability had been replaced by chaos. Only those of great wealth whose stock losses could be tolerated without undue inconvenience and only those very few who did not have to worry about margin calls to cover their indebtedness to brokers and banks could wait out the storm with equanimity.

On October 24, the bubble created by the largest number of stockholders in American history was about to burst. There had been warnings that the economy was far from sound. The Florida land boom had collapsed the year before. The agricultural depression of 1920-1921, which had continued throughout the 1920's, had contributed to the failure of nearly a thousand banks—usually state banks in rural areas not under federal control and unable to offer guarantees to their depositors. Margin percentages had been going up, especially since Labor Day; construction and industrial production were down and unemployment was increasing. Nevertheless, people had continued to have faith in their "fictions," at least until September when the market began to quake mildly. By the week before October 24, the crevasse had opened wide. On Saturday, October 19, stocks lost in a few hours the gains of preceeding months. Monday the 21st had brought a minor rally, but offered little solace to stockholders. Tuesday afternoon witnessed the loss of all the gains that had been made on Monday and Tuesday morning. All this had happened before, but the market had always rallied. This was what people expected on Wednesday. It did not happen. Instead a record number of shares—six million—were sold on October 23, and stock sellers took a record loss.

Still people did not give up hope, even though the opening of trading indicated rapidly declining prices. It was assumed briefly that a heroic stand by the organized buying of the great financiers would turn the tide. After all, Pierpont Morgan had halted the Panic of 1907 by such remedial action. The bankers did meet at noon, and, although records of that meeting are unavailable, Shachtman ascribes selfish motives to the actions taken by the bankers. Essentially, the author believes, they were playing for time. They decided to buy certain key stocks at prices just below the current market levels. This would provide the confidence and temporary stability to attract other smaller buyers back into the market. The bankers' pool could then sell many less desirable stocks without suffering intolerable losses. They were, in other words, going to prop up the market temporarily for their own interests and not for those of the general investing public.

Before the bankers could meet, however, the panic was well under way. The bankers' broker, Richard Whitney, made a theatrical entrance onto the floor of the exchange at 1:30 P.M. and began buying the several stocks to which the bankers had previously agreed, including United States Steel, General Motors, and American Telephone and Telegraph. Whitney's actions generated a brief rally and made Whitney an overnight celebrity, but only temporarily stopped the downward momentum which gained force the following day. Shachtman performs a valuable service in aiding the student to understand a major reason for the magnitude of the panic in the emphasis he places on the lack of information available to the investor. From the beginning of trading, the ticker tape ran behind; by the end of the trading day it was a full three hours late. Without information, especially outside the Wall Street area, judicious decisions could not be made, since the investor was in no position to know the prices of his stocks at a precise moment. On the basis of his knowledge only that a downward trend had been established, he could do little more than try to divest himself as quickly as possible, if possible. This was especially true if he had bought on margin—which was true of most buyers—and was subject to a margin call by his broker. Thus the snowballing effect of the panic was created and gained momentum. In his closing chapter, Shachtman traces the "five weeks of downs" that made it clear that the events of October 24 were not aberrations.

One of the great assets of this book, as previously mentioned, is the considerable attention the author devotes to the impact of the Crash on individual people, both great and small. Their reactions to the happenings on the 24th are traced throughout the book, and in the epilogue the author summarizes by individual the immediate- and long-term effects of the Depression. Thus by personalizing an event that is often treated abstractly, the author provides a poignancy and immediacy that makes his work more forceful than a simple narrative of the crisis on Wall Street. Indeed, although he has drawn on the available literature in both books and periodicals of the period, Shachtman has also included in his research personal interviews with nearly a score of individuals as well as letters solicited from more than five hundred people from throughout the nation who were directly affected by the Crash and its aftermath.

Furthermore, Shachtman has not forgotten groups often neglected in treatises on the subject: farmers, laborers, blacks, and children. In addition, he has not failed to tackle, at least briefly, the international political impact of the Crash and the resultant Depression. It was as a result of the Crash that reparation loans from the United States to Germany were terminated, thus creating widespread unemployment in Germany that helped to facilitate the ascendancy of Hitler. Further encouragement to Hitler's expansionist ambitions were created by the Crash's restrictive effect on America's military budget which rendered the United States militarily unprepared in the decade preeceding World War II.

Without question, this is a valuable work. Although Shachtman does demonstrate a sometimes annoying anti-Wall Street bias, and although his explanations of the purely economic and financial factors associated with the Crash are no replacements for those found in John Kenneth Galbraith's *The Great Crash, 1929*, he has produced an excitingly written book that gives the Crash a badly needed immediacy that it has failed to enjoy previously. Hopefully a paperback edition will be published. It should be very popular and useful as supplementary reading on the secondary and college level.

J. Stewart Alverson

THE DEAD ZONE

Author: Stephen King (1947-   )
Publisher: The Viking Press (New York). 372 pp. $11.95
Type of work: Novel
Time: 1953 and 1970-1979
Locale: Various small towns in Maine and New Hampshire

After reviving from an accident-induced coma and discovering that he has clairvoyant powers, Johnny Smith is inexorably drawn against his will into a violent confrontation with a dangerous would-be American Hitler

> *Principal characters:*
> JOHNNY SMITH, a reluctant psychic
> SARAH BRACKNELL, his girl friend, later Mrs. Walter Hazlett
> HERB SMITH, his father
> VERA SMITH, his mother, a religious fanatic
> DR. SAM WEIZAK, his doctor
> GEROGE BANNERMAN, a rural sheriff
> FRANK DODD, a psychotic murderer
> ROGER CHATSWORTH, a millionaire
> CHUCK CHATSWORTH, his son, Johnny's private student
> GREG STILLSON, an unscrupulous, ambitious politician

Ever since 1976, when the film version of *Carrie* lifted his first novel from relative obscurity to public acclaim and sales approaching four million copies, Stephen King has been acknowledged as America's foremost "horror" writer. Each of his succeeding novels (*Salem's Lot*, 1975; *The Shining*, 1977; *The Stand*, 1978; and *The Dead Zone*), as well as his one collection of short stories (*Night Shift*, 1978), have been best-sellers. By the end of 1979, approximately ten million copies of King's books had been published; it is expected that that number will double in 1980. With perhaps only slight exaggeration, the New American Library promotion department calls him "the best-selling author in the world in 1980."

However, all of this does not guarantee King status as an important writer; quite the opposite is true: no popular genre writer, the critical assumption goes, especially one so flagrantly successful in the commercial markets, can at the same time be a serious artist. While the critical establishment may, after some time, give reluctant posthumous credit to the occasional Dashiell Hammett or Raymond Chandler, or periodically allow a Kurt Vonnegut or Ray Bradbury to escape the "category" ghettos, it is harder for a successful horror writer to be so honored than for that proverbial camel to pass through the needle's eye. Hence, the reaction of many critics to *The Dead Zone* is curious: they thoroughly enjoy it; they praise its plotting and characterization; they come to the brink of calling it an important work; and then, remembering who they are and what they are dealing with, they pull back and downgrade the novel as merely a popular work, an entertainment.

However, *The Dead Zone* is a first-rate serious work, as are all of King's other novels. King has found in the horror and science fiction genres the vehicles through which he can present his insightful, disturbing vision of modern America. His novels no more resemble those in the current flood of second-rate neo-Gothic trash than the fiction of Ernest Hemingway can be likened to the cruder hard-boiled pulp writers of the 1930's. A further irony is that, despite the horror story label, only one of King's novels, *Salem's Lot*, is a traditional story of supernatural terror. The others deal with themes and elements more commonly associated with science fiction—telekinesis (*Carrie*), ESP (*The Shining* and *The Dead Zone*), and almost-the-end-of-the-world scenarios (*The Stand*).

Yet the fact that King has never been categorized as a science fiction writer is not surprising. In mood, tone, atmosphere, and emphasis, he is worlds apart from all but a few science fiction authors (such as, perhaps, Tom Disch, J. G. Ballard, and Harlan Ellison in some of his works). Similar to all writers of real merit, King stakes out his own distinct territory. He *uses* the genres; he is not bound by them. The paranormal or supernatural aspects in his novels dramatize and intensify conflicts that are already present in the characters and situations. At the center of his works are potent dramas of human crises, provocative analyses of contemporary American society and culture, and a dark, troubling vision of man's place in the modern world.

Hence, the holocaust provoked by Carrie White's telekinetic powers is not a spectacle of gratuitous violence but the inevitable explosion of social, sexual, and religious tensions latent in small-town America; it can be compared to the riot scene that ends Nathanael West's *The Day of the Locust*. The mass vampirism in *Salem's Lot* is a concrete manifestation of the underlying corruption which pervades that isolated, ingrown, puritanical New England region. The supernatural presences that are inadvertently evoked by Danny Torrance's ESP in *The Shining* are images of evils endemic to our times. *The Stand* offers us a surrealistic allegory of good and evil in the modern world, and the unwanted gift of clairvoyance simply forces the hero of *The Dead Zone* to confront the problems of personal obligation, moral responsibility, and violence in this dangerous, difficult era.

Johnny Smith has his first ESP experience following a fall on the ice at the age of five, but the talent remains more or less latent until one night seventeen years later when he takes his girl friend, Sarah Bracknell, to the county fair and wins more than five hundred dollars spinning the Wheel-of-Fortune. His extraordinary good luck immediately turns bad; after leaving Sarah at her home, Johnny is almost killed in a traffic accident. He languishes in a coma for five years, and upon reviving discovers that his psychic powers have become overt and powerful, if somewhat erratic. When he touches a person or object, waves of shock surge through his body and images flood his mind; in most instances they are images from the past, but in a few extreme cases, they are frightening visions of the future.

It is appropriate that the Wheel-of-Fortune scene immediately precedes the accident that sends Johnny into his coma: *The Dead Zone* is a novel about fate, accident, choice, and responsibility. Is Johnny Smith's unique talent a gift, a curse, or both? Can he avoid the implications of his talent and live normally, or does it place special obligations on him? Are his talent and "mission" mere accidents in a blind universe, or do they suggest some purpose? In following Johnny Smith's checkered, problematic career, King explores all of these questions, although he gives no final answers to any of them. Nor are such questions the most important element in the novel; it is the human dilemma that most interests the author. Above all, *The Dead Zone* is the story of the ambiguous, perhaps tragic, fate of Johnny Smith.

When Johnny awakens from his five-year coma, he finds himself totally cut off from the world he had known. The political and social scene is entirely different: the Vietnam War has become history; Watergate has come and gone; Ford has replaced Nixon in the White House; campus agitation has given way to quiescence. On the personal level, things have altered even more drastically: Johnny's job and prospects are long gone; his father and mother are constantly bickering, primarily because she has turned into a religious fanatic (a toned-down version of Carrie White's mother); and, most upsetting of all, his girl friend Sarah has married and had a son.

Given the time lost and the physical debilitation, the return to normal after such an experience would be difficult for anyone, but it is Johnny's psychic abilities that prove to be the real barrier. As he recovers, he inadvertently reveals his gift a number of times—to his doctor, to his physical therapist, and to Sarah when she visits him. In every case, the result is the same: however helpful his information proves to be, it stimulates fear rather than gratitude. As his powers become known, he is looked upon as a freak, a charlatan, or both. After he leaves the hospital, the pattern established there repeats itself again and again in the outside world.

At the same time another theme grows in the book—the idea that there is a vague but real pattern and purpose in Johnny's actions. The wheel-of-fortune motif is picked up soon after he emerges from his coma, especially in his mother's enunciations of her son's mission. Although Vera Smith is clearly insane and most of her rantings are religious gibberish, her statements about her son's gift and his obligation to use it to "further God's plan" strike a realistic note in the context of Johnny's life. This sense of design is reinforced by King's (perhaps heavy-handed) foreshadowing of other pieces in the apparent puzzle: frequent references to a series of unsolved murders; vignettes from the career of Greg Stillson, an ambitious and unscrupulous politician on the make; an enigmatic scene between a lightning-rod salesman and a cocktail lounge owner; and a series of images of violence and destruction—always seen through a mysterious blue filter—that persistently surface to plague Smith from the "dead zone" of his consciousness.

This is not to say that Johnny is simply swept along by events. He clearly chooses the course of action he takes, even though he comes to realize that it will probably lead to his own destruction—and this is what gives the book much of its power. In many ways he resembles a version of the traditional epic hero. He is the average man (note his name) who is singled out for a specific, if ambiguous, task and given the special ability needed to carry it out—a talent that also prevents him from functioning as a normal member of society. Unprepared emotionally or morally for his mission, Smith at first tries to deny and avoid it. The main conflict in the story lies in the inner turmoil the hero experiences, and its real climax occurs when the protagonist accepts his obligations and sets out to carry them through.

However, by setting the hero in the modern world and confronting him with contemporary moral, social, and political issues, King gives power and immediacy—as well as ambiguity—to his hero's dilemma. Three times Smith's psychic abilities lead him to confront violence, once with a psychotic serial murderer, once with a mass disaster that could have been avoided, and once with a dangerous politician who threatens to become an American Hitler. Each time, he initially rejects his vision and then changes his mind when events force him to face the practical and moral consequences of his inaction. Each of these crises requires a greater personal commitment, makes heavier demands upon him physically and emotionally, further estranges him from society, and increasingly places the burden of solitary responsibility on his shoulders. Even Johnny's single idyllic afternoon of lovemaking with Sarah only emphasizes the gulf between his life and an ordinary existence.

As the tests become more difficult, the questions of choice and responsibility become more crucial; Johnny's decisions are never made easily, nor are the results of these choices clearly predictable. King adroitly maintains such a fine balance between necessity and surprise that all the novel's important events seem both inevitable and unexpected. When Smith accepts an invitation to use his powers to track a killer, he is acting as an arm of the law. When he has a premonition that a fire will kill all the members of his tutee's high school graduating class, the primary responsibility for averting the tragedy—and the guilt for not doing so completely—falls on his millionaire employer. However, when he meets Greg Stillson, the ruthless politico, the traumatic, terrifying vision provoked forces him to choose between committing personal violence and abandoning mankind to a horrendous fate; and his must be an act that can be shared with no other human being. Having been given godlike powers, Johnny Smith must finally make a godlike decision, and then hope that his human frailty will not betray him.

Stephen King brings all of these variables together in a potent, unexpected conclusion, one that resolves all of the intricacies of the plot, but leaves the larger questions unanswered—appropriately so, since they are questions which are fundamentally unanswerable. As a character study and as an "idea" novel, *The Dead Zone* is a memorable reading experience, as well as being a most exciting, furiously paced narrative. Although it may lack some of the social/psychological complexity of *Carrie* or the density of setting and atmosphere of *Salem's Lot* or *The Shining*, *The Dead Zone* is a serious, stimulating novel in which Stephen King once again demonstrates that there is nothing incompatible between commercial success and artistic vision.

Keith Neilson

DECADENCE
The Strange Life of an Epithet

Author: Richard Gilman (1925-   )
Publisher: Farrar, Straus and Giroux (New York). 180 pp. $8.95
Type of work: Literary and linguistic history
Time: Primarily 1850 to the present
Locale: England and France

A history of the uses to which the word "decadent" has been put in the last hundred and fifty years, especially in literary and artistic contexts

Although Richard Gilman brings an impressive reputation to the writing of *Decadence: The Strange Life of an Epithet*, his credentials may initially seem off the mark for the task he has attempted. As author of books and essays on the theater, drama critic at *Commonweal*, *Newsweek*, and *The New Republic*, Professor of Drama at Yale and CUNY, he seems little fitted by training or experience to undertake a study that is essentially linguistic—the history of the meaning of a complex word, *decadence*. Gilman knows that he might appear less than qualified, but tries to turn that flaw into a virtue by approaching the problem from what could be a fresh perspective. He soon finds that words such as *decadent* are difficult to define, since they have no fixed referent, such as *horse* and *millimeter* do. Moreover, the meanings of words like *decadence* seem to change almost unpredictably, depending on who uses them. Although he finds little aid in his search through dictionaries, he writes that this changeableness in the word is something likely to be appreciated by the specialist in lexicography or linguistics.

All this is true, indeed; but the immediate question is, why did Gilman not consult the experts whose acumen he praises? If we suppose, for the sake of argument, that Gilman managed to locate and consult every word written on the meaning of *decadence*, there still may be a large gap in the underpinnings of this book: the last generation has seen no lack of work on the theoretical study of meaning in language, on *how* words mean, and on how and why that meaning changes. Yet Gilman makes no reference to those studies; if he has consulted and either profited from or rejected them, we find no evidence of it here.

More seriously, the decision of either the author or the publisher to dispense with such tools of scholarship as footnotes and bibliography has handicapped the book. Too often, the bookbuyer, and more importantly, the opinionmakers, approach the question of a book's publisher with a certain kind of snobbery: a book from a university press is likely to be thought of beforehand as crabbed, esoteric, dusty, and cluttered with the impedimenta of scholarship such as footnotes, references, and bibliography. It is not that this is true in every case, of course, but simply that this prejudice will face a book from a university press: if a study of Sanskrit verbs appeared, it would not be from a large commercial publisher. On the other hand, we are likely to assume that the "really important" book will be a serious study of wide interest produced by one of the prestigious commercial presses, of which Farrar, Straus and Giroux is certainly one. In the average customer, this attitude shows little more than a deep misunderstanding of what scholarship is; but when the same attitude exists among those people who are important forces in the cultural life of a society, then the likely result is a shallowness of intellectual life, a sort of laborious reinventing of the wheel, as one retraces well-worn paths with an air of fresh discovery.

Someone with that attitude decided that *Decadence* would not have its pages sullied with footnotes, nor its conclusion clogged with a bibliography, and that decision was a great disadvantage to the book, although it may well please those who think of the external forms of scholarship as dry and point-less. The book is designed for reading, not for learning; for example, the author supplies no footnotes—not even ones that simply supply references. Thus, we find statements such as: "As Renato Poggioli has written in *The Theory of the Avant-Garde*, 'the most facile and frequent motif of hostile criticism is to accuse all avant-garde art of decadence.'" This sort of comment causes no problems only for the reader who can recall from memory who Poggioli is, and when his book was written, since only that reader can supply the date of publication needed to put the comment in its historical perspective. Those who wish to check the relevance of the quotation by examining its context are also out of luck since the lack of a page number for the quotation means that even an owner of Poggioli's book has to thumb through the whole work to find the quotation in question. As the comment stands, Gilman does not incorporate Poggioli's work, he only invokes it, either as an authority or as an especially well-wrought statement of the idea. Nor does the book contain a bibliography that would allow this and scores of similar examples to be cited and located. Consider one last example: "'It is the corollary of this conception of a model performance,' the art historian E. H. Gombrich has said, 'that once the problem has been mastered the only alternatives are imitation or decline.'" Some small percentage of the readers of *Decadence* may know that Gombrich is an art historian (a piece of information that Gilman supplies), but will even those few readily place the quotation, without even a title to identify it? It may not always be wise to assume that the reader has the same familiarity with the subject that the author has, yet it is an assumption more likely to be found in a "popular" book than in a "scholarly" one.

However, if the form of *Decadence* is deficient, what about the content? Gilman may offer arguments of real weight, insights of real value, even if the book is hard to use. One must disagree with Gilman to make this conces-sion, since he seems to reject the possibility of separating form and content; but that theoretical problem is not of importance here, so let us consider what Gilman has to say.

He begins the book with an investigation of the etymology of *decadent*, and notes that its meaning in the classical period was "a declining, a falling away," and more interestingly, finds that the word was never used by the Roman historians to describe their own civilization. Gilman can see, though, how the word could have been used to describe Imperial Rome (as it was used later): an apocalyptic turn of mind will find the notion of a decline from a golden age congenial, and this idea will join with an analogy between a civilization and an individual to lead very naturally to the perception of societies in terms of rise, maturity, and decline. Gilman's real interest in the word, however, begins with the nineteenth century, when, as he discovers, it was applied to individuals for the first time; he asks what is the key question in the book: if decadence means a falling away of power, talent, or originality, how is it possible for some of the most talented and original minds of the time to believe in decadence, to accept it, to embrace it?

Gilman supplies the answer: those minds did not perceive decadence in the sense of the historical definition; they saw the word and used it in a different way, and Gilman works hard to establish what that vision and that meaning was. This is to say, simply, that the meaning of the word changed. For Flaubert, Baudelaire, and others, the word comes to mean a rejection of the Romantic idea of the natural, a rejection of the notion of progress, and a movement of human values in a new direction.

Gilman's description of decadence as a literary movement strikes one as convincing and well-documented, and one can hardly doubt that these writers meant what Gilman says they meant when they used the word. Yet Gilman is bothered by some recent and not-so-recent uses of the word that he characterizes as "strange, illiterate, and hyperbolic." If an English critic is quoted as calling Baudelaire "decadent," the critic is faulted for using the term as a sign of moral disapproval. Since Gilman has no problem with other terms of moral disapproval, his objection must lie in the critic's use of this word, without regard to its etymology. If, however, the critic misuses the word by giving it a different meaning, why do the French and English Decadents themselves not misuse the word? They certainly have a nonetymological meaning in mind when the word is self-applied, as it was, for example, in the title of Anatole Baju's journal, *Le Décadent*.

The historical exploration of the root of the modern word is largely beside the point if Gilman's purpose is to look at the uses of the word in the last one hundred and fifty years; one feels more than a hint of the groundless notion that the etymological meaning of a word is the "real" meaning, and that later changes can only be corruptions.

Part of the problem may lie in a notion that Gilman himself exposes. He describes the idea, found in primitive cultures, that there is a magical relationship between names and things, and the subconscious belief that this idea produces: that if a word exists, there must be a corresponding thing. No one doubts that the primitive relationship described actually existed; there is abundant evidence for it. Nor can it be denied that this same feeling regarding words and names still has a widespread life among the näive today (although how widespread it is is a qustion to be investigated, not a principle to be assumed).

Gilman's task in the book could have been made easier and the clarity of his arguments improved if he had first of all established the present understanding of the relationship between words and things: that a word does not stand for a thing, but rather stands for an idea or conception of something that may or may not exist in reality. This is, of course, the reason why we can have names for things that once existed but no longer do, such as *Oscar Wilde*; for things that do not exist, but could possibly exist, such as *unicorn*; and for things that neither do nor can exist, such as *time machine*. Not making this distinction causes unnecessary problems for Gilman: having established a definition of *decadence* that satisfies him, Gilman considers someone like Wilde and finds it difficult to reconcile the definition and the actions or works of the man. He therefore concludes that *decadent* is a term misapplied to either Wilde's works or life. If the grounds of the argument were shifted just a bit, and it were realized that the person who applied the term was not characterizing Wilde but his own understanding of Wilde, the difficulty might not disappear, but we would have a better idea of where the real problem lies—not in the behavior of the person described, but in the understanding of the person describing.

Gilman objects that the word *decadence*, in the mouths of detractors of Wilde and others, did not describe a fact, but made a value judgment. There is nothing startling in this process: words such as *knave* and *gossip*, for example, begin as neutral, unoffensive terms and end as insults, and it is not hard to see how a word like *decadent* would go through the same semantic shift. Nor is there any great mystery in the fact that the word meant something different to the French Symbolists and their English followers than it did to those who were alarmed by their beliefs and behavior. Hardly a name for a group, sect, party, or cult does not mean something different to those inside than to those outside it. To describe a particular practice as "socialist," for example, means one thing in Leningrad, another in Nairobi, and still another in Dallas.

Gilman is harshly critical of C. E. M. Joad's 1948 book, *Decadence*; the British philosopher had attempted the same job—to define the word—yet (if Gilman's account is accurate) Joad strayed away just as Gilman has, but on the opposite side of the road. Joad appears to have defined *decadence* satisfactorily in the usage of those who (like Richard Le Gallienne or T. S. Eliot) satirized or criticized the Decadents. For the reasons outlined above, it comes as no surprise that Joad's definition does not describe the Decadents' work or fit their lives, since he was not defining actions and objects, but particular conceptions of actions and objects. Yet Joad no doubt thought that he had established the definitive treatment of decadence. In fact, it is characteristic of arguments on matters like these that one party establishes a meaning of a word and claims that all other meanings are erroneous, inaccurate, or foolish.

The possibility remains that all parties to the controversy are right: that when the critics call Baudelaire, Huysmans, or Wilde "decadent," they are using the word accurately to name what they consider an adverse moral effect of the works of those writers; and that when the writers themselves rejoice in the term "decadent," they too are using the word accurately to label a movement to bring new areas within the sphere of artistic treatment. If the multiple, even contradictory, meanings of the word make life more difficult for the lexicographer, that is the nature of the language.

Walter E. Meyers

THE DECLINE OF BISMARCK'S EUROPEAN ORDER
Franco-Russian Relations, 1875-1890

Author: George F. Kennan (1904-   )
Publisher: Princeton University Press (Princeton, New Jersey). 466 pp. $25.00
Type of work: History
Time: 1875-1890
Locale: Europe

A work which traces Russia's diplomatic alignments as she broke away from her German alliance in order to pursue her Balkan ambitions with more independence

Principal personages:
OTTO VON BISMARCK, German Chancellor
NIKOLAI GIERS, Russian Foreign Minister
ALEXANDER III, Russian Czar, 1881-1894
M. N. KATKOV, Russian journalist and publicist
ALEXANDER VON BATTENBERG, Prince of Bulgaria
JULES GRÉVY, President of France, 1879-1887

George Kennan has written a masterful account of the diplomacy preceding the Franco-Russian alliance of 1894 which deserves to be read by all students of the period. Kennan set himself a large task, one which commands the attention of Westerners to the present: he asks how it was possible for the nations of Europe to slaughter one another during the four long years of World War I. It would be too much to say he has answered this puzzle, but he has portrayed a world of intrigue, ambition, and aggressiveness which at least carries one toward an understanding of the mind-frame which sent Europe's youth to an early and ugly death.

Beyond this larger concern comes the more specific job of describing the hesitant rapprochement between Paris and Moscow which led to their treaty of 1894. Much of this story is familiar, yet Kennan is a master diplomatist, and he has made the motives of the European foreign offices extremely clear; he shows that, far from being inevitable, the Franco-Russian alliance was fashioned with tedious craftsmanship throughout many years. Most importantly, Kennan shows the importance of the treaty. It was not just a defensive treaty to protect France from the ascendant and exuberant German Empire; it was an offensive alliance designed to facilitate Russian expansion in the Balkans, eventually to the Bosporus. As a result, it was a portentous event, for Russian aims made conflict in the Balkans highly probable. By agreeing to it, France was tying herself to a policy which virtually accepted the possibility of war sooner or later.

Germany under Otto von Bismarck was the third actor in the story of the Franco-Russian treaty; in fact, without Bismarck, there might have been no Franco-Russian alliance. It was only recently that France and Russia had been enemies; no one had forgotten Napoleon's invasion in 1812, and more recently the two countries had squared off on the Crimean peninsula, contesting rival claims to the Levant. With the unification of Germany under Bismarck's aegis, however, a new threat arose which superseded the old conflicts. France, of course, had been soundly thrashed by Prussia in 1870-1871, and now had all the more reason for fear, with Prussia dominating all of non-Austrian Germany. She therefore needed an ally in order to assure her national security, not to mention her hopes of regaining Alsace-Lorraine.

Russia, on the other hand, had no natural enemies. Her weakness lay in her authoritarian political and social structure and in her backward economic system. Given this perspective, France, with her republican government and her willingness to harbor Russian political exiles, was far from being the ideal ally. The staunch monarchical principle prevailing in Germany and Austria-Hungary was more congenial to Russian views. Bismarck, for his part, realized that he need fear France only if she could ally herself with one of the other continental powers. Thus, from the first, he directed his very considerable powers to the goal of keeping his Western neighbor at an arm's length from the empires of the East. The Franco-Russian alliance was not a natural occurrence as sometimes thought, and it is to Kennan's merit to have pointed out that it was formed to satisfy offensive purposes as well as the more commonly accepted defensive ones. By concentrating predominantly on the Russian side of the event, Kennan explains Petersburg's motivation for the alliance and the implications the treaty held for the peace of Europe.

The one flaw in Bismarck's plan to isolate France lay in Russia's desire to seize the Black Sea straits at Constantinople, which controlled her access to warm water. Inside Russia, several powerful interest groups supported this ambition, including the Russian Orthodox Church, the Pan-Slav chauvinists, and the Asiatic branch of the Foreign Office. Achieving this goal, however, meant gaining a dominant position in the Balkans, which in turn threatened the vital interests of the Austro-Hungarian Empire. With large numbers of South Slavs incorporated in the Empire, events in the Balkan peninsula were of importance to Vienna, and Russian control was unacceptable. Here was a conflict of significance, and it was to perplex Bismarck as long as he was in office.

In the 1870's, France was in a weakened position after having lost the Franco-Prussian war and was not ready to be anybody's ally. Furthermore, the Austro-Russian confrontation was not particularly acute at this point, so it did not require great pains for Bismarck to keep his friends from each other's throats. The revolt of the Slavs in Bosnia-Herzegovina in 1875, however, made the situation more acute. For two years, one group of Christians after another rose up against the Muslim power which had dominated the area for centuries. When the Turks repressed them in turn, the resulting publicity, such as the furor over the Bulgarian atrocities, created pressure among Christian Europe to intervene. Even distant England was affected.

It was in Russia, however, that the indignation was at its greatest pitch.

With a similar language, ethnic background, and religious orientation, many Russians considered themselves the protectors of the South Slavs. There were also those who viewed the turmoil as an occasion to further national ambitions in the area. By 1877, these circumstances pushed St. Petersburg into war, and a full-scale invasion of the Balkans was mounted.

Although the Turks proved more resistant than was expected, the Russians finally broke their lines and, in the spring of 1878, reached the environs of Constantinople. This advance frightened the British, for the last thing London wanted was the competition for world trade routes which would ensue if the Russians gained access to the Mediterranean. Therefore, Disraeli sent a fleet to the Bosporus and threatened war if any further movement was made. Czar Alexander II agreed to stop, but the peace treaty he arranged with the Ottoman Empire created a large Bulgarian state which included Thrace, bordering the Aegean. Fearing Bulgaria would become a Russian satellite, Britain found this provision unsuitable and demanded a revision. With war looming, the Russians retreated and agreed to an all-European Congress to be held in Berlin to discuss the situation. Presided over by Bismarck, the Congress of Berlin reduced the size of Bulgaria, returned Thrace to Turkey, and divided the smaller Bulgaria into two sections.

Clearly the nation primarily responsible for the reduction of Russian gains was Great Britain. Yet Austria too was anxious to curb Petersburg's influence in the Balkans and so supported London, while Bismarck in turn agreed with Vienna. Thus, even though Germany was far from having caused the Russian humiliation, Petersburg resented its action, perhaps irrationally, because it was supposed to be a friend. When the Germans and the Austrians signed a treaty in 1879, it became even more clear in Russia that expansionist tendencies in the Balkans would run into German opposition.

Bismarck's decision to ally Germany with Austria has been regarded as one of his more far-reaching diplomatic moves, for it basically established alignments for World War I. He chose Austria for a variety of reasons. Like France, Austria needed an alliance, and so there was a great risk that these two powers would get together if Germany stood aloof. The alliance bolstered Germany's security position; there were affinities of language and culture, and it secured the volatile conflicts in Eastern Europe. Nevertheless, it did bring Berlin into Balkan politics and complicated relations with Russia.

For the time being, however, Bismarck was able to coordinate his different interests. The Russian Czar was the nephew of the German emperor, and the two rulers had a close relationship. In 1881, Bismarck succeeded in getting the Czar and the German and Austrian Emperors to form the League of the Three Emperors, solidifying his position in Europe. 1881, however, was also the year in which Alexander II was assassinated, and his son, Alexander III, proved much less easy for Bismarck to handle. For one thing, Alexander III was in sympathy with the Pan-Slavs and was therefore sensitive to their criticism of the German connection. Second, the relationship established between Russia and Bulgaria was deteriorating. Alexander III felt this foreign policy failure as a personal insult and again, perhaps irrationally, resented Bismarck for not doing more to help.

For Kennan, the Bulgarian question is the key to the development of Russian diplomatic objectives in the 1880's, and he devotes a considerable portion of his book to this problem. The Congress of Berlin had divided Bulgaria into two parts, one still nominally ruled by the Sultan and the second to be in the Russian sphere of influence. This latter Bulgarian entity chose Alexander von Battenberg as its ruler. Battenberg was to be advised by Russians, giving the Russian bureaucracy control over the new state. As time went on, however, Battenberg proved less and less willing to listen to this advice, which made him more and more popular with his Bulgarian subjects. The early 1880's recorded a series of Russian setbacks, each one infuriating Alexander III, who developed an intense hatred for Battenberg.

When the League of the Three Emperors treaty came up for renewal in 1884, the Bulgarian situation had not yet come to a head, and so the Russians agreed to continue it. Then, in 1885, Bulgarian patriots staged a coup in which they united the country's two sections. Ordinarily, such an event would have pleased the Czar, but since it benefited Battenberg, it only made him more angry. Consequently, in 1886, the Russians arranged successfully to overthrow the Bulgarian prince, but soon afterward a Bulgarian countercoup took place. Although Battenberg refused to return, Bulgaria nevertheless had effectively escaped Russian control.

Throughout this experience, Germany had remained friendly to Petersburg, although Austria took delight in the Russian discomfiture, and even went so far as to say it would not tolerate further intervention. When the Three Emperors treaty came up again for renewal in 1887, the Pan-Slavists decided that their problems in the Balkans were the fault of Germany and that the treaty should be abandoned. Alexander III, deeply offended by the setback in Bulgaria, grasped this argument as a convenient rationalization, and, despite the opposition of his foreign minister, N. K. Giers, agreed to break the alliance.

Russia was now in the market for a new ally who could back up her Balkan ambitions. France, finally recovered from 1870-1871, had also begun thinking in offensive terms, evidenced in the ephemeral popularity of General Boulanger, and was now ready to enter into a Russian connection. France, naturally, wanted Russian support in case of an attack by Germany, but as Kennan makes clear, the price for Russian help was acceptance of her Balkan strategy. Since this strategy was aggressive in nature, the burgeoning Franco-Russian alliance in fact threatened war. In order to avenge her defeat in 1870-1871, France was willing to tie her star to a country which was expansionist, thus imperiling the peace of Europe.

The volume concludes in 1890, before the treaty was actually finalized. The negotiations leading to this accomplishment and the dynamics of the relationship between the odd bedfellows, France and Russia, will be the subject of a forthcoming volume by Kennan.

Stuart Van Dyke, Jr.

THE DEVIL'S HORSEMEN
The Mongol Invasion of Europe

Author: James Chambers (1923-   )
Publisher: Atheneum Publishers (New York). Illustrated. 190 pp. $11.95
Type of work: History
Time: 1216-1287
Locale: Asia and Eastern Europe

  A narrative history of the thirteenth century Mongol invasion of Europe and the Near East

>   *Principal personages:*
>   CHINGIS KHAN, the first Mongol invader of Europe
>   BATU, Khan of the Golden Horde
>   BELA IV, King of Hungary
>   KUBILAI KHAN, grandson of Chingis
>   SUBEDEI BAHADUR, chief Mongol military strategist
>   MARCO POLO, the most famous of the European visitors to the
>   Mongols

In the Polish city of Kraców, every hour on the hour, a trumpet calls an alarm to its citizens, but the trumpet call is never completed. It sputters and dies out, as if the trumpeter had been suddenly struck dead. In fact, a trumpeter was once struck dead, on March of 1241, by a Mongol arrow. The present-day trumpeter at Kraców is the last reminder of the thirteenth century Mongol invasion of Europe, an invasion that once threatened to reach the Atlantic and the Mediterranean, but of which no other sign now remains. What actually happened—or nearly happened—has more often been ignored than told. What impelled these Asiatic tribes so recently welded into nationhood to leave their ordinary precincts and seek victories in strange lands is also a matter worthy of careful speculation. Perhaps most interesting of all is the question of how these semisavage tribesmen were able to defeat the cream of European chivalry.

James Chambers is at his best in telling the exciting and incredible story of the invasions. In 1218, the governor of the near Eastern province of Otrar murdered the friendly ambassador and merchants of the first Mongol caravan to arrive as a result of a commercial treaty. The ruler of Khwarizm, Muhammad II, supported the actions of his governor, murdering a second ambassador sent by the Mongols in the interests of justice and sending back that ambassador's severed head. Chingis Khan, the Mongol leader, could brook no further insult and unleashed a devastating war under the direction of his military leaders, of whom Subedei was the greatest. Under Subedei, each of whose campaigns was a "masterpiece of original and imaginative strategy," a victorious war against Muhammad was followed by an extended reconnaissance of Europe. After this reconnaissance came the invasion of Europe, the subjugation of Russia, and the disintegration of Hungary. Just before the

Mongols were to invade Austria, the great Khan died. By tradition, the leaders of the invasion returned to Asia, and a defenseless Europe was saved by accident. Later, the Mongols invaded the Near East, sacking the city of Baghdad. Again, their supreme leader died (August 12, 1259), and again the military leaders returned to Asia. Both Islam and Christendom had been saved, not by their own resources, but by chance.

Although he tells their story well and clearly, Chambers is far less competent at delving into the motives of the Mongols, which stem directly from their warlike and ambitious natures. The provocation of Muhammad was real, but it was significant only in that it opened a door to the possibility of easy victories and plunder and territory for the taking. Batu, the grandson of Chingis, became immensely rich through conquest. This Khan of the Golden Horde ruled an empire that stretched from the Carpatheans to the Urals—an enormous territory; blood, gold, and land were not means to an end for the Mongols, but ends in themselves. War was all they knew and cared about. Outside of its sphere, they achieved nothing and left nothing. Their military leaders were brilliant and ruthless; the men under them "could suffer without complaint and kill without pity."

It seems incredible that these primitive and ruthless Mongol tribesmen could have achieved what they did militarily, for they were fighting not defenseless peasants and townsmen, but the best products of European and Islamic chivalry. Chambers supports, but does not make vivid, the reasons for the long record of Mongol success. He shows how part of their easy triumph was due to the feudal nature of the forces arrayed against them. When a resourceful ruler like Bela IV of Hungary tried to defend his country effectively, he was defeated by the treachery and dissention of his own people. Mostly, however, the Mongols won because of their endurance, their weaponry, and their military tactics and strategy. This endurance was phenomenal: inaccessible deserts were crossed; mountain passes five feet deep in snow were traversed. In his endurance, moreover, the soldier was complemented by his mount, the Przevalsky horse. The main weapon of the soldier was the bow—not the longbow of the English, but the recurved composite bow made of horn and sinew. This bow had a pull of one hundred and sixty pounds, over twice that of the longbow, and a range of three hundred and fifty yards— a fifth of a mile. Armed with such a bow, mounted on his stoical Przevalsky horse, steadied by its stirrups, his arrow release timed so as to avoid interference of the horse's gallop, the Mongol cavalryman could unleash a deadly hail of arrows from a mobile platform. Their mobility made the Mongol archers difficult to hit; mobility also facilitated arrow recovery, since rearming was absolutely essential to maintain steady firepower. This cavalry firepower was supplemented by the artillery and its catapulting rocks and rockets. There was no infantry.

Mobile firepower did not exist for its own sake but as part of well-thought-out military strategy. For instance, a vanguard of cavalry would attack and seemingly fall back in disarray. The European knights would give chase, only to fall victims to a prepared Mongol ambush. For such strategies the European knights, with their heavy armor and their close-quarters weapons, were ill-equipped. Ready to fight bravely with another armored man on another horse, they were outmaneuvered, surrounded, and annihilated. On this matter of Mongol military strategy, Chambers is weakest, and the book suffers from a lack of clear military maps.

When Marco Polo, the most famous of European travelers to Cathay, returned from the court of Kubilai Khan, he brought with him stories of gunpowder and printing; but of the Mongol art of war, medieval Europeans learned nothing. Europeans continued to annihilate one another and their brutality on occasion equaled, though it never exceeded, that of the Mongols. Not until the twentieth century, however, was the West ready to learn the mobile combat lessons of the Mongols. Even then, only generals as forward-thinking as Patton and Rommel listened with care.

Alan G. Gross

D. H. LAWRENCE'S NIGHTMARE
The Writer and His Circle in
the Years of the Great War

Author: Paul Delany (1937-   )
Publisher: Basic Books (New York). Illustrated. 420 pp. $15.95
Type of work: Literary biography
Time: 1914-1918
Locale: England

An account of literary England during World War I which focuses on Lawrence's experience and seeks an answer in it to the question of why Lawrence wrote his masterpiece, Women in Love, *toward the end of the war*

Principal personages:
D. H. LAWRENCE, the English novelist
FRIEDA LAWRENCE, his wife
JOHN MIDDLETON MURRY, the English author
KATHERINE MANSFIELD, his wife and an author in her own right
BERTRAND RUSSELL, the English philosopher
LADY OTTOLINE MORRELL, his lover
LADY CYNTHIA ASQUITH, patroness of the arts and daughter-in-law of the English politician

Recently, a veritable industry has arisen chronicling the life of literary England at the beginning of the twentieth century. The number of books about the Bloomsbury circle—its members and their interlocking relationships—has reached epidemic proportions. In the last year or so, the focus has shifted to the years of World War I, that nightmare which so clearly marks the emergence of a distinctively modern consciousness in the arts. The acknowledged masterpiece in this field is Paul Fussell's *The Great War and Modern Memory*, a splendid piece of literary and social history. Fussell's concern in that book is with the impact of the war on the imaginations of English writers, especially those who participated in the war and who, if they survived, found their perceptions of history and mankind irrevocably altered. Paul Delany's painstaking account of D. H. Lawrence's experiences during the war years, as its title suggests, is intended to be another chapter in that story. His starting point is the fact that Lawrence, whose feelings toward his native country were mixed at best, came to England in 1914 only intending to stay for a brief time. Instead, while he was there, the war began, and Lawrence was effectively trapped, finding himself unable to leave the country until the cessation of hostilities. As a result, he was plunged into a profound personal crisis, one which he almost did not survive.

Delany's chief undertaking in this book, therefore, is to chronicle Lawrence's wartime experiences in England. These included the banning of his recently completed novel, *The Rainbow*, an event which meant, among other things, that Lawrence would face financial difficulties as well as public suspicion and scorn throughout the war years. The fact that he was married to a woman of German extraction and opposed the English war effort added little to his welcome among his own countrymen. As a result, Lawrence spent the majority of the war years living in a succession of small cottages in rural England which appealed to him primarily because they were cheap to rent and kept him out of the public eye. Delany's account of Lawrence's wanderings, heightened by the inclusion of photographs of each cottage and refuge, makes for a vivid and moving story.

Delany's second objective in this book, which he also achieves admirably, is to chronicle Lawrence's psychological ups and downs during his years of entrapment throughout the war. His skillful interweaving of excerpts from letters and diaries, coupled with quotations from Lawrence's works which transformed many of these events into fiction or philosophical reflection, presents a graphic picture of a deeply troubled, lonely, yet angry and embittered man who was systematically denied the one thing he wanted most: to leave the country. As a result, Lawrence clung to friends and sought to involve them in schemes for utopian communities; he railed against the war and against English efforts at winning it. When his friends found they could not follow him in all his schemes nor share in his feelings about the war, he turned on them bitterly, thus making his sense of loneliness all the greater. At the fringes of this story is precisely that same Bloomsbury group with which so many other writers have dealt, although Lawrence was never close to it. Upset by its sexual irregularities and disturbed by its tolerance of homosexuality, Lawrence nevertheless had to deal with it because it held much of the power in English literary circles tied up in its intricate and interlocking patterns of relationships. Readers of this book will perhaps find reported here a slightly different picture of the Bloomsbury set than they have received from other sources.

Delany has a third item on his agenda, but one which does not find in this book as satisfactory a treatment as his other concerns. Just as the war began, Lawrence was putting the finishing touches on *The Rainbow*, his first major work after *Sons and Lovers*. At the end of the war, he was finishing his next major novel, *Women in Love*, which Delany believes is Lawrence's masterpiece. *Women in Love* is a dramatically different book, a work one would not have predicted Lawrence would write next on the basis of the evidence presented by *The Rainbow*. Delany, therefore, attempts to show that Lawrence's war experiences contributed to this dramatic shift in style and approach. The author's approach is to analyze carefully the kinds of things Lawrence was writing and the kinds of experiences he was having while trapped in England. He is able to see in many of Lawrence's encounters with his friends and acquaintances the germs of characters and episodes in *Women in Love*. For example, he finds in Lawrence's experiences with John Murry and with an English farmer the origins of some of the homoerotic themes in

Women in Love. He also finds, in Lady Cynthia Asquith and other members of the Bloomsbury group, inspirations for other characters in that novel.

Delany's argument is unconvincing. Details of a writer's life often bear striking resemblance to details of character and episode in his fiction, yet the process of transformation, the turning of fact into fiction, remains an elusive and mysterious process. In fact, access to this sort of information must be achieved with caution: the work of fiction stands on its own, with its own integrity and coherence, and can often be drained of its power if we seek to label this or that fictional character with the name of an actual person. We run the risk of diminishing a fictional personage to what we know of its real counterpart, a process which deprives the author of the real mark of his genius—the ability to create believable, fictional worlds out of whatever experience he might choose.

Even so, if Delany were able to illuminate Lawrence's creative process, the ways he used real people and events by transforming them into his fictional world, he might teach us something about Lawrence. Unfortunately, however, this dimension of Delany's work all too often amounts merely to noting parallels between fictional characters and real people.

However, to point this out is to raise only a small reservation about Delany's book, which stands up well in terms of how he achieves his other aims. He gives us a vivid, gripping, and often painful account of Lawrence during the war. He tells us more about the mood of the artistic community in England in those years than anyone else has, and he adds to it a strongly written sense of how the larger populace responded to its artists during a critical period in English history. For what he has given us, we must be grateful.

John N. Wall, Jr.

A DREAM OF GREATNESS
The American People 1945-1963

Author: Geoffrey Perrett (1940-   )
Publisher: Coward, McCann & Geoghegan (New York). 893 pp. $16.95
Type of work: History
Time: 1945-1963
Locale: The United States

A social and political history of the United States from 1945 to 1963

> *Principal personages:*
> HARRY S TRUMAN, thirty-third President of the United States, 1945-1953
> JOSEPH R. MCCARTHY, United States Senator and Chairman of the Permanent Subcommittee on Investigations, 1954
> HENRY A. WALLACE, Vice-President of the United States, 1940-1945
> THOMAS E. DEWEY, Republican candidate who lost to Truman
> JULIUS AND ETHEL ROSENBERG, arrested as spies in 1950
> DWIGHT D. EISENHOWER, thirty-fourth President of the United States, 1953-1961
> JOHN F. KENNEDY, thirty-fifth President of the United States, 1961-1963

Geoffrey Perrett is an energetic researcher and writer. The present work is a sequel to his comprehensive *Days of Sadness, Years of Triumph: The American People, 1939-1945* (1973), which tried to capture the complexity and scope of life in the country during World War II. *A Dream of Greatness* is even larger and more ambitious, almost nine hundred pages of information, anecdotes, character sketches, and opinions about a period that is considered fairly dull and barren and commonly viewed through a haze of nostalgia. Perrett, however, argues that these were particularly exciting years, a time when Americans believed they were destined for "greatness." This was not a time when there were "the bland leading the bland," but rather when "America represented, to the ordinary people at home and overseas, vigor and daring—thinking big, acting big."

Americans emerged from World War II full of hope, but were soon faced with staggering problems—economic dislocations, unemployment, labor unrest and strikes, inflation—and a conservative mood in Washington. President Harry Truman, a complex man admired by Perrett, was unable to extend New Deal programs. While the author devotes some space to such traditional topics, he is more interested in the state of public schooling (he criticizes the Life Adjustment curriculum for its antiintellectualism), the expansion of higher education, the growth of suburbs, the expansion of consumer spending, and changing dress styles. After the sacrifices and hardships of the previous decade and a half, Americans were eager to spend their money. They were not so eager to confront social and economic problems. Blacks faced extreme segregation and hostility in the South and North, despite the war's democratic rhetoric and President Truman's limp attempts to promote racial equality, such as desegregating the military in 1948. This is an example of Perrett's style, alternating descriptions of optimistic and positive aspects of society with others that reveal the nagging persistence or creation of serious problems.

Against the background of domestic stresses and strains, Perrett develops the unfolding of the Cold War. While historians have been arguing about whether the United States or the Soviet Union was most responsible for increasing world tensions, the author comes down on the side of the former, simplifying in the process the meaning of the Truman Doctrine and the Marshall Plan, both aimed at halting Communism in Europe. The attack on Communism abroad was matched by an internal crusade, led by the President, to purge the country of supposed subversives. This is another topic that has fascinated historians in recent years as it has become more and more evident that Senator Joe McCarthy did not initiate the Red Scare that has since carried his name. He was preceded by union leaders, right-wing Congressmen in the House UnAmerican Activities Committee (such as Richard Nixon), and many others. Many people were queried and punished, including Alger Hiss. Perrett defends Hiss, while believing that he acted somewhat foolishly. Truman's established procedures for screening government employees resulted in the dismissal of two thousand civilian employees, innocent victims of the country's fears, as Perrett readily admits.

While most of the country was moving in a conservative direction, there were a handful going against the tide. Former Vice-President Henry Wallace and a small group of mavericks organized the Progressive Party in 1948 to offer a left alternative to the nation. Perrett is most critical of the party, "a doomed cause," for not purging its Communist supporters and in general being too weak and divided to do much good except help the Republicans by taking votes from Truman. The Democrats' acceptance of a civil rights plank in the platform also alienated a large chunk of Southerners, who broke off to form the States Rights Party. However, Thomas Dewey, the Republican candidate, was unable to parlay these disaffections into a victory, for the small turnout of voters gave Truman an upset. The President's second administration was as rocky as the first. 1949 was not a good year, the Soviet explosion of an atomic bomb being followed by a Communist victory in China, the North Korean invasion of South Korea in June, 1950, and the arrest of nine accused spies, including Julius and Ethel Rosenberg, the previous month. In this climate, Truman's liberal domestic programs got nowhere, and anti-Communist hysteria became more shrill. The Rosenbergs were not alone, by far, in being caught in Washington's far-flung anti-Communist net, but they were the most controversial. They paid for their alleged crimes with their lives, while others escaped with prison sentences, deportation, lost jobs,

ruined reputations, and other serious inflictions. Perrett believes Julius Rosenberg was guilty of atomic espionage, although he admits that the trial was
highly emotional and the judge fanatical in his belief that the Rosenbergs
were responsible for the fifty thousand American casualties in Korea. The
stage was set for Senator Joe McCarthy.

The Red Scare did not start in the 1950's, but it reached its most virulent
form during these years. Perrett covers the topic in some depth in a chapter
aptly entitled "The Long Night of McCarthyism." The crusade was marked
by mistakes, stupidities, and a vindictiveness that ruined many lives. For the
author, it was "a dreary, silly business." Offsetting such activity, however,
were technological innovations that enriched peoples' lives, such as television,
FM radio, and new Hollywood film styles. Not that the entertainment industry
was immune from the purges, for blacklisting was widespread and content
was heavily influenced by Cold War propaganda. There then emerged on the
scene a sober, immensely popular war hero, Dwight Eisenhower, to lead the
Republican Party and the country into an era of optimism and security. Perrett
has nothing but praise for Ike, whose two terms in office were characterized
by peace and prosperity. He ended the fighting in Korea and supported the
attack on Joe McCarthy. The fading away of the Red Scare by mid-decade
demonstrated, to Perrett, that in the end Americans were committed to the
defense of democratic freedoms. Many suffered, but the country survived,
only to find itself pervaded by conformity—in thought, in dress, and in almost
every other area. "This blandness, eschewing strong preferences, avoiding
sharp differences of belief, was part of the tepid lake of conformity which
appeared to seep in everywhere," Perrett writes. He constantly attempts to
balance the virtues of American democracy with its obvious liabilities in this
period. Life was good, if not great.

Trying to capture the diversity of life in the 1950's, Perrett discusses a broad
range of topics: rock and roll music, teenage rebels, Beat life, organized
crime, race relations, the start of the civil rights movement marked by the
Brown v. *Board of Education* case, the Montgomery bus boycott, the emergence of the Reverend Martin Luther King, religion, the space race, public
schooling and the expansion of higher education, art, business, unions, farmers, and foreign policy—on all of which he has personal views and comments.
The country, like its President, had more problems than necessary, but less
than many believed. The country was ripe, however, for energetic new leadership, and it got it by a squeak.

For Perrett, John F. Kennedy was more style than substance, just the
reverse of Eisenhower. Surrounding himself with young, vigorous advisers,
including his brother Robert, the President was nevertheless quite conservative, and he made many blunders, including the Cuban invasion. Despite
his reluctance to change society, the country was discovering that serious
problems existed, such as poverty, discrimination, and decaying cities. Ken-

ncdy grudgingly reacted, pushed by grassroots organizing, particularly among civil rights workers in the South. He supported new civil rights legislation. Throughout the country there was an awakening, the stirrings of a women's movement, growing radicalism among college students who protested the Cold War, HUAC, and injustice. In the midst of these activities, Kennedy brought the country to the brink of war in order to force Russian missiles out of Cuba. Perrett agrees with those who see this as an excessive response that could have destroyed the country, "but the Kennedy Administration knew no other style." His increasing aid to the faltering government in South Vietnam was equally misguided. He blundered, but also represented the last vestiges of American optimism. With his death in late 1963, Perrett concludes, "Americans reeled toward the future, instead of reaching out to seize it."

In his broad, sweeping account of American life between World War II and the death of John F. Kennedy, Perrett reveals the country's warts as well as its virtues. He concludes, however, that "out of the restless energy, the revival of optimism and self confidence, arose countless opportunities for expansive, generous, brave spirits to express themselves freely." The period produced great men, such as Truman, Eisenhower, and Kennedy, that have not been matched since. An open society survived despite McCarthyism. Such interpretations seem to contradict much of the book's evidence and certainly a large amount of recent scholarship. The problem was not that American society was bland, but that it was perhaps continuing to cause more problems than it was solving because of the needs of American capitalism and the general conservative temper of the ruling elites. Take, for example, the country's foreign policy. It was not just anti-Communist, it was aggressively interventionist even before Kennedy's Bay of Pigs fiasco. Perrett completely ignores the CIA-led coup in Iran that restored the Shah to power in 1953 and the CIA's other secret activities throughout the world that are only now coming to light. He glosses over our shortsighted China policy and substantial intervention in South Vietnam antedating the French defeat in 1954 and continuing throughout the decade. Also there is little in the book about United States intervention in the affairs of Latin American countries in the name of supporting American business interests. Indeed, the needs of American corporations dictated much of American foreign policy, an interpretation that Perrett ignores in his haste to emphasize the democratic motives of the country's leaders.

Similar problems affect the author's interpretation of social and cultural activities. Perrett points out the deadening influence of the anti-Communist crusade on arts and culture, but he does not seem to comprehend the scope of the problem. Some have argued that film, literature, drama, and other aspects of the arts were dealt a staggering blow by the purges and blacklists, set back years because so much creative talent was obliterated. This was true in many other aspects of life as well. There were voices of dissent throughout the decade, but they were muted, only to reappear with a vengeance in the 1960's. Perrett does not adequately explain why this resurgence occurred, other than somehow attributing it to Kennedy; but there was more to it than this.

Perrett has written a widely ranging history of a crucial period in American history, a period too long ignored. However, by intermixing the trivial and the important, and giving so many opinions about so many events, individuals, trends, and activities, the reader often gets lost. More seriously, by generally painting a rosy glow over the period, he misses much that was harmful and dangerous, despite his periodic criticisms. A more critical eye would have explored the connections between the military-industrial-political complex that Eisenhower warned the country about, and how these connections controlled both domestic and foreign policy. This is a rich, yet ultimately flawed, work.

Ronald D. Cohen

DUBIN'S LIVES

Author: Bernard Malamud (1914-   )
Publisher: Farrar, Straus and Giroux (New York). 362 pp. $10.00
Type of work: Novel
Time: The early 1970's
Locale: Upper New York State; New York City; and Venice, Italy

A story of a biographer who lives other men's lives in order to find his own

Principal characters:
WILLIAM DUBIN, a biographer
KITTY, his wife
FANNY BICK, his lover
GERRY, his stepson
MAUD, his daughter

William Dubin, once a composer of obituaries, has found his vocation and his identity as a biographer. Responding to the pathos of unrealized possibilities, he began with *Short Lives*. Later he wrote biographies of Lincoln, Mark Twain, and Thoreau; and at the opening of Bernard Malamud's novel, he has just begun a life of D. H. Lawrence. "Everybody's life is mine unlived. One writes lives he can't live," Dubin jots down in a note to himself. In *Dubin's Lives*, Malamud portrays Dubin's struggle to break free of others' lives and live one more completely his own.

As the novel begins, sometime early in the 1970's, Dubin is living an existence partly Thoreau's and partly Lawrence's. One therefore notices the likenesses in these odd, original, nature-loving, sexually incomplete writers. Drawn to both, Dubin lacks their strongly directed commitment to a certain way of life that for them represents living fully. Dubin, for example, loves nature and had once been passionately affected by it like a young Wordsworth; but now, living a retired life in the countryside of northern New York State, he must remind himself to observe his surroundings as he partakes of nature during his daily walk, regularized as either the short walk or the long walk. "William Dubin, visitor to nature, had introduced himself along the way but did not intrude." Though not much given to meditation on the external world, Dubin, like Thoreau, is trying to learn how to live his life. Like Lawrence, he has taken on another man's wife—the husband was dead, but Kitty had not ceased to belong to him—and won through to a relationship that seems solid, though there are tensions. Yet Dubin still tends to see himself as a stephusband.

Dubin composes by imagining he is writing about himself, and so as he begins his book about Lawrence, he finds his life joining Lawrence's—though with reservations. With something like a Lawrentian attempt at fully living, Dubin begins a sexual adventure with a twenty-two-year-old girl. The story follows a conventional course: Dubin is at first reluctant to entrust much of himself to the girl; next, upon losing her, he experiences torments of desire for her, then he loves her fully (while suffering sexual impotence with his wife); and at the end of the book, he runs home to his wife with a heart full of love. Although his lover has suggested he spend half the week with her and the other half with his wife, the implication is that he is making a new beginning toward loving his wife as fully and completely as Lawrence believed necessary.

Malamud tells the story with a wealth of naturalistic detail and wry humor that give an illusion of utter realism. The beginning of William and Fanny's affair, for example, is a frustrating, funny, hideously unromantic fiasco. Fanny, a college dropout, has wrecked her car on the way to the Big Apple after a disillusioning experience at a Zen commune. She becomes acquainted with Dubin when she takes a job cleaning his house; he invites her to meet him in New York, but she loses the name of the hotel. He then takes her to Venice, where her flamboyant sexuality lights up the city, but he never manages to make love to her. The first night she gets sick, and he cleans her up. To Dubin's distaste, Fanny's conversation seems to turn inevitably to his wife, Kitty, despite Dubin's desire to keep Kitty as untouched by their conversation as he hopes she will be by this affair. Also, Dubin is distracted by worrying whether a young girl he caught sight of with an older man may be his daughter Maud. He returns late from searching for Maud to find Fanny copulating on a hotel room rug with a gondolier.

Hurt and angry, Dubin dismisses Fanny and flies to Sweden to look up his stepson, an army deserter; this adventure is equally frustrating and shabby. Dubin takes a fall in the street and bangs up his knees. Painfully he searches for and locates his stepson, who has discarded Dubin's name and taken back his original surname, rejecting his stepfather along with the army, the United States, and any normal existence. Bitter and uncommunicative, Gerald rebuffs Dubin in every possible way. The last scene of the chapter has Dubin wretchedly pursuing his son down the street calling his name, while a hopeful prostitute trails behind. This many-toned European excursion in which Dubin experiences anticipation, pleasure, guilt, injured vanity, frustration, shame, and anguish is a rich slice of intensely observed, intensely felt real life.

One becomes aware, however, that Dubin, realistic though he seems, is also living his way through an intricate web of literary allusions. He is living other writers' lives and other writers' creations. When he talks to himself, as he frequently does, he tends to mumble quotations from Thoreau, Lawrence, Coleridge, Samuel Johnson, Shakespeare, and other major authors. When he begins to take cold showers in the morning, he does so as therapy recommended by Carlyle. Eventually, even Kitty Dubin begins to identify with Jane Welsh Carlyle, the unhappy wife of an impotent biographer. A melancholy piece of music heard in the silence of an extremely cold night brings thoughts of Schubert and of Keats ("The Eve of St. Agnes"), two short lives collapsed together. Fanny Bick, of course, hints at Fanny Brawne, and Dubin's long period of agonized desire for her after their parting in Venice suggests Keats's ambivalent feelings of longing and fear with respect to Fanny Brawne as well as the misery of the bewitched knight at arms in "La Belle Dame Sans Merci." Moreover, Dubin's daughter quotes to him part of Keats's sonnet "To Fanny," the lines about living as a "wretched thrall," unable to work, in "idle misery," exactly chiming with Dubin's hopeless and unhappy condition at the time.

Certain events in the novel, moreover, suggest scenes in other literary works. Lost in the snow at night, Dubin finds it "easy" to sit under a tree, but he fears "the woods filling with snow," as Malamud recaptures Robert Frost's suggestions of the lure of death. On a contrasting occasion, Fanny in bed with Dubin decorating her lover's body with a flower is an obvious reference to *Lady Chatterley's Lover*. Somewhat less obvious are the reminiscences of Lawrence's "Shades of Spring." Like Syson in Lawrence's story, Dubin and Fanny make their way over a wall, through a field of wildflowers, and into a wood. Both authors hint at Edenic associations in the setting and in the characters. Like Adam, the man names the flowers—he knows the names of things—and the woman learns from him. He is analytical; she is simple and sensuous. In Malamud's novel the couple pass first through an apple orchard; they seat themselves, relaxed and calm, near a quarry pond "as if they had no prior history," and later Dubin watches as Fanny picks flowers: "Fifteen or more billion years after creation, the biographer thought, here's this sea of wild flowers on earth and amid them this girl picking white daisies." The world is fallen—and the apples that hang in the orchard are worm-eaten—still, to make love in spring in this wild garden suggests a primal health and innocence.

Out of the rather banal story of an aging man having an affair with a hippie girl, a story individuated by a mass of well-observed detail and made complex by myriad literary references, a mythic tale emerges. Fanny is a life-affirming woman whose element is water. In the city of canals, where she appears so voluptuously beautiful, she makes love first with a gondolier and then with the captain of a watertaxi. Later, the prelude to sexual consummation is the scene at the deep quarry pool inside the wood, inside the wildflower garden. In love with Fanny, Dubin experiences in her company the sensation of a fountain inside him, "flowers of splashing water." For Dubin, a man in middle-life finally willing to be himself, the relationship with Fanny means not just a renewal of youth but a finding of self. As the book moves through a two-year cycle of seasons, Dubin meets Fanny in late summer, loses her in fall, suffers through a frigid winter, finds her again in spring, and loves her in summer. The seasonal patterning allows Malamud to suggest natural rebirth in the spring meeting and also to set on either side of the period of loving two periods of intense deprivation, one freezing cold, the other hellishly hot. The novel ends at the beginning of another spring.

Dubin, who was drawn to Lawrence and Thoreau because both wrote of death and resurrection, thus lives through two times of mock-death, of agony, and of sterility (in the first he cannot write; in the second he is impotent). Each period is brought to a climax by a stunning scene which is both actual and metaphorical: in the first, in a blinding blizzard, assailed by wind and snow, he is in an unknown place, his brain pierced by snow, unable to see. At length he is rescued by his wife. In the second scene, his car out of gas and he is lost again; he stumbles over an open grave, is attacked by a ferocious Cerberus, and is shot at by an angry farmer. This time he is rescued by Fanny. After each sojourn in a living hell, Dubin experiences a rebirth.

Against Dubin's effort to find his life are set the efforts of others: Fanny, who develops in the course of the novel from a promiscuous, undirected child to an independent, purposeful woman; the bitter stepson Gerry, who leaves Sweden for spy-training in Soviet Russia and eventual fear and penury; Dubin's daughter Maud, who drops out of college and becomes pregnant by a married black professor; and finally Dubin's wife Kitty, who is honest, attractive, generous, and kind but rather dissatisfied with her lack of accomplishment. She suffers from insomnia, she still dreams of her dead doctor-husband, she reads his psychiatric handbook in an effort to understand Dubin's problems, and each time she leaves the house she comes back to sniff the gas burners. She cannot live her life easily and without fears. Although their stories are not fully told, one perceives at the end of the book signs of hope for all of these characters.

The signs are vague, however, and somewhat vague also in the case of Dubin. Much of his story has been suggested in dialogue, in symbol, and in metaphor. His emotional distance from his wife is often conveyed by having her speak directly, while his answer is given in indirect discourse: "He said he couldn't go then. Circumstances weren't right." Symbolically, his episodes of misery and sterility begin with dieting. His pain is expressed in epigram: "If your train's on the wrong track every station you come to is the wrong station." His alienation from his wife is expressed as two separate locked houses, full of locked rooms; and his guilt is described as a pile of rocks he wears for a hat.

However, despite indirection and allusiveness at times, the pattern of Dubin's story is fairly clear. Son of a madwoman and a waiter, later a stepfather and stephusband, almost friendless, Dubin is a man who had learned to live to himself. He controlled his life, his work, and his wife's existence. He loved her and wanted to share himself with her but found himself out of touch as he lost his self among the lives he re-created in his writing. Yet in living the lives of others (with reservations), Dubin finally finds his way to his own life. He knows that he did not pick Lawrence as his subject; rather, Lawrence picked him because there was something Lawrence wanted Dubin to know. Through a selfish concentration on his own concerns, Dubin fails in his first chance to learn through Fanny, but later, he begins to live more fully, to surrender himself to the blood, as Lawrence bade, and even to feel like a god.

Across the street from the window before which Fanny stood naked is a synagogue where, on the second floor, Jews could be seen praying. The emblematic scene expresses Dubin's reservation and his guilt; and guilt brings on impotence with Kitty, inadequacy in his relationship with Fanny, and a second descent into a hell. Then, reunited with Fanny, Dubin's life blooms once more. At the end of the novel, as he runs back to his wife, holding his half-erect phallus, another emblematic scene suggests that he will find it possible to let his life bloom again with Kitty—or at least that his life will begin to put out a few leaves. Through responding to others' lives, he has, it seems, renewed or found his own.

Guilt, pain, and mythic renewal of life are themes that have been treated by Malamud before (*A New Life* is the most obvious example). However familiar its theme, *Dubin's Lives* is a fine book because it is splendidly written and because Dubin becomes a highly sympathetic character. Unheroic and lonely, his self subdued and absorbed by the lives of others, Dubin nevertheless possesses a pungent humor and a capacity for suffering one must respect.

Mary C. Williams

THE DUKE OF DECEPTION
Memories of My Father

Author: Geoffrey Wolff (1937   )
Publisher: Random House (New York). Illustrated. 275 pp. $12.95
Type of work: Memoir
Time: Primarily 1937-1970, including some flashbacks to earlier times
Locale: Various locations in the United States, including Connecticut, California, New York, Alabama, and Florida

A touching and harrowing memoir of a son's quest to come to terms with the paradox that was his father

Principal personages:
GEOFFREY WOLFF
ARTHUR SAMUELS WOLFF, his father, the "Duke"
ROSEMARY WOLFF, his mother
TOBY WOLFF, his brother

In *The Duke of Deception: Memories of My Father*, Geoffrey Wolff has taken on the task of justifying in his own mind the life of his father. His investigation cracks the lies and con games that created a barrier between family, friends, and the general public, and he feels better because he realizes that there was love and concern through all the hard times. The memories are disturbing, breathtaking, bitter, twisted, and tangled with guilt, but are always measured against the love between father and son. This memoir opens with the author learning of his father's death in 1970 in a seedy California apartment. With this knowledge, Wolff unravels for himself and the reader the enigma that was his father. The book is part memoir, part autobiography, and part biography of Arthur Samuels Wolff—the father—and the heritage which molded him.

With a stammer, Arthur "Duke" Wolff spoke to his son Geoffrey and admonished him for shortcomings, directed him in how to be a gentleman. Duke Wolff expected his son to be a gentleman and nothing less. It was necessary on all occasions to put on airs, and to make a good impression. Duke's opinions were rigid, although he was patient in training his son to his code. He taught Geoffrey how to shoot, box, handle a boat, and appreciate jazz, among other gentlemanly arts. Besides the tips on the proper way a gentleman should handle himself, there were Duke's stories, stories that had been concocted as a self-defense mechanism. These tales were about being schooled at Groton, going on to Yale, then being a fighter pilot in the Eagle Squadron (American volunteers who served in the Royal Air Force), and being involved in gripping World War II adventures. These stories were of a type to make a son proud of his father, but they were all lies, or, at best, half-truths. Duke was a man frustrated by the reality of being a Jew, which he blocked out of his history because he saw no advantage to this reality.

No matter how interesting, harrowing, or intriguing his real history was, it was not good enough for Duke Wolff. It had to be molded to suit his criteria for being "successful." It had to sustain him, to furnish him with the nourishment necessary to survive in a world which he perceived as a threat. This led him to become a confidence man. The result of this choice wreaked havoc on himself, his family, and anyone who came in contact with him. This bluff only lasted for awhile; then it was time to move on to new territory and create new excuses for his lot in life.

The early sections of *The Duke of Deception* are gripping in their descriptions of the actual heritage Arthur Wolff was born into but refused to acknowledge. His father was a noted doctor, the chief of the medical board of Mt. Sinai Hospital when it opened in Hartford, Connecticut, in 1923. His range of expertise was wide, and he held posts as chief of the surgical staff, gynecology, and the laboratory. Yet he was a fierce man, not to be crossed, who had little time for his son. He expressed his affection through material gifts instead of time, thus early instilling in Duke the notion that objects are supposed to make up for the time not spent with an offspring. As the author explains, "My father spent time, the truly precious gift, on me; but even so he thought of possessions as the fundamental, material manifestations of love." Although Geoffrey could feel the love his father felt for him in a gift, such was not the case with Arthur and his father. Arthur was filled with insecurity and fear, which led him to suck his thumb long past the age when he should have outgrown the habit and to stammer when talking. Whatever charm he possessed did not impress his father in the least, so he began to skirt the truth and to create an imaginative world which covered up the fact that his father had for the most part given up on his son. Boarding schools, with all their ironfisted rules, attempted to shape Arthur into what would be considered respectable, but their authority was not tempered with concern. Performance seemed to be the only thing that counted. Arthur became the "Duke," he was going to perform, to put on a show in a guise he created for himself. Imagination was an easy tool to wield for him.

The author next focuses on his mother, Rosemary, and the time he spent with her while preparing this book. Through the use of a tape recorder, endless hours of their question and answer sessions were recorded for Wolff to ponder and analyze. These interviews are an account of Rosemary and Duke's marriage that is honest, unsentimental, and free of bitterness. Rosemary was initially drawn to Duke out of desperation over her own home conditions, which were marred by an intolerable father. She was a dreamer who believed that a big break would come to rescue her from a tragic fate. As a teenager she went to Beverly Hills High School, where she tried to look like Carole Lombard and waited to be "discovered" for the movies; she was selected to be queen of a Rose Bowl float, but there were no calls from the movie studios. When she was sixteen, her family moved to Hartford, Connecticut; not soon after the move, her mother died. Her father was brutal:

"he spanked my mother after dinner every night on the principle that while he didn't wish to trouble himself with specifics, she must have been guilty of *some* misdemeanor that day." By the time Rosemary met Duke, she was ready for anyone to replace her father and take her away from her present set of circumstances. When the author pressed his mother on whether she ever loved Duke, she answered, "No, I never loved him. Not in the conventional sense."

Moving from place to place became common for the Wolff family. Geoffrey was born in Hollywood in 1937, and by the time he was four, the family was headed east for New York. He notes that out of the first twelve years of his life, his father lived with him and his mother for only six. The constant traveling was partly because Duke was always looking for a better job and partly because he was restless. It was like a fever, something that built up within him and took over completely. Escape for him was easier than dealing with hard decisions. Charm and bluff carried Duke from job to job, from one scheme to the next. He had no actual job qualifications; they were part of his created history. The surprising thing is that he was never fired for incompetence. He got into trouble and lost positions because of bad debts and arrogance.

By World War II, Arthur was working for North American and was sent to London as Assistant Chief Designer to insure that the RAF Mustang airplanes ran efficiently. For fourteen months he soaked up English manners only to be tossed out of the country by North American because of credit problems. He moved on to other aircraft companies one step ahead of his past. While working for Bechtel, McCone and Parsons in Birmingham, Alabama, Duke came up with one of his wildest schemes: hiring midgets for aircraft construction because their size would allow them to fit in "places inaccessible to grosser persons." The midgets were ultimately let go, and not soon after, Duke was again out of a job.

The pace of Wolff's narrative throughout the account is even and does not break stride. Whether relating biographical material on his mother or father, recalling his own unique childhood, or looking back as an adult at his father and coming to terms with the relationship, Wolff is sensitive and daring. He never flinches or avoids unpleasant topics, such as the fact that both his parents took lovers; their marriage continued, however, and they had another son, Toby.

The childhood of Geoffrey, and later that of Toby, comprise the core of *The Duke of Deception*. The things that fathers and sons do together, and what they never get a chance to do, swell in importance as the book continues. Wolff acknowledges that his father "instructed" him and that he did this out of love. Duke felt that it was necessary to live well and to have luxury items no matter how much into debt he had to go. He coped as best he could, but friction increased between him and his wife until each took refuge in love affairs that led nowhere. Rosemary wearied of facing people to whom her husband owed money. The family was often forced to change residence and start a new life; Geoffrey and Toby had to make new friends and adjust to new schools.

In the late 1940's, Duke was sent to Turkey by his employer with the stipulation that he stay out of debt or he would be fired; he was accustomed to being warned and receiving ultimatums. He had certain salable skills, but his carelessness always seemed to get him into trouble. Nevertheless, companies still took the bait and hired him, only to fire him later. Faith in the family kept him going; Rosemary threatened to leave him and did so on various occasions, but he never had a doubt that she would return. "He was a sentimental man, and I think he believed that because he loved my mother, he could make her love him back. He believed too in The Family, that we all belonged together."

Wolff has movingly and courageously sifted through his father's life and the lives affected by it, especially his own, and labeled the conflicts that exist between all fathers and sons. It becomes clear that regardless of the shortcomings of either, it is hard to tell where the father leaves off and the son begins. Wolff's personal memoir seeks the answer to this universal dilemma.

Jeffry Michael Jensen

THE DU PONT FAMILY

Author: John D. Gates
Publisher: Doubleday & Company (Garden City, New York). 358 pp. $11.95
Type of work: Biography
Time: 1799 to the present
Locale: Delaware

Offers a basic overview of one of America's most influential and wealthy family's contributions to its state and nation

> Principal personages:
> PIERRE SAMUEL DU PONT DE NEMOURS, the founder of the American branch of the du Pont family
> IRÉNÉE DU PONT, his son
> LAMMOT DU PONT, a Union sympathizer during the American Civil War
> PIERRE DU PONT, his son
> ALFRED DU PONT, both the Company's savior and its rebel

John D. Gates's *The du Pont Family* is an admittedly modest family history that is long on anecdote and praise and short on real critical analysis. Author Gates, a former Wilmington, Delaware, newsman, is, as he notes, partial to the du Ponts, having at one time married into the family and having been on friendly terms with several family members. Believing the du Ponts to have been unduly abused by past critics such as Ralph Nader, he sets out to "right the balance," only to end up overpraising his subjects. Moreover, his book suffers from an overabundance of monetary facts and figures and a corresponding paucity of explanation and elaboration. The most satisfactory way to approach *The du Pont Family*, therefore, is to treat it simply as a collection of fascinating anecdotes bogged down in places by dreary lists of financial information. Nevertheless, Gates's early chapters do a fine job of establishing the cultural and social milieu of the first du Ponts: patriarch Pierre Samuel du Pont de Nemours, who founded the company bearing the du Pont name, and his son Irénée, who advanced its fortunes.

Unlike most immigrants, Pierre Samuel du Pont was financially well-to-do and had a secure position among France's elite when he took his large family from France to the infant United States in 1799. His interest in gunpowder making was not his chief interest; he also had visions of establishing a Utopian colony in the wilderness to be called Pontiana, a venture which proved impossible to fund. Even though the family had considerable resources upon which to draw, funding for the proposed powder works also proved difficult, owing to the sheer magnitude of the project. Irénée du Pont was able to secure the needed money to build sizable facilities in Delaware by borrowing heavily from various sources; and he not only kept the family in business, but was also able to expand its operations. The plant he built was a first-class concern in which worker safety was a priority (although any powder mill of the time was inherently unsafe). Around it, he built a village for his employees in which amenities such as gardens and cow pastures were provided.

Later du Ponts added to the size and scope of the family's commercial empire. Among them was Alfred Victor, Irénée's eldest son, who followed his own concise advice: "Make it safer. Make it better." In spite of a number of explosions (which he deeply lamented) at his powder plants, Alfred got along well with workers, never driving them to strike his company. One possible reason for this rapport was the unusual amount of contact between du Pont children and those of du Pont Company employees, many of whom played and went to school together.

Alfred may have been loved by his workers and may have worked hard at his job, yet it took his energetic brother Henry to "make things happen" in the years preceding and directly following the Civil War. Known for his John D. Rockefeller-like cheapness and shrewdness, "Boss Henry" ruled strictly yet benevolently. Although the approach of the war would divide the du Ponts for the first time, Henry made certain that the company—and his home state of Delaware—were kept in the Union ranks.

The du Pont Company flourished dramatically during the Civil War and was able to pay old debts and expand its operations. After the war, it dominated the powder trade, especially after its directors formed the Gunpowder Trade Association from the "Big Three" powder manufacturers of the day, thus achieving a stranglehold on industry prices. Gates, however, overlooks the ethical implications of this kind of trust-formation, choosing instead to concentrate on other matters.

Still later, in 1902, the du Pont Company grew greatly in power and wealth in the hands of Pierre, Coleman, and "Colonel Henry" du Pont, who took the advice of Alfred I and decided to capture control of their rival powder company, Laflin and Rand, in a $5.5 million deal. Following some intricate (and possibly illegal) maneuverings, the company executed the takeover, after which they controlled the entire powder industry without any competition from other companies. By creating a monopoly, the du Ponts in 1911 fell afoul of the new Sherman Antitrust Act, under which they were sued by the federal government. The outcome of the suit was momentous: du Pont was forced to sell two of its assets, although retaining all of the stock and half of the bonds in those companies as well as all of the smokeless powder division. Out of the proceedings were born the Hercules and Atlas powder companies.

From 1906 to 1916, the du Ponts prospered as never before, due in large part to the Great War of 1914-1919, in which millions of tons of gunpowder were used. By 1916, however, the family was plagued by the falling-out of Frank du Pont's sons, Philip and Eugene, who, in turn, caused other family members to take sides. This dispute signaled the end of the family harmony which had been preserved for over a century, and more importantly, heralded the beginning of an era during which fewer du Ponts would take an active interest in their namesake company, instead abdicating their power to out-siders.

The first du Ponts to arrive in the United States possessed traits that all successful business people share—single-minded dedication to their work and supreme belief in their abilities. Generation after successful generation fol-lowed Pierre's lead, building upon the original gunpowder company base until du Pont became synonymous with chemical production in the United States. Such products as nylon, teflon, dacron, rayon, and a host of others made by the du Pont Company have made life easier and more pleasant for millions of people.

While company building and moneymaking were high on the list of prior-ities, they were not the sole concerns of the du Ponts; public service followed close behind, especially during the first half of the twentieth century, when art museums, public highways, and colleges were freely given to the people of Delaware by various family donors. The tradition of public service began early when Pierre Samuel du Pont, a friend of President Thomas Jefferson, helped negotiate the Louisiana Purchase with Napoleon of France. Bargaining with the Emperor was difficult and tricky, and without du Pont's help, the purchase might never have been accomplished, according to Gates. Almost as important as patriotic acts have been those acts of charity and philanthropy which have made du Ponts the "first citizens" of Delaware, such as their bequeathing to the public some of the most magnificently manicured grounds and gardens in North America: those of the Longworth estate. Other highly visible contributions have been the University of Delaware, which du Pont funding helped establish and maintain; the Unidel Foundation founded by Amy du Pont; the decorative arts gallery at the Winterthur estate; and the Eleutherian Mills-Hagley Foundation which supports a museum and a library of business. In addition, millions of dollars have been used to create con-servation districts, parks, and other outdoor facilities, as well as to revamp Delaware's aging, dilapidated school system and build new schools. For a brief time, old people left without money to exist on were taken care of through du Pont generosity.

In fact, few areas of Delaware life have been left untouched by du Pont influence; Delaware's current governor, Peter (Pete) du Pont, for example, continues the family tradition of conspicuous service. This sense of belonging to Delaware is strong among many family members, although du Ponts have distributed themselves among thirty-seven states, the District of Columbia, and ten foreign countries. Nevertheless, family cohesion is a myth perpetuated by outsiders, who tend to think of the du Ponts as some sort of monolithic group. There may have been a certain amount of family unity at one time, but it has long since vanished.

Hardly any du Ponts remain in the upper echelons of their namesake company today. The last important position (Senior Vice-President) was held by Irénée du Pont, Jr., until his recent retirement; and scarcely any du Pont children are coming up in the ranks. According to Gates, what happened to the du Pont family is similar to what has happened to many large, family-run companies: after a few generations, the young do not care about the business and, having an ample income, begin spending rather than making money. The younger du Ponts, like younger Rockefellers and Mellons, are overshadowed by their awesome forebears, the family tycoons. This does not mean that the current du Pont generation lacks vigor and drive, but simply that its successes do not match in scope those achieved by their grandparents and great-grandparents.

The achievements of the du Ponts during the nineteenth and early twentieth centuries were impressive; equally impressive is the manner in which they assembled their fortunes, which set them apart from some of the other great American families. When great wealth came to them following World War I, the du Ponts followed their earlier inclinations and kept to themselves, living in graceful châteaus in Delaware where they entertained the gentry with restrained elegance, rather than gaudy display. Their preference for Delaware over New York left them open to charges that they were a "provincial" family out of touch with the greater world of glamour and fashion. In addition to their penchant for the quiet and undemonstrative life in Delaware, the du Ponts historically have tended to socialize—and even marry—mainly among themselves. At the same time, however, each family member has wanted to be known for his or her individual achievements rather than for du Pont family achievements, a leaning which accounts for the lack of a family "voice" on political and financial matters. Thus paradoxically, du Ponts associate with one another, yet do not band together in any formal way to make unified decisions. With each generation this tendency toward individualism has grown more intense.

The du Ponts have succeeded in changing the tenor of American life, sometimes in obvious and other times in subtle ways. Pierre Samuel du Pont's gunpowder, for example, helped win the American Revolution, just as Lammot's saltpeter helped win the war for the Union in 1865 and Irénée's influence over Napoleon made America one third larger than she previously had been. And today, the du Pont's production of synthetic fibers, plastics, and chemical additives has contributed to vast changes in contemporary life. Unfortunately, Gates's biography, while full of intriguing observations about the passions, foibles, and successes of the du Ponts, is ultimately lacking in depth. The author's lack of insight, combined with his avoidance of questions of ethics, make the book less of an achievement than it otherwise might have been.

Anne C. Raymer

DUST BOWL
The Southern Plains in the 1930s

Author: Donald Worster (1941-   )
Publisher: Oxford University Press (New York). Illustrated. 277 pp. $14.95
Type of work: History
Time: 1930-1939
Locale: The United States

A pathbreaking integration of environmental and social history that discusses the dust storms that devastated parts of the southern plains during the 1930's

It has been some fifty years since Walter Prescott Webb published his monumental *The Great Plains*. This great work—which studied the social, economic, and institutional adjustment of settlers to this water-short region—was the first to demonstrate comprehensively the interrelationships of ecology and civilization. In the ensuing five decades, the plains environment has held the fascination of historians such as Henry Nash Smith, Eugene Hollon, Edward Everett Dale, and Frederick Rathjen. Scores of books and articles have been published on this semihumid, still relatively underpopulated region — perhaps more than on any other section of the country.

It is surprising that yet another landmark book could be written about this well-trodden subject. However, Donald Worster, Associate Professor of American Studies at the University of Hawaii, has made a major contribution to American history in *Dust Bowl*. This book pushes back the frontiers of conservation and environmental history in many important ways, and it marks the fulfillment of scholarly promise Worster demonstrated in his other fine books, *Nature's Economy* and *American Environmentalism*. With this publication, he makes a strong claim for being the most worthy inheritor of Walter Prescott Webb's mantel.

The *Dust Bowl* is a well-written, thoroughly documented synthesis of human and ecological events. Man's misuse of the fragile plains environment resulted in suffocating "black blizzards" during the 1930's that swept away topsoil and destroyed homes, farms, and entire local economies. America's heartland paid a terrible price for ignoring environmental determinants. An intriguing dimension of the book is that it represents a native son's coming to terms with a catastrophe that touched his own family, since Worster's parents lived through the Dust Bowl years. The author's strong identification with his subject is manifest throughout this moving history, which is illustrated with more than fifty startling photographs of the people and places affected by the holocaust.

Dust Bowl is based not only on extensive library research, but on conversations with farmers, store owners, and government officials who had memories of blowing dust indelibly imprinted on their minds. Its fourteen chapters are divided into five major sections that each offer a different dimension of the subject. The first two, "A Darkling Plain" and "Prelude to Dust," describe the human dislocation that resulted from the 1930's drought and years of abusive agricultural practices. The next two parts, "Cimarron County, Oklahoma" and "Haskell County, Kansas," enable the reader to view the phenomenon in microcosm. Survivors offer firsthand accounts of the storms that virtually tore their communities apart. The final section, "A New Deal for the Land," describes the federal relief programs that attempted to ameliorate suffering and cushion the shock of depression and drought. The efforts of federal conservationists to foster better dryland farming practices is also described in this section.

Since the late nineteenth century, the once-superb grasslands of Kansas, Colorado, New Mexico, Oklahoma, and Texas were plowed and planted with wheat and other crops. A ceaseless tide of farmers migrated to the region and transformed millions of acres of prime grazing land into marginal farmland. Until the 1930's, agriculture in this region was largely successful due to generally adequate rainfall; but when the wet cycle ended and the drought commenced, the disturbed soil blew away—often as much as a foot of this resource that it took nature thousands of years to produce. The resultant storms shielded out the sun as far away as Chicago and dusted the decks of ships hundreds of miles out in the Atlantic Ocean.

Worster suggests that the causes of the Dust Bowl, like those of the Depression, lay in America's economic institutions and ethos. He also implies that this case study of environmental disaster has important implications for our own age, when drought, starvation, and ecological abuse are threatening the world.

Most historians have noted, like Worster, that this darkest moment in the history of the southern plains took some fifty years to make. Rather than viewing it as an aberration caused by unwise men, however, Worster suggests in his Introduction that it "came about because the culture was operating precisely the way it was supposed to." The author's fundamental assumption is that Americans have devastated their richly endowed continent with a ruthless, unrelenting efficiency unmatched by any other civilization. The sodbusters, therefore, literally "busted" the environmental rules that governed the arid region. Many ecological catastrophes such as earthquakes and tornadoes are nature's work; other human tragedies are the products of exploitation, poverty, and disease. In contrast, Worster contends that the Dust Bowl was the inevitable outcome of a culture that deliberately and self-consciously set itself the task of dominating and exploiting the land for all it was worth.

The basic thesis point of the book is that the two major traumas of the 1930's—Dust Bowl and Depression—were interconnected as well as coincidental. Few historians have noted this subtle yet obvious fact. Worster convincingly argues that the same society produced them both for similar reasons and suggests that these two phenomena revealed basic weaknesses in the traditional culture of America: one in ecological terms, the other in economic.

The book further contends that capitalism is the root cause of the ecological genocide that swept the southern plains. The author recognizes that the white pioneers carried with them a cultural baggage of religious ideas, family institutions, and social traditions that either reinforced or in some cases moderated the dominant American economic ethos. In the settler's attitude toward the land, however, capitalism was the major defining influence. Rather than following the Jeffersonian ideal of the self-sufficient, agrarian hero, American agriculturists came to view farming—on the plains and elsewhere—as a business, the object of which was not simply to make a living but to make money. Thus, the notion that there were ecological limits to what man could do to the land was as abhorrent as the idea of economic controls. The plains were extensively plowed and planted and turned into highly mechanized factory farms that yielded huge harvests.

Worster draws an interesting parallel between the Wall Street barons of the 1920's, who ignored the shaky foundations of the stock market, and the plains operators who ignored the environmental limits of their enterprise. The Dust Bowl came about because there was nothing in the plains society to check the growth of marginal commercial farming; every risk was taken to make a profit.

The author cautiously notes that other societies with contrasting economic institutions have blundered into environmental disasters. Nevertheless, he recklessly concludes that the American Dust Bowl of the 1930's suggests that a capitalist-based society has a "greater resource hunger than others, greater eagerness to take risks, and less capacity for restraint." This point seems rather strained. Modern societies throughout the world have ravaged nature regardless of economic philosophies and institutional frameworks. Ecological exploitation seems a common phenomenon of the industrial and postindustrial ages, and perhaps the author should have broadened his conceptual scope.

One of Worster's best chapters deals with the response of writers, artists, and musicians to the Dust Bowl. A circle of brilliant people, such as John Steinbeck, Dorothea Lange, and Woody Guthrie, saw the larger significance of the drought and wind. They found in the dust storms a potent symbol for a wider, national predicament that suggested the need for sweeping reform. The Dust Bowl was seen as a microcosm for an entire continent that had been ravaged by economic ambition. It also marked the death knell of the Jeffersonian assumption that to till the soil was to be in harmony with nature. The lined faces of refugees from the drought were a sharp contrast to the shared belief that farmers were happy, healthy, and virtuous. These victims, often stereotyped as "Okies," became the symbolic archetypes of hard times, a warning to the rest of the nation that the retribution for abusing nature was, as Woody Guthrie called the storms, "a curtain of black rolled down."

The writers and artists were the first to observe that the holocaust was not an act of God. The factory farm, just as its counterpart industries in the cities, were based upon exploitive capitalist principles. Through this image of displaced persons, dust drifts, and dead livestock ran a common thread of tractors, banks, and large-scale commercial farming. In city and town alike, there was a sense of rampant decay and loss, provoked by an economic system that eroded the most cherished human ideals: individual freedom of choice, material sufficiency for all, and a sense of oneness with nature. Thus, the causes of the Dust Bowl were deeply entrenched in the American economic ethos. Throughout the book, Worster adheres to the vision of John Steinbeck and other pessimistic radicals of the 1930's.

The most vivid portions of the book are the two Kansas and Oklahoma case studies. The photographic legacy of the Dust Bowl provided by Arthur Rothstein and Dorothea Lange—two Farm Security Administration photographers—is a national treasure. Their pictures of Cimarron County, in the Oklahoma Panhandle, captured a community that was eroded, depopulated, broke, and on relief. Cimarron was at the very center of the blow area, and the dozens of stark photographs, emphasizing loss and incalculable ruin, became the quintessential drought images. Rothstein's photograph of a man and two boys scrambling to find shelter from the stinging dirt in a half-buried outbuilding, adorns the pages of many American history textbooks. Worster offers ample documentation to prove that the reality was every bit as forlorn and traumatic as the black and white images.

By almost every economic indicator, Cimarron County was in collapse by 1933. The fundamental demise of wheat-based agriculture pulled down everyone in the community who ultimately depended on the farmer and his crops —schoolteachers, implement dealers, railroad workers, grocers, and so on. The 1931 wheat harvest of $1.2 million fell to seven thousand dollars in 1933 and did not recover during the entire decade. By 1939, the value of all crops harvested—wheat, corn, hay, and feed grains—was one-fifth of what it had been ten years earlier. During the same period, the average value of a Cimarron farm declined in worth from $16,600 to $9,200. Banks failed, local businesses signed National Recovery Act agreements to shore up shaky employee wages, and citizens petitioned congress for other emergency aid. In the meantime, the farm population experienced a forty percent decline.

Worster stresses that most Cimarron residents did not espouse national planning, permanent government land regulation, and other long-term reforms to insure that the black blizzards would not reoccur; they simply wanted relief from what were regarded as temporary economic and climatic aberrations. Most asked for and got assistance, but the requests were circumscribed by intense pride and devotion to the principle of self-sufficiency. There were no confessions of failure, and the gospel of work remained enshrined as a positive good. The word "relief" connoted a temporary arrangement in keeping with the American tradition of assisting the victims of accidental circumstances. Thus, the trials of adjustment and survival did not alter basic assumptions.

When the rains returned in the 1940's, Cimarron residents congratulated themselves on having handled the disaster so well. Those who left the area were regarded as misfits and suitcase farmers who had neither the intelligence nor resolve to "stick it out." The farmers, therefore, refused to acknowledge their role in creating or intensifying the dust storms. They regarded the 1930's as a freakish act of God unlikely to strike again. In the midst and wake of disaster, the common human reaction was for the people to cling ever-tightly to their value structures. Prevalent notions of success and the means of achieving it were not shaken, and Dust Bowl denizens soon returned to seeking agricultural and commercial success in traditional ways.

To the Northeast in Haskell County, Kansas, the situation was much the same, even though Sublette, the county's main town, was on the fringes of the Dust Bowl. The flow of grain to the county's grain elevators virtually ceased due to drought and a plunging crop market. Worster makes an interesting comparison between the Kansas farmers and big city unionists. The entry of New Deal rural welfare programs into Haskell's economic life brought about a new type of agriculture. Pressures of circumstances caused farmers to band together to keep afloat. All over the county groups of federal employees inspected farms, disbursed funds, and wrote reports. Extension agents were hired to explain and administer federal programs, and farmers formed pressure groups to keep open the flow of funds from Washington.

The author does an excellent job of defining the basic paradox of the farmers. They regarded themselves as much businessmen as manufacturers; yet they expected the government to assist them to avoid the fate of family-operated factories. The AAA and other relief programs reinforced the agrarian myth that the family farm was a cherished repository of human virtue that should be protected at any cost. Nothing helped the farmer to confront a basic dilemma: whether a business-run small farm was truly compatible with traditional small-scale agrarian values. The welfare state actually prevented the alteration of the nonresident tenure, factorylike business administration, and market speculation that dominated the county. Thus, the ecologically erosive capitalistic monolith was propped up.

Worster uses Haskell County to suggest that even before the storms came the people of the region had not achieved a sense of place and environmental adaptation. There had not been enough time for those things to develop. Since the sod was first broken, communities such as Haskell were subjected to the basic forces of change—mobility, a drive for affluence, and enthusiasm for technological innovation. They failed to adjust themselves to the semiarid plains and were tantalized by urban markets, fashions, and living standards. By the 1930's, Kansas farmers were other-directed hostages of industrial society, rather than inner-directed humans with a strong self-identity and sense of community. Local institutions could not effectively compete against the outward pull of the mass consumer society.

The fundamentally weak societal structure badly fragmented during the Dust Bowl years, but once again the response was to strive even harder to achieve traditional bourgeoisie goals. Basically, the people who stayed sought to end the interlude of environmental upheaval by continuing to exploit the land and turn it into cash. By the end of the 1930's, they were still unable to meet nature on its own terms, acknowledge its limits, and shape their culture by its imperatives.

Worster is curiously harsh in his treatment of the New Deal planners and ecologists that attempted to come to grips with the realities of dryland farming. These dark-suited, academic experts were, according to the author, too timid in their analyses of the problems and proposals for solutions. Most of these reformers were not interested in the preservation of nature and failed to recognize that, if an ecological balance was to be achieved, fundamental economic assumptions would have to be challenged.

Thus, the highly educated agronomists regarded their new techniques as simply an advancement of good businesslike farming. They suggested that operators who accepted their advice would achieve success in the long run. The Dust Bowl to them was simply a case of bad agricultural management practices and poor farming techniques. Remedy the plainsmen's incompetence, they believed, and the crop factories would be overhauled and set going again. The economic rewards of the great plow-up would be restored, but not at the risk of ruining land and capital. New Deal agronomy, therefore, was a renewed commitment to making the land pay off.

Worster claims that New Deal agricultural conservation made little lasting impact on the southern plains, but in this assessment he is wrong. The type of ecologically sensitive reforms suggested by the author were not undertaken, and the area remained committed to expansion. However, the region is a far cry from what it was forty or fifty years ago. Shelterbelts, improved cultivation techniques, groundwater irrigation, terraces, crop rotation, and other methods are used to insure that another Dust Bowl will not reoccur. Rather than succumb to the dictates of nature, the area's residents have adopted techniques that have transformed the plains into an economically stable habitat. The pessimistic conclusions of the author regarding impending environmental disasters seem badly overdrawn. He should have given the plainsmen greater credit for learning from their Dust Bowl experiences.

Worster's strong economic and ecological point of view occasionally distorts his judgment and leads him to shaky conclusions. Nevertheless, these excesses do not seriously detract from his prodigious research, lucid prose, and keen insights into societal and environmental dynamics. The *Dust Bowl* is an important, seminal book. It may inspire a new generation of historical writing on the plains, just as Walter Precott Webb did a half-century ago.

Michael C. Robinson

THE DUST BOWL
Men, Dirt, and Depression

Author: Paul Bonnifield
Publisher: University of New Mexico Press (Albuquerque). Illustrated. 232 pp. $12.50
Type of work: History
Time: 1930-1940
Locale: The Southern Plains

A history of the dust bowl based on local accounts

Paul Bonnifield's *The Dust Bowl* is a bold reappraisal of the history of a region generally viewed as one of the most severely depressed parts of the United States during the 1930's. Notwithstanding unrelenting bouts of catastrophic weather, soil erosion, and the migration of more than 350,000 area residents, Bonnifield contends that the Depression of the 1930's was no more seriously felt in the dust bowl of the Southwest Plains States than in other more urban regions of the nation. The author even suggests that times were actually better in the dust bowl than in other areas. His account is based on newspaper articles, government reports, and interviews with residents with whom he is deeply sympathetic. Ironically, Bonnifield concludes that government programs traditionally credited with forestalling complete economic and social collapse actually contributed to agricultural decline and hindered locally conceived approaches to recovery.

Bonnifield's study begins with a survey of the history of the "heartland" of the dust bowl since the late nineteenth century. He defines the dust bowl geographically as the area encompassing the Northern Texas Panhandle, Northeastern New Mexico, Southeastern Colorado, Southeastern Kansas, and the Oklahoma Panhandle. He portrays the harsh life of the region's pioneers or "Sooners," so named for their rush to claim land prior to official government sale. Despite initial hard times experienced by the Sooners of 1890, abundant rainfall, railroad construction, and extensive oil and gas exploration ushered in an era of prosperity during the first two decades of the twentieth century, dubbed the "good years" by Bonnifield. However, in view of the disastrous events of the 1930's, Bonnifield astutely compares the ultimate fate of many of the Sooners and their descendants with the experience of their predecessors, the native Americans.

In Bonnifield's opinion, the agricultural practices of the Sooners of 1890 and their children were partially responsible for the economic disaster and social dislocation of the Depression era in the dust bowl. During the "good years" of the early twentieth century, the heartland of the dust bowl steadily developed as a wheat-growing area. Spurred on by the opening of an international market during World War I the region's agriculture expanded even more rapidly as a result of technological innovation of the 1920's. The introduction of a revolutionary new plow and the extensive cultivation of specialized wheat and sorghum feed crops such as maize, kafir, and feterita, however, left dust bowl farmers ill-prepared to cope with meteorological calamities and economic hard times of the mid-1930's. Extreme pulverization of farm soil by new implements and misplaced conservation emphasis on water erosion instead of wind erosion left the region easy prey to severe storms known as "rollers" (windstorms) and "snusters" (snow and dust storms), which occurred with terrifying frequency during the 1930's. According to Bonnifield, the introduction of the technically advanced Angel One-Way Plow contributed to the economic malaise by permanently displacing many small independent farmers, tenant farmers, and agricultural workers from the labor force.

Human suffering left in the wake of technological advancements of the 1920's was far surpassed by outright devastation caused by the extreme weather of the 1930's. Bonnifield claims that the heartland of the dust bowl was relatively unscathed by the economic hardship suffered by the rest of the country from the Stock Market Crash of 1929 until 1933. During these years, grain markets remained buoyant, and the cycle of wet weather characteristic of the first two decades of the early twentieth century persisted. In 1931, for example, the region harvested the largest wheat crop ever recorded. However, in a technically impressive section of the book, the author explains the cyclical change to drought that dominated the meteorological history of the dust bowl during the mid- and late-1930's.

Bonnifield's account of the "dirty thirties" starkly portrays the ecological disequilibrium that accompanied and fueled economic hard times in the dust bowl of the mid-1930's. Beginning in 1933, precipitation fell to dangerously low levels, and the worst harvests ever were recorded. Severe wind and snow storms blew dust and dirt from soil pulverized down to the pan by modern plows. The author quotes the editor of Kansas' *Morton County Farmer*, who observed the onslaught of a dust storm in 1934 in vivid terms:

> We can see nothing out our windows but dirt, every time our teeth (or the dentists, or maybe you have your store teeth paid for) come together, you feel dirt and taste it; haven't heard a thing for hours, my ears are full, can't smell, my nose is full, can't walk, my shoes are full but not of feet.

Compounding the misery occasioned by dust storms, plagues of rabbits, rodents, and insects periodically swept the dust bowl during the 1930's. Bonnifield makes a strong point of showing the complete lack of preparedness on the part of the federal government to deal with an economic and ecological crisis of such magnitude. The initial advice of then Secretary of the Interior, Harold Ickes, to disaster stricken farmers to simply abandon their homes, was justifiably perceived as insensitive by area residents. Only in 1935, when six deaths caused by "dust pneumonia" occurred in Baca County, Colorado, did the plight of dust bowl residents attract significant national attention and plans for relief.

Bonnifield sharply criticizes federal approaches and methods of recovery in the dust bowl. Despite its recent history as a wheat producing region, the author notes that government attitudes reflected traditional views of the area as possessing agriculturally marginal land more suited for cattle grazing than for crop cultivation. The Taylor Grazing Act of 1934 heralded the federal government's plan to turn the dust bowl back to grassland and presaged the massive efforts of later "Agricultural Adjustment Acts" both to resettle vast numbers of small "submarginal" farmers on government owned land and to change the region's economy to one based on livestock raising. Similar to the Indians before them, the author concludes that dust bowl farmers were "tempted with removal," "improvement in civilization," and "a shift in land ownership."

In Bonnifield's view, government relief efforts fell short of original expectations and failed to assist those families most in need. Federal jobs programs in small towns and cities in the region were inadequately funded and administered. Many farmers who were resettled found the federal government unwilling to relinquish water and mineral rights to the land and, at times, were denied vital "feed and seed loans" originally promised them. Small farmers of 150 acres or less could ill-afford to repay even the modest terms of low interest federally subsidized loans offered, and many were simply driven from productive farmland by foreclosure. Millions of acres of such farmland were bought by the government at deflated prices while several hundred thousand dust bowl residents, known as "Okies," took to the road.

By the late 1930's, the dust bowl had suffered the worst effects of the Depression and extreme weather and, according to Bonnifield, was on its way toward recovery. He cites the return of more normal patterns of rainfall and improvements in the nation's economy as important factors in recovery, but also attaches considerable significance to the "brave farmers" own response to the crisis. Local farmers did not accept the government's definition of "submarginal" land as one based on size of acreage instead of productivity and were in the vanguard of developing implements and techniques to combat wind erosion. Widespread opposition to the government's attempt to create a pastoral economy in the dust bowl led citizens to vote down the proposed soil conservation districts and thwart the "missionary spirit" of agricultural planners.

Despite the author's assertion that life was no worse in the dust bowl and perhaps better there than elsewhere during the Depression of the 1930's, the evidence he cites in support of this view is unconvincing. Bonnifield quotes a disparate disarray of statistics to support his claim, such as the number of newspaper ads, postal receipts, school closings, and new car sales, but neglects systematic analysis of more fundamental economic indicators such as wages, prices, mortgage foreclosures, and individual bankruptcies. He cites the statistic that the Oklahoma Panhandle registered a net loss of eight thousand people between 1930 and 1940 but does not provide similar statistics for the "heartland" subject to his inquiry. Systematic analysis of federal census records is not indicated in the book, and the author's relatively low estimate of 350,000 emigrants from the region is questionable.

Despite its shortcomings, *The Dust Bowl* is a valuable contribution to the history of our country during one of its bleaker eras. Bonnifield's use of oral history, interviews, and letters of local residents, seems to portray life as it really was during that time and lends the book an overall style of authenticity. *The Dust Bowl* is a tribute to local residents who refused to abandon hope and continued to persevere through hard times.

Sheldon A. Mossberg

EARL WARREN
The Judge Who Changed America

Author: Jack Harrison Pollack
Publisher: Prentice-Hall (Englewood Cliffs, New Jersey). Illustrated. 386 pp. $14.95
Type of work: Biography
Time: 1891-1974
Locale: The United States

The biography of the 14th Chief Justice of the United States Supreme Court, who presided when the Court made some of its most controversial decisions of this century

> *Principal personages:*
> EARL WARREN, Chief Justice of the United States Supreme Court, 1953-1969
> NINA PALMQUIST MEYERS, his wife
> DWIGHT D. EISENHOWER, the President who appointed Warren Chief Justice
> LYNDON B. JOHNSON, the President who appointed Warren to head the commission to investigate the assassination of President John F. Kennedy
> HERBERT BROWNELL, Eisenhower's Attorney General

The biography of a public figure is valuable if it explains and fairly evaluates the person's contributions and if it provides insight about the path to achievement. In addition, a well-written biography can be entertaining reading. Jack Harrison Pollack gives a detailed, colorless account of the events and achievements of Earl Warren but does not make an evaluation of his contributions. Although his treatment is generally sympathetic, it is fair to the extent that facts are accurately presented and some criticisms given. Pollack looks for forces in Warren's life which might explain his career but does not reach a satisfactory answer. Instead, he conveys a sense of puzzlement about the great impact that Warren had upon his time. Pollack suggests that it was Warren's extraordinary commitment to the common virtues that explain his impact.

Certainly, there was nothing unique in Warren's early life that foreshadowed the impact he would have in his adult life. Pollack attempts briefly to develop the theme of "Viking genes" to explain Warren's venturesome spirit, but he soon seems to realize that this theory will not do. To find factors that provide some understanding of the man, the best that can be done is to examine the family background in which Warren grew to maturity. Ordinary virtues were a predominant feature of Warren's childhood; his family environment was marked by love, mutual respect, close companionship, and unity. Much of the unity was provided by the parents' concern for the nurturing of their children. Warren's father took special care to impress upon his son the deprivation of poverty and to devise a plan which would enable him to get an education.

Having grown up in this kind of home, it is not surprising that Earl Warren's own wife and children would be the center of his life. Pollack gives the impression that Warren, although he did not marry until he was thirty-four, gave no thought to such matters until he met and married, in 1925, the widow Nina Palmquist Meyers, his lifelong companion. While Pollack stresses the importance of Warren's family, he portrays only a campaign-poster picture of the ideal family and does not give the reader any sense of the quality or depth of the family relationship. Pollack is doubtless on sound ground when he relates Warren's personal experiences as a father of three daughters to the difficulty he had leading the Supreme Court in the obscenity cases to a position that would stand the test of time, yet later Justices have fared no better in dealing with this issue.

Another contributing factor to Warren's career was the great pleasure he took from his association with others. It was during his years at the University of California at Berkeley that the genial, self-confident, companionable Earl Warren began to emerge. Soon after his graduation from law school, he became president of the Young Lawyers Club and naturally developed an interest in politics. He made contacts which led to his appointment as deputy city attorney of Oakland. From there, he moved to the district attorney's office and became district attorney of Alameda County at thirty-four.

As district attorney, Warren made a reputation as a hard-working, effective prosecutor. Between 1927 and 1930, he was prosecuting corruption in other law-enforcement agencies, and a special target was the sheriff of Alameda County. Warren was frustrated because witnesses would not testify before the grand jury either because they were afraid or were bribed. In an effort to create pressure on the witnesses from the public, he released information that the grand jury had received to the local paper. Although this act violated a basic principle that proceedings before a grand jury are secret, Warren narrowly interpreted the state statute and took the position that the law stated the grand jury could not release testimony but that it did not say anything about the district attorney. This action clearly violated accepted practice, and Pollack reports that Warren was not proud of this episode. Another case of District Attorney Warren's which had irregularities involved the murder of the chief engineer of the SS *Point Lobos*. One of these irregularities was the apparent holding of the accused overnight for questioning without legal counsel—a procedure which was declared unconstitutional by the Supreme Court when Warren was Chief Justice.

These incidents may explain, at least in part, the direction in which Chief Justice Warren took the Supreme Court in a series of extremely controversial decisions regarding due process for criminal defendants under the Bill of Rights. Pollack quotes Warren after his retirement from the Supreme Court as saying that interrogation methods now ruled illegal were common when he was a district attorney. It was perhaps this knowledge that caused Warren to recognize a need for strict procedures to protect criminal defendants.

While district attorney of Alameda County, Warren was active in Republican politics and ran successfully for the office of Attorney General. Soon his political ties and activities extended outside California. He was a delegate to the Republican National Convention in 1928 and 1932, and in 1936, he was chairman of the California delegation. Meanwhile, he was establishing a reputation as an outstanding Attorney General, and in 1940, he was elected president of the National Association of Attorneys General. Following his service as California Attorney General, he was elected Governor in 1942 and reelected for two additional terms. The fact that Governor Warren won both the Democratic and Republican primaries in his race for Governor in 1946 attests to his success and popularity. Being such a strong Governor in the large state of California inevitably made him an important political figure on the national scene. He was temporary chairman and keynote speaker at the 1944 Republican Convention, although he refused to be the vice-presidential candidate.

Although Warren had rejected second place on the ballot with Thomas Dewey in 1944, he was Dewey's vice-presidential running mate in 1948. Not only was the outlook better for the Republicans that year, but Warren, who had some presidential aspirations, also understood that if he ever expected to be the party's nominee for president, he could not refuse the vice-presidential spot in 1948. As the 1952 National Convention approached, Dwight Eisenhower and Robert Taft were the front-runners for the Republican nomination. Warren again headed the California delegation and hoped a deadlock would open the way for his nomination. However, when such a deadlock did not occur, he swung his support to Eisenhower and campaigned for him.

Pollack indicates that although he campaigned for Eisenhower, Warren was aware of differences in their political ideas. Nevertheless, when he decided not to run for a fourth term as Governor of California, he informed Eisenhower and his aide Herbert Brownell of his decision. Pollack suggests Warren's future depended upon a good position in the Eisenhower Administration such as Attorney General or Supreme Court Justice. Thus, when Eisenhower informed Warren that he was appointing Brownell Attorney General, he also told him that he planned to offer him the first available vacancy on the Supreme Court. At the time, there was speculation that Associate Justice Felix Frankfurter would soon resign.

There had been conjecture about the role Richard Nixon played in Earl Warren's elevation to the Supreme Court. It has been suggested that it was to Nixon's political advantage to get Warren on the Court in order to remove him from his own path to the presidency. Pollack relies upon the authority of Justice William O. Douglas for his information of the visit of Vice-President Nixon and Senate Majority Leader William F. Knowland to President Eisenhower on behalf of Warren's appointment to the Supreme Court. Among other reasons, they argued that the appointment would remove Warren as an obstacle to Eisenhower's renomination in 1956. Yet the series of events leading to the appointment, which are carefully detailed, indicate that Warren and Eisenhower agreed that Warren's position in the party and his campaign efforts on Eisenhower's behalf entitled him to a high-level appointment. Therefore, it was natural that Eisenhower promised Warren to appoint him to the first vacancy on the Supreme Court.

As it turned out, the first vacancy did not occur as a result of Frankfurter's resignation but because of the death of Chief Justice Fred M. Vinson. Pollack recounts the details of Eisenhower's deliberations, which included the possibility of elevating an Associate Justice to the position of Chief Justice and appointing Warren Associate Justice. Warren, however, insisted that he had been promised the first vacancy. Eisenhower sent Brownell to California to meet with Warren, and even though there is a difference of opinion about the length of the meeting, Pollack reports that Warren held out for Chief Justice. Despite this, Pollack is reluctant to present Warren as actively seeking the appointment and prefers to imply that it simply came to him.

The political background and skills which led to Warren's appointment to the Court also explain much of his behavior as Chief Justice. Pollack correctly stresses that Warren was not an outstanding legal scholar and that explanations for his achievements on the Court must be sought elsewhere. For example, the amazing unanimity of the decision in the controversial school desegregation case of *Brown* v. *Board of Education* attests to his political skill and leadership ability. However, it was not the school desegregation case that Warren considered the most important decision of the Court during his tenure, but the reapportionment cases. Again, a politician who had run for office many times and had served three terms as Governor would appreciate the importance of the apportionment of representation. So great was Warren's faith in fair representation that he felt the problems of racial discrimination would have been avoided if a "one man, one vote" system had been in effect.

Chief Justice Earl Warren had a great impact on his times, not only because of the Supreme Court decisions but also because of his leadership of the commission to investigate the assassination of President John F. Kennedy. This assignment did not come automatically to a Chief Justice of the Supreme Court, but was one which President Lyndon Johnson prevailed upon Warren to take in addition to his other duties. No doubt Johnson was motivated by a desire to have a person of the highest prestige head the commission and thereby give credibility to the report. Pollack recounts the criticisms of the handling of the investigation. The most important were the failure to examine the FBI and CIA files and the refusal to allow other members of the commission to examine the pictures and X rays of Kennedy after he was shot. The commission was also criticized for its less than thorough interrogation of Marina Oswald. Pollack concludes that, despite the weaknesses of some procedures of the commission, the determination that only Lee Harvey Oswald was involved in the assassination has not been successfully refuted.

Although Pollack presents a reliable and factual account of Earl Warren's life, his book falls short of depicting a judge who changed America. He does not adequately evaluate Warren's contributions or analyze the impact he had upon his times.

Doris F. Pierce

THE EDWARD HOAGLAND READER

Author: Edward Hoagland (1932-   )
Edited, with an Introduction, by Geoffrey Wolff
Publisher: Random House (New York). 399 pp. $12.95; paperback $4.95
Type of work: Essays

A richly varied selection from the work of one of America's finest essayists, with subjects ranging from New York City to the wilderness of British Columbia

Essayists characteristically come late to the discovery of their gift. William Hazlitt was thirty-five, the author of several philosophical and political treatises, when, having finally given up his ambition to become a painter, he began to find his vocation as an essayist. De Quincey was thirty-six when he began his harried career as a professional writer; to feed his eight children he churned out hundreds of essays, sketches, reviews, and assorted journalism, including the quirky, utterly individual pieces for which he is still read. Edward Hoagland was thirty-four and had recently published his third novel— a "failure," he has said, both critical and artistic—when, in the summer of 1966, he began *Notes from the Century Before*, a journal covering two months and many miles in British Columbia. Since then he has published three collections of essays—*The Courage of Turtles* (1971); *Walking the Dead Diamond River* (1973); *Red Wolves and Black Bears* (1976)—and another travel book, *African Calliope: A Journey to the Sudan* (1979). Unremarkable as a novelist, Hoagland has found himself as an essayist, as an observer of the familiar and the exotic: he is one of the finest contemporary American writers.

For *The Edward Hoagland Reader*, Geoffrey Wolff has selected twenty-one essays from the three previously published collections, and he has also added three brief excerpts from *Notes from the Century Before*. Although Hoagland is often labeled a naturalist, *The Edward Hoagland Reader* is more or less equally divided between nature pieces—on bears, wolves, mountain lions; on the wilderness of British Columbia—and pieces on other subjects, including the routine of a tugboat, the fate of the circus, and partisan accounts of New York City. Some of the most ambitious essays in the book have no easily identifiable journalistic subject. (It is no surprise to read in Wolff's excellent Introduction that Hoagland is that rare beast, a professional writer who does not write on "assignment.") Essays such as "Home Is Two Places" and "Other Lives," which Wolff has chosen to begin and end the book, framing his other selections, are complex meditations on contemporary life, virtuoso pieces in the manner of modernist fiction: Hoagland shifts focus abruptly, suppressing the connections between topics, trusting the reader to fill in the blanks. *The Edward Hoagland Reader* is a substantial, representative selection, an excellent introduction to Hoagland's work.

Hoagland's great gift is to see clearly, and describe what he sees so that his readers see too. This gift is not common. "Hundreds of people can talk for one who can think," Ruskin said, "but thousands can think for one who can see." For Hoagland as for Ruskin, perception has absolute value. The object of the perception does not matter as much as the fact that something is being freshly seen. Thus, in the course of comparing his father to Eisenhower (in whose Administration his father worked), Hoagland writes that "each had a Chinese face lurking behind the prosaic American bones which materialized inchmeal as he aged and died." This perception does not lead to any conclusion, does not have a point, one might say, but it creates the shock of recognition: one sees the aging Eisenhower with uncanny vividness. Such odd, surprising, wonderfully accurate perceptions are likely to turn up on any page of Hoagland's.

If Hoagland is a master of the odd detail, his vision is equally adequate to sustained, large-scale description. To demonstrate this power, it would be sufficient to quote any sizable chunk from "River-Gray, River-Green," a description of thirty thousand salmon, "each as long as my arm, stymied and dying in the droning roar" of the Tahltan River in British Columbia. In this excerpt from *Notes from the Century Before*, Hoagland's excellence is not just a matter of precision, although that is no small feat: he has to deal freshly with a subject which has often been described and filmed, and he has to avoid sentimentality. He meets the first challenge with striking similes which, however surprising, are never merely verbal fireworks obscuring their ostensible subject. The leaping salmon "were like paper airplanes thrown into the hydrant blast." The language always urges the reader to *see*: "These were the sockeyes. Their bodies have a carroty tint on top of the back at spawning time, often quite bright, and their heads turn a garish green. They wear a lurid mascaraed look, a tragedian's look, as if dressed for an *auto-da-fe*." While he doesn't hesitate to express his feelings—"I felt like a witness at a slow massacre"—Hoagland banishes sentimentality with smart-guy similes and colloquial language. Feasting eagles revel "like bank robbers who had broken into the vault"; feasting gulls sit by the water, "so fat that by now they ate only the eyes."

For a writer who has nothing more sensuous to work with than words on paper, description requires more than visual imagination, more than a perceptive eye. The sound and texture of his words, their heft, but above all, the rhythm of his sentences will determine the extent to which the writer succeeds in making his readers *see*. Just how verbal textures and rhythms work is a mystery, but Hoagland—like any gifted writer—knows *what* works, and the shapes of his sentences would not be despised by any contemporary novelist. He is an artist in his own territory. This quality of his work again requires quotation; a brief passage will have to suffice. In a long essay called "Americana, Etc.," Hoagland describes the Orleans County Fair in Vermont, which included several "cunnilingual girlie shows." Here, Hoagland is describing the operator of two of the shows: "He was stocky, in his forties, and enjoyed confiding to the crowd how tough the life was on the girls, a pair of whom were at his side like two leashed minks, dancing in the heat and cold." How the rhythm of this passage, particularly of the last phrases, helps to deliver all that Hoagland sees on that stage is difficult to specify, but any reader should feel the effect.

As an artist, Hoagland works in the no man's land of the personal essay. If his essays are more distinguished by their fidelity to the natural world than are the works of his great predecessor, De Quincey, they are nevertheless personal essays, often as richly idiosyncratic in their language and as confidently scornful of abecedarian logic as "The English Mail Coach." Moreover, Hoagland has turned his observer's eye on himself with a candor which exceeds that of *Confessions of an English Opium Eater*.

It is possible to piece together a kind of autobiography from the essays collected in *The Edward Hoagland Reader*: along with the mundane details, such as the schools he attended—Deerfield Academy and Harvard—Hoagland also informs the reader about his first love affair, "with a Philadelphian, a girl of twenty-seven." He came by stages, he says, to "the habit of beating her briefly with my belt or hairbrush before we made love, a practice which I have foregone ever since." Such confessions—rather cool reports, that is, in which Hoagland observes Hoagland's intimate moments, however unflattering they might be—are never prolonged, but crop up abruptly here and there. The same essay—"The Threshold and the Jolt of Pain"—includes Hoagland's longest discussion of his stuttering: "Being in these vocal handcuffs," he concludes, "made me a desperate, devoted writer at twenty."

By his own account, Hoagland is an exemplary modern artist, alienated from his fellows, cooly detached from himself—and he has the artist's wound: his apparently incurable stutter; but too often, Hoagland seems to be merely cashing in on the vogue for lacerating but juicy revelations. This exploitation of intimacy is also evident when he speculates in a rambling way about his father's sexual life: his father "probably was sexually faithful, although I think he fooled himself about the nature of certain avuncular relationships he had; when one young woman married he tore her honeymoon picture in half."

More is at stake in such passages than an acquiescence to current fashions. Hoagland has a commitment to what might be called the ugly truth. In "The Problem of the Golden Rule," he describes his hesitance to intervene when he saw a baby-sitter "or whatever she was" standing next to a phone booth, "feasting her eyes" on the spectacle within: her charge, a boy of two or three, trapped in the booth, unable to open the spring door, screaming in panic and thumping the glass. Now the characteristic Hoagland touch: "I was seething, partly because I found that some of the woman's sexual excitement had communicated itself to me, which was intolerable, and partly because my cowardice in not interfering was equally outrageous."

What are Hoagland's implications here? By identifying a sexual element in this little drama, Hoagland proves his willingness to tell the ugly truth—and proves his sophistication. (Would another observer have seen "sexual excitement" in the woman's cruelty? Was it there to be seen?) However, at a deeper level, the ugly truth implied by Hoagland's narrative is this: there was a kind of complicity, he suggests, between himself and the woman. This is a peculiar way to arrive at the Golden Rule. Hoagland concludes the essay by mentioning an incident in which he did take action, "gesticulating sternly" to drive some robbers off a nearby rooftop. "They waved back as they went down the stairs," he says, "like people who've escaped a fall." This curiously sentimental conclusion reinforces the theme of complicity which runs through the essay; it is not to be confused with "there but for the grace of God go I." Hoagland's "ugly truth" allows him to blur the question of moral responsibility in a manner both cynical and sentimental. We are all in one boat, like Hoagland and the robbers who wave back at him.

Yet at its best, Hoagland's work reawakens the child's sense of wonder at the great world, touches deep memories and longings. Millions of children have read about tugboats but few have ever seen one. Hoagland spends a day on a tugboat every year. He has worked in the circus. He has followed the routine of a wildlife biologist whose whole ambition is to understand bears—he practically lives with them. (Another child's dream magically fulfilled.) Wherever he goes, Hoagland describes what he sees, both with clarity and in his own lively idiom.

John Wilson

EDWARD VII
Prince and King

Author: Giles St. Aubyn (1921-   )
Publisher: Atheneum Publishers (New York). Illustrated. 555 pp. $19.95
Type of work: Biography
Time: The mid- to late-nineteenth and early twentieth centuries
Locale: Great Britain and Continental Europe

A painstakingly researched and deftly written study of Edward VII which emphasizes his intelligence and diplomatic abilities while at the same time showing him to be the jolly and robust king of legend

> *Principal personages:*
> EDWARD VII, King of England and Emperor of India, 1901-1910
> QUEEN VICTORIA, his mother, Queen of England, 1837-1901
> PRINCE ALBERT, his father, Prince of Saxe-Coburg-Gotha and the Queen's Consort
> KAISER WILHELM (WILLIAM II), Kaiser of Prussia and Germany, 1888-1918

Currently head of Eton School's Department of History and the author of such well-received studies as *The Royal George: The Life of H. R. H. Prince George, Duke of Cambridge, 1819-1904* and *Infamous Victorians*, Giles St. Aubyn lends credence to the long-held popular notion that England's Edward VII was a large-souled monarch who ably led his nation and Commonwealth of colonized nations into the twentieth century. Certainly it cannot be said that St. Aubyn hides his enthusiasm for King "Bertie," whom he regards much as the anonymous balladeer did who called him "a King . . . from head to sole,/ Loved by his people one and all."

Even the most cursory glance at the author's eighteen-page selected bibliography will convince the reader that St. Aubyn knows his subject in considerable depth. His biography of Edward is authoritative without being dull and analytical without being nitpicking. In it, he proves that Edward summoned sufficient courage and insight to rid himself of those suffocating constrictions of spirit foisted on him by his father, Prince Albert, and mother, Queen Victoria. Instead of turning out to be the prig his father hoped he would be, he became a pleasure-seeker; rather than a solemn utterer of pieties, he became an ebullient, charming statesman; rather than a Germany worshiper, he preferred France; and rather than be a stay-at-home like his mother, he cultivated a love of travel and outdoor life. As a result, Edward outstripped his emotionally and physically cloistered parents, truly becoming the hale, lively king of legend.

As the author points out, it was incredible that young Albert Edward (as he was known during childhood and his regency period), so emotionally vulnerable as a youth, could survive the death of his beloved father and, even more remarkably, the emotional freeze that set in between him and his mother.

Victoria, looking for someone to blame for her adored Albert's early death, found her scapegoat in Albert Edward; she spurned his affection and often chose to ignore him completely. The atmosphere of the great houses and palaces in which he grew up was gloomy, if not funereal; and this gloom, combined with Victoria's sour cast of mind, made life for the boy hard to bear. Yet bear it he did; astonishingly, he did not turn into himself and shut out the rest of the world, but insistently looked to the time when he could escape Victoria and her melancholia.

The Queen's already substantial consternation about her son increased when she discovered that her tutors could do little with him; as a student, he seemed to be a failure. What he lacked in scholarly diligence he made up for in what his companion, Charles Carrington, later was to call "pluck," a characteristic he was to display for the rest of his life.

Despite the Queen's discontent with her son's progress at school, she did allow him to venture abroad so that he might become better acquainted with the ancient splendors of Rome and other things he avoided studying about. It was on such a tour as the one taken in 1859 that Edward learned not only to behave properly in the presence of foreign dignitaries but to appreciate the elegance, wit, and beauty of women, a pleasure frowned upon by Her Royal Majesty. Edward's high spirits and ready jests made him the center of attention wherever he traveled, whether it was to visit Austria's Crown Prince Metternich or King Louis Philippe of France. His curiosity about the countries he visited flattered his hosts, most of whom hoped to see more of him. Needless to say, the grand tours of Europe released the young heir apparent from the tyranny of his mother and taught him to appreciate the wider world beyond Windsor and Buckingham Palace. Additionally, the friendships he made while on tour would come in handy when he did become King.

After leading a fairly restricted life at Oxford University, Edward looked for a likely marriage partner at age sixteen and found her in the person of Princess Alexandra, daughter of Prince Christian of Denmark. As always, St. Aubyn does a fine job of portraying all of the treachery and behind-the-scenes maneuvering that went on to get Alexandra and "Bertie" together (Queen Victoria did not approve of her son's marrying someone other than a German). The wedding of 1863 served to unite members of European monarchies, most of whom were related to one another, in a way similar to that of Edward's grand funeral in 1910, their last happy meeting before world war struck. Yet even in 1863, certain cracks in Europe's monarchical system were apparent.

Especially apparent and stressed throughout this biography was the rift between Albert Edward and his nephew, the mercurial William II of Germany, who was, from the start, jealous of England and all things English. St. Aubyn makes clear that it was William (later Kaiser Wilhelm) who was responsible for creating tensions between Germany and England which were to lead to World War I; in this, he is being fairly traditional in approach, for many historians blame William's this-way-that-way attitude for driving nations to war. Like other historians, St. Aubyn finds that the reason behind William's inconsistent behavior was his feeling of inferiority when around his uncle.

Edward for some time had felt that the German court was excruciatingly dull; William's inconsistent actions and angry charges made him even less inclined to visit Germany which, in turn, caused William to become more insulted and rejected. Such antagonism toward Germany would have infuriated Edward's teutonic father, for Prince Albert thought of practically nothing else save England, Germany, and the ties that he imagined they enjoyed.

As Edward developed into a social lion, he visited France with increasing enthusiasm, treating that nation as a kind of spiritual homeland. When he was elsewhere (especially visiting the drab, lifeless courts of the Scandinavian monarchs), he longed for the voluptuous pleasures of Paris. Such feelings were shared by Princess Alexandra, who also appreciated the gaiety of Continental life. It was France that gave Edward his first opportunity to be a playboy regent in the manner of forebear William IV. Rather than disapprove of his conduct, a good portion of his British public loved him for it, finding in him the common touch missing in his austere, aloof mother. Abroad, he made countless friends among aristocrats and commoners alike. As a diplomat, he had no peer; in fact, as St. Aubyn notes, it was "Bertie" who reversed the negative attitude the French public had maintained toward Great Britain by voicing his approval of republicanism and French culture. (Of course, such praise for France met with disgust in Berlin.)

Although other historians may think differently, St. Aubyn believes Edward to have been an open minded appreciator of all classes of people, much to the chagrin of some of those close to him. His subjects' opinions were of importance to him, and he took the trouble to listen to what they had to say. Such consideration made him one of the most fondly remembered modern rulers of Britain. As Prince and King, Edward listened not only to fellow British citizens but also to his overseas subjects. As St. Aubyn has it, Edward (no doubt because of all the traveling he did in India and elsewhere in the Empire) was as popular in the colonial world as he was at home. It was this personal esteem which that world had given him that he converted into respect for the "mother country." Although St. Aubyn does not say it, he implies that without Edward's personal popularity working for Britain, the Empire might not have held together as long as it did in this century.

Living as he did during what has been termed the "British century" (which actually did not end until 1914 when World War I broke out), Edward was able to view the world as few persons have ever been able to view it. A modern day Alexander the Great, Edward surveyed an Empire upon which, in fact, "the sun never set"; his pride in that Empire was deep and abiding and he felt privileged to live at the "floodtide" of British imperialism.

On the domestic scene, Edward took an active role in home affairs, conferring on taxes or parliamentary politics with various politicians. Conservative by nature, Edward distrusted liberals and liberalism and yet was able to keep in contact with all of the eminent figures of his age: William Gladstone, Benjamin Disraeli, Arthur Balfour, Lord Randolph Churchill, Henry Campbell-Bannerman, and even the greatest liberal of them all, David Lloyd George. Most at home with Gladstone, whom he highly regarded, Edward felt least comfortable with Lloyd George, whom he believed to be a Welsh radical. Therefore, unlike Queen Victoria, who kept herself far from what she considered the unseemly turmoil of the political arena, Edward relished what was going on in Parliament and served as an avid adviser to whomever needed his advice. For the most part, leaders of Parliament were happy to have such assistance from their monarch.

After Prince Albert's death in 1861, Edward had to wait forty years to become King, the longest wait any regent in British history had endured. His reign, though short (1901-1910), was later to be looked back upon with considerable nostalgia as a time of peace and relative prosperity when England was unquestionable ruler of the waves, the world's leading power, and colonialist without peer. Germany and the United States were still emerging powers, formidable yet not as powerful as Great Britain. As King, Edward sought to reconcile the sometimes feuding members of his family, some of whom were powerful monarchs themselves. Ominously, it was Wilhelm of Germany, his nephew, who was the most difficult to calm, since, as was previously noted, Wilhelm hated Edward and felt inferior to him. So it was with considerable distress that Edward viewed not only his own problem with Wilhelm but also Wilhelm's problem with cousin "Nicky," Czar Nicholas of Russia.

Sometimes, however, Edward was able to make diplomatic headway. In 1904, for example, Edward made every attempt to better Anglo-Russian relations (which had been poor for some time) by meeting with Baron Isvolsky of the Czar's court. Later, in June, 1908, he paid a visit to Czar Nicholas himself, despite a loud outcry from outraged subjects who saw the Czar as the embodiment of foreign treachery and deceit.

To St. Aubyn, the King could never be accused of any lack of conviction or courage, for whenever Edward decided something was important enough to argue for, he argued, no matter how powerful was his opponent. From this biography, one gathers that it was Edward alone who, for a time, managed to glue together the bickering nations of Europe—a difficult and painful task at best. To do it, he used his charm and considerable negotiating ability.

With all of the diplomatic skill in the world, however, it would not have been possible for Edward to keep Kaiser Wilhelm content. Wilhelm meant for Germany to be the new Britain and thereby to end the nagging feelings of inferiority that tormented him. He built upon the army and navy created by former leader Count von Bismarck, and threatened both France and Britain with them. Edward, though appalled by his nephew's warlike preparations, did not—and, to be fair, could not—anticipate the horrors that Wilhelm's war would bring about. For, as a product of the relatively serene nineteenth century, Edward could not envisage such things as the rise of socialist revolution, bringing with it the deaths of Czar Nicholas and his family, nor the destruction power-mad Germany would wreak upon Belgium and northeastern France.

Though he did support the Royal Navy's refurbishing, Edward, for his part, chose to cling to diplomacy of the most personal sort to keep nation from fighting nation. When he died in 1910, a way of life came to an end and, as it has become clichéd to say, a new era was ushered in. While alive, Edward personified the British nation as it wanted to be perceived: alert, robust, adventurous, and forthright in its dealings with the world. Dead, he personified the spirit of an age long on ceremony, decorum, and decency and short on bad manners, sword-waving fanaticism, and democracy.

St. Aubyn's life of Edward is superbly researched and masterfully written. Though at times overpraising Edward and failing to investigate his darker side, the author has given readers a remarkable account of the Prince and King who ruled (for the most part, at least) wisely and well.

John D. Raymer

THE EIFFEL TOWER AND OTHER MYTHOLOGIES

Author: Roland Barthes (1915-1980)
Translated from the French by Richard Howard
Publisher: Hill and Wang (New York). 152 pp. $9.95
Type of work: Essays

A collection of essays which uncover the layers of meaning structured beneath the surface of twenty-nine "myths"

Accused of being "a geyser of pishposh" and "famous for remarks which mean nothing," and acclaimed as "one of the foremost literary critics in France" and "a brilliant polemicist, a formidable rhetorician, an ingenious, mercurial man of letters," Roland Barthes has indeed had a significant impact on the modern literary world. The tragedy of his death early in 1980—the result of an automobile accident—will not be soon forgotten. If not for being the forerunner of French structuralist theory, a respected literary critic (a label he would have gladly relinquished), a leading practitioner of *la nouvelle critique*, or the authority on semiological linguistics, Barthes most certainly will long be remembered as the perceptive and lucid author of *Mythologies* (1972), *A Lover's Discourse* (1978), and, now, *The Eiffel Tower and Other Mythologies*.

Barthes wrote the twenty-nine essays collected here in a three-year span from 1954 through 1956. A portion of these essays appears in *Mythologies*, which stands in refreshing contrast to his early theoretical works, *Writing Degree Zero* and *Elements of Semiology*. Also included in *Mythologies* is the title essay, "The Eiffel Tower," which Barthes originally wrote as an introduction to a volume of photographs of the Tower. *The Eiffel Tower and Other Mythologies* makes available for the first time to English-speaking readers "The Eiffel Tower" and the complete "mythologies" series.

In the title essay, the reader finds an adoring, even sentimental Barthes discussing "the universal symbol of Paris." He begins with the simple statement "the Tower is friendly" and proceeds to unfold its myriad meanings. A structure touched by every Parisian glance, it is "reduced to that simple line whose sole mythic function is to join, as the poet says, *base and summit*, or again, *earth and heaven*." Beyond its mythic function as an object, "it becomes a lookout in its turn when we visit it. . . . The Tower is an object which sees, a glance which is seen." Barthes uses a system of polarities to define the Tower, and it functions both as the extremes and as the unifying force. Hence, for Barthes, the Tower is a "total monument," at once a glance, object, metaphor, and symbol. Yet to complete this "infinite circuit of functions," the Tower, he claims, "must escape reason." The Eiffel Tower represents pure meaning—it exists as a playground for the imagination. "The first condition of this victorious flight is that the Tower is an utterly *useless* monument." Barthes explains later that "use never does anything but shelter meaning."

"The Eiffel Tower" displays Barthes at his best. Devoid of the abstruse language and neologisms which belabor his theoretical works, Barthes rejoices here in divulging the multilayered meanings of a well-known landmark. He tantalizes and spurs the imagination with his acute perceptiveness and his spontaneous insights. Affectionately rendered unforgettable by Barthes's formidable intellect and poetic ability, the image of this monument will always "be something other and something much more than the Eiffel Tower."

In his other essays, Barthes's topics range from major events such as the Tour de France bicycle race, the Paris flood of 1955, and the Billy Graham crusade in France, to political rhetoric and international affairs, to literature, language, and the arts (a Buffet painting, the New Theater, a Marlon Brando film). The unifying factor behind each of these phenomena is that they are all "mythologies"—phenomena whose multilayered meaning is not obvious, not "clearly apparent." Mythologies are "empty realities" for Barthes. Their assumed, simple definitions hide the true underlayer of complex meanings. Barthes finds societal mythologies too easily ignored, or worse, accepted at their face value; it is such intellectual laziness that Barthes combats in these essays. In each, he confronts the obvious and reveals the underlying structure of meaning in an effort to replenish that "empty reality."

There are myths of sentiment, myths of judgment, and myths of reason; there are myths created when a "difference" or "meaning" is reduced to a "universality." Barthes attributes this reduction to the machinations of the petit bourgeoisie—he makes no attempt to subdue his Marxist philosophies. He states, "the petit-bourgeois flourish consists in eluding qualitative values, in opposing processes of transformation by a statics of equalities." An easy system of simplification and static generalities, "the whole petit-bourgeois mythology implies the refusal of alterity, the exaltation of 'kind.'" We live in a world that changes constantly and, for Barthes, the inquisitive, open mind accepts change instead of evading it; change, differences, progress, and decay are all part of nature. Unfortunately, Barthes falls prey to his own criticism of static thought when he too easily includes the bourgeoisie in his attacks on "mythologies." However, his bias rarely interferes with either his astute insights or the development of the text.

Barthes's training as a semiologist and linguist provides a solid background for the essays dealing with word myths and language. In the powerful and perspicacious essay "African Grammar," Barthes exposes the meaning of a few terms used in political rhetoric—"words [that] have no relation to their content, or else a contrary one." Political language mollifies and obfuscates reality. Amplified nouns and destroyed verbs all serve in an ingenious political cover-up. In his dogged search for meaning, Barthes powerfully identifies that which obscures it. A primary obstacle in the search lies in the concept of "good sense." "Good sense is the watchdog of petit-bourgeois equations: it blocks up any dialectical outlets, defines a homogeneous world in which

we are at home, sheltered from the disturbances and the leaks of 'dreams.'"
We protect ourselves from the rigors of thought and change through good
sense. "We know the war against intelligence is always waged in the name
of *good sense*." Again and again Barthes warns us against using "simplicity,"
"innocence," and "good sense" as excuses for not having ideas, intellectual
laziness, and for falling into the "admirable security of nothingness."

Practicing the flexibility of mind he preaches, Barthes does not confine his
essays to forceful assaults on the everpresent "mythologies." "The Eiffel
Towel" reveals his adoration of certain myths and exposes a sensitive, even
whimsical, tone. Turning disaster into festivity in "Paris Not Flooded,"
Barthes draws a parallel between the mobilization and cooperation of the
citizens to Noah's Ark: "For the Ark is a happy myth: in it humanity takes
its distance with regard to the elements, concentrates itself and elaborates
the necessary consciousness of its powers, making disaster itself provide evidence that the world is manageable." Barthes defends New York City against
false accusations in "Buffet Finishes Off New York," another essay which
reveals a playful, spontaneous, and humorous side of Barthes, who has often
been described as cold, dry, and didactic.

No matter what tone Barthes employs or what approach—supportive or
combative—he chooses, he always demands the close attention of his readers.
Thinking is a commendable activity not only for writers but for readers as
well. A passive reader accepts the myth that literature has only one dimension—the meaning which appears on the surface. For Barthes, reading is as
much an activity as writing and is a crucial process in the creation of literature.

Thus, it is understandable that Barthes's work is not considered easy reading. Structurally similar, all the essays of the collection develop, as it were,
inwardly. They are not direct syntagmatic chains of events in which the narrative moves through space and time; instead, each essay is one complete
digression. The sentence and paragraph structures varying from short statements to long passages (some sentences constitute more than twenty lines)
layered with signification, underline the sense of digression. Barthes takes
an "event" (be it the Eiffel Tower or a famous murder trial) and muses,
meditates, explores, and examines that "event." In the process, he destroys
facile, superficial boundaries until the event can no longer be perceived in
a single dimension. Barthes leads the reader through the obvious exteriors
and into perceptive observation with a voice that is personal (the narrative
stance is always in the first person and generally plural) yet authoritative,
accessible yet intellectual. He provides the strong lead of a master teacher,
while continuously insisting upon the reader's aggressive participation. He
challenges readers to use their powers of insight and instinct to broaden their
point of view, even (or especially) when regarding the most common phenomena.

Barthes's erudite theories of literary criticism and language are overshadowed by the swift and spontaneous insights of the essays. Barthes is an unconventional critic, author, and reader whose cogent observations reveal a new world of understanding. Long after his systems and theories have been confined to academic history, his insistence on mental activity, piercing and perceptive insights, and the pleasure of literature will remain to enhance our thinking.

Dawn Paige Dawson

THE EIGHTH DAY OF CREATION
The Makers of the Revolution in Biology

Author: Horace Freeland Judson
Publisher: Simon and Schuster (New York). Illustrated. 686 pp. $15.95
Type of work: Science

A recent history of molecular biology which not only deals with scientific research but also with the ethical questions and personal stories involved

Judson's book is surely monumental. Claiming to be a rather extensive popular scientific history of three decades of progress in molecular biology, it is successful. The book has three major units—one each on DNA, RNA, and protein. These substances are large macromolecules found in the cells of living organisms: they are intimately and essentially involved in biological function. Judson sees correctly that an important part of the recent revolution in biology is the successive refinement to smaller and smaller levels where function is related *specifically* to structure. The three major units of Judson's book illuminate the diverse strands of differing lines of research; at least five different scientific disciplines were involved in the attainment of our present understanding—physical chemistry, crystallography, genetics, microbiology, and biochemistry. Thus, things that were obvious to a person coming from one disciplinary perspective were not so to another. An example would be the approach of George Gamov, who came from physics to molecular biology, and whose papers, while erratically brilliant, were seen to be fundamentally wrong in their basics by the dean of theoretical molecular biologists, Francis Crick. Time and again Judson illustrates the importance of the interdisciplinary perspective and how the narrowly disciplinary approach actually is obstructive.

Judson's book does not cover only the scientific side of the development of molecular biology, however; it would probably have been dull reading indeed had he done no more than recount which discoveries and breakthroughs came when. Instead, Judson deals with the associated human drama as well. Thus we learn of the frustration of blind alleys, disputes of scientific priority, ingenious and exhilarating experiments, failures of nerve and imagination, ethical questions, serendipity, tragedy (Rosalind Franklin), comedy (James Watson being made the butt of a joke), jealousy, pettiness, and glory. Even if one were totally uninterested in the science in Judson's book, he could still enjoy the human story while skipping over the more technical scientific language (although Judson has done an excellent job of explaining some very difficult science).

In preparing this fairly fine-print, 686-page work, the author contacted, recontacted, and followed up on interviews which, in most cases, he tape recorded. In fact, long entries in his text consist of transcriptions from these tapes (sometimes the entries are too lengthy). All in all, Judson interviewed about 130 persons, and from the roughly three dozen major figures, he gained repeated interviews sometimes after intervals of years.

Some of the actors in the molecular biology story have seen their names come close to becoming household words despite the complexity of their theories and subject matter—James Watson, Francis Crick, and Linus Pauling, for example. Others are less familiar, if familiar at all to the general reader (and perhaps even to some younger contemporary researchers in molecular biology). Such others, and some of them are Nobel laureates as are Watson and Crick, are Monod, Jacob, Perutz, Franklin all of whom it would be tedious to list here. All of these persons made necessary if not sufficient contributions to our current understanding of how events run their courses on the level of the very small in living beings—in other words, of the molecular interactions among nucleic acids and proteins. What was discovered through the labor and thought of these investigators was that coded "information" is to be found in specifically determined form in DNA (deoxyribonucleic acid) arranged as constituents of chromosomes in the nuclei of cells. RNA (ribonucleic acid) "reads off" or *transcribes* this information and transfers it to specialized organelles (ribosomes) outside of the cell nucleus where the "information" is *translated* in the manufacture of proteins. The proteins thus formed carry out myriad functions in the cell, including catalytic activities in metabolism, and also serve as activators and inactivators of the DNA itself (switching genes on and off).

Why did Judson spend ten years of research, interviewing, and writing to bring out this book? The subtitle of the work contains the word "revolution." To say that there has been a recent molecular revolution is not an understatement. The implications of the "molecular revolution" are both awesome and promising. Witness the attention paid to biological matters by the popular media (although in its dealings with molecular biology the popular media have usually misrepresented the implications of molecular biology theory, and more often, those of the molecular biology technology; the errors are also those of premature optimism). Put another way, had these persons who gave us understanding of the structure and function of DNA, RNA, and protein *not* made their contributions, we should not be speaking and writing of Recombinant DNA production of insulin, interferon, and atmospheric nitrogen-fixing ability in green plants not now possessing such capacity. Also, considerable sums of investment capital have been sunk into companies actively engaged in causing the fruits of molecular biological technology to be borne from the theoretical tree grown up over the last three decades.

For a time the forward movement of research in molecular biology was forced to a halt. From about 1973, some in the molecular biology research community began to look into the possibility that undesirable and perhaps dangerous "new" organisms might be produced by research made possible by the theoretical molecular revolution. Some even envisioned new diseases loosed upon unsuspecting humanity. A degree of moratorium on some kinds of DNA research was self-imposed by the molecular research community, and, ultimately, the federal government's National institutes of Health imposed research guidelines specifying certain levels of physical and biological containment. These guidelines have been progressively relaxed as dangers once thought possible have been deemed extremely remote.

The Eighth Day of Creation will at times seem confusing to those with little or no biological background. At times, Judson relates the sequence of events leading to a particular theoretical breakthrough or crucial experiment; at other times, however, he writes as if the *preliminary* stages of the sequence seem to be definitely established, then demolishes them two paragraphs or two pages later. It is indeed fascinating to see the hypotheses tested and abandoned and blind alleys explored, but to do this with each and every developmental strand in each of the major categories of DNA, RNA, and protein makes the book lengthier than it need be. For this reason the reader should be forewarned that there is a "correct" way in which to read the book: it must be done at least a chapter at a time. The chapters are long, but each is by and large a self-contained story—in fact, a self-contained detective story. To leave off in the middle of a chapter may necessitate partial or total rereading of the chapter; an occasional date in parentheses would have been helpful. Perhaps this problem will be remedied in future editions.

Judson makes some major points concerning the molecular revolution and scientific revolutions in general and concludes that the subject of which he has written does not conform to the popular model of scientific revolutions developed by Thomas Kuhn. Molecular biology did not involve the replacement of one scientific theory by another (there was nothing to replace); rather, it involved an extension and enrichment of existing theory. What Judson terms the "standard view" of the history of the molecular revolution holds that the "revolution" consisted of coming to see that not protein but nucleic acids were the bearers of the genetic information. Judson says that this is true but misleading and tends to obscure the *real* revolution, which was the refinement of the idea of *biological specificity*. The biological macromolecules which form in long chains are specific in the sequences of their constituent elements. Second, biological function on the molecular level is specific to the structural configuration of large macromolecules. Finally, one-dimensional specificity (DNA's linear specificity of information) translates to three-dimensional specificity (proteins manufactured at the command of RNA-transmitted "information").

Judson has pointed out that as a result of the molecular revolution, we have now seen biology become much more specific; function has been related to structure at the molecular level where distances between components of complex structures are measured in millionths of an inch. Such views are far advanced from the nineteenth century unifying principle of biological evolution (which has been extended and enriched by the molecular revolution), but still further removed from the mere natural history that could be said to be characteristic of biology before that science was unified by the evolutionary principle.

Judson's book bears a 1979 date. Hence, it is reasonable to assume that since research goes on apace, some things may have changed since its publication. Such is the case. As recently as April of 1980, the so-called "central dogma" of Francis Crick came under challenge when an apparent exception materialized. The central dogma states that the coded information for the synthesis of protein are transcribed from DNA to RNA. In a particular species of toad it appears that a part of a gene (DNA) not only acts as the code but controls the transcription as well. Another dogma recently challenged is the "one gene, one protein" assertion. Some viruses apparently are undogmatic because they manufacture more than one protein type from only one gene. This, however, is uncommon. Such exceptions actually may bear out the rule. Further, there is the recent discovery of "intervening sequences" in higher organisms. Their significance is yet to be worked out, although, as one might expect, there are ample hypotheses floating about. Perhaps Judson in a few years will give us an exciting sequel to *The Eighth Day of Creation*.

This work is difficult but rewarding reading. The benefits and general worthiness of the book far outweigh its shortcomings, and it is safe to say that it has rendered obsolete almost everything else written on the historical development of molecular biology. It is likely that some books that were in the process of being written have been abandoned, perhaps half-finished. To repeat, the book is monumental.

Robert L. Hoffman

ELEANOR OF AQUITAINE

Author: Desmond Seward
Publisher: Times Books (New York). Illustrated. 264 pp. $10.00
Type of work: Biography
Time: The twelfth century
Locale: France and England

A biography of Eleanor of Aquitaine which suffers from the lack of documented facts available on the subject

> *Principal personages:*
> ELEANOR OF AQUITAINE, Queen Consort of Louis VII of France and Henry II of England, mother of Richard I and King John of England
> LOUIS VII, first husband of Eleanor, King of France, father of Philip Augustus
> HENRY II, King of England, father of Richard I and King John
> RICHARD I, King of England and famous crusader
> KING JOHN, his brother, King of England
> PHILIP AUGUSTUS, King of France, successful rival of John for John's French possessions

Because of the immense accumulation of data in the late twentieth century, the lives of recently dead contemporary figures are a boon to the historical biographer. Newspaper and magazine stories, recollections of friends and enemies, official papers, speeches, and news conferences are only some of the sources for interpretations and reinterpretations. In addition, private papers are steadily being revealed to the public through time, the treachery of close associates, and often acrimonious lawsuits. Thus new evidence is constantly available to alter the view of the recent past. As one goes back in time, however, the amount of data begins to thin out and become unreliable. Before the eighteenth century, there is a real paucity of historical information; by the Middle Ages, the thin stream of reliable facts has been reduced to a trickle. This lack is compounded in the case of those who seem more important to modern historians than they did to their contemporaries. Poets such as Shakespeare and Chaucer and queens such as Eleanor of Aquitaine, were given more contemporary historical attention than most of their peers, but not so much as modern historians would like. Moreover, these few older records often create problems because older historians generally had a very different idea of truth than their modern counterparts. Rumors, gossip, and the recollections of old men, all distorted by an author's political or religious bias, were the basis of history for the Elizabethans, and, to an even greater extent, for the Angevins, of which Eleanor of Aquitaine was one.

This attitude toward history changed by the nineteenth century. By then, history had become scientific, but biographies of half-known figures of the past still suffered. Nineteenth century biographers of Shakespeare, not satisfied by the few facts of the playwright's life—documents like his baptismal record and his will—wrote volumes filled with psychological conjecture based on an analysis of the plays and sonnets and larded with sermonizing founded on Victorian standards of conduct.

Twentieth century biographers were wisely wary of such shabby procedures—not wary enough, however, to avoid conjecture of a new sort. Marchette Chute's biography of Shakespeare may be fairly taken as a model of this new school of conjectural biography, a school to which Desmond Seward's *Eleanor of Aquitaine* clearly belongs. Chute avoids the high-minded meandering of the nineteenth century, but substitutes for this fiction a new fiction of her own. For example, nothing is known of Shakespeare's youth; however, something is known about Elizabethan grammar schools. No one knows whether Shakespeare attended grammar school, but children of his class generally did, and the knowledge demonstrated in his writing is not inconsistent with a grammar school education. Therefore, it is concluded that Shakespeare probably went to grammar school, most likely studied certain subjects, and so on. After nineteenth century romanticizing, this method of conjecture may seem a welcome relief. Large sections on Elizabethan grammar schools, or everyday life in Elizabethan London, are followed by sentences such as "Shakespeare probably went to a grammar school of this sort" or "This was the London in which Shakespeare lived."

The difficulty with this approach to historical biography can be seen when its methods are transposed to the present day. Supposing nothing were known about any well-known contemporary literary figure—say, Ernest Hemingway. Would one be regaled in a biography with long sections on Spain during the Civil War, followed by the sentence, "This is unquestionably the Spain that Hemingway knew and that inspired *For Whom the Bell Tolls*"? Likewise, speaking of Henry II's desire to possess Toulouse, Desmond Seward says:

> Henry looked hopefully at the great and rich county of Toulouse. Cut off from Capetian France by the Massif Central, Toulouse had once been part of greater Aquitaine. It was especially important in that through it ran the trade routes so vital for Aquitaine's prosperity, the waterways and Roman roads that connected the duchy with the Mediterranean. Its possession would be the ultimate rounding off of the Angevin empire, which without it would be strategically unsound. *Eleanor may well have encouraged Henry to assert the rights to Toulouse that she inherited from her grandmother* [italics added].

Actually, Seward has no knowledge of any connection between his subject and the stated facts, but this lack of knowledge never deters him. Concerning the revolt of Henry's sons against their father, he says, "Even if there is no firm documentary evidence, all circumstances point to Eleanor as the architect of an ingenious plot."

The general level of Seward's speculations is quite low. Even though he is skeptical of the reliability of chronicles, he quotes from them with unseemly enthusiasm. He states, for example, that the *Annals of Margan* contain "an extremely plausible account" of King John's murder of his nephew. Nor is he above the trivial psychologizing that explains Richard I's homosexuality by saying that "it is not too much to suppose that the queen was one of those excessively dominant mothers who transform their sons into little lovers."

What we really know about Eleanor deserves little more than a paragraph entry in an encyclopedia. An heiress to Aquitaine, she married Henry II after an unsuccessful union with Louis VII of France. She bore Henry many children, two of whom—Richard and John—became kings of England. Henry's sons revolted against him, and the King had reason to believe Eleanor was involved in this rebellion; he therefore imprisoned her. She managed to outlive him however, as well as most of her contemporaries, dying at the age of eighty-two. In the latter part of her life, she seems to have been helpful to John and Richard—and especially to Richard during his absence from England to participate in the Crusades. Ultimately, her Angevin empire was lost to Louis VII's son by another marriage, Philip Augustus, because of John's political and military ineptness.

Eleanor combined intellect, charm, religious devotion, guile, ruthlessness, and greed for power in a manner typical of her family and, indeed, of feudal nobility. She was a remarkable woman, avoiding her most probable fate of mere dynastic pawn. Would that it were possible to know more about her; unfortunately, it is not, and Seward's tissue of conjecture, although it whets, cannot satisfy waiting appetites.

Alan G. Gross

THE ELEPHANT MAN

Author: Bernard Pomerance
Publisher: Grove Press (New York). 71 pp. $8.95; paperback $2.95
Type of work: Drama
Time: 1884-1890
Locale: London; one scene in Belgium

A moving, provocative play that chronicles the last six years in the life of the grossly deformed "Elephant Man," John Merrick, and his relationship with his benefactor, Sir Frederick Treves, an eminent Victorian physician

> *Principal characters:*
> JOHN MERRICK, the "Elephant Man"
> FREDERICK TREVES, Merrick's benefactor, a surgeon and teacher
> CARR GOMM, administrator of the London Hospital
> MRS. KENDAL, an actress
> ROSS, Merrick's manager
> BISHOP WALSHAM HOW, Merrick's religious counselor
> THE PINHEADS, three female freaks whose heads are pointed

John Merrick (1863-1890) was most likely given the label "Elephant Man" by a shrewd carnival pitchman in order to lure the customers, but his actual physical appearance defied such a simple metaphorical description. In the scene that introduces Merrick to the audience, his doctor and benefactor, Frederick Treves, describes him more concretely:

> The most striking feature about him was his enormous head. Its circumference was about that of a man's waist. From the brow there projected a huge bony mass like a loaf, while from the back of his head hung a bag of spongy fungous-looking skin, the surface of which was comparable to brown cauliflower . . . . Another mass of bone . . . protruded from the mouth like a pink stump, turning the upper lip inside out, and making the mouth a wide slobbering aperture. The nose was merely a lump of flesh . . . . The back was horrible because from it hung, as far down as the middle of the thigh, huge sack-like masses of flesh covered by the same loathsome cauliflower stain. The right arm was of enormous size and shapeless . . . . The right hand was large and clumsy—a fin or paddle . . . . The other arm was remarkable by contrast. It was not only normal, but was moreover a delicately shaped limb covered with a fine skin and provided with a beautiful hand . . . . From the chest hung a bag of the same repulsive flesh . . . . The lower limbs had the characters of the deformed arm . . . unwieldy, dropsical-looking, and grossly mis-shapen. There arose from the fungous skin growths a very sickening stench which was hard to tolerate . . . .

The facts are these: Treves discovered Merrick in 1880 in a freak show, studied him briefly, and then sent him and his manager off with a business card. Two years later, when Merrick was found abandoned and destitute in London, Treves's card was the only identification on his person. This led authorities to the doctor, who agreed to take responsibility for the apparently imbecilic freak. Once permanently housed at the London Hospital, however, Merrick proved to be a sensitive, intelligent, artistic individual who, under

Treves's tutelage, emerged as a social being, even a minor celebrity. Always in precarious health, however, Merrick died unexpectedly in his sleep. Perhaps it was the result of an attempt to sleep "normally," a posture which, by forcing the full weight of the oversized head onto the weak neck and spine, caused a fatal dislocation.

Treves chronicled Merrick's story in his moving, beautifully written memoirs, *The Elephant Man and Other Reminiscences* (1923). In 1971, Ashley Montagu reprinted Treves's essay along with an extended medical, psychological, and philosophical analysis of the elephant man phenomenon. Dramatist Bernard Pomerance, in turn, became fascinated by the story of Merrick's plight and wrote a play that has been an outstanding commercial and critical success both in London and on Broadway; during its opening season in New York, it won all of the major theater awards, including three Tonys, three Obies, the Drama Desk Award, and the New York Drama Critics Circle Award.

However, for all of its power and poignancy, the story of the Elephant Man would seem to hold little promise as a subject for any creative interpretation, let alone a hit play. How could an audience be expected to identify and sympathize with a character so physically repulsive that public viewing of him was banned and the mere sight of him provoked riots? How could the feelings, ideas, and experiences of such a man be communicated when the nature of his disfigurement rendered him "utterly incapable of the expression of any emotion whatsoever" as well as slurred his speech to the point where he could be understood only by those who learned his personal language? Pomerance's answer is not to try to tell Merrick's story, but to write a play about it. *The Elephant Man* works in the theater because of the adroit, sensitive ways in which the dramatist theatricalizes his material.

The play is structured in twenty-one brief, well-paced scenes. In Brechtian fashion, a projected title prefaces each scene ("Police side with Imbecile Against the Crowd," "Even on the Niger and Ceylon, Not This," "Mercy and Justice Elude Our Minds and Actions"). The atmosphere is fortified by a cellist, dressed in tails, who sits at the side of the stage playing Bach and Elgar. Most importantly, the actor playing Merrick does the role without makeup and with only minimal gestures and slightly stylized speech to suggest the Elephant Man's impairments of movement and voice. "Any attempt to reproduce his appearance and his speech naturalistically—*if* it were possible—" the playwright states, "would seem to me not only counterproductive, but, the more remarkably successful, the more distracting from the play."

The Treves lecture that introduces Merrick is illustrated by a series of slides depicting the original. These grotesque images must satisfy the audience's view of Merrick's deformity. A tension is created in the viewer's mind between the humanity of the freak, as seen in the "normal" actor, and the awfulness of his real physical appearance, as projected in the slides. The audience's focus is turned away from Merrick's deformity toward his relationship to society in general, to other individuals, and to himself. He thus emerges from the play less as a freak than as an outsider and a kind of noble savage.

The aspect of Merrick's personality that most impressed Ashley Montagu was his sweet, affirmative disposition. Despite his horrendous appearance and the harrowing experiences Merrick had been subjected to prior to being rescued by Treves, he expressed no bitterness over his plight toward the society that had ostracized and brutalized him, toward the particular individuals who had taken advantage of him, or toward the God/Fate that had given him such a grotesque body in the first place. He craved, appreciated, and responded to all human contact; he worshiped God piously. The major act of his life was to construct an elaborate paper model of St. Phillips Church. The model, pictured in Montagu's book, becomes the play's dominant metaphor.

Pomerance convincingly carries that view of Merrick into the play. As presented, Merrick's innocence and simplicity are not the products of ignorance, but are innate character traits. He knows perfectly well what he is, and he is extremely sensitive to the attitudes and motives of those around him—sometimes even more so than they are. It is this self-awareness that makes Merrick's plight so poignant. He is more than simply a victim; he takes on aspects of the tragic hero.

Similar to that of many such heroes, his situation veers close to the comic. The ludicrous contrast between his existence and his longings (the inappropriate props he surrounds himself with, such as clothing which he is physically incapable of wearing and the artifacts of a dandy, and his romantic imagination, fed on popular novels and *Romeo and Juliet*) can be seen as comic and, from another angle, as mawkishly sentimental. However, Pomerance carefully balances his material between the emotional and the cerebral. The distancing devices, rapid pacing, and carefully controlled language keep us from a too-close involvement; the emotional potency of the material and our admiration for the principals keep our emotions sensitized. Consequently, when Pomerance wants to stimulate a strong visceral reaction, he can do so with great theatrical intensity. The two scenes that demonstrate this most forcefully deal with Merrick's contact with a beautiful woman, the actress Madge Kendal.

It is not surprising that Merrick's dream of being normal centered on women. One of the many small, cruel ironies of his life was that, besides his left arm, the only other part of his body unaffected by his disfigurement was his genitals; in every way, physically and emotionally, he was a sexually mature adult male. He read romantic novels voraciously, worshiped women as a species, and probably adored every individual female he met. Pomerance focuses all of this desire and frustration into Merrick's relationship with one woman, the aforementioned Mrs. Kendal. Scene Ten concludes with Merrick shaking hands with the vivacious actress. "Do you know," Treves tells her, "he's never shook a woman's hand before?" as Merrick sobs soundlessly, uncontrollably. In the second, even more potent scene, Mrs. Kendal strips for the Elephant Man. He is awestruck; Treves, who enters suddenly, is shocked; the audience is profoundly moved.

However, it is with such scenes that purists might cavil with Pomerance's use of historical material. Neither episode in fact ever happened as dramatized. The handshake was given Merrick by a young widow of Treves's acquaintance; the stripping scene is pure fiction. There is no way of knowing, of course, how close Pomerance's stage creation is to the real John Merrick, but sufficient data exists about the other historical figures to establish a distance between the playwright's conceptions and the persons upon which they were based. In Pomerance's version, they are not so much real figures as representative Victorian types—or perhaps contemporary types in Victorian garb. Thus, Pomerance is able to use the Elephant Man as a metaphor and a mirror—a metaphor for the outsider and his relationship to society, and a mirror in which the characters and the audience members see themselves reflected.

This latter thematic device is explicitly presented in Scene Twelve, titled "Who Does He Remind You Of?" Each of Merrick's visitors verbalize their identification with him: to Mrs. Kendal, he is an actor who uses props to make himself, but who remains sensitive and vulnerable—"like me," she adds; to Carr Gomm, he is a practical man who willingly accepts being exploited; the Bishop sees him as a devout believer who "struggles with doubt"; and to Treves, the most complicated figure in the play, he is a divided, paradoxical soul. As the physician states to himself:

> That, as he rises higher in the consolations of society, he gets visibly more grotesque is proof definitive he is like me. Like his condition, which I make no sense of, I make no sense of mine.

It is in the complex, ambiguous relationship between Merrick and Treves that the real center of the play can be found. The urbane, articulate Treves, revealed in his memoirs and discussed by Montagu, projects little of the neurosis and self-doubt that characterizes the Treves of the play. However, a completely stable, sensible Treves would have turned the work into, at best, a moving case history. Pomerance's Treves gives the play its dramatic tension and thematic implication. The doctor is as important a character as Merrick, and only by understanding them both, and their relationship, can one fully appreciate the power and meaning of the play.

Treves's self-doubt is evident in the short first scene, before Merrick even enters the play. The doctor subsequently rescues Merrick as a humanitarian and scientific gesture, but as their relationship develops, it takes on subtle, contradictory implications. The Elephant Man becomes many different things to his benefactor—an unfortunate to be helped, a natural curiosity to be studied, a child to be shaped and educated, a terminal patient to be reconciled to death, a living symbol of an arbitrary universe, a heroic example of courage and optimism in the face of adversity, a foolish self-deceiving romantic, and a catalyst for the doctor's own guilt and self-recriminations. The rigidly puritanical Treves tells Merrick that rules are for "your own good" and banishes Mrs. Kendal for her indecent exposure; the self-critical modern Treves openly doubts all Victorian certainties and admits that Mrs. Kendal's banishment was the result of his possessiveness, not his ethics. The "mirror" that Merrick holds up to Treves is a progressively disturbing one.

These paradoxes are crystallized near the play's conclusion in two climactic dream sequences. Although a number of popular drama critics have dismissed these scenes as intrusive and dramatically unconvincing, they actually define the themes of the play in powerful surrealistic visions. Sensing that he has failed in his handling of the Mrs. Kendal incident, Treves goes into an uneasy sleep. He dreams that he is the freak in his normality, Carr Gomm is his manager, and John Merrick is his physician. Merrick, standing upright and speaking clearly, delivers a highly charged speech about the doctor to the audience of pinheads; the speech is a perfect inversion of the lecture which Treves had previously made about Merrick. The talk is also a stinging denunciation of Treves's Victorian morality, hypocrisy, and rigidity. The speech concludes with the statement that "the wretched man when a boy developed a disabling spiritual duality, therefore was unable to feel what others feel, nor reach harmony with them." The pinheads call for an immediate cure. Merrick shakes his head sadly: "the truth is, I am afraid, we are dealing with an epidemic."

Perhaps Pomerance's ironical conclusion that Merrick's hideous appearance covered a pure soul, while the glossy, attractive Victorian surface projected by Treves and his circle concealed hypocrisy, corruption, and deception, is too facile and does not do justice to the rich, ambiguous texture of the play as a whole. Moreover, for all the intellectual potency of the themes, *The Elephant Man* still communicates its greatest power as a story of particular individuals subjected to intense psychological and emotional pressure. Yet the Elephant Man as a distorting mirror in which we catch a glimpse of ourselves is a memorable theatrical idea. The grotesque reflection forces us not only to look at our own images, but also to see beneath the surface.

Keith Neilson

THE END OF THE WAR IN ASIA

Author: Louis Allen (1922-   )
Publisher: Beekman/Esanu Publishers (Brooklyn Heights, New York). 306 pp. $24.95
Type of work: History
Time: August 15, 1945-early 1946
Locale: Southeast and East Asia

Shows the impact of Japanese occupation in Asia during World War II and the role of Japan's defeat and surrender on the history of postwar Asia, stressing the rise of Asian nationalism and the origins of political division in areas such as Korea and Vietnam

> *Principal personages:*
> SUBHAS CHANDRA BOSE, Bengali nationalist and collaborator
> SUKARNO, Indonesian nationalist leader
> HO CHI MINH, Vietnamese nationalist and Communist leader
> MAJOR GENERAL DOUGLAS GRACEY, Saigon surrender administrator
> LIEUTENANT GENERAL JOHN R. HODGE, Seoul surrender administrator
> SYNGMAN RHEE, Korean nationalist leader
> KIM IL-SUNG, North Korean leader and Russian client
> CHIANG KAI-SHEK, Chinese nationalist leader
> MAO TSE-TUNG, Chinese Communist Party leader

This book is an insightful analysis of the important impact of Japan's defeat on Asia. "Wars," writes Louis Allen, "do not come to a clean end," and Japan's war in Asia was no exception. For, although World War II ended the short-lived Japanese empire in 1945, the old, prewar order in Asia never revived. For one thing, Western colonialism in Asia ended with the war, and Japan's surrender, far from marking a clean break in history, actually denoted the beginning of a significant transition to a new Asia based on nationalism and independence.

Allen has not written just a military history: he stresses political and diplomatic aspects of Japan's surrender, and even touches occasionally on the human element. For example, the plight of Japanese settlers in Manchuria is described in harrowing detail. Allen organizes his broad subject geographically in two large divisions. The first section on Southeast Asia includes chapters on what are now called Burma, Thailand, Indonesia, and Vietnam. The second section on East Asia deals with the surrender in Korea, Manchuria, and China proper, where the Japanese military and administrative structure was more intact. This approach is well chosen since Japanese occupation policy, indigenous political development, and the military situation differed greatly between Southeast Asia and East Asia. This regional diversity also led to a difference in the nature and outcome of Japanese surrender. It would be difficult to make useful generalizations about the meaning of Japanese occupation and surrender without, as Allen has demonstrated, examining each area separately.

One topic that cannot be treated strictly in terms of Japanese occupation is the story of the Bengali political leader, Subhas Chandra Bose, and the Indian National Army (INA). Major Fujiwara Iwaichi and other Japanese military personnel working through secret organizations in Southeast Asia developed plans to appeal to Indian aspirations for independence from British rule. In the Malaya-Singapore campaign, around twenty-five thousand of some sixty-five thousand captured Indian troops were recruited by Fujiwara and his Indian collaborators to form anti-British military units. In contrast to their cautious policy in occupied areas such as Indonesia, the Japanese, since they did not occupy India, were willing to support the concept of Indian independence for their own purposes. With the possible exception of Wang Ching-wei in China, Bose was the most prominent Asian politician in occupied Asia, although he did not operate within his own national territory. The INA was not an important military factor in the war, and most Indians remained loyal to the British raj. However, the postwar New Delhi trials of the INA officers, which were intended as an object lesson by the British Army, became a focal point of aroused Indian nationalism. They helped speed the path toward independence in 1947.

In Southeast Asia, the surrender of Japanese forces in the field and the return of European colonial powers were awkward logistical and political exercises. Indonesia, for example, was promised independence by the Japanese late in the war, and the occupation had organized and trained an Indonesian military force. On August 17, 1945, with Allied victory apparent, the Japanese permitted the leader of the nationalists, Sukarno, to declare independence. British military forces which landed to take charge were ignorant of nationalist aspirations in much of occupied Asia, and they were urged by the Dutch government not to recognize the Indonesian Republic. Indonesians seized weapons and ammunition because Japanese troops were either unable or unwilling to obey Allied directives to keep the peace until an orderly transition of power could be effected. Most of their arms fell into Indonesian hands, and Japanese military training, especially in night fighting, helped Indonesians launch their four-year successful struggle for independence. As in other parts of Southeast Asia, some Japanese deserters remained behind and blended into the culture, but there were also reprisals against Japanese troops and civilians. About one thousand were massacred in Indonesia.

The author's analysis of the Vietnamese situation is one of the most interesting and complex subjects covered. During the war, the United States gave logistical support to a Vietnamese popular front guerrilla force led by Ho Chi Minh. This force, the Viet Minh, tried to take over military and administrative control in the brief power vacuum left between Japanese capitulation and Allied-French reoccupation in August, 1945. The Allies had other plans, adumbrated at the Cairo meeting and later, including a postwar Tongkin (North Vietnam) under the control of Chiang Kai-shek.

One of the most momentous decisions was to divide Vietnam at the 16th parallel, a decision partly determined by military logistics. The north was to be administered under General Wedemeyer as part of China operations and the southern region by Mountbatten's South-East Asian Command. Because the new Labour Government in London was hostile to forcefully stifling Asian nationalism, the local command faced an untenable situation. Japanese administrative power vanished, French and Vietnamese in the Saigon area attacked one another, and the seeds were sown for future suspicion and bitterness. Major General Douglas Gracey, in charge of Saigon after September 13, 1945, found himself in a Byzantine political situation, without sufficient British and Indian troops to keep order. Once again Japanese forces were reluctant to intervene when requested, fearing later reprisals from the local population.

This situation was a common dilemma in former colonial possessions. Indigenous nationalism had been fomented by European departure in 1941 and Japanese occupation propaganda. Nationalist forces were determined to resist the return of their former colonial rulers without some assurances of a definite timetable for independence. In the face of this political reality, France and the Netherlands did not have military forces ready to reassert their control immediately after the Japanese acceptance of the Potsdam Declaration on August 15, 1945. This led to the awkward expediency of using Japanese troops and military administration already in place to ensure a smooth transition. In colonies such as Burma, local political figures such as Ba Maw took no part in truce negotiations.

Postwar division was partly a result of military *fait accompli* and surrender policy in Korea as well as Vietnam. In June, 1945, the Allies had hinted at independence "in due course" for the former Japanese colony, but on August 10, 1945, the immediate problem was determination of Soviet and American zones of occupation in Korea. Lacking informed opinion, Far Eastern Advisers in the War Department selected the 38th parallel as a dividing line. It had previously been defined as a naval operations boundary when the Soviet Union entered the war against Japan on August 9, 1945. The Soviets accepted the proposal, although the Americans were worried they might insist on a larger occupation zone since they had troops on the peninsula. Although the American advisers were unaware of its possible significance, the Russians and Japanese before the outbreak of war in 1904 had discussed the 38th parallel as a potential division, and the Soviets in August, 1945, may have viewed the proposal as a tacit recognition of their right to a sphere of influence in North Korea.

On September 6, 1945, the United States advance party arrived in Seoul.

The American zone was administered by Lieutenant General John R. Hodge, who was forced to rely on Japanese troops commanded by General Abe Nobuyuki in order to control Korean demonstrations in Seoul on September 8. Hodge had no briefing on the seriousness of the traditional enmity felt between Japanese and Koreans, and the United States was seen by Korean nationalists as a new colonial power. In North Korea, the Soviets installed Kim Il-sung and the 38th parallel soon became a closed border. In the south, Syngman Rhee emerged as the most prominent political leader. Korea, with the breakdown of negotiations in Moscow in December, 1945, had already embarked on its future, divided by the tensions of the Cold War and the diktats of military occupation following Japan's defeat.

In Manchuria, the Soviet forces brought from Europe in the late spring and summer of 1945 quickly overran the weakened Kwantung Army on August 9. Nevertheless, several diehard factions vowed to fight to the death until an Imperial emissary arrived on August 16 to persuade them to accept the reality of Japan's defeat. The fate of the some six hundred thousand Japanese soldiers captured in Manchuria was particularly harsh. They were taken to Siberia as forced labor, and repatriation did not begin until 1947, dragging on into the 1950's. Many never returned.

Occupation of Manchuria by the Soviet Union gave that country an opportunity to manipulate the postwar military situation in China. Chiang Kai-shek had been reserving his forces for years in anticipation of Japanese defeat and a showdown with Communist forces. He intended quickly to reoccupy Chinese cities with Kuomintang troops to preempt Communist takeover. This goal was supported by the Japanese Commander in Chief in China, Okamura Yasuji, a hardline anti-Communist general who served as a military adviser to Chiang in China's 1945-1949 Civil War. The U.S.S.R., on the other hand, saw to it that Japanese arms captured in Manchuria fell into Communist hands. Lin Piao was allowed to enter Manchuria at the head of weakly armed Communist troops from North China to seize Japanese supplies.

In October, 1945, negotiations between Chiang and Mao Tse-tung broke down. General Wedemeyer aided the KMT by transporting nationalist troops to strategic areas and ordering United States Marines to occupy Peking, Tientsin, and other points until Chiang could get his forces in place. In December, 1945, General George Marshall tried unsuccessfully to establish a national conference to avoid further conflict in China, but it is likely that both Chiang and Mao wanted to take their chances in a civil war.

Allen also relates the difficult repatriation program in Asia, as some six million former Japanese soldiers and civilians were transported back to Japan, while Korean laborers were returned to their homeland. Marine shipping capacity had been reduced to one-eighth the prewar level, making this program difficult to implement rapidly.

A book which ambitiously attempts to deal with the entire area of Asia inevitably risks some shortcomings. Allen does not deal with the Philippines, perhaps because American troops were already occupying much of the archipelago by August, 1945. Still, the contrast with other parts of Asia would be illuminating, and it cannot be questioned that Japanese occupation during the war and the Philippine resistance movement played an important role in the politics of postwar independence in that country. His failure to deal with Malaya and Taiwan is even more puzzling.

Although the author refers the reader to an excellent study of Wang Ching-wei and other Chinese collaborators, J. H. Boyle's *China and Japan at War 1937-1945* (1972), his analysis of the Chinese theater is the least satisfying section of the book. The general reader may be satisfied, but a specialist would require a much more detailed analysis of Japan's inconsistent and uncoordinated dealings with Chiang and puppets like Wang Ching-wei. Allen's bibliography, as one would expect from an author who has already published significant works on the Asian war such as *Japan: The Years of Triumph* (1971) and *Sittang: The Last Battle* (1973), is an excellent guide to his subject for those wishing to pursue particular aspects of the conflict and its end. He was not able to include Joyce C. Lebra's *Japanese-Trained Armies in Southeast Asia: Independence and Volunteer Forces in World War II* (1977), which appeared after his book and covers some of the same ground. He also neglects some sources such as M. A. Aziz's *Japan's Colonialism and Indonesia* (1955).

These, however, are minor faults; overall the book is well researched in both English and Japanese sources, and it draws as well on Allen's own participation at several surrender negotiations, serving as a young Japanese language specialist in the British Army at the time. The most important contribution of this work is that it proves that wars do not come to a clean end. It fills in the historiographical gap created by earlier military studies which deal with the war and end with Japan's defeat, and other books which analyze postwar Asian history, often without due attention to the transition studied by Allen. He succeeds in showing that a clean break did not occur, for echoes of occupation and surrender policy still reverberate in Asia today. All too often, the brief but extremely important transition has been neglected. This book should be required reading for all who wish to understand the full impact Japan has made on postwar Asian history.

Richard Rice

END TO TORMENT
A Memoir of Ezra Pound by H. D.

Author: H. D. (Hilda Doolittle)
Edited by Norman Holmes Pearson and Michael King
With the poems from *Hilda's Book* by Ezra Pound
Publisher: New Directions (New York). 84 pp. $8.50
Type of work: Memoir
Time: The twentieth century

A memoir of Ezra Pound in journal form, similar to the author's journal of her psychoanalysis with Freud

End to Torment takes its title from a letter which Norman Holmes Pearson wrote to H. D. in April, 1958; the indictment against Ezra Pound for high treason had just been dropped, and Pound's release from St. Elizabeth's—the asylum in Washington, D. C., where he had been confined since 1945—was imminent. The indictment was dropped because Pound was judged to be permanently, incurably insane. Pearson wrote to H. D.: "And now another canyon has been bridged by Ezra's end to torment. . . ." Later, when H. D. sent the manuscript of this book to Pound in Italy, he found "a great deal of beauty" in it, but added this postscript: "Torment title excellent, but optimistic." He lived another fifteen years, withdrawing into the anguished silence which so many visitors described. In addition to H. D.'s memoir, New Directions has included in this volume the early poems by Pound collected in "Hilda's Book," which he wrote for Hilda Doolittle before she became "H. D. Imagiste."

Not a memoir composed in tranquillity, but a journal of piercing memories all related to Ezra Pound, *End to Torment* jumps back and forth between the distant past, the present, and the recent past. There is beauty in it, as Pound said, but there is also much anguish in reading *End to Torment*: H. D.'s own as she probes her memory; the reader's pity—not condescension—at the sad spectacle she sometimes makes, sorting through lives and events as if through a Tarot deck, desperately seeking patterns, occult affinities. There is the tragedy of Ezra Pound; so much has been written about that, but H. D.'s imagistic discontinuous glimpses deepen our understanding, as many volumes have failed to do.

The publication of *End to Torment* follows by five years the reissue (with considerable additions) of H. D.'s *Tribute to Freud*. Earlier, New Directions reissued her *Trilogy* written during World War II (*The Walls Do Not Fall*, *Tribute to the Angels*, *The Flowering of the Rod*), which some readers regard as her finest work. Other works have also been published by New Directions, and there are a number of manuscripts still awaiting publication, including several novels. Eventually the body of this work should correct the notion that her art flared and died with Imagism.

H. D. began writing *End to Torment* in March, 1958, in Kusnacht, Switzerland, where she was recovering from a serious fall. (She remained a semi-invalid until her death in 1961.) She finished in July, and the last entry records, via Pearson's report to her, Pound's departure for Italy. She keeps to the journal form throughout, darting from image to image, experience to experience, as she did in the "Advent" section of the *Tribute to Freud*. Transitions are abrupt or nonexistent, and part of the pleasure of reading the book is in making the associative leaps with her, yet she can also exasperate with hermetic or merely precious musings (as she does more often in the latter stages of the memoir). Although the memoir is not a record of psychoanalysis, H. D. was spurred to pursue her recollections of Pound by her physician, Dr. Erich Heydt, the chief doctor of a nearby clinic. Her "tea sessions" with him—he called on her three or four times a week—during which she would often show him what she had just written, and he would question her further about her memories, give many of the entries a connecting thread.

The memoir begins with characteristic abruptness, with chiseled beauty: "Snow on his beard. But he had no beard, then. Snow blows down from pine branches, dry powder on the red gold. 'I make five friends for my hair, for one for myself.' " Let the reader scorn this who has never remembered first kisses. H. D.'s recollection has the content of any dusty romantic novel, but the telling is jagged, and not without irony: she catches young Ezra Pound pleased with himself in one sentence.

The first entry is dated March 7, 1958, more than fifty years after the meeting in the winter woods which she recalls. From our even greater distance, it is difficult to connect this scene with any of the familiar images of H. D. or Ezra Pound: H. D., hermetic, tormented, bisexual; Pound, holding court at St. Elizabeth's. Yet in 1905 she was Hilda Doolittle, eighteen years old, daughter of a professor of astronomy. Pound was nineteen, "a young, more robust Ignace Paderewski," already writing poems but chiefly notorious around the University of Pennsylvania for his eccentric behavior: he told a professor that Bernard Shaw was more important than Shakespeare; he wore flashy socks deemed inappropriate for a freshman.

It is a lost world which H. D. evokes, beginning with their first kisses, "the frost of our mingled breath." Her memories have more evocative power—and more pathos—because they alternate with her awareness of the present. Her attempt to see the Ezra Pound of 1905 and the Pound of 1958 together from one viewpoint is quite explicit. The distance between herself in 1905 and in 1958 is more implicit: her bisexuality is hinted at obliquely, as in her reference to Balzac's *Séraphita*.

The story which she begins in the first entry comes out in bits and pieces, with much backtracking, and with prodding from Dr. Heydt. The recollections come in fragments, but with increasing intensity, until the story is complete:

Pound and H. D. were engaged. Her parents disapproved. Her father discovered them "curled up together in an armchair" and asked Pound to leave. It would be easy to dismiss the whole business as absurd, particularly the father's "discovery," but the young girl did not have the benefit of our liberated perspective. H. D. returns to this scene of "discovery" just after she has told Erich Heydt how she became "H. D.," styled "Imagist" by the inspired fiat of Pound. She tells him she has been "hiding" the memory of herself and Pound "standing before my father, caught 'in the very act' you might say. For no 'act' afterwards, though biologically fulfilled, had had the significance of the first *demi-vierge* embraces." This intense recollection brings to an end the first movement of the journal.

On one level, then, the memoir is a poignant evocation of lost love, a sad and beautiful variation on that inexhaustible theme. Moreover, H. D. seems to suggest—however obliquely—that if she and Pound had married, she might have escaped some of the suffering of her later years. A boy with red-gold hair reminds her of the child they might have had. Yet in another passage, after speaking of the "rigor mortis" she felt fifty years earlier when Pound left for Europe ("my poetry was not dead but it was built on or around the crater of an extinct volcano"), she says "Ezra would have destroyed me and the center they call 'Air and Crystal' of my poetry."

However, if she is sometimes ambivalent toward Pound, H. D. writes about him with a passion which is both moving and saddening. This passion can be curiously impersonal, when she seems to see Pound as a bearer of light and energy, a chosen one whose gift transcends his all-too-human failings. (He often appears extremely callous in these pages, not malicious but apparently oblivious to the pain he is causing others.) After several friends criticize Pound, denounce his Fascist contacts, his St. Elizabeth's crowd, H. D. thinks: "There is no argument, pro or con. You catch fire or you don't catch fire." Yet she is also able to laugh at an account of the poet with his peanut butter jars. Only when H. D. begins to identify with Sheri Martinelli, a young painter who was close to Pound during his time at St. Elizabeth's, does the emotion in the memoir seem false, somehow contrived. The editors chose to call Martinelli "Undine," which is quite confusing: there are several references to her in the later *Cantos*, and Pound wrote a florid introduction to a small book of her paintings. H. D's identification with Martinelli peaks when Pound "abandons" her after the indictment is dropped, and prepares to leave for Italy.

H. D. asked Norman Holmes Pearson to give Dorothy Pound a rose for her when Dorothy and Ezra boarded the *Cristoforo Colombo* in New York. The last entry in the memoir consists mostly of Pearson's letter describing the send-off on shipboard; he mentions that Pound lectured him on college entrance exams for half an hour and showed him "Canto XCIX." The rose, Pearson told Pound, was "for the *Paradiso*." That is how H. D. chose to conclude her memoir. It is a very strange, moving, private book. It is difficult to say how much of the strangeness lies in H. D.'s restless inward-turning mind, and how much in the conventions of our day, according to which we are expected to probe to the bone of any life which attracts our attention.

John Wilson

ENDLESS LOVE

Author: Scott Spencer (1945-   )
Publisher: Alfred A. Knopf (New York). 418 pp. $10.95
Type of work: Novel
Time: The late 1960's
Locale: Chicago and New York

A novel couched in relentless realism which tells of a boy's continuing, obsessive, and destructive compulsion toward loving a girl and her family

> *Principal characters:*
> DAVID AXELROD, the boy who narrates his story of painful, possibly insane love
> JADE BUTTERFIELD, the girl David loves
> ANN BUTTERFIELD, her mother
> HUGH BUTTERFIELD, her father
> ROSE AND ARTHUR AXELROD, David's parents

Scott Spencer is an astonishingly perceptive and powerfully skilled young writer who had two successful novels to his credit before he was thirty. His *Last Night at the Brain Thieves' Ball* (1973) and *Preservation Hall* (1976) won him both the praise of critics and a widening audience; both works demonstrate his profound identification with the problems experienced by persons of genuine emotion who are fronted by an uncaring and false society. In each, he made his people, their language, their thoughts, and their times come vitally alive. Now, in *Endless Love*, Spencer allows his vision of that problem to mature in a story which is consistently fascinating in its narrative range and often—even in our callous age—shocking in its intensity of emotion.

Endless Love is a novel of compulsion. The epigrammatic title, which comes from Delmore Schwartz's poem "I Am a Book I Neither Wrote nor Read," foreshadows the obsessive, trancelike effect this novel has. The novel's narrator is an original. His passion and his crime are unlearned behaviors; they simply are, and he unblinkingly reports his having done them. Told in the first person, his narration is about obsession and displays a relentless, unnerving momentum. The story, which could have become merely a mawkish tale of adolescent love or an attack on women's demands for security or another denunciation of contemporary American society, instead succeeds in communicating complex attitudes and asking sophisticated philosophical questions. If a sociologist fifty years from now wanted to know what representative families were like in the 1960's, this novel would faithfully answer most of his questions.

Spencer's energy and psychological insights in *Endless Love* are impressive. Between the lines, through the novel's events, the author asks, "What is love in our time? What is the family? What do they mean to each other? What ought they to be. . . . What will they be allowed to be . . .?" Sadly but truthfully, he reports the effect our harsh and changing circumstances have had on families. He reveals a deep sympathy for people who care, who can still be touched despite all their defenses, escapes, and alienations. Spencer's complex and daring theme seems to be that the emotion of love, when it is most pure—that is, when it is most conscious of itself, most exclusive of external restraint—is truly obsessive and inevitably destructive, a threat to society's other forms such as the family; it is thereby labeled by society not as love, but as sickness. As a result, love must be diluted; it is too nakedly powerful, and therefore must be controlled and redefined. It must, in other words, be made into a lie; if it is not, it conflicts so glaringly with all other concerns in life as to destroy them and, finally, itself. The concept of over-powering, Romantic love simply cannot be tolerated by our emotionally dulled society, which seeks above all to maintain a comfortable status quo; thus, any passionate, consuming love is seen as insane and labeled criminal. Throughout his novel, Spencer conveys a sadness at this loss of passion between individuals. He describes a world of slums and high rises and empty political maxims which has no room in it for the beauty of passionate gestures or for the destructive fire of obsessive love.

Specifically, this disturbing novel tells the story of society's attempt to quell the love of young David Axelrod for Jade Butterfield. Sensitive to the lack of warmth between his own parents, David falls wildly, ecstatically in love with Jade and, moreover, with her family. He is attracted to the easy and casual human warmth and joy he sees them give one another. They seem to him natural, beautiful, and excitingly vital in contrast to his own background of isolation and strictness. His rapport with Jade leads to an intense sexual relationship; they live together, making seemingly endless love in the But-terfield's home, with the family's knowledge and seemingly casual approval. David's world now seems perfect; he is secure and wants life to go on this way forever.

Of course, it cannot go on forever. When Jade's father decrees David's banishment, the boy feels unjustly treated, doubly bereft. There has been no beauty or passion in his life prior to his relationship with the Butterfields; he has come to love them and their vigorous, profligate ways. Joined with them, his life has taken on substance; he needs their life-style to be his and to include him. From David's point of view, he is justified in burning the But-terfields' home because he has planned to save them from the flames, thus winning their gratitude and reinstating himself in their lives; of course, society sees his actions as criminal and insane.

From that point on, David is truly isolated. All of society's strengths are brought to bear to reshape him: there are legal measures; there are the years in psychiatric hospitals; there are people who cannot speak to him. When the novel concludes, David has been altered by others' insights enough to think he might be mad, but he does not care. He has learned to live on two levels: one which is acceptable to the outer world, and another which is acceptable, and accessible, only to himself. On the latter level, he is no longer concerned with anyone's definition of madness; it simply is of no consequence. He sees his love, Jade, everywhere; he cannot have her in the real world, but he has her in his own.

Spencer illustrates a disturbing thesis: that we sometimes have passions we must resist, yet which we cannot deny without destroying ourselves. There is no true middle ground between the extreme views—both false—of sexuality and passion as a destructive curse, and as a healing blessing. The novel's question is enormous: is society sound in protecting itself from the extreme passion it does not understand? Is the passion itself some sort of cosmically biological joke? Is the emotion of love itself a madness? *Endless Love*, uncompromisingly realistic and artful in its treatment of this quandary, should make a lasting place for itself in the realm of truly daring and effective books.

Thomas N. Walters

THE ENGLISH CIVIL WAR
Conservatism and Revolution 1603-1649

Author: Robert Ashton (1924-   )
Publisher: W. W. Norton and Company (New York). 453 pp. $24.95
Type of work: History
Time: The seventeenth century
Locale: England

A reconsideration of the factors that contributed to the outbreak of civil war in seventeenth century England, and of the developments during the war which ultimately led to the overthrow and execution of the Stuart king, Charles I

> *Principal personages:*
> CHARLES I, King of England and Scotland, 1625-1649
> WILLIAM LAUD, Archbishop of Canterbury, 1633-1645
> JOHN PYM, prominent Parliament leader against the King
> EDWARD HYDE, Earl of Clarendon, moderate royalist adviser to King Charles
> OLIVER CROMWELL, Parliamentary General, later Lord Protector
> DENZIL HOLLES, Presbyterian spokesman in the Parliament

At a point well into *The English Civil War*, Ashton makes a statement which seems to express the fundamental thesis of his study: "Most of the Members of Parliament," he writes, "who came up to Westminster in 1640 . . . aspired, if anything, to put the clock back rather than innovate: to restore what they thought of—however mistakenly—as the traditional local ways of doing things as against royal centralizing innovation." Thus it is Ashton's basic contention that the Stuart kings were the perceived revolutionaries of the early seventeenth century, not the Puritans, parliamentarians, and common lawyers, and that by attempting innovations in church and state, the Stuart kings and their agents aimed at subverting the constitution and imposing absolutist, divine right monarchy upon the kingdom. It was to preserve their traditional local rights and the constitution of church and state that many of the king's subjects were forced to take up arms and ultimately to bring down the monarchy.

Ever since the arrival of James I from Scotland in 1603, there had been mounting hostility and division between "Court" and "Country" in England. This unrest stemmed from several sources. One of the most significant was the sweeping assertion by King James of the authority of the monarchy: "the state of monarchy is the supremest thing on earth . . . and kings sit on God's throne." Although James assured his new English subjects that he did not intend to be a tyrant, nevertheless as God's vice-regent on earth, he would be sole master of the kingdom and a surrogate, but loving, father to his people. Moreover, King James inculcated his absolutist divine right theories into his son and successor, Charles I, so much so that Charles eventually paid with his own life for his firm adherence to those doctrines.

Adding to the growing dislike of the country gentry of England toward the Stuart kings was the emergence of a distinctive "court culture" which represented a divergence from traditional English ethos and aesthetics. Most historians have passed over the Stuart court culture rather lightly; Ashton places considerable emphasis upon the court culture as a source of division between the kings—particularly King Charles—and their subjects. King Charles, as is well known, was an outstanding connoisseur and patron of fine arts, as were several of his courtiers. On the face of it, that would have been unobjectionable except the King showed a proclivity for the work of foreign, especially Roman Catholic, artists. This was encouraged by Charles's Catholic wife, Henrietta Maria, and that was what much alarmed the English Protestants of the country. Protestant suspicions were further aroused by similar foreign novelties in architecture and music as part of the court culture. To the Puritans and ordinary country gentlemen, the creations of the royal architect Inigo Jones were as offensive as polyphonic music, organs, and choirs in church services. All those, it seemed, were pointing the court culture in the direction of Rome; nor was that all. The masques, the banquets, the pageantry of the court, and the supposed sexual immorality that presumably flourished at the courts of James and Charles much offended the Puritans and the sober country gentry. In short, contemporaries tended to "identify the Country with the maintenance of traditional standards and the Court with cultural, political, religious and numerous other varieties of innovation."

The growing dichotomy between court and country was also expressed in the matter of local administration, focusing particularly on the office of Lords Lieutenant. These were men whose function it had long been to represent the Crown in their districts, and their districts to the Crown. In line with their bent toward centralism, the Stuart kings attempted to enlarge the first function of the Lords Lieutenant—representation of the Crown in their districts. During the 1620's, the Lords Lieutenant and their deputies were, as agents of the Crown, ordered to carry out such measures as the billeting of soldiers in private homes, demanding forced loans from the gentry, and even imposing martial law although England was nominally at peace. The unpopularity of those measures and of the Lords Lieutenant would find expression in the celebrated Petition of Right presented to King Charles in 1628 by the Parliament. Charles accepted the Petition, agreed to end those practices, and then dismissed the Parliament.

For the next eleven years, from 1629 to 1640, Charles would not summon a Parliament. The King resumed the centralizing efforts, including the resumption of some of the measures he had promised would be halted in the Petition of Right. Without the forum of a Parliament to air their grievances, the country was largely unheard during that time of royal "personal rule," but they nursed their complaints and would act on them when the Parliament was called again.

There was also the intensifying religious quarrel between the Puritans and Archbishop William Laud, Primate of All England. Laud, a good and honest man, aimed only at restoring "church government as it hath been in all ages and all places. . . ." However, that was seen by the Puritans as another dangerous innovation—tending toward the bringing of Popery into the English church and linking it to its secular adjunct, divine right monarchy. By 1640, after a decade of Laud and his Armenian policies, an embittered Puritan would declare that the Archbishop was the "sty of all the pestilential filth that hath infected the state and government of this church and common wealth . . . the cause of all our miseries." Although rightly cautioning against ascribing great and complex events to single causes, Ashton does hold that if any one person can be said to have been responsible, by his policies and actions, for the fall of the Stuart monarchy, that person was William Laud. Laud's actions alienated a growing number of religious Puritans, sending some fleeing to find religious sanctuary in New England, and others to arms to defend the "antient constitution" of church and state, as they understood it.

Puritanism thus joined other issues and other grievances against the King and his Archbishop when Charles finally summoned a Parliament in 1640 after the eleven-year personal rule. Indeed, in the minds of many members of the new Parliament, including Oliver Cromwell, it was the reformation of religion in a more puritanical direction that became the prime issue, and later, the chief "ground of the Parliament's taking up arms."

Part II of *The English Civil War* traces the critical events from the sessions of the Short and Long Parliaments, to the breakdown of efforts by parliamentary and royalist moderates to reach an accommodation, the first and second civil wars, and the royalist defeat and the execution of King Charles in 1649.

For over a year (1641-1642) the major issue in controversy between the King and Parliament was not reformation of religion; it was the effort by a "middle group" of parliamentarians, led by John Pym, to force the King to accept parliamentary approval of the appointment of royal ministers. Pym's principal targets in this controversy were King Charles's chief minister, the Earl of Strafford, and Archbishop Laud. Strafford and Laud were the joint architects of the policy called "thorough" which had meant the imposition of absolutist royal authority during the period of the personal rule. Pym issued a series of petitions and statements of grievances during that year, culminating with the Grand Remonstrance which outlined all of the complaints of the Parliament against the Crown and the policy of "thorough." King Charles, with the advice of Edward Hyde, the Earl of Clarendon, countered with appeals to the moderates in Parliament in which he agreed to make reformations in church and state while holding firmly to the royal prerogative in choosing Crown ministers.

Then, on January 4, 1642, came the famous event in which the King with a troop of soldiers entered the Parliament chambers to arrest Pym and four other members. That reckless attempt at a coup showed the "true face of the court" to the majority in the Parliament. It brought increased support to Pym, it undid the previous work of the Clarendon royalist group to modulate court and country differences, and, worst of all, it was a failure since Pym and the other "birds had flown" before the King could arrest them.

Pym returned to carry through the Parliament two fateful measures: the attainder and subsequent execution of Strafford and Laud, and the Militia Ordinance which placed control of the military forces and the appointment of the Lords Lieutenant, in the hands of the Parliament. With that, the die was seemingly cast; only civil war between King and Parliament remained as the arbiter of their differences. In August, 1642, King Charles raised the royal standard at Nottingham summoning all loyal subjects to repair to it, while the Parliament called on the nation to join with them in defending the reforms that had already been made. Thus, the fighting of the first civil war began.

There were extremists in both camps who welcomed the conflict as the clearest and cleanest way of resolving the outstanding issues. However, for most Englishmen to side wholly with the King or with the Parliament posed a cruel dilemma, and, indeed, many would assert they were fighting for the restoration of both King and Parliament working together in their traditional manner. A substantial number of men remained—or tried to remain—neutral in the fighting, refusing to commit themselves either to the side of the an- nointed King or to the Parliament which appeared to want to turn their world upside down. Interestingly, one group that generally remained neutral in the civil wars were the Roman Catholics of the country (not of the court); those country Catholics could not see that a victory for either Laudian Armeninism or antipapal Puritanism would benefit them or their Church. Most numerous and notable of the neutralists during the war were the so-called "clubmen," voluntary groups that formed in many counties to "preserve ourselves from plunder and all other unlawful violence." The clubmen defended their lands and lives against the depredations of both the royalist and the parliamentary forces, and at the same time they worked to reconcile the conflict, and end it.

Those neutralists also represented the continuing manifestations of localism versus centralism. In the name of local rights they resisted the tax collections, the military levies, and the civil authority which both the King and the Par- liament sought to impose upon them during the war.

As the civil war progressed, new divisions emerged within the Parliament and within its armies. Quarrels erupted between the Presbyterian right wing in the Parliament, represented by Denzil Holles, and the Independents, of which Oliver Cromwell became the best-known. The Presbyterians sought to replace the Laudian episcopal church system with a representative synodal arrangement of the Scottish pattern while the Independents desired a system of autonomous "free" churches. Also appearing were disputes between the Parliament and the Scots who had allied in the first civil war to bring down the King, but then disagreed on the English church settlement. In the parliamentary armies other factions developed, of which the most alarming to the conservative army commanders were the Levellers who were demanding a rough kind of political democracy.

All the while, as the fighting went on, so did negotiations and conferences, seeking to reconcile the royalists with the parliamentarians, the Scots with the English, the Presbyterians with the Independents, the Levellers with the army grandees. Seeing his opportunity in these divisions and in the failures of negotiations, King Charles joined with the Presbyterians and Scots to bring down the Independents in the second civil war, but that effort was doomed and led to his fall and ruin in 1649. Yet, as Ashton sees it, the removal of King Charles and the establishment of the republican Commonwealth afterward did not inaugurate a new era. Rather, for the great majority of Englishmen, it was a "return to the pristine English freedoms which had been usurped by the innovating kings."

The English Civil War is not a book for the casual reader or the beginning student. It is a scholarly study filled with references, concepts, and names that probably would have little or no meaning for the reader without a substantial background knowledge of seventeenth century England. The writing is clear, but the book is densely packed with information. The bibliography, while not extensive, is judiciously selected. Interested readers might study some of the standard works mentioned in the bibliography before turning to *The English Civil War* itself. If that suggestion were followed, then a student would surely find much of interest in this book, and an excellent source for further interpretation and analysis of that most turbulent and tragic age.

James Pringle

ESSAYS IN FEMINISM

Author: Vivian Gornick (1935-   )
Publisher: Harper & Row Publishers (New York). 234 pp. $10.00
Type of work: Essays

A group of essays written over the past decade upon current feminist issues

Most people would agree that the status of women in American Society has undergone some change during the past half century, although the degree of change would unquestionably be a matter hotly debated. Even more hotly debated is the central question of whether the changes in status, those already achieved and those still sought by militant feminists, are beneficial to either women or American society. Even without the self-conscious agitation for change which has become so stridently vociferous during the past decade, women's place in the social and economic order has been evolving at an uneven pace for as long as the industrial revolution has been in progress. Economic pressures, expanding demand for cheap labor, and increased schooling have effectively though inadvertently cooperated to swell the ranks of working women, and to increase the awareness of women as to their position in the social order.

Tradition, religion, laws, and history have prescribed and presumed that women should be silent, passive, and submissive to men. The changes wrought by the industrial revolution and universal public education stimulated a series of changes in the life-styles and the thinking of American women.

Early feminist militancy was primarily vocal or physical. Marches, strikes, and speeches were the principal means of agitation and the most effective methods of impact both upon opponents of change in women's status and upon the vast dormant body of women who had heretofore been guided in their thinking and actions by the precepts of the aforementioned guardians of the status quo: tradition, religion, laws, and history. However, with the expansion in education, labor-saving devices which increased leisure time, and inexpensive and abundant printing and publishing resources, advocacy of feminist causes has more and more been disseminated through the printed word.

During the past decade, this volume of writings about women has increased from a trickle to a torrent. Fiction and nonfiction, drama, essays, political tracts, poetry, biography, history, how-to books, and journals have come to focus in great numbers on the subject of women, their place, their potential, and their personalities. Of course, as the writings of advocates of women's liberation have proliferated, so have the writings of those opposite points of view, but scarcely in any proportionate volume. Or perhaps authors of the vast bulk of printed materials simply accept the traditional status of women as given, and not a matter of interest or argument.

The energy and efforts of writers espousing the women's rights cause must be directed both at educating, arousing, and encouraging change while simultaneously attacking and exposing what writers call the demeaning and unfair conditions associated with "woman's place." One clear and impassioned voice which has been advocating the cause of women through essays and books is that of Vivian Gornick. Her latest book is this collection of essays which originally appeared in the *The Village Voice*, the *New York Times Magazine*, *Ms*, and other periodical publications between 1969 and 1978. As her writings have spanned this pivotal decade in the women's movement, they have a special historical relevance. She speaks to the present and the future, remembering always the past. She describes new patterns of behavior, new attitudes, and new values as American women are in the process of sweeping changes in their life-styles. The scope, if not the momentum, of the changes is increasing daily. Her thoughtful, provocative, and always stimulating descriptions and commentaries on the issues and activities which constitute feminism are gathered here in a volume which speaks powerfully and well to her view of modern woman's experience.

The psychology of women, as it has been shaped by society, and as it is being newly defined and altered by self-conscious women today, is a recurring theme throughout Gornick's essays. Her essay "Consciousness" narrates the interchanges and revelations that occurred at a consciousness-raising session of a half dozen women in 1970. The session is presented as a model for such groups, which can be initiated and developed anywhere that a group of women feels such a need for psychological support and self-examination. The dialogue speaks to several problems in the lives of the women. Their mutual help in analyzing their underlying assumptions and motives, their frank confessions of their fears and mistakes, and their sympathetic support coupled with candid perceptions can convey to the reader a sense of the bonding which women experience as a sustaining force in their lives, arising out of such sessions. The essay is decidedly melodramatic, but it does have impact.

The essay "Boesman and Lena: About Being a Woman" is a moving essay celebrating the discovery of a woman's soul as staged in a dramatic presentation in New York. It deals with the slave mentality, the subjugation to a man, the fear of hunger, and all the assorted threats and stresses of life which overwhelm Lena. Vivian Gornick vividly and with the clarity of sympathetic perception describes the action in terms of the transformation that is occurring within the psyche of this woman as she comes to terms with her situation and with her self.

Two of the essays, "Why Women Fear Success" and "Why Radcliffe Women Are Afraid of Success," deal with a psychological phenomenon which is currently receiving some attention, since it was revealed just a few years ago. It speaks to the fears of both men and women because it deals with the social expectations of both, and with the discomfort or even anxiety one experiences when expected behaviors and customary outcomes do not materialize. The essays express a joy and fervent hope that women and men will come to see women's aggressiveness as normal and necessary for the development of a complete and wholesome personality. Women, Gornick urges, need the striving for, and expectation of, success just as much as men do; for it is exactly such striving and such orientation toward success that develops the personality in the most complete way. The essays are developed with a well-reasoned logic and are supported by researches of psychologists. The effect of dependence has been stultifying on women; it has kept them at an immature state of personality development and in a state of fear of change or of independence.

Indeed, the most pervasive message informing this series of essays is that the crucial task of feminism is self-knowledge; social and political issues will work themselves out as women gain the inner strength of self-understanding and self-realization. Gornick's essays are alive with the passion of conviction, and her writing is sometimes more polemical than polished. However, she also has a well-sustained ring of conviction to her prose which gives even her more melodramatic and radical statements a reason for being.

The essays which deal specifically with the relationships between men and women—relationships of love, kinship, marriage, rivalry, and those which deal with their differences and likenesses as our culture has defined and established them—reveal a bitterness and anger which animates them and which gives them the usefulness of partisan tracts. However, this manifest hostility negates any semblance of objectivity. Her statements are reactions, animated by indignation at the attitudes of men, and the treatment they consequently have accorded to women.

Vivian Gornick is, as she says, a radical. Her essays exhort women and men alike to redefine women in the most liberating sense. She wants all women to define themselves and to shape their own lives, taking full responsibility for themselves. She wants men to cooperate in this process by accepting women as equals in the human experience. She insists on women's potential, on their capabilities, and on their urgent need to achieve the status of equality. Women, she reiterates constantly, are being emotionally and intellectually crippled by the restrictions and indignities which are imposed by society as a matter of course.

The biographical essays in this collection are about women novelists such as Virginia Woolf and Agnes Smedley, about political activists and political writers such as Alice Paul and Dorothy Thompson, and about strong personalities such as Rahel Levin Varnhagen. These essays are designed to present role models of strong women, to analyze their lives and to indicate how they achieved the successes they did, how they developed these strengths which motivated them, and what their weaknesses were—especially how their careers and their personalities were negatively influenced by the traditional expectations of the woman's role in the world and with respect to men.

Gornick mentions the abrasiveness and sometimes hostile nature of these women's personalities. These characteristics, she indicates, were necessary in order for the women to achieve success in a culture which discouraged and deplored such "unfeminine" behavior. If women must behave in socially unacceptable ways to achieve their personal fulfillment, then so be it. She urges women to accept and to champion the right to freedom of expression of all other women, no matter that lesbianism, abrasiveness, and aggressiveness are behaviors sure to arouse condemnation in a society dominated by males, who feel (and probably are) threatened by such manifestations of women's independence.

An important point made by these essays, and one which probably especially needed to be made during the early years of the 1970's, is that the movement toward women's liberation should not become narrowly issue-oriented. The author worries over the appearance of fragmentation, divisiveness, and precious time and energy wasted on bickering about which issues to stress and what definitions must be imposed upon the language. She urges that there is room for all, that the central issue is freedom to develop, freedom to choose, and the acceptance of responsibility along with this independence. She urges political and legal reform, but by no means considers these crucial in the way that personal development and self-knowledge are crucial.

Gornick's analysis of heroines in literature, especially in the final essay, "Female Narcissism as a Metaphor in Literature," incisively probes the personalities of women crippled by social restrictions and by their fears of breaking these bonds. Such women, she demonstrates, are pathetic because they remain infantile, unfulfilled, and unrealized.

Now, in the second half of the twentieth century, Gornick and many other women are decrying the state of civilization, which so demeans and retards the female half of humanity. Through her writing, and through the efforts of many dedicated women and their organizations, she sees changes occurring which can transform women's lives and enhance the quality of life for us all. Gornick speaks with the shrill voice of a radical, with the uneven quality of writing which comes of haste and passion; but she also speaks with conviction, considerable knowledge, and sufficient idealism to lift these essays far above the level of a mere carping attack on the status quo.

Betty Gawthrop

THE EXECUTIONER'S SONG

Author: Norman Mailer (1923-   )
Publisher: Little, Brown and Company (Boston). 1,056 pp. $16.95
Type of work: Novel
Time: 1976-1977
Locale: Utah

The story of Gary Mark Gilmore from his parole in April of 1976 until his execution by a firing squad on January 17, 1977

> *Principal characters:*
> GARY GILMORE, a convicted murderer
> NICOLE, his girl friend
> LAWRENCE SCHILLER, winner of the rights to the story

Norman Mailer has been, by dint of personality as well as overt effort, the most public American man of letters since Ernest Hemingway. Indeed, his popular reputation relies as much upon his acts as upon his words. Behind the public persona of Mailer, however, behind the macho posturing, the obnoxious braggadocio, and the quixotic political ventures, there has always lurked a writer of great ability, a writer who is frequently very good and who, even in failure, is usually at least interesting. Mailer made his early mark as a writer of fiction, most notably with *The Naked and the Dead*. More recently he turned to "new journalism," filtering contemporary events through the prism of his unique and sharply honed consciousness. In a series of books and magazine articles, he explored such subjects as space shots and Vietnam protest, always bringing to his material a passionate self-involvement and making his own perceptions and reactions the focal point of his approach.

The Executioner's Song is "new journalism" of a different order. Mailer is again dealing with real-life materials, but this time he effects an almost naturalistic tone of detachment and objectivity. Not only does he remove his own consciousness from the immediate narration of his story, but he also goes to considerable pains as his story progresses to shift the consciousness among the characters in his tale. Among his achievements in this book is Mailer's almost uncanny ability to locate an idiom, a nuance of speech, or a shade of expression which subtly but deftly reveals the character through whose eyes and ears a segment of the narrative is being perceived.

The raw material of *The Executioner's Song* is the nine-month period between the April, 1976, parole of Gary Gilmore from prison and the January 17, 1977, death of Gilmore at the hands of a Utah firing squad. From this raw material Mailer has fashioned a compelling and often gripping narrative with an astonishing array of finely etched characters.

Mailer tells his tale in two parts. The first and better part, "Western Voices," focuses on Gilmore the man, following him from his release from prison, through his halfhearted and unsuccessful attempt to make it on the outside, his cold-blooded and pointless murders of two unarmed and unresisting men, his unremarkable trial and sentence of death, and, finally, to his decision to renounce the appeals process and to demand that the state carry out the death sentence which it had imposed. It was this act which separated Gilmore from the dozens of other inmates of death row who were waiting out the tedious business of the appellate courts and which suddenly turned Gary Gilmore into a household name, an instant celebrity who was the subject of front-page stories and six o'clock news reports. It was likewise this act which attracted to Utah dozens of legitimate journalists as well as scores of hucksters and hustlers trying to make a buck from the merchandising of Gary Gilmore.

This shabby saga of media hype and amoral profiteering was largely the work of slickers from the East coast and is the focus of the second part of the book, "Eastern Voices." This subject matter is inherently less interesting than that of "Western Voices," and Mailer's decision to devote several hundred pages to Gilmore the media event causes the pace of the book to slow appreciably. Fortunately, Mailer returns to Gilmore the man for the last hundred and fifty pages, in which he recounts the approach of execution day and, finally, of Gilmore's last hours, the execution itself, the ensuing autopsy and cremation, and the maudlin memorial service and sprinkling of ashes which concluded Gary Gilmore's journey on earth.

Mailer's technique is rather like that of an impressionist painter who applies to his canvas seemingly random splotches of color which become coherent shapes only as the observer backs away and lengthens his perspective. Mailer's "random splotches of color" are short, clipped paragraphs in which he shifts from scene to scene, from character to character, gradually bringing vividly to life not only Gilmore but also the others—relatives, friends, lawyers—who were part of the story. Characters too numerous to name materialize in the book as unique, living individuals, and in each case, the reality comes from Mailer's accurate choice of the right anecdotes, the right quotations, the right physical descriptions to set the characters apart from each other and to make them real.

Three characters dominate the book. First, of course, is Gilmore—a complex, enigmatic man, intelligent, artistic, loving, at times almost poetic in his utterances, but possessed in his soul of a terrible, indefinable malignancy which propelled him inexorably toward destruction of himself and others. Time and again one must stifle an urge to reach into the pages of the book and to shake Gilmore back to reason, back to a recognition of the folly of his behavior, of the disastrous and finally fatal consequences of his acts. Next is his lover, Nicole. Twice married, twice divorced, twice a mother while still a teen, and yet somehow innocent and naïve, she seems at times to sleepwalk through a life of pointless promiscuity, poverty, and emotional distress, at other times flaring up with rage and indignation. Finally, there is Larry Schiller, who won the bidding war for the story. He is glib, devious, amoral, and ruthless, and yet shrewdly accurate in his insights and perceptions. It is he who provides the central consciousness for much of the story, and it is apparently he who gathered much of the material for the book and who arranged for Mailer to organize it.

It is to Mailer's credit that he studiously avoids traps into which he could easily have stepped. First, he resists the temptation to use the book as a soapbox from which to preach on capital punishment, prison reform, or myriad other topics. In fact, an advocate interested in such public issues can find persuasive but inconclusive evidence for either side of the debate. For example, advocates of capital punishment can point to a man with abundant natural gifts and ample opportunities who kills indiscriminately and remorselessly. Opponents of the death penalty, however, can argue equally plausibly that, depsite his sins, Gilmore possessed valuable human qualities which could have been nourished. In short, the book would have been seriously weakened had Mailer digressed from the details of his case study and attempted to use his materials to argue a cause. Similarly, Mailer wisely avoids the pitfall of sentimentality. Much of Gilmore's personality and of his relationship with Nicole is the material of which pulp romances are made.

However, Mailer is not able to avoid another problem inherent in this curious genre of "new journalism." The problem is implicit in the book's subtitle: "A True Life Novel." Putting aside mere quibbles about the academic definition of a "novel," there remain serious questions of just what to make of this long and interesting work. By combining real life materials with novelistic techniques—invented dialogue as well as the obvious selection and arrangement of material—Mailer has created a hybrid which contains neither the objective approach to truth of the best nonfiction nor the soaring flights of the imagination which are the lifeblood of serious fiction. For example, Mailer quotes copiously from Gilmore's letters, mostly intimate outpourings to Nicole. In an afterword, however, Mailer admits to selecting excerpts from the letters in order to show Gilmore "at a level higher than his average." It is disconcerting to think that the author frequently made conscious choices aimed at falsely presenting a character. Thus, once the first doubt arises regarding the true reporting of facts about a character, it becomes difficult not to approach the entire work with considerable skepticism. One yearns to know where the real Gilmore, Nicole, and Schiller end and where the Mailer imagination begins.

Recalling the seemingly endless spate of Gilmore stories in the press and adding to those this lengthy book, it is tempting to nod in agreement with the Utah journalist who, according to Mailer, muttered: "Can you believe the attention this cheap punk is getting?" Yet one does not begrudge Gilmore this book as one would perhaps begrudge him a serious biographical treatment because the stuff of Gilmore's life in the hands of a literary craftsman of Mailer's ability is a heady combination. Even if *The Executioner's Song* is ultimately consigned to some literary subgenre, it does not alter the fact that Mailer has used his outstanding skills to create a fascinating, powerful, and moving reading experience which evokes the entire range of human emotions and which consumes the reader's attention—perhaps against his will. It is surely correct to say that a book is better tested by the enchantment it exercises upon a reader's mind than by the facility with which it eases into a convenient literary category. Measured against this standard, Mailer has written a very good book.

L. W. Payne

FAMILIAR TERRITORY
Observations on American Life

Author: Joseph Epstein
Publisher: Oxford University Press (New York). 204 pp. $11.95
Type of work: Essays

A collection of essays by the editor of The American Scholar *which stress wit and clarity of thought in commenting on American life*

The openness and multitudinousness of American culture make Joseph Epstein, the editor of the distinguished journal *The American Scholar*, uneasy. Urbane, reasonable, and deferent, his discontent, however, breeds no zeal. Unlike Aristides, the fifth century B.C. soldier and democratic politician who was purportedly ostracized from Athens because the citizens tired finally of hearing him called "The Just," and under whose name he first wrote the essays collected in *Familiar Territory* for *The American Scholar*, Epstein is not a reformist. Like the exiled Aristides (and this may be the joke behind the use of the *nom de plume*), he stands outside the corridors of cultural power and fashion, if we take them to run through the literary establishment of New York. He edits his journal from Evanston, Illinois, and Northwestern University, where he also teaches, a vantage he finds, despite its location, companionable.

The familiar essay, as practiced by Epstein, is not designed to catch fashion's eye. With its antecedents in Addison and Steele, Dr. Johnson, William Hazlitt, Charles Lamb, George Orwell, E. B. White, and Joseph Wood Krutch, it is written at a leisurely pace without the apocalyptic urgency that so often characterizes contemporary prose. Besides, the familar mode is frequently and generously humorous. Speaking from no other authority than the essayist's taste and prejudice, it does not make any large demands on the reader, its territory never seriously encroaching upon that staked out by the professionals of psychology, politics, sociology, linguistics, literature, or philosophy, although it touches upon all these subjects. Nor is it interested in gaining backers for a cause, but only in establishing a common ground of experience with the reader. Or, as Epstein himself says in the Preface:

> In the end the true job of the familiar essayist is to write what is on his mind and in his heart in the hope that, in doing so, he will say what others have sensed only inchoately. . . . How often the essays in this book will accomplish this is for their readers not for their author to say. But when it does happen, it is like calling out in the desert and having a voice answer back. At such times above all others does the familiar essay breed content.

The desire to breed content rather than contempt is one mark of Epstein's studied indifference to a fashion, long in the ascendancy, that calls for the pundit to ridicule the reader's desire for solace. His recognition of the reader's need for a consolation that derives from finding company in a writer, along with his willingness to fulfill that want, sets him apart from those who aim at either alarming or alienating the reader. This is not to say that he himself is satisfied with the way things are. Quite the contrary, American manners and mores, the subject of these essays, grieve him. This unease of spirit prompts him, though, to seek to comfort like-minded others, as well as himself.

If his own pleasure is derived from being understood and confirmed in his experience by responsive readers, it also resides, as he says, in the act of writing itself. If the satisfaction the reader gains from the prose of *Familiar Territory* is anything like his own in composing it, Epstein is indeed a pleasured writer. His style does not please by shocking us, or by its lyrical sweeps, or by elaborate metaphor and syntax, those characteristics of journalists such as Tom Wolfe and Hunter Thompson. However, it does delight us with its wit, its clarity of structure and language, and its use of apt and recognizable quotations from Dr. Johnson, Dickens, Mencken, and Orwell, among others. His achievement comes, moreover, in having created a "voice," a quality difficult to define, having to do with that word full of useful ambiguity, "sincerity." It is also a style impossible to illustrate through brief quotation, since its effect is cumulative, only moving us to an admiration of its eloquence after a sufficiently long acquaintance.

In his magisterial study of Matthew Arnold, Lionel Trilling wrote: "Style is character, it is the quality of a man's emotions made apparent; then, by an inevitable extension, style is ethics, style is government." This being so, Epstein's style, meticulous in its observation of standard forms of composition, expression, and correctness and in its abhorrence of eccentricity in language and rhythm, is his moral response to a culture that has little patience with any inherited forms, whether of social manner, dress, sexual mores, or language, all subjects of his bemusements. Indeed, contemporary American culture, characterized by its ignorance and misuse of language, its appetite for the ephemeral and trivial, and its obsession with change and variety, expresses its hatred of any kind of limit, together with a desire for existence without any of its conditions. We are, according to Epstein in his animadversion "Running and Other Vices," "self-absorbed perfectibilitarians," a particularly apt phrase. We prefer the life of the senses to mind; experience to innocence; relativity of values or democratization to hierarchy; and the self-indulgence of youth to the forbearance of maturity. In consequences of our choices, we have made a culture without order or tranquility, and, paradoxically, without pleasure, or at least without the joys of "life at the quotidian," which has been forgone in favor of the life of the bizarre—or at the boutiques.

Epstein's description of the American character is by no means unfamiliar. These same attributes, although in an earlier stage of development, were recognized by Alexis de Tocqueville in the 1830's, and by Henry Adams somewhat later, as well as by a number of social observers and satirists in this country. In *Democracy in America*, for example, we read of the early settlers following similar paths of escape from the past, present, and social and moral limitations. Our country was conceived in liberty and the pursuit of happiness, after all, and we have found those ends where we will. And, besides, we inherited no sufficiently strong institutions to check effectively the excesses of our national bent, as the British did to restrain their modern zeal for liberation. Puritan morality, together with the old bourgeois ethic of work, duty, and family, did hold us in bounds, at least at times, and until after World War II. Indeed, it was the tension that arose between the drive for liberation and the restraints of middle-class religion and family that once gave our culture, and our literature, its provocative and complex drama. Now, it would appear, we have thrown off these encumbrances. Propelled by the superabundance and distribution of our great wealth, we have leaped the ethic of the past and landed in a brave new world without imperatives.

It is this newly created "counterculture," and particularly the ways in which the sons and daughters of the bourgeois have embraced it, that elicits Epstein's discontent, as well as a wry humor designed to maintain some balance in the whirligig of the moment. The descendents of the patriarchs and matriarchs, who ten years ago or so took to the streets, protesting domestic and international injustice, are now at work, liberating us from the inconveniences of manners and morals. They are also busy making the schlock that jams the bookstores and the boutiques and constitutes our television programs and movies. Contemptuous of the disciplines of art and history, our tastemakers and their followers glut themselves on the entertainment of the moment, "cure" themselves with Pop psychology, and consume anything that might shock the old middle class (as if it existed any longer), somehow convinced that being so "with it" is to be authentic and free.

If the counterculture were confined to the creation and the consumption of junk, it might be easier to tolerate. What discomfits Epstein, however, is that the current liberation movement has made significant incursions into the University, at one time a refuge against such vulgarities. Its walls, alas, are no longer ivied or unbreached. Also in his most powerful essay of the collection, "Sex and the Professors," the only one in which bemusement gives way to something approaching disgust, he describes how the Academy has adopted the mores of youth and the moment, betraying mind, reason, and its duty to teach in the process. Assuming that the large majority of his readers are themselves academics, he is probably not so much interested in breeding content here as he is in calling into embarrassing question the whole moral character of the American professoriat.

He puts the questions bluntly: "Do professors often sleep with their students? Are professor-student liaisons now rather a commonplace aspect of academic life? If they are what does this say about the quality of academic life today?" Anyone who has been around the University during the last generation could not but agree with his affirmative answers to the first two questions. Yet his response to the last question would not, I believe, draw a clear consensus. The new freedom of sexual congress between students and teachers, in Epstein's view, has corrupted pedagogy; but he sees the breakdown of that fragile taboo as a symptom rather than a cause of the professors' general retreat from the authority of the mind and history, which they at one time represented, in a hysterical rush to worship at the altar of youth and to deny that they are really different from everyone else. Nor is it merely, as he continues, that "Faculty-student sex is unprofessional, but it is also wrong." Those professors who ignore the lesson of the Socrates who rejected the advances of Alcibiades have joined the "Gadarene."

Epstein's conclusion is painfully true; but it must be pursued another step, one he is not willing to take, although he considers it. He does not think the corruption touches the students, but only the "quality of academic life" and the professors. It is difficult to see why the students should be immune to the corruption. On the contrary, in joining their teachers in bed, often looking for self-affirmation and therapy, and not always innocently either, they too have jumped into the sty. The effect on all those involved is a withering of the spirit. Certainly, the professors commit the greater wrong by taking advantage of their more vulnerable students, and by failing to love them in their refusal to provide the knowledge that makes personhood possible. Violence done to souls and minds, rather than ignorance, is the unforgivable academic sin.

However the subject, once opened, must be taken yet another step, an inquiry the familiar essay possibly does not accommodate, suggesting an inherent limitation of the form. One must ask why, at last, the contemporary professor has abrogated his authority, just as one must wonder why Americans, as Epstein describes them, dread jokes, enlist in every faddish psychological movement in the hope of absolute fulfillment, and exercise and diet with a devotion verging on the hysterical. It has everything to do, as he knows, with the pathological fear of death that has overtaken us. While he alludes to this underlying cause, he does not investigate it with any thoroughness. It is not, as he would surely say, the place, since such a question demands a seriousness inappropriate to the familiar essay. It is the place, and it is certainly the time, for an act of grace on the part of the writer, an offering of sympathy and understanding which Epstein never makes. For if Americans are running from the ultimate weight of death in their search for perfection and in their demand for an endless variety of experience, then in the interest of affection and truth, criticism and judgment must be suspended, at least long enough to acknowledge the pain and sadness these antics, however reprehensible, bespeak. Epstein, for example, in ridiculing those silly Dandies, "Wearing sunglasses, helmets of hot-combed hair, [and] sprayed mustaches," never pauses to wonder how much anxiety and hurt lie behind their "disguises," as he calls them.

It is not that he is incapable of imaginative sympathy. In his first book, *Divorced in America*, he tells of his experiences with Parents Without Partners, an organization for the divorced. At one of their meetings, he is able to get beyond the members' forced good humor, their Babbittry and zeal for organization, to recognize their clumsy struggle for happiness. As he concludes, "No one in this room has overcome hope, and alongside this fact all criticisms seem trivial." If there is too much at stake to allow Epstein to suspend criticism entirely when faced with the "self-absorbed perfectibilitarians" or with the "TV Johnnies" or with the Calibans of the Academy, there is not so much that he can ignore that they are more than creatures of culture. There is, in short, another and nobler way of breeding content among those who share his experience of a demeaning culture. That is to extend, without condescension, consolation in the form of an understanding and an acknowledgment of the cruel, fundamental situation that all undergo. The felicitous pleasures provided by wit, style, and clarity of perception, all abundantly available in *Familiar Territory*, and all themselves protections against the existential cruelty, are not the best a writer can confer. The best is wisdom founded on the affections, a wisdom such as Saul Bellow's Mr. Sammler gives to all those caught up in our present absurdity.

David Kubal

FIELD WORK

Author: Seamus Heaney (1939-   )
Publisher: Farrar, Straus and Giroux (New York). 66 pp. $8.95
Type of work: Poetry

The fifth collection by an Irish poet of resourcefulness and power, Field Work *is a collection of genuine importance and a harbinger of even more important work to come*

Seamus Heaney has been widely praised since his first book of poems appeared in 1966. He is now fifty years of age, and serious critics are calling him the finest Irish poet since Yeats. It is Heaney's good fortune to have combined a reverence for the earth—its farms, bogs, and men—with an extraordinarily subtle command of poetic technique. In other words, much of what he has to say gives the impression that it would be worth saying badly; yet he has the skill to say it uniquely and durably.

Field Work ranges over the earth with love, humor, anger, and regret, in a wide variety of forms. The book tends to fall into three parts, two sets of some dozen poems, each separated by a ten-sonnet sequence. Several of the poems in the first section confront the Irish "trouble." In "Sibyl," the second part of a poem called "Triptych," someone answers the speaker's "What will become of us?" by saying that "unless forgiveness finds its nerve and voice," the very form of the people is bound to change, in "Saurian relapses":

> "My people think money
> And talk weather. Oil-rigs lull their future
> On single acquisitive stems. Silence
> Has shoaled into the trawlers' echo-sounders.
>
> The ground we kept our ear to for so long
> Is flayed or calloused, and its entrails
> Tented by an impious augury.
> Our island is full of comfortless noises."

The best of the poems arising from this tragic subject is "Casualty," an astonishingly deft portrait of a fisherman and drinking companion blown to bits one night when he was out during a curfew. The surprising technical fact is that the poem is cast in something over a hundred lines of iambic trimeter—not a measure that comes readily to mind when one is casting about for something elegiac. The flexibility of this meter, in Heaney's hands, is considerable; it is achieved partly by skillful variation of the meter itself, and partly by a subtle variation in the rhyme scheme, which begins by being regular and audible, and then shifts in the direction of slant rhyme and unpredictable placement. The regularity is most obvious at the beginning of the poem:

> He would drink by himself
> And raise a weathered thumb

Towards the high shelf,
Calling another rum
And blackcurrant, without
Having to raise his voice,
Or order a quick stout
By a lifting of the eyes
And a discreet dumb-show
Of pulling off the top;
At closing time would go
In waders and peaked cap
Into the showery dark,
A dole-kept breadwinner
But a natural for work.

The friendship between this fisherman and the speaker of the poem is somewhat tenuous; the speaker, "always politic/ And shy of condescension," is reluctant to let their conversations in pubs hover too long over poetry, even when the fisherman has introduced the subject. He prefers to let the talk drift to what the fisherman knows; as this point is made, the predictability of rhyme diminishes, and the fisherman meets his end, just three days after "they shot dead/ The thirteen men in Derry."

The poem continues with a leisurely and moving description of the funeral of the Derry thirteen, and then goes again over the death of the fisherman. The poem ends, not with the fisherman's funeral, but with a recollection of a day spent in his boat:

To get out early, haul
Steadily off the bottom,
Dispraise the catch, and smile
As you find a rhythm
Working you, slow mile by mile,
Into your proper haunt
Somewhere, well out, beyond . . .

Dawn-sniffing revenant,
Plodder through midnight rain,
Question me again.

Much of this poem's power comes from its sense of proportion, its right placement of emphasis. That the fisherman was a victim of tragic hostilities is important, but this is not primarily a poem about the Irish trouble; it is an elegy for a man whose character has been reimagined with such affection and fullness that the cause of his death takes its place as something always in the background, pervasive, implacable, and unjust, but not powerful enough to obliterate the sense of humanity and love that informs these lines.

"Glanmore Sonnets" is a rich and rewarding sequence. Heaney has found, as any living poet must, his own way of working within this demanding form. The pressures of such work are both technical and historical; one can hardly sit down to write a sonnet in total obliviousness to what others have done with the form. But for some, this realization has been crushing, productive of rebellion against meter and of such manifestos as Robert Bly's wonderful idea that "The sonnet is where old professors go to die." The assumption in such cases is that one must forge ahead, making a kind of poetry which gives evidence of progress over the old modes.

The trouble with this assumption is that the materials of a craft do not outlive their usefulness all by themselves: they have to be replaced to the general satisfaction of most practitioners. In technology, this process is more easily visible than in the arts: dynamite is better than black powder, the steam drill was better than John Henry. But the line of Whitman, for example, is not demonstrably better for all purposes than the sonnet.

All this is prompted partly by a remark Heaney made during a reading at the Library of Congress in 1979. He introduced a poem by saying, "Now I should like to read you a little sonnet," then paused, looked up as if he had caught himself in some mistake, and added, "Why should one say 'little sonnet'? They're all the same size—ten by fourteen." As Heaney thus acknowledged, an advantage of the sonnet is that its venerable history makes choosing it a kind of statement in itself. So when a poet calls something "Glanmore Sonnets," we can immediately detect a stance toward the poetic traditions of his language. And, if the poet is skillful enough, he can convince us that writing sonnets is not a way of competing with Shakespeare, Words-worth, or Yeats; it is a way, to paraphrase Eliot, of collaborating with them in the development of a tradition.

The narrative situation of Heaney's sequence is, in terms of external events, not very complex. A poet and his wife have gone to live in a rural section of County Wicklow; Heaney himself lived there for four years, after his departure from Belfast in 1972. From Heaney's earlier books we may have learned that farm life has meant much to him, though he is hardly a man for whom farming is a whole way of life. These sonnets portray the Glanmore interlude as a period of coming to terms with the land and of accommodating the poetic voice to what rises from the land. There are two or three faint suggestions that life in the country, at least as the poet was trying to live it, might have been something of a strain on his wife, as in "Sonnet III," which begins with the evocation of birdsong and glimpses of deer:

> I had said earlier, "I won't relapse
> From this strange loneliness I've brought us to.
> Dorothy and William—" She interrupts:
> "You're not going to compare us two . . .?"
> Outside a rustling and twig-combing breeze
> Refreshes and relents. Is cadences.

The subtle alternation of full rhymes and slant rhymes here is characteristic of the entire sequence. In an isolated example such as the passage above, the total effect of this kind of rhyming is hard to see; but what happens is not unlike what often happens in the full rhymes of Pope's couplets. When there is a likeness of sound alone, the effect may be pleasing enough; but sometimes there will be an ironic juxtaposition of meanings as well. By sprinkling half-rhymes and full rhymes almost equally throughout the sequence, Heaney is able to create similar surprises even when the rhymes are inexact.

This particular device is appropriate to the themes of the sequence; the poems constitute an exploration, a patient and waiting search for the words that will make poems, and for evidence that the poet has chosen his life responsibly. Such overt concern with poetry as a subject has been the death of many a skillfully wrought poem, but the balance here between internal and external lives, like the balanced rhyming technique, gives the poems a tension which keeps them alive.

The poems which follow "Glanmore Sonnets" are somewhat miscellaneous in effect; it is apparent that a variety of events, images, and people have triggered further exploration of the themes enumerated above. Some poems, like "Field Work," seem too private, too nearly inaccessible; others, however, are immediate and powerful. "A Dream of Jealousy" is a fine vignette of a man, his wife, and another woman, trying to be civilized about desires that are generally thought to be illicit. "An Afterwards" is a scarifying vision of the poet in Dante's ninth circle; his wife, touring the area with Vergil's wife, says

> "I have closed my widowed ears
> To the sulphurous news of poets and poetry.
> Why could you not have, oftener, in our years
>
> Unclenched, and come down laughing from your room
> And walked the twilight with me and your children—
> Like that one evening of elder bloom
> And hay, when the wild roses were fading?"

The image of Dante's ninth circle is powerfully evoked in this poem, but not so powerfully as in "Ugolino," a translation from Dante which concludes *Field Work*. Heaney has selected the end of "Canto XXXII" and the beginning of "Canto XXXIII," the horrifying story of Count Ugolino and Archbishop Ruggiero; it is the episode in which Ugolino and his children were imprisoned and starved to death. Like most successful translators of Dante, Heaney has not attempted to retain the *terza rima*, but rhymes only the first and third lines of each tercet. He also omits the stanza breaks. Amidst many felicities in this translation, there are a few phrases which seem forced, as if Heaney had not entirely come to grips with the fact that several centuries lie between Dante and himself; furthermore, Heaney's use of slant rhyme sometimes seems, in this instance, to have been a last resort—the well-known "translator's rhyme" that plagues any of us who work with rhymed originals. But the power of Dante's story is undiminished by these small distractions; "Ugolino" is a suggestive conclusion to this volume.

When a poet falls to translating, it is often because he is casting around for something to do. *Field Work* is a splendid collection, but there are indications that it marks a significant turning-point in Heaney's career. Less single-mindedly intense than his earlier books, sometimes faltering slightly, it is nevertheless a solid achievement which at the same time presages even better work to come.

Henry Taylor

5TH OF JULY

Author: Lanford Wilson (1937-   )
Publisher: Hill and Wang (New York). 128 pp. $11.95
Type of work: Drama
Time: The evening of July 4 and morning of July 5, 1977
Locale: The Talley farm near Lebanon, Missouri

Disillusioned Berkeley ex-radicals struggle to find new meaning and direction for their lives in the late 1970's

> *Principal characters:*
> KENNETH TALLEY, JR., a legless Vietnam veteran
> JED JENKINS, his lover
> JUNE TALLEY, his sister
> SHIRLEY TALLEY, her illegitimate daughter
> JOHN LANDIS, a childhood friend of the Talleys
> GWEN LANDIS, his sensual, erratic wife
> WESTON HURLEY, composer friend of the Landises
> SALLY FRIEDMAN, Ken and June's aunt

Although Lanford Wilson is the second most frequently produced American playwright (Tennessee Williams is first), his name was little known to the general public beyond the confines of the New York theatrical scene until the Broadway success of his most recent play, *Talley's Folly* (as yet unpublished)—a fact that says more about the state of American theater and its place in the cultural spectrum than it does about Wilson's work.

A quick comparison between Wilson's career and that of Edward Albee, America's last "important" playwright, demonstrates the point. Despite its brevity, Albee's first play, *The Zoo Story* (1958), made him fairly well-known as the most significant "Off-Broadway" dramatist of the late 1950's. Since the peak of Off-Broadway activity coincided with Albee's best works, his reputation soared, although his productivity was modest. In 1962, he made the move to Broadway with *Who's Afraid of Virginia Woolf?*, which became the most famous and successful serious American play of the 1960's, as well as one of the decade's better-known films. Since then, although only two of his plays, *Tiny Alice* (1965) and *A Delicate Balance* (1966), have achieved any degree of critical and/or commercial success, Albee is still well known and seriously regarded.

By the time Lanford Wilson came to New York in 1962, however, theatrical production costs had soared, innovation and experimentation were dead, and "Off-Broadway" had become almost indistinguishable from its slightly richer big brother. But Wilson found a new milieu, "Off-Off-Broadway," where coffee shops, storefronts, basements, church naves, and the like had been converted into noncommercial stages, and original, experimental work was emphasized. Here a playwright could work free of commercial pressures and of the temptations of fortune or fame. Wilson's second produced play, *The*

Madness of Lady Bright (1966), became the first real Off-Off-Broadway "hit," and since that time he has produced a most impressive body of work.

The best-known of these works include *Balm in Gilead* (1965), the first original full-length play done Off-Off-Broadway; *The Rimers of Eldritch*, winner of the Vernon Rice-Drama Desk Award as the best Off-Broadway play of 1967; *The Hot l Baltimore*, winner of the New York Critics Circle and Obie Awards for Best Play of the 1972-1973 season, and later adapted for a short-lived ABC-TV series; and *The Mound Builders* (1975), another Obie Award winner and subsequent PBS television production. Yet for all of that, only in 1980, with *Talley's Folly* a certified Broadway hit, can Lanford Wilson be said to have finally achieved success.

5th of July, produced Off-Broadway in 1978 and published in 1979, is the first of a trilogy about the Talley family and the first of several projected plays to be set in Lebanon, Missouri, Wilson's hometown. It chronicles the attempts of the Talley children, who came to maturity during the social and political chaos of the late 1960's and early 1970's, to put their disoriented, disillusioned lives together and find new directions for themselves as they precariously enter middle age. *Talley's Folly* takes place thirty years earlier when Sally Talley, a high-spirited, rebellious WASP spinster of thirty-one, is wooed and won by Matt Friedman, a forty-two-year-old Jewish refugee accountant. Sally Talley Friedman, a sixty-seven-year-old widow in *5th of July*, provides the primary connection between the two plays. The final play in the trilogy is slated for production late in 1980.

In *5th of July*, Wilson demonstrates the method that he has so effectively developed over the past few years, an approach that clearly reflects his commitment to "ensemble creativity." In 1969, he and a number of his colleagues founded the Circle Repertory Company, which has since thrived, to some extent because of its fine productions of his plays. Wilson regards the Circle Rep players as true collaborators, and much of his work seems tailored to their talents; he has, he says, "a kind of mild aversion to working alone that everybody at Circle Rep comes by honestly."

In some ways Wilson is a very old-fashioned playwright, in others a most contemporary one. His approach to characterization and theatrical techniques fixes him squarely in the American realistic tradition of (early and late) Eugene O'Neill, the Elmer Rice of *Street Scene*, Clifford Odets' social plays, and the best works of William Inge, Arthur Miller, and Tennessee Williams— although the dramatist he most resembles is Anton Chekhov. But if his methods are traditional, his insights are thoroughly contemporary. He writes, he has said, "for that decently intellectual, politically aware social realist out there that I think the intelligent half of America is," and his characters are absolutely attached to their time and place, be it 1944 or 1977. Yet Wilson is never a social or political polemicist. His focus is always on the effects that sociopolitical currents and pressures have on his characters as individuals and how they shape their needs, actions, and directions.

As is the case with Tennessee Williams, a dramatist with whom he has been compared (and with whom he has worked, as collaborator on "The Migrants," a CBS-*Playhouse 90* script, and as librettist for Lee Hoiby's music in the operatic version of *Summer and Smoke*), the Chekhovian influences on Wilson are obvious. The action in many of his plays, especially those with a half dozen or more characters, may seem undirected, almost aimless. Characters talk, ruminate out loud, go about ordinary tasks, establish relationships, and reveal their foibles and preoccupations. The talk is believable, clever, and interesting, filled with bits and pieces of insight and information. The characters are vivid, very real, and quite sympathetic. But the design of the whole and the direction of the action is not always clear, and the emotional intensities seem muted. Frequently the individuals, or even couples, seem isolated, wrapped up in their own worlds with little connection to others or to any overtly developing plot line. Then subtly, beautifully, it all comes together in revelations that are powerful and memorable, but without the histrionics of a Williams or Albee; it is more like a Joyce epiphany than an O'Neill climax.

Although the play takes place during the evening of the 4th and the morning of the 5th of July, 1977, the title refers to much more than the time of year: it is the day after the "patriotic celebration" of the late 1960's and early 1970's. The Vietnam War is ancient history; Ken Talley's potential high school students "don't even know where Vietnam is." The moral fervor, the protests, the hopes, and the anger have been long dissipated, forgotten, or barely remembered with a bitter nostalgia. Yet the people are left, no longer young, and with half a lifetime yet to live. *5th of July* focuses on a small group of onetime "Berkeley radicals" who have returned, without convictions or directions, to the family homestead, the rundown Talley farm near Lebanon, Missouri. All have been severely damaged by their experiences.

Ken Talley, Jr., began as a protester, but eventually answered the draft, served in Vietnam, and had both legs blown off. His disillusioned sister June, having sent her illegitimate daughter to live with her Aunt Sally during the years she was riding the protest circuit, now tries to establish a viable relationship with that daughter, Shirley, now fourteen. Visiting them at the Talley farm are Gwen and John Landis, companions of the radical years, who separated from the Talleys shortly before Ken's induction into the Army. Gwen, a very rich, erratic, oversexed, would-be singer, has been physically, emotionally, and morally burned out by sex, alcohol, drugs, and feverish living. Her husband, John, seemingly the least damaged by time and pressures, hovers about her like a predatory bird. They have ostensibly come to the Talley farm not only for a friendly reunion, but also to buy the property and turn it into a "recording studio away from Nashville."

Bracketing the revolutionary generation are two other important characters, Sally Friedman, the Talley's sixty-seven-year-old aunt, and June's daughter Shirley. Sally has returned to the farm in order to dispose of the ashes of her late husband before moving to a California retirement community. Shirley chafes at the dull Lebanon milieu, while constantly proclaiming her devotion to life, to art, to the future, to herself, and to everything other than the values and life-style of her mother.

Like Chekhov's *Uncle Vanya*, it is the intrusion of the "sophisticated city folk" into the rural environment that upsets the delicate balance that has previously prevailed. But, also like the Chekhov play, the corrupting influence is unobtrusive and ambiguous; it emerges slowly and does not so much challenge the other characters as it brings into focus their own latent weaknesses and inner crises. The Landis offer to Ken Talley promises a chance to get off the farm and evade, or at least put off, the personal tests that lie in front of him. To Shirley they offer some glamour and a possible escape. To both June and Ken they offer a return to the unfulfilled possibilities of their youth and, perhaps inadvertently, a chance to come to terms with the vital questions in that past that have remained, not only unanswered, but even unasked.

The one emotion that can sentimentalize, even destroy, a play like *5th of July* is self-pity, an easy emotion for a playwright to indulge in under the guise of "sensitivity" (as in much of O'Neill and Tennessee Williams). The characters in *5th of July* have none of it. Ken blames nobody, person or government, for his misfortune, and June has no sentimental apologies or recantations for her ex-radicalism. Even Gwen, a much less sympathetic figure, mutes her self-pity with self-deprecating wit and irony.

But if they have accepted the facts of their pasts, the Talleys do not yet know what to do with their futures. Ken has been offered a teaching job at Lebanon High School. He is, he admits, "terrified" at the prospect. Can he face the world—the *young* world, one that could not care less about Vietnam "heroes"—on crutches? A single visit to the school left him quaking. He also worries about his homosexuality, which is an obvious, although unemphasized, fact of his life. However, Ken knows that his expressed fears about community acceptance are only rationalizations; it is his own doubts about himself that he must overcome. Similarly, June must come to terms with her daughter's illegitimacy if she is to break down the barriers between them, while Shirley must understand her mother's actions in order to accept them; she must get over the notion that her birth was the result of a casual, promiscuous coupling.

John Landis unintentionally brings these questions to light. Loved by all, he has loved nobody. The disappointment Ken felt when John and Gwen went to Europe without him was the primary reason he ignored his antiwar convictions and let himself be drafted. In the climactic scene of *5th of July*, Ken learns that it was John, not Gwen, who betrayed him by leaving precipitously. John's offer to buy the Talley farm at a ridiculously low price is only incidental to his real purpose—to get Shirley for a "visit" to Nashville. John almost confesses to being her father, but backs off from that responsibility in front of the girl. Seeing that, Shirley begins to look at June in a new light and accept some of the things she has said. At the crucial moment, Shirley rejects John and says she "will live in St. Louis with my mother."

On that line John pushes himself by Ken, accidentally knocking him to the floor. That theatrical image crystallizes the play. John is the villain, but nobody really cares. He has survived the disillusionment of the 1960's because he has never cared about anybody but himself, an attitude that has not altered with time. He loved and left both Ken and June because they could give him nothing; he literally pursued and captured Gwen because of her money, and he uses her weaknesses to keep her dependent while he manipulates her life to suit the corporate interests that want to keep her out of the way.

Ken, of course, is able to rise from the floor and face the tests he must. He has a responsibility to himself to do so and "responsibility" is one of the two key words in the play, the other being "survival." Ken and June will survive because they accept responsibility for their own lives and because they can force themselves to make the best of them. Sally, who decides to reject California in favor of the Talley farm, has long shown herself to be a tough old bird. Shirley shows great promise, with a touch too much of adolescent romanticism, perhaps, but with much of her mother's strength showing through. But Gwen will survive only as long as artificial worlds are created for her to live in, and John will survive the way all parasites do, only as long as his host animal does. In the end we rejoice with the characters who will survive and, unpleasant though they may be, lament those who will not. No other current American playwright creates characters as believable, provocative, and sympathetic as Lanford Wilson.

The underlying theme—that man must look into himself rather than to external things or causes or events for his own strength and direction—is hardly a new one, but Wilson gives it fresh verve and intensity in *5th of July*. The theme is most memorably summarized in the conclusion of a science fiction story which has been written by a young boy that Ken is tutoring. In the final moments of the play, Ken reads it to the audience:

> ". . . After they had explored all the suns in the universe, and all the planets of all the suns, they realized that there was no other life in the universe, and that they were alone. And they were very happy, because then they knew it was up to them to become all the things they had imagined they would find."

Keith Neilson

FIVE FOR SORROW, TEN FOR JOY

Author: Rumer Godden (1907-   )
Publisher: The Viking Press (New York). 262 pp. $10.95
Type of work: Novel
Time: The early to late twentieth century
Locale: England and France

A story, told in flashbacks, of a woman's career including her trial for murder, her service in World War II, her life as a prostitute and a madame, and finally, her life as a nun

> *Principal characters:*
> LISE, the protagonist
> PATRICE, her lover and mentor
> VIVI, a woman who succumbs to the evil side of her nature

This latest novel by British writer Rumer Godden explores a number of themes with which she has dealt in many of her previous fictions. In some respects, *Five for Sorrow, Ten for Joy* recapitulates ideas and concerns about which Godden has written through her entire lengthy career. This interesting, intriguing novel, while not one of her best books, might in some ways be considered a summation of the obsessions with which this always fascinating and thoughtful writer has wrestled in volume after volume.

Once again, as in several earlier novels, Godden uses the cloistered setting of the Catholic convent as the vehicle to express her themes. In *Black Narcissus* and *In This House of Brede*, she wrote with authority and compassion of the cloistered life and of the women who chose— or were chosen—for it. Perhaps few other writers have expressed so vividly or felt so deeply both the attractions and the pains of this austere, rigorous, and constantly *giving* way of life, a style of existence which necessarily is endured and celebrated within walls. Now, in her most recent book about the agonies and joys of the religious life, Godden plunges through scenes of depravity in the outer world in order to make yet more vital the mystery and wonder of the inner world of the cloister.

Freedom in confinement has long been a theme which fascinates Godden. The inner freedom found when confined by the strangeness of an alien culture, the peace discovered through trial and error in the holy life, the gradual alleviation of torment when confined against one's will in a man-made prison—in novel after novel, Godden has woven these threads through her fictional narratives. In *Five for Sorrow, Ten for Joy*, the protagonist, Sister Lise, has experienced all of these kinds of bondage and has made her way to the ultimate freedom, the triumphant peace of selflessness. The many themes which weave in and out of the story are heightened by the author's flashback technique, through which the stages of Lise's life come to be seen as a whole.

Good and evil, treated both as opposing forces and as different sides of each human personality, have been one of Godden's major concerns since her first published writings. The problem of the so-called "incorrigible" personality appeared as far back as *Black Narcissus*, was approached from different points of view in books as varied as *An Episode of Sparrows* and *The Peacock Spring*, and was fully analyzed in *In This House of Brede*. These "evil" personalities struggle, either to dominate or to overcome their inclinations; some triumph over their worse elements, while others, such as Vivi, in this novel, succumb to the evil side of their natures. Always, their struggle is portrayed with compassion and precision.

Closely aligned with this theme is that of the individual's awakening, be it the awakening of a young person to the wonders of the world and the possibilities of life, or the awakening of a lost soul to the glory of virtue and God. This theme was explored in *The Greengage Summer*, *The Battle of the Villa Fiorita*, *The River*, *An Episode of Sparrows*, and in both of the previous convent novels. Many of Godden's characters achieve inner peace only after a long battle and only after they learn the importance and necessity of certain values—most fundamentally, duty and responsibility. Lise, for example, anticipates that the convent will be peaceful, but finds instead that it is a place of constant self-denial, of joyous obedience, of work for others, and of satisfaction in doing one's duty before all else.

When Lise is tried in court for the murder of her lover and mentor, Patrice, the theme of responsibility is symbolized by the great tapestry hanging on the wall which depicts the childking Louis XIII on his throne, wearily holding his sceptre as he is offered the crown by his mother, Marie de Medici. The boy's responsibility is burdensome, yet he accepts it as inevitable. The message is that no one can escape his or her responsibilities without destroying that part of themselves which is fundamental and worthwhile.

The theme of duty and work is richly documented in the descriptions of the seasons at the convent. Godden lovingly describes the work which comes with each season: the planting, the spreading of manure, the pruning and digging, the harvesting and preserving, the storage of fodder, the milking, the manufacturing of cheese and butter. In these simple, homely tasks, the characters find a peace and a joy which is missing from more ambitious endeavors; and these tasks represent the duties which each person must master before he can find lasting happiness and tranquility.

Perhaps the greatest example of duty, of its difficulties and rewards, is seen in Lise's courage when she is sent by the convent to visit inmates in the same prison in which she was a convict fifteen years earlier. The return to those bleak walls is painful for Lise, but she realizes that she must endure the pain and triumph over it, both for the sake of her own soul, and for the sakes of the women prisoners who need what she has to offer them. Duty is related to charity, and sometimes the two are one. After her years in the outside world, Lise finds it difficult to learn about charity, but eventually the concept permeates her being, as she discovers the riches inherent both in giving and in receiving charity, and in feeling charity toward others.

Lise is transformed several times in this tale of her life, first when she is discovered by her own Svengali, like Botticelli's *Birth of Venus*, rising from a fountain in Paris. Later, another of her transformations is symbolized by the birth of a butterfly, beautiful and delicate, but short-lived. Lise is known by many names during her many different incarnations. Born Elizabeth Fanshawe in England, she becomes Lise the Army driver during World War II, then Lise Ambard, the high-class prostitute, then Madame Lise Ambard, the proprietor of one of the best "houses" in Paris, and, after her face is scarred, "La Balafrée." Then she is a numbered convict in prison, and finally, she becomes "Soeur Lise"—Sister Lise. Each name represents another stage in the pilgrimage of her life.

Many comparisons are drawn and implied between the nuns and the prostitutes and the female convicts: all of them are "out of the ordinary world," living lives different from those of most women. They are confined by their "superiors," told what to do, and required to lead disciplined existences, for better or for worse. Each must find satisfaction in areas in which most women would never look. They learn to sublimate certain dreams and desires, to endure hardship, and to find their happiness where they can.

This is a rich book, a sensitive and intelligent story firmly based in a philosophical and moral code. If the structure is somewhat forced and the style less pure and true than in the best of Godden's novels, *Five for Sorrow, Ten for Joy* nevertheless remains an important and a rewarding book.

Bruce D. Reeves

FRANKLIN D. ROOSEVELT AND
AMERICAN FOREIGN POLICY, 1932-1945

Author: Robert Dallek (1934-   )
Publisher: Oxford University Press (New York). 657 pp. $19.95
Type of work: History
Time: 1932-1945
Locale: The United States

A comprehensive, chronological survey of the foreign policy ideas and actions undertaken by the Franklin D. Roosevelt Administrations

> *Principal personages:*
> WINSTON CHURCHILL, Prime Minister of England, 1940-1945
> CORDELL HULL, United States Secretary of State, 1933-1944
> FRANKLIN D. ROOSEVELT, President of the United States, 1933-1945
> JOSEF STALIN, Premier of the Union of Soviet Socialist Republics, 1924-1953
> SUMNER WELLES, United States Under Secretary of State, 1937-1942

Franklin D. Roosevelt and his presidential policies have been the subject of intense controversy and speculation virtually from their inception. No president of the twentieth century, with the possible exception of Richard M. Nixon, has been more vehemently opposed as well as supported during his term of office, and the controversies have remained vibrant in academic circles nearly half a century after the fact.

Robert Dallek is, in one respect, simply another voice of analysis surveying the much-debated Roosevelt Administrations. Yet Dallek's work here is a viable addition to the collection of FDR studies in that it offers a relatively compact, yet comprehensive, one-volume look at Roosevelt's foreign policies. Beyond this, however, Dallek has also benefited from an advantage that previous Roosevelt scholars did not enjoy: namely, the 1970's release of a vast quantity of United States and British records on foreign relations in the 1930's and 1940's.

One might have expected Dallek to employ this new information in pursuit of a radically revisionist view of traditional assumptions associated with Roosevelt and the motives at work in his policies. Instead, Dallek has consciously avoided any attempt to drastically reevaluate the Roosevelt personality and has similarly excluded frequent criticism or praise, preferring instead to let the course of events speak for itself. The author makes it clear early in the text that he accepts the fact, as others such as Rexford Tugwell did, that Roosevelt's personal style of decisionmaking was without any underlying tow of patterned coherence. While Roosevelt has been said to have "brokered" the New Deal, much the same could be concluded from his foreign policy approaches. Although conscious of presenting a public image of determination, Roosevelt frequently annoyed his closest advisers with his reluctance to be frank and direct regarding his real views.

Interestingly, Dallek does devote an initial chapter to a fast-paced survey of Roosevelt's prepresidential life. At first glance, the effort would seem to be a mere cosmetic gesture designed to familiarize the uninitiated with Roosevelt's youth and early political experiences. On closer reading, particularly in conjunction with the main body of the text dealing with the presidential years, this opening sketch establishes many of the consistent features which do surface in Roosevelt's foreign policy.

The more or less aristocratic nature of Roosevelt's upbringing tailored him toward an appreciation of international relations based upon personal observation through overseas trips. As Dallek points out, of all previous presidents, only John Quincy Adams could claim to have such a firsthand familiarity with the foreign scene as an integral part of his impressionable youth. In addition, Roosevelt's schooling at Groton under Endicott Peabody added a touch of classic liberalism bathed in Christian humanism. A deep sense of moral obligation to the world at large became a key component of the Roosevelt perspective. While Roosevelt demonstrated early a seemingly uncharacteristic tendency to emulate cousin Theodore's public career and viewpoints, contact with the Woodrow Wilson Administrations left a more permanent mark.

From Wilson's determined struggle for a League of Nations, Roosevelt rekindled the notion that America had a moral commitment in a chaotic world to offer its leadership and objective goodwill in search of a stable peace. That Wilson was unable to propagate this role and place the United States in the midst of international dealings was a lesson not lost on Roosevelt. While clearly supportive of the internationalist view, Roosevelt also witnessed the futility of the Wilson efforts to lead American opinion in a direction it did not wish to go. Dallek implies that Franklin Roosevelt's abandonment of Teddy Roosevelt-style jingoism in favor of moral persuasion in world affairs had more to do with his appraisal of the political temperament of the American public than with any deep-seated conviction. When moral leadership ran aground during the latter days of the Wilson Presidency, Roosevelt became even more convinced that one eye fixed upon domestic moods was a vital necessity in any successful foreign policy.

Although his observation of the Wilson era had convinced Roosevelt that public opinion could never be ignored in the determination of national policy, he also had become more firm in his own convictions regarding the inherent wisdom of internationalism. On this point, Dallek's presentation fails to steer a coherent course. Impressions are left which clearly suggest that Roosevelt was willing to recant any public statement in order to remain within the vanguard of public opinion. Yet strong implications are equally offered which present Roosevelt as a figure who repeatedly felt hemmed in by opinion from doing what he instinctively believed to be the national interest. It is entirely possible that Dallek's seemingly inconsistent approach to Roosevelt in this regard is, in fact, a calculated effort on the author's part to highlight the very truth of Roosevelt's flexible style. Even the polio seizure from which Roosevelt suffered is treated by Dallek in much the same way that Roosevelt himself seems to have dealt with it—as an inconvenience. No suggestion is made that the handicap in any way manifestly altered Roosevelt's views or demeanor.

Beyond this brief but insightful opening presentation, Dallek provides a chronological history of the Roosevelt Presidency and its foreign policies, from the lame-duck period of late 1932 to the President's death in early 1945. The most expressive coverage is directed toward the pre-Pearl Harbor years and also the closing months dominated by Yalta. In this respect, Dallek again is not really deviating from tradition as scholars have long found these periods of Roosevelt's foreign policy to be more controversial than the pursuit of wartime strategies. The war years of 1941 to 1945, as Dallek presents them, offer only further evidence that the Allied camp occasionally did not agree on the most opportune approach for bringing about the Axis defeat.

Dallek is particularly impressive in his treatment of Roosevelt during the period from 1933 to December 7, 1941. The portrait which emerges is one of a frustrated president curbed by public and congressional opinion that was itself a legacy of the disillusioning experience of World War I. The fact that Roosevelt, although frequently annoyed at his inability to seize upon opportunities for action aimed at safeguarding the peace, was nevertheless willing to honor the national consensus as he read it indicates that he believed foreign policy to be a continual struggle for influence. Roosevelt tended to move cautiously in foreign affairs while seeking to educate a majority which would support his evaluation of proper United States actions in a growingly hostile world.

Of some interest is Dallek's observation that the period from 1933 to 1935 was one of "public indifference" more than isolationism. The extent of this public apathy is felt to have given Roosevelt a relatively free hand in policy, leading to such steps as recognition of the Soviet Union. The fact that recognition of Russia produced little direct consequence to the United States and, in turn, little public comment, suggested to Roosevelt that he could do more. It was a mistaken belief.

If a turning point could be singled out in which public indifference became vehement isolationism, Dallek offers Roosevelt's efforts in 1935 to secure Senate approval of United States involvement in the World Court. To Roosevelt and his equally internationalist-minded Secretary of State, Cordell Hull, United States entrance into the World Court seemed to present a basically harmless policy of fostering international goodwill and communication. Instead, the Senate consent never materialized and fell victim to an unleashing of pent-up United States bitterness and resentment over everything from outstanding World War I debts to fear of United States involvement in another foreign war. Dallek maintains that both Roosevelt and Hull viewed this failure as the turning point, signaling an end to Roosevelt's freedom of action in foreign affairs. After 1935, United States opinion became a sentinel of isolationism, everwatchful for executive actions liable to pull the nation into deeper involvement in the spreading world crisis. In particular, tough neutrality legislation emerged in Congress which Roosevelt the politician could not ignore.

While Roosevelt would have preferred to place the United States clearly on the side of collective security arrangements with the world's democratic nations, the American mood would have none of it. Dallek believes that the public, as well as Congress, were more mindful of Roosevelt's growing executive clout in foreign affairs than in domestic matters. Fears that a determined president could jeapordize the peace far outweighed any concerns that his domestic policies might transform the American system into a socialist state or a dictatorship. Dallek draws a portrait of the American temperament, by 1935, as being convinced that United States involvement in World War I was a mistake brought on by the freedom of action extended to Wilson as Chief Executive.

Under the circumstances, Roosevelt sought to maintain a vigil which enabled him to comment upon world developments within the constraints of the national mood. By honoring public opinion and continuing his fight against the domestic Depression, Roosevelt at least hoped to stabilize democracy at home. Hopefully, too, these actions could be indirectly employed as a beacon to others in the international community that militant and extreme governmental systems were not the only recourse. In order to retain his posture of leadership, Roosevelt had taken to promoting the rhetoric of isolationism himself, at least for domestic political consumption. Although dismayed by the Ethiopian invasion, the Spanish Civil War, and the Sino-Japanese conflict, the President was always aware that there were very genuine boundaries beyond which he dared not go, even in his speeches.

Still, Roosevelt rarely missed an opportunity to test the limits of isolationist opinion, seemingly in the hope that public observation of foreign events would produce a change in attitude. Dallek dwells upon the celebrated "Quarantine the Aggressors" speech given by Roosevelt in Chicago in 1937 as being symptomatic of Roosevelt's approach. The author maintains that Roosevelt's speech was not designed to encourage specific actions by the United States, such as embargos and military sanctions. Instead, Dallek notes that Roosevelt subsequently told the press that he merely wished to place the United States in pursuit of peace, but was unsure as to what kind of program to promote. In addition, Dallek reminds the reader that initial reaction to the speech was warmly supportive rather than hostile, temporarily raising Roosevelt's hopes that aggression overseas might finally have caught the public's attention. The mood was short-lived, however, as public reaction to the *Panay* incident in China amply demonstrated shortly thereafter.

Occasionally, Roosevelt would consider options presented to him by others which sought added maneuverability for a hemmed-in administration. Sumner Welles, Under Secretary of State to Cordell Hull, suggested a plan of "general agreements" in which involved nations would be encouraged to adopt "fundamental norms" of international conduct. The hopelessly vague semantics of such a notion are presented as an illustration of the Administration's desperation over being unable to play a meaningful role.

It is rare for Dallek to offer an overt opinion within the confines of his presentation here, but he is candid on the subject of the German and Austrian Jewish refugees, firmly believing that Roosevelt could have exerted greater leadership by appealing to American humanitarianism. Although he does add that United States public and congressional opinion certainly opposed any modification of existing immigration laws (in fact, from March through December of 1938, polls indicated that such opposition rose from seventy-five to eighty-three percent), Dallek feels that the President did not act simply because the Jewish refugee question was not a priority matter.

While United States opinion was clearly angered by the Axis aggression which spread deeply through Europe after the fall of Poland, Roosevelt's level of support for the surviving democracies continued to require caution. Dallek suggests that there was little Roosevelt could realistically do until events abroad altered the public mood. He admitted as much to Lord Tweedsmuir, Governor General of Canada, in mid-September of 1939, by commenting that, "I am almost literally walking on eggs."

As criticism of Roosevelt is only randomly spliced into Dallek's work, praise is also sporadic. Whatever foreign policy errors emerged during the Roosevelt Presidency are blamed on domestic and international constraints rather than on Roosevelt's personal shortcomings. However, the author's observation that Roosevelt's wartime leadership contributed to undemocratic practices and a more arbitrary use of executive power is hardly a revelation. John Adams, James Polk, Abraham Lincoln, and Woodrow Wilson would all pass the test as presidents prior to Roosevelt who resorted to the use of executive authority in order to meet the demands of wartime leadership.

In summary, it can be said that Dallek's work is at its most convincing when he allows events to speak for themselves. Once the tone is altered in favor of the author's personal assumptions, a more questionable presentation results. The view that Roosevelt was not, as some would claim, naïve about Russian intentions in 1945 is an observation supported by the notion that Roosevelt sought to maintain a genuine line of communications with Josef Stalin despite obvious ideological differences. To offer the suggestion, however, that President Roosevelt would have moved more quickly to confront the Russians than Truman did is at best a theory which can never be finally tested.

What Dallek does provide is a compelling look at the scope of events from 1932 to 1945 as seen from the vantage point of an American president never fully in control of the agenda. It offers a study of the limitations of presidential power more than the grand portrayal of executive dominance.

Terry Alan Baney

FROM *BROWN* TO *BAKKE*
The Supreme Court and School Integration: 1954-1978

Author: J. Harvie Wilkinson III (1906-   )
Publisher: Oxford University Press (New York). 368 pp. $17.95
Type of work: History
Time: 1954-1978
Locale: The United States

A historical analysis of desegregation tracing the court cases and the impact of the decisions on society

> *Principal personages:*
> EARL WARREN, Chief Justice of the Supreme Court presiding at the time of the *Brown* case
> ORVAL FAUBUS, Governor of Arkansas, Southern demagogue
> LOUISE DAY HICKS, Boston demagogue at the time of forced busing
> MARCO DEFUNIS, the plaintiff in the first affirmative action suit before the Supreme Court
> ALLAN BAKKE, the plaintiff in the second affirmative action suit before the Supreme Court
> WARREN BURGER, Chief Justice of the Supreme Court at the time of the *Bakke* case

Because it has been twenty-five years since the Supreme Court under Chief Justice Earl Warren declared Southern segregation in public schools illegal, there is a definite need for a retrospective analysis of the legal history of desegregation and its social and political repercussions. *From* Brown *to* Bakke is such an analysis. With a genuine dispassion that does not shun the complex truth, J. Harvie Wilkinson III outlines the legal history of segregation that preceded *Oliver Brown* v. *Board of Education of Topeka* as well as the efforts to further desegregation that followed that momentous decision. To anyone who has lived through the confusion of the last twenty-five years of social strife and legal striving, Wilkinson's book will come as a welcome gift of clarity and insight.

Many times, as Wilkinson makes clear, the future legal history of the Supreme Court can be read in the dissents of its past justices and the arguments of its losing counsel. In his 1883 dissent in the *Civil Rights Cases* Justice Harlan had said of the fourteenth amendment: "there cannot be, in this republic, any class of human beings in practical subjection to another class, with power in the latter to dole out to the former just such privileges as they may choose to grant. . . ." In the more famous *Plessy* v. *Ferguson*, Plessy's counsel made the point that the doctrine of separate but equal made no sense. In other words, separate was inherently not equal, although it took the Supreme Court over a half century to strike at the segregated society over whose erection it had so benignly presided.

Although *Brown* was important, it was deliberately bland and was furthermore peculiar in its implicit contention that the public school, and education generally, could be both the vehicle to strike down segregation and the certain avenue for betterment for the black race. Bland or not, *Brown* was defied. When the Court ordered the South to proceed "with all deliberate speed," Southerners held back stubbornly. First there was the absolute defiance of such demagogues as Governor Orval Faubus in Little Rock, Arkansas. Then the South learned to substitute foot-dragging for fireworks. The Court has been much criticized for a formula that became an excuse for tokenism. Wilkinson points out, however, that Southern segregation was probably too entrenched for the South to move quickly without severe disruption.

More to be criticized was the Court's reluctance to expound clear integration guidelines. In ignoring its responsibility for clarity, the Court encouraged unseemly diversity among lower court judges and continued foot-dragging on the part of local Southern authorities. In Prince Edward County, for example, there were no public schools at all for four years. Although whites went to private academies, for many blacks there was no schooling at all. Slowly, the Court became exasperated, but it was still exasperation without guidance. Finally, in the mid-1960's, a move toward affirmative action could be seen. The Department of Health, Education and Welfare promulgated integration guidelines and the use of white-black statistics as proof of desegregation became more common. It was this use of statistics, combined with the Court's growing loss of patience, that led to massive integration of Southern schools by means of busing. The results were mixed: calm prevailed in Charlotte, chaos in Richmond.

Finally, inexorably, massive public school integration through busing moved North. Wilkinson dwells carefully on the spectacular ironies of this development. In the South, segregation was *de jure* and did not have to be proved; in the North, it was *de facto*, the result of urban housing patterns, and an elaborate case had to be made. Even when segregation was proved, desegregation might have little effect, since Northern cities became more and more black as the years passed. Thus, Northern busing, which excluded white suburbs, placed an unfair and increasingly pointless burden on poor whites and blacks, a circumstance which led to a frightening eruption of violence in Boston, violence abetted by such demagogues as Louise Day Hicks. The logical remedy was to include those suburbs in busing plans, as Judge Roth ordered in Detroit. The Supreme Court struck his opinion down. By now, the Court, presided over by more conservative spirits such as Chief Justice Warren Burger, was in full though slow retreat from the results of its earlier temerity.

The author's extended discussion of *Brown* and its aftermath puts *Allan Bakke* v. *University of California at Davis* in its proper perspective. Everyone knew that *Bakke* was coming. In an earlier case, *DeFunis*, the Court had retreated on technical grounds from making a decision. Marco DeFunis objected to his exclusion from a law school on the basis of paper credentials demonstrably superior to those of minority candidates who were nevertheless admitted. Allan Bakke's complaint was parallel, except that it concerned medical school admission. The Court hemmed and hawed; affirmative action was acceptable, but not quotas, and Bakke should be admitted. As Wilkinson firmly but diplomatically implies, affirmative action makes sense when it means helping minorities to achieve higher goals. It makes no sense when it means admitting or hiring minorities with patently inferior credentials. Worst of all, perhaps, it insults the talented black: " . . . the current official government doctrine seems to be that we black people, and some other selected minority groups, are by definition inferior, and therefore must be permanently monitored and controlled—by quotas and racial balancing acts, by racial apportionment and reverse discrimination."

For Wilkinson, *Bakke* is an addendum to *Brown*, "a symbol of how far toward racial justice we still have to go [and] how far since *Brown* we [have] come." *Bakke* reveals an American consensus on the issue of racial justice: no sane, realistic person questions its necessity. Sane, realistic persons of good will can differ markedly, however, on the means. Some may say that affirmative action is currently one necessary road to social justice; others, that it is the pious equivocation of the self-deceived and self-righteous.

Alan G. Gross

THE GENERATION OF 1914

Author: Robert Wohl (1936-   )
Publisher: Harvard University Press (Cambridge). Illustrated. 307 pp. $17.50
Type of work: History
Time: 1900-1933
Locale: Great Britain, France, Italy, Germany, and Spain

A study of the development of generational consciousness among young European intellectuals during the first three decades of the twentieth century

> *Principal personages:*
> PIERRE DRIEU DE LA ROCHELLE, a French poet of World War I and later a convert to Fascism
> HENRY DE MONTHERLANT, the French novelist who wrote about his experience in World War I
> JEAN LUCHAIRE, the French writer who advanced theories of generational consciousness during the 1920's
> HENRI MASSIS, the French writer who propounded his theories of generational consciousness in the years immediately prior to World War I
> GIOVANNI PAPINI, an Italian journalist and critic
> BENITO MUSSOLINI, the Italian socialist who broke away to found the Fascist Party; Dictator of Italy, 1922-1943
> ANTONIO GRAMSCI, the Italian journalist and intellectual who helped found the Italian Communist Party
> ADOLFO OMODEO, Italian World War I memoirist and later opponent of Fascism
> SIEGFRIED SASSOON, British army officer and poet of World War I
> GÜNTHER E. GRÜNDEL, the German writer who propounded theories of generational consciousness during the 1920's
> ERNST JÜNGER, German veteran of World War I whose postwar memoirs glorified the war experience
> KARL MANNHEIM, Hungarian-born German sociologist
> JOSÉ ORTEGA Y GASSET, Spanish journalist and professor of philosophy

During the late 1960's in the United States, there was considerable discussion of the so-called "generation gap" between those who had reached maturity just before World War II and those who had come of age during the Vietnam War. In his scholarly, carefully reasoned new book, *The Generation of 1914*, Robert Wohl, a Professor of History at the University of California at Los Angeles, looks closely at another period in which theories of generational uniqueness were widely held among intellectuals: the years from 1900 to 1933. Since these theories appeared simultaneously in more than one country, the author has used a comparative approach, conducting research in the literatures of five languages. Wohl has, for the first time, applied the methods of intellectual history and collective biography to the study of the problem of generations. In so doing, he sheds light on the origins of World

War I, on the effects of the war on those who fought it, and on the rise of Communist and Fascist movements in Europe during the period between the two world wars.

The outbreak of World War I in the summer of 1914, which shattered more than forty years of peace among the Great Powers of Europe, has often been seen as a turning point of modern European history. Among European intellectuals of the first three decades of the twentieth century, it came to be widely believed that all those who had lived through the Great War of 1914-1918, and who had been born in the years between 1880 and 1900, constituted a cohesive bloc with a consciousness radically different from that of their elders. What was the reality behind this belief?

To determine what reality lay behind the idea of a "generation of 1914," the author has studied the writings of the young intellectuals of France, Germany, Spain, England, and Italy. These men, some of them well-known, others obscure, were all born between 1880 and 1900. They all belonged to the tiny elite of educated Europeans, those who had a secondary or higher education. They were almost all males from the middle strata of society who made their living by writing, chiefly as journalists and poets. The chosen writers either explicitly set forth theories of generational consciousness, as did the Spanish philosopher José Ortega y Gasset and the German sociologist Karl Mannheim, or reflected such consciousness in their writings, as did the French war writers Henry de Montherlant and Pierre Drieu de la Rochelle, the British war poet Siegfried Sassoon, and the German war memoirist Ernst Jünger. The sources used by the author for the study of their thoughts are novels, poems, memoirs, autobiographies, philosophical essays, university lectures, recorded conversations, and interviews with surviving intellectuals of the period and with the friends and families of those intellectuals already deceased.

Wohl has excluded some countries that did participate in the Great War, such as Russia and the United States. He has included Spain, a country which remained neutral throughout the conflict, because of his belief that the economic dislocations produced by the war accelerated the coming of a political crisis in that country. While maintaining a European perspective, Wohl is careful not to ignore the national peculiarities of generational thought. Thus, he shows that, while Continental Europeans produced much theorizing about the problem of generations, the Englishmen produced none. Instead, generational consciousness in England was expressed solely through poetry, novels, memoirs, and letters. In Spain, the only major proponent of generationalist theory was the renowned philosophy professor, José Ortega y Gasset, who relied chiefly on lectures and speeches to spread his ideas.

Since his subject does not easily yield to a straightforward narrative form, Wohl's book is organized topically rather than chronologically. Chapters One through Five deal with the phenomenon of generational thinking in each separate country, while Chapter Six presents the author's general conclusion. The idea of a cohesive "generation of 1914," Wohl concludes, was a myth, albeit one that was both widely believed and politically significant. As much divided the men of this generation as united them.

Generational consciousness, Wohl points out, had already begun to grow among the intellectual youth of major European countries during the decade prior to the outbreak of war in 1914. During the decade prior to the war, the rise of a new avant-garde culture, the speed of technological change, and the growth in numbers of young people whose parents could afford to send them to secondary school and university, had all contributed to this new sense of separateness among youth. Throughout Europe, poets and social critics such as Henri Massis in France, José Ortega y Gasset in Spain, and Giovanni Papini in Italy had all hailed the arrival of a new generation which would carry out the task of regenerating the hopelessly decadent society bequeathed by its elders.

Although the coming of the war did not create generational consciousness, it did, the author believes, "fortify and strengthen" it. For it was, by and large, the young males who fought the Great War, while it was the men of the older generation who headed the warring governments. The old division between young and old was reinforced by the new division between the combatants of the front and the noncombatants of the rear.

Paradoxically, however, it had been precisely the young intellectuals of Europe who had greeted the coming of the Great War with the greatest enthusiasm. This may seem demented to the modern reader, but Wohl succeeds in making such a response seem comprehensible. Young European intellectuals, accustomed to long years of peace and material comfort, had seen in war the only hope of renewing a tired old society and of creating a new sense of national unity. Since 1815, all European wars had been brief and progressive in their effects. Accustomed to safety, the intellectual young had longed for risk and danger. Only a general war, they had believed, was capable of creating the new man, more heroic and less materialistic, whom they had wished to see replace those two self-seeking creatures of the existing society, the bourgeois and the proletarian. This enthusiasm for war was found among the intellectual youth of all major European countries.

When young intellectuals, arriving at the front as junior officers, began to experience the reality of trench warfare, some disillusionment did set in. The prolonged agony of the Western Front bore little resemblance to prewar fantasies of knightly courage. Dugout upon dugout faced each other, year in, year out, separated by miles and miles of barbed wire. Instead of man-to-man, hand-to-hand fighting, there were impersonal exchanges of machine gun fire. Survival depended more on luck than on the heroism and prowess so admired by prewar youth. The young intellectuals, Wohl shows, now began to realize fully the horror and brutalization imposed by combat.

Yet, the attitude of most of the combatant intellectuals toward the war was, the author demonstrates, one of ambivalence. While abhorring the slaughter, many intellectuals also enjoyed the simplification of life, the chance for escape and adventure, the heightened sense of national unity, and the comradeship across class barriers offered by the Front.

The Front experience had led many intellectuals to believe that peace, when it came, would bring with it the dawn of a new era. Surely, they believed, class barriers would be eliminated, and a new and lasting peace among nations would be achieved. Wohl shows how, by the end of 1920, most of these illusions had been shattered by the realities of post-Armistice Europe. Most revolutionary upheavals were suppressed, the old politicians remained in power, and the Versailles Peace reflected the old imperialism rather than the new dreams of reconciliation among nations.

Despite the disillusionment, however, generational thinking continued to flourish among European intellectuals. Wohl describes how, during the 1920's, such men of "weak political instincts" as the German writer Günther E. Gründel, the French writer Jean Luchaire, and the Spanish philosopher José Ortega y Gasset dreamed aloud of the creation of a new political coalition based on generation rather than on class. These aspirations, the author argues, were doomed from the very beginning to failure.

For the so-called "generation of 1914," Wohl shows, never constituted a cohesive bloc. Some of its members had had families and careers when the war broke out, while others were just reaching adulthood when the war ended. Articulate, middle-class intellectuals experienced the war differently from those who were less educated. Furthermore, even those members of the generation who shared very similar experiences did not necessarily think alike. Some veterans became ardent militarists, while others became equally fervent pacifists. Among the young intellectuals there were, even within the same country, sharp divisions of political opinion. Some writers of the generation of 1914, such as the Frenchman Pierre Drieu de la Rochelle, turned towards Fascism; but this was by no means universal. In the homeland of Fascism, Italy, one intellectual of this generation, the socialist journalist Antonio Gramsci, became a founder of the Communist Party; while yet another young intellectual, the veteran and war memoirist Adolfo Omodeo, ultimately became an anti-Fascist liberal. Wohl points out that many young intellectuals, such as the French war writer Henry de Montherlant, seemed to have no politics at all. The only belief that appears to have united all young European intellectuals, the author implies, was a general skepticism about the validity of nineteenth century political remedies in a twentieth century world.

While demonstrating that the idea of a politically unified "generation of 1914" was a myth, Wohl also shows that this myth did have certain "practical and political consequences" in Europe during the years between the two world wars. Admirers of the Bolshevik Revolution used the generational idea in order to cause a split in the European Socialist Parties and the founding of Communist Parties. The former Italian socialist, Benito Mussolini, exploited the generational idea in order to win support for his creation of a Fascist dictatorship in Italy in the 1920's. In the England of the 1930's, the advocates of appeasement of Nazi Germany presented themselves as the legitimate representatives of the generation of men who had fought in the trenches. Both the policy of appeasement pursued by England and the aggressive and expansionist foreign policy pursued by Nazi Germany and Fascist Italy were, Wohl argues, both "expressions, in their own ways, of the generation of 1914 and of the lessons learned on the battlefields of the Great War." Thus, while there may not have actually been a cohesive war generation, the fact that so many people believed there was one is in itself of some historical significance.

Why did intellectuals continue for so long to espouse generationalism? Wohl stresses the sociological, rather than the psychological, origins of generationalist thought. He does not see theorizing about generational consciousness as the natural and inevitable expression of the perennial revolt of sons against fathers. Instead, he sees such theorizing as a reflection of the class interests of a very specific social group, the middle-class intellectuals.

Thus, the author sees the idea of a "generation of 1914" as a project of domination by which young intellectuals hoped to gain supremacy over other social groups. Generationalism, these young intellectuals believed, would pave the way for rule by an intellectual elite, instead of by the contending parties of the bourgeoisie or the proletariat. This project of domination, the author argues, was realized only in Italy, and there only for a brief moment. Wohl criticizes the intellectuals of the generation of 1914 for deriding as materialistic the ambitions of workers and peasants for a better life, and for clinging for far too long to "the fantasy of heroic action."

Wohl sees signs of elitism not only among the Continental European theorists but also among their much less theoretically inclined English counterparts. In England, the young intellectuals of the post-1918 years often argued that it had been the losses of young talent in the slaughter of the trenches which had doomed England to decline. The idea, the author believes, is "elitist nonsense." It is true, he admits, that a disproportionate number of young men of university education and upper-class background were killed at the Front, although the overall losses of England were not unusually great. The author believes that the role of England in the world, and the role of the upper class within England, were bound to decline anyway, as new powers emerged in the world and as new social forces emerged in England itself. The myth of the "lost" generation was, Wohl argues, a necessary solace for members of the old elite, troubled over the economic stagnation and political decline of post-1918 England.

While conceding that most young European intellectuals, with their elitist desire for a "neoconservative revolution," did not often join the frequently quite plebeian Fascist parties, the author does place a great deal of responsibility for the success of Fascism in Italy and Germany upon their shoulders. Fascism, with its promise to subordinate both capitalism and the working class to the rule of a national-minded elite, was, Wohl argues, the "great temptation of the generation of 1914." Fascism also gave them the hope that their privileges and way of life would be protected against any attack from the masses. The author concludes that the intellectuals of the generation of 1914, by their incessant criticism of the liberalism and socialism inherited from the nineteenth century, created a "cultural climate, and hence a political climate," in which Fascist movements could attract support. This, Wohl declares, was probably "the most important contribution" of the generation of 1914 to interwar European politics.

By 1948, Wohl shows, most of the dreams of the generation of 1914 had been shattered. Barely twenty years after the end of World War I, another World War had broken out which drastically reduced the power and influence of all the states of Western Europe. Fascism, which had captured the imaginations of at least some of the intellectuals of the generation of 1914, had shown itself, during World War II, to have been one of the most brutal political movements in history. While many Communists were dedicated anti-Fascists, the post-1945 Communist parties acted as mere puppets of Russian imperialism. It was the United States, the bastion of that commercial, capitalist civilization so despised by many of the intellectuals of the generation of 1914, which dominated the world after 1945.

Wohl's book is stimulating and subtle, but it raises almost as many questions as it answers. By studying generational thinking in Europe, Wohl is able to explain why all the major countries of Western Europe had Fascist movements during the period between the two world wars. He does not and cannot explain, however, why Fascist leaders succeeded so spectacularly in coming to power in Germany and Italy, and failed so dismally in England. Nor does Wohl explain why pacifism was so strong in interwar France, while a desire for military revenge was so widespread in post-1918 Germany. To answer these questions requires a deeper investigation of the political and social history of the individual countries, not just the history of their intellectual elites.

While Wohl's book is indeed profound and highly original, it is likely to appeal to the scholar rather than the general reader. In general, the author writes well; his chapter on England is especially clear and easy to understand. All too frequently, however, the author inundates the reader with names, producing a feeling of intellectual indigestion. At one point, for example, he reels off a list of ten major figures of turn-of-the-century avant-garde European culture, without identifying a single one of them except by name. Unless the reader has a great deal of background in the intellectual history of Continental Europe, he can be easily bewildered by Wohl's discussion of one little-known thinker after another.

There are relatively few aids for the reader. Although there are photographs of most of the thinkers discussed in the text, there is no map of the Western Front, nor is there any photograph of the trenches, although there is an artist's conception of them. The copious footnotes are placed at the back of the book, making it inconvenient for the reader to consult them. There is no separate bibliography.

Nevertheless, reading *The Generation of 1914* is well worth the effort. For it was not so long ago that Americans were being told, by the most serious of social critics, that only the "new" generation, with its shining ideals of peace and love, could repair the damage wreaked by its materialistic, militaristic elders. Wohl's book helps put such generational thinking in a broad historical perspective.

Paul D. Mageli

GERMAN REARMAMENT AND THE WEST
1932-1933

Author: Edward W. Bennett (1923-   )
Publisher: Princeton University Press (Princeton, New Jersey). 569 pp. $35.00
Type of work: History
Time: 1932-1933
Locale: Geneva, Switzerland; Berlin, Germany

A history of the Geneva disarmament conference in 1932-1933, seen in the light of the politics of clandestine German rearmament and the divergent reactions of the Western nations

Principal personages:
ANDRÉ TARDIEU, French War Minister, January-February, 1932; Premier, February-May, 1932
HEINRICH BRÜNING, German Chancellor, March, 1930- May, 1932
KURT VON SCHLEICHER, German Defense Minister; Chancellor, December, 1932- January, 1933
JOHN SIMON, British Foreign Secretary, 1931-1935
JAMES RAMSAY MACDONALD, British Prime Minister, 1929-1935
ADOLF HITLER, German Chancellor from January, 1933
EDOUARD DALADIER, French Premier, December, 1932- October, 1933
CONSTANTIN VON NEURATH, German Foreign Minister, 1932-1938

Some of the more important and vexing questions of the period between the two world wars are examined in *German Rearmament and the West*. The elements of continuity and change in German foreign policy from the Weimar Republic to Hitler have often been debated; the stability of the international order established by the Treaty of Versailles has often been contested. Questions have also been raised on the position of Britain and France and their acquiescence in the face of unilateral revision of the Versailles system. All of these matters in their turn are related to the breakdown of the European balance of power and the origins of World War II, as, during the 1930's, the dictators moved to overthrow the existing international order while the Western powers wavered between acceptance of and resistance to the actions of the revisionist states. In Bennett's work, some of the underlying themes of this period are displayed against the personalities and events that figured in one of the turning points of interwar diplomacy; his use of many of the German, British, and American archival materials also permits a modification of some of the traditional views on the aims and tactics of the various powers.

One of the first areas in which conflict arose was on disarmament, where the ideals of Western statesmen clashed with the aims pursued by defeated Germany; German rearmament eventually marked the first stage in the breakdown of the Allies' hopes for an enduring peace, and the advent of German Nazism signaled a change in the political and diplomatic climate in interwar Europe. Hence it is Germany that is at the center of Bennett's study.

For Germany, the peace treaty of 1919 had imposed territorial losses and a reparations burden that were the cause for widespread resentment; moreover, the German Army was restricted to 100,000 soldiers, and tanks, heavy artillery, and military aircraft were prohibited. With the tacit consent of many civilian political leaders, the German defense ministry engaged in some measures of clandestine rearmament, such as the accumulation of forbidden weapons and the training of volunteers for short-term service, with a view toward their eventual mobilization as military reserves. Such programs, devised to provide for Germany's needs in a possible military confrontation, acquired a logic and momentum of their own, quite apart from the efforts of German diplomacy to obtain a place of respect in international relations. Undeterred by such considerations, beginning in January, 1931, military leaders had drafted several expansion plans, the most ambitious of which would require a budget of one billion marks. Furthermore, since at about this time the Nazi Party had grown to a major political force, some of its paramilitary contingents were allowed to serve in the volunteer units to further supplement the regular army.

With German politicians and military men divided among themselves, but for the most part working toward some form of rearmament, the Western powers reacted as suited their particular views of national security. Both the British and the French intelligence services had enough information on German rearmament to realize that treaty infractions had taken place, but German military aims and the scope of German planning remained unclear. Unable to obtain a military alliance or other firm commitments from the British, France had adopted an essentially defensive posture with its armed forces prepared largely for a possible conflict with Germany. The nominal strength of the French Army, with colonial troops, was at least five times that of the German forces as defined by the Versailles Treaty; with a superiority in matériel, and also in the military aircraft that the Treaty had denied Germany, France held a definite advantage over its former adversary.

Nevertheless, the severity of its losses during World War I and uncertainty on the diplomatic orientation of its former allies left France as a conservative force intent largely on preserving the existing situation. Britain was still in some ways inclined to act in consultation with its former ally, but also remained open to a policy of reconciliation elsewhere in Europe. The British Army had been reduced to a small expeditionary force after the war, and attention was given largely to Britain's naval superiority; efforts were also made to maintain parity with France in aircraft. To a greater extent than in Germany or France, financial considerations were vital for British military planning, and with its war debts and the chronic economic crisis that affected Britain during the interwar years, military expenditures were maintained only at reduced levels. As Bennett points out, a characteristic posture for German leaders was to seek the support of military commanders, while British decisionmaking depended to a corresponding extent on the advice of financial experts.

On February 2, 1933, an international conference on disarmament was convened in Geneva under the aegis of the League of Nations, and by April formal proposals were considered. While American involvement in European security questions had been intermittent, questions of armaments levels also affected the United States, and hence an American proposal, the first read before the conference, dealt with the limitation of weapons of aggressive land warfare. This appeal was resisted by French Premier André Tardieu, who was fearful of a forced reduction of France's military establishment. Speaking for Germany, Chancellor Heinrich Brüning called for equality of rights between conference participants, and in consultation with the British and American delegates, efforts were made to reach a Franco-German reconciliation on the disarmament question. It has often been maintained that, had Tardieu and Brüning been able to resolve the questions between them, an accord might have been reached. Bennett demonstrates, however, that on the one hand, Brüning's own account of his efforts in Geneva emphasized the nationalistic aims he had hoped to achieve by gaining assent for some of the measures of rearmament planned by his military staff, and on the other hand, while the Anglo-American representatives had shown some sympathy for Brüning's public position, no changes in the existing armaments situation were contemplated without the assent of France. In any case, by May, 1932, an impasse was reached when both Tardieu and Brüning fell from office after elections in France and Germany.

Subsequent sessions of the conference were affected by the conflicting currents of German military-diplomatic policy, and here Bennett points out some of the efforts in Berlin to work behind the scenes for an armaments convention in keeping with the current stage of military planning. Kurt von Schleicher, the German Defense Minister, publicly indicated Germany's dissatisfaction with its military inferiority and hinted that, with or without a disarmament accord, Germany would seek to redress the military imbalance. Privately, Schleicher and his associates were concerned with the implementation of a five-year plan of military expansion to begin in April, 1933, and his pronouncements were meant to daunt foreign opinion; his threats, however, were met by protests from the other major conference members. In the process Schleicher had undercut the German foreign ministry, whose efforts to have accepted the principle of equality of rights were viewed with some scepticism and suspicion. In spite of this show of German inflexibility, the danger of a Franco-German breach prompted British Foreign Secretary Sir John Simon to offer some gratification for long-standing German claims that weapons forbidden Germany under the Versailles Treaty might be acquired as "samples." Although with the express misgivings of the French government, the British also proceeded with a new plan advanced by Prime Minister

James Ramsay MacDonald which, in general terms, declared that the conference should work for equality of rights under a system of security for all nations.

From the German point of view it appeared that Schleicher, who had recently become chancellor, had succeeded in his attempts to promote German rearmament on the international stage, and the MacDonald plan was accepted by Germany on December 11, 1932. Nevertheless, military circles were uneasy with the possibility that future German military strength would have to be accommodated to the levels prescribed by other nations. On the domestic level, political instability had reached serious dimensions, and the paramilitary units of the Nazi Party had begun to threaten civil disturbances. Although Schleicher had thought that he could gain Nazi support to promote his position against the left-wing parties, he was unable to cope with the economic disarray of the German state and the specter of internal upheaval should the Nazi Party remain outside the government. Under Nazi pressure, Adolf Hitler was made Chancellor on January 30, 1933, although, as Bennett maintains, the position of the general staff was not of decisive importance in his ascendancy. Rather, it was thought that Hitler would be able to ensure domestic stability and prevent political dissensions from undermining public order. Hitler did accept the military plans that Schleicher and his associates had originally formulated, and by April additional funds were made available for rearmament measures.

The subsequent breakdown of the disarmament talks arose not so much from Hitler's plans and prejudices as from a series of encounters that revealed the open discrepancies that had existed all along between Germany's diplomatic and military positions, and between its aims at the disarmament conference and the objectives of the other powers. During the spring and summer of 1933, Britain continued to promote the MacDonald plan, and the United States put forward a proposal for the renunciation of aggressive war. France, under Premier Edouard Daladier, was unwilling to accept such measures without provisions for international inspection and, if possible, the imposition of sanctions against any violators of a uniform armaments convention.

Hitler at first was inclined to follow the course of Foreign Minister Constantin von Neurath, who wished Germany to continue with the disarmament negotiations. Bennett demonstrates that the position of the military staff that rearmament be pursued in any case was supported when dispatches from the military attaché in London seemed to indicate that the British were to propose a lengthy probationary period that would considerably postpone German military expansion. It was reported from Geneva that the other powers suspected Germany of violating many points of the Versailles Treaty. In response, Hitler resolved to take matters into his own hands before the Western powers could act, and, on October 14, 1933, he announced that, since Germany had been unable to obtain release from the restrictions imposed at Versailles, it would leave the Geneva disarmament conference and would terminate its membership in the League of Nations. This measure, Hitler's first diplomatic gamble, surprised and stunned the Western nations, while opening the way for major rearmament under the Third Reich. At the same time, Hitler's presentation of the German case and his argument that Germany could not be denied military rights already held by the Western powers left Britain and France without an effective response.

Bennett's conclusions, as derived from the evidence for this period, are both revealing and disturbing. The influence of German military pressures upon politics, rather than changes in German government, was the opening wedge that ultimately permitted the restoration of German military strength, and it was this element of continuity that figured in Hitler's first major foreign policy initiative. Disunity among the Western powers, however, and an unwillingness on the part of the British and the Americans to countenance measures that would have preserved the military balance limited the courses of action open to the West. Thus, the first major test of wills between the powers left the military-political order of interwar Europe the more readily subject to the demands and claims of the revisionist states.

John R. Broadus

GHOST STORY

Author: Peter Straub (1943-   )
Publisher: Coward, McCann & Geoghegan (New York). 483 pp. $10.95
Type of work: Novel
Time: Milburn, a small town in Upstate New York; also Berkeley, the Deep South, and Panama City, Florida
Locale: The mid- to late-1970's and 1929

A young author, a teenaged boy, and the elderly members of a social club confront a mysterious, hidden, pervasive evil force

> Principal characters:
> DONALD WANDERLEY, a young novelist
> FREDERICK ("RICKY") HAWTHORNE, a seventy-year-old lawyer
> SEARS JAMES, his partner
> LEWIS BENEDIKT, a playboy in his sixties
> DR. JOHN JAFFREY, a prominent Milburn physician
> STELLA HAWTHORNE, Frederick's promiscuous wife
> PETER BARNES, a high school student
> ANNA MOSTYN, an attractive, mysterious, dangerous "young woman"
> GREGORY BATE ("BENTON"), a strange, deadly "ghost"
> FENNY BATE, his younger brother, also a "ghost"

Ghost Story is not, it turns out, about "ghosts" at all. Its originality of concept is one of the reasons why Peter Straub's horror novel was not only the best of its kind in 1979, but must also be ranked as one of a handful of modern dark fantasies that have transcended the limits of the genre to establish themselves as significant works of art.

Perhaps the uniqueness of Straub's novel can be most clearly seen by a brief comparison with another excellent contemporary dark fantasy, Stephen King's *Salem's Lot* (1975). The basic plots of these two works are quite similar: a young, introspective, troubled writer comes to a small, provincial Eastern town where he encounters a mysterious and unnatural menace. Viewed with suspicion and hostility by the local authorities, he nevertheless manages to recruit a small group of converts, most notably a bright teenaged boy, to do battle with the evil before it destroys them and overwhelms the town. After a harrowing and protracted conflict, the menace is finally vanquished, but not before much of the town has been ravaged and most of the hero's allies killed. However, in *Salem's Lot* the menace is vampirism; in *Ghost Story* it is a new (or at least obscure) species of evil capable of destroying its adversaries in new and different ways. The qualities and tools needed to fight the vampires in *Salem's Lot* are well known; the creatures in *Ghost Story* demand new tactics and weapons. Therefore, once we know what we are dealing with in *Salem's Lot*, the novel takes a thoroughly predictable shape, but even after the evil in *Ghost Story* has been unmasked, defeating it remains difficult and problematic. Moreover, Stephen King narrates *Salem's Lot* in a thoroughly straightforward manner, while Peter Straub approaches his material indirectly and experimentally, keeping us off balance and constantly surprised, as much by his manipulations of narrative technique as by the originality of his concepts. Thus, for all of the skillful plotting, excellent characterization, and fine writing in *Salem's Lot*, it never becomes more than a first-rate vampire story. *Ghost Story*, on the other hand, breaks new ground in the horror genre.

Ghost Story opens with a short "Prologue" that frames the narrative. Donald Wanderley, the protagonist, is driving south with a female child he has apparently kidnapped. Wanderley is obviously distraught, harried, and frightened; he carries a knife which he constantly fingers as he debates using it on his captive. The child, however, is calm, self-possessed, and strangely ironical in her responses to her captor. Even as Wanderley drives toward the Pacific, his mind wanders. Images from memory blur into hallucinatory scenes. Names, events, and scattered details from the story are tossed out as tantalizing hints. For a few moments he thinks he is in New York City. Later, walking alone in a strange Southern town, he suddenly comes upon his brother's tombstone. Back at the motel he feverishly quizzes the girl: "What are you?" he demands. "I am you," she answers him as the Prologue ends. The same question and answer occurs every time a doomed character has his/her final confrontation with "it," and in this exchange lies much of both the novel's power and its meaning.

This short, brilliant Prologue prepares the reader for what is to come, both in substance and in technique. It provokes obvious questions: why is he kidnapping the child? Who is she? What will he do with her? What could bring a man to consider murdering a ten-year-old? Also what awful sequence of events has led them to this strange confrontation? All such questions must wait, of course, until the end of the book, but this opening lingers in the mind as we move through this long and complex dark fantasy.

The technical adroitness of that opening sequence—the sudden jumps in time and place, the instant breakdown of objective reality into apparent hallucination, the pervasive sense of nightmare—sets the reader up for things to come. While, as with *Salem's Lot*, even the best modern horror tales tend to be conventional and straightforward in presentation, with at most an occasional flashback, flashforward, or dream sequence to vary the chronological presentation, *Ghost Story* is given to us in fragments. The primary story, which takes place in the late 1970's, is continually broken up by other bits and pieces of narrative: stories within stories, time shifts, scenes, images events—real and imagined—from the past, glimpses of the future, seemingly irrelevant incidents and details, bizarre yet realistic hallucinations, and terrifying nightmares. Not only does Straub create that required sense of unknown supernatural menace but he also blurs the distinctions between reality and illusion so effectively that the horror seems to be as much from within as without.

Despite this fragmentary approach, however, *Ghost Story* is never arbitrary or chaotic; its underlying structure is, in fact, quite stable. One of the real pleasures of the book lies in seeing how these apparently unrelated bits and pieces gradually come together to form a coherent, powerful whole. Straub takes two basic plot lines, the first concerning Don Wanderley and the second centering on the "Chowder Society," counterpoints them for a while, and then merges them. Thus, once he has established his narrative spine, he can bring in a host of minor characters and play their lesser dramas out against his larger background without ever losing the main thrust of his story.

Having introduced us to Wanderley in the Prologue, Straub shifts his focus to the "Chowder Society" as he begins the novel proper. The Chowder Society consists of four elderly gentlemen who represent the elite of Milburn society— Frederick Hawthorne and Sears James, law partners, Lewis Benedikt, a well-to-do playboy, and John Jaffrey, a prominent physician. For over thirty years the small group has met regularly, dressed in formal attire, drunk fine whiskey, and told one another ghost stories. The group had had one additional member, Edward Wanderley, a writer and uncle to Don, who has been dead over a year at the point the narrative begins. The mysterious, sudden death of Edward during a party thrown in honor of a visiting actress named Ann-Veronica Moore, followed by a sequence of weird experiences and terrifying "shared" nightmares, have induced the men to summon the nephew, Donald Wanderley, in an effort to analyze and explain their doubts and fears.

The names "Hawthorne" and "James" are not, of course, accidental or arbitrary; they are deliberate attempts to evoke the great masters of American dark fantasy, Nathaniel Hawthorne and Henry James. Direct and oblique references to both are scattered throughout the novel. The most important of these references occurs early in the book at a Chowder Society meeting when Sears James tells a "true" ghost story about an experience he had had as a rural schoolteacher prior to his taking up law. The story is an ingenious lower-class variant of *The Turn of the Screw*, stripped of its psychological ambiguities, but following the same basic story line. In his version, Sears James assumes the role of the governess, two of his students, Fenny Bate and his sister, Constance, replace the children, and Fenny's older brother, Gregory, stands in as the demonic spectres. As in the Henry James original, the "ghost," Gregory Bate, returns to continue his undescribed but clearly perverse relationship with the youngsters. At great personal risk Sears James vows to defend them against "his"—"its"—intrusion. He apparently succeeds in saving the girl, but again, as in the classic version, at the moment of final confrontation the boy dies. Of course, in *Ghost Story*, the tale of the Bate brothers does not end with Sears James's recollections: they reappear through-out the novel, confront all of the major characters, wreak havoc on Milburn, and help to carry out the insidious designs of the primary malevolent force, "the woman."

In keeping with the best horror fiction, *Ghost Story* combines a sense of progressing evil with the gradual unraveling of a first-rate mystery. The Chowder Society members are vulnerable not only to external menaces, but to their own consciences as well. As the fragments of narrative coalesce, we learn not only about the malevolent forces that are currently devastating Milburn, but also of the strange events that preceded them.

At the center of each man's story is a woman and a guilty secret associated with her. As a group, the Chowder Society feels guilty for having "killed" Eva Galli, the first of the dangerous females, when they were young men. Lewis Benedikt blames himself for his wife's suicide because he left her, rather than himself, to tend a strange child named Alice Montgomery. Donald Wanderley feels himself responsible for the death of his brother—also an unexplained suicide—having put him in contact with yet another mysterious female, Alma Mobley.

Thus, the key to the mystery and the ways to fight against it lie in the men's personal histories. They must come to terms with their own pasts, first by reliving them in order to understand their meanings, and then by finding the strength to break free of them. Those that can, survive; those that cannot, die. The arrival of Donald Wanderley provides the stimulus for this encounter with their personal histories, but it is not until they recruit Peter Barnes, a teenager, and hence a man without a past, that they are able to fight effectively in the present.

The central revelation of the novel is the realization that, however different they may seem in appearance, age, personality, and circumstance, these women—Eva Galli, Anna Mostyn, Alma Mobley, Ann-Veronica Moore, Alice Montgomery, Amy Monckton, Angie Maule—are all the same person—or "thing." The most frightening aspect of the relationship that each man establishes with his particular version of "her" is that "she" uses their own personalities, needs, guilts, and fears to damn them: that is the primary meaning of the "I am you" accusation each female makes to her intended victim. In the end, however, it is by accepting this insight that the men are able to retaliate.

"We chose to live in your dreams and imaginations because only there you are interesting," "she" tells the group on a tape left for them to hear. "You are at the mercy of your human imaginations, and when you look for us, you should always look in the places of your imagination. In the places of your dreams." The taped voice is meant to taunt and convince them of their opponent's omnipotence, but it has the opposite effect. The group is galvanized into action, formulates a plan, and, by following clues found in their memories and associations, confronts the creatures, beginning with the Bate brothers and ending with the woman.

With the exception of the last bloody fight with the Bate brothers—the weakest scene in the book—all the climactic episodes take place in hallucinatory dream sequences. Rather than a palpable enemy, each major character, and a number of important minor ones, meets his own past and his dead friends and loved ones, in a jumble of scenes, characters, sounds, smells, and images that climax with his death or, if he can break through the nightmare to act, his deliverance. These moments of terror in *Ghost Story* are among the most harrowing in dark fantasy because of the intense identification we feel with the character and because we face not only supernatural malevolence, but also a powerful disorientation of reality itself. In a nightmare there is no place to hide.

In the final analysis, most horror fiction fails because stereotyped supernatural beings are simply dropped into a landscape full of predictable characters. In *Ghost Story*, however, the characters are real, believable human beings whose fates are closely related to their own unique makeups (the best way to test the literary merit of a horror story is to subtract the horror and see what is left). Ghosts are often encountered in the novel, but they are not traditional ghosts. Victims are frequently drained of blood, but the villains are not traditional vampires. Gregory Bate resembles a wolf and ravages his victims, but he is not a traditional werewolf. All the evil creatures behave demonically, but none is a traditional demon. Instead Straub posits a species of being that, by combining the traits of such typical menaces, offers a common explanation for them all. Probably the most disturbing aspect of his creatures is that Straub has taken one of our most cherished romantic notions—the "dream girl"—and inverted it. The most frightening myth lurking beneath the surface of *Ghost Story* is that of the succubus, the beautiful, tantalizing, idealized woman who turns suddenly, in the midst of sexual ardours, into the ravaging, devouring monster.

Straub uses many traditional horror-story devices, but in original and vivid ways. *Ghost Story* is not simply the best of recent dark fantasies, it is a veritable synthesis of the genre. Straub has said that "the novel refers back to the classic American novels and stories of the genre by Henry James and Nathaniel Hawthorne." It is probably this "classic" dimension, given a striking contemporary twist, that sets *Ghost Story* apart from the plethora of mostly indifferent horror and occult works that have inundated the market in the past few years.

Keith Neilson

THE GHOST WRITER

Author: Philip Roth (1933-   )
Publisher: Farrar, Straus and Giroux (New York). 180 pp. $8.95
Type of work: Novella
Time: 1956
Locale: Rural Massachusetts

An autobiographical novella concerning a young Jewish writer's search for a spiritual father

> *Principal characters:*
> NATHAN ZUCKERMAN, a young writer
> E. I. LONOFF, a middle-aged reclusive writer
> HOPE, his wife
> AMY BELLETTE, Lonoff's former student

Twenty years after launching his up-and-down career with the prize-winning novella *Goodbye, Columbus*, Philip Roth has come up with another brief novel that could become a modern classic. Although its themes might restrict its audience, its assured craftsmanship and sustained control are remarkable—especially since the book is so patently autobiographical.

There are, to be sure, echoes from Roth's early work: his Newark childhood, his Jewish *angst*, his sometimes sensational sensualism, and his tendency to shock. There is even an unnecessary masturbation scene and a smothering Jewish mother who must be escaped, not to mention his familiar literary passions: Kafka, Joyce, and Chekhov. Obviously Roth has not yet recuperated from his graduate seminars in contemporary fiction and criticism.

The plot of the novella is simplicity itself. Nathan Zuckerman, who is much like Roth in 1956 (he is also borrowed from the previous autobiographical and somewhat patchy *My Life as a Man*), spends a day and a half with the famous older Jewish writer E. I. Lonoff in his reclusive home in the Berkshires. Here he meets Hope, the unhappy gentile wife of the self-denying artist, as well as Amy, a beautiful and mysterious former student of Lonoff, and promptly falls in love with the alluring and talented girl. After a dramatic encounter the next morning, he and the girl go their separate ways—he to write down frantically all he had imagined and spied on during his pilgrimage to his literary master (which is this novel), while the unflappable Lonoff is left to patch up his shaky marriage and pursue his lonely art—which is revealed to the naïve young writer as "a terrible triumph."

Roth himself has revealed his intentions in *The Ghost Writer*: to record the surprises in store for one who sets out to live the life of a dedicated artist. This seems broad and vague enough; it certainly encompasses most of the action here—even the exacting demands endured by Hope, the artist's long-suffering wife.

There are, however, other approaches. Unless one accepts the thesis that Thomas Wolfe wrote at his best in the novella form, one would see little kinship between Wolfe's untidy and overwritten autobiographical novels and Roth's carefully balanced and understated fiction. Yet one recalls that Leslie Fiedler once wrote that "all Southerners are honorary Jews." Perhaps it is a commentary on Wolfe's current reputation to note that nothing has been made of his influence on *The Ghost Writer*. Yet it is palpable, and Roth intends for his reader to be aware of it. After all, Nathan Zuckerman in the earlier *My Life as a Man* wrote that when he went off to college he read *Of Time and the River*, and it changed his life. (He also later says that he outgrew the Southern novelist.) Here, young Nathan lists Wolfe as his favorite novelist when he was in high school. It is possible, then, that Wolfe suggested the overriding theme of *The Ghost Writer*, the quest for a spiritual father. One recalls that this theme was suggested to Wolfe after his first novel—by Maxwell Perkins, who became his spiritual father and was immortalized in *You Can't Go Home Again*—just as Nathan is turning his abortive search into a work of art here.

Perhaps, too, Wolfe's turbulent life and writing suggested another important motif to Roth: the attack on the artist by his own people who feel betrayed and become outraged when they find themselves vividly portrayed, warts and all, in his fiction. In Part II, "Nathan Dedalus," Roth writes:

> Hadn't Joyce, hadn't Flaubert, hadn't Thomas Wolfe, the romantic genius of my high-school reading list, all been condemned for disloyalty or treachery or immorality by those who saw themselves as slandered in their works? As even the judge knew, literary history was in part the history of novelists infuriating fellow countrymen, family, and friends.

In spite of Roth's referring to his persona as "Nathan Dedalus," Wolfe seems the most significant name of the three, because he made extensive, even obsessive, literary use of the attacks made on him by his family and acquaintances after the publication of *Look Homeward, Angel*. This is not to minimize the influence of the others, for, of course, Flaubert is Roth's stylistic model, not Wolfe with his romantic, dithyrambic prose.

Another way of reading *The Ghost Writer*—not the best way, surely—is as a summary of the Jewish literary situation in the 1950's. Not only has Roth used chunks of his own life—his middle-class childhood in New Jersey, his study at the University of Chicago, his army experience, his stay at Yaddo, and the flap over his first stories such as "Epstein" and "Eli, the Fanatic" (and later *Portnoy's Complaint*)—but some other major characters are also based on real-life figures; or, more precisely, they are rather obvious composites. Although Roth has denied that he had anyone in mind other than his younger self, it is impossible to read the book as straight fiction, and this proves to be distracting at times. For instance, just as Nathan's master E. I. Lonoff begins to seem a faintly disguised portrait of Isaac Singer, the light shifts and he becomes the reclusive J. D. Salinger, then Bernard Malamud, who teaches part-time at a college, as does Lonoff here. Although Lonoff looks like Singer, at times he takes on the majesterial quality of Henry James, whose story "The Middle Years" provides "the madness of art" subtheme and is quoted at length in the second part of the novella.

And it is much the same with the flamboyant and successful Felix Abravanel, whose many wives and court battles contrast so obviously with Lonoff's retiring life and lack of critical attention. Just when he seems so clearly based on Saul Bellow, especially in the recalled scene of consternation when he shows up for a college lecture with his shiksa mistress, a detail is added, and Abravanel becomes Norman Mailer. To further complicate matters, he is described as looking somewhat like Thomas Wolfe—tall, with a head much too small for his body. (There is, of course, an inside joke here, for Wolfe was anti-Semitic.) And so it goes with Knebel, the editor of an influential Jewish quarterly. No doubt the book kept the New York literati buzzing for weeks when it first appeared in two issues of the *New Yorker*.

This distraction aside, however, the style and structure of *The Ghost Writer* are nearly unimpeachable. The whole novella is based on a series of contrasts, such as the love for the real father versus the love for the spiritual master and the untidiness and turbulence of life versus the order and design of art. Nathan and Amy are contrasting individuals, for they both look to Lonoff as a father; Amy, who wants to marry him, calls him Dad-da, and young Nathan admits, "I had come . . . to submit myself for the candidacy as nothing less than E. I. Lonoff's spiritual son . . . [though] of course, I had a loving father of my own. . . ." Moreover, all four major characters create a fantasy that is doomed: Lonoff admits to wanting a year in Florence with a young woman (when Amy offers to make this a reality, like a character in his own fiction he inevitably refuses); his wife Hope wishes to escape to Boston; Amy fantasizes about her escape to Europe with Lonoff as her husband; and Nathan imagines that the mysterious Amy is in reality Anne Frank, whom he will marry, thus proving to his doubting and disturbed family that he is even more Jewish than they are—in spite of what they label as anti-Semitic in his apprentice stories.

Part III, "Femme Fatale," seems the least effective of the novella's four parts, perhaps because of the trendiness of the Holocaust material. At any rate, after masturbating while fantasizing about Amy Bellette, young Nathan imagines an entire past for the mysterious displaced woman from Fetching. In his fantasy she becomes Anne Frank, who has miraculously escaped the death camp, and while hiding her identity from her father, becomes the prize creative-writing student of Lonoff, whom she appealed to by letter, just as Nathan had. This fantasy of Nathan seems overly long, but no doubt Roth would justify it by suggesting that it shows the fertility of Nathan's imagination, which is to stand him in good stead in his career as a writer.

No such questions can be raised about the climax, "Married to Tolstoy."

It is dramatic, economical, and, above all, convincing. The next morning, in the cold light of day, all fantasies are dispensed with. In a final confrontation of hosts and guests at breakfast, all of the thematic patterns are brilliantly woven together. Hope, rebelling against the deadly restrictions of her marriage to the monklike artist, offers him to Amy, who leaves, only to be followed on foot by the doomed wife. Nathan, appalled and chastened (he is called "boy" by his master), realizes the absurdity of his youthful need for a mentor and faces up to the demands of his own life as an artist. "There is his religion of art," Hope cries to Amy, "rejecting life. *Not* living is what he makes his beautiful fiction *out* of! And you will be the person he is not living with!"

The Ghost Writer is an accomplished novella, Philip Roth at his richest and most controlled. If the novella has a flaw other than its Anne Frank material, it is the lack of freshness in the episodes dealing with Nathan's squabble with his parents and his Jewish critics. This is merely a fictionalized version of parts of Roth's *Reading Myself and Others*. Perhaps in the future he should not follow Norman Mailer so readily in writing advertisements for himself. In any case, his fiction is far superior to the early accounts, much of which should be left to talk-show gossip.

Guy Owen

GIVING GOOD WEIGHT

Author: John McPhee (1931-   )
Publisher: Farrar, Straus and Giroux (New York). 261 pp. $9.95
Type of work: Essays

Five journalistic essays published individually between 1975 and 1979

"Buckley has a way of tracking down the secret joys of the city," says J. Anthony Lukas, Pulitzer Prize-winning reporter and world-class pinball player, after squaring off against his colleague from the *New York Times* in an explosive pinball match at Circus Circus peepshow emporium on West Forty-second Street. This talent for discovery characterizes John McPhee. In the five essays collected here, which include "The Pinball Philosophy" featuring the Buckley-Lukas shootout, McPhee tracks down the joys hiding in the familiar and reveals them with contagious delight.

These essays are studies of actual events: truck farmers hold an open-air market; journalists play a game of pinball; the scientific community plans a nuclear power plant; eight men take a canoe trip in the Maine woods; a chef works in the kitchen of his roadside inn. Yet in reporting these events, McPhee does not limit himself to assembling an abundance of data, however interesting, and finding the instructive historical and social perspective; he uses the novelist's techniques of dramatic action, character development, and imagery to give vitality and texture to the stories.

The dramatic shape of each essay emerges from the movement inherent in the event itself. In "Giving Good Weight," an account of New York City's outdoor Greenmarket, the action follows the truck farmers from city to country and back to city, alternately building to an urban frenzy and slowing to the rural calm of unending labor. "The Atlantic Generating Station," the story of the attempt to develop the first ocean-borne nuclear generating station, gathers suspense as research efforts spread and intensify, eventually involving tens of millions of dollars and the talents of hundreds of people.

The other three essays begin with a concentrated factual narrative locating place and time and setting the tone, and then proceed to climax and denouement. "The Keel of Lake Dickey" reaches its climax when the canoeing party negotiates the St. John River's Big Rapid, where a man has died twelve days before and where the party now encounters a capsized canoe and two men being thrashed by the river. "Brigade du Cuisine" tells of the art and philosophy of the pseudonymous chef "Otto." "He would like to be known for what he does, but . . . his wish to be acknowledged is exceeded by his wish not to be celebrated. . . ." The action builds up slowly as Otto shops and makes preparations: "The great thing is the *mise en place*. . . . You get your things together." It reaches a crescendo at the dinner hour when, in fevered activity grown reflex and coordinated from years of training, Otto whirls out coulibiac of salmon, quenelles of veal and shrimp, paella, and osso bucco behind doors that conceal him from the dimly lit dining room where guests speak in low voices.

McPhee's character portraits highlight American virtues. Hard work, generosity, courage and ingenuity are implicitly applauded as McPhee depicts his characters doing what they do best, or most love to do, and permits the dictates of the task to reveal the strength and talent necessary for the execution. The truck farmers in "Giving Good Weight," who labor ninety hours a week and diversify their farms to lure the college-educated young back to the family, pass the hat one market day when an elderly customer loses her money, and regularly close their eyes to the extra ears of corn in the bag when they charge for a dozen. "I sort of favor Brooklyn," says Yash Labanowski, who hauls his produce in from the mucklands near the New York-New Jersey border. "I give them two pounds always for a pound and a half."

The source and historical depth of these American virtues is suggested by contrapuntal references to our forebears. Alvina Frey, a truck farmer who dislikes herbicides and mechanization and wears sweaters that look soft and expensive, still farms the land that her Saxon grandmother cleared and planted and draws water from the well her grandmother dug. Helen Hamlin, wife of game warden Curly, kept a journal of their life in the 1930's on the banks of the St. John River. As the party in "The Keel of Lake Dickey" reaches the ruins of the Hamlin's cabin, having endured the cold and rain for days and anticipating the upcoming rapids, McPhee recalls these journal entries. "Forty degrees below zero sounds cold," wrote Helen, who could shoot the rapids and would travel rivers in the middle of the night. "It is cold—a dry suffocating cold. The coldest I ever experienced was fifty-four below."

Though attractive in their strength of character, the people of the stories are not sentimentalized. Reflecting on the pressures that compromise him, a prosperous truck farmer says, "Yeah, this is some business. . . . We have friends in New Jersey, and they hope we'll have a cyclone, or a flood. We hope they'll have a hurricane. Things like that drive the prices up for the lucky ones." The few moments of pathos which the stories permit themselves are understated. Anne, chef Otto's wife and pâtissiére-en-chef, spent her early childhood in Latvia, from which her family fled before the advancing Russians. Hidden in the countryside, she was told never to give her name. "To this day, she recoils inwardly when someone asks her name."

Nor are the wilderness and land which McPhee frankly loves treated with sentimentality. His dispassionate attitude is like that of Tom Cabot (of the Boston Cabots who talk only to God), one of the canoeing party in "The Keel of Lake Dickey" who is well-credentialed as a nature advocate, having climbed Mt. Katahdin in 1927 on skis and having coauthored, decades ago, the first guidebook to New England canoeing. But Cabot is "part aesthete, part Wall Street, and he can take his scenic settings or leave them alone. He knows both sides of the wilderness argument, and he is not always with nature in its debate with man."

The debate between man and nature is an explicit theme of "The Atlantic Generating Station" and is given even-handed treatment as McPhee allows the evidence to speak for itself. This essay is an impressive demonstration of McPhee's journalistic talents. In describing the numerous factors which were researched and evaluated in planning the nuclear power plant which was to be stationed in the Atlantic off the coast of New Jersey, he writes of conversion of the traditionally nomadic skilled labor force into stationary assembly line workers; historical precedents for ocean-borne generators; the construction of a shipyard large enough to build the hulls (an estuarine island was purchased); engineering of the huge breakwater (the difficulty being solved by reference to the South African children's game of knucklebone); the impact of maritime law; and the influence of governmental regulations and lawsuits by environmentalists. He describes the meticulous research of the scientific community: ichthyologists, physical oceanographers, seismologists, geologists, chemists, meteorologists, hydrologists, and general and marine ecologists. ("They knew the exact distance—eleven and two tenths miles—from the site to the nearest dairy cow.") He has fun with hypothetical natural and man-made disasters in every conceivable combination. He even considers the insurance costs of floating the $375 million station from Florida to its northern site: "Setting the premium for such a voyage calls for, if nothing else, wit."

Solid as the research foundation of the essays is, data assembly plays a secondary role to the interplay of human events. The project manager of the Atlantic generating station and an officer of the Audubon Society meet at the University of Florida in the immense laboratory where a scale model of the generator and its ocean site have been built.

> And now here they were, paths crossed, a Turk educated in Illinois and an Irishman from Oxford, standing in an artificial ocean in Florida and joining the issue of a floating nuclear power plant off the coast of New Jersey and aspects of it that conceivably could concern the world.

McPhee's apt and often surprising imagery likewise pulls the essays into the camp of creative writing. With one phrase he draws a portrait (her hair was "professionally reorganized as a gold hive"); depicts a character type (of the corporate echelon men: "Their silvered hair is perfect in coif. It appears to have been audited."); describes a scene in nature: "Downriver more hills of avalanchine ice, pale green, crashing, tumbling, tearing the banks, splitting the sunlight into rainbows." He evokes the taste and smell of nature's bounty: "Onions. Onions. Multilayered, multileveled, ovate, imbricated, white-fleshed, orange-scaled onions. . . . Leaf after savory mouth-needling sweet-sharp water-bearing leaf to the leaf flowering stalk that is the center and the secret of the onion." McPhee takes such a delight in America's bounty that he recites it in litanies. "Greengage plums. Ruby Red onions. Yellow crookneck squash. Sweet white Spanish onions. Starking Delicious plums." The plurality of New Yorkers passing through the Greenmarket is just as cornucopian. "Greeks. Italians. Russians. Finns. Haitians. Puerto Ricans. Nubians. . . . Jews by the minyan, Jews of all persuasions. . . ."

Although his treatment of his subjects readily reveals his attitudes, McPhee is reticent about interjecting his presence into the essays. He appears in the stories only to establish the point of view: as the taciturn pepper seller in "Giving Good Weight," as Lukas' quiet companion in "The Pinball Philosophy," and as the receptive but unrecorded journalist in "The Atlantic Generating Station" and "Brigade du Cuisine." McPhee is his most self-revelatory in "The Keel of Lake Dickey," in which, as one of the company canoeing the St. John, he rationalizes his fear of shooting a rapid: "This is a canoe trip, not a rodeo. . . . For us, just being out here is the purpose of the journey, and not shooting like spears to hit God knows what and where."

McPhee finds humor in the irony which people create for themselves: chef Otto, who samples all things he touches, both raw and cooked, protests that he eats nothing but a couple of cucumbers a day. "His way of not eating comes to roughly eight thousand calories a day." He finds it in sudden contrasts: Lukas, product of Eastern pre-prep and prep schools, comes across Tom Buckley at Circus Circus and "reaches for his holster." He finds it in the anecdotes his characters tell. His historian's perceptions of the attributes of our age seek out humor as well. The flow at the mouth of the St. John River turns around and rushes back on itself. When the French explorers discovered this river on the feast of John the Baptist in 1604, McPhee tells us, and saw this phenomenon, they "could have called it the Reversible River. Instead, they called it St. John."

McPhee uses irony as effectively in sharpening political issues as in creating humor. In "The Keel of Lake Dickey," he discloses his anger over the waste of the Dickey Dam that "plugs" the pristine and mighty St. John to give a couple of hours of electricity a day. "That's all. . . . Never mind that it would give New England roughly one percent of its electricity. Never mind that it would almost surely cost, in the end, a billion dollars. It would provide pollution-free, Arab-free, indigenous New England power."

Since 1964, McPhee, who is a staff writer for the *New Yorker* and lives and teaches in Princeton, has published more than a dozen collections of essays concerning a variety of topics presented by his interests in art, science, history, geography, sports, and food. The richness of the five essays collected in *Giving Good Weight*, like those that preceded, derives largely from McPhee's talent for coupling the novelist's power to discern and release the human spirit with the journalist's skill to think like a scientist, historian, and philosopher. Edward Hoagland has called him the most versatile journalist in America. L. E. Sissman has ranked him with H. L. Mencken and A. J. Liebling. This book of essays again demonstrates the justice of that praise.

Angelika Kuehn

THE GNOSTIC GOSPELS

Author: Elaine Pagels (1943-   )
Publisher: Random House (New York). 182 pp. $10.00
Type of work: Intellectual and theological history

Lucid exposition and analysis of the so-called Gnostic gospels, comprising texts discovered some thirty years ago at Nag Hammadi in Egypt, by a leading historian of Gnosticism and Christian origins

Digging for "sabakh," a soft soil used in Upper Egypt for fertilizer, an obscure Arab peasant uncovered in 1945, near the village of Nag Hammadi, a large reddish earthenware jar. With his mattock he smashed the top of the jar to discover inside thirteen papyrus books bound in leather. Some of the outer leaves of these books were later carelessly burned, but the bulk of the manuscripts was eventually sold to antiquities dealers, smuggled out of Egypt, or retained by the Egyptian government and placed in the Coptic Museum in Cairo. Following more than thirty years of controversy among scholars, museums, and universities over the property and publication rights to these documents, the American scholar J. M. Robinson finally published in 1977 a complete edition of *The Nag Hammadi Library.* Although philologists are still vigorously laboring over many unresolved problems in dating, reconstructing, and evaluating the texts, the work as a whole is now available to scholars and general readers alike. Identified as Gnostic writings from the first three centuries of the Christian era, the Nag Hammadi manuscripts consist of fifty-two texts that are without question the most significant archaeological discovery of our time. Like the discovery of the Dead Sea Scrolls, which have made possible a convincing reconstruction of first century Zadokite Judaism and have revealed links to Christian origins, the Gnostic Writings, or "gospels," have been hailed as primary evidence that enables Biblical scholars to reconstruct a previously misunderstood connection between Gnosticism and early Christianity.

Elaine Pagels' *The Gnostic Gospels,* winner of the 1980 American Book Award for Religious History, is a penetrating study of the theological significance of the Nag Hammadi texts. Like Edmund Wilson's popular study, *The Scrolls from the Dead Sea* (1955), Pagels' book exposes for a general audience in fairly nontechnical language the basic conceptual framework of the texts. With directness, vigor, and scholarly precision, she treats several major questions that lay readers would like to ask about the gospels. Are the writings relevant to Christian Scriptures? Should the Gnostics, a sect described as heretical by the early Church Fathers, be identified in any way as Christians? And did the Gnostic gospels influence the dogma or structure of the Catholic Church? During the course of her study, Pagels answers these three questions in the affirmative. However her work, unlike Wilson's book addressed to the common reader, goes well beyond a straightforward exposition of recent scholarship. In matters of Biblical (Hebrew) scholarship, Wilson was an amateur (a word used in the original, nonpejorative sense); Pagels, Head of the Religious Studies Department at Barnard College, Columbia University, is a distinguished scholar of Gnosticism with a specialized knowledge of early Church social and theological history. Her work can be read on two levels: on the popular, as a clear account of the Gnostic texts and their significance; and on the scholarly, as a persuasive argument that establishes Gnosticism as a profoundly important movement influencing and countering orthodox (that is, Catholic) Christian doctrine and ecclesiastical organization.

For the general reader, *The Gnostic Gospels* reveals an aspect of theological history that had long been buried. Before the discovery of the Nag Hammadi texts, scholars had known about the Gnostics from only a few scattered fragments of their writings or, from an adversary's viewpoint, condemnations of that sect by the Church Fathers. Tertullian and Irenaeus, among others, had described the Gnostics as blasphemous, heretical, and wicked. Quoting parts of the Gnostic texts, almost always in concert with their own fierce denunciations, the Fathers had represented the sect as apostate from the true faith. On the basis of massive evidence from the Nag Hammadi texts, however, readers now can judge for themselves the main concerns of Gnostic theology and philosophy. It is evident that the Gnostics were not exclusively, as scholars had previously believed, a Hellenistic-oriented sect dabbling with Christian notions; instead, they were assuredly Christians representing a minority movement that challenged the hierarchy and many dogmas of the fledgling Church.

Documenting her case with sound evidence derived from the early social history of the universal Church, Pagels shows how the Gnostic gospels threatened the majority viewpoint on at least six major theological points (to each of which she devotes a chapter): that Christ's Resurrection should be considered as a symbolic instead of historical event; that no direct Apostolic line of succession should be traced, as proof of divine authority, from Peter to the bishops of the Church; that God the Father has a feminine aspect as Grace; that Christian martyrdom is not a necessary test of salvation; that the universal Church lacks power to guide congregants to spiritual wisdom; and finally, that the surest guide to spirituality is self-knowledge, Gnosis as God-knowledge. As a Church historian, Pagels argues that such a challenge by the Gnostics threatened both the political and theological supremacy of the Apostolic line. To establish upon a secure foundation their spiritual authority, the early Church Fathers reacted against the Gnostics by sharply dogmatizing their own positions. As a result, therefore, of nearly two centuries of antagonism between majority and minority Christian viewpoints, the victorious Catholic theologians formulated a number of arguments partly in opposition to Gnostic teachings.

For the general reader, Pagels' discussion of early Church history not only illuminates the social and intellectual background of the Gnostic gospels; but her analysis also throws a powerful light upon the canon of Christian Scriptures. She proves, for example, that many "gospels"—not merely the four Gospels of the New Testament—had been extant during the first two centuries and were available both to Christian and Gnostic-oriented communities. Also, she suggests that the selection of texts for the authorized Bible may have been a process involving political as well as theological considerations. More startling to the general reader, perhaps, are Pagels' remarks, presented casually as though they were common knowledge, upon the authorship of the Greek Scriptures. "Few today believe," she writes, "that contemporaries of Jesus actually wrote the New Testament gospels. Although Irenaeus, defending their exclusive legitimacy, insisted that they were written by Jesus' own followers, we know virtually nothing about the persons who wrote the gospels we call Matthew, Mark, Luke, and John." Or she describes as "pseudo-Pauline" the Timothy letters ascribed in the New Testament to Paul. To be sure, Pagels has no intention of shocking or antagonizing the lay reader. Her problem is one of communicating to a larger audience of intelligent persons a body of information understood by only a relatively small number of theological scholars who have sufficient technical linguistic mastery of the original writings to examine them as documents.

For this specialized group of scholars, Pagels contributes a major unifying thesis—that the Gnostic gospels can best be understood in their historical setting as a reaction to political forces within early Christianity. Outside the scope of her study are a number of other significant matters: the relationship between the Gnostic gospels and Hellenistic philosophy; between the gospels and Eastern (especially Hindu but also Zoroastrian) religions; between the gospels and first and second century Judaism; between the gospels and mystic cults of various kinds from Persia to Egypt; and between the gospels as they survived in oral tradition and the sixth century Koran, with its apparently Gnostic-influenced view of Jesus. Also Pagels leaves to other scholars some intriguing questions on the exact dating of texts. She quotes, presumably with assent, Harvard professor Helmut H. Koester's suggestion that the Gospel of Thomas, compiled *circa* 140, may include some sayings of Jesus even older than those of the Gospels of the New Testament, "possibly as early as the second half of the first century." If that judgment is accurate, the Gospel of Thomas would contain materials, Pagels writes, "as early as, or earlier than Mark, Matthew, Luke and John." Such an assessment, obviously, would require a substantial rethinking of New Testament data in the light of Gnostic influence. Yet Pagels usually avoids speculation on subjects outside her own specialty as a social historian of Gnosticism and early Christianity.

Within this highly technical field, she understands and expresses with admirable precision the general message of the Gnostic texts, details the intellectual background of their composition, and contrasts them to orthodox Christian writing. In addition, she shows how the Gnostic gospels, although centuries old, still have modern-day relevance. For these judgments she is bound to incite the most heated dissent among fellow scholars. Although Pagels insists that she does not, "as the casual reader might assume, . . . advocate going back to gnosticism—much less that I 'side with it' against orthodox Christianity," her argument does establish an attractive picture of the Gnostics. She sees their independence in many ways resembling that of the historical Protestant movement. With their emphasis upon the light of individual conscience as opposed to the authority of dogma, their opposition to hierarchical ecclesiastic structure, and their "insistence on the primacy of immediate experience" instead of the offices of the Church for salvation, the Gnostics appear to have links to other liberal Christians, both of the past and the present. Moreover, in their insistence upon a strong spiritual role for women, their celebration of the "greatness of human nature," and their high valuation of self-awareness as the beginning of enlightenment, they seem to resemble modern identity-searchers in a world of psychological stress.

Although Pagels may be guilty of exaggerating a case for the relevancy of the Gnostics to current theological problems, her book clearly demonstrates how the origins of Christianity and Gnosticism had a common root. "If we go back," she writes, "to the earliest known sources of Christian tradition—the sayings of Jesus (although scholars disagree on the question of *which* sayings are genuinely authentic), we can see how both gnostic and orthodox forms of Christianity could emerge as variant interpretations of the teaching and significance of Christ." To explore fully these variant interpretations, Pagels' book performs the admirable service of showing how and why the two forms of Christianity diverged into competing traditions.

Leslie B. Mittleman

GÖDEL, ESCHER, BACH
An Eternal Golden Braid

Author: Douglas R. Hofstadter
Publisher: Basic Books (New York). Illustrated. 777 pp. $18.50
Type of work: Essay

An entertaining and enriching discussion of the mechanisms of human thought and of Artificial Intelligence which uses drawings by Escher, music by Bach, and ideas from logic, biology, mathematics, and computer programming

Perhaps more frequently than he realizes (although that is difficult to accept), Douglas Hofstadter uses the verbs "evoke" and "provoke," or their adjectival forms, in his complex weaving of strands of mathematics, music, art and philosophy into an interdisciplinary "golden braid." Those two verbs summarize his attempt to evoke correspondences between and among formal systems (starting with Gödel's Theorem), DNA, the brain (as hardware), the mind (as software), Bach canons and fugues, Escher prints, Artificial Intelligence, and computers. To provoke such connections, the author has developed a format which is almost as unique as the ideas he pursues.

In his Introduction, Hofstadter defines *ricercar* (an Italian word originally meaning "to seek") as a designation, in Bach's time, of "an erudite kind of fugue, perhaps too austerely intellectual for the common ear." *Gödel, Escher, Bach*, too, in format is "a kind of fugue," but Hofstadter's goal is to present the information in such a way that it will not be "too austere." Whether he succeeds or not, of course, will depend upon the individual reader and the amount of time and thought the reader wishes to give to this large volume, but the author deserves praise for his innovative manipulation of words and graphics, even if the words become almost too cute and too sprinkled with puns after a while. For example, a section which concerns a computer language, SHRDLU, is entitled "SHRDLU, Toy of Man's Designing," an almost painful pun upon Bach's "Jesu, Joy of Man's Desiring."

Yet whatever cuteness is here is controlled, is intended. The author does not play with words merely because he does not know how to make his way out of a verbal or semantic blind alley, as is the case with many punsters. Rather, he plays with words because he is an assistant professor of computer science and a mathematician who, not incidentally, set the type for the book himself—on a computer, of course. Thus, as indicated above, it is difficult to accept that he would not know how many times certain words are used in his book; he may well have a printout of the frequency of occurrence of every word in the 777 pages. Thus all words are controlled by the author, controlled in a double sense of creation and of technology. On the other hand, he may not have such a printout. The methodical, boring counting of words, a purely mechanical process which a computer does so much better than humans with limited, wandering attention spans, may be too rudimentary a program for Hofstadter to bother writing. (The occasional old-fashioned, reactionary humanist who happens to read this book, then, may even take a kind of perverse pleasure in the occasional apparent typographical error in such a controlled manuscript—until he encounters Hofstadter's offhand comment that computers can be *programmed* to make seemingly *random* errors.)

To make complex intellectual concepts more easily understood, the author precedes each chapter with a "Dialogue" involving Achilles and a Tortoise— an idea taken from Zeno via Lewis Carroll—along with occasional visits from a Crab, a Sloth, and, in the final Dialogue, the Author himself. These Dialogues present, metaphorically, the ideas to be discussed later. Whether the reader can follow the more abstract, formal presentations of number theory and formal systems of logic and the structure of DNA or not, he usually can grasp the author's intentions from the Dialogues.

Another example, which may be nothing more than verbal cleverness or may be brilliance, comes in a discussion of "recursion," in other words, "nesting and variations on nesting," a variation of the process in computer terminology of the "pushdown stack," here called "push, pop, and stack." When a machine or the brain "pushes," it suspends operations on a task, without forgetting the place in the operation where the functioning stopped, in order to take on a new task. The first task is "stacked," that is, stored away temporarily. When the machine "pops," it returns to the first task, using the "return address" established for it in the stack. An image the author does not use but which visualizes the process is of several airplanes "stacked" over an airport awaiting instructions to land, to complete the suspended operation. We all operate with this "push, pop, and stack" process in conversations as we interject asides and parenthetical comments. The brilliance—or cleverness—in the present book comes as Hofstadter discusses the process in several long, involved sentences full of "stacked" ideas.

Apart from the entertaining side excursions, there are, perhaps, two main ideas which permeate the book: the Epimenides paradox and the potential abilities of Artificial Intelligence.

The Cretan philosopher Epimenides once said "All Cretans are liars." At a different level, this becomes "I am lying" which becomes "This statement is false." If it is a false statement, then it is true; if it is a true statement, however, how can it be false? This Epimenides paradox "rudely violates the usually assumed dichotomy of statements into true and false." Such a paradox becomes, for Hofstadter, a "Strange Loop," a phenomenon which occurs "whenever, by moving upwards (or downwards) through the levels of some hierarchial system, we unexpectedly find ourselves right back where we started." This paradox can be applied to the comment above about intentional "errors" in a computer program. Is a "mistake" a mistake when it is planned? Can a true/false statement be applied in this case? Are there statements of truth which cannot be proved?

Such a strange loop led Kurt Gödel to develop his "Incompleteness Theorem" in response to *Principia Mathematica*, proposed by Bertrand Russell and Alfred North Whitehead as a way to "prove" all true statements of number theory. Gödel's statement, as paraphrased by Hofstadter, is "All consistent axiomatic formulations of number theory include undecidable propositions." That is, some "truths" cannot be proved. If one proves one's system in terms of that system, it is like pulling one's self up by one's own bootstraps—another strange loop.

Gödel's statement in 1931 came just before the development of the electronic digital computer. The Londoner Charles Babbage (1792-1871) was the first person to propose an "Analytical Engine," a complex system of interlocking geared cylinders which would store data and use it to compute and, perhaps, to make rational decisions. He died before such a machine was ever built, but his friend, Lady Ada Lovelace (Lord Byron's daughter) was aware he was proposing a machine which approached mechanized intelligence, especially if the engine could react on the basis of something other than numbers. Babbage himself recognized such a possibility, and said such a machine would be "eating its own tail," or, in contemporary computer terminology, such a machine acting in such a way would alter its own program. Lady Lovelace did say, however, the "Analytical Engine has no pretensions whatever to *originate* anything. It can do whatever we *know how to order it* to perform." Today, one would not make quite such a strong statement, and it is here the author moves into the most important issue of this book, important for all persons, not just mathematicians and computer programmers: Artificial Intelligence (AI), thinking and reasoning done by machines.

The "Computer-Which-Can-Think" is the contemporary equivalent of Mary Shelley's Frankenstein's monster, the stereotyped man-made, mechanical humanoid. Whereas the creature Dr. Frankenstein created in his laboratory was slow and awkward and had finite powers, the monster computers from IBM or Univac or any of a half-dozen other "laboratories" deftly perform their functions in terms of seconds or microseconds, and they may be infinite in their powers once they learn to "eat their own tails." Such self-referencing computers are the ones which show up in science fiction novels and films, such as "HAL," the evil computer in Stanley Kubrick's *2001: A Space Odyssey*.

Beyond self-referencing, which computers already can do—for example, by comparing an accumulation of data during a program function against a predetermined end point for computation—Hofstadter muses about computers being able to "jump out of the system." Human beings cannot "transcend" themselves; that is, they cannot step out of their own skins to achieve true objectivity. They can, however, move out of ruts in thinking and perceive new approaches or solutions to problems. This stepping out is based upon new connections of the subsystems of the brain (hardware). It still operates on basic principles which the mind (software) has implanted. By the same token, Hofstadter theorizes that a computer, which can modify its program— "but such modifiability has to be inherent in the program to start with"—still is unable to violate its own instructions. Those who would create Artificial Intelligence today must face a basic problem: how to tell an inflexible machine to be flexible.

It is self-referencing, however, which allows us as humans to carry out routine functions, to solve problems, and to be creative. As the mind self-references, so, too, would AI in a computer, but just as it is difficult to determine the locus of a nonmechanical function in the biological structure, so, too, would it be difficult to know where or how to place such functions in a program for AI. That AI will be developed, the author does not doubt.

When it comes, what kind of intelligence will it be? Will it be a "super-intelligence" which will neither be able to nor desire to communicate with humans? If it desires such communication, will we understand? Even the experts can only theorize at this point.

On this basis, Hofstadter argues that there is no such thing as "computer music." For a computer to compose as Bach or Chopin, "it would have to have known resignation and world weariness, grief and despair, determination and victory, piety and awe." No machine does that today. Music produced by a computer ultimately is composed by the programmer; thus, the machine is a tool for a human idea, not a creative element in the composition. "It is a simple and single-minded piece of software with no flexibility, no perspective on what it is doing, and no sense of itself." Only with AI, with self-referencing, with emotion can a machine—not its program—compose music.

While discussions of AI, strange loops, and other terms and catch-phrases— TNT ("Typographical Number Theory"), isomorphism ("an information-pre-serving transformation"), contracrostipunctus ("a study in levels of mean-ing"), and Hofstadter's Law ("It always takes longer than you expect, even when you take into account Hofstadter's Law")—make for complex reasoning and interpretations relative to mathematics, there also are a great many profound, but humorous, comments in relationship to music and art.

Hofstadter uses thirty-five drawings by M. C. Escher (1902-1972), the Dutch graphic artist who created "some of the most intellectually stimulating drawings of all time." It is not surprising that Hofstadter would be drawn to Escher's works which are based upon paradox, illusion, and double meanings. Thus Escher's "Mobius" strips become visual representations of strange loops, as do his "Waterfall," where water seems to flow uphill to power its own waterwheel, and his "Drawing Hands," where two hands draw themselves. These are all self-referencing images.

The works of J. S. Bach, especially his "Crab Canon" which goes back into itself, are also representations of the strange loop and self-referencing. In the last measure of the "Art of the Fugue," written just before Bach died, there is a four-note melody which transcribes in the German notation system as B-A-C-H. If that melody is augmented in a certain way it comes out as C-A-G-E, that is, John Cage, composer of modern, aleatoric ("found") music. In one of the Dialogues, Achilles comments on this augmentation phenomenon and pursues it further, pointing out that "when you augment CAGE over again, you get BACH back, except jumbled up inside, as if BACH had an upset stomach after passing through the intermediate stage of CAGE." To this the Tortoise answers: "That sounds like an insightful commentary on the new art form of Cage." Cage as well as abstract, that is, non-referencial, art express little if anything to Hofstadter, who feels they "exist as pure globs of paint, or pure sounds, but in either case drained of all symbolic value."

Gödel, Escher, Bach is a work like a Bach canon, full of symbolic values. It gains new meaning with each new experiencing of the work. It is a work which requires a return or a replaying to achieve understanding. Significantly, it ends with the word "ricercar."

Hofstadter's comments relative to understanding the origin of life might apply also to the reader's ability to understand totally his book. "For the moment, we will have to content ourselves with a sense of wonder and awe, rather than an answer. And perhaps experiencing that sense of wonder and awe is more satisfying than having an answer—at least for a while."

John C. Carlisle

GOOD AS GOLD

Author: Joseph Heller (1923-   )
Publisher: Simon and Schuster (New York). 447 pp. $12.95
Type of work: Novel
Time: The present
Locale: New York City and Washington, D. C.

A witty and ironic account of a professor's attempt to come to terms with his Jewish background and get a government job in Washington

Principal characters:
> BRUCE GOLD, a middle-aged Jewish college professor of English
> BELLE GOLD, his wife
> SID GOLD, his older brother
> JULIUS GOLD, his father
> RALPH NEWSOME, aide to the President of the United States
> ANDREA CONOVER, a beautiful Protestant woman with whom Gold
> has an affair
> PUGH BIDDLE CONOVER, her influential and anti-Semitic father

This is Joseph Heller's third novel. His first, *Catch-22*, a blackly ironic depiction of the airman's lot in World War II, has achieved the status of a modern classic. Faced with that kind of success in his initial effort with fiction, Heller then published *Something Happened*, a straightforwardly told and often depressingly realistic depiction of modern family life. After *Catch-22*, this was not what Heller's wider readership was expecting, and so the work has received a mixed, generally lukewarm response. In *Good as Gold*, Heller returns to the vision of *Catch-22*, that life is basically a black comedy in which logic and rationality have little to do with the outcome of things, and in which appearance matters far more than substance. Our hopes, dreams, and desires are prisoners of an order which is outrageous, yet we are trapped beyond escape. If *Good as Gold* occasionally seems a thin book, it is not because of any fault in the clarity of Heller's vision, but perhaps because he himself senses the inherent futility of his central character's situation.

Since, in *Good as Gold*, Heller transfers the central vision of *Catch-22* from its original World War II setting to post-Watergate Washington, it might be helpful to review briefly the central irony of Heller's first novel. Set on an island off the coast of Europe during the war, *Catch-22* involves a number of members of a bomber squadron who fly frequent missions against Nazi Germany. Every mission is fraught with the danger of being killed, yet the bomber crews are supposed to have regular periods of rest after a set number of missions. Their commanding officer, however, tries to curry favor with his superiors through constantly raising the number of missions each man must fly before he is eligible for his leave. The consequences for the morale and mental health of the bomber crews are devastating, to say the least. There is, however, one way out; if a man is certified to be insane, he may be granted his leave at any time. Unfortunately, there is a catch, Catch-22; the only way a man may be declared insane is to request the diagnosis, but to make such a request is a sign of sanity. And so the missions go on.

Instantly recognized as an apt description of the nature of military life, *Catch-22* found a wide readership, especially during the Vietnam War. For many nonmilitary people, the basic situation in *Catch-22* has seemed equally applicable to civilian life, especially in regard to the functioning of large bureaucracies such as major corporations or governments. What Heller has done in *Good as Gold* is to make this vision explicit, on two levels. On the one hand, Gold, the central character, finds a whole series of Catch-22 situations facing him as he seeks employment in the federal government. On the other hand, he finds a similar problem arising in the context of his own extended family. *Good as Gold* does represent one advance over *Catch-22*, however, in its exploration of causality. In Heller's war novel, the bomber crews are captives of their government; none would choose to be in the Army Air Corps if given a say in the matter. In *Good as Gold*, on the other hand, the central character quickly discovers the nature of what he has to do to gain employment in Washington, yet voluntarily persists in his efforts. Heller's challenge in this novel is to make Gold's motivation believable; he locates that motivation in Gold's family situation.

What Gold is after in Washington is a government job. An English professor, a partner in a marriage of long standing, Gold feels early in the novel that his career and his marriage are both fast approaching a dead end. Abandoning any pretension to a scholarly career, he has taken to writing essays on public affairs that get published in journals nobody reads. His relationship with his wife has gone stale, and he has entered into a series of affairs. His father, brother, and sisters constantly tease and bate him at family suppers. His children only seem to cause endless bickering and disappointment. As a result, the chance at a job in Washington appears a convenient escape: "He had no doubt he would be disowned by his father, brother, and sisters and rejected by his children. The future looked bright."

Yet what Gold must do to get the job would sap the energies of a lesser man. Urged to find an influential patron, Gold starts an affair with Andrea Conover, whose father has committed perjury before Congress for five straight administrations and thus is admired for his altruism. She will not marry him until he has the government job; however, he cannot get the job until he marries her. Along the way, Gold puts up with a seemingly endless onslaught of anti-Semitic abuse from her father, who is willing to help as long as Gold withstands the abuse.

The novel moves through a series of scenes which alternate between Gold's interfamily squabbles in New York and his pursuit of the ever-elusive job in Washington. There, he is constantly encouraged and also put off by Ralph Newsome, a presidential aide who copied Gold's papers in college. According to Newsome, Gold is always close to the job, yet never seems close enough to get it. Newsome's style parodies Washington jargon: "I can just about guarantee that you'll get the appointment you choose as soon as you want, although I can't promise anything. We'll want to move ahead with this as speedily as possible, although we'll have to go slowly."

A subtheme amidst all this *Catch-22*-like posturing is Gold's attempt to come to terms with his Jewish background. Assaulted for a racial and religious identity he often wishes to disavow, Gold also is trying to write a book on the Jewish experience in America, for which he has received a large advance. One of Heller's satiric targets in this book seems to be the Jewish intellectual community in New York, men whom Gold despises on the one hand, but to whom he looks for publishing outlets on the other. A major figure, because of Gold's fascination with him, is Henry Kissinger, whose career in Washington Gold would like to replicate, yet whose character Gold finds beneath contempt.

Much of this book depicts Jewish family life, a subject familiar in modern fiction from the works of Philip Roth, Saul Bellow, and others who present the same kinds of ironic, double bind-type situations which, at least in Heller's depiction, are operative in the intrigues of Washington politics. Heller's America is a land filled with fools and knaves; the saving grace of the book is that Heller's central character is at home in such company and knows it.

In *Good as Gold*, Joseph Heller is witty, clever, and often downright funny. If this novel suffers in comparison with *Catch-22*, it is because the earlier novel has a richer, more interesting, and even more bizarre cast of characters. Here, in a more limited world, the novel's basic joke, although a good joke, sometimes wears thin through constant repetition. In short, *Good as Gold* is better appreciated if read in a series of short sittings, rather than all at once. This work will not become the bible for disillusioned Washington bureaucrats, but it may well allow those who must live with the effects of bureaucracy to find redemptive humor in its complexities.

John N. Wall, Jr.

THE GOOD WORD & OTHER WORDS

Author: Wilfrid Sheed (1930-   )
Publisher: E. P. Dutton (New York). 300 pp. $10.95
Type of work: Essays and reviews

*A lively critic of American and English literature and culture offers a stimulating
collection of essays and reviews covering the decade of the 1970's*

When Wilfrid Sheed is not writing novels (his latest being *Transatlantic
Blues*), he writes criticism, and vice versa. He is a transplanted Briton who
moved with his parents to the United States in 1940. He returned to England
in 1946 for his university years; but, having taken a liking to America during
his adolescence, he later made another westward crossing of the Atlantic to
establish his home here. His experience of life and education in both England
and America gives him a special advantage in his critical writing about such
authors as Cyril Connolly and Evelyn Waugh, on the one hand, and Edmund
Wilson and James Thurber, on the other.

The Good Word & Other Words is a collection of fifty-two critical essays
published (except for one) during the 1970's in the *New York Times Book
Review*, the *New York Review of Books*, and elsewhere. Most of them are
either book reviews or essays on British and American literature. The thirty-
four brief essays in Part One all appeared first in the *New York Times Book
Review* in Sheed's column "The Good Word." They cover a wide range of
literature and subliterature—since Sheed the novelist draws from many diverse sources for his satiric presentation of life and character, Sheed the critic
cannot be expected to restrict himself to the "best" literature.

"Edmund Wilson, 1895-1972" is both a memoir for a departed friend and
a tribute to a major American critic. Wilson, says Sheed, "set a standard of
scholarship-as-adventure that has vivified even his enemies and helped lib-
erate academic diction from the slithy pedants for the next generation." One
can imagine the liveliness of Sheed's own writing as perhaps having been
influenced by his early reading of Wilson's essays in the *New Yorker* that he
fondly recalls in his closing paragraph.

Certainly, his comment that Wilson's criticism "can sometimes be read as
a play of voices" may also be applied to Sheed's, in which the critic's voice
is often followed by another, unidentified but clearly distinct. To illustrate:
writing on authors' coming out of their closets—to reveal their homosexuality
or their sectarian or political beliefs, for example—Sheed warns of the trou-
bles that may be caused by those who welcome the uncloseted to their ranks.
"Partisans want their writers out of the closet all right, but on a very short
leash. Just say that you're happy, Ivan, in spite of the mistreatment, and we'll
handle the publicity." As he is nearing the end of a "meditation on the
difficulty of resolving novels these days to anyone's moral pleasure," he brings
up the matter of national differences in a concern for honor: "The French,

who like to think of themselves as the wickedest people on earth, would tell you that Americans are . . . childishly obsessed with honor. These things happen, my friend. We are men of the world, no?"

Sheed makes no pretense of being a "heavyweight" reviewer. "I leave that to the professors," he might say. He flicks a right, jabs with the left, and dances away. He even engages now and then in a little sparring with other critics, as in "Howe's Complaint," in which he takes on Irving Howe for having professorily chided Philip Roth for being superficial and funny in *Portnoy's Complaint*. Sheed himself grants Roth talent only but he feels that Roth, "not precisely a satirist nor exactly a pure humorist," still did pretty well in *Portnoy's Complaint*. "Criticism is a contact sport," says Sheed, but he rarely attempts any knockout blows. He is in the sport for the fun of it, to exercise his mind and perhaps to pass on to his readers some commonsense observations. If his opponents get a bruise here or there, they will soon recover.

Having published novels himself and having written them with an aim at more than mere commercial gain, Sheed is well aware of the plight of the "literary" writer competing with hacks, hoping to attract some discerning readers while he looks longingly at the hacks' sales figures and perhaps listens to the hacks themselves being interviewed on talk shows where they and their host promote their latest "smasheroo." "Four Hacks" is a funny parody interview with Irving Trustfund, Peaches Smedley, Percy Fang, and Alder-shott Twilley in which Sheed concludes that all hacks, while varying greatly in quality, "share a certain turbid homogeneity of thought and phrase which perhaps explains their popularity." In "Genre Writers" he returns to the hacks, discussing the attempts that have been made to "smuggle" such writers as P. G. Wodehouse, Ross Macdonald, and James M. Cain into literature. They are only done a disservice though, since "when they are approached as major writers they lose all their strength and don't even seem as good as they are. The first extravagant phrase kills them like frost."

Although published respectively in 1972, 1975, and 1973, three essays on George Orwell, Cyril Connolly, and Evelyn Waugh have been grouped together in *The Good Word & Other Words*, and one is given the opportunity to compare and contrast these British writers who were contemporaries. "The necessary element of perversity in Orwell's work," says Sheed, "was that he wrote best about the things he hated." Connolly, who developed a fine style as a young man, grew lazy and became a disappointment in his later years, when he wrote mainly book reviews. He was never a good critic, thinks Sheed, "because among other things, he could not pan a friend . . . [and] for all his surly independence, he could not make the *assertions* that criticism requires." Connolly was not prolific and this was a blessing. "He left us, like Jane Austen and E. M. Forster, wanting just one more." Many critics have written of Evelyn Waugh's snobbery, which he flaunted for most of his life.

In Sheed's Waugh essay, which he subtitles "No Snob Like a Snubbed Snob," he portrays Waugh as a sham snob filled with "self-loathing, strong and dolorous, with the force of genius behind it." As for Waugh's posthumously published diaries, Sheed remarks: "There are no theatrics of repentance, and no luxuries of self-analysis, only a mumbled resolve to do better. . . . You can't really hate a man like that."

Sheed is Catholic, but this does not seem to bias his critical views. In fact, one forgets his Catholicism until he mentions it or refers to his early training, as he sometimes does. He recalls "how we used to jump for joy when an author converted to Rome, and how we'd automatically promote him two literary notches. . . . G. K. Chesterton has barely recovered yet from the stuffing and mounting the Catholics gave him." Generally, Sheed appears to take his religion lightly. He sometimes jokes about it or refers to or quotes non-Catholic criticisms, as when he cites Edmund Wilson—in a consideration of Evelyn Waugh's *The Loved One*—"asking in what way California funeral practices were sillier than lighting candles for the dead."

Although born in England of an Australian father and an English mother, Sheed has lived so long in the United States that he writes as if he is a native-born American, with only an occasional aside regarding his English origin. When he writes "our" or "us," as he frequently does, he means "our country" or "us Americans."

After a two-week visit to Eire following a governmental tax concession to creative artists, Sheed writes on it as a great place for bad writers, since the government has "made their gushings virtually tax-free." He warns though that a writer "may be threatened by dense clouds of smug" after a one-book success. As for Americans escaping the sharp tax bite at home, they should remember that while they are saving money they are also losing contact with the mainstream of fast-moving American life and thus their subject areas will be limited. Lacking external stimuli they must fall back upon their inner resources.

One of the best of Sheed's essays is the last, entitled "Frank Sheed and Maisie Ward: Writers, Publishers, and Parents," in which he sketches affectionate and often amusing portraits of his mother and father, who began a small, mainly Catholic, publishing house in England and later established an American branch. Sheed dedicates his book "To my father, who put me on to all this."

The essays in Part Two of *The Good Word & Other Words*, which originally appeared in various newspapers, magazines, and books, reflect Sheed's varied activities during the 1970's as movie reviewer, literary critic, and political reporter. "America and the Movies" briefly surveys the recent development of a considerable body of criticism treating the cinema as a fine art. Sheed takes a few potshots at critics Michael Wood and Richard Schickel for their books *America in the Movies* ("funny") and *The Men Who Made the Movies* ("boyish"), but he has high praise for Walter Kerr's *The Silent Clowns*, which analyzes the stream of comedies turned out before movies gained a voice. The oddly titled "Toward the Black Pussy Cafe" (the meaning is cleared up in the last sentence of the essay) is an excellent examination and assessment of the comic genius of W. C. Fields, a rare classic comedian who survived the shift in the 1930's from silent films to the talkies (Harold Lloyd and Buster Keaton did not). In "I Am a Cabaret," Sheed looks at the several versions of Christopher Isherwood's *Berlin Stories*—from the play *I Am a Camera* to the movie *I Am a Camera* to the stage musical *Cabaret* to the movie musical *Cabaret*, in all of which changes were introduced—and he concludes that, "If we must have adaptations, complete disregard for the originals is the safest rule."

Two essays in Part Two were originally written as introductions to new editions of P. G. Wodehouse's *Leave It to Psmith* and James Thurber's *Men, Women and Dogs*. Sheed bluntly says that, "Wodehouse wrote first and last for money. If he finally became a sort of artist, it was only because it paid to." In an earlier essay he had treated Wodehouse as an inspired hack whose characters were derived from English music halls. Now he sees *Leave It to Psmith* (1923) as a transition book between the author's writing for the theater and the long series of comic novels which brought Wodehouse international fame and a large fortune during his long life. In the novel, writes Sheed,

> The elements are ramshackle, . . . but they are all there, ready to be shaped over the next twenty years into a comedy so narrow and fastidious, so lacking in strain and the clown's need for approval, and so ruthlessly unadulterated by other emotions that they deserve to be called classic art.

As Wodehouse's comedy could only have come from his being an Englishman, so Thurber's could only have been the product of an American. "Thurber was a marvelous comic writer," says Sheed, "but alone among such he was able to sketch the phantasmagoric goo from which his ideas came." The comedy in *Men, Women and Dogs* becomes "black magic" through Thurber's words and drawings combined, and Sheed is thankful that Thurber assembled the book before his blindness became complete and his humor darkened and turned bitter in his last years.

Published four years apart, the essays on Ernest Hemingway and F. Scott Fitzgerald are companion pieces in which Sheed writes of the physical and artistic decline of the two men who had been friends in their youth but who later became estranged, partly because of Fitzgerald's alcoholism and partly because of Hemingway's surly ingratitude. Yet when both were young they portrayed their era with brilliance. "Anyone interested in the tone of American writing in the twenties, that sense of a party going wrong, of sudden tears and dash for the bathroom, must accept both these men, in a harmony they could never create for themselves. Together, they make one hell of a writer."

Like other books of its kind, *The Good Word & Other Words* is best read a few essays at a time. Sheed's wit, his refreshing observations on the two cultures he knows best, English and American, and his critical judgments on twentieth century authors can then be both absorbed and enjoyed as they deserve.

Henderson Kincheloe

GOSHAWK, ANTELOPE

Author: Dave Smith (1942-   )
Publisher: University of Illinois Press (Chicago). 127 pp. $7.95; paperback $3.95
Type of work: Poetry

A stunning collection of poems of landscape, as it was, is, and should be, that combines music and passion, the internal and external realities that dignify poetry and distinguish it unquestionably from prose

Goshawk, Antelope is the fourth major volume of poems by Dave Smith in this decade. The first three, *Mean Rufus Throw Down* (1972), *The Fisherman's Whore* (1974), and *Cumberland Station* (1976), are informed by a sense of place—his boyhood growing up on the eastern shore of Virginia and in Maryland—which serves, as Smith has said, "an inevitable function in my poetry" without which "I could not write. . . ." This work bears the vigorous stamp of his love of the poetry of Richard Hugo and James Wright, by Smith's admission: "When I read a book of poems, I look first to see if there are poems about rivers and oceans. . . . I want to know people who, in such places have always held the hand of Death, and want to shake my hand." In this early work, much of the *duende*, the tragic sense of life, the oblique angle of vision, and the fictional sequences find their upward thrust to arc in *Goshawk, Antelope*.

Beginning with an epigraph from William Styron's *Lie Down in Darkness*, this volume demands much of the reader. It moves through time like a dreamer; it is lyrically exhilarating, passionate, and rich with musical hauntings. It appeals strongly to the nonverbal, primitive level of response. It is enormously likable. It eludes definition and explanation.

About poetry, Smith has stated: "Poetry is not language. It is language made. A unique. I call it a dialect." Poetry, he goes on to say, is not artifact, a coin to be bitten and then discarded. *Goshawk, Antelope* more than any of Smith's work, *is* this poetry. It is airy, it soars, it reiterates, it darts and speeds and hurriedly stops in midair, like the goshawk that weaves itself through so many of these poems. Rarely, when it is opaque, it fails, but most often it succeeds because of Smith's skill. The poems remind one of Walt Whitman, for Smith, too, is a poet of wholeness, and of Robert Penn Warren, and particularly of Robinson Jeffers. Reminders of Jeffers' dark prophetic voice abound, in Smith's natural symbolism, his vaulting of the wild and the violent, his sense of doom, and his strong images. But *Goshawk, Antelope* is more than influences. Smith's is an original voice, combining physical and psychological realities, projecting human character, and juxtaposing the bizarre with the unsentimental truths of life. He also affirms in a particular language of delight, and, at times, ecstasy. There is never any danger, as there is with so many of Smith's contemporaries, of confusing his poetry with prose.

Each of the book's four sections takes its title from the section's initial poem. Smith establishes himself in the first section, "Messenger," as a poet of sounds rather than silences. He excells in the statement of emotion which recollects and asserts itself so strongly that it hardly seems to need the poet, seeming to spring full-grown from his heart. "Raw Light, Mountain Lake," which is set, as are so many of Smith's poems, in the Western United States with its mountains and deserts, achieves lyricism.

Among the diverse significances attached to the goshawk is the use of the goshawk as memory, which apparently for the poet is a function of the male principle. In "Goshawk, Antelope," the antelope appears as the female, soft, hesitant, receptive, the immovable rooted one, the mother and giver, "changeless beneath the sudden whistle of gray." The speaker sees "the accusing goshawk face of my father," thus bringing out of the wind and the earth his two dominant symbols and the recurring and intermingling themes of life and death. Here Smith uses alliteration, harsh sibilants, and abrupt monosyllables to contrast with breathy h's and liquid l's, as he brings his news to the "dream-contending world." Throughout, Smith works with compound adjectives and compound adjective-noun forms reminiscent of Gerard Manley Hopkins, Dylan Thomas, and Jeffers, turning the stock epithets of Greek epic and English narrative ballad into new coin with an old ring.

> I saw memory. He came
>
> out of the strange clouded horizon like the dark of whipped
> phone wires and the quiet of first feathering shingles
> in storm or in the hour of burial,
>
> and dropped into absence where the antelope stood alive
> at the fence of barbed wire, horns lifted slightly,
> hovering on hooves' edge as if bored with the prospect
> of leaps, long standing and still.

Often voices of anger or anguish, such as those of mother and son, repudiate what is written in books as false or unusable "truth." In "Between the Moon and the Sun," as well as in "Apples in Early October," the remembering boy relearns pain and its causes, mortality, "the apple's brown ache," and "the faint sweet bloodscent of rot" by eating green apples: "though the books warned us, we still/eat green apples and cramp our bellies." The authority of experience is more eloquent than dictum, and Smith writes a good deal about his effort to define his calling and his problem as a poet: to make the words accessible, but not to make things and ideas captive in words. Even what is known of "the yawning toybox of the universe" must be known and known again, and still the mystery is beyond understanding:

> . . . and I will show the world without

> dreams, starless, mouthing itself, and the apples
> growing black with nothing to tell us. Nothing.

The message keeps coming, transmitted over the vibrating wires of memory; Smith tries throughout the volume to break the code, knowing he never will. In "Willows, Pond Glitter," the death of a sunfish, "each scale set into position by/secret and implacable desire," sets in motion a series of questions: "what I have seen and you have seen and nobody/understands, that enormous hunger."

> I swear I will come back if you can tell me what it means
> to hear the world belch its ugly answers clear as the truth
> a child would be too scared to lie about.

Gradually, through poem after poem, the theme of death is developed, the knowledge growing that what happens to others will happen to us. There are dreams of dying, night dreams, and daydreams. In "Dreams in Sunlit Rooms," the speaker visualizes "a pit as black as the secret bubble of a coal lamp," and asks himself, "and is your child only sleeping/as precise as a glass statue this glary morning?" As this section ends, the poet takes up a new variation on the same theme, but a significant variation on which the poetic direction turns. The slow thread of guilt and acceptance of involvement in the facts of death, both real and imagined, begins to bind the human to the philosophic dilemma. For with complicity comes love, and with love comes forgiveness, both asked for and given.

In "The True Sound of the Goshawk," the poet as remembering boy recalls throwing clods of dirt thoughtlessly at a swooping hawk, "that strange gesture which is like the swoop/of love." Then something like penitence, something like "I am you," passes between the boy and the bird:

> . . . I did not know
> why she cried out but began to howl
> my child's tears
>
> as if I knew what she knew, that the heart tears open
> like the goshawk's mouth when it sees at last
> what it has come for, . . .

Such nameless atrocities and the avoidable cruelties lead to apology for even what was not done, but would have been. For example, the speaker in "Under the Scrub Oak, a Red Shoe," remembers with love a girl and himself:

> I did not mean
>
> whatever I said, but said it because she was so small, she
> could not hide her fear and shivered on her back.

Smith is a reclaimer, as Jeffers said in "Triad," who wishes "not to play games with words/His affair being to awake dangerous images/And call the hawks." Cycle upon cycle, the natural and the human are recalled and narrated in that larger world that Jeffers knew, and Smith knows.

Goshawk, Antelope moves toward synthesis, for if the poet cannot affirm, he can at least bring the world together and hold it in his poem, making it new and finely wrought, if not better. Seeing a child fighting death, being sustained by tubes and hope, in "Hospital Memory During Storm," he doubts there is any possibility that scientist or poet will ever take away "from that room, the awful pus of death." He concludes that "passion/if you once believe in it, is a way of hope," the world offering "no guarantee but of loss and life." The disappointments and the sins of youth—riding a horse nearly to death, eating poisoned green grapes for a girl he cannot have and waiting to die—jostle one another in the poet's memory.

"The White Holster" is an extended poem rich in redundancies of rhythm and wonder which speaks of a boy receiving at Christmas from his mother a gun, with the blessings of his soldier-father. Here as frequently, family motifs emerge out of the natural landscape—this time a bleak and lonely Christmas. The joy, the connectedness of love, and the unity of all the poet feels are restated in sensual and erotic terms in "Sea Change: The Rented House at Seal Rock, Oregon." Waking from a dream of childhood, the speaker tumbles into the present and the sound of seals playing. Turning to the woman beside him, he thinks:

> This is what I have waited for, the body
> of joy buoyant with forgiveness, all
>
> bodies seal-sleek rising from the fracturing waters.

The third section, "Settlement," begins with a moving narrative of childhood, and before, of ancestry with its hard needs and demands. In a metaphorical sense, these poems move toward attempts to settle things—debts incurred, needs for forgiveness and for love—and toward a return even for a moment to some lost land of innocence, as seen in the poem "In the Yard, Late Summer":

> . . . knowing ourselves
> wingless and bestial, we wait
> for the sun to blow out,
> for the return of that first
> morning of pink blossoms
> when we saw the dark stains
> of our feet printing
> what we were on that
> dew-bed of the world.

In the closing section, "The Round House Voices," memories of the poet's father, grandfather, and family are captured with words, poor as they are, which in a sense stay mortality.

Smith testifies to what all great poets since Sophocles have known: we are nothing, yet we are everything. What has been forgotten is revitalized here, as Smith offers simple, ancient answers made exquisite by language, made current by passion, and given veracity by music.

Agnes McDonald

GREAT DAYS

Author: Donald Barthelme (1931-   )
Publisher: Farrar, Straus and Giroux (New York). 172 pp. $7.95
Type of work: Short stories and dialogues
Time: Primarily the present
Locale: Primarily the United States

A collection of fragments—stories, dialogues, situations—in which the author ex-
periments with the limits of language in narrative

Donald Barthelme has always been one of the most experimental and
innovative writers in the *New Yorker* stable. Yet, as such, he operates within
the mainstream of modern American fiction, and *New Yorker* fiction in particular. What characterizes American fiction since World War I has been an
obsession with experimentation, with the basic task of defining and redefining
over and over, with each successive attempt, the nature of fiction—the nature
of narrative, of the novel, and of the short story. The distinctive *New Yorker*
contribution to this long-running experiment has been an obsession with style,
with the nature of what language artfully arrayed can achieve when put to
the service of narrative expression. Especially in the seven dialogues in *Great
Days*, Barthelme has dispensed with all the trappings of narrative—setting,
description, plot, action, characterization—and instead has left himself only
dialogue to work with. This radical jettisoning offers him the chance to explore, in all its purity, one sort of language, while raising questions about the
nature of fiction and the limits of language for expressing that fiction.

The reader looks, in Barthelme's dialogues, for the kinds of indirect trans-
mission of information that would make possible constructing the dramatic
context of these interchanges. There are clues—a street reference here, an
allusion to action outside the dialogue there—but they are so brief and so
much a part of the private worlds of reference known to the conversants but
hidden from the reader that they frustrate rather than inform. Instead, one
is finally drawn to the language of the dialogues themselves, to the allusive
juxtapositions of sound and image, the ironic turns of phrase and shifts in
subject. It is as though these conversations, always, seemingly, between two
persons, are overheard by the reader who can neither see the conversants
nor their surroundings. When all external references are lacking, all one has
left is the words themselves. To borrow a term from the visual arts, we might
say that Barthelme has created a verbal experiment in minimalism, to see
how little is necessary to make a story.

What we are given, therefore, consists mainly of fragments—of speeches,
of ideas, of images—and of the interplay of those fragments as they are
arranged on the page and experienced sequentially by the reader. Since one
overhears conversations all the time in restaurants, theaters, and other public
places, it would be unfair to accuse Barthelme of being "unrealistic"; on the

other hand, to strike out all contextual information is to reduce such conversations to a purely verbal experience, an abstract verbal experience analogous to the way our experience of an abstract painting is an experience of paint, of the medium of artistic expression. There is no way to be clearer than to examine a specimen, taken from the end of the "Great Days" dialogue:

> —There's a thing the children say.
> —What do the children say?
> —They say: Will you always love me?
> —Always.
> —Will you always remember me?
> —Always.
> —Will you remember me a year from now?
> —Yes, I will.
> —Will you remember me two years from now?
> —Yes, I will.
> —Will you remember me five years from now?
> —Yes, I will.
> —Knock knock.
> —Who's there?
> —You see?

One could see in this a painful moment of recognition that love is fleeting, that commitments are at best for the moment; and perhaps that is what Barthelme gives us. Yet if we look hard, we realize that we do not know where "what the children say" stops and dialogue between the two conversants resumes. At the same time, we must note that the final ironies of the passage result from the juxtaposition of two kinds of language use: the asking and giving of commitments and the ritual language of a trite, childish joke form. More likely, what this passage is about is the potential of language for creating relationships or breaking them. The implicit relationship created by the "knock knock" joke form is one in which the script for both parties, at least to a point, is known in advance: the intricacies of this form that comes at the end are delightful. To say "knock knock" is to create expectations, both of a set script and also of a variation. The ritualized expression of love and commitment shares certain elements with the joke form; the second voice plays along with both set patterns, only to find that it has been set up for a break in both scripts. What effect this ending of the "Great Days" dialogue has comes from the breaking-down of ritual and the accompanying ironies that language collapse entails.

While such dialogue-based verbal gymnastics make up seven of the offerings in this volume, there are also nine other, somewhat more conventional, stories. Here, we are on more familiar ground, in the sense that we have characters, plots, and settings, at least of a sort. When, in "The Death of Edward Lear," however, the figure of the nonsense writer merges with the image of the central character in Shakespeare's tragedy, we know that these stories are in their own way as experimental as the dialogues. Other stories find Hokie Mokie, the newly crowned King of Jazz, besting his first rival; Mr. Lynch coolly murdered in a parlor game; a Swedish army officer having a dreadful day; and Cortes and Montezuma walking hand-in-hand down by the docks. Throughout, the pervasive tone is cool and ironic; do not ask Barthelme to be too engaged in the worlds of his fictions.

What Barthelme is doing in *Great Days* is raising some very serious questions about the nature of language, especially literary language. Whether he, finally, is a poser, or a poseur, is yet another question. What is clear is that his work appeals to a certain kind of mind, a mind that appreciates the deftly drawn irony, the self-consciously verbal text, and the work that is aware it is a literary artifact. For that mind, *Great Days* is richly rewarding.

John N. Wall, Jr.

GROUNDWORK

Author: Robert Morgan (1944   )
Publisher: Gnomon Press (Lexington, Kentucky). 56 pp. $8.50
Type of work: Poetry

A fourth collection by a young poet with a vision of nature and culture as a continuum

Robert Morgan is a profoundly ecological poet with a vision of endless variety in the unity of nature. More than that, his vision does not assume a realm of nature and a separate sphere of the human. In his view, the made world of culture and technology (what folklorists call the "cultural landscape") consists of scheme, strategies, and accommodations that parallel those in the natural, organic world of plants and animals.

Three previous collections—*Zirconia Poems* (1969), *Red Owl* (1972), and *Land Diving* (1976)—have presented people behaving and coping essentially as do plants, insects, and animals. In *Red Owl*, for example, a well is described as a root sunk by people to maintain a hold on the land. The well is a tree with leaves of men. In "Copse," from *Land Diving*, a boundary between field and woods where plants grow crowded resembles a state line where fugitives gather for getaways in first one direction, then another.

In *Groundwork*, Morgan has moved further into the human realm, dealing increasingly with local characters, anecdotes, superstition, and legend in such poems as "Flying Snake," "Mountain Bride," "Reuben's Cabin," "Death Crown," and "Devil's Courthouse." Yet all his work to date is groundwork because he is concerned with how all living things cope and find solutions to basic problems: getting food, keeping warm, wintering over, reseeding themselves, surviving, and, if they are lucky or do something right, prevailing. The bear in "Den Tree" and the pigeons in "Pigeon Loft" are like the worm in "Weed Above Snow" from *Red Owl* in that they are examples of strategies for keeping warm and secure. Reuben's cabin resembles the bear's den tree, the pigeon's loft, and the worm's bulb in the weed stalk. Reuben's behavior is buzzard behavior. His cabin, stitched together out of odds and ends up high in a place near Buzzard Rock, is his nest. (Buzzards are known for the slapdash nests they build.) It is not irrelevant that squirrels have stolen the innards of Reuben's couch to line *their* nests. Reuben, the squirrels, the pigeons, and the bear are all coping in their own way, surviving like the "Ice Worm" from *Land Diving* that has figured out a way to live on glaciers in Antarctica.

The mink in "Sport" that kills forty-six chickens is one in its strategy with the panther that eats the baby in "Huckleberries," with the "Flying Snake," and with the snakes in "Mountain Bride." The observer-predator of "Burning the Hornet's Nest" is behaving like the mink and like the panther. The lichens in "Appalachian Trail" resemble mountain climbers attaching their crampons to rocks. The people in "Fear" who live close to the fire in their clearings, isolated and immersed in superstition, have their parallel in the strategy of lichen, grass, rockfern, and fruit trees in "Huckleberry Bald": they all play close and root deep.

Morgan's metaphors connect things in such a way as to present a whole which contains not only nature but culture and technology as well. The process of storing up energy is similar for plants, insects, animals, and people. The bear in "Den Tree" has stored up acorn fat and lies in the hollow tree like a banked coal. Canned peaches in the cellar in "Canning Time" are stored energy, a vegetal battery people will draw on later. This metaphor appears in the earlier *Land Diving* in "Frozen Lake," where trout swim alert, like juice in a battery: the lake is a battery; nature has its technology. Also technology resembles and aids natural processes. A kitchen stove in *Red Owl* is presented as a digestive tract, a motor, a vehicle for translating vegetable heat from the past to the present.

In the continuum of nature-culture-technology, as Morgan presents it, levels interpenetrate complexly. The "upper rooms" of "Burnoff" resonate with "Upstairs at the Country Store," where coffins lie stacked like canoes, ready when a death occurs to be launched into "cellar undercurrents." In "Canning Time," however, the canned peaches on cellar shelves underground are life-sustaining. The paradox is part of Morgan's vision, summarized in "Affliction," from *Land Diving*, in which blight-stricken chestnut trees that keep sending up sprouts are said to be like people in that they are forever attempting to ascend and, like people, are "immortal/only in dirt."

Because Morgan uses place names, local lore, and legends in this collection, *Groundwork* will be more closely associated with the history and culture of the Appalachian South than have his previous collections, and rightly so. In "Bricking the Church," Morgan compresses into a striking symbol much of the social and cultural history of the Appalachian South. The church, built originally of logs in the settlement period, then later covered with unpainted lumber, with white clapboards, and finally with a veneer of brick, is described as having grown successive rings, like a tree. As the church's doctrine has softened, it has put on a hard shell "for weathering the world." Social significance may also be attached to "Trash" which is caught up by wind and scattered while rooted oaks stand unmoved nearby.

Certain poems in *Groundwork* lack the wonderful economy and compression of the earlier *Red Owl* and *Land Diving*. The loss of compression is most noticeable in the relaxation of the line, which may be the result of Morgan's working more frequently in the narrative mode. When the poems work as narratives (as in "Mountain Bride") and when they work as ideational lyrics, they work extremely well. When narrative and lyric impulses appear to be at odds in the same poem and when details are not subsumed by metaphor (as in "Baptism by Fire," "Lost Flower," and "Devil's Courthouse"), the result is less satisfactory.

Morgan's poems, however, are like the strategies of his plants, animals, and people: some work, some do not. It is inappropriate to speak of Morgan's progress from collection to collection because his vision is not linear. Morgan sees everywhere, as Emerson put it, "circular power returning to itself." Such a vision results in poems that, read in any sequence, always spell the same thing. Instead of progressing, Morgan is presenting an increasingly rich and complex articulation of levels and interpenetrations. To accomplish this, he must try different ways of doing things. He knows that accomplishment is no guarantee of success in the future, but he also knows that initial failures may be ultimately fruitful. In "Praying Through," the last poem in *Groundwork*, Morgan says:

> The detours guide,
> the side trips and dead-ends
> like pruning
> strengthen and confirm the main
> stalk of your going out.

Jim W. Miller

THE HABIT OF BEING

Author: Flannery O'Connor (1925-1964)
Edited, with an Introduction, by Sally Fitzgerald
Publisher: Farrar, Straus and Giroux (New York). 617 pp. $15.00; paperback $6.95
Type of work: Letters
Time: 1948-1964

A collection of letters written by Flannery O'Connor over a period of sixteen years, and edited sensitively by one of her intimate friends

Principal personages:
FLANNERY O'CONNOR, important American author of short stories and two novels
REGINA CLINE O'CONNOR, her mother
SALLY FITZGERALD, close friend to O'Connor
ROBERT FITZGERALD, her husband and close friend to O'Connor
MARYAT LEE, playwright and O'Connor's devoted friend
CECIL DAWKINS, professor and admirer of O'Connor's work
JOHN SELLY, Editor in Chief of Rinehart Publishing Company

Book reviewers were not among Flannery O'Connor's favorite people. They invariably have "hold of the wrong horror," she bristled early in her career when she saw her stories reviewed as horror stories. Again toward the end of her life, after eighteen years of writing, she summarily dismissed "the racket that's made over a book and all the reviews. The praise as well as the blame—it's all bad for your writing."

O'Connor's possible disapproval notwithstanding, this book deserves a racket of praise. It is a masterful collection of letters that she wrote to friends, acquaintances, publishers, and agents—to anyone, in fact, who felt compelled to write to her, no matter for what reason. They sparkle in a chiaroscuro of feelings, are full of sometimes delightful, sometimes provocative insights, and flow in a style that is forceful, precise, and although on occasion amusingly oblivious to correct spelling, free from the usual ugly infelicities and clichés. Sally Fitzgerald, one of O'Connor's most intimate friends, has edited them with superb, unobtrusive scholarship. Her pithy comments and explanations provide helpful information and sustain the letters' continuity. On all counts, *The Habit of Being* is a remarkable event in this genre of literature.

Appropriately, the collection begins with a letter in which O'Connor, in 1948, introduces herself to Elizabeth McKee, who was to become her lifelong agent and friend. Twenty-three years old at the time, she had already published one story, and two others had been accepted for publication. The last letter is dated July 28, 1964, six days before her death at the age of thirty-nine. During the sixteen years spanned by this collection, she came to be considered by her admirers as one of the finest short story writers in the English language, and by her critics as, at best, bizarre.

In contrast, O'Connor's life was transparent. She was born an only child in Savannah, Georgia, in 1925, and when she was twelve, moved to Milledgeville, and central Georgia town, where her father died three years later. She was graduated with a B. A. degree from Georgia State College for Women (now Georgia State College) in Milledgeville; received a Master of Fine Arts degree from the State University of Iowa; and after having spent some time at Yaddo, a retreat for writers and artists in Saratoga Springs, New York, lived for two years in the country home of the Fitzgerald family in the woodlands of Connecticut. When, after her return to Milledgeville in 1950, it was discovered that she suffered from *lupus erythematosus*—an incurable but controllable disease of metabolic origin and varying severity—she and her mother moved to the nearby family farm, "Andalusia." There she spent her life, most of it on crutches, until she succumbed to the disease twelve years later.

O'Connor's letters abound in vivid descriptions of life at "Andalusia," reflecting the extraordinary power of observation that characterizes all of her work. Nothing she sees is trivial to her, and with the turn of a phrase she elevates the commonplace to an event of significance. "I have twenty-one brown ducks with blue wing bars. They walk everywhere they go in single file." As an avocation, O'Connor raised peacocks, "something that requires everything of the peacock and nothing of me," and she also painted. To the poet Robert Lowell, she wrote that her mother preferred that she paint rather than write. Her mother, Regina Cline O'Connor, is ubiquitous in O'Connor's correspondence, whether she reports on life at "Andalusia," her work, or her reading. Almost without exception, Regina stars in wickedly funny stories or is referred to in humorous quips, but the lighthearted tone reveals more than it conceals an abiding affection.

Whereas in O'Connor's stories the dependency of family members on one another in the intimacy of day-by-day living is often governed by sentiments ranging from indifference and irritation to open resentment and murderous hate, she embraces her own necessary dependency on her mother not only with good humor but also with an attitude amounting to creative delight. To the playwright Maryat Lee she complains playfully, "My parent took advantage of my absence to clean up my room and install revolting ruffled curtains. I can't put the dust back but I have ultimated that the curtains have got to go, lest they ruin my prose." To another friend she describes an afternoon as "a full horror as my mother elected to remove the rug from under me & my furniture and put another one down. Everything was wiped up with turpentine water & I am waiting for the seven other devils. . . ."

O'Connor was reticent about the disease that made her dependent on others and severely limited her movements and her social life, but when she talked about it, she often adopted the same tone of self-mockery. "You didn't know I had a DREAD DISEASE didja?" she asked Maryat Lee more than a year after their correspondence had begun:

> Well I got one. My father died of the same stuff at the age of 44 but the scientists hope
> to keep me here until I am 96. I owe my existence and cheerful countenance to the
> pituitary glands of thousands of pigs butchered daily in Chicago Illinois at the Armour
> packing plant.

One of the rare instances where she drops the guard of self-deprecation is also one of her most moving passages. "I have never been anywhere but sick. In a sense sickness is a place, more instructive than a long trip to Europe, and it's always a place where there's no company," she confesses to a correspondent who became her closest confidant, identified in the book only as "A." "Success is almost as isolating and nothing points out vanity as well."

As guarded as she could be about the things concerning her private life, there are two things about which she wrote with a candor that occasionally amounts to a fierce assertiveness: her work and her faith as a deeply committed Roman Catholic. Her comments on her own work, and that of others which she reads voraciously, could serve, collectively, as an instructive and delightfully entertaining guide to the novelist's craft. She is "a full-time believer in writing habits," she tells a fellow novelist, Cecil Dawkins; "I write only about two hours every day because that's all the energy I have, but I don't let anything interfere with those two hours, at the same time and the same place." She warns "A" not to write exercises: "Experiment but for heavens sakes don't go writing exercises. You will never be interested in anything that is just an exercise. . . ." She is exacting of her work-in-progress, sending drafts to friends and asking for, and accepting willingly, their advice. But she draws the line where she feels the integrity of her writing is being questioned. To John Selby, Editor in Chief of the Rinehart publishing firm, she sends this scathing rebuke:

> I can tell you that I would not like at all to work with you as do other writers on your
> list. I feel that whatever virtues the novel [*Wise Blood*] may have are very much connected
> with the limitations you mention. I am not writing a conventional novel, and I think that
> the quality of the novel I write will derive precisely from the peculiarity of aloneness, if
> you will, of the experience I write from. . . . In short, I am amenable to criticism but
> only within the sphere of what I am trying to do; I will not be persuaded to do otherwise.

The peculiarity or "aloneness" of the experience to which she alludes here, and from which all of her writing flows, is her faith, a faith nourished and formed by the teachings of the Catholic Church. She is at her most eloquent and profound when she writes to "A" about the perceived interdependency of her work, her faith, and the Church. "I write the way I do because (not though) I am a Catholic," she tells "A." Elsewhere in their correspondence, she expresses the conviction that her writing talent is a gift and that "the direction it has taken has been because of the Church in me or the effect of the Church's teaching, not because of a personal perception or love of

God. . . ." She progressively defines and redefines this awareness of her unique vocation. "Your freshman who said there was something religious here [in *Wise Blood*] was correct," she writes to Cecil Dawkins in May, 1957. "I take the Dogmas of the Church literally. . . . The only concern, so far as I see it, is what Tillich calls the 'ultimate concern.' It is what makes the stories spare and what gives them any permanent quality they may have."

Flannery O'Connor reveals herself in her letters as one of the rare writers who seems to have been spared the torture of self-doubt about her talents and her work. She wrote because, as she once told a student, "I am good at it," and as openly as she confesses delight in the stories she particularly likes, she expresses misgivings about others whose publication she always regretted. Yet there is a curiously melancholic sentence at the end of a long letter she wrote one year before her death to a nun: "I appreciate and need your prayers," she writes. "I've been writing eighteen years and I've reached the point where I can't do again what I can do well, and the larger things that I need to do now, I doubt my capacity for doing."

We will never know to what heights of literary perfection and quality O'Connor could have risen. She left a modest body of work—two brief novels, thirty-one short stories, and a few essays—that has enriched and ennobled American literature. Now we possess, in addition, in *The Habit of Being*, an unsolicited testimonial to her life, and we may well come to count that which O'Connor never intended for publication as her most splendid gift.

Heinz R. Kuehn

HANNAH ARENDT
The Recovery of the Public World

Editor: Melvyn A. Hill
Publisher: St. Martin's Press (New York). Illustrated. 362 pp. $14.95
Type of work: Essays

Essays on Hannah Arendt's political and philosophical thought

The essays in Melvyn Hill's collection, *Hannah Arendt: The Recovery of the Public World*, include both appreciative commemorations of Arendt's unique place in American intellectual life and critical appropriations of her thought. The writers bring a variety of perspectives to bear on Arendt's work: they are both academic theorists and nonprofessional political thinkers; they are philosophers, professors of political theory, and architects; they are Marxists, structuralists, and idealists. All have found in Hannah Arendt's work some exemplary or engaging or provocative quality: Hill's collection is a record of their engagements with this thinker.

Perhaps because this collection has been published so soon after Arendt's death, and perhaps because so many of the writers represented in it knew her personally, the commemorative rather than the critical aspects of the collection are the most evident and striking. This commemoration takes three forms: tributes to Arendt's temper of mind, to the main trends of her thought, and to her distinct method.

Many of the writers in Hill's collection find in Arendt's reflections on her experience as a Jew in Nazi Germany, in Occupied France, and in exile in the United States, an exemplary response to the central problems of the twentieth century: the problems of totalitarianism and of thinking politically in an age when traditional patterns of political thought have collapsed. Moreover, Arendt's refusal to classify herself as either liberal or conservative, her abstention from any ideological commitments, and her stubborn independence saturate her intellectual project with moral significance, as if the refusal of commitment were a refusal to collaborate with the disasters of modern politics, and instead expressed a willingness to take responsibility for one's own explorations. Thus, the writers in this collection give their works such titles as "The Pathos of Novelty: Hannah Arendt's Image of Freedom in the Modern World" (James Miller), "Thinking Without a Ground: Hannah Arendt and the Contemporary Situation of Understanding" (Stan Spiros Draenos), and "The Abyss of Freedom—and Hannah Arendt" (J. Glenn Gray). Such titles are the elegiac tribute paid by analytic writers to an ethical thinker.

Such a tribute is especially striking given Arendt's understanding of the relation between theory and action. Arendt refused to compromise the autonomy of either political theory or of communal political reflection; as a result, she renounced any project of influencing political affairs. Thus, at the

1972 Toronto conference on her work, some exchanges from which conclude this volume, Arendt responds to the question of how she would instruct a political actor: "No. I wouldn't instruct you, and I think that this would be presumptuous of me."

In spite of this renunciation, however, for writers in this collection, Arendt's work suggests possibilities of action and engagement and forges a connection between reflection and practical political work. Thus, editor Melvyn Hill invokes Arendt's own term, "storytelling," to describe her work, and asserts that "Storytelling keeps this 'understanding heart' alive, so that when one acts one does so in the full recognition of the world that makes freedom possible, and with respect for the citizens with whom one shares it." Hill's collection, then, commemorates Arendt as a moral thinker in two ways: she thinks as an ethical being; and her thought is of ethical consequence.

Much of the ethical force of Arendt's work is expressed in her investigations of language, especially of the traditional language of political discourse, which she examines as an instrument of disclosure. For many of the writers in this volume, recovering and working through the differentiations of Arendt's language is a way of commemorating and preserving her thought. It is the distinction between "labor," the production of consumable necessities of life, and "work," the production of durable objects, the creation of a world of man, that has attracted most attention from the authors represented in this collection. Mildred Bakan, in "Hannah Arendt's Concepts of Labor and Work," and Bikhu Parekh, in "Hannah Arendt's Critique of Marx," both provide explications of this distinction. Both also confront her understanding of labor with Marx's. Both writers, while critical of Arendt's subordination of labor to work and to political activity, find her distinction illuminating, not as a tool for classifying actions, but as a way of disclosing what is at stake in different modes of living the *vita activa*. To distinguish labor from work is, for these writers, to ask certain useful questions about the relationships between public and private worlds. The distinction between labor and work has also attracted the attention of Robert Major and Kenneth Frampton; their treatments of this theme will be considered later in this review.

Other essays in this volume, including the examination by Peter Fuss of "Hannah Arendt's Conception of Political Community" and the essays by Miller and Draenos cited above, treat the distinction between the political and the social. Whether either of these distinctions is entirely satisfactory, of course, is an open question, a question which emerges again and again in the exchanges collected at the end of the volume. A respondent insists that the political and the social cannot, in practical situations, be consistently distinguished; Arendt replies tartly that they certainly can, and distinguishes the social problem of providing decent housing, about which "there shouldn't be any debate," from the political problem of whether housing should be integrated. A few pages later, we read C. B. Mcpherson's complaint: "She defines a lot of key words in ways unique to herself: you know, social *versus* political (a rather special meaning to the word 'social'), force *versus* violence (a quite special meaning to the word 'force')." And, in a few more pages, Mary McCarthy will propose, in a startling metaphor, that "each distinction is like a little house," a "free space" with its own architecture and furnishings, sheltering a discrete idea. As so often with Arendt, what is distinctive in her thought is provocative for both her adherents and her critics.

In raising the question of Arendt's use of language, we have already opened the topic of the third commemorative or celebratory theme of this collection: Arendt's distinctive method. Three essays in the collection are explicit investigations of method; all three merit fairly close examination. They are Kenneth Frampton's "The Status of Man and the Status of His Objects: A Reading of *The Human Condition*," Robert Major's "A Reading of Hannah Arendt's 'Unusual' Distinction Between Labor and Work," and Miller's essay on Arendt's concept of freedom. All three articles walk the thin line between commemoration, performed in Arendt's sense as an act of memory preserving the significance of a deed for a different time and place, and critique, an investigation that penetrates a writer's thought in order to extend what is incomplete and identify what is missing in it.

Frampton's essay is the most surprising of the three. Writing as an architect interested in issues of urban planning, he makes use of the distinction between labor and work to consider the differences between "building" and "architecture," an examination which is made more concrete by Frampton's discussion of the historical roots of this distinction in the Renaissance. Frampton's essay reminds us how deep are the roots of the process of "deskilling the work force" described by Harry Braverman in *Labor and Monopoly Capital*. His discussion transforms Arendt's categories; Frampton ends by suggesting connections between the themes of *The Human Condition* and the concerns of two thinkers, Marcuse and Habermas, for whom Arendt had little fondness. But this transformation is not covert. Frampton has "thought through" Arendt's terms in a fruitful way.

Robert Major examines the ways that specialist readers—and Arendt herself—have "misread" the labor-work distinction. Major's essay is an unusual but accessible application of structuralist methods normally applied to the analysis of literature to a political text. He considers what forms of preunderstanding by specialist readers lead them to distort or neglect Arendt's text, and finds that "commitment to the self, i.e. 'subjectivity,' and to self actualization" is the hallmark of such readings. This analysis of misreading is more helpful than Bernard Crick's testy and defensive remark, in his essay "On Rereading *The Origins of Totalitarianism*," that Arendt's critics "Have either not read her closely or else are just using other formulations of the origins and conditions of totalitarianism, often crude, rigid, and deterministic." What is most audacious in Major's essay, however, is his hypothesis that Arendt "misreads" her own text, misunderstanding the nature of the body that sustains and is sustained by labor, seeing that body sometimes as a mere object in the world, and only fitfully as a living being.

James Miller's essay, "The Pathos of Novelty: Hannah Arendt's Image of Freedom in the Modern World," begins with the experience of puzzlement and resistance which so many readers of Arendt report, and attempts to work through the text to construct an understanding of her method. Miller examines *On Revolution*, noting Arendt's odd analysis of American history expressed in her image of the Constitution as a document rooted in confidence in the people, allowing himself to be puzzled by her amalgamation of the councils of the French Revolution to the Russian soviets. Miller, however, does not end his reading here, with an easy critique of Arendt's data. Noting that "for one thing, it is scarcely credible that she simply suppresses contrary evidence, since such evidence occasionally figures in her own text," Miller invokes Walter Benjamin's "Theses on the Philosophy of History" to argue that Arendt's is a revolutionary conception of history as a series of stories, stories which crystallize moments of freedom, preserving them as living memories. Miller presents an interesting reading of *On Revolution* in these terms and concludes that, while Arendt's analysis neglects a good many crucial issues, her method "provides a model for using the past to think about the possibilities of the present."

The essays by Frampton, Major, and Miller all attempt to make sense of the resistant and anomalous elements of Arendt's thought by establishing a context within which her odd distinctions and her unique method are illuminating. This strategy is more successful than the alternate method of "regularizing" her thought into traditional forms, the strategy pursued by Michael Denneny in his essay, "The Privilege of Ourselves: Hannah Arendt on Judgment," which attempts to anticipate what Arendt would have written had she lived to complete her manuscript on *Judging*, which was to have formed the third section of *The Life of the Mind*. Denneny seems to be unaware, however, of the difficulties of translating Kant's *Critique of Judgment*, a work on aesthetics, into political and ethical terms. He neglects the subtle set of distinctions which allows Kant to see the judgment of taste as a joint labor of the subjective cognition and objective reason as they collaborate in the individual's perception of a work of art, conceiving of taste rather as a joint labor between the individual's subjectivity and the imagined "objective" response by a group. Such a flattening of Kant's concept does not help us to "think through" his distinctions; it reduces Kant, and by implication Arendt, to a sociologist of literature.

This collection, then, includes a great variety of work. Although most of the writers are sympathetic to Arendt's project, it is by no means an attempt to create what editor Melvyn Hill would call a "school of Arendtians." Hill's collection is, however, the most substantial contribution to the study of

Arendt's thought since Canovan's *The Political Thought of Hannah Arendt*. Its value for both beginning students and scholars is substantially increased by two contributions by Elisabeth Young-Bruehl: a short sketch of Hannah Arendt's life and work, which serves as an excellent introduction to the themes of the collection, and a very full chronological bibliography of the works of Hannah Arendt. The thirteen pages of this bibliography, listing titles on subjects as diverse as St. Augustine and W. H. Auden, speak as eloquently as any of the essays in this collection, demonstrating the range and power of Arendt's thought.

Susan Wells

HERBERT HOOVER
A Public Life

Author: David Burner (1937-   )
Publisher: Alfred A. Knopf (New York). 433 pp. $15.95
Type of work: Biography
Time: 1874-1964
Locale: Primarily the United States and particularly Washington, D. C.

A biography of the thirty-first President of the United States

> *Principal personages:*
> HERBERT HOOVER, thirty-first President of the United States, 1929-1933
> WOODROW WILSON, twenty-eighth President of the United States, 1913-1921
> WARREN G. HARDING, twenty-ninth President of the United States, 1921-1923
> JOHN CALVIN COOLIDGE, thirtieth President of the United States, 1923-1929
> AL SMITH, Governor of New York, who lost presidential election to Hoover in 1928
> FRANKLIN D. ROOSEVELT, thirty-second President of the United States, 1933-1945
> THEODORE ROOSEVELT, twenty-sixth President of the United States, 1901-1909
> HARRY S TRUMAN, thirty-third President of the United States, 1945-1953

This biography of Herbert Hoover corrects commonly held views of the man who occupied the American presidency during the Great Depression. Hoover received the censure of the electorate for his failure to pull the nation out of the Depression, and his reputation never recovered. This biography salvages his place in history to some extent and reveals that he was a far more complicated individual than the failures of his presidency would indicate and that he did try to come to grips with problems of twentieth century American development that have yet to be solved.

Hoover graduated as a member of Stanford University's first class (1895) and went on to a career as a mining engineer. Most of his jobs were overseas, and eventually he toiled on four continents. He lectured and wrote on his work and thereby acquired a considerable reputation in engineering and business circles. He established himself as a consultant on the problems of managing and operating corporate businesses and from offices in London and various American cities advised concerns around the world on their financial and managerial problems. He was a very wealthy man by the time of World War I.

Hoover had a Quaker upbringing which manifested itself in a lifetime of strong social concern. Caught in the Boxer Rebellion in June 1900 in China, he organized relief work for the foreign community there; in London, when World War I broke out in 1914, he plunged into relief activities for Americans fleeing the European Continent. This work branched out into attempts to do something for the people of Belgium who had been overrun by the German armies. Hoover became chairman of a privately organized Belgian relief commission which fed the Belgians in spite of severe obstructions on the part of both the Allies and the Germans. After the United States entered the conflict in 1917, President Woodrow Wilson selected Hoover to head America's food effort, and, under Hoover's leadership, the United States fed not only itself but the Allied armies and peoples as well. Half a million tons of food and aid worth a hundred million dollars was delivered to thirty European countries during the war and its aftermath, all under Hoover's direction and administration. In 1927, when Hoover was Secretary of Commerce, he directed relief efforts necessitated by the Mississippi River floods, and after World War II he again directed European famine relief programs.

Hoover's mobilization of American food resources and his European relief work made him the foremost American hero of World War I; he could have had the 1920 Democratic presidential nomination, but sensing the Democratic Party to be doomed by its association with Wilson, the problems stemming from the conflict, and the peace, he declared himself a Republican and supported the Harding-Coolidge ticket. After the election he was offered the position of Secretary of Commerce in the Harding-Coolidge Administration, which he accepted and held from 1921 to 1929. This position gave Hoover the opportunity to undertake on a national and even an international scale what he had previously done in private business and war relief work. He proceeded to reorganize and expand the Department of Commerce, so as to rationalize major segments of the American economy. Little escaped Hoover's reforming hand; domestic and international business activities were grouped under appropriate Commerce sections and elaborate studies undertaken to determine what the government could do to aid and regulate these businesses in their orderly growth and development. Appropriate government programs were then instituted.

Hoover's reputation as food administrator during the war was enhanced by his work at the Department of Commerce during the prosperous 1920's, and he could not be denied the 1928 Republican presidential nomination. In that year Hoover reached the zenith of his popularity; perceived to be the epitome of an American success story—the poor orphan lad who had become a professional and business success, a millionaire, and a public servant—he was swept into the presidency on a tide of prosperity, while his Democratic opponent, Governor Al Smith of New York, was rejected by the majority of Americans as nothing more than an urban and ethnic politician. In 1928, Hoover was clearly the candidate who favored expanding the powers of government over the economy and the public believed his promises of permanent prosperity.

As President, Hoover continued his work of ordering and rationalizing the economy, but the Great Depression took hold of the country and his efforts went unnoticed. Significant as Hoover's reforms had been during the 1920's, he had never sought to reorder the nation's economic and financial structure, which was the basic cause of the Depression. During the 1920's, great segments of the population had not participated in the decade's prosperity; the working and agricultural classes were in fact in a depression long before the crash in 1929. Thus the prosperity of the 1920's was a prosperity of the urban middle and upper classes, and these classes invested heavily in a banking and financial system that was poorly structured, managed, and regulated. The Depression set in with the collapse of the New York Stock Market in 1929 and gradually spread through the economy; the middle and upper classes could no longer absorb the productivity of American industry, and everything ground to a halt. Unemployment and bank failures grew as people took their money out of the banks to pay for life's necessities; confidence collapsed, and Hoover faced a national and international crisis. Europe had largely recovered from the ravages of the world war on the basis of American credit, and with the Depression this credit dried up, dragging Europe down along with the United States.

Hoover's solution to the problem was to work harder at reviving the nation's financial structures in order to revive business and employment. Scores of new government programs were introduced, and government spending soared. Among the better-known Hoover agencies were the Reconstruction Finance Corporation, which refinanced major units of business and government, and the Federal Farm Board, which tried to lift agricultural prices but met with what must be judged total failure. Revival did not occur, and people lost confidence in Hoover's leadership as unemployment and misery grew. Demands arose that the President attack the unemployment problem directly with massive federal relief programs, but Hoover, despite a lifetime of administering relief to foreigners, took the position that individuals and localities would have to help themselves through the crisis and that the federal government could not get directly involved in the administration of relief to individuals. Hoover had always insisted that the government could do much to order and aid economic development by extending all sorts of help to businesses and various organizations, thereby enabling the latter to do a job themselves, but he drew a firm line when it came to injecting government into the actual operations of business. He believed that if this line were breached and if government entered directly into the ordinary life of the country, then bureaucracy would take over and individual liberties and initiatives would be lost. Hoover's position was philosophically sound, but given the scale of suffering, people could not accept such arguments and felt him callous, particularly in view of his previous relief work. On his part, Hoover was by training an engineer and an administrator, not very articulate, a miserable speaker, and hence not suited to sell what basically was an unpopular program to start with.

Hoover became associated with the Depression and became the butt of a thousand jokes. He had spent his life attempting to build up the world economy and thereby to further social justice, and when his redoubled efforts met with failure the Depression only grew worse, causing the public to heap all the blame on his head, he was deeply hurt. He did not have the background, training, temperament, nor imagination to understand that American society had reached one of its historic turning points and that new solutions would have to be entertained. It was all beyond his grasp.

Hoover's successor, Franklin D. Roosevelt, continued Hoover's work of restructuring and rationalizing the economy's major segments in the New Deal, but he also set up direct relief programs and took the nation off the gold standard. Hoover warned that abandoning the gold standard would give the government and the people open-ended financial means (this was Roosevelt's intention) and that this, coupled with governmental responsibility for individual welfare, would result in ruinous inflation and strangling bureaucracy. His attacks on the New Deal assumed a bitterness which probably sprang as much from the wound of being blamed for the Depression as from a fear of Roosevelt's excesses. Hoover's only opportunity to make the best of the New Deal reforms was to serve, at President Truman's request, as head of two federal commissions following World War II which successfully eliminated much waste and inefficiency in the federal bureaucracy.

Hoover's Quakerism gave him a pacifist tendency, and he was convinced that the United States would be better off if it stayed out of foreign quarrels as much as possible. During his presidency he repudiated the right of the United States to interfere in the internal affairs of Latin American states, proclaimed by Theodore Roosevelt, and he was slow to encourage American involvement in the war against Hitler, though once it came he supported it wholeheartedly. After World War II, he adopted a militant anti-Communist stance which overshadowed his call for a retreat of American power to the North American continent and the rejection of any "world policeman" role for the United States. Hoover clearly believed that the American people should place firm limits on what their government should be allowed to do at home and abroad, and he warned that if such limits were not established, bureaucratic strangulation, inflation, and defeat would be the inevitable results. His presidency must be judged a failure, but he foresaw where his successors would take the country.

Jack L. Calbert

HITLER VS. ROOSEVELT
The Undeclared Naval War

Author: Thomas A. Bailey (1902-   ) and Paul B. Ryan (1913-   )
Publisher: The Free Press (New York). Illustrated. 303 pp. $12.95
Type of work: History
Time: 1939-1941
Locale: Germany, the United States, and the North Atlantic

A study of the undeclared German-American naval conflict which lasted from 1939 to 1941

> *Principal personages:*
> FRANKLIN D. ROOSEVELT, President of the United States, 1933-1945
> SIR WINSTON CHURCHILL, Prime Minister of Great Britain, 1940-1945
> ADOLF HITLER, Führer of Germany, 1933-1945
> BURTON K. WHEELER, Senator from Montana and a leading isolationist politician
> ROBERT A. TAFT, Senator from Ohio, another leading isolationist politician
> CHARLES A. LINDBERGH, famous aviator and prominent spokesman for isolationism
> CHARLES A. BEARD, renowned historian, another prominent spokesman for isolationism

During the Vietnam War, the question of the right of an American president to conduct an undeclared war became a controversial one. In *Hitler vs. Roosevelt*, Thomas A. Bailey and Paul B. Ryan closely examine an earlier and equally controversial exercise of executive power in the realm of foreign policy: President Franklin D. Roosevelt's undeclared naval war against Nazi Germany. Their new book deals with the politics and diplomacy of that undeclared war, which lasted from the German invasion of Poland until the Japanese bombing of Pearl Harbor.

Although neither author participated in the events of the period, both lived through those years. Thomas A. Bailey was a Professor of Diplomatic History at Stanford University, while Paul B. Ryan was a young naval officer. Bailey is now retired, while Ryan is presently a Research Associate at Stanford University. The two men have collaborated to produce a book which is not only scholarly but also well-written and easy to follow.

To prepare *Hitler vs. Roosevelt*, the authors have made use of all existing secondary sources, as well as some previously unexploited primary ones. The captured German documents of the period, which became available after World War II, are used with especially great skill. As a former naval officer, Ryan was able to obtain access to documentary sources in Washington, D.C., which were not readily available to civilian researchers.

On September 1, 1939, the German invasion of Poland plunged Europe into World War II. In Chapters One through Six, Bailey shows how, from the beginning of the war up to the fall of France to the German armies in June of 1940, President Franklin D. Roosevelt grew steadily firmer in his determination to resist the aggressive policies of the German dictator Hitler and his Japanese and Italian allies. Although Roosevelt took no overt measures against Nazi Germany during this time, he did manage to secure a partial revision of the Neutrality Acts.

The three Neutrality Acts of 1935, 1936, and 1937 had reflected the staunch determination of the United States Congress to prevent American entanglement in any future European war. The first two of these acts had absolutely forbidden the sale or transport of arms to any belligerent country. The third Neutrality Act allowed commodities that could be made into arms to be sold to foreign purchasers, if they paid for cargoes with cash and hauled them in their own ships.

On November 4, 1939, after American citizens had been involved in two unfortunate incidents involving German submarines, the United States Congress revised the Neutrality Acts. Foreign purchasers of munitions could now take them away in their own ships on a cash-and-carry basis. This change benefited Hitler's archenemy, Great Britain, which still controlled the seas. At the same time, however, the revised Neutrality Act established danger zones, extending far out to sea from the waters of the warring states. Into these waters American ships were forbidden to sail. This latter provision, included to pacify the American foes of foreign involvement, would long hamper Roosevelt's efforts to aid Hitler's foes.

Once France had fallen, Roosevelt resolved to take stronger measures against the Nazi menace. In Chapter Seven, the authors tell the story of Roosevelt's first major break with American neutrality: the "Destroyers-for-Bases Deal" of September 2, 1940. This executive agreement, concluded between President Roosevelt and British Prime Minister Winston Churchill, was designed to circumvent existing American laws, which forbade the direct gift of American arms to any one of the warring sides. By the terms of the agreement, the United States Government gave several overage destroyers to Great Britain in return for the right to build military bases on various Western Hemisphere islands possessed by Great Britain.

In Chapter Eight, Bailey and Ryan give the background of the next major step toward war: the Lend-Lease Act. Roosevelt first broached the idea of Lend-Lease at a presidential press conference on December 17, 1940, shortly after his reelection to a third term. He urged that the United States, instead of selling arms to Britain, should simply give needed arms to that country, with the understanding that these arms should be replaced once the war was over. This proposal was designed to help a desperate Britain which could no longer afford to pay for arms. The survival of Britain, the President declared in a radio address on December 29, was vital to the defense of the United States.

Roosevelt did not convince everybody. When the Lend-Lease Bill was introduced into Congress on January 10, 1941, it ran into heavy opposition from such isolationist politicians as Senator Burton K. Wheeler of Montana and Senator Robert A. Taft of Ohio. In addition, the famous aviator Charles A. Lindbergh and the renowned historian Charles A. Beard testified against the bill. These men predicted that passage of the bill would eventually lead the United States into war. It was, therefore, not until March 11, 1941, after two months of prolonged and exhausting debate, that the bill was finally passed into law.

During the debate over the Lend-Lease Bill, Roosevelt had promised that British ships carrying Lend-Lease goods to Britain would not be escorted by ships of the United States Navy. He did not, the authors make clear, keep this promise for long. In Chapters Nine through Fifteen, they show how, from April through November, 1941, Roosevelt, making full use of his powers as Commander in Chief of the Armed Forces, steadily led his country deeper and deeper into an undeclared war.

During these months, Roosevelt took what the authors view as a series of deliberately unneutral measures. On April 4, 1941, he had American officials sign an agreement with the Ambassador of German-Occupied Denmark, allowing the United States to occupy the Danish colony of Greenland. Although the Nazi-dominated government in Copenhagen repudiated the agreement, the first American troops arrived in Greenland on June 4. In July, United States Marines occupied Iceland, which was about three times closer to the European continent that it was to North America. In the same month, Roosevelt unilaterally extended the North Atlantic safety zone for American shipping to include the waters around Iceland, even though Hitler had made it clear that he considered these waters to be part of his blockade zone. It was in July, too, that Roosevelt, without asking Congress for permission, quietly ordered ships of the United States Navy to escort all the way to Iceland any ships that requested such protection. Soon, clashes between American ships and German submarines (U-Boats) were taking place.

On September 4, 1941, the United States destroyer *Greer* became involved in a clash with a German submarine. On September 11, President Roosevelt, in a fiery radio address to the nation, presented this incident as an unprovoked German attack. In doing so, the authors make clear, the President was guilty of misrepresentation, since it is uncertain whether it was the American or the German commander who fired the first shot. Using the *Greer* incident as a justification, Roosevelt announced that he was ordering ships of the United States Navy to attack the U-Boats, those "rattlesnakes of the Atlantic," whenever they showed themselves in waters deemed vital to American national security. Thus, the President had proclaimed an undeclared shooting war.

In October, two American destroyers—the *Kearny* and the *Reuben James*—were torpedoed by German submarines, with considerable loss of American lives. Taking advantage of the public anger produced by these incidents, Roosevelt succeeded in persuading Congress to remove the last remaining legal obstacle to his policy of offering all aid to Britain short of officially entering the war. In November, 1941, both Houses voted, by narrow majorities, to repeal the Neutrality Act of 1939. Henceforth, the United States Navy would be free to escort British ships all the way to Britain. The danger zones, into which American ships had been forbidden to sail, were abolished. While technically still a neutral country, the United States had become a de facto ally of Britain.

Roosevelt, Bailey and Ryan argue, wished to aid Britain as much as possible, but not to engage the United States in an all-out land war against Nazi Germany. Rebutting the accusations of such revisionist historians as Charles A. Beard, the two authors emphatically deny that Roosevelt deliberately provoked the Japanese attack on Pearl Harbor in order to drag the United States into war. According to Bailey and Ryan, Roosevelt genuinely hoped to avoid the necessity of sending an American expeditionary force to Europe, since he did not believe that the United States was sufficiently prepared militarily for a land war on the Continent. Furthermore, the authors point out, he was acutely aware of the need for the unanimous support of public opinion at home in the event of war. Roosevelt gambled that the German dictator wished to avoid an all-out war also.

Bailey and Ryan demonstrate that the other fencer in this suspenseful naval duel, Adolf Hitler, was an equally cautious man. Making expert use of captured German documents, the authors show that Hitler exercised prudence and restraint in the face of American provocation, placing a short leash on those German naval officers who pleaded for harsher retaliation against the United States Navy. The German invasion of Soviet Russia, launched on June 22, 1941, did not prove to be the easy conquest Hitler had expected. Thus, with his armies fully occupied on the Russian front, Hitler knew that he could ill afford to tangle with the American forces as well. He remembered all to well the decisive role played by the American Expeditionary Force in defeating the German Army during World War I, in which he himself had fought as a common soldier. It was not until December 11, 1941, four days after the Japanese bombing of Pearl Harbor, that Hitler, in a vain attempt to win Japanese assistance in the war against Russia, declared war on the United States.

The authors frankly admit that President Roosevelt was not always "unduly" bothered by "old-fashioned morality" in his efforts to give all aid short of war to beleaguered Britain; yet, they are quite sympathetic to Roosevelt's somewhat unorthodox use of executive power in the realm of foreign policy.

They do not condemn him for his dissembling, but instead praise him for his bold leadership. They applaud his willingness to take the initiative in dealing with that "homicidal maniac," Adolf Hitler. For, Bailey and Ryan assert, it is the president, and not "the windy body known as Congress," who bears the ultimate responsibility of judging what constitutes the American national interest at any given time.

While generally well-reasoned, the book does have some flaws. It seems exaggerated to speak repeatedly of a "personal feud" between Hitler and Roosevelt, two men who never met each other. The two authors, moreover, fall into a seeming contradiction in their treatment of the problem of American public opinion. On the one hand, they argue that Roosevelt's deliberate deception of the American people over the submarine incidents was absolutely necessary for the success of his plan to aid Britain, since isolationist sentiment at home was too strong to permit him to gain support for his policy in a more honest fashion. On the other hand, they also argue, chiefly on the basis of contemporary public opinion polls, that a strong majority of Americans favored aid to Britain even at the risk of war. Perhaps, as the authors themselves suggest, the American people simultaneously wanted two mutually exclusive things: peace and the survival of Britain. The apparent contradiction between a strongly pro-British public opinion and a politically powerful isolationist movement does, however, require more explanation than the authors give.

Hitler vs. Roosevelt contains numerous aids for the reader who is not an expert on the history of the period. Maps of the North Atlantic sea-lanes show exactly where the clashes between American ships and German submarines took place. American newspaper cartoons of the period are reprinted to illustrate the various shades of contemporary opinion on foreign policy within the United States. The fine collection of photographs includes photographs of Hitler, Roosevelt, and Churchill, as well as photographs of some of the ships involved in the incidents in the North Atlantic. The back of the book contains a brief list of primary and secondary sources and several pages of footnotes.

Paul D. Mageli

THE ILLUSION OF TECHNIQUE
A Search for Meaning in a Technological Civilization

Author: William Barrett (1913-   )
Publisher: Anchor Press/Doubleday (Garden City, New York). 359 pp. $12.95
Type of work: Philosophy

A theoretical study of modern man's mania for techniques and technical systems

In *The Illusion of Technique: A Search for Meaning in a Technological Civilization*, William Barrett, author of *Irrational Man*, champions the cause of liberty in the modern world. His book is, he says, "an attempt at a connected argument for human freedom," and it is apparent that this argument is directed forthrightly at B. F. Skinner and other behavioral scientists who would seek to thrust upon man a "technology of behavior."

Divided into three sections, each of which centers upon a major philosopher, the main part of Barrett's study is taxing even for the most sophisticated reader. Wittgenstein, Heidegger, and William James are his foci, each of whom represents a type of modern philosophizing: respectively, analytic philosophy, phenomenology/existentialism, and pragmatism. In addition, Barrett adds a fourth, briefer section which endeavors to give a glimpse of the future. Stylistically, his study speaks one moment in sharp, everyday prose; at other times, it appears in dense, philosophic ruminations; on occasion, it drifts into rhapsody and metaphor. Its style, then, is a self-conscious illustration of "open-endedness," one of the book's major arguments about the nature of language and resulting human freedom.

Early in *The Illusion of Technique*, Barrett pits against closed systems (his example is the mathematical logic of *Principia Mathematica*) such open systems as ordinary language (which Wittgenstein embraced in *Tractatus Logico-Philosophicus*). What these systems illustrate for Barrett is the choice between enslavement and liberty. A behaviorist, he argues, seeks to regulate a subject's mental life by shaping it as a series of bodily responses. That is, he does not obliterate the inner life (far less does he wed it to the outer life) so much as he renders it inconsequential. Yet it is apparent that in daily life, the most lasting, meaningful changes of human behavior come from within, prompted by a transformation in the "inner person." They are, in short, acts of the will. This conflict, stripped to its essentials, is for Barrett one between "technique" (a closed, methodological system) and "choice" (an open, freedom-flexing indeterminacy). Thus, Wittgenstein's rejection of mathematical logic and his eventual accommodation of ordinary language is seen here as a movement from a closed to an open world—a world of flexibility, potentiality, and alternative choice.

It is in the first quarter of his study (entitled "Technique") that Barrett uses the example of Wittgenstein to engage the problem of man's self-enclosure.

His thesis, set out both here and in the preceding lucid Prologue, is that man has bound himself with Blake's "mind-forged manacles" by gradually crafting a mechanical world in which he is both physically and philosophically a mechanical human. His technology, at whose altar he has come to worship, is itself a demigod in a pantheon, the Lord of which is Technique.

By "technique," of course, Barrett means the attitude of mind so familiar to us all in a world of self-help books and "how to" manuals on everything from acquiring instant wealth to achieving surefire orgasm—the attitude that for every problem there is a system, a methodology which will work if only we learn to use it properly. At its most trivial, though still dangerous, level, we see this attitude of mind in the standardized-testing mania which infects American schools and colleges and in such programmed-learning schemes as those for teaching university students how to write a decent essay. They are fundamentally noncreative, closed systems. Our belief in their efficacy, Barrett would argue, is a dominant myth of our time, akin to a Frankenstein monster. At its most serious level, he adds, we see this attitude of mind in behaviorism and Communism. The former, in effect, hypothesizes that some technique can readily shape humans, whatever situation arises in their lives. The latter is straightforward indoctrination in obedience. Both fail to understand that any attempt to turn a human into a closed system is bound to beget a zombie, not a creative intelligence. The very essence of man is not his limitation or enclosure, but his sense of participation and belonging in a universe of "Being." Technique, then, may achieve momentary victories. Over the long run, it may even succeed in crafting our oblivion; but by its very nature, it does not seek to preserve the elements of our humanness.

In the second part of his book, where he turns to the concept of Being by drawing liberally upon Descartes and Heidegger, Barrett posits freedom as a possibility for man. This second part is detailed and tough, not always as lucid as one could wish, but filled with those "swoops and darts" of insight that Barrett finds so characteristic of Wittgenstein.

Beginning with Descartes, Barrett surveys the idea of man's living in two worlds—the inner (subjective) and outer (objective)—and so being fraught with the doubt that arises from a divided consciousness. Yet even here, as in the phenomenology of Husserl, man's will is manifest in the free choices it makes: to pursue nature's secrets, despite the doubt of physical reality, or (in Husserl) to "bracket" the very idea of objective reality as though it were not now significant. What follows next is far and away the most "poetic" section of *The Illusion of Technique*—a strange, rhapsodic interlude entitled "Homeless in the World," wherein Barrett tries to wrest into clarity the idea of our coming into light, into illumination, into the revelation that we are part of universal Being. In some ways this is the heart of his study. It encroaches upon something that elsewhere in his book he refers to as the region of the inarticulable; yet here, interestingly, it is language that Barrett uses to suggest the sense of our "Being-in-the-world." Just as we grope with the actualities and possibilities of language toward illumination in a sentence, so language evidences a world of Being. It is neither physical nor mental in its reality but some medium between both. Adds Barrett: ". . .our difficulty in grasping it is exactly of the same order as our difficulty in grasping Being, which, like language, eludes and embraces both these categories at once." A "technician," of course, would have no understanding of this nature of language, but Being is precisely what technical man cannot conquer, Barrett remarks.

At the risk of oversimplifying the argument: technology does not seek to *be*; it seeks to dominate. It objectifies the stuff of the world, humans included, in order to control it. As a result, technicians (especially behaviorists) have as their aim a preoccupation with spreading power, and so deeply embedded is this technical framework in our lives that we permit that power to flourish though it is without wisdom or purpose. Yet as subjects, rather than objects, we feel a genuine loss of Being, an anxiety or alienation that has become thoroughly characteristic of our modern lives. So Barrett's essential point is that we are not yet lost. Although technique looms as the enemy of human freedom, man possesses a moral will which lies at the very center of his identity. Further, it is a will with which he directs the events and judgments of his actual life.

The remainder of *The Illusion of Technique* seeks to explore this concept of will. In some ways, of course, Barrett's idea is terribly commonplace, but, as he is quick to point out, that in no way disqualifies its truth. And shorn of its philosophical trappings, we recognize it as a truth that all too often we try to avoid. Ravage our physical world as we will, pile machines and buildings one upon the other, dominate our fellow man, contrive schemes for government—still, the very fact of our Being, of our existing, is the mystery before which we pale.

By focusing on William James, Barrett draws together the sense of mystery and the concept of the moral will. He begins by pointing out James's crisis of 1870 as recorded in his diary: "I will go a step further with my will, not only act with it, but believe as well; believe in my individual reality and creative power." The first step toward freedom is in believing that freedom is possible, for out of belief there come actions which confirm that belief.

Yet any such assertion of the moral will inevitably leads toward religion, as Barrett notes, especially in an age of nihilism. James, then, is treated as a religious thinker—but one who speaks for religion rather than from within it. What Barrett advocates, in contrast, is that one get "within" religion— and this cannot be done by willing oneself to be religious or by dogmatically asserting one's belief, since in truth we probably do not know *that* we believe much less what we believe. We get "within" religion by repeating ritual and by cultivating a sense of the mystic. The ritual may be as simple as making the sign of the cross; whatever it is, it serves not to state a conviction but, through repeated use, to develop a conviction that there is purpose and meaning to existence, an intensely personal value which transcends the social goals of determinism or Marxism. If the value of life is nothing more than achieving these goals or simply indulging pleasure and avoiding pain, how does one explain the last runner in an agonizing race who crosses the finish line long after the crowd has left, the sun has set, and there is no one to see him break the non-imaginary tape? This example is Barrett's own, and in a way it suggests perfectly how the apparently irrational, meaningless, futile, absurd actions of our lives are at once acts of the moral will by which we declare a faith in transcendent value.

The last sixty or so pages of *The Illusion of Technique* form a very personal utterance. Here Barrett suggests that for modern civilization there is no more important task than to recapture a sense of the mystic. What he means by this, it appears, is that man needs to reject his domineering, power-seeking will and his wholesale indulgence of closed systems long enough to rediscover the "Being" with which he is one. Again, while Barrett's point may seem mundane, he clearly drives at the truth which is desperately in need of re-affirmation. "Mysticism" is not a practice whereby we gain access to an ethereal, other-worldly realization the secret of which somehow is possessed by a guru. It is not some grand cosmic consciousness or spiritual state into which we plunge ourselves as if into a river. It is certainly not a rarefied state of mind and spirit accessible only to the select few. As Barrett reminds us, mysticism was once a natural condition of mankind. It was revealed in man's sense that he, too, was part of the trees, rocks, and plants that inhabit the world of Being. Modern biological materialism simply cannot speak of man in these terms any more than determinism can comprehend him as something other than a finite organism whose only meaning lies in repeating obedient, unchosen response. What genuine mysticism offers, then, is a kind of religious reawakening in which there may lie an understanding of life's value:

> The mystic reclaims and redeems this instinctual source of life for us. We live from the same instinct that keeps the rat struggling in his trap. But who is to say that the struggle of the rat is not holy? Mysticism is instinct lifted to the level of faith and love. The mystic represents that point in evolution where consciousness, a perilous offshoot of the whole process, rejoins and affirms the great flood of life that has produced it.

Yet is this reawakening a possibility in our modern world? Even if one concedes its necessity, as surely we must, have not technique and the tech-nological world so embedded themselves into our lives that we cannot go beyond them? It would appear that Barrett wants to answer optimistically. He wants to insist that technology is not in itself an evil, that what harms mankind is the belief in more technology as the simple solution to our planet's problems. Further, he wants to claim that the real answer is quite within the grasp of everyone: it is to rediscover the bond of life which holds all things together. How does one do that? Not by schemes or by vast abstract concepts, but by settling on the simple, evident things of life to which we find ourselves attached—a pet we love, a plant we water, a bird whose brilliant colors fascinate us, a rock whose very attitude or expression changes with the seasons and its surroundings.

In the Epilogue to *The Illusion of Technique*, Barrett intensifies his personal message by drawing us to the walks he takes, the things he sees, the doubts and affirmations that alternately occupy the mind of one who reflects on the reality of death. In the background of these pages, however, we sense that all is not well. Fences are built, which obstruct Barrett's free ambling through the woods; in the public world, slogans replace thought, inner vision yields to prepackaged television images, the deep and agonizing problems of life persist in the face of more freeways, real estate's newest Tract Heaven, and the President's latest in a series of Programs-to-end-Inflation. In short, we sense that the reawakening may not be possible, despite Barrett's conviction that man will never permit his freedom to be eradicated. (He has just finished reading *The Gulag Archipelago*.) The fact remains that B. F. Skinner is probably just as widely read as Solzhenitsyn, and as Barrett himself acknowledges, there is something menacing and foreboding in the utterly nonhuman Utopia which behaviorism promises us. There is also something frighteningly immediate about it, if only because it can promise near-instant success.

It is now more than three hundred years ago that John Milton, ever England's greatest champion of liberty, declared: "I cannot praise a fugitive and cloistered virtue, unexercised and unbreathed, that never sallies out and sees her adversary, but slinks out of the race. . . ; that which purifies us is trial, and trial is by what is contrary." He was, of course, stating in *Areopagitica* another version of his oft-repeated notion that man is a coward who prefers "easy bondage" to "strenuous liberty." While Barrett does not turn to Milton (or to any writers, really, other than the existentialists), he might well have done so, for the point to be made is his own. It is difficult to live. It can even be painful and horrifying. Yet in the end, to eliminate life's trial by manipulating behavior or genetics is fundamentally no different from eluding trial by persistent, cowardly avoidance. That is not "life" at all but something ignoble, unpraiseworthy, and irreligious.

David B. Carroll

THE IMPROPER BOSTONIAN
Dr. Oliver Wendell Holmes

Author: Edwin P. Hoyt (1923-   )
Publisher: William Morrow and Company (New York). Illustrated. 319 pp. $12.95
Type of work: Biography
Time: 1809-1894
Locale: Cambridge, Massachusetts

A popular biography of the medical professor and man of letters, now remembered for a handful of poems such as "Old Ironsides"

> *Principal personages:*
> OLIVER WENDELL HOLMES, medical professor and man of letters, the father of the Supreme Court justice
> LOUIS PASTEUR, the famous French scientist
> JAMES T. FIELDS, editor of the *Atlantic Monthly*, in which much of Holmes's work was published
> RALPH WALDO EMERSON, famous author of essays and friend of Holmes
> HENRY WADSWORTH LONGFELLOW, famous poet and friend of Holmes
> JAMES RUSSELL LOWELL, poet and friend of Holmes

Of the two Oliver Wendell Holmeses—father and son—the father seems the less important and the more interesting, while Oliver Wendell Homes, Jr., the legal thinker and Supreme Court justice, remains of stellar importance in the development of American jurisprudence. His father, the medical professor and writer, is remembered as the author of much forgotten prose and some unforgettable poems.

The useful or amusing if evanescent prose and the immortal if minor verse form the appropriate testament of a man of talent. Oliver Wendell Holmes was a man of genius saddled with the achievements of a man of talent; but Edwin Hoyt in *The Improper Bostonian* ignores this fascinating facet of his subject's life. Hoyt's journalistic survey of the elder Holmes is amusing reading that skirts the edges of, but deliberately does not penetrate the mystery of Holmes's relative failure. Hoyt portrays an incurable, insecure egotist coping in his chosen careers of medicine and literature, but he stops short of analysis.

The son of a strict Calvinist preacher, Holmes had no use for his father's bleak religious view, but he would not take a stand against it. He conformed; after his father's church split away in controversy, he continued to attend that church. When studying medicine in Paris, supported by his father, he studied hard, taking care to amuse himself quietly in ways that would certainly have distressed his father had he known. Instead of being honest, Holmes wheedled money out of his father by means of the most outrageous hypocritical twaddle:

"Were I a parent . . . I should consider no sacrifice too great . . . and I should hesitate long before I would say to him, pale and fatigued with study—leave Europe forever, the only one among your companions who has not been beneath the dome of St. Peter's."

Holmes's inability to take stands and follow through and his willingness to live independently while stopping short of real emancipation were manifested clearly in his medical career. Early in his thirties, Holmes, the astute medical researcher, discovered that the chief carriers of puerperal (childbed) fever were physicians themselves. By not observing what today would be considered ordinary sanitary precautions, physicians were literally murdering the women whose childbirths they attended. This was startling and important news, but many physicians rejected it, choosing murder over soap and water. Holmes knew he was right, but because he lacked the courage of his convictions, because he would not take a strong stand, thousands of women died unnecessarily. This early espousal of unpopular attitudes followed by retreat after the first serious opposition was a persistent pattern throughout Holmes's medical career, from his objection to deplorable hospital conditions to his later flirtation with the issue of women and blacks attending medical school.

In his literary career, Holmes dabbled. Unlike his close friends—James Russell Lowell, Henry Wadsworth Longfellow, and Ralph Waldo Emerson—Holmes regarded himself as a literary amateur. A favorite of James T. Fields, the editor of the *Atlantic Monthly*, Holmes wrote and published essays, novels, and poems, most of which appeared in that magazine. A small sheaf of his poems still deserves high praise: The fervent "Old Ironsides," the introspective and lyrical "The Chambered Nautilus," and the boisterous "The Deacon's Masterpiece" are deservedly remembered. Holmes's essays, of which "The Autocrat of the Breakfast Table" is the finest flowering, are the unmemorable distillations of his forgotten conversations. His novels—*Elsie Venner, The Guardian Angel, A Mortal Antipathy*—reveal more about their author than about their characters. Of the three, none was a critical success, and only one, *The Guardian Angel*, was a publishing success. In literature, as in medicine, Holmes fell short. He longed to be remembered but felt that he was not destined for immortality. Shortly before his death, he wrote on a picture autographed for writer William Winter's son: "Ten—twenty—perhaps even thirty years from now—somebody may be interested to hear you say that you received this picture from the hands of the original; sometimes writers are remembered even as long as that."

Edwin P. Hoyt's *The Improper Bostonian* is an interesting book about a fascinating life; it provokes thought not only about a minor nineteenth century literary figure, but also about the way personality can circumscribe and even stultify talent. While Hoyt's account raises these questions, it does not speculate any further about them. The author's restraint seems a conscious decision in pursuit of a wider audience; inevitably, more thoughtful readers will feel amused rather than instructed, soothed rather than challenged.

Alan G. Gross

IN BETWEEN THE SHEETS AND OTHER STORIES

Author: Ian McEwan (1948-   )
Publisher: Simon and Schuster (New York). 153 pp. $8.95
Type of work: Short stories

A gripping collection of short stories that, through detailed narration, unite the real and the bizarre worlds

Ian McEwan's voice, as is always necessary in short fiction, is distinctive, and his technique is controlled. If, after two collections of stories and one brief novel, McEwan is not yet a major writer, he gives every indication that he could become one. His flaws are those of youth, self-indulgence, and subject matter, rather than of craft or intelligence. *In Between the Sheets and Other Stories* is an intriguing, sometimes challenging, and generally superior collection of stories, the work of a craftsman on his way to becoming an artist.

McEwan's subject matter is not enticing. He often indulges a fascination for the squalid and the sickening; his imagination tends to dwell on freaks, sexual aberrations, and bizarre fantasies. Nevertheless, other writers have created literature from such subject matter. The question which the reader must ask (and which McEwan must ask himself) is: do these preferences of subject matter add up to an authentic vision of life and of the world, or are they a quirk of youth or of the desire to be different?

As V. S. Pritchett has pointed out, McEwan is a master of styles and structures who is able to muster a variety of feelings through his strange tales. He possesses intellectual resources sufficient to enable him to open up his claustrophobic stories and suggest worlds beyond them. Perhaps the underworld in these stories is the first view we are experiencing of a new artist's unique perceptive faculties.

McEwan's strength lies in his ability to create a scene or a character out of precise, perfectly chosen details. Even his more fanciful or bizarre stories are rooted in concrete, meticulously described details. He also possesses invention and humor, a flair for irony, and a gift for satirical parody, but without the well-chosen details which make us *believe* his stories—at least while we are reading them—these other gifts would be futile. McEwan has been compared to Kafka and Beckett. He is not yet in their league, but he does possess their understanding that it is necessary in direct proportion to the degree of fantasy in a tale to tie the fantasy to reality with homely, immediately comprehensible details.

McEwan's novel, *The Cement Garden,* a short, bizarre work which tells the humorous and terrifying story of a most unusual London family, is successful largely because of the dryness of its tone and its ironic attention to detail. The stories in *In Between the Sheets and Other Stories* lead the reader into a world still more bizarre, violent, and filled with sexual fantasies and erotic dreams; in these stories, the deformed and maimed play major roles, deliberately perverse and disgusting images abound, and an audacious black humor runs throughout. Often strange images and shocking scenes are used to symbolize McEwan's themes; for example, the Americanization of Britain is represented in the story "Pornography" by the shifting of the pornography shop to entirely American stock, because it is "better" and more salable. It is unclear, however, what is being symbolized by O'Byrne's contradictory relationships with Pauline, whom he dominates, and Lucy, who dominates him.

Pathetic, lost, frightened individuals swarm through McEwan's stories, struggling to survive, to find a moment of happiness, to achieve some kind of satisfaction in their existence, however brief or tenuous. These characters are often portrayed humorously, but a shift in plot or tone inevitably provides the thrust which carries the story into the grim, bizarre literary realm which McEwan seems determined to carve out for himself. The Ape in "Reflections of a Kept Ape," five-foot-tall Harold with his built-up shoes and thick-lensed glasses in "Pornography," and ugly and precocious little Charmian in the title story are three examples of these bizarre yet ultimately meaningful characters, and there are many others.

The first story in the collection, "Pornography," veers from what promises to be a comical account of the lives of two brothers running a Soho pornography shop, in which nervous customers try to get as many free glances of the pornography as they can before they are asked to buy or vacate, to a sickening tale of sexual revenge. The precise observation of the Soho grubbiness, the cheap lodgings and filthy baths, the nasty smells and cheap drink, develops into a story of the archetypal fear of the sexual adventurer: castration. But does this sordid tale possess a larger significance? The implications are there in the pornography store, O'Byrne's venereal disease, the infiltration of the influence of America, and the final act of emasculation. Is it the British male who is being castrated, or even the entire British nation? While the symbolism in the story is insistent, it is not entirely clear.

"Reflections of a Kept Ape" is a story at once more subtle and more bizarre. A first-person narration by a pet monkey which has been seduced by a young woman who has written a best-selling novel, the story presents a picture of faded lust and broken promises. The varied style of the prose, the flexibility of the tone, and the pathetic irony all indicate a craftsman in control of a strange but effective tale. The Ape is a Romantic, but his mistress, Sally Klee, is an opportunist, a "modern" woman. Even her name, a combination of Sally Bowles and the painter Klee, indicates her sleek, modern, ruthless incompetence. Perhaps the significance of this story lies in the fact that the Ape is capable of feeling more genuine and complicated emotions than is his mistress (mistress in *both* senses of the word). Some kind of relationship seems to be implied between Sally's sterility as an author and her affair with the ape, but he is a much more appealing character than she is, as well as a more noble individual. The reader cannot help feeling—despite a natural reluctance to accept an ape as a "lover"—that the beast has come out the worst in this affair. The world of Ian McEwan is a world in which conventional morality and sentiments have been turned on their heads.

The basic fable in the story "Dead as They Come" has been told before by other writers, but McEwan twists it so that it fits into his own fictional universe. The story of the rich man who falls in love with a beautiful female mannequin in a shop window is made believable and pathetic by McEwan's half-vulgar, half-elegant rendering of detail. The protagonist of this story is a man with an obsession, as are most of McEwan's characters. The first-person narration adds verisimilitude to an improbable story. When the protagonist speaks of his dummy (and *to* her) as if she were a human woman (even naming her *Helen*, after the most famous beauty of all time), the tone of his voice manages to make a ridiculous and unbelievable situation touching and almost tragic. The reader is drawn into his passion, sympathizing as he attributes human emotions to a wooden dummy.

The narrator/protagonist of "Dead as They Come" is searching for peace and tranquility, even if only, at last, in death. He is not the only character in this collection to be engaged in such a quest. He mistakenly thinks that he has found peace and happiness with this silent, beautiful female, and he does not allow for the intrusion of the outside world. There is no peace in the real world, McEwan seems to imply; there is no rest, no permanent happiness for the living.

The title story draws an uneasy comparison between a nine-year-old girl grimly working in a cheap restaurant and the spoiled daughter of the protagonist and her perverse young friend. One child is forced to labor to stay alive, but Miranda and Charmian (again McEwan's names, both from Shakespeare, are not accidental) are free to indulge in secret vices. Miranda's father, separated from her mother, assuages his guilt by sending her money. The story is about fear and what it can do to human relationships. In some ways, the tone of the narration is reminiscent of F. Scott Fitzgerald's stories about his relationship with his daughter (such as "Babylon Revisited"), but McEwan's tone takes a perverse turn and adds a different, unique shape to his story. In a McEwan story, children are no longer sexual innocents and are as likely as the adults to be deformed, perverse, and evil.

"Two Fragments: March 199-" is an evocation of a half-destroyed London on the eve of the next century. The narration does not make clear whether the scene of destruction is the result of war or revolution, but it deliberately avoids the conventional melodramatic portrait of catastrophe, preferring to concentrate on the dull, ordinary events in people's lives within this altered world. We see government offices smoldering in a deteriorating wilderness and witness the scrounging for food and shelter. We see people eating polluted fish from a polluted Thames and traipsing on pointless journeys across a desertlike city landscape. This is a world in which lovers find rest by recalling the bygone era before the catastrophe, remembering such commonplace events as visits to the old zoo, now a closed ruin, and football matches.

Again, the traditional image of childhood and innocence is shattered in this story. The protagonist's daughter asks about sex, but her innocence is only theoretical. What she already has witnessed, what she witnesses during the course of the story, and what she is sure to witness in the future, have deprived her of innocence in any real sense of the word. No one living amid the violence and devastation portrayed in this story could long remain innocent. Even this story set in the future is rich in closely observed details, in precisely drawn vignettes, scenes, and actions which anchor the fantasy in a constructed reality. This quality of a concrete fairy tale also pervades the story called "Psychopolis," which presents the British view of Southern California as a land of narcissists, beaches, and Doggie Diners.

Ian McEwan is a storyteller to watch, a writer who relishes the interplay of reality and fancy, who is intrigued by the banal as well as by the grotesque, and who compulsively studies inner realities hidden beneath façades. His voice is distinctive, his craft controlled, as seen in this collection of unusual, impressive stories indicative of an original talent.

Bruce D. Reeves

IN EVIL HOUR

Author: Gabriel García Márquez (1928-   )
Translated from the Spanish by Gregory Rabassa
Publisher: Harper & Row Publishers (New York). 183 pp. $8.95
Type of work: Novel
Time: The late 1950's
Locale: The Caribbean coast of Colombia

An account of a small town that reacts violently when confronted with the disparity between its image of itself and what it actually is

> *Principal characters:*
> THE MAYOR
> FATHER ÁNGEL
> JUDGE ARCADIO
> THE DENTIST

Gabriel García Márquez sets *In Evil Hour* in an indefinite time and place, but given his description of the mysterious setting, we can assume it to be a town in his native lowlands along the Caribbean coast of Colombia during the late 1950's. The action thus occurs during that tempestuous period of Colombian history known as *La Violencia*, a period of anarchic struggle between factions roughly paralleling the traditional Colombian Liberal and Conservative parties. Most of the novel, however, takes place during a long lull in the hostilities while the town is experiencing an uneasy peace and wondering when the general killing will begin anew. This foreboding, in the effective imagery of García Márquez, pollutes the very environment of the unnamed community which suffers from the humidity, rains, and floods of its tropical climate. The floods leave carcasses strewn about the town, at one point befouling the air with the stench of a dead cow. The foreboding is such that even in the church a dead mouse is found floating in the holy water.

Within this ominous environment García Márquez develops his plot around the mysterious appearance, on doors throughout the town, of posters lampooning the unmentionable "secret" sins of the inhabitants. These lampoons, though seemingly innocuous gossip, so terrorize the townspeople that their fear of the posters becomes synonymous with their fear of the impending civil strife. Subliminally, the townspeople know that open criticism such as the lampoons represent could lead to violence because individuals and groups will go to any length to avoid or avenge public humiliation. Exposure of imperfections or supposed imperfections forces the targets of such criticism to compare their public image of themselves with "reality," a comparison that can prove psychologically unbearable when it reveals an apparent disparity. The reaction of individuals and groups to such public shame, especially their political reaction, is the central theme of *In Evil Hour*.

Dealing as he does with the psychology of a community, García Márquez presents us with a cross section of the town's population: laborers, shopkeepers, aristocrats, professionals, and government officials. While this multitude leads to some confusion and shallowness in characterization, the major figures—the mayor, Father Ángel, Judge Arcadio, and the dentist—achieve a good degree of complexity despite the brevity of the novel. Structurally, these figures, together with some of the minor characters such as the doctor and the barber, functon, by nature of their occupations, as links between the town's different social groups and, consequently, between the novel's different episodes. Presented as the townspeople engage in their daily activities, these realistic episodes each center on the lives of two or three characters and reveal the reasons why these individuals do or do not fear the mysterious lampoons. The plot, therefore, while superficially exhibiting the episodic quality of daily life, is unified by the common concern over the posters and builds to a climax as everyone wonders what will be done about the lampoons and whoever is posting them.

The first important incident to result from the posters occurs early in the novel when César Montero, a rich lumberman, who reads of his wife's "infidelity," openly murders her alleged lover. Publicly shamed by the lampoon placed on his door, Montero reacts violently because he finds an ostensible and unbearable discrepancy between his image of himself as a man and the "reality" of himself as a cuckold. Ironically, his wife has actually been faithful, but this only serves to show the power that public humiliation can have over its victim. While the lumberman and his family suffer the shame in this incident, his open murder of a fellow citizen threatens to shame the authorities who during the lull in *La Violencia* have been trying to restore the people's confidence in the local and national governments' abilities to maintain the peace. Thus, the lampoons indirectly threaten the image that the political establishment has projected, an image of a lawful system, itself resorting to violence only when absolutely necessary.

The members of the town's political establishment are among the novel's major characters: the mayor, Judge Arcadio, and, since the Catholic Church remains a strong political institution in Colombia, Father Ángel, the priest. At first, even after Montero's crime, they dismiss the lampoons as a silly prank, changing this attitude only after the tension in the town becomes intolerable. Until then, the civic leaders' vested interest in preserving the community's image as a pacified town prevents them from seeing that the lampoons portend the resurgence of social and economic hostilities that have been repressed during the period of political peace. Father Ángel prefers to believe that he has succeeded in shaping, especially through the power of censorship granted him by the state, a parish exemplary in its spiritual harmony. He refuses to believe that the posters' accusations of sin have much merit; to do so would expose him as a failure. Judge Arcadio, enjoying a government salary and a meaningless title, would rather not disturb the status quo by investigating the problem of the silly lampoons. The mayor, who also heads the police, would like most to maintain the peace since he has learned to use his office to enrich himself quietly; and to use his police powers against the posting of mere gossip would seem an undue and even illegal use of force.

While the civic leaders ignore the lampoons, the town's wealthy citizens, the chief targets of the posters, become increasingly tense since they make the most pretensions to respectability. The Asís and Montiel households, besides the Montero family, exemplify the reaction of the upper class to the lampoons. Rebeca Asís, like the wife of César Montero, is accused of adultery. Her husband, Roberto, less impulsive than Montero, doubts the truth of the poster, but begins making unexpected appearances at his home should the rumored lover arrive there. Rebeca, together with the other wealthy ladies of her church group, implore Father Ángel to condemn the lampoons from the pulpit, but the priest continues to deny the seriousness of the situation. Only after he discovers that Roberto's shame may actually lead to another killing does Father Ángel decide to denounce publicly the posting of and overreaction to lampoons. In the meantime other families shamed by the public posting of their own sins react by leaving town. Among those preparing to flee is the widow Montiel, an extremely rich woman whose wealth accrued from the unsavory financial and political practices of her dead husband. Before she can leave, however, the lampoons drive the widow insane, and she attempts suicide.

In contrast to such violent reactions are the nonchalant attitudes of other members of the population: the wealthy Don Sabas, Judge Arcadio's "wife," the dentist, and the poor. An unscrupulous rancher, womanizer, and traitor to his former political allies, Don Sabas has one redeeming virtue: his shamelessness. He tolerates the lampoons because there is no disparity between his public image and reality; he never pretends to be respectable. Because of this, García Márquez presents him as a less reprehensible character than the hypocrites who make up the rest of his class. Similar to Don Sabas in this respect is Judge Arcadio's common-law wife, who, despite the entreaties of Father Ángel, refuses to pressure her lover into marrying her. Since Arcadio saved her from poverty and loves her, she does not fear gossip; interestingly, a lampoon against her never appears. Her attitude reflects that of the town's poor who, struggling against disastrous floods and economic exploitation, at best find the current upper-class concern with respectability amusing.

Of the novel's characters, the dentist fears the lampoons least simply because he has high ideals and lives up to them. Both during the peak of *La Violencia* and during the uneasy interlude of peace, he has steadfastly opposed the forces now in control of the town. Having refused to leave town when the government was intimidating its opponents with gunfire, he worries little about mere lampoons, despite the qualms of his wife. However, because of his integrity and continued political opposition, the dentist threatens the government's recent conciliatory image; in a sense his presence is a lampoon against the state, exposing its oppressive nature. This becomes apparent when the dentist, in protest against the government, refuses the mayor treatment for a terrible toothache. Desperate, the mayor and his policemen break into the dentist's office and force him to extract the tooth. This violent reaction to the dentist's protest belies the government's peaceful image, revealing the state's tyrannical nature and prefiguring the renewal of open warfare.

While the mayor carried out his attack on the dental office under cover of night, the increasing tension in town caused by the posters finally leads him to take openly repressive measures to find the person disturbing the nerves of the community. Having been convinced of the lampoons' demoralizing effect by Father Ángel, the mayor orders a curfew requiring that all citizens remain in their homes at night between the hours of eight and five. Despite this decree, the lampoons continue to appear, and it becomes obvious that more than one person is posting them. After a while, the mayor even suspects that the local men recruited to enforce the curfew may themselves be tacking up posters. He begins to realize that respect for his authority has declined. When a youth is caught, not posting lampoons, but actually distributing fliers critical of the government, the outraged mayor, fearing rebellion, places the town completely at the mercy of the police, who are in fact nothing but hired killers. Faced with open criticism of the regime, the mayor abandons his government's conciliatory image, reveals its oppressive character, and moves to crush the sources of free speech.

The first to die from the state's renewed attempts to silence criticism is the youth arrested for distributing forbidden propaganda. Tortured to reveal the sources of the fliers, he dies in his cell after attempting to "escape." Hoping to preserve whatever remains of the government's nonviolent image, the mayor refuses to allow an autopsy; he fails, however, to get judicial sanction for this act when Judge Arcadio flees town to avoid any connection with the shameful murder. With this crime *La Violencia* begins anew, as the police ransack the town, seeking fliers, finding weapons, and filling the jail. Opposition arises, and men flee into the jungle to join guerrilla bands. Stunned by the violence resulting from the seemingly innocuous lampoons, Father Ángel becomes virtually comatose, unable to accept the evil reality of what he thought to be an exemplary town.

Yet in spite of the renewed bloodshed, the novel ends with the cessation of the rains and the breaking of a brilliant day. Because of the oppressive mood powerfully perpetuated by García Márquez through most of the novel, we actually feel relieved when the violence finally breaks out. At least the immorality and injustices are out in the open where they can be recognized and combatted. Exposed by the open criticism of the lampoons and fliers, and by their own violent reaction to that criticism, the upper class cannot feign respectability, nor the government, legality, while imposing their control over the community.

John R. Chávez

IN QUEST AND CRISIS
Emperor Joseph I and the Habsburg Monarchy

Author: Charles W. Ingrao (1928-   )
Publisher: Purdue University Press (West Lafayette, Indiana). 278 pp. $12.95
Type of work: History
Time: 1705-1711
Locale: Austria

A study of the Habsburg Monarchy and its emperor during a critical time in the Monarchy's history

> *Principal personages:*
> JOSEPH I, Emperor of the Holy Roman Empire, King of Hungary, King of Bohemia, and Archduke of Austria
> CHARLES VI (III), Joseph's brother, claimant to the Spanish throne and Emperor, 1711-1740
> LEOPOLD I, Joseph's father and Emperor, 1658-1705
> PRINCE EUGENE OF SAVOY, President of the War Ministry and Commander of the Austrian armies
> JOHN CHURCHILL, Duke of Marlborough, British Commander
> CHARLES THEODOR OTTO SALM, Joseph's tutor and close adviser
> JOHANN WENZEL WRATISLAW, influential adviser of Joseph

Until twenty years ago, studies in English on the Habsburg Monarchy were rare indeed. Since then, however, the number of such studies has multiplied at an impressive rate, and their quality has improved remarkably as well. In eighteenth century Habsburg history, most of the recent works have focused on the reigns of Maria Theresa (1740-1780) and her son Joseph II (1780-1790)—and with good reason. These rulers both recognized some of the fundamental weaknesses in the Habsburg Monarchy and instituted substantial changes in its political, economic, and social structure in order to make possible its survival in the world. Within the last few years, however, scholars writing in English have applied their skills to the lesser-known members of the dynasty who preceded their more illustrious descendents. The results have been such welcome biographies as John P. Spielman's *Leopold I*, Derek McKay's *Prince Eugene of Savoy* (not a Habsburg or a ruler, but the skillful servant of the family for fifty-three years), and the subject of this review, Charles Ingrao's *In Quest and Crisis: Emperor Joseph I and the Habsburg Monarchy*.

Joseph I became Emperor of the Holy Roman Empire and sovereign of the Habsburg lands for a brief but critical time in their history. When he assumed the throne, the Habsburg Monarchy was beset by foreign threats and internal rebellion that had begun during the reign of his father, Leopold I. In 1701, the Monarchy had become involved in the War of the Spanish Succession, which some scholars regard as the first European war with world-wide dimensions and repercussions. The war had begun with the death of the Spanish King, Charles II, a Habsburg but of the Spanish branch of the family. On his deathbed, Charles had willed his entire inheritance, including Spain proper and the Spanish possessions in Italy, Belgium, and the Americas, to Philip of Anjou, grandson of Louis XIV, the greatest and most feared monarch of his day. To prevent Spain from becoming a tool of French policy, Britain, the Netherlands, Portugal, Savoy, the Habsburg Monarchy, and most of the states of the Holy Roman Empire formed a coalition and declared war on Louis XIV and his grandson. The ensuing conflict featured four main battlegrounds for the Austrians: Belgium, Southern Germany, Italy, and Spain itself, where the allied candidate for the Spanish throne, Joseph's brother Charles, tried to assert his claim by force. A war of this magnitude would have been serious enough by itself for any state to face, but only two years after it began, the Habsburg Monarchy was threatened by an internal crisis equally perilous: a revolt in Hungary. The uprising began in northern Hungary and soon spread throughout the land. The government seemed unable to stop it, since it dared not grant the concessions demanded by the rebels and could not recall sufficient troops from the battlefields in Western Europe to suppress it by force.

When Joseph became Emperor, the War of the Spanish Succession was four years old and the Hungarian rebellion, two years old, and neither was going particularly well for the Monarchy. One reason was the failure of Joseph's father to come to grips with the problems at hand. A pious and devout man, Leopold believed that the interests of his dynasty would ultimately be defended by God, and no amount of human exertion could replace His efforts. Consequently, Leopold had failed to make the military and financial efforts necessary to prosecute the war effectively. When Joseph assumed the throne, the war in Italy was going badly, the armies everywhere were short of money and matériel, and the Hungarian rebellion was becoming increasingly serious. One must admit that the Habsburg forces had done well in southern Germany, where nine months before Leopold's death, they and their British allies had scored a stunning victory over a combined Franco-Bavarian army at Blenheim (Höchstädt), a victory that led to the Austrian conquest of Bavaria and the reduction of the German Front to one of secondary importance for the remainder of the war.

Despite the success at Blenheim, Joseph at his accession faced formidable dangers indeed, and Ingrao's book tells in detail how he dealt with those dangers. Dividing his study along topical rather than chronological lines, the author examines Joseph's efforts at reforming the administration and especially at improving the Monarchy's finances, his policies toward the German states, his efforts to subdue the Hungarian uprising, his conquest of most of Italy, and finally his difficulties in dealing with his allies, especially during the latter years of the war when the temptation for each government to conclude a separate peace with France became so great. The topical approach may be the only way to deal effectively with the reign of Joseph I, which was so short and beset by such disjointed problems, but it has its pitfalls as well. Each of the chapters provides a wealth of detailed information; in some places the reader can follow the Habsburg response to a crisis almost memorandum by memorandum. As he makes his way through each chapter, however, the reader often forgets what he has read before. Deep in the heart of the chapter on Italy, for example, might be a fleeting reference to some event occurring concurrently in Germany which had been discussed two chapters previously. So much information has been offered since then, however, that the reader finds himself frantically and often unsuccessfully trying to remember what the German event involved. When finished with the book, he has a firm grasp on the problems and solutions within each of the topics, but the overall picture remains cloudy.

The main purpose of Ingrao's study is to guarantee Joseph I his rightful place in the decisionmaking and policy-formulating processes of the Habsburg government of the time. Since the nineteenth century, historians have tended to slight Joseph, not only because of the shortness of his reign, but also because of the presence during it of that illustrious servant of the Habsburgs, Prince Eugene of Savoy. Whereas the Prince has been the subject of numerous biographies in many languages, including a three-volume work by Alfred von Arneth published in the 1860's and a five-volume work by Max Braubach published in the 1960's, Professor Ingrao's book is the first biography of Joseph in any language since the late eighteenth century. The Emperor is indeed an intriguing figure, in many ways more like Louis XIV than like any of his fellow Habsburgs. Unlike his father, brother, or even his celebrated niece Maria Theresa, Joseph was not a religious enthusiast excessively concerned about the interests of Roman Catholicism. In the Italian campaign he did not hesitate to make war on the pope when it seemed in the interest of the state to do so, and in Silesia he did not shirk from restoring the rights of Protestants in order to mollify a bellicose king of Sweden. He was no moralist either. A lover of the chase, he pursued both beasts and women with considerable passion, another trait that separates him from the prudery of the Habsburg family. Finally, his doodlings on the minutes of the council meetings—featuring drawings of hangings, fencing matches, and the faces of his ministers—offer a picture of a ruler most of us find fascinating.

Despite these insights, Ingrao admits that his subject is often hard to characterize. Joseph left behind little personal correspondence, which is usually the treasure chest of biographers, and so the author has had to glean his subject's personality from the often sterile official papers that abound in the archives. Such a task is difficult, and the author has performed it well. Yet the man in many ways remains elusive. Joseph was a Francophobe virtually from birth, sharing his father's fear of Louis XIV and his humiliation at the frequent French successes at Habsburg expense in the late seventeenth century. Moreover, he was educated by incipient German nationalists such as

H. J. Wagner von Wagenfels, who called upon his fellow Germans to rally around the Habsburgs as the leaders of Germandom against French cultural and political arrogance. The reader is surprised at and intrigued by the thought that in the early eighteenth century there might have been a Habsburg who not only appreciated the latent power of German nationalism but also wished to mobilize and to lead it. When Joseph became Emperor, however, he shunted aside thoughts of Germandom to pursue Habsburg dynastic concerns, notably in Italy and Hungary. One wonders why; and Ingrao offers no really satisfactory answer. In one place he suggests that Joseph "appreciated the logic of favoring tangible dynastic advantages"; in another that "it was only inevitable that he refocus his attention on purely dynastic concerns"; and in a third that he "had inevitably matured to the realities of his dual role as emperor and Habsburg monarch." Such explanations suggest that no satisfactory answer can be found.

One reason that Joseph's character does not emerge more clearly in his decisions concerning policy was the very multitude and immediacy of the problems he faced. The details of the book argue that Joseph and his advisers faced such serious, daily questions for which they had to find answers that they lacked the opportunity to analyze carefully the long-range goals of the state and to formulate strategies to reach them. Vienna's aims during the reign of Joseph were the containment of Louis XIV and the suppression of the rebellion in Hungary. Policy was based largely on the dangers and opportunities that emerged from these two serious and immediate concerns. For some scholars, this suggests a foreign policy of opportunism, for others *Realpolitik*, and for still others *raison d'état*. Whether these words in themselves suggest different policies or whether they can all describe the same one is itself a subject of considerable debate.

Ingrao laments the shortness of Joseph's reign and strongly suggests that, had he lived longer, the Habsburg Monarchy would have been much better prepared for the crises it faced later in the century. He mentions plans for internal reforms that Joseph pursued which were similar to those implemented later by Maria Theresa and Joseph II and suggests that Joseph I might have had still others in mind that would have strengthened the state considerably. In fact, the author not only regrets Joseph's untimely death, but also regrets the accession of his brother, Charles VI. Charles, the only Habsburg who ruled between 1657 and 1792 who has not yet been blessed with an enthusiastic biographer, appears as perhaps the greatest misfortune in the entire history of the Monarchy.

This book is a fine addition to the study of Habsburg history. More clearly than any other book in English, it identifies the policies of the Monarchy during the War of the Spanish Succession and the rebellion in Hungary. And more clearly than any other work in any language, it identifies the role of Joseph I in the formulation of those policies. The author has employed a great number of archival and printed sources, and his documentation is impressive. A particularly splendid addition is five detailed maps which every student of eighteenth century history will value. A particularly glaring omission is the absence of a bibliography; since Ingrao includes more than one thousand notes, a bibliography should definitely have been provided. Its omission may be the fault of the publisher and not the author, however, because Ingrao admits at the beginning of his work that certain deletions were required for publication, and the bibliography may have been one of the casualties. Nevertheless, this is a fine book which fills admirably a serious gap in Habsburg studies of the early modern period.

Karl A. Roider, Jr.